BRADSHAW'S

CANALS AND NAVIGABLE RIVERS

OF

ENGLAND AND WALES.

A HANDBOOK

OF

INLAND NAVIGATION

FOR

MANUFACTURERS, MERCHANTS, TRADERS,

AND OTHERS:

Compiled, after a Personal Survey of the whole of the Waterways,

BY

HENRY RODOLPH DE SALIS,

Assoc. M. Inst. C.E.,

Director: Fellows, Morton, & Clayton, Ltd.,
Canal Carriers.

LONDON:

HENRY BLACKLOCK & CO. LTD., PROPRIETORS AND PUBLISHERS OF BRADSHAW'S GUIDES,
59, FLEET STREET, E.C.; AND ALBERT SQUARE, MANCHESTER.

1904.

Published in Great Britain in 2012 by Old House books & maps
Midland House, West Way, Botley, Oxford OX2 0PH, United Kingdom.
44-02 23rd Street, Suite 219, Long Island City, NY 11101, USA.
Website: www.oldhousebooks.co.uk
© 2012 Old House. Printed (twice) in 2012.

A CIP catalogue record for this book is available from the British Library.

ISBN-13: 978 1 90840 214 1

Originally published in 1904 by Henry Blacklock & Co, Fleet Street, London.

Printed in the UK by CPI Group (UK), Croydon CR0 4YY.
12 13 14 15 16   11 10 9 8 7 6 5 4 3

Publisher's note
This is an exact facsimile of the edition published in 1904, and any spelling
or typographical errors in this book were present in the original.

PREFACE.

THIS work, to use a well-worn phrase, needs no apology for its appearance. The cost of carriage must always be a matter of the first importance to a commercial community, and it is not too much to say that the steady growth of our commercial prosperity is largely due to the growth of our system of internal communications.

Previous to 1761, when the Bridgewater Canal was opened from Worsley to Manchester, the internal trade of England was chiefly conveyed by pack horse, the few roads which existed were in a very bad condition, and inland navigation was almost entirely restricted to the naturally navigable rivers.

The success of the Bridgewater Canal inaugurated what may be called the Canal Era, which attained its height during the latter part of the eighteenth century. Then came the Railway Era, which commenced with the opening of the Liverpool and Manchester Railway in 1830, and at length in 1845, 6, and 7 completely destroyed any chance which there might have been at that time of a homogeneous system of inland navigation by placing during those three years no less than 948 miles of waterways under railway control.

Whatever may be said on the question of the unfair starving and stifling of canals by railways, there is no doubt that in the first place the canals had largely to thank themselves for it. In many cases the canal companies forced the railways to purchase or lease their undertakings at substantial prices before constructing their lines.

Canals in their day reached a far greater pitch of prosperity than the railways have ever attained to, but they suffered fatally, and do so now, from the want of any serious movement towards their becoming a united system of communication. Each navigation was constructed purely as a local concern, and the gauge of locks and depth of water was generally decided by local circumstances or the fancy of the constructors without any regard for uniformity. The same ideas of exclusiveness appear to have become perpetuated in the system of canal management; there is no Canal Clearing House, and with few exceptions every boat owner has to deal separately with the management of every navigation over which he trades. It is only since 1897 that the four canal companies forming the route between London and Birmingham have made arrangements by which through tolls can be quoted by the Grand Junction Canal Company, who own the largest portion of this route.

No doubt, to some extent, profiting by the experience of canals, the railways have avoided such errors ; had they not done so they could never have reached their present high standard of efficiency.

In these days of keen competition, manufacturers and merchants must consider every possible saving that can be effected, and the question which has been mooted from time to time of some comprehensive scheme for the improvement of our waterways may well continue to receive earnest attention. Even in the present imperfect state of the system as a whole, many tons of traffic might with advantage be conveyed thereon which are now carried by railway at increased cost.

One contributory cause of this is that there has not been, until now, any book of reference concerning our Inland Waterways in which could be found the most ordinary information concerning places to which cargoes can be sent, and under what circumstances. The difficulty of obtaining such information when required has in most cases been considerable, especially when relating to a waterway not in the immediate vicinity. With a view to supplying this deficiency, the Author has undertaken the production of this work after a survey of the whole of the navigable inland waterways of England and Wales, extending over eleven years, carried out in all seasons and all weathers, and amounting to a mileage travelled over the navigations of over 14,000 miles.

The Author tenders his grateful thanks to numerous Directors, Managers, and Engineers of Navigations for much assistance rendered, and especially to his friend Mr. W. H. Wheeler, M.I.C.E., of Boston, who, having made commencement of a similar Work, gave to the Author the result of his labour in that direction.

The greatest care has been taken to insure the accuracy of the information contained in this Work, and no responsibility can be accepted for any errors which may be contained therein.

CONTENTS.

(1)—EXPLANATION OF TERMS USED IN THIS WORK.

The expression " navigable " in this Work means navigable for the purposes of trade ; waterways which can only be used by rowing boats, &c., for pleasure purposes are not dealt with.

Indented places in distance tables.—Where names of places appearing in tables of distances are indented, as Wards Mill, thus :—

> Thornes Flood Lock
> Wards Mill
> Broad Cut

it signifies that the names of the places so indented are situated on a short branch, dock, or backwater off the direct line of the navigation.

In the lists of locks, locks whose numbers are bracketed together form a flight of locks, that is to say, they are not more than 400 yards apart.

In the dimensions of the maximum size of vessels that can use the various navigations, the expression " not limited " when applied to the figures of length and width signifies not limited by the length or width of any locks or works of the navigation. In some cases where the maximum length of vessels is determined by bends in the navigation, these figures are also given separately.

The figures of the times of high water and the rise of the tides at places frequented by sea-going vessels are mostly taken from the Admiralty Tide Tables ; the figures relating to places more inland have been specially obtained for this Work. The figures of the rise of the tides are the heights above Low Water of Spring Tides, unless otherwise stated.

(2)—CANAL NAVIGATIONS AND RIVER NAVIGATIONS.

Inland navigations may be divided into two classes—canal navigations and river navigations ; and there are also navigations composed of varying amounts of both of these classes.

Canal navigations have the advantage of providing still water for the passage of craft, the only movement of the water whch takes place being that due to lockage or the entrance of water feeders which is generally insignificant.

On river navigations, the advantage given by the current to vessels going down stream does not compensate for the disadvantage they encounter from the same cause when going up stream. The strength of the current in our navigable rivers above the tideway varies considerably, the chief cause in general being the amount of water coming down the river at the time, and, locally, the area of the channel of the river and the slope or inclination of the surface of the water, due to the fall of the river bed. The velocity of the current in the non-tidal portion of any of the navigable rivers in England as a rule finds its maximum at between three to four miles an hour ; the flow of the River Severn from Stourport to Gloucester has never been measured to exceed four miles an hour.

The maximum velocity of current, about six miles an hour, is found at Hazelford, fourteen miles below Nottingham on the Trent, on a section of the river about three-quarters of a mile long known as Hazelford Inway.   Just below Hazelford Ferry the river divides into two channels round what in times of full water is an island.   In ordinary times the left-hand channel, called the Inway, which is the navigation channel, takes the whole of the flow of the river, and it is then that its full force is felt.   In times of full water the right-hand channel comes into operation to the relief of the Inway.

The traffic on river navigations is more liable to be interrupted by floods and drought than that on canal navigations.   When the banks of a river overflow, although there is plenty of water in the channel, the surrounding country being submerged, it becomes a trackless waste, where risk of the navigator losing his way is great, and headroom under bridges is much diminished.

Weeds also exercise an effect on the depth of water at the top of reaches in rivers according to the season.   Given a river with a moderate flow which is the same throughout the year, and that consequently maintains the same level of water at the bottom of a reach, the water at the top of that reach would be higher in summer than in winter because of its retardation by the full-grown weeds, which in winter will have died down.

The traffic on river navigations is not stopped by frost as soon as it is on canals, running water of course freezing less quickly than still water.   Although the course of some of the canals is extremely tortuous, river navigations, following as they do in great part natural channels, generally have a longer course from point to point than canals.   As an instance may be noticed the alternative routes from Abingdon-on-Thames to Latton in Wiltshire, which existed prior to the Wilts and Berks Canal becoming unnavigable.

By the navigation of the River Thames from Abingdon to Inglesham is 41½ miles, and thence by Thames and Severn Canal to Latton is 8½ miles, total 50 miles, and by Wilts and Berks Canal throughout from Abingdon, via Swindon, to Latton was 34½ miles.   Stonar Cut, a short cut less than one furlong in length, and which is not navigable, unites two elbows of the River Stour (Kent) near Sandwich ; to navigate from one end of this cut to the other it is necessary to go over 5½ miles round the river through Sandwich, although it should be mentioned in this case that scarcely any trade on the river goes above Sandwich.

On rivers having weirs in which there is removable tackle, navigation is often assisted by the system of " flashing," or, as it is sometimes called, " flushing."   A head of water is allowed to accumulate in a reach, and it is then used to replenish successive lower reaches by keeping the weir at the bottom of each reach shut in and drawing tackle in the weir at the top of the reaches, such operation keeping pace with the movements of the boats so assisted.

Canal navigations have also the advantage over most river navigations in the matter of pilotage. Any ordinary canal boatman can find his way in safety over a canal on which he has never travelled before, but if his journey extend over rivers the extra cost of a man with local knowledge to pilot him is often incurred. For instance, it would not be advisable to send a man over the Upper Thames, or down the Trent below Nottingham, who was a stranger to the navigation. So convinced was James Brindley, the early Canal Engineer, of the superiority of canal over river navigations that on one occasion, when under examination by a committee of the House of Commons concerning one of his schemes, to a member who enquired of him of what use he considered navigable rivers, he is said to have answered " to supply canals with water."

Again, there are navigations and portions of navigations which may be described as intermittent, that is, those on which the passage of the trade is confined to spring tides owing to there not being sufficient depth of water on neap tides to navigate a paying load, as, for example, the River Dee to Chester, to which city paying loads can only be navigated during about one week in the month. The Louth navigation in Lincolnshire is also another instance, as the entrance to it from the North Sea through the sands of Tetney Haven has only sufficient water for loaded Yorkshire keels trading from Hull for about two weeks during the month.

(3)—HAULAGE.

(a) *Hauling by Horses.*

Hauling by horses is still the system most in use on the general body of the inland waterways, and in it must be included hauling by mules, which is rare, and by pairs of donkeys, or, as they are termed, " animals," which are much used for boats on the Stroudwater Canal and the Worcester and Birmingham Canal, and also for the stone boats on the Shropshire Union system. Horse towing-paths are, as a rule, provided on all canals, and on rivers above the region of the strong ebb and flow of the tide.

Canal towing-paths vary considerably, from the well-appointed and well-metalled way to the neglected track—often in winter nothing but a slough of mire, and bounded by a hedge so overgrown as seriously to curtail the width necessary for the passage of the horse.

River towing-paths, unlike those belonging to canals, are usually not fenced off from the adjacent land, being provided with gates set to close automatically by their own weight at the points of passage through the various boundary fences. In the large group of waterways of the Bedford Level and district an antiquated substitute for these gates is in general use in the shape of stiles, some of them as high as 2ft. 7in., over which horses towing have to jump, giving themselves frequently nasty knocks in so doing. It is not creditable to the various authorities in this district that such inconvenience to horses is allowed to continue, especially seeing that in so doing they stand alone among all the other inland navigations of England.

River towing-paths are often not the property of the navigation, but consist merely of the right of passage for the purpose of towing, an annual rent in some cases being paid for the privilege. The towing-path of the River Severn was constructed as a separate undertaking from the naviga- tion, the portions above and below Worcester being owned by two different independent companies. The towing-path, or " haling way " as it is there termed, of the River Ouse (Bedford) from Denver Sluice to King's Lynn is vested in the Ouse Haling Ways Commissioners, there being also separate authorities in charge of the river banks and also of the navigation between these places.

When the towing-path changes from one side of the navigation to the other, means for transferring horses to the opposite bank are necessary. In the case of canals, bridges are always provided for this purpose, and are known as " roving " bridges. On rivers, bridges are not always so conveniently placed ; for instance, lighters coming out of the Middle Level, bound, say, for Ely, on arrival at Salters Lode Sluice, the junction of Well Creek with the River Ouse (Bedford), have to send their horses two miles round by Downham Bridge to get them to the opposite side of the river. In the absence of bridges, ferry boats, which are in some cases owned and worked by the navigation, as on the Upper Thames, take their place. In the Bedford Level and district the gangs of lighters often take with them, in tow behind the last lighter, a special small boat for ferrying over the horses, known as the " horse boat." Horses are sometimes ferried over on the boat or barge itself, as on the River Trent and River Stour (Suffolk). The latter river is the only navigation remain- ing in the country where the old system of transferring the horses from one side of the river to the other on the vessels themselves, without stopping them, is still in use. The system may be worth describing as a relic of times gone by, and as being one which requires special training of the horses.

The traffic on this river is conducted by lighters of a type closely resembling the Fen lighters of the Bedford Level, being about 47ft. long and 10ft. 9in. beam. They always travel in pairs, chained together one behind the other; the fore end of the fore lighter has a deck sufficiently large to afford standing room for the horse ; wood strips are fastened to the deck both fore and aft and across it, and a covering of litter is placed on the top to afford foothold. At the point of the towing-path crossing the river two piers or jetties are built out, one from each bank, con- structed so as to give deep water alongside their extremities, but they are not placed opposite each other, one always being some few yards further up or down stream than the other. When a crossing has to be made, the towing-line is cast off on approaching the first pier and the horse is walked to the pier head, the lighters are steered alongside the pier head, and as they pass the horse jumps on to the fore end of the fore lighter, the lighters are then steered sharp over to the pier on the opposite side of the river, on passing which the horse jumps out ready to resume work.

Constable's picture of " Flatford Mill " in the National Gallery gives an excellent representation of the lighters in use on the River Stour.

Fords, now happily almost extinct, are also another means of crossing horses from one bank of a river to the other ; and the Rivers Nene, Ouse (Bedford), and Larke still furnish examples of them. Fords in a navigable river, it need hardly be said, are very unsatisfactory : they require to be maintained at a certain height, so that the average depth of water may not be too much for fording purposes or too little for navigation, but any abnormal shortness of water is sure to cause obstruction to the latter.

The following are about the average speeds attained by a narrow or monkey boat hauled by a horse in a narrow boat canal in fair order :—

1 narrow boat loaded, hauled by one horse, about 2 miles per hour.

1	,,	,, empty,	,,	,,	,,	,,	3	,,	,,	,,
2	,,	boats loaded,	,,	,,	,,	,,	$1\frac{1}{2}$	,,	,,	,,
2	,,	,, empty,	,,	,,	,,	,,	$2\frac{1}{2}$	,,	,,	,,

In Section XI. of this Work the existence of a towing-path or not to a navigation is always noted, as also, in the event of the towing-path not being continuous throughout the navigation, the points of commencement and termination.

(b) *Bow hauling or hauling by men.*

There is but little bow-hauling done now, and what there is is restricted to occasional use for quite short distances. It may, for example, sometimes be seen on the Bungay Navigation, North Walsham and Dilham Canal, and Aylsham Navigation—non-tidal waterways of the Norfolk Broad District—when the wind is unfavourable for sailing, as there are no horse towing-paths, and the navigations are not wide.

When a pair of narrow boats are worked through a narrow boat canal by one horse, on arriving at locks the horse usually takes the first boat, leaving the second one to be bow-hauled through the locks by the crew.

In the early days of canals the bow-hauling interest must have been very strong, as we find clauses inserted in Acts of Parliament enacting that barges on certain navigations shall be "haled" by men only. Traffic on the River Trent was thus restricted until the year 1783, when two Acts of Parliament were passed containing clauses which permitted horse haulage throughout the navigation from Burton to Gainsborough.

In a paper on the past and present condition of the River Thames read before the Institution of Civil Engineers, January, 1856, by Mr. Henry Robinson (Minutes of Proceedings, Inst. C. E., vol. 15, p. 198), we read :—" The traffic on the Upper Thames was in the last century principally conducted by large barges carrying as much as 200 tons each, and hauled against the stream by 12 or 14 horses, or 50 or 80 men ; these men were usually of the worst possible character, and a terror to the whole neighbourhood of the river."

The River Avon Navigation (Warwickshire) from Stratford-on-Avon to Tewkesbury was constructed without a horse towing-path, and must have been worked by bow haulage. At the present time the trade on the lower navigation from Evesham to Tewkesbury is conducted by steamer, the upper navigation from Evesham to Stratford-on-Avon being derelict.

(c) *Sailing.*

Sailing is suitable for districts where the country is flat, with long reaches of water without locks, and where there are few trees to break the wind; it is also a valuable assistance to drifting with the tide or stream when the wind is favourable.   Traffic in the Norfolk Broad District, consisting of the Rivers Yare, Waveney, and Bure, and their communicating Dikes and Broads, is conducted entirely by sailing vessels, termed "wherries"; haulage by horses is quite unknown, and in no case are there any horse towing-paths provided.

Sailing is also extensively practised on the large expanse of waterways navigated by the Yorkshire keels.

Other vessels which use sails are principally Medway sailing barges, Severn trows, the black flats of the River Weaver, and the barges navigating the River Teign, Stover Canal, and Hackney Canal.

(d) *Drifting with the Tide or Stream.*

Drifting on the ebb or flow of the tide, or down stream in the non-tidal portion of a river, is usually supplemented by sailing, steam, or horse haulage, as otherwise progress would be needlessly slow.   Dumb barges and lighters, however, in spite of the increase in the number of steam tugs, still continue on the Thames in the neighbourhood of London, drifting with the tide and controlled as far as they can be by sweeps or long oars, but always ready to blunder into whatever may cross their path.

Vessels drifting must of necessity be very unmanageable, as a rudder is practically useless unless the vessel is travelling faster than the water in which it floats.

(e) *Haulage by Steam or other Mechanical Power.*

Although successful installations of electrical haulage are in use on portions of the continental waterways, they have not as yet been established in this country.   Oil engines have been tried but have never, passed much beyond the experimental stage.

Steam haulage is in use to a greater or less degree on all the principal rivers—the Tyne, the Humber, the Ouse (York) up to York, the Trent up to Nottingham, the Witham up to Boston, the Nene up to Wisbech, the Ouse (Bedford), the Cam, the Larke up to Mildenhall, the Brandon River or Little Ouse occasionally up to within three miles of Thetford, the Yare up to Norwich, the Colne up to Colchester, the Thames usually as far up as Reading but occasionally to Oxford, the Medway up to Maidstone, the Stour (Kent) up to Sandwich, the Ouse (Sussex) up to Lewes, the Arun up to Arundel, the Parrett up to Bridgwater, the Avon (Bristol) up to Bristol, the Severn up to Stourport, the Avon (Warwickshire) up to Evesham, the Dee, the Mersey, and the Weaver.

Steam haulage is in use on all the Ship Canals, namely, the Manchester Ship Canal, the Gloucester and Berkeley Ship Canal, and the Exeter Ship Canal, but on the last named the Exeter Corporation, the owners of the canal, being also the proprietors of the horses used for hauling, charge for horse haulage whether required or not. The other canals on which steam haulage is in use are the Aire and Calder Navigation main line from Goole to Wakefield and Leeds ; the Leeds and Liverpool Canal from Leeds to Liverpool ; the Bradford Canal; the Manchester Ship Canal Co.'s Bridgewater Canal ; the Rochdale Canal ; the Shropshire Union Canals between Ellesmere Port and Chester ; the through route between London and Birmingham, consisting of the Regents Canal, Grand Junction Canal, portion of the Oxford Canal, the Warwick and Napton Canal, and the Warwick and Birmingham Canal ; the through route between London, Leicester, and Nottingham, consisting of the Regents Canal, Grand Junction Canal, Leicester Navigation, Loughborough Navigation, River Trent, and the portion of the Nottingham Canal between Lenton Chain and Trent Lock, Nottingham ; the London level of the Grand Junction Canal—that is, between Paddington and Cowley Lock, including the Slough Branch—locally for the brick, manure, and refuse traffic ; the Glamorganshire Canal from Cardiff to Melin Griffith ; and the Stow-market and Ipswich Navigation from Ipswich to Bramford. Some side-wheel paddle steamers are still at work on rivers, but on canals the screw propeller is alone used.

The first steam boat employed on canals appears to have been the " Bonaparte," tried by the Duke of Bridgewater and Fulton, the American engineer, on the Bridgewater Canal, some time between 1796 and 1799 (Smiles' " Lives of the Engineers"), but it does not appear to have been successful on account of the injury caused to the canal banks by the wash, and the Duke dying soon afterwards its use was discontinued.

At first sight it may appear surprising that the use of steam haulage has not become more general on the main body of the waterways of this country, especially considering the expense and risk of epidemic incurred in keeping large numbers of horses, but the true reason is that so few of the canals are at all adapted for it. The ordinary " narrow " or " monkey" boat, with a capacity of about 30 tons, with which the bulk of the inland trade of the country is conducted, is quite small enough already without further deduction on account of engine room space ; to work at a profit such vessels fitted up as steamers it is necessary to tow at least one boat after them. In a barge canal this works well enough, as the two boats can pass the locks together; but in a narrow boat canal, delay is caused by having to lock twice at every lock, and the towed or " butty " boat has to be hauled in and out of locks by the crew. Again, the working of traffic by steam tends to concentrate boats together at one place at the same time. Were steam haulage universal on some of our narrow canals delay and inconvenience would be constantly caused by the abstraction of sundry locks of water from the short pounds at one time without any corresponding replenishment from the pound above, thereby causing temporarily a serious reduction of the navigable depth.

Steam haulage, like sailing, is favourably adapted for long pounds of water without locks, which unfortunately are the exception and not the rule in this country, a fact very much apt to be overlooked by inventors of systems of mechanical haulage. Contrary to what is often supposed, steam haulage on the ordinary narrow boat and barge canals adds but little to the speed of vessels over horse haulage ; whatever horse power may be developed, the rate of progress is limited by the ease with which the water can get past the vessel as it travels, which is governed by the proportion of the cross section of the waterway to the immersed section of the vessel, subject to the proviso that, with a given immersed section of vessel and a given section of waterway, the waterway which has the most water beneath the vessel and the sides of which more closely approximate to the vertical will give the best result. Any attempt to increase the speed beyond what the section of the waterway permits merely causes a waste of power, heaps up the water in front of the vessel, creates a breaking wave highly injurious to the banks of the canal, and renders the vessel more difficult to steer.

Steamers have the advantage over horse-hauled boats in being able to travel continuously night and day to destination when provided with two sets of men ; continuous travelling by horse boats necessitates changes of horses at intervals, where, of course, stables must be established, with the additional disadvantage that a horse used by many men is not so well taken care of as one which always works for the same boatman.

The question of injury caused to canal banks and works by the wash of steamers is a very vexed one, opinions on the matter differing widely. As a rule, steamers are allowed on all canals owned by independent companies, those canals on which they are prohibited being mostly owned by railway companies.

In 1859 some coal owners trading on the Ashby-de-la-Zouch Canal proposed hauling boats by steam, the long level of thirty miles without a lock constituting this canal being especially favourable for the purpose. The Midland Railway Company, the owners of the canal, however, refused to allow the boats to pass on the ground of the damage which might be caused to the banks by the steamer, and proceedings were instituted in Chancery to test the rights of the case. The Master of the Rolls directed, with the consent of both parties, that a series of experiments should be carried out by Mr. Pole, an eminent engineer, to ascertain what effects were produced by the use of the proposed steamer. The result of the experiments showed that no wave of an injurious character appeared up to a speed of three miles an hour, and that between three and three and a half miles an hour a breaking wave appeared occasionally in curves and shallows. Mr. Pole accordingly recommended that steamboats should be admitted on the canal subject to such a limitation of their speed as would avoid the production of an injurious wave ; and this recommendation was made an order of the Court of Chancery (Minutes of Proceedings of the Inst. C. E., vol. 26, p. 17).

The Severn is the navigation where the greatest number of vessels are towed together at one time. Between Gloucester and Worcester as many as two dozen narrow boats are sometimes towed behind one tug, the boats being in two parallel lines.

To those wishing to go further into the subject of mechanical haulage on canals, the following papers, &c., are recommended, " Mechanical Propulsion on Canals," by Leslie S. Robertson (Proceedings of the Inst. Mech. E., No. 2, 1897) ; " Speed on Canals," by F. R. Conder, 1884 (Minutes of Proceedings of the Inst. C. E., vol 76, p. 161); " Steam Power on Canals," by W. B. Clegram, 1866 (Minutes of Proceedings of the Inst. C. E., vol. 26, p. 1) ; " Notes on Canal Boat Propulsion," by W. H. Bailey (Proceedings of the Fourth International Congress on Inland Navigation, held at Manchester, 1890) ; " Remarks on Canal Navigation illustrative of the Advantages of the use of Steam," by William Fairbairn, 1831.

(4)—APPLIANCES FOR OVERCOMING CHANGES OF LEVEL.

(a) *Locks.*

A lock, as is generally known, consists of a pit or chamber built usually in brick or masonry, and provided at both ends with a gate or gates and suitable sluices, whereby the level of the water in the lock chamber can be made to correspond as required with the level of the navigation at either end.

Although locks were apparently known to the Venetians as far back as 1481, the first lock constructed in England seems to have been on the Exeter Canal, some time between 1675 and 1697. This canal was completed from Exeter to Topsham in 1566 by John Trew, a native of Glamorganshire (Smiles' "Lives of the Engineers"), and according to an article on Inland Navigation written for the "Edinburgh Encyclopædia," 1830, by the eminent engineer Thomas Telford, the canal as originally constructed appears to have been an open cut, the locks not having been added until over a century later. Mr. Telford goes on to say, that Misterton Soss on the River Idle, constructed by Vermuyden about 1630, was probably the first lock with a chamber built in England ; but Misterton Soss has not now, and so far as the Author can ascertain never has had, more than one pair of navigation gates, and consequently hardly comes within the definition of a lock, but is merely a sluice or staunch to maintain the level of the water in the river above the Soss when the tide is low, the passage of vessels only taking place on the levels of the tide.

Lock chambers, as already stated, are generally constructed in brick or masonry, but there are some few exceptions to be met with. The two locks on the Shropshire Union Canal at Beeston, near Chester, have their sides formed of cast-iron plates bolted together, owing to their being built on a stratum of quicksand. Some locks, mostly on old river navigations, are to be found constructed of timber, and another old type of lock not yet totally extinct has sloping turf sides, with a few piles or old railway metals driven vertically along the foot of the slope to confine the vessels when locking down to their proper limits, so as they do not settle down on to the turf slope. This latter type of lock takes a long time to fill, and consumes a great deal of water, especially in dry weather, as there is considerable soakage into the sides. Lock gates are almost invariably constructed of timber, having the back of the heel post of semi-circular form so as to work in a hollow quoin when opening and shutting. Occasionally, however, cast-iron gates are found, as in the case of some of the bottom gates of locks on the Oxford Canal. Gates working on hooks and rides instead of in hollow quoins are of very early design, and may still be seen on the Rivers Stort, Larke, and Stour (Suffolk).

Lock gates of the portcullis or guillotine type, made to open by being raised vertically, are to be seen at Kings Norton, near Birmingham, where the stop lock of the Stratford-on-Avon Canal, close to its junction with the Worcester and Birmingham Canal, has both top and bottom gates of this pattern, the fall of the lock being only about four inches. Similar gates are also in use for the bottom gates only of the nine small locks on the Old Shropshire Canal Section of the Shropshire Union Canals, between Wappenshall Junction and Trench. The above are the only examples of this type of gate in the country.

The ordinary shape of a lock is naturally rectangular, so as to consume no more water than is necessary, and exceptions to this shape are very rare. Wyre Lock on the Lower Avon (Warwickshire) Navigation is formed of a diamond shape; on the Upper Avon (Warwickshire) Navigation, now derelict, Cleeve Lock was of a diamond shape and Luddington Upper Lock was circular. Cherry Ground Lock, or, as it is locally termed, "sluice," six miles below Bury St. Edmunds, on the portion of the River Larke now closed for traffic, was built somewhat in the form of a crescent moon.

Examples of a large number of locks per mile are 58 in 16 miles between Worcester and Tardebigge on the Worcester and Birmingham Canal, in which are included the famous flight of 30 at Tardebigge, which is the greatest number in one flight in the United Kingdom. There are also 74 locks in 20 miles between Huddersfield and Ashton on the Huddersfield Narrow Canal, and 92 in 32 miles between Manchester and Sowerby Bridge on the Rochdale Canal.

The largest canal lock in the United Kingdom is the large entrance lock to the Manchester Ship Canal at Eastham, which measures 600ft. by 80ft. In passing, it may be mentioned that the Lady Windsor Lock of Barry Docks is supposed to be the largest and deepest of any lock in the world, it measures 647ft. long, 65ft. wide, and is 59½ft. deep from quay wall to invert. The smallest locks in use in the country for trade are the nine locks on the Old Shropshire Canal between Wappenshall Junction and Trench, referred to above, and which pass boats measuring 70ft. by 6ft. 2in.

Locks, as a rule, are not constructed to give a greater fall each than from 6 to 8 feet, as otherwise they would use an excessive amount of water, and the bottom gates would become of abnormal size. Excluding for the moment the locks of the Manchester Ship Canal, the single canal lock having the greatest fall in the country, so far as the Author has observed, is No. 6 lock from Merthyr Tydfil on the Glamorganshire Canal, which has a fall of 14ft. 6in. Tardebigge top lock on the Worcester and Birmingham Canal would appear to come next with a fall of 14ft. Three of the Manchester Ship Canal locks, however, have falls in excess of the above, namely, Latchford, Irlam, and Barton, the falls of which are respectively 16ft. 6in,. 16ft., and 15ft.

The provision of an adequate supply of water to canals is often an expensive matter. Each time a vessel passes through a summit level or highest pound of a canal it consumes two locks of water, that is to say, a lock full at each end, which has to be replaced, but which amount of water will, theoretically at any rate, suffice for working all the locks for the passage of that vessel below the highest lock on each side of the summit level. To maintain the supply of water to the summit level of a canal impounding reservoirs are generally provided to store the rainfall from as large an area as possible for use as required, the supply from the reservoirs being often supplemented by pumping from wells and from streams where available.

A lock of water may cost anything from nothing upwards. In evidence given in 1892 before Lord Balfour of Burleigh, Mr. Hubert Thomas, general manager of the Grand Junction Canal, stated that a lock of water pumped from the Artesian Well to the Tring Summit of the Canal cost. £1. 4s. 8d., and a lock from the Cowroast Well 13s. 7d., the average capacity of a Grand Junction Canal Lock being reckoned as 56,000 gallons.

Mr. G. R. Jebb, engineer to the Birmingham Canal Navigations, stated with regard to that system of canals, that the average cost of water per lock was 2s. 4d., the average capacity of these locks being reckoned as 25,000 gallons each.

Economy in the use of lockage water can be obtained (1) by sub-stituting lifts or inclined planes for locks ; (2) by pumping back the water from the lowest to the highest level. This is done on the Birmingham Canal Navigations at Ocker Hill, where six beam engines are available for pumping back from the Walsall to the Wolverhampton level, also on the north side of both Tring and Braunston summits of the Grand Junction Canal, and at Hillmorton on the Oxford Canal ; (3) by the system of duplicate locks as described below ; (4) by the use of locks with side ponds. The principle of the side pond is that instead of allowing the whole of the water to escape into the lower pound when emptying a lock, the upper portion of the water contained in the lock chamber is allowed to flow into a pond or ponds at the side, placed at a level or levels intermediate between that of the water when the lock is full and empty. The water thus collected in the side ponds is used to replenish the lower portion of the lock when it is required to again fill it, instead of the whole of the water being drawn from the top pound of the canal. The number of side ponds usually employed is from one to three.

" Waiting turns " is a system sometimes practised in dry weather at a flight of locks to economise water. The system is that boats are not allowed to follow each other indiscriminately, but that for every boat that goes down the locks one shall also come up, and vice versa, thus making sure that the maximum amount of traffic is passed for the water consumed. Where the traffic is heavy the duplicate system of locks is made use of, as on the Regents Canal main line, on the Trent and Mersey Canal from the north end of the summit level at Hardings'Wood down to Wheelock, and at Hillmorton three locks on the Oxford Canal near Rugby. On this system, instead of one lock a pair of locks are provided side by side, the one being usually full when the other is empty. Supposing an ascending boat to have entered the empty lock from below, and a descending boat to have entered the full lock from above, when the gates have been closed the water from the full lock is allowed to discharge across into the empty one till both have run level, thus leaving only half a lock of water to be drawn from the top pound for the ascending boat, and the same quantity to be discharged into the bottom pound for the descending boat. Each lock consequently acts as a side pond for the other.

Staircase locks, or as they are sometimes termed " Risers," are locks arranged in flight without any intermediate pools, so that the top gates of one lock are also the bottom gates of the lock above. This arrangement of locks is used where the slope of the ground to be surmounted is steep, but it has the disadvantage that vessels which are over half the size the lock will contain cannot pass each other when in any locks so con-structed. The five staircase locks at Bingley on the Leeds and Liverpool Canal are fine examples of the type. They give a total lift of 59ft. 2in.

Five is the maximum number of locks arranged together on this plan which can be found in this country, but two locks together are often met with on canals, and are usually called double locks.

Mr. G. R. Jebb, in a paper on the "Maintenance of Canals" read before the Society of Arts Conference on Canals, 1888, gives the following interesting information on a point connected with the consumption of lockage water. "A boat locking down from the higher to the lower level requires a lock full of water minus the amount it displaces ; a boat locking up from the lower to the higher level requires a lock of water plus the amount it displaces ; thus, it will be seen that a loaded boat requires more water than an empty one when locking up hill, and that an empty one requires more water than a loaded one when locking down hill."

Throughout the main body of the barge and narrow boat canals, the lock gates and paddles (the latter also variously known as " slats," " slackers," and " cloughs,") are invariably operated by manual labour. The rack and pinion is the usual gear for opening and closing paddles, the spindle of the pinion having a square on the end to take a portable crank or windlass carried by the boatmen ; sometimes the crank is a fixture on the spindle of the pinion, which has the disadvantage of enabling unauthorised persons to interfere with the paddles. In a few localities, gear which requires the use of a handspike is still in existence, and there are also paddles operated by a fixed lever, as the " jack cloughs " of the locks on the Leeds and Liverpool Canal.

On navigations where the traffic is not large it is generally the rule to leave all locks empty, so that when locking up hill each lock must be drawn off after the boat has passed. This ensures that the water in the pounds is held by the top gates of each lock, which are less likely to leak than the bottom gates, being much smaller.

(b) Navigation Weirs or Staunches.

Navigation weirs, called in the Eastern Counties " staunches," are of necessity peculiar to rivers on account of the amount of water they consume in working. They are at best but rude and primitive contrivances, having the sole merit of being cheap, and can only exist where the traffic is small, as their use entails what is practically, to use a railway phrase, single line working. The system consists in providing, instead of a lock, an opening for the passage of vessels through a weir which can be opened or closed at will, so that the water of the river can be penned back in the reach above or allowed to run level, or nearly so, with the water in the top of the reach below. The passage of the water from the higher to the lower level is also assisted by sundry side sluices in addition, which are opened for the purpose when required. The opening or closing of the navigation passage is effected either by a gate or gates similar to those of a lock, or a shutter or " clough," which is wound up vertically by suitable gear, or, in the case of three of the navigation weirs still in use on the Upper Thames, by removing a number of the rimers and paddles of which the weir consists and opening a portion of the bridge specially constructed to swing aside for the purpose.

Thus it will be seen that the change of level from one reach to another is accomplished by allowing the two reaches to run together approximately level instead of, as in the case of the lock, by raising or lowering the level of the water in the lock chamber to correspond with either reach as required. Navigation weirs or staunches, except on the Upper Thames, stand normally open or "drawn," being only closed or "set" when required to be brought into use.

In navigating down stream on a river provided with staunches, a man must be sent in advance to set the staunch, and sufficient water allowed to accumulate before the vessel can enter the reach of water held up by that staunch.   On arrival of the vessel at the staunch it is drawn, and the vessel passes into the next reach.   Going up stream the vessel passes through the staunch, which is then set, and the vessel must then wait until sufficient water accumulates to allow of a passage into the next reach above, when the staunch is drawn, and left in its normal position. The process of allowing the water to accumulate can generally be hastened by drawing water from the reach above, but it must be remembered that in going up stream all water thus drawn decreases the navigable draught in the reach the vessel is about to enter, while when going down stream the reverse takes place, putting only any vessel which may be following to a disadvantage, which of course in most cases is not held to be a matter of great consequence.

There are at present thirty-three navigation weirs or staunches in existence in England, of which twenty-seven termed staunches are situated in the Fen Country or on its tributary rivers ; the other six, which are termed weirs, consist of four on the Thames between Oxford and Lechlade, and two on the Lower Avon Navigation (Warwickshire) between Tewkesbury and Evesham.   Of the staunches in the Eastern Counties, three are on the Ouse (Bedford) between Bedford and Offord, ten on the Nene between Northampton and Peterborough, eight on the Little Ouse, or Brandon River between its junction with the Ouse (Bedford) and Thetford, one on Lakenheath Lode a branch waterway from the last named river, and five on that portion of the River Larke still open for traffic between its junction with the Ouse (Bedford) and Icklingham.   The longest reach of water held up by a staunch is that above Crosswater Staunch on the Little Ouse or Brandon River, which has a length of four miles.   Orton Staunch on the River Nene, two miles above Peterborough, holds up a reach of water three miles long ; in dry weather lighters going up stream are sometimes detained here a whole day waiting for a staunch of water to accumulate, and instances have been mentioned when the delay has amounted to a week.   It has been narrated to the Author how, years ago, lighters trading on the River Nene between Wisbech and Peterborough would sometimes surmount the shallows by the use of a set of "staunching tackle" carried with them.   An empty lighter would be securely moored broadside across the stream, which would not be much wider than the length of a lighter, stout stakes would be driven at intervals across the river along the side of the lighter which faced up stream.   Against the stakes wattled hurdles would be laid, and over the hurdles, again, a large canvas sheet, the bottom of which was trodden down into the mud at the bottom of the river, thus forming an improvised staunch.

(c) *Lifts.*

Lifts are of two kinds : vertically ascending lifts and inclined plane lifts.   At the present time there are only three lifts in use in this country : the vertical lift at Anderton, near Northwich, the property of the River Weaver Navigation Trustees, which enables vessels measuring 72ft. by

14ft. 6in. to be transferred from that navigation to the Trent and Mersey Canal; the inclined plane lift at Trench, on the Old Shropshire Canal, belonging to the Shropshire Union Railways and Canal Co., which passes tub boats measuring 19ft. 9in. by 6ft. 2in.; and the Grand Junction Canal Co.'s inclined plane lift at Foxton, on the Leicester section of that Canal, which can pass barges measuring 72ft. by 14ft.

The Anderton hydraulic lift, which was opened for traffic July, 1875, consists of two caissons supported and raised by hydraulic rams ; the motive power is chiefly obtained by gravity, an arrangement of syphons regulating the water in the ascending caisson so that the additional weight of the descending caisson raises the former. The total lift is 50ft. 4in. A full account of the lift will be found in the Minutes of Proceedings of the Inst. C. E., vol. 45., p. 107.

The Trench incline plane lift, which was constructed towards the close of the eighteenth century, consists of two lines of rails laid parallel to each other, on each of which runs a trolley raised and lowered by a wire rope, and capable of carrying one tub boat at a time. The descending trolley assists in balancing the weight of the ascending one, the extra power required being supplied by a stationary winding engine. The length of the inclined plane is 227 yards, and the vertical rise is 73ft. 6in.

The Foxton inclined plane lift, which was opened for traffic April, 1900, consists of two caissons, each mounted on ten wheels, and running on five rails parallel to each other. The caissons are wound up and down the inclined plane laterally by wire ropes, and here again the one helps to balance the other, the extra power required being obtained from a stationary winding engine. The length of the inclined plane is 307ft., and the vertical rise is 75ft. 2in. An account of the lift, with illustrations, will be found in " Engineering " of 25th January, 1901.

Among canal lifts which have gone out of use may be mentioned the Tardebigge lift, erected on the Worcester and Birmingham Canal in 1809, and the seven lifts on the section of the Grand Western Canal between Taunton and Loudwell, constructed from 1834 to 1836, and closed in 1867 (Transactions of the Inst. of C. E., vol. 2). All these lifts were of the vertically ascending type, and their remains are cleared away. Of disused inclined plane lifts may be mentioned the Coalport lift, almost a counterpart of the Trench lift, with the exception that the trolleys were hauled up by chains instead of wire ropes. This inclined plane was constructed towards the close of the eighteenth century, and went out of use in 1902. It is 300 yards long, and has a vertical rise of 213ft., and is still to be seen almost intact. On the Bude Canal, only the first 2 miles of the canal, which are still open for traffic, were made navigable for barges, the remaining 40 miles (closed by Act of Parliament of 1891) were navigable only by four-ton tub boats, and on this portion all changes of level were accomplished by inclined planes. The boats, which measured 20ft. long by 5ft. 6in. beam and 2ft. 9in. deep, were fitted with four iron wheels, each of 14in. diameter, projecting out beyond the boat's side,and which ran in rails of channel section up and down the inclined planes. The first inclined plane was at Marhamchurch, a little over two miles from Bude, where the boats were hauled up and down by a water wheel. The next incline beyond (Thurlibeer) was worked by a pair of balanced tubs, the descending one being filled with water. The machinery at all the inclined planes has been removed.

The Monkland incline plane lift at Blackhill in Scotland, completed in 1850, resembled somewhat the Grand Junction lift at Foxton of later date, but with the difference that the caissons were constructed to move end on, and ran on two rails each only instead of, as in the case of the Foxton lift, moving laterally and running on five rails each.

(5)—TUNNELS.

The first main line canal tunnel constructed in England was Harecastle Old Tunnel, 2897 yards long, on the summit level of the Trent and Mersey Canal. It was commenced by James Brindley in 1766 and finished in 1777, five years after his death. The latest work in canal tunnelling in the country is Netherton Tunnel, 3027 yards long, on the Birmingham Canal Navigations. It was commenced on 28th December, 1855, and completed within two years and eight months. Harecastle and Netherton Tunnels, besides being the examples of tunnels of the earliest and latest dates, are also the instances of extremes as regards sectional area ; the minimum height above water level and the minimum width at water level of the two tunnels are.: Harecastle 5ft. 10in. and 8ft. 6in., and Netherton 15ft. 9in. and 17ft. waterway, or 27ft. including the two towing-paths.

In the tunnels of early date, towing-paths were never constructed, and, except where steam haulage is in use, the method of propelling boats through such tunnels down to the present time is either " shafting " or " legging." Shafting consists of pushing with a long pole or shaft against the top or sides of a tunnel while walking from forward to aft along the boat, and is generally only used in short tunnels. Legging is performed by two men, one on each side of the boat, who lie down on the fore end on their backs and push against the tunnel sides with their feet. If the tunnel is too wide to admit of their reaching the side walls with their feet from the boats deck, boards projecting over the boats side termed " wings " are brought into use for them to lie on. Sometimes, when the roof of a tunnel is low, one man can leg an empty boat lying down on the top of the cabin. Legging is hard work, and in former days used to be performed by women as well as men. At the tunnels where the traffic is good professional leggers are in attendance, who take their turn assisting boats through as required. At Harecastle Old Tunnel one may be engaged for 1s. 6d. for the passage through, which will take about three hours. At Lappal Tunnel, on the Dudley Canal of the Birmingham Canal Navigations, which is 3795 yards long, assistance is given to the legging of the boats by causing a flow of water through the tunnel in the direction in which they are travelling. A few yards from the western end of the tunnel there is a stop gate across the canal, and also a pumping engine for raising water from the west side of this stop gate to the east side when required. The traffic is allowed three hours alternately in each direction to pass through the tunnel. When the trade is about to pass from west to east, the stop gate at the west end of the tunnel is closed, and the engine begins lifting water from its west side to its east side. This causes a stream to flow from west to east through the tunnel, and raises the level of the water in the pound as far as Selly Oak, distant five miles, to a total amount of about six inches in the three hours. When the trade is about to pass from east to west a paddle is drawn in the stop gate, and the water allowed to run level again, thus causing a current through the tunnel in the opposite direction.

The construction of canal tunnels of any considerable length with towing-paths for horse haulage in this country was only commenced shortly before canal construction practically terminated, consequently there are but few examples of such tunnels to be found. Among the principal are Netherton and Coseley on the Birmingham Canal Navigations, Harecastle New Tunnel—parallel to Harecastle Old Tunnel on the Trent and Mersey Canal—and Chirk Tunnel on the Ellesmere Canal of the Shropshire Union Canals.

Steam haulage is in regular use through Blisworth and Braunston tunnels on the Grand Junction Canal; Foulridge and Gannow tunnels on the Leeds and Liverpool Canal; Westhill, Shortwood, and Tardebigge tunnels on the Worcester and Birmingham Canal; Preston Brook, Barnton, and Saltersford tunnels on the Trent and Mersey Canal; and Islington tunnel on the Regents Canal. In all the above cases the steam tugs are driven by screw propellers, except in the case of the tug working through Islington tunnel, which hauls on a submerged chain.

Departures from the ordinary practice may be noticed in the case of Preston Brook, Barnton, and Saltersford tunnel tugs, which are fitted with a projecting pair of wheels on each side so as to act as fendoffs, and which run along the tunnel wall when the tug is moving; also in the case of tugs working the Foulridge and Gannow tunnels, which are double-ended boats, thus obviating the necessity of being turned round after completing each passage through the tunnel.

CANAL TUNNELS OF ENGLAND AND WALES UPWARDS OF 100 YARDS IN LENGTH.

No.	Name	Canal	Length in Yards
1	Standedge	Huddersfield Narrow	5456
2	Sapperton	Thames and Severn	3808
3	Lappal	Birmingham Canal Navigations—Dudley Canal	3795
4	Dudley	Birmingham Canal Navigations—Dudley Canal	3172
5	Norwood	Chesterfield	3102
6	Butterley	Cromford	3063
7	Blisworth	Grand Junction	3056
8	Netherton	Birmingham Canal Navigations	3027
9	Harecastle (New)	Trent and Mersey	2926
10	Harecastle (Old)	Trent and Mersey	2897
11	West Hill	Worcester and Birmingham	2750
12	Braunston	Grand Junction	2042
13	Foulridge	Leeds and Liverpool	1640
14	Crick	Grand Junction	1528
15	Preston Brook	Trent and Mersey	1239
16	Greywell	Woking Aldershot and Basingstoke	1200
17	Husbands Bosworth	Grand Junction	1166
18	Berwick	Shropshire Union	970
19	Islington	Regents	960
20	Saddington	Grand Junction	880
21	Shortwood	Worcester and Birmingham	608

CANAL TUNNELS OF ENGLAND AND WALES—*Continued.*

No.	Name	Canal	Length in Yards
22	Barnton	Trent and Mersey	572
23	Tardebigge	Worcester and Birmingham	568
24	Gannow	Leeds and Liverpool	559
25	Gosty Hill	Birmingham Canal Navigations—Dudley Canal	557
26	Savernake	Kennet and Avon	502
27	Chirk	Shropshire Union	459
28	Shrewley	Warwick and Birmingham	433
29	Saltersford	Trent and Mersey	424
30	Hincaster	Lancaster	380
31	Ashford	Brecon and Abergavenny	375
32	Coseley	Birmingham Canal Navigations—Main Line	360
33	King's Norton	Stratford-on-Avon	352
34	Hyde Bank	Peak Forest	308
35	Maida Hill	Regents	272
36	Newbold	Oxford	250
37	Snarestone	Ashby	250
38	Dunhampstead	Worcester and Birmingham	236
39	Whitehouses	Shropshire Union	191
40	Woodley	Peak Forest	176
41	Drakeholes	Chesterfield	154
42	Armitage	Trent and Mersey	130
43	Leek	Trent and Mersey	130
44	Cardiff	Glamorganshire	115
45	Edgbaston	Worcester and Birmingham	103

(6)—BRIDGES.

The type of overline canal bridge most commonly found in this country is the single-arch brick or stone bridge having the towing-path carried under it alongside the waterway. In districts affected by subsidences due to mining operations, iron girder bridges are largely used, as they can be more readily raised when the headroom under them diminishes.

Throughout the waterways of the Fen Country, the towing-path, or as it is there termed the " haling way," is not carried under the bridges, but horses towing have to have their tow lines detached on nearing bridges and reattached again on the far side. A remarkable type of bridge is to be found on the Stratford-on-Avon Canal, designed to save the expense of constructing the towing-path under it, and at the same time to obviate the inconvenience of casting off and reattaching the tow line. These bridges consist of two iron brackets, each projecting half across the canal from an abutment of brickwork on either side. The two brackets do not touch each other over the centre of the canal by something less than an inch, the bridge being thus completely cut in two in the middle transversely. Instead, therefore, of having to detach and reattach the tow line, when the horse and boat are about equidistant from the bridge on either side, the horse is slacked up and the tow line is dropped through the slot left between the two halves of the bridge.

B

Opening bridges or movable bridges are of two kinds, those which open by turning aside on a centre, sometimes called "turn bridges," and those which open by lifting upwards and are balanced by counter-weights.

Opening bridges are cheaper in first cost than the fixed brick or stone bridge, but cost more to maintain. They are not generally adopted except for special situations. Large numbers of them are, however, to be found on the southern portion of the Oxford Canal between Fenny Compton and Oxford.

(7)—AQUEDUCTS.

The earliest canal aqueduct constructed in England was that at Barton, opened on the 17th July, 1761. It was built by James Brindley for the Duke of Bridgewater to carry the Bridgewater Canal from Worsley to Manchester across the River Irwell, about five miles west of Manchester. This aqueduct, built of stone, was about 600ft. in length and 36ft. in width at the top, the waterway being 18ft. wide and about 4½ft. deep carried in a puddled channel across the structure. It remained in use and in a good state of preservation until 1893, when it was superseded by the present Barton swing aqueduct, designed by Sir E. Leader Williams, and necessitated by the portion of the bed of the River Irwell below being absorbed into the Manchester Ship Canal. The main girders of the swinging portion of the present aqueduct are 234ft. long, the waterway being 19ft. wide and 6ft. deep. The aqueduct is always swung full of water, there being gates at each end and also at the shore ends of the canal which can be closed at will. The total weight of the swinging span and of the water contained therein is about 1600 tons.

For an account of the circumstances attending the construction of the old Barton aqueduct see Smiles' "Lives of the Engineers"; and for an excellent illustrated description of both old and new aqueducts, and the Manchester Ship Canal in general, see "Engineering" of the 26th January, 1894, from which the above figures of dimensions are taken.

Another notable canal aqueduct is Lancaster aqueduct, completed by Rennie in 1796 at a cost of £48,000, which carries the Lancaster Canal over the River Lune near Lancaster. It is 600ft. long, and consists of five arches of 75ft. span each. The mortar (pozzolana earth) used in its construction was brought from Italy (see Smiles' "Lives of the Engineers").

Two other remarkable aqueducts are those of Chirk and Pontcysyllte, completed by Telford, the former in 1801 at a cost of £20,898, and the latter in 1803 at a cost of £47,069, for the Ellesmere Canal, now portion of the Shropshire Union Railways and Canal Company's system. Chirk aqueduct, over the River Ceriog, consists of ten arches, each of 40ft. span, and is 710ft. long. The waterway was originally carried across this aqueduct in a puddled channel.

Pontcysyllte aqueduct over the River Dee, four miles north of Chirk, is 1007ft. long, and consists of a cast-iron trough for the canal with towing-path and iron side railings carried on nineteen arches. For further particulars and illustrations of these two aqueducts, see Smiles' "Lives of the Engineers," and the "Life of Thomas Telford," written by himself, 1838.

A remarkable instance of road, canal, and railway, on three different levels, is to be seen near Hanwell in Middlesex. Here the short aqueduct carrying the main line of the Grand Junction Canal over the Great Western Branch Railway from Southall to Brentford is also surmounted by the bridge carrying the high road from Greenford to Osterley Park. The three ways of communication make approximately angles of 60 degrees with each other at their point of crossing, and an imaginary plumb line could be drawn to intersect all of them.

(8)—TIDES.

In navigable waters, under the influence of the ebb and flow of the tide, traffic, as a rule, has to be conducted in the same direction as that in which the tidal current is moving at the time. The difference of level of the tide at high and low water, the velocity of the tidal current, the distance inland to which the periods of ebb and flow extend, and the further distance to which the effect of the tide is felt by backing up the land water, vary very much. It must always be remembered that the tide is greatly affected both as regards the time of high and low water and the height to which it rises or falls by the wind. For instance, a wind blowing with a flood tide will cause it to be earlier and to rise higher, whilst a contrary wind will produce the opposite effect. In rivers also the amount of land water coming down the river considerably affects the time and height of the tide at any given place.

The greatest tidal range in the British Isles, and apparently also in the world, is found at Chepstow, on the River Wye. Here the average range of a spring tide is 38ft. and of the maximum recorded tide 53ft. It used to be commonly held that the tide in the Bay of Fundy exceeded that of the Bristol Channel, but it appears recently to have been proved to the contrary. The Bristol Channel tide can also apparently claim to have the greatest velocity of flow of any in England. The tide flowing past Sharpness Point on the Severn, the entrance to the Gloucester and Berkeley Ship Canal, is at times credited with a velocity of twelve knots (nearly fourteen miles) per hour.

Great Yarmouth has the smallest tidal range of any port in England. At the mouth of the River Yare the average rise of spring tides is only six feet and of neap tides four feet six inches. With regard to the distance inland to which the influence of the tide reaches, it may be mentioned that on the Thames high spring tides sometimes flow to Kingston Bridge, a distance of 68 miles from the Nore. The River Ouse (York) is tidal up to Naburn Locks, 5¼ miles below York and 55 miles from Hull, and on the River Ouse (Bedford) spring tides affect the level of the water as far as Brown's Hill Staunch (now a lock) above Earith, and about 42 miles from the estuary.

When the tide flowing up a river to a weir rises to the same height as the reach of water above the weir the tide is said to "make a level." Where the tide, owing to its rising considerably above the normal level of the inland waterways, has to be shut out by sea doors, as in the Fen Country, two levels are made at every tide—the level of the flood tide, or as it is termed "the first level," and the level of the ebb tide or "the back level." These levels are of great assistance in passing trade, as so long as the level lasts both top and bottom gates of the lock can be open at the same time, thus affording an easy passage from one reach to the other.

The phenomenon of the first of the flood tide flowing up a river in the form of a tidal wave, or as it is termed " Bore " or " Aegre," is met with in certain of the rivers at spring tides whose channels suddenly contract from wide estuaries, thus causing the advancing water to be heaped up. The term "bore" is applied to this wave when it occurs in rivers of the West Coast of England, while "aegre" is the term used in the case of the rivers of the East Coast. The bore is seen in the Severn, the Parrett, the Avon (Bristol), the Dee; and the aegre in the Trent and the Welland. An Aegre used to occur in the Witham below Boston, but the deepening of the channel has now removed the cause of its origin. Various statements have from time to time appeared as to the height of these tidal waves. In one case an aegre on the Trent which sunk two narrow canal boats at Gainsborough in 1898 was credited with a height of from 8 to 10 feet, but it may generally be accepted that the height of these waves in the case of any of the rivers of England finds its maximum at from three to four feet.

An excellent short description of the phenomenon of the tides in general will be found in Whittaker's Almanack.

(9)—PRINCIPAL TYPES OF VESSELS USED IN INLAND NAVIGATION.

(a) *Non-Sailing Vessels.*

" Narrow " boats or " monkey " boats are by far the most numerous class of vessel engaged in inland navigation. They are from 70ft. to 72ft. long by from 6ft. 9in. to 7ft. 2in. beam, and draw from 8in. to 11in. of water when empty, loading afterwards about 1in. to 1 ton.

The ordinary type of long-distance travelling narrow boat carries from 25 to 30 tons, and is built with rounded bilges. The narrow boats in use on the Severn and in a few other localities for short-distance traffic are built with square bilges, and carry up to 40 tons. This latter class of boat requires more power to haul, as it offers more resistance to the water, and also has the disadvantage of not being able to " carry a top," as the boatmen say, that is, they become top heavy in loading sooner than a boat with rounded bilges.

A modification of the narrow boat is found in Yorkshire, where there is a type of short boat about 58ft. long by 7ft. beam, made for the purpose of passing the short locks of the Huddersfield Broad Canal and Calder and Hebble Navigation and the narrow locks of the Huddersfield Narrow Canal.

Another small type of narrow boat is found on the Shropshire Union Canals, being made to pass the small locks between Wappenshall Junction and Trench ; these boats measure 70ft. long by 6ft. 2in. wide, and draw, when empty, about 12$\frac{1}{2}$in., and when loaded with 17$\frac{1}{2}$ tons, about 2ft. 8$\frac{1}{2}$in.

When an ordinary full sized narrow boat is fitted up as a steamer, the reduction in cargo carrying capacity amounts to about ten tons.

Wide boats are boats of a size intermediate between the narrow boat and the barge; they are from 70ft. to 72ft. long by from 10ft. to 11ft. beam, and draw, when empty, about 11in. or 12in., loading afterwards about $\frac{3}{4}$in. per ton to a maximum of about 50 tons. This type of boat is found chiefly on the Grand Junction Canal. The term "boat" in Yorkshire is also applied to a class of vessel built on the lines of a Yorkshire keel, but without masts and sails, and which as a rule do not navigate tidal waters.

Barges comprise a large number of vessels of widely varying dimensions, the largest of which, sailing barges of course excluded, are probably the Thames barges such as navigate the Surrey Canal, which admits of dimensions of 105ft. in length, 17ft. 9in. beam, and 4ft. 9in. draught.

Barges measuring 90ft. long by 16ft. beam, and drawing from 5ft. to 5ft. 6in., can navigate the River Lee to Enfield Lock, some of them carrying as much as 90 tons. The Regents Canal can pass barges 79ft. long by 14ft. 6in. beam with a draught of 4ft. 6in.

In all the above measurements of length the rudder is included.

A barge such as would pass Cowley Lock on the Grand Junction Canal, measuring 72ft. long without rudder and 14ft. 3in. beam, would draw about 16in. when empty and carry 70 tons on a draught of 51in. loading—therefore, about 2 tons to 1in.

Leeds and Liverpool Canal short boats, which are the maximum size which can pass between Leeds and the bottom of the 21st lock at Wigan, measure about 62ft. long by 14ft. 3in. beam, and draw when empty about 1ft. 2in.,and when loaded with the maximum load of 45 tons about 3ft. 9in.

When these boats are constructed for use as steamers they are built so as to measure about 1ft. shorter and 3in. less in width than the above dimensions, the reduction in cargo-carrying capacity amounting to nearly 15 tons.

Thames lighters, or as they are termed by the watermen and lightermen "punts," are swim-ended vessels, that is, they have flat sloping ends; their dimensions average about the same as those of the barges, but they do not travel far away from the river. Their advantage is that they are less damageable than barges, most of them having no helm; those fitted with helms are termed "rudder punts."

Bridgewater Canal lighters are of the same size as the Mersey flats, but are open vessels, and do not travel on the Mersey estuary. Their maximum load is about 50 tons.

Mersey flats are from 68ft. to 70ft. in length by from 14ft. 3in to 14ft. 9in. in beam. Their draught when empty is about 1ft. 10in., and they load afterwards about 2 tons to 1in. to a maximum load in open water of about 80 tons.

Weaver flats are usually about 90ft. in length by 21ft. beam, and draw up to 10ft 6in. of water with a load of about 250 tons, as when not exceeding these dimensions four can lock together through the locks on that river. Some of these flats are fitted up as steamers and others are plain flats for towing by steamers; there are also the No. 1 flats (sailing flats), which are now greatly reduced in number owing to the increase of the steam traffic on the river.

Aire and Calder Navigation compartment boats, or " Tom Puddings," are oblong iron boxes towed on the Aire and Calder Navigation by steam tugs in trains, the length of the train varying from any number of the compartments up to a maximum of thirty-two. Attached to the fore end of the first boat in the train is a short wedge-shaped boat called the " Dummy Bows," for the purpose of cleaving the water, and which carries no cargo. The old system of working these boats was by pushing them in front of the tug and steering them by two wire ropes which were passed along the train, one on each side. The ends of the ropes were connected to gear on the deck of the tug, by which either of them could be heaved in while the other one was slacked out ; the use of these wire ropes has, however, been discontinued, the boats being now towed in the ordinary manner. The measurement of these compartment boats is about 20ft. in length by 16ft. beam and 7ft. to 7ft. 6in. deep; they carry 35 tons on a draught of 6ft.

Chelmer and Blackwater Navigation barges measure about 58ft. 6in. long by 16ft. beam. Their maximum load is about 27 tons with a draught of 2ft. 2in. There are only one or two of these barges fitted with cabins, as the length of the navigation is only thirteen miles.

Glamorganshire Canal, Aberdare Canal, Brecon and Abergavenny Canal, and Monmouthshire Canal boats measure about 60ft. long and about 8ft. 6in beam, drawing when empty about 13in., and loading afterwards about 1in. to 1 ton. Their usual load is about 20 tons.

The majority of these boats are without cabins.

Neath Canal and Tennant Canal boats measure about 60ft. long by 9ft. beam, and draw when empty about 9in., loading afterwards about 1in. to 1 ton. Their average load is 20 tons and the maximum 24 tons.

None of these boats have cabins, all of them are double ended, the rudder being transferred from one end to the other as required.

Swansea Canal Boats measure about 65ft. long by 7ft. 6in. beam, and draw when empty about 12in to 13in., loading afterwards about 1in. to 1 ton up to 20 tons.

None of these boats have cabins, all of them are double ended, the rudder being transferred from one end to the other as required.

Fen lighters are usually about 42ft. long by from 9ft. to 10ft. beam at bottom to from 10ft to 11ft. beam at deck, and draw when empty about 12in. They load a little more than 1in. to 1 ton, drawing about 3ft. 6in. when loaded with 25 tons. Owing to the beam at bottom being less than that at deck, the immersion is of course greater per ton for the first portion of the cargo loaded than for the last.

Fen lighters are only met with on the waterways of the Bedford Level and tributaries ; they invariably navigate in gangs of about five lighters, the stern post of one lighter being tightly coupled to the stem of the next by a " seizing chain." All the lighters in a gang except the first are fitted with poles projecting over the bows like bowsprits, the second lighter is fitted with a longer pole than any of the others, called a " steering pole," by means of which a man or men standing on the first lighter steer the whole gang unaided. Two ropes called " fest ropes," one from each side of the lighter, and passed round the fore end of the steering pole, are used to steady the pole as required when steering. The third and remaining lighters in a gang are fitted with shorter poles called "jambing poles," whose fore ends are attached to either side of the lighter in front by ropes called "quarter bits." All Fen lighters do not have cabins, but it is usual for one lighter in each gang to be provided with a cabin, and such lighter is termed a "house lighter."

River Stour (Suffolk) lighters measure about 47ft. long by 10ft. 9in. beam, and draw when empty about 12in. and when loaded with 13 tons about 2ft. 5in. They closely resemble the Fen lighters, and always work in gangs of two, the stern post of the fore lighter being coupled to the stem of the after lighter by a "seizing chain," and the gang being steered from the fore lighter by a "steering pole" fixed to the after lighter.

The locks on the River Stour can take in the two lighters at one time, and as each lighter can carry about 13 tons the capacity of the gang is about 26 tons. The after lighter contains the cabin, and is termed a "house lighter," as in the case of the Fen lighters.

Upper Trent boats measure about 74ft. long by 14ft. 2in. beam, and draw when empty about 20in. forward and 14in aft, or an average draught of about 18in. When loaded with 32 tons the average draught is 30in., and with 75 tons 53in.

These boats, as will be noticed from the above dimensions, carry a good load on a small draught, as the upper portion of the River Trent has often but little depth of water. They would be quite unsuitable for carrying on the Lower Trent traffic, as this necessitaties navigating the Humber in order to reach Hull. Upper and Lower Trent traffic is often transhipped at Newark, but Upper Trent boats in no case ever go below Keadby.

Tyne wherries are the type of vessel in general use for conducting the local traffic on that river. They vary in size from 30 to 100 tons, and are usually towed by steam tugs.

Tub boats are in use on the Shrewsbury Canal of the Shropshire Union Railways and Canal Company, and on the Duke of Sutherland's Canal, for carrying coal from Lilleshall pits up to and including Shrewsbury. Much of this traffic, however, which used to come by tub boats down the Trench Incline, is now sent by tramway to the end of the Humber Arm of the Newport Branch, where it can be loaded direct into narrow boats.

Similar tub boats are also still at work on the Shropshire (Coalport) Canal, carrying coal and iron stone from the head of the canal to Blissers Hill Blast Furnaces. The above boats measure about 19ft. 9in. long by 6ft. 2in. beam by 3ft. deep, drawing when empty about 3in. and loading afterwards about 4in. to 1 ton to a maximum load of 5 tons. They are towed by horses in trains of as many as 20 boats together, and are steered by a man walking along the towing-path, who keeps the foremost boat in the middle of the canal by pushing against it with a long shaft.

On the portion of the Bude Canal in Cornwall which is still open for traffic, between Bude and Hele Bridge, some of the tub boats which used to carry the traffic on the old tub boat canals above Marhamchurch Incline continue in use.   These boats measure about 20ft. long by 5ft. 6in. beam and 2ft. 9in. deep, and draw about 4in. when empty, loading afterwards about 4in. to 1 ton up to a maximum load of 4 tons.   They work in trains, but, unlike the Shropshire tub boats, the first boat in each train has a pointed bow instead of being flat ended.   Steering is effected by a man standing in the bow of the second boat and prizing with a handspike between the after end of the first boat and the fore end of the second boat, so as to force them out of the straight line as required.

(b) Sailing Vessels.

Medway sailing barges are built in sizes ranging from 65 to 150 tons, the usual large size barge being about 120 tons.   A 65-ton barge such as would pass the locks in the London District of the Grand Junction Canal would gauge the same as an ordinary barge with the addition of about 4 tons extra in respect of the mast, spars, sails, and gear.

Yorkshire keels measure about 57ft. 6in. to 58ft. long and from about 14ft. 2in. to 14ft. 8in. beam, and draw when empty from about 2ft. to 2ft. 6in., loading afterwards between 5½in. and 6in. per 10 tons up to a maximum draught of about 6ft. to 6ft. 9in. with a load of about 80 to 100 tons at this draught.

Yorkshire keels like Fen lighters are built of less beam at the bottom than at the deck, and similarly the immersion is greater per ton for the first portion of cargo loaded than for the last.

Severn trows measure about 70ft. long by 17ft. beam, and draw when empty from between 3ft. to 4ft., they carry about 120 tons on a draught of from 8ft. 6in. to 9ft. 6in.

Lower Trent boats measure from 70ft. to 80ft. long by from 14ft. to 14ft. 6in. beam, and draw when empty about 15in. to 17in., loading afterwards from about 8in to 9in. per 20 tons up to a maximum of from 80 to 100 tons.

No. 1 flats are vessels trading up the River Weaver from Liverpool and district.   Their numbers are now much reduced owing to the growth of steam traffic on the river.   For average dimensions, &c., see Weaver flats—(a) Non-Sailing Vessels.

Norfolk wherries vary in size from 12 to 83 tons.   A 12-ton wherry measures about 35ft. long by 9ft. beam, and would draw when empty about 2ft. and when loaded with 12 tons about 3ft. 3in.   A 20-ton wherry is a size of which many are in use, they measure about 54ft. to 56ft. long by 13ft. to 14ft. beam, and draw when empty about 2ft. and when loaded with 20 tons about 4ft.

The largest wherry ever built is supposed to be the "Wonder" of Norwich, which measures 65ft. long by 19ft. beam, and draws when empty about 3ft. and when loaded with 83 tons nearly 7ft.

River Teign, Stover Canal, and Hackney Canal barges, which are mostly engaged in taking china clay from the Newton Abbot district to Teignmouth for shipment, measure about 56ft. long by 13ft. 6in. beam, and carry 30 tons with a draught of about 3ft. forward and 3ft. 9in. aft.

(10)—TABLES OF PRINCIPAL THROUGH ROUTES OF INLAND NAVIGATION IN ENGLAND AND WALES.

Revised and enlarged from a table of through routes handed to the Parliamentary Select Committee on Canals, 1883, by the late Mr. E. J. Lloyd.

London to Liverpool—Route No. 1.

Navigations.	From	To	Miles.	Locks.	Maximum Size of Vessels that can use the Navigation.	Approx Draught of Water.
Regents Canal ..	Limehouse ..	Paddington ..	8½	12	80′ 0″×14′ 6″	4′ 6″
Grand Junction Canal ..	Paddington ..	Braunston ..	100¾	90	72′ 0″×14′ 3″	3′ 8″
Oxford Canal ..	Braunston ..	Napton ..	5½	1*	7′ 0″	3′ 8″
Warwick & Napton Canal	Napton ..	Budbrooke .. (Near Warwick)	14¼	25	72′ 0″× 7′ 0″	3′ 8″
Warwick & Birmingham Canal	Budbrooke ..	Birmingham .. (Warwick Wharf)	22	34	72′ 0″× 7′ 0″	3′ 8″
Birmingham Canals ..	Birmingham ..	Aldersley ..	16¾	43	71′ 6″× 7′ 1½″	3′ 6″
Staffordshire & Worcestershire Canal	Aldersley ..	Autherley ..	0½	—	— —	4′ 0″
Shropshire Union Canals	Autherley ..	Ellesmere Port ..	66½	46	71′ 6″× 6′ 10″	3′ 3″
Manchester Ship Canal ..	Ellesmere Port ..	Eastham ..	3¼	1	600′ 0″×80′ 0″	26′ 0″
River Mersey ..	Eastham ..	Liverpool ..	6	—	— —	26′ 0″
		Total ..	244	252		

* Stop Lock.

London to Liverpool—Route No. 2.

Navigations.	From	To	Miles.	Locks.	Maximum Size of Vessels that can use the Navigation.	Approx. Draught of Water.
River Thames ..	Limehouse ..	Brentford ..	16	—	— —	4′ 0″
Grand Junction Canal ..	Brentford ..	Braunston ..	93¾	102	72′ 0″×14′ 3″	3′ 8″
Oxford Canal ..	Braunston ..	Hawkesbury ..	23¼	4	72′ 0″× 7′ 0″	3′ 8″
Coventry Canal ..	Hawkesbury ..	Fazeley ..	21½	14	72′ 0″× 6′ 10″	3′ 6″
Birmingham Canals ..	Fazeley ..	Whittington ..	5½	—	— —	3′ 6″
Coventry Canal ..	Whittington ..	Fradley ..	5½	—	— —	3′ 6″
Trent & Mersey Canal ..	Fradley ..	Preston Brook ..	67	59	72′ 0″× 7′ 0″	4′ 0″
Bridgewater Canal ..	Preston Brook ..	Runcorn ..	5¾	10	71′ 11″×15′ 0″	4′ 4″
Manchester Ship Canal ..	Runcorn ..	Eastham ..	12	1	600′ 0″×80′ 0″	26′ 0″
River Mersey ..	Eastham ..	Liverpool ..	6	—	— —	26′ 0″
		Total ..	256¼	190		

London to Liverpool—Route No. 3.

Navigations.	From	To	Miles.	Locks.	Maximum Size of Vessels that can use the Navigation.	Approx. Draught of Water.
River Thames ..	Limehouse ..	Brentford ..	16	—	— —	4′ 0″
Grand Junction Canal ..	Brentford ..	Braunston ..	93¾	102	72′ 0″×14′ 3″	3′ 8″
Oxford Canal ..	Braunston ..	Napton ..	5½	1*	7′ 0″	3′ 8″
Warwick & Napton Canal	Napton ..	Budbrooke .. (near Warwick)	14¼	25	72′ 0″× 7′ 0″	3′ 8″
Warwick & Birmingham Canal	Budbrooke ..	Birmingham .. (Warwick Wharf)	22	34	72′ 0″× 7′ 0″	3′ 8″
Birmingham Canals ..	Birmingham ..	Aldersley ..	16¾	43	71′ 6″× 7′ 1½″	3′ 6″
Staffordshire & Worcestershire Canal	Aldersley ..	Haywood ..	21	12	72′ 0″× 6′ 9″	4′ 0″
Trent & Mersey Canal ..	Haywood ..	Preston Brook ..	54¼	54	72′ 0″× 7′ 0″	4′ 0″
Bridgewater Canal ..	Preston Brook ..	Runcorn ..	5¾	10	71′ 11″×15′ 0″	4′ 4″
Manchester Ship Canal ..	Runcorn ..	Eastham ..	12	1	600′ 0″×80′ 0″	26′ 0″
River Mersey ..	Eastham ..	Liverpool ..	6	—	— —	26′ 0″
		Total ..	267¼	282		

* Stop Lock.

London to Hull—Route No. 1.

Navigations.	From	To	Miles.	Locks.	Maximum Size of Vessels that can use the Navigation.	Approx. Draught of Water.
Regents Canal ..	Limehouse ..	Paddington ..	8½	12	80′ 0″×14′ 6″	4′ 6″
Grand Junction Canal ..	Paddington ..	Leicester ..	137¾	125	72′ 0″× 7′ 0″	3′ 8″
Leicester Navigation ..	Leicester ..	Loughborough ..	15¾	11	70′ 0″×14′ 6″	3′ 6″
Loughboro' Navigation	Loughborough ..	Mouth of River Soar	9¼	7	72′ 3″×14′ 3″	3′ 6″
River Trent ..	Mouth of River Soar	Lenton Chain ..	7¾	2	81′ 0″×14′ 6″	3′ 6″
Nottingham Canal ..	Lenton Chain ..	Trent Lock .. (Nottingham)	2½	3	82′ 0″×14′ 0″	3′ 6″
River Trent ..	Trent Lock .. (Nottingham)	Trent Falls ..	81¼	4	81′ 0″×14′ 6″	3′ 6″
River Humber ..	Trent Falls ..	Hull ..	18	—	— —	12′ 6″ to 18′ 0″
		Total ..	281¾	164		

London to Hull—Route No. 2.

Navigations.	From	To	Miles.	Locks.	Maximum Size of Vessels that can use the Navigation.	Approx. Draught of Water.
River Thames ..	Limehouse ..	Brentford ..	16	—	— —	4′ 0″
Grand Junction Canal ..	Brentford ..	Braunston ..	93¾	102	72′ 0″×14′ 3″	3′ 8″
Oxford Canal ..	Braunston ..	Hawkesbury ..	23¼	4	72′ 0″× 7′ 0″	3′ 8″
Coventry Canal ..	Hawkesbury ..	Fazeley ..	21½	14	72′ 0″× 6′ 10″	3′ 6″
Birmingham Canals	Fazeley ..	Whittington ..	5½	—	— —	3′ 6″
Coventry Canal ..	Whittington ..	Fradley ..	5½	—	— —	3′ 6″
Trent & Mersey Canal ..	Fradley ..	Derwent Mouth	26¼	17	72′ 0″× 7′ 0″	3′ 6″
River Trent ..	Derwent Mouth	Lenton Chain ..	9½	4	81′ 0″×14′ 6″	3′ 6″
Nottingham Canal ..	Lenton Chain ..	Trent Lock (Nottingham)	2½	3	82′ 0″×14′ 0″	3′ 6″
River Trent ..	Trent Lock .. (Nottingham)	Trent Falls ..	81¼	4	81′ 0″×14′ 6″	3′ 6″
River Humber ..	Trent Falls ..	Hull ..	18	—	— —	12′ 6″ to 18′ 0″
		Total ..	305½	148		

London to the Severn (Avonmouth Docks)—Route No. 1.

Navigations.	From	To	Miles.	Locks.	Maximum Size of Vessels that can use the Navigation.	Approx. Draught of Water.
River Thames ..	Limehouse ..	Reading ..	76¾	22	120′ 0″×17′ 0″	4′ 0″
Kennet and Avon Navigation	Reading ..	Hanham ..	86½	106	73′ 0″×13′ 10″	3′ 6″
River Avon ..	Hanham ..	Avonmouth ..	14¼	2	— —	6′ 6″
		Total ..	177½	130		

London to the Severn (Sharpness Docks)—Route No. 1.

Navigations.	From	To	Miles.	Locks.	Maximum Size of Vessels that can use the Navigation.	Approx. Draught of Water.
River Thames ..	Limehouse ..	Inglesham .. (near Lechlade)	146½	47	100′ 0″×14′ 0″	3′ 6″
Thames & Severn Canal	Inglesham ..	Stroud ..	28¾	44	70′ 0″×11′ 0″	3′ 6″
Stroudwater Navigation	Stroud ..	Saul ..	7	11	70′ 0″×15′ 6″	5′ 0″
Gloucester & Berkeley Ship Canal	Saul ..	Sharpness ..	8½	—	— —	14′ 0″
		Total ..	190¾	102		

LONDON TO THE SEVERN (Sharpness Docks)—ROUTE No. 2.

Navigations.	From	To	Miles.	Locks.	Maximum Size of Vessels that can use the Navigation.			Approx. Draught of Water.
River Thames ..	Limehouse ..	Brentford ..	16	—				4′ 0″
Grand Junction Canal ..	Brentford ..	Braunston ..	93½	102	72′ 0″	×14′	3″	3′ 8″
Oxford Canal ..	Braunston ..	Napton ..	5½	1*		7′	0″	3′ 8″
Warwick & Napton Canal	Napton ..	Budbrooke .. (near Warwick)	14¼	25	72′ 0″	× 7′	0″	3′ 8″
Warwick & Birmingham Canal	Budbrooke ..	Kingswood ..	7½	21	72′ 0″	× 7′	0″	3′ 8″
Stratford-upon-Avon	Kingswood ..	King's Norton ..	12½	20	72′ 0″	× 7′	0″	3′ 6″
Worcester & Birmingham Canal	King's Norton ..	Worcester ..	24½	58	71′ 6″	× 7′	0″	4′ 0″
River Severn ..	Worcester ..	Gloucester ..	29	2	135′ 0″	×22′	0″	8′ 6″
Gloucester & Berkeley Ship Canal	Gloucester ..	Sharpness ..	16½	1	140′ 0″	×22′	0″	14′ 0″
		TOTAL ..	219¼	230				

* Stop Lock.

LIVERPOOL TO THE SEVERN (Sharpness Docks)—ROUTE No. 1.

Navigations.	From	To	Miles.	Locks.	Maximum Size of Vessels that can use the Navigation.			Approx. Draught of Water.
River Mersey ..	Liverpool ..	Eastham ..	6	—	—	—		26′ 0″
Manchester Ship Canal..	Eastham ..	Ellesmere Port..	3½	1	600′ 0″	×80′	0″	26′ 0″
Shropshire Union Canals	Ellesmere Port..	Autherley ..	66½	46	71′ 6″	× 6′	10″	3′ 3″
Staffordshire & Worcestershire Canal	Autherley ..	Stourport ..	25½	31	72′ 0″	× 6′	9″	4′ 0″
River Severn ..	Stourport ..	Gloucester ..	42	5	87′ 0″	×15′	6″	6′ 0″
Gloucester & Berkeley Ship Canal	Gloucester ..	Sharpness ..	16½	1	140′ 0″	×22′	0″	14′ 0″
		TOTAL ..	159¼	84				

LIVERPOOL TO THE SEVERN (Sharpness Docks)—ROUTE No. 2.

Navigations.	From	To	Miles.	Locks.	Maximum Size of Vessels that can use the Navigation.			Approx. Draught of Water.
River Mersey ..	Liverpool ..	Eastham ..	6	—	—	—		26′ 0″
Manchester Ship Canal..	Eastham ..	Runcorn ..	12	1	600′ 0″	×80′	0″	26′ 0″
Bridgewater Canal ..	Runcorn ..	Preston Brook ..	5½	10	71′ 11″	×15′	0″	4′ 4″
Trent & Mersey Canal ..	Preston Brook ..	Haywood ..	54½	54	72′ 0″	× 7′	0″	4′ 0″
Staffordshire & Worcestershire Canal	Haywood ..	Aldersley ..	21	12	72′ 0″	× 6′	9″	4′ 0″
Birmingham Canals ..	Aldersley ..	Birmingham .. (Worcester Wh'f)	15	24	71′ 6″	× 7′	1½″	3′ 6″
Worcester & Birmingham Canal	Birmingham ..	Worcester ..	30	58	71′ 6″	× 7′	0″	4′ 0″
River Severn ..	Worcester ..	Gloucester ..	29	2	135′ 0″	×22′	0″	8′ 6″
Gloucester & Berkeley Ship Canal	Gloucester ..	Sharpness ..	16½	1	140′ 0″	×22′	0″	14′ 0″
		TOTAL ..	189½	162				

LIVERPOOL TO HULL—ROUTE No. 1.

Navigations.	From	To	Miles.	Locks.	Maximum Size of Vessels that can use the Navigation.			Approx. Draught of Water.
Leeds & Liverpool Canal	Liverpool ..	Leeds ..	127¼	91	62′ 0″	×14′	3″	3′ 9″
Aire & Calder Navigation	Leeds ..	Goole ..	34	13	120′ 0″	×17′	6″	7′ 6″
River Ouse ..	Goole ..	Trent Falls ..	8	—	—	—		12′ 6″ to
River Humber ..	Trent Falls ..	Hull ..	18	—	—	—		18′ 0″
		TOTAL ..	187¼	104				

Liverpool to Hull—Route No. 2.

Navigations.	From	To	Miles.	Locks.	Maximum Size of Vessels that can use the Navigation.	Approx. Draught of Water.
River Mersey ..	Liverpool ..	Eastham ..	6	—	— —	26′ 0″
Manchester Ship Canal..	Eastham ..	Runcorn ..	12	1	600′ 0″×80′ 0″	26′ 0″
Bridgewater Canal ..	Runcorn ..	Manchester ..	28½	10	71′ 11″×15′ 0″	4′ 4″
Rochdale Canal ..	Manchester ..	Sowerby Bridge	33	92	72′ 0″×14′ 2″	4′ 0″
Calder & Hebble Navigation	Sowerby Bridge	Wakefield ..	21½	35	57′ 6″×14′ 1″	5′ 0″
Aire & Calder Navigation	Wakefield ..	Goole ..	32	11	120′ 0″×17′ 6″	7′ 6″
River Ouse ..	Goole ..	Trent Falls ..	8	—	— —	12′ 6″ to 18′ 0″
River Humber ..	Trent Falls ..	Hull ..	18	—	— —	
		Total ..	159	149		

Liverpool to Hull—Route No. 3.

Navigations.	From	To	Miles.	Locks.	Maximum Size of Vessels that can use the Navigation.	Approx. Draught of Water.
River Mersey ..	Liverpool ..	Eastham ..	6	—	— —	26′ 0″
Manchester Ship Canal..	Eastham ..	Runcorn ..	12	1	600′ 0″×80′ 0″	26′ 0″
Bridgewater Canal ..	Runcorn ..	Manchester ..	28½	10	71′ 11″×15′ 0″	4′ 4″
Rochdale Canal ..	Manchester ..	Manchester ..	1¼	9	72′ 0″×14′ 2″	4′ 2″
Ashton Canal ..	Manchester ..	Ashton ..	6¾	18	70′ 0″× 7′ 0″	3′ 3″
Huddersfield Narrow Canal	Ashton ..	Huddersfield ..	20	74	70′ 0″× 7′ 0″	3′ 6″
Huddersfield BroadCanal	Huddersfield ..	Cooper Bridge ..	3¾	9	58′ 0″×14′ 2″	4′ 6″
Calder & Hebble Navigation	Cooper Bridge ..	Wakefield ..	13	20	57′ 6″×14′ 1″	5′ 0″
Aire & Calder Navigation	Wakefield ..	Goole ..	32	11	120′ 0″×17′ 6″	7′ 6″
River Ouse ..	Goole ..	Trent Falls ..	8	—	— —	12′ 6″ to 18′ 0″
River Humber ..	Trent Falls ..	Hull ..	18	—	— —	
		Total ..	149¼	152		

Birmingham to London.

Navigations.	From	To	Miles.	Locks.	Maximum Size of Vessels that can use the Navigation.	Approx. Draught of Water.
Warwick & Birmingham Canal	Birmingham .. (Fazeley Street)	Budbrooke .. (near Warwick)	22	34	72′ 0″× 7′ 0″	3′ 8″
Warwick & Napton Canal	Budbrooke ..	Napton ..	14¼	25	72′ 0″× 7′ 0″	3′ 8″
Oxford Canal ..	Napton ..	Braunston ..	5½	1*	7′ 0″	3′ 8″
Grand Junction Canal ..	Braunston ..	Paddington ..	100¾	90	72′ 0″×14′ 3″	3′ 8″
Regents Canal ..	Paddington ..	City Basin ..	4½	5	80′ 0″×14′ 6″	4′ 6″
		Total ..	147	155		

* Stop Lock.

Birmingham to Liverpool—Route No. 1.

Navigations.	From	To	Miles.	Locks.	Maximum Size of Vessels that can use the Navigation.	Approx. Draught of Water.
Birmingham Canals ..	Birmingham .. (Worcester Wh'f)	Aldersley ..	15	24	71′ 6″× 7′ 1½″	3′ 6″
Staffordshire & Worcestershire Canal	Aldersley ..	Haywood ..	21	12	72′ 0″× 6′ 9″	4′ 0″
Trent & Mersey Canal ..	Haywood ..	Preston Brook ..	54¼	54	72′ 0″× 7′ 0″	4′ 0″
Bridgewater Canal ..	Preston Brook ..	Runcorn ..	5¾	10	71′ 11″×15′ 0″	4′ 4″
Manchester Ship Canal..	Runcorn ..	Eastham ..	12	1	600′ 0″×80′ 0″	26′ 0″
River Mersey ..	Eastham ..	Liverpool ..	6	—	— —	26′ 0″
		Total ..	114	101		

Birmingham to Liverpool—Route No. 2.

Navigations.	From	To	Miles.	Locks.	Maximum Size of Vessels that can use the Navigation.	Approx Draught of Water.
Birmingham Canals ..	Birmingham .. (Worcester Wh'f)	Aldersley ..	15	24	71′ 6″× 7′ 1½″	3′ 6″
Staffordshire & Worcestershire Canal	Aldersley ..	Autherley ..	0½	—	— —	4′ 0″
Shropshire Union Canals	Autherley ..	Ellesmere Port ..	66½	46	71′ 6″× 6′ 10″	3′ 3″
Manchester Ship Canal ..	Ellesmere Port ..	Eastham ..	3¼	1	600′ 0″×80′ 0″	26′ 0″
River Mersey ..	Eastham ..	Liverpool ..	6	—	— —	26′ 0″
		Total ..	91¼	71		

Birmingham to Hull.

Navigations.	From	To	Miles.	Locks.	Maximum Size of Vessels that can use the Navigation.	Approx. Draught of Water.
Birmingham Canals ..	Birmingham .. (Worcester Wh'f)	Whittington ..	21	38	71′ 6″ 7′ 1½″	3′ 6″
Coventry Canal ..	Whittington ..	Fradley ..	5½	—	— —	3′ 6″
Trent & Mersey Canal ..	Fradley ..	Derwent Mouth	26¼	17	72′ 0″× 7′ 0″	3′ 6″
River Trent ..	Derwent Mouth	Lenton Chain ..	9½	4	81′ 0″×14′ 6″	3′ 6″
Nottingham Canal ..	Lenton Chain ..	Trent Lock .. (Nottingham)	2½	3	82′ 0″×14′ 0″	3′ 6″
River Trent ..	Trent Lock .. (Nottingham)	Trent Falls ..	81¼	4	81′ 0″×14′ 6″	3′ 6″
River Humber ..	Trent Falls ..	Hull ..	18	—	— —	12′ 6″ to 18′ 0″
		Total ..	164	66		

Birmingham to the Severn (Sharpness Docks)—Route No. 1.

Navigations.	From	To	Miles.	Locks.	Maximum Size of Vessels that can use the Navigation.	Approx. Draught of Water.
Worcester & Birmingham Canal	Birmingham .. (Worcester Wh'f)	Worcester	30	58	71′ 6″× 7′ 0″	4′ 0″
River Severn ..	Worcester ..	Gloucester ..	29	2	135′ 0″×22′ 0″	8′ 6″
Gloucester & Berkeley Ship Canal	Gloucester ..	Sharpness ..	16½	1	140′ 0″×22′ 0″	14′ 0″
		Total ..	75½	61		

Birmingham to the Severn (Sharpness Docks)—Route No. 2.

Navigations.	From	To	Miles.	Locks.	Maximum Size of Vessels that can use the Navigation.	Approx. Draught of Water.
Birmingham Canals ..	Birmingham .. (Worcester Wh'f)	Black Delph ..	13	10	71′ 6″× 7′ 1½″	3′ 6″
Stourbridge Canal ..	Black Delph ..	Stourton ..	5	20	70′ 0″× 7′ 0″	4′ 0″
Staffordshire & Worcestershire Canal	Stourton ..	Stourport ..	12¼	13	72′ 0″× 6′ 9″	4′ 0″
River Severn ..	Stourport ..	Gloucester ..	42	5	87′ 0″×15′ 6″	6′ 0″
Gloucester & Berkeley Ship Canal	Gloucester ..	Sharpness ..	16½	1	140′ 0″×22′ 0″	14′ 0″
		Total ..	88¾	49		

BIRMINGHAM TO THE SEVERN (Sharpness Docks)—ROUTE No. 3.

Navigations.	From	To	Miles.	Locks.	Maximum Size of Vessels that can use the Navigation.			Approx. Draught of Water.
Birmingham Canals ..	Birmingham .. (Worcester Wh'f)	Aldersley ..	15	24	71'	6" × 7'	1½"	3' 6"
Staffordshire & Worcestershire Canal	Aldersley ..	Stourport ..	25	31	72'	0" × 6'	9"	4' 0"
River Severn ..	Stourport ..	Gloucester ..	42	5	87'	0" × 15'	6"	6' 0"
Gloucester & Berkeley Ship Canal	Gloucester ..	Sharpness ..	16½	1	140'	0" × 22'	0"	14' 0"
		TOTAL ..	98½	61				

(11)—THE WHOLE OF THE NAVIGABLE WATERWAYS AND THEIR CONTROLLING AUTHORITIES IN ALPHABETICAL ORDER, WITH REFERENCES AND CROSS REFERENCES FROM THE NAMES OF THE NAVIGATIONS TO THEIR CONTROLLING AUTHORITIES AND *VICE VERSA*, AND THE FOLLOWING INFORMATION ABOUT EACH ONE:—

(a) Short description, main line from——————to——————, branches from——————to——————, &c.

(b) Proprietors or Controlling Authority, Officers, and Offices, and whether the Proprietors themselves act as Carriers or not.

(c) Table of Distances of Places on the Navigation, giving all cases of bonus mileage allowed under Act of Parliament.

(d) Locks.

(e) Maximum size of Vessels that can use the Navigation

　　　Length.

　　　Width.

　　　Draught.

　　　Headroom.

(f) Tunnels—their size, method of working, and working hours.

(g) Towing-path.

(h) Tidal Information.

(i) Types of Vessels using the Navigation, and notes as to Steam Traffic.

ABBEY CREEK—*see* River Lee.

ABERDARE CANAL—*see* Glamorganshire and Aberdare Canals.

ACLE DIKE—*see* River Bure.

(1)—RIVER ADUR.

(a) Short Description.

The navigation of the River Adur may be said to commence at Upper Beeding Bridge near Bramber, as, although the river is navigable on spring tides for some distance further up, there is practically no trade carried on above this point.

From Upper Beeding Bridge the river proceeds by Old Shoreham, New Shoreham, and Kingston-by-Sea to the sea at Southwick, all in the county of Sussex, forming below the Norfolk Bridge, New Shoreham, the western arm of Shoreham Harbour.

There is but little trade done above the cement works at Beeding Chalk Pit.

The course of the river channel between Beeding Chalk Pit and the Norfolk Bridge, New Shoreham, is among shifting sand banks.

The eastern arm of Shoreham Harbour communicates through a lock at Southwick with a floating basin or canal, extending for 1¾ miles eastward to Portslade and Aldrington.

(b) Proprietors, Officers, and Offices.

The upper portion of the river down to Beeding Chalk Pit is under the jurisdiction of the Trustees of the River Adur Navigation as a Drainage Authority.

Clerk : G. A. Flowers.

Office : High Street, Steyning, Sussex.

From Upper Beeding Chalk Pit to Old Shoreham Bridge the river is an open navigation, having no controlling authority, and from Old Shoreham Bridge to the Harbour Mouth is under the jurisdiction of the Shoreham Harbour Trustees.

Clerk : Cranfield Baguley.

Harbour Master and Engineer : A. J. Catt.

Offices : Southwick, near Brighton.

(c) Distance Table.

	Miles.	Fur.
Upper Beeding Bridge to—		
Beeding Chalk Pit, Cement Works, and L. B. & S. C. Rly. Bridge (Horsham and Shoreham Line)	1	2
Old Shoreham Bridge	3	4

(1)—RIVER ADUR—*continued.*

	Miles.	Fur.
Upper Beeding Bridge to (*continued*)—		
L. B. & S. C. Rly. Bridge (Brighton and Portsmouth Line)	4	1
Norfolk Bridge, New Shoreham, and upper extremity of the western arm of Shoreham Harbour.	4	3
Kingston-by-Sea Wharf	5	4
Junction with eastern arm of Harbour.. ..	5	7
Mouth of River	6	0

(*e*) *Maximum size of vessels that can use the navigation.*

Length.—Not limited.

Width.—Not limited.

Draught.—There is about 21ft. of water over the bar at the mouth of Shoreham Harbour at high water of spring tides, and about 16ft. at high water of neap tides. Barges drawing 4ft. can navigate up to Beeding Bridge and beyond on spring tides, but on neap tides only as far as the cement works at Beeding Chalk Pit on this draught.

Headroom.—Unlimited up to Norfolk Bridge, New Shoreham, above there Upper Beeding Bridge is the lowest on the navigation. It is a low single-arch bridge, and forms a great obstruction to the passage of craft.

(*g*) *Towing-path.*

There is no towing-path, navigation being only conducted on the ebb and flow of the tide.

(*h*) *Tidal Information.*

The navigation is tidal throughout.

High water at Shoreham, 2hrs 24min. before London Bridge.

Spring tides rise .. .. 18ft.
Neap ,, ,, ... 13ft. 3in.

High water at Beeding Bridge about one hour after Shoreham.

(*i*) *Types of vessels using the navigation.*

Small barges varying from about ten tons carrying capacity up to forty tons.

(2)—RIVER AIRE.

(*a*) *Short Description.*

The portion of the River Aire dealt with in this section is that part which is situated between Weeland and the mouth of the river at Asselby Island, the junction with the River Ouse, all in the West Riding of the county of Yorkshire, and being the only navigable portion of the river not under the jurisdiction of the Aire and Calder Navigation.

(2)—RIVER AIRE—*continued.*

Prior to 1826, when the Knottingley and Goole direct canal of the Aire and Calder Navigation was completed, all the main line traffic between Leeds or Wakefield and Goole passed over the River Aire between Knottingley and Asselby Island, but now there is but little navigation remaining, such as there is being merely local traffic.

(b) *Proprietors, Officers, and Offices.*

This portion of the river is an open navigation, having no controlling authority.

(c) *Distance Table.*

	Miles.	Fur.
Weeland, junction with River Aire—under jurisdiction of the Aire and Calder Navigation—(No. 3d), to—		
Snaith	3	4
Rawcliffe	7	2
Newland	8	6
Airmyn	11	0
Asselby Island, junction with River Ouse (No. 81)	12	0

(e) *Maximum size of vessels that can use the navigation.*

Length.—Not limited.

Width.—Not limited.

Draught.—There is a navigable draught of from 10ft. to 4ft. 6in. from Asselby Island to Snaith according to the tide, and above Snaith to Weeland there is an average draught of about 5ft. 6in. on the tide.

(g) *Towing-path.*

There is no towing-path, navigation being only conducted on the ebb and flow of the tide.

(h) *Tidal Information.*

This portion of the river is tidal throughout (*see* Tidal Information):— Goole, River Ouse (No. 81), and Haddlesey Old Lock, River Aire, under jurisdiction of Aire and Calder Navigation (No. 3d).

(i) *Types of vessels using the navigation.*

Yorkshire keels. Steam keels occasionally use the navigation up as far as Snaith.

---

(3)—AIRE AND CALDER NAVIGATION.

(a) *Short Description.*

The navigation consists of—the main line of the Aire and Calder Navigation (Nos. 3a1, 2, and 3), being (No. 3a1) from a junction with the Leeds and Liverpool Canal just above Victoria Bridge, Leeds, to Castleford, (No. 3a2) from Wakefield Old Wharf to Castleford, (No. 3a3)

C

(3)—AIRE AND CALDER NAVIGATION—*continued.*

from Castleford to Goole, where there is a junction through the docks
with the River Ouse ; the Barnsley Canal from a junction with the main
line at Heath Lock to Barugh Wharf near Barnsley ; the Selby Branch
from a junction with the main line at Bank Dole, Knottingley, following
the course of the River Aire to Haddlesey, and thence by canal to Selby,
where there is a junction with the River Ouse ; the continuation of the
River Aire from Haddlesey to Haddlesey Old Lock, and thence down
the tideway to Weeland, where it joins that portion of the River Aire
which is an open navigation—*see* River Aire (No. 2) ; the Dewsbury Old
Cut from a junction with the Calder and Hebble Navigation at the foot
of Double Locks to Savile Town, Dewsbury.

The whole course of the navigation is situated in the West Riding
of the county of Yorkshire.

The Undertakers of the Aire and Calder Navigation are also the
conservators of the River Ouse from a point 100 yards below Hook
Railway Bridge, near Goole, to the junction of that river with the River
Humber at Trent Falls ; joint proprietors with the Leeds and Liverpool
Canal Company of the Bradford Canal ; and joint proprietors with the
Sheffield and South Yorkshire Navigation Company of the Aire and
Calder and Sheffield and South Yorkshire Junction Canal.

(b) Proprietors, Officers, and Offices.

The Undertakers of the Aire and Calder Navigation.
Manager : Thomas Marston.
Secretary : Samuel Barraclough.
Office : Dock Street, Leeds. Telegrams : " Navigation, Leeds."
    Telephone : No. 530.
Agent : Goole, W. E. Grayburn.
Harbour Master : Goole, Captain Bowman.
The proprietors act as carriers.

(c) Distance Table.

Main Line (No. 3a1) Leeds to Castleford.

	Miles.	Fur.
Junction with Leeds and Liverpool Canal Main Line (No. 58a), and Leeds Bridge, to—		
Leeds North and South Side Wharves	–	2
Crown Point Bridge	–	4
Nether Mills Wharf	–	4
Island Stone Wharf	–	4
New Dock Basin	–	4
Fearn's Island	–	6
Varley's Ware Mill	–	6
Victoria Chemical Works	–	6
Low Fold Mill Wharf	–	6
Taylor's Forge	1	0
Whittaker's Wharf	1	0
Suspension Bridge	1	0
Airdale Chemical Works	1	0
Goodman Street Mills	1	2
Goodman Street Wharf	1	2
Hunslet Wharf	1	4

(3)—AIRE AND CALDER NAVIGATION—*continued.*

Junction with Leeds and Liverpool Canal Main
Line (No. 58a), and Leeds Bridge, to
(*continued*)—

	Miles.	Fur.
Knostrop Turn Bridge ..	1	6
Thwaite Wharf	2	0
Thwaite Forge	2	0
Waterloo Colliery ..	2	0
Leeds Sewage Works	2	2
Thwaite Mills	2	2
Thwaite Mills Wharf ..	2	2
Elmore Copper Works ..	3	0
Chemical Works (Brotherton's)	3	2
Rothwell Haigh Staiths and Wharf ..	3	2
Bullough Bridge..	4	2
Woodlesford Mills	5	2
Woodlesford Lock and Wharf..	5	2
Woodlesford Pottery ..	5	2
Swillington Bridge Wharf	5	4
Fleet Mills ..	6	4
Fleet Bridge	6	4
Savile Colliery Basin ..	7	0
Astley Cut Staiths..	7	6
Caroline Bridge Wharf ..	7	6
Kippax Lock ..	8	4
Allerton Haigh Staith (Locke & Co.)..	8	6
Allerton Wharf ..	9	0
Allerton Bywater Staiths	9	0
Castleford Junction, junction with main line (Nos. 3a2 and 3a3) ..	10	0

Main Line (No. 3a2), Wakefield Old Wharf to Castleford.

Wakefield Old Wharf to—

	Miles.	Fur.
Green's Economiser Works	–	2
Kilner's Glass Bottle Works ..	–	2
Chemical Works (Read, Holliday, & Sons) ..	–	4
Cement & Chemical Works (Brotherton&Co.)	–	4
Wakefield Old Lock ..	–	4
Fall Ing, junction with Calder and Hebble Navigation Main Line (No. 17a) ..	–	4
Wakefield Corporation Depot ..	–	6
Junction with Barnsley Canal (No. 3b)	1	0
Kirkthorpe Dam ..	2	0
Broadreach Lock	1	4
Parkhill Upper Staith ..	2	0
Parkhill Coal Staiths ..	2	0
Stanley Ferry Wharf & Basin (Victoria and Lofthouse Collieries)	2	6
Stanley Aqueduct	2	7
St. John's Colliery Basin and Wharf ..	3	0
Birkwood Lock ..	3	4
Lindley Swing Bridge ..	4	0

(3)—AIRE AND CALDER NAVIGATION—*continued*.

	Milos.	Fur.
Wakefield Old Wharf to (*continued*)—		
King's Road Lock	4	4
King's Road Wharf	4	4
Foxholes Side Lock	4	4
Low Bottom Boat (Charlesworth's)	5	0
Bottom Boat (Charlesworth's)	5	2
Foxholes (Wood's Colliery)	5	0
Nordon's Bridge	4	6
Penbank Bridge	5	0
Woodnook Lock	5	6
Altoft's Lock	5	4
Altoft's Basin	5	6
Fairies Hill Lock	6	0
Whitwood Basin (Briggs')	6	0
Popplehole Staith	6	2
Methley Bridge Wharf	7	0
Pottery Bridge	7	6
Clokie's Flint Mill	7	6
Ford Bros' Pottery	7	6
Calder Chemical Co.	7	6
Clokie's Pottery	7	6
Breffit's Bottle Works	7	6
New Staith (Schofield's)	8	0
Castleford Junction, junction with Main Line (Nos. 3a1 and 3a3)	8	0

(*Castleford Mere* bracketing Clokie's Flint Mill through New Staith (Schofield's).)

In calculating distances for rates and tolls, the Stanley Aqueduct is to be taken as equal to an extra distance of two miles.

Main Line (No. 3a3), Castleford to Goole.

	Miles.	Fur.
Castleford Junction, junction with Main Line (Nos. 3a1 and 3a2), to—		
Castleford Junction Flood Lock	–	0
Castleford A. & C. Chemical Works	–	2
Ashley Patent Bottle Co.'s Wharf	–	2
Lumb & Co.'s Bottle Works Wharf	–	2
Castleford Mill Wharf	–	4
Castleford Mills	–	4
Castleford Bridge Wharves	–	2
Castleford Wharf	–	2
Ryebread Glass Works (Breffit's)	–	4
Castleford Gas Works	–	6
Bulholme Clough Lock	–	6
Wheldale Basin	1	2
Wheldon Sand Pit	1	6
Wheldon Lime Staith	2	0
Fryston Basin	2	4
Fairburn	3	2
Brotherton Wharf	4	4
Ferrybridge Wharf	5	2
Ferrybridge Lock and Basin	5	2
West Riding Pottery	5	4
Ferrybridge Pottery	5	6

(3)—AIRE AND CALDER NAVIGATION—*continued.*

	Miles.	Fur.
Castleford Junction, junction with Main Line (Nos. 3a1 and 3a2), to (*continued*)—		
Mill Bridge Wharf	5	6
Knottingley Mills	6	0
Jackson's Bridge	6	4
Bendhill's Lime Staith	6	4
Knottingley Glass Bottle Works	6	4
Cow Lane Bridge	6	6
Shepherd's Bridge	6	6
Bank Dole Junction, junction with Selby Branch (No. 3c).	7	0
Toll Bar Bridge	7	0
Kellingley Bridge Wharf	7	6
Stubb's Bridge Wharves	8	4
Whitley Bridge Wharves	10	2
Whitley Lock	11	0
Heck Bridge Wharf	12	2
Heck Basin	12	4
No. 1 Swing Bridge (Booty Lane Bridge)	12	4
No. 2 Swing Bridge (Gibson's Bridge	13	0
Pollington Bridge Wharf	14	2
Pollington Lock	14	4
No. 3 Swing Bridge (Barker's Bridge)	14	6
Crowcroft Bridge	15	0
No. 4 Swing Bridge (Balncroft Bridge)	15	4
Southfield Wharf (Hagg Lane)	16	2
Junction with Aire and Calder and Sheffield and South Yorkshire Junction Canal (No. 4).	16	6
Beever's Bridge Wharf	17	4
Newbridge Wharf	18	4
Rawcliffe Sugar Works	20	2
Rawcliffe Bridge Wharf	20	6
Goole Waterworks Pumping Station	20	6
Rawcliffe Pulp Works	21	0
Ibbotson's Wharf	21	4
No. 5 Swing Bridge and Beverley's Wharf	22	0
Waterhouse's Wharf	22	0
No. 6 Swing Bridge (Smith's Bridge)	22	6
Dunhill's Wharf	22	6
Goole Cooperage Works	23	0
Goole Timber Pond (Dog and Duck)	23	2
Goole Tillage Works	23	2
Goole Alum Works	23	2
Goole Repair Yard	23	2
Illingworth, Ingham, & Co.'s Timber Works	23	4
Goole, Doyle Street Basin	23	4
Goole Old Timber Yard, Wharf, and Pond (Maude's)	23	4
Goole Flour Mill	23	4
Goole Sugar House Wharf	23	4
Goole Bridge	23	4
Entrance Locks to Goole Docks, and Junction with River Ouse (No. 81).	24	0

(3)—AIRE AND CALDER NAVIGATION—*continued.*

Barnsley Canal (No. 3b).

	Miles.	Fur.
Heath Lock, junction with Main Line (No. 3a2), to—		
Sandal Sewage Works	–	4
Agbrigg Bottom Lock and Wharf	–	4
Agbrigg Wharf	–	4
Oakenshaw Bridge	1	2
New Sharlston Colliery Basin	1	6
Walton Lock No. 4	1	6
,, ,, No. 6	2	0
,, ,, No. 8 (Low Town Wharf) ..	2	2
,, ,, No. 11 (Yard Lock) ..	2	4
,, ,, No. 15	2	6
Walton Hall Bridge	3	0
Clay Royd Bridge	3	6
Haw Park Wharf	4	0
Cold Hiendley Bridge Wharf	4	6
Notton Bridge and Wharf	5	4
Ryhill Main Colliery Staith	5	4
Monckton Main and Hodroyd Colliery Basin	6	2
Senior Lane Bridge	6	4
Royston Bridge Wharf..	7	0
Wharncliffe Wood Moor Colliery Staith ..	7	2
Carlton Bridge Wharf	7	6
Carlton Main Colliery Basin	8	2
Farfield Bridge	8	4
Burton Bridge Mill	9	0
Burton Bridge Wharf	9	0
Monk Bretton Colliery Staith	9	2
Day's Bridge	9	4
Littleworth Bridge	10	0
Cliffe Bridge Wharf	10	2
Junction with Dearne and Dove Canal,Sheffield and South Yorkshire Navigation (No. 91d1)	11	0
Redfearn Bros. Glass Bottle Works	11	4
Harborough Hill Bridge	11	4
Barnsley Old Mill Wharf	11	4
Barnsley Bridge Wharves	11	4
New Gawber Colliery	12	0
Smithie's Bridge Wharf	12	2
Greenfoot Bleach Works	12	6
Day House Bridge	13	4
Barugh Basin	14	0
Barugh Wharf	14	2

Selby Branch (No. 3c).

	Miles.	Fur.
Bank Dole, junction with Main Line (No. 3a3), to—		
Aire Tar Works	–	2
Robinson's Tar Works	–	2
Bank Dole Lock	–	4
Beal Bridge Wharf	2	4

(3) AIRE AND CALDER NAVIGATION—*continued.*

	Miles.	Fur.
Bank Dole, junction with Main Line (No. 3a3), to (*continued.*)—		
Beal Lock	2	6
Birkin Wharf	3	6
Commencement of Selby Canal and Haddlesey Flood Lock, junction with River Aire (No. 3d).	6	4
Haddlesey Wharf (Selby Canal)	6	4
Paper House Bridge	7	2
Gateforth Landing	7	6
Burton Bridge	8	4
Burn Bridge Wharf	9	2
Brayton Bridge Wharf	10	2
Selby Stone Bridge	11	2
Selby Stone Bridge Wharf	11	2
Selby Swing Bridge Wharf	11	4
Selby Lock and Junction with River Ouse (No. 81)	11	6

River Aire (No. 3d).

	Miles.	Fur.
Junction with Selby Branch (No. 3c), to—		
Haddlesey Old Bridge Wharf	–	2
Haddlesey Bridge Wharf	–	4
Haddlesey Old Lock	–	6
Temple Farm	2	2
Temple Hirst	4	0
Weeland, junction with River Aire (No. 2)	4	6

Dewsbury Old Cut (No. 3e).

	Miles.	Fur.
Double Locks, junction with Calder and Hebble Navigation — Main Line — (No. 17a), to—		
Dewsbury Corporation Gas Works	–	2
T. Turner & Co.'s Glass Bottle Works	–	4
J. Crowther & Sons' Coal Wharf	–	6
W. Hodgson & Sons' Timber Yard	–	6
Savile Town Wharf	1	0

(d) *Locks.*

Main Line, Leeds to Castleford (No. 3a1).

1. Leeds
2. Knostrop.
3. Thwaite.
4. Fishpond.
5. Woodlesford.
6. Lemonroyd.
7. Kippax.

Fall from Leeds.

Wakefield to Castleford (No. 3a2).

1. Wakefield Old.
2. Broadreach.
3. Birkwood.
4. Kings Road.
5. Woodnook.

Fall from Wakefield.

(3)—AIRE AND CALDER NAVIGATION—*continued.*

Castleford to Goole (No. 3a3).

1. Castleford Flood Lock.
2. Bulholme Clough.
3. Ferrybridge.
4. Whitley.
5. Pollington.
6. Goole.

Fall from Castleford.

Barnsley Canal (No. 3b).

1. Heath.
2. Agbrigg bottom.
3. Agbrigg top.
4. ⎫
to ⎬ Walton.
15. ⎭

Rise from Heath Lock.

Selby Branch (No. 3c).

1. Bank Dole.
2. Beal.
3. Haddlesey Flood Lock.
4. Selby.

Fall from Bank Dole.

River Aire (No. 3d).

1. Haddlesey Old.
Fall from junction with Selby Branch.

(e) *Maximum size of vessels that can use the navigation.*

Main Line (No. 3a1, No. 3a2. from Fall Ing, junction with Calder and Hebble Navigation to Castleford, and No. 3a3).

	Ft.	In.
Length	120	0
Width	17	0
*Draught	7	6
Headroom(Nos. 3a1 and 3a3)	12	9
,, (No. 3a2)	11	6

* For draught of water of vessels into Goole Docks, *see* River Ouse (No. 81).

Main Line (No. 3a2, from Wakefield Old Wharf to Wakefield Old Lock).

	Ft.	In.
Length	64	0
Width	14	6
Draught	6	0

Barnsley Canal (No. 3b).

	Ft.	In.
Length	78	6
Width	14	6
Draught	6	0
Headroom	10	0

Selby Branch (No. 3c).

	Ft.	In.
Length	78	6
Width	16	6
Draught	6	0
Headroom	11	0

3)—AIRE AND CALDER NAVIGATION—*continued.*

River Aire (No. 3d).

						Ft.	In.
Length	..	..	..	..	..	78	6
Width	..	..	..	..	..	16	6
Draught, average on the tide	..	..	..	5	6
Headroom	..	..	..	..	..	11	0

Dewsbury Old Cut (No. 3e).

Length	..	..	..	..	..	57	6
Width	..	..	..	..	..	14	1
Draught ..	..	..	..	..	..	5	0
Headroom	..	..	..	..	..	9	0

(g) *Towing-path.*

There is a towing-path throughout the navigation.

(h) *Tidal Information.*

The portion of the River Aire (No. 3d) from below Haddlesey Old Lock to Weeland is under the influence of the tide, the average rise and fall at the lock tail at spring tides being about 3ft., and at neap tides practically nil.

(i) *Types of vessels using the navigation.*

Aire and Calder Navigation compartment boats, Yorkshire keels, boats, &c.

Steam haulage is in use to a considerable extent on the main line for towing the trains of compartment boats.

———

(4)—AIRE AND CALDER AND SHEFFIELD AND SOUTH YORKSHIRE JUNCTION CANAL.

(a) *Short Description.*

The canal commences by a junction with the main line of the Sheffield and South Yorkshire Navigation shortly above Bramwith Lock, and runs in a north-easterly direction to a junction with the main line of the Aire and Calder Navigation near Sykehouse, all in the West Riding of the county of Yorkshire.

(b) *Proprietors, Officers, and Offices.*

The canal is the joint property of the Undertakers of the Aire and Calder Navigation and of the Sheffield and South Yorkshire Navigation Company.

Office : Dock Street, Leeds.

(4)—Aire and Calder and Sheffield and South Yorkshire Junction Canal—*continued.*

(c) *Distance Table.*

	Miles.	Fur.
Bramwith, junction with Sheffield and South Yorkshire Navigation — River Dun Navigation—(No. 91b1), to—		
Sykehouse Lock..	3	4
Junction with Aire and Calder Navigation— Main Line—(No. 3a3)	5	4

(d) *Locks.*

1. Sykehouse.

Fall from Bramwith.

(e) *Maximum size of vessels that can use the navigation.*

	Ft.	In.
Length	120	0
Width	17	6
Draught	7	6
Headroom	Not limited.	

(g) *Towing-path.*

There is a towing-path throughout the navigation.

(i) *Types of vessels using the navigation.*

Aire and Calder Navigation compartment boats and Yorkshire keels.

Steam haulage is in use for towing the trains of compartment boats.

---

(5)—River Ancholme Drainage and Navigation.

(a) *Short Description.*

The river commences to be navigable at Bishopbridge, whence it proceeds in a northerly direction past the town of Brigg to a junction with the River Humber at Ferriby Sluice, all in the county of Lincolnshire. The navigation above Harlam Hill Lock is not much used.

(b) *Proprietors, Officers, and Offices.*

The Commissioners of the River Ancholme Drainage and Navigation.

Clerk : Frank C. Hett.

Engineer : Alfred Atkinson.

Office : 11, Bigby Street, Brigg, Lincolnshire.

Toll Collector : William Robinson, 6, Market Place, Brigg.

(5)—River Ancholme Drainage and Navigation—*continued.*

(c) *Distance Table.*

	Miles.	Fur.
Bishopbridge to—		
Owersby Landing	1	4
Atterby Landing	2	0
Harlam Hill Lock	2	4
Snitterby Bridge	2	6
Brandywath	4	0
Redbourne Old River	6	2
North Kelsey Landing	6	4
Hibaldstow Bridge	6	6
Cadney Bridge	7	6
Southern junction with navigable loop line of Old River Ancholme through Brigg, 1¾ miles long	9	4
Brigg, Town and New Bridge	10	2
Northern junction, with navigable loop line of Old River Ancholme through Brigg, 1¾ miles long	10	6
Castlethorpe Bridge	11	4
Broughton Bridge	12	4
Worlaby Landing	13	4
Bonby Landing	14	6
Appleby Landing	16	0
Saxby Bridge	16	2
Scabcroft	17	2
Horkstowe Bridge	17	6
Ferriby Sluice, junction with River Humber (No. 49)	19	0

(d) *Locks.*

1. Harlam Hill. 2. Ferriby.
Fall from Bishopbridge.

(e) *Maximum size of vessels that can use the navigation.*

	Ft.	In.
Length.—Below Harlam Hill Lock	80	0
Above ,, ,, ,,	69	0
Width.— Below ,, ,, ,,	19	0
Above ,, ,, ,,	16	0
Draught.—Ferriby Sluice to Brigg	6	6
Brigg to Brandywath	6	0
Brandywath to Bishopbridge	4	0
Headroom.—Ferriby Sluice to Brigg	15	6
Brigg to Bishopbridge	10	2

(g) *Towing-path.*

There is a towing-path throughout the navigation, but it is not much used, as sailing is the principal means of propulsion used by vessels.

(i) *Types of vessels using the navigation.*

Yorkshire keels and billy-boys.

ANGLESEY BRANCH CANAL—*see* Birmingham Canal Navigations, Wyrley and Essington Canal.

ANSON BRANCH CANAL—*see* Birmingham Canal Navigations, Walsall Canal.

ANT, RIVER—*see* River Bure.

ARRAM BECK—*see* River Hull.

---

(6)—RIVER ARUN.

(a) *Short Description.*

The river commences to be navigable at Greatham Bridge near Pulborough, whence it proceeds by Amberley, Arundel, and Ford to the sea at Littlehampton, all in the county of Sussex.

There is a fair trade done up the river from Littlehampton as far as Arundel, but not much above Arundel.

In former days the Wey and Arun Junction Canal, from the River Arun at Newbridge to the River Wey a short distance above Guildford, formed a through route of inland navigation from Littlehampton to the Thames, but owing to the opening of the Mid Sussex Line of the L. B. & S. C. Railway the traffic on the canal fell off, and it was closed by Act of Parliament of 1868.

(b) *Proprietors, Officers, and Offices.*

The upper portion of the river from Greatham Bridge to Arundel Bridge is under the jurisdiction of the Commissioners of Sewers for the Rape of Arundel.

Clerk : Arthur Holmes.

Office : Maltravers Street, Arundel, Sussex.

From Arundel Bridge to the mouth of the harbour at Littlehampton the river is under the jurisdiction of the Commissioners of the Port of Arundel.

Clerk : Arthur Holmes.

Office : Maltravers Street, Arundel.

Harbour Master : Captain Sewell.

Office : Littlehampton.

(6)—River Arun—*continued.*

(c) *Distance Table.*

	Miles.	Fur.
Greatham Bridge to —		
Junction of Old Arun Navigation Canal (derelict)	—	7
Bury Wharf and Ferry..	3	1
Houghton Bridge and Amberley Station (L. B. & S. C. Rly.)	4	2
South Stoke	6	4
Offham Bridge	7	5
Arundel Bridge	9	7
L. B. & S. C. Railway Bridge, Ford (Brighton and Portsmouth Line)	12	5
Junction of Old Portsmouth and Arundel Canal (derelict)	12	6
Littlehampton Ferry	15	0
Littlehampton Harbour Mouth	15	6

(e) *Maximum size of vessels that can use the navigation.*

Length.—Not limited.

Width.—Not limited.

The length of vessels navigating between Littlehampton and Arundel should not exceed 110ft. on account of the bends in the river.

Draught.—There is about 16ft. 6in. of water over the bar at the mouth of Littlehampton Harbour at high water of Spring tides, and about 12ft. at high water of Neap tides. Vessels drawing 14ft. of water can navigate from Littlehampton to Arundel on Spring tides.

From Arundel to Houghton Bridge, Amberley, there is a draught of about 8ft. on the tide, and from Houghton Bridge, Amberley, to Greatham Bridge of about 4ft. on the tide.

(g)—*Towing-path.*

There is a towing-path from Arundel Bridge to Littlehampton Ferry only. Navigation is conducted on the ebb and flow of the tide.

(h) *Tidal Information.*

The navigation is tidal throughout.

High water at Littlehampton about 2hrs. 38mins. before London Bridge.

Spring tides rise	16ft.
Neap ,, ,, ...	11ft. 6in.

High water at Arundel 1hr. 5mins. after Littlehampton.

Spring tides rise	10ft.
Neap ,, ,, ...	7ft.

High water at Greatham Bridge about 3hrs. after Littlehampton.

(6)—RIVER ARUN—*continued.*

(i) Types of vessels using the navigation.

Sea-going vessels of between 300 and 400 tons burden can navigate up to Arundel.   Barges of 100 tons carrying capacity can navigate up to Houghton Bridge, Amberley ; and barges of from 30 to 35 tons carrying capacity can navigate up to Greatham Bridge.

ARUNDEL, COMMISSIONERS OF THE PORT OF—*see* River Arun.

ARUNDEL, COMMISSIONERS OF SEWERS FOR THE RAPE OF—*see* River Arun.

ASHBY CANAL—*see* Midland Railway.

ASHTON CANAL—*see* Great Central Railway.

———

(7)—RIVER AVON (Bristol).

(a) Short Description.

The portion of the River Avon dealt with in this section is that part which is under the jurisdiction of the Corporation of the City of Bristol, and which extends from the tail of Hanham Lock through the City of Bristol to the Estuary of the River Severn at Avonmouth, forming throughout the boundary between the counties of Gloucestershire and Somersetshire.

(b) Proprietors, Officers, and Offices.

The Docks Committee of the Corporation of the City of Bristol.

Secretary and General Manager : F. B. Girdlestone.

Office : Queen Square, Bristol.   Telegrams : " Girdlestone," Bristol.

Engineer : W. W. Squire.

Office : Underfall Yard, Cumberland Basin, Bristol.

Telegrams : " Docks Engineer, Bristol."   Telephone No. 129.

Harbour Master : Captain J. Turner.

(c) Distance Table.

	Miles.	Fur.
Tail of Hanham Lock, junction with Kennet and Avon Navigation (No. 43a), to—		
Hanham Colliery Wharf	—	4
Conham	2	0
Netham Lock	4	0
Bristol, Marsh Bridge, junction with Bristol Floating Harbour through Marsh Bridge Lock	5	1

(7)—RIVER AVON (Bristol)—*continued.*

Tail of Hanham Lock, junction with Kennett and Avon Navigation (No. 43), to (*continued.*)—

	Miles.	Fur.
Bristol, Totterdown Lock	5	2
Bristol Bridge	5	6
Bristol, Bathurst Basin, junction with Bristol Floating Harbour through Bathurst Basin Lock	6	2
Bristol, Cumberland Basin, junction with Bristol Floating Harbour through Cumberland Basin Lock	7	5
Clifton Suspension Bridge	8	0
Pill	12	2
Avonmouth, junction with Avonmouth Docks and Estuary of River Severn (No. 89a) ..	14	2

(d) Locks.

1. Netham.   2. Totterdown.

Fall from Hanham.

(e) Maximum size of vessels that can use the navigation.

Maximum size of vessels that can navigate up to Bristol Floating Harbour through Cumberland Basin :—

	Ft.	In.
Length	320	0
Width	58	0
Draught—Up to Cumberland Basin, on Spring tides, about	32	0
„ Up to Cumberland Basin, on Neap tides, about	22	0

„ Vessels drawing over 22ft. on entering Cumberland Basin must lighten to that extent before entering the Floating Harbour

Headroom—Practically unlimited ; Clifton Bridge 240ft. above river.

Maximum sizes of barges that can navigate up to the tail of Hanham Lock :—

	Ft.	In.
Length	102	0
Width	18	0
Draught	6	6
Headroom	8	0

(g) Towing path.

There is a towing-path from Hanham Lock to Marsh Bridge, Bristol.

(7)—RIVER AVON (Bristol)—*continued.*

(h) *Tidal Information.*

This portion of the river is tidal throughout.

High water at Avonmouth Docks about 5hrs. after London Bridge.

Spring tides rise	36ft. 6in.
Neap „ „	25ft.

High water at Cumberland Basin, Bristol, about 15mins. after Avonmouth.

Spring tides rise	31ft. 6in.
Neap „ „	20ft.

High water at Hanham about 1hr. after Avonmouth.

Spring tides rise	4ft.
Neap „ „	1ft.

The tidal wave or " bore " is encountered in the river below Bristol at Spring tides—*see* Section 8, Tides.

(i) *Types of vessels using the navigation.*

Sea-going vessels navigate up to Bathurst Basin, Bristol.

Barges and narrow boats navigate up to Hanham Lock.

AVON RIVER (Bristol), portion included in Kennet and Avon Navigation —*see* Great Western Railway.

---

(8)—RIVER AVON (WARWICKSHIRE) LOWER NAVIGATION.

(a) *Short Description.*

The navigation commences at Evesham and proceeds by Fladbury and Pershore to Tewkesbury, where it forms a junction with the River Severn.

The whole course of the navigation is in the county of Worcestershire excepting a small portion which forms the boundary between that county and the county of Gloucestershire.

There is very little trade done on the river at the present time.

The Upper Avon Navigation from Evesham to Stratford-on-Avon fell into decay, and ceased to be navigable about the year 1873.

(b) *Proprietors, Officers, and Offices.*

The Trustees of the late Edmund Thomas Perrott, Esq., being :—
A. R. Hudson, Esq., Pershore, and A. W. Byrch, Esq., Evesham.

Manager : W. A. Salsbury.

Office : Bridge Street, Pershore.

(8)—RIVER AVON (WARWICKSHIRE) LOWER NAVIGATION—*continued.*

(c) *Distance Table.*

Evesham to—					Miles.	Fur.
Chadbury Lock ..	..	..	..	..	3	0
Fladbury Lock ..	..	..	..	..	5	4
Fladbury Weir ..	..	..	..	..	6	0
Wyre Lock	..	..	..	..	12	0
Pershore Lock ..	..	..	..	..	13	0
Pershore Weir ..	..	..	..	..	13	4
Nafford Lock ..	..	..	..	..	18	2
Eckington Bridge	..	..	..	..	19	6
Strensham Lock	..	..	..	..	22	2
Bredon ..	..	..	..	..	24	4
Tewkesbury Lock	..	..	..	..	28	0
Tewkesbury, junction with River Severn—						
Main line—(No. 89a).	..	..	..	28	2

(d) *Locks.*

1. Chadbury.
2. Fladbury.
3. Fladbury Weir (Navigation Weir.)
4. Wyre.
5. Pershore.

6. Pershore Weir (Navigation Weir.)
7. Nafford.
8. Strensham.
9. Tewkesbury.

Fall from Evesham.

(e) *Maximum size of vessels that can use the navigation.*

					Ft.	In.
Length ..	..	..	..	..	70	0
Width ..	..	..	..	..	14	6
Draught : Tewkesbury to Fladbury, about ..					4	6
„ Fladbury to Evesham, about		..			3	6 to 4ft.
Headroom ..	..	..	..	..	8	0

(g) *Towing-path.*

There is no towing-path on any part of the navigation.

(i) *Types of vessels using the navigation.*

Narrow boats and trows. One steamer habitually trades to Evesham Mill with grain.

AYLESBURY BRANCH CANAL—*see* Grand Junction Canal.

AYLSHAM NAVIGATION—*see* River Bure.

BARKING CREEK—*see* River Thames.

BARNES' DIKE—*see* River Yare

BARNSLEY CANAL—*see* Aire and Calder Navigation

D

BASINGSTOKE CANAL, or LONDON AND HAMPSHIRE CANAL (old names for the Woking, Aldershot, and Basingstoke Canal).

BEDFORD, DUKE OF—*see* Thorney River.

BEDFORD LEVEL CORPORATION, THE, are the controlling authority in respect of that portion of the River Ouse (Bedford) known as the Hundred Foot, or New Bedford River, the sluice or lock known as Hermitage Sluice, situated at the commencement of the Old West River, River Ouse (Bedford) at Earith, are the owners of the site of Denver Sluice, the appointers of the Sluice Keeper, and were the original builders of the Sluice, and maintain (jointly with the South Level Drainage and Navigation Commissioners) the sluice or lock at the entrance to Reach Lode.

BEESTON CUT—*see* River Trent.

BENTLEY Canal—*see* Birmingham Canal Navigations.

BERKELEY SHIP CANAL—*see* Sharpness New Docks and Gloucester and Birmingham Navigation Company, Gloucester and Berkeley Ship Canal.

BETHELL, WILLIAM, ESQ.—*see* Leven Canal.

———

(9)—BEVERLEY BECK.

(a) Short Description.

The beck commences in the town of Beverley, and runs in an easterly direction for a distance of six furlongs to a junction with the River Hull—Main Line—(No. 48a) at Grove Hill, all in the East Riding of the county of Yorkshire.

There is a good trade on the navigation.

(b) Proprietors, Officers, and Offices.

The Corporation of the Town of Beverley.

Town Clerk : James Mills.

Office : Lairgate, Beverley.

Collector of Dues : R. Needham, Beck Side, Beverley.

(d) Locks.

1. Grove Hill.

Fall to River Hull.

(9)—BEVERLEY BECK—*continued.*

(e) *Maximum size of vessels that can use the navigation.*

						Ft.	In.
Length	..	..	..	..	..	65	0
Width	..	..	..	..	..	17	6
Draught	..	..	..	..	..	7	0

(g) *Towing-path.*

There is a towing-path throughout the navigation.

(i) *Types of vessels using the navigation.*

Yorkshire Keels.

BEVERLEY, CORPORATION OF THE TOWN OF—*see* Beverley Beck.

BEVILS LEAM—*see* Middle Level Navigations.

BILSTON BRANCH CANAL—*see* Birmingham Canal Navigations—Walsall Canal.

---

(10)—BIRMINGHAM CANAL NAVIGATIONS.

(a) *Short Description.*

The Birmingham Canal Navigations comprise a large system of canals, with numerous branches situated in South Staffordshire, East Worcestershire, and North Warwickshire, having a total mileage of 159 miles. The principal places served are :—Birmingham, Smethwick, Oldbury, Dudley, Brierley Hill, Tipton, Wednesbury, Wolverhampton, Wednesfield, Walsall, Bilston, Darlaston,' Lichfield, Cannock, and Fazeley. The system is a very complicated one, owing to many improvements and fresh canals which have been added to it from time to time.

The old main line from Birmingham to Aldersley Junction was originally 22 miles in length. Its deviations from the course of the present main line included the Icknield Port Road Wharf Loop Line, the Soho Branch Loop Line, the Old Main Loop Line from Smethwick Junction to Tipton Factory Junction, and the Wednesbury Oak Loop Line. A large portion of the district is subject to subsidences due to coal mining operations, which cause the maintainance of the canals to be very difficult and expensive.

A portion of the Dudley Canal—Line No. 2 (No. 10f2)—between Parkhead Junction and Blackbrook Junction has been closed since March, 1898, owing to heavy subsidences.

The Bilston and Willenhall short branches leading out of the Walsall Canal (No. 10k1) between Moxley Stop and Bug Hole Wharf are also closed, as well as a portion of the Spon Lane Branch of the Titford Canal (No. 10c4).

(10)—BIRMINGHAM CANAL NAVIGATIONS—*continued*.

The Wolverhampton level extends from Smethwick Top Lock to Wolverhampton, Birchills, and Ogley Top Lock, and includes the portion of the Dudley Canal from Tipton to Parkhead, the Wednesbury Oak Loop Line, Lord Hay's Branch, the Cannock Extension, and the Daw End and Anglesey Branches.

The Birmingham level extends from Paradise Street, Birmingham, to Tipton Factory Bottom Lock, and includes the Netherton Tunnel Branch Canal, and the portion of the Dudley Canal between Parkhead Bottom Lock and Selly Oak, and the Wednesbury Old Canal and branches.

The Walsall level extends from the bottom of Riders Green Locks to Walsall Junction, and includes the Anson Branch, and also the Tame Valley Canal to the top of Perry Barr Locks.

By Act of Parliament, the Birmingham Canal Company passed in 1846 under the control of the London and North Western Railway Company, the latter guaranteeing to the Canal Company a minimum dividend of four per cent on their capital.

(b) *Proprietors, Officers, and Offices.*

The Company of Proprietors of the Birmingham Canal Navigations.

Clerk : William Hutton.

Assistant Clerk : Charles Watkins.

Chief Office : Paradise Street, Birmingham.

Engineer : George R. Jebb.

Assistant Engineer : C. H. Nias.

Office : Paradise Street, Birmingham.

Assistant Mechanical Engineer : C. W. Robinson.

Office : Ocker Hill Works, Tipton.

(c) *Distance Table.*

Main Line (No. 10a1).

	Miles.	Fur.
Birmingham, Paradise Street, to—		
Worcester Bar, junction with Worcester and Birmingham Canal (No. 90b)	–	1
Farmer's Bridge, junction with Birmingham and Fazeley Canal (No. 10p1)	–	4
Junction with Oozells Street Branch (No. 10a2)	–	7
Eastern junction with Icknield Port Road Wharf Loop Line (No. 10a3)	1	0
Western junction with Icknield Port Road Wharf Loop Line (No. 10a3)—left, and eastern junction with Soho Branch Loop Line (No. 10a4)—right	1	1

(10)—BIRMINGHAM CANAL NAVIGATIONS—*continued.*

	Miles.	Fur.
Birmingham, Paradise Street, to (*continued*)—		
Winson Green Railway Station L. & N. W. Rly.	1	5
Western Junction with Soho Branch Loop Line (No. 10a4)	1	7
Smethwick Junction, junction with Old Main Loop Line from Smethwick Junction to Tipton Factory Junction (No. 10c1) ..	2	7
Bromford Junction, junction with Spon Lane Locks Branch (No. 10c3)—right, and junction with Parker Branch (No. 10a5)— left	4	7
Pudding Green Junction, junction with Wednesbury Old Canal (No. 10j1)	5	5
Albion Junction, junction with Gower Branch (No. 10d)	6	1½
Dunkirk Junction, junction with Dunkirk Branch (No. 10a6)	6	2
Dudley Port Junction, junction with Netherton Tunnel Branch Canal (No. 10e)	6	6
Junction with Dixon's Branch (No. 10a7) ..	7	3
Watery Lane Junction, junction with Tipton Green and Toll End Communication (No. 10i)—right and left	7	7
Tipton Factory Junction, junction with Old Main Loop Line from Smethwick Junction to Tipton Factory Junction (No. 10c1), and top of Tipton Factory Locks.. ..	8	3
Bloomfield Junction, southern junction with Wednesbury Oak Loop Line (No. 10b1) ..	8	5½
Coseley Tunnel, south end	9	1
Deepfields Junction, northern junction with Wednesbury Oak Loop Line (No. 10b1) ..	10	0
Parkfields Basins	10	6
Rough Hills	12	0
Horseley Fields Junction, junction with Wyrley and Essington Canal (No. 10q1)..	13	0
Wolverhampton, Albion Wharf, Fellows, Morton, & Clayton Ltd.—Canal Carriers	13	2½
Wolverhampton, top of 21 locks	13	4
Aldersley Junction, junction with Staffordshire and Worcestershire Canal—Main Line—(No. 95a), and bottom of 21 locks..	15	1

Oozells Street Branch (No. 10a2).

Junction with Main Line (No. 10a1) to—		
Oozells Street Wharf	–	2

Icknield Port Road Wharf Loop Line (No. 10a3).

	Miles.	Fur.
Eastern Junction with Main Line (No. 10a1) to—		
Icknield Port Road Wharf	–	3
Western Junction with Main Line (No. 10a1)..	–	6

(10)—BIRMINGHAM CANAL NAVIGATIONS—*continued.*

Soho Branch Loop Line (No. 10a4).

	Miles.	Fur.
Eastern Junction with Main Line (No. 10a1) to—		
Junction with Soho Branch, ¼ mile long to Soho Wharf..	–	5
Winson Green Wharf	–	7
Western Junction with Main Line (No. 10a1)..	1	2

Parker Branch (No. 10a5).

Length from junction with Main Line (No.10a1)	–	2

Dunkirk Branch (No. 10a6).

Length from junction with Main Line (No. 10a1)	–	2

Dixons Branch (No. 10a7).

Length from junction with Main Line (No. 10a1)	–	6

Wednesbury Oak Loop Line (No. 10b1).

Bloomfield Junction, southern junction with Main Line (No. 10a1), to—		
Junction with Ocker Hill Branch Canal (No. 10b2)	1	2
Wednesbury Oak	1	6
Bradley Locks Junction, junction with Bradley Branch Canal (No. 10h)	2	0
Pothouse Bridge Wharf	3	0
Capponfield	3	3
Deepfields Junction, northern junction with Main Line (No. 10a1)	4	2

Ocker Hill Branch (No. 10b2).

Junction with Wednesbury Oak Loop Line (No. 10b1) to—		
Ocker Hill, Birmingham Canal Co.'s workshops and pumping station	–	5

Old Main Loop Line from Smethwick Junction to Tipton Factory Junction (No. 10c1).

	Miles.	Fur.
Smethwick Junction, junction with Main Line (No. 10a1), to—		
Junction with Engine Branch, Smethwick (No. 10c2), and top of Smethwick Locks..	–	4
Spon Lane Wharf and Junction, junction with Spon Lane Locks Branch (No. 10c3) ..	1	4
Oldbury Locks Junction, junction with Titford Canal (No. 10c4)	2	4

(10)—Birmingham Canal Navigations—*continued.*

	Miles.	Fur.
Smethwick Junction, junction with Main Line (No. 10a1), to (*continued*)—		
Junction with Houghton Branch Canal (No.47)	2	5
Southern junction with Oldbury Loop Line (No. 10c5)	2	6
Northern junction with Oldbury Loop Line (No. 10c5)	3	1½
Brades Hall Junction, junction with Gower Branch (No. 10d)	3	5½
Aqueduct over Netherton Tunnel Branch Canal	4	3
Fellows, Morton, & Clayton Ltd.—Canal Carriers—Dudley Port Wharf and Warehouse (Dudley, distant 1½ miles)	4	7
Tipton Junction, junction with Dudley Canal (No. 10f1)	5	4½
Tipton Green Junction, junction with Tipton Green and Toll End Communication (No. 10i)	5	6
Tipton Factory Junction, junction with Main Line (No. 10a1)	6	0

Engine Branch, Smethwick, (No. 10c2).

	Miles.	Fur.
Length from junction with Old Main Loop Line (No. 10c1)	–	5

Spon Lane Locks Branch (No. 10c3).

	Miles.	Fur.
Spon Lane Junction, junction with Old Main Loop Line (No. 10c1), to—		
Top of Spon Lane Locks	–	1
Bromford Junction, junction with Main Line (No. 10a1)	–	3

Titford Canal (No. 10c4).

	Miles.	Fur.
Oldbury Locks Junction, junction with Old Main Loop Line (No. 10c1), to—		
Top of Oldbury Locks, and junction with Spon Lane Branch, one furlong in length, rest abandoned	–	3
Langley Green Wharf	1	1
Junction with Portway Branch, 6 furlongs in length, to Birchy Field Wharf and Portway	1	2
Titford Pool Wharf	1	3½
Causeway Green	1	6

Oldbury Loop Line (No. 10c5).

The old course of the Canal round Oldbury.

	Miles.	Fur.
Southern junction with Old Main Loop Line (No. 10c1) to—		
Northern junction with Old Main Loop Line (No. 10c1)	1	0

(10)—BIRMINGHAM CANAL NAVIGATIONS—*continued*.

	Miles.	Fur.
Gower Branch Canal (No. 10d).		
Brades Hall Junction, junction with Old Main Line (No. 10c1), to—		
Bottom of Brades Hall Locks	–	2
Albion Junction, junction with Main Line (No. 10a1)	–	4
Netherton Tunnel Branch Canal (No. 10e).		
Dudley Port Junction, junction with Main Line (No. 10a1), to—		
North End of Netherton Tunnel	–	4
Windmill End Junction, junction with Dudley Canal (No. 10f2)	2	7
Dudley Canal—Line No. 1 (No. 10f1).		
Tipton Junction, junction with Old Main Loop Line (No. 10c1), to—		
North End of Dudley Tunnel	–	3
Junction with Pensnett Canal (No. 85), and top of Parkhead Locks	2	1
Parkhead Junction, junction with Dudley Canal—Line No. 2 (No. 10f2)—bottom of Parkhead Locks and top of Blowers Green Lock..	2	3
Woodside Junction, junction with Two Lock Line Canal (No. 10g)	3	1
Brierley Hill, top of Delph Locks	4	1
Black Delph Wharf, bottom of Delph Locks, and junction with Stourbridge Canal—Main Line—(No. 99a)	4	4
Dudley Canal Line No. 2 (No. 10f2).		
Parkhead Junction, junction with Dudley Canal—Line No. 1 (No. 10f1), to—		
Blackbrook Junction, junction with Two Lock Line Canal (No. 10g)	–	6
Primrose Hill Wharf	1	5
Junction with Withymoor Branch Canal (No. 10f3)	2	1
Southern junction with Bumble Hole Branch Canal (No. 10f4)	2	3
Windmill End Junction, junction with Netherton Tunnel Branch Canal (No. 10e), and northern junction with Bumble Hole Branch Canal (No. 10f4)	2	5
Rowley Wharf	4	0
Waterfall Lane Wharf	4	1
Old Hill and northern end of Gosty Hill Tunnel	4	3
Haywood Wharf, Halesowen	5	5
Lappal Wharf, and west end of Lappal Tunnel	7	0
Harbourne Wharf	10	4
Selly Oak, junction with Worcester and Birmingham Canal (No. 90b)	10	6

(10)—Birmingham Canal Navigations—*continued.*

Withymoor Branch Canal (No. 10f3).

	Miles.	Fur.
Length from junction with Dudley Canal—Line No. 2 (No. 10f2)	–	2

Bumble Hole Branch Canal (No. 10f4).

A loop line, 4 furlongs in length, from southern junction to northern junction with Dudley Canal—Line No. 2 (No. 10f2)—at Windmill End.

Two Lock Line Canal (No. 10g).

	Miles.	Fur.
Woodside Junction, junction with Dudley Canal—Line No. 1 (No. 10f1), to— Blackbrook Junction, junction with Dudley Canal—Line No 2 (No. 10f2)	–	3

Bradley Branch Canal (No. 10h).

	Miles.	Fur.
Bradley Locks Junction, junction with Wednesbury Oak Loop Line (No. 10b1), and top of Bradley Locks, to— Moorcroft Junction, junction with Walsall Canal (No. 10k1)	–	7

Tipton Green and Toll End Communication (No. 10i).

	Miles.	Fur.
Tipton Green Junction, junction with Old Main Loop Line (No. 10c1), to— Watery Lane Junction, junction with Main Line (No. 10a1)—right and left, and bottom of Tipton Green Locks	–	3
Toll End Wharf, and bottom of Toll End Locks	1	2
Toll End Junction, junction with Walsall Canal (No. 10k1)	1	4

Wednesbury Old Canal (No. 10j1).

	Miles.	Fur.
Pudding Green Junction, junction with Main Line (No. 10a1), to— Riders Green Junction, junction with Walsall Canal (No. 10k1)	–	5
Junction with Ridgacre Branch Canal (No. 10j2)	1	2
Golds Green	2	2
Termination of Canal	2	5

Ridgacre Branch Canal (No. 10j2).

	Miles.	Fur.
Junction with Wednesbury Old Canal (No. 10j1) to— Junction with Dartmouth Branch Canal (No. 10j3)	–	$4\frac{1}{2}$
Junction with Halford Branch Canal (No.10j4)	–	$5\frac{1}{2}$
Termination of Canal	–	6

(10)—Birmingham Canal Navigations—*continued.*

Dartmouth Branch Canal (No. 10j3).

	Miles.	Fur.
Length from junction with Ridgacre Branch Canal (No. 10j2) to—		
Termination near Balls Hill	–	5

Halford Branch Canal (No. 10j4).

Length from junction with Ridgacre Branch Canal (No. 10j2)	–	4

Walsall Canal (No. 10k1).

	Miles	Fur
Riders Green Junction, junction with Wednesbury Old Canal (No. 10j1), and top of Riders Green Locks, to—		
Great Bridge, junction with Haines Branch (No. 10k2), and bottom of Riders Green Locks	–	6
Junction with Danks Branch (No. 10k3) ..	1	0
Toll End Junction, junction with Tipton Green and Toll End Communication (No. 10i) ..	1	1
Junction with Lower Ocker Hill Branch (No. 10k4)	1	2
Junction with Tame Valley Canal (No. 10n) ..	1	3
Junction with Gospel Oak Branch (No. 10k5)..	2	$0\frac{1}{2}$
Junction with Monway Branch (No. 10k6) ..	2	$1\frac{1}{2}$
Moorcroft Junction, junction with Bradley Branch Canal (No. 10h)	2	3
Moxley Stop	3	0
Bug Hole Wharf	4	2
Darlaston Green Wharf	4	6
Junction with Anson Branch (No. 10k7) ..	5	1
Walsall Junction, junction with Walsall Branch Canal (No. 10 l)	6	7
Walsall Public Wharf	7	0

Haines Branch Canal (No. 10k2).

Length from junction with Walsall Canal (No. 10k1) to termination of canal near Dudley Port.	–	5

Danks Branch Canal (No. 10k3).

Length from junction with Walsall Canal (No. 10k1) to junction with Tame Valley (No. 10n)	–	5

Lower Ocker Hill Branch Canal (No. 10k4).

Length from junction with Walsall Canal (No. 10k1)	-	1

(10)—Birmingham Canal Navigations—*continued.*

Gospel Oak Branch Canal (No. 10k5).

	Mile	Fur.
Length from junction with Walsall Canal (No. 10k1) to—		
Lea Brook Wharf, Gospel Oak	–	4

Monway Branch Canal (No. 10k6).

Length from junction with Walsall Canal (No. 10k1) to near Wednesbury	–	3

Anson Branch Canal (No. 10k7).

Junction with Walsall Canal (No. 10k1), to—		
Junction with Bentley Canal (No. 10m1)	–	1
Termination of Canal at Reed's Wood, near Bentley	1	3

Walsall Branch Canal (No. 10l).

Birchills Junction, junction with Wyrley and Essington Canal (No. 10q1), to—		
Birchills Wharf, and top of Walsall Locks ..	–	2
Walsall Junction, junction with Walsall Canal (No. 10k1), and bottom of Walsall Locks	–	7

Bentley Canal (No. 10m1)

Wednesfield Junction, junction with Wyrley, and Essington Canal (No. 10q1), to—		
Junction with Nechells Branch Canal (No. 10m2), and bottom of Bentley Locks 1st flight	–	6
Monmore Green Wharf	1	3
Spring Bank Wharf	1	7
Short Heath, and bottom of Bentley Locks 2nd flight	2	2
Junction with Anson Branch Canal (No. 10k7)	3	3

Nechells Branch Canal (No. 10m2).

Length from junction with Bentley Canal (No. 10m1)	–	3

Tame Valley Canal (No. 10n).

Junction with Walsall Canal (No. 10k1) to—		
Junction with Danks Branch Canal (No. 10k3)	–	2
Golds Hill Wharf	–	3
Holloway Bank Wharf	1	0
Newton Junction, junction with Rushall Canal (No. 10o)	3	4
Hamstead Wharf	4	3

(10)—BIRMINGHAM CANAL NAVIGATIONS—*continued.*

	Miles.	Fur.
Junction with Walsall Canal (No. 10k1), to (*continued*)—		
Barr Top Lock Wharf, and top of Perry Barr Locks 1st flight	5	4
Perry Barr Wharf	6	4
Witton Stop, and top of Perry Barr Locks 3rd flight	7	7
Salford Junction, junction with Birmingham and Fazeley Canal (No. 10p1), right and left, and junction with Birmingham and Warwick Junction Canal (No. 11).. ..	8	4

Rushall Canal (No. 10o).

	Miles.	Fur.
Longwood Junction, junction with Daw End Branch of Wyrley and Essington Canal (No. 10q4), and top of Rushall Locks, to—		
Bell Wharf	1	4
Newton Junction, junction with Tame Valley Canal (No. 10n)	2	6

Birmingham and Fazeley Canal (No. 10p1).

	Miles.	Fur.
Farmers Bridge, junction with Main Line (No. 10a1), to—		
Junction with Newhall Branch Canal (No. 10p2), and top of Farmers Bridge Locks..	–	1
Aston Junction, junction with Digbeth Branch (No. 10p3), and top of Aston Locks ..	1	4
Bloomsbury Wharf	2	2
Salford Junction, junction with Birmingham and Warwick Junction Canal (No. 11)— right, and junction with Tame Valley Canal (No. 10n)—left	3	2
Erdington Wharf	5	1
Minworth Stop, and top of Minworth Locks ..	6	2
Minworth Wharf..	7	3
Griffiths Dock Wharf	7	6
Dunton Wharf, between 1st and 2nd Locks, Curdworth	9	4
Bodymoor Heath Wharf	11	3
Curdworth Stop, bottom of Curdworth Locks	12	1
Fazeley Junction, junction with Coventry Canal (No. 24)	15	0
Hopwas	17	6
Whittington Brook, junction with Coventry Canal—detached portion (No. 24) ..	20	4

Newhall Branch (No. 10p2).

	Miles.	Fur.
Length from junction with Birmingham and Fazeley Canal (No. 10p1)	–	2

(10)—Birmingham Canal Navigations—*continued.*

Digbeth Branch Canal (No. 10p3).

	Miles.	Fur.
Aston Junction, junction with Birmingham and Fazeley Canal (No. 10p1), to—		
Junction with Warwick and Birmingham Canal (No. 115)	–	6
Bordesley Basin	–	7

Wyrley and Essington Canal (No. 10q1).

	Miles.	Fur.
Horseley Fields Junction, junction with Main Line (No. 10a1), to—		
Heath Town Wharf	–	7
Wednesfield Junction, junction with Bentley Canal (No. 10m1)	1	2
Wednesfield Wharf	1	6
Devil's Elbow Wharf	2	5
Olinthus Wharf	3	1
Short Heath Wharf	4	7
Sneyd Junction, junction with Sneyd and Wyrley Bank Branch Canal (No. 10q2)	6	2
Birchills Junction, junction with Walsall Branch Canal (No. 10 l)	8	0
Harding's Wharf	9	2
Goscote Wharf	10	3
Teece's Bridge Wharf	11	2
Junction with Lord Hay's Branch Canal (No. 10q3), near Little Bloxwich	11	7
Pelsall Junction, junction with Cannock Extension Canal (No. 10r)	12	7
Highbridge Wharf	14	1
Catshill Junction, junction with Daw End Branch Canal (No. 10q4)	15	3
Junction with Anglesey Branch (No. 10q5), and top of Ogley Locks	16	3
Redcap Wharf	18	0
Danks Wharf	18	4
Pipe Hill Wharf	19	0
Lichfield Basin Wharf	21	1
Twenty-fourth Lock Wharf	21	5
Paper Mill Wharf	22	2
Huddlesford Junction, junction with Coventry Canal—detached portion (No. 24)	23	4

Sneyd and Wyrley Bank Branch Canal (No. 10q2).

	Miles.	Fur.
Sneyd Junction, junction with Wyrley and Essington Canal (No. 10q1), to—		
Junction with Old Essington Locks line of canal, now abandoned	–	7
Broad Lane Wharf	1	2
Landywood Wharf	2	6
Wyrley Wharf	3	4

(10)—BIRMINGHAM CANAL NAVIGATIONS—*continued.*

Lord Hay's Branch Canal (No. 10q3).

	Miles.	Fur.
Length from junction with Wyrley and Essington Canal (No. 10q1) to—		
Newtown Wharf..	–	7

Daw End Branch Canal (No. 10q4).

	Miles.	Fur.
Catshill Junction, junction with Wyrley and Essington Canal (No. 10q1), to—		
Clayhanger Wharf	–	1
Black Cock Wharf	–	6
Aldridge Wharf	2	4
Daw End Wharf	4	0
Longwood Junction and Wharf, junction with Rushall Canal (No. 10o)	5	2

Anglesey Branch Canal (No. 10q5).

	Miles.	Fur.
Junction with Wyrley and Essington Canal (No. 10q1) to—		
Burntwood Road Wharf	1	1
Anglesey Wharf, and eastern end of Cannock Chase Reservoir	1	4

Cannock Extension Canal (No. 10r).

	Miles.	Fur.
Pelsall Junction, junction with Wyrley and Essington Canal (No. 10q1), to—		
Wyrley Grove Wharf	–	5
Norton Common Wharf	1	5
Norton Basin	2	0
Norton Green Wharf	2	5
Silvester Wharf	3	2
Rumour Hill Junction, junction with Churchbridge Branch Canal (No. 10s)	4	1
Leacroft Wharf	4	5
Hednesford Basins	5	6

Churchbridge Branch Canal (No. 10s).

	Miles.	Fur.
Rumour Hill Junction, junction with Cannock Extension Canal (No. 10r), and top of Churchbridge Locks, to—		
Churchbridge Junction, junction with Hatherton Branch Canal of Staffordshire and Worcestershire Canal (No. 95c), Churchbridge Wharf, and bottom of Churchbridge Locks	–	5

(10)—BIRMINGHAM CANAL NAVIGATIONS—*continued.*

(d) Locks.

Main Line (No. 10a1).

1
to } Tipton Factory.
3.

Rise from Birmingham.

4
to } Wolverhampton.
24.

Fall from Birmingham.

Old Main Loop Line from Smethwick Junction to Tipton Factory Junction (No. 10c1).

1
to } Smethwick.
3.

Rise from Smethwick Junction.

Spon Lane Locks Branch (No. 10c3).

1
to } Spon Lane.
3.

Fall from Spon Lane Junction.

Titford Canal (No. 10c4).

1
to } Oldbury.
6.

Rise from Oldbury Locks Junction.

Gower Branch (No. 10d).

1
to } Brades Hall.
3.

Fall from Brades Hall Junction.

Dudley Canal—Line No. 1 (No. 10f1).

1
to } Parkhead.
3.
4.—Blowers Green.
5
to } Delph.
12.

Fall from Tipton.

Two Lock Line Canal (No. 10g).

Two Locks.
Rise from Woodside Junction to Blackbrook Junction.

(10)—Birmingham Canal Navigations—*continued.*

Bradley Canal (No. 10h).

1
to } Bradley.
9.

Fall from Bradley Locks Junction.

Tipton Green and Toll End Communication (No. 10i).

1
to } Tipton Green.
3.

4
to } Toll End.
10.

Fall from Tipton Green Junction.

Walsall Canal (No. 10k1).

1
to } Riders Green.
8.

Fall from Riders Green Junction.

Walsall Branch Canal (No. 10l).

1
to } Walsall.
8.

Fall from Birchills Junction.

Bentley Canal (No. 10m1).

1
to } Bentley 1st flight.
6.

7
to } Bentley 2nd flight.
10.

Fall from Wednesfield Junction.

Tame Valley Canal (No. 10n).

1
to } Perry Barr 1st flight.
7.

8
to } Perry Barr 2nd flight.
11.

12
and } Perry Barr 3rd flight.
13.

Fall from junction with Walsall Canal.

Rushall Canal (No. 10o).

1
and } Rushall 1st flight.
2.

3
to } Rushall 2nd flight.
9.

Fall from Longwood Junction.

(10)—BIRMINGHAM CANAL NAVIGATIONS—*continued.*

Birmingham and Fazeley Canal (No. 10p1).

1 to 13. } Farmers Bridge.

14 to 24. } Aston.

25 to 27. } Minworth.

28 to 38. } Curdworth.

Fall from Farmers Bridge.

Digbeth Branch Canal (No. 10p3).

1 to 6. } Ashted.

Fall from Aston Junction.

Wyrley and Essington Canal (No. 10q1).

1 to 8. } Ogley 1st flight.

9 to 12. } Ogley 2nd flight.

13 to 18. } Ogley 3rd flight.

19.—Ogley 4th flight.

20 to 23. } Ogley 5th flight.

24 to 28. } Ogley 6th flight.

29 and 30. } Ogley 7th flight.

Fall from Horseley Fields Junction.

Sneyd and Wyrley Bank Branch Canal (No. 10q2).

1 to 5. } Sneyd.

Rise from Sneyd Junction.

Churchbridge Branch Canal (No. 10s).

1 to 13. } Churchbridge.

Fall from Rumour Hill Junction.

E

(10)--BIRMINGHAM CANAL NAVIGATIONS—*continued.*

(e) *Maximum size of vessels that can use the navigation.*

						Ft.	In.
Length	..	..	..	..	..	71	6
Width	..	..	..	..	..	7	1½
Draught	..	..	..	..	..	3	6

Headroom.—The standard headroom is 8ft. 6in., but this is subject
by temporary reduction to 6ft. 6in. in consequence of subsidences due to mining operations. The lowest headroom is
that through Dudley Tunnel, which is 5ft. 9in.

(f) *Tunnels.*

Main Line (No. 10a1).

Coseley—

				Ft.	In.
Length	..	..	360 yards		
Minimum height above water level ..	..	..		15	3
Minimum width at water level	..	..		15	9
Minimum width at water level, including both towing-paths..	..	..	..	24	9

Towing-path both sides;   boats enter from either end at any time.

Netherton Tunnel Branch Canal (No. 10e).

Netherton—

				Ft.	Iŗ
Length	..	..	3027 yards		
Minimum height above water level ..	..	..		15	9
Minimum width at water level	..	..		17	0
Minimum width at water level, including both towing-paths ..	..	..	..	27	0

Towing-path both sides; boats enter from either end at any time.

The tunnel is lighted by gas lamps.

Dudley Canal—Line No 1 (No. 10f1).

Dudley—

				Ft.	In.
Length	..	..	3172 yards		
Minimum height above water level ..	..	..		5	9
Minimum width at water level	..	..		8	5

No towing-path; boats " legged " through.

Boats enter from Tipton end at 5-0 a.m., 11-0 a.m., and 5-0 p.m.,
and from Parkhead end at 8-0 a.m. and 2-0 p.m.

Dudley Canal—Line No. 2 (No. 10f2).

Gosty Hill—

				Ft.	In.
Length	..	..	557 yards		
Minimum height above water level ..	..	..		7	4
Minimum width at water level ..	..	..		8	1

No towing-path; boats " legged " through.

(10)—Birmingham Canal Navigations—*continued.*

Dudley Canal—Line No. 2 (No. 10f2).

	Ft.	In.
Lappal—		
Length .. .. 3795 yards		
Minimum height above water level	6	0
Minimum width at water level	7	9

No towing-path; boats "legged" through, assisted by flushing—*see* Section 5, Tunnels.

Boats enter from Lappal Wharf end at 4-0 a.m., 10-0 a.m., 4-0 p.m., and 10-0 p.m., and from Selly Oak end at 7-0 a.m., 1-0 p.m., and 7-0 p.m.

(g) Towing-path.

There is a towing-path throughout the navigation, except through certain of the tunnels enumerated above.

(i) Types of vessels using the navigation.

Narrow boats. In addition to the ordinary narrow boats, there are a large number of open narrow boats without cabins in use for local traffic, which are termed "day boats."

Birmingham and Fazeley Canal—*see* Birmingham Canal Navigations.

Birmingham and Liverpool Junction Canal—*see* Shropshire Union Canals.

————

(11)—Birmingham and Warwick Junction Canal.

(a) Short Description.

The canal commences by a junction with the Warwick and Birmingham Canal at the bottom of Bordesley Locks, and terminates at Salford Bridge, where it forms a junction with the Tame Valley Canal and the Birmingham and Fazeley Canal of the Birmingham Canal Navigations. The whole course of the canal is situated in the parish of Aston, Birmingham.

(b) Proprietors, Officers, and Offices.

The Company of Proprietors of the Birmingham and Warwick Junction Canal Navigation.

Secretary : G. J. Blunn.

Engineer : William Salt.

Office : Fazeley Street, Birmingham. Telegraphic Address : "Canals, Birmingham."

(11)—BIRMINGHAM AND WARWICK JUNCTION CANAL—*continued.*

(c) Distance Table.

	Miles.	Fur.
Bordesley, junction with Warwick and Birmingham Canal (No. 115), to—		
Park Wharf, Saltley : Fellows, Morton, and Clayton, Ltd., Canal Carriers	1	0
Saltley Gas Works	1	2
Saltley Road Bridge and Saltley Station ..	1	3
Salford Bridge, junction with Tame Valley Canal (No. 10n), and Birmingham and Fazeley Canal (No. 10p1)	2	5

(d) Locks.

1
to } Garrison.
5.
6.—Salford.

Fall from Bordesley.

(e) Maximum size of vessels that can use the navigation.

	Ft.	In.
Length	72	0
Width	7	0
Draught	4	7
Headroom	8	0

(g) Towing-path.

There is a towing-path throughout the navigation.

(i) Types of vessels using the navigation.

Narrow boats.

BLACK HAM DRAIN—*see* Middle Level Navigations.

BLACKBROOK BRANCH CANAL—*see* London and North Western Railway, St. Helens Canal.

---

(12)—BLACK SLUICE DRAINAGE AND NAVIGATION, *alias* THE SOUTH FORTY-FOOT DRAIN.

(a) Short Description.

The drain commences to be navigable at its top end at Guthram Gowt, and, proceeding by Donington Bridge and Swineshead, terminates by a junction with the tidal River Witham at Boston, about one mile below the Grand Sluice, all in the county of Lincolnshire.

There is not much trade done on the drain, what there is being almost entirely confined to the section between Donington Bridge and Boston.

(12)—BLACK SLUICE DRAINAGE AND NAVIGATION, *alias* THE SOUTH
FORTY-FOOT DRAIN—*continued.*

(b) Proprietors, Officers, and Offices.

Black Sluice Commissioners.

Clerk : Benjamin Smith.

Offices : Horbling; and Donington, near Spalding.

Deputy Clerk : Richard Bothamley.

Office : Donington, near Spalding.

Engineer and Surveyor : F. Sanderson-Robins.

Office : 5, Horncastle Road, Boston.

(c) Distance Table.

	Miles.	Fur.
Guthram Gowt to—		
Neslam Bridge	6	3
Donington Bridge	8	3
Swineshead Railway Station	14	0
Hubberts Bridge Railway Station	17	3
Boston, junction with River Witham (No. 124)	21	0

(d) Locks.

1.—Boston.

Fall to River Witham.

The lock is provided with sea doors, as the tide in the River Witham
rises above the level of the water in the drain.

(e) Maximum size of vessels that can use the navigation.

	Ft.	In.
Length	72	0
Width	19	6
Draught—to Donington Bridge	8	0
Draught above Donington Bridge gradually decreases towards Guthram Gowt to ..	4	0

(g) Towing-path.

There is a towing-path throughout the navigation.

(i) Types of vessels using the navigation.

Barges. Steam haulage for the purpose of trade is not allowed.

BOARDMANS BRIDGE BRANCH CANAL—*see* London and North Western
Railway, St. Helens Canal.

BOROUGHBRIDGE AND RIPON CANAL—*see* North Eastern Railway, River
Ure Navigation.

BOSTON HARBOUR AND DOCK COMMISSIONERS—*see* River Witham.

BOW CREEK—*see* River Thames and River Lee.

(13)—BRADFORD CANAL.

(a) Short Description.

The canal commences at Canal Street in the City of Bradford, and proceeds by Frizinghall to a junction with the main line of the Leeds and Liverpool Canal near Shipley, all in the West Riding of the county of Yorkshire.

(b) Proprietors, Officers, and Offices.

The canal is the joint property of the Leeds and Liverpool Canal Company and of the Undertakers of the Aire and Calder Navigation.

Secretary : Robert Davies.

Office : Pall Mall, Liverpool.

(c) Distance Table.

	Miles.	Fur.
Bradford, Canal Street Wharf, to—		
Spinkwell Locks ..	–	4
Bradford Corporation Gas Works	–	4
Oliver Locks	1	0
Frizinghall Wharves	1	4
I. Holden and Son, Grease Works	1	6
Cragg End Locks	2	0
Pricking Locks ..	2	2
Midland Dye Works	2	4
Windhill Lock ..	2	6
Junction with Leeds and Liverpool Canal—		
Main Line (No. 58a)	3	0

(d) Locks.

1 and 2. Spinkwell (Staircase).

3 and 4. Oliver (Staircase).

5 to 7. Cragg End (Staircase).

8 and 9. Pricking (Staircase).

10.—Windhill.

Fall from Bradford.

(e) Maximum size of vessels that can use the navigation.

	Ft.	In.
Length	61	0
Width	14	4
Draught, average about	3	8
Headroom	8	0

(g) Towing-path.

There is a towing-path throughout the navigation.

(13)—BRADFORD CANAL—*continued.*

(i) *Types of vessels using the navigation.*

Leeds and Liverpool Canal short boats—*see* Section 9, Types of Vessels, (a) Non-Sailing Vessels.

BRADLEY BRANCH CANAL—*see* Birmingham Canal Navigations.

---

(14)—BRANDON RIVER, *alias* LITTLE OUSE RIVER.

(a) *Short Description.*

The navigation commences at the Town of Thetford, and proceeds through Brandon to a junction with the River Ouse (Bedford) at Brandon Creek.

The navigation throughout the greater part of its course forms the boundary between the counties of Norfolk and Suffolk, a short length, however, at the lower end is situated entirely in the county of Norfolk.

The portion of the navigation under the jurisdiction of the Thetford Corporation is in a very indifferent condition, most of the staunches are out of order, and will not hold up the water.

(b) *Proprietors, Officers, and Offices.*

From Thetford to Wilton Bridge the river is under the jurisdiction of the Corporation of the town of Thetford.

Town Clerk : John Houchen.

Office : Thetford.

From Wilton Bridge to Brandon Creek the river is an open navigation, with no controlling authority ; but the Bedford Level Corporation cut the weeds over this length, and the South Level Drainage and Navigation Commissioners maintain Crosswater Staunch.

(c) *Distance Table.*

Thetford Bridge to—	Miles.	Fur.
Thetford Staunch	–	4
Thetford Middle Staunch	1	7
Turfpole Staunch	2	6
Fison's Vitriol and Manure Works	3	3
Croxton Staunch	3	6
Santon Staunch	5	2
Santon Downham	5	7
Brandon Bridge	8	6
Bran Staunch	9	1
Shipwash Staunch	10	5

(14)—Brandon River, *alias* Little Ouse River—*continued*.

	Miles.	Fur.
Thetford Bridge to (*continued*)—		
Wilton Ferry	12	1
Wilton Bridge	13	0
Crosswater Staunch	16	4
Junction with Lakenheath Lode (No. 54) ..	17	0
Brandon Creek, junction with River Ouse (No. 79b)	22	4

(d) Locks.

1. Thetford Staunch.   (Navigation Weir.)
2. Thetford Middle Staunch.   ,,
3. Turfpole Staunch.   ,,
4. Croxton Staunch.   ,,
5. Santon Staunch.   ,,
6. Bran Staunch.   ,,
7. Shipwash Staunch.   ,,
8. Crosswater Staunch.   ,.
            Fall from Thetford.

(e) Maximum size of vessels that can use the navigation.

	Ft.	In.
Length.—Not limited	—	—
Width	12	6
Draught.—Very uncertain	—	—
From Brandon Creek up to Fison's Vitriol and Manure Works, about	3	0
From Fison's Vitriol and Manure Works to Thetford, about	2	0

(g) Towing-path.

There is a towing-path throughout the navigation.

(i) Types of vessels using the navigation.

Fen lighters.

Brecon and Abergavenny Canal—*see* Great Western Railway.

Brewery Cut Branch Canal—*see* Great Northern Railway, Nottingham Canal.

Breydon Water—*see* River Yare.

Bridgewater Canal—*see* Manchester Ship Canal Company, Bridge water Canal.

Bridgwater, Corporation of the Town of—*see* River Parrett.

Bridgwater and Taunton Canal—*see* Great Western Railway.

BRINKLOW WHARF BRANCH CANAL—*see* Oxford Canal.

BRISTOL, CORPORATION OF THE CITY OF—*see* River Avon (Bristol).

BROADWATER BRANCH NAVIGATION—*see* River Nene.

BROMLEY BRANCH CANAL—*see* Great Western Railway, Stourbridge Extension Canal.

BRUE, RIVER—*see* River Parrett.

BUCKINGHAM BRANCH CANAL—*see* Grand Junction Canal.

---

(15)—BUDE CANAL.

(a) *Short Description.*

The portion of the canal now remaining open for traffic commences at the foot of the old Marhamchurch Inclined Plane, between Helebridge and Marhamchurch, and proceeds in a northerly direction to its termination at Bude Harbour, all in the county of Cornwall.

Prior to 1891, when power to abandon was obtained by Act of Parliament, there were about 40 miles of canal only navigable for tub boats, extending from the top of the Marhamchurch Incline further inland. This consisted of a line to Red Post, North Tamerton, and Druxton, a branch from Red Post to Brendon and Blagdonmoor, and another branch from Brendon to Alfardisworthy Reservoir.

(b) *Proprietors, Officers, and Offices.*

The Urban District Council of Stratton and Bude.
Clerk of the Council : R. A. Foster-Melliar.
Office : The Strand, Bude, Cornwall.

(c) *Distance Table.*

	Miles.	Fur.
Head of canal at foot of the Old Marhamchurch Incline to—		
Helebridge	–	1
Whalesborough Lock	–	5
Rodd's Bridge Lock	–	7
Bude Swing Bridge	1	7
Bude Sea Lock, entrance to canal from the sea..	2	1

(d) *Locks.*

1. Rodd's Bridge.   2. Whalesborough.   3. Bude Sea Lock.
Fall from head of canal.

(e) *Maximum size of vessels that can use the navigation.*

Vessels not exceeding 100ft. in length by 25ft. in width, and drawing 10ft of water on Spring tides and about 6ft. on Neap tides, can use the first quarter mile of the canal above Sea Lock. Barges measuring 50ft. in length by 13ft. in width, and drawing 3ft. 6in. of water, could navigate the canal up to Helebridge, but there are none in use at the present time.

(15).—BUDE CANAL—*continued.*

(g) *Towing path.*

There is a towing-path throughout the navigation.

(h) *Tidal Information.*

The tide flows to Sea Lock, Bude.

High water at Bude Harbour is 3hrs. 47min. after London Bridge.

Spring tides rise	..	..	..	..	23ft.
Neap „ „	..	..	..	..	17ft.

(i) *Types of vessels using the navigation.*

Small coasting vessels use the first quarter mile of the canal.

Tub boats measuring 20ft. in length by 5ft. 6in. in width, and carrying four tons on a draught of 20in., are the only vessels using the remainder of the canal.   Four of these can pass the locks at one time.

BUMBLE HOLE BRANCH CANAL—*see* Birmingham Canal Navigations, Dudley Canal.

BUNGAY NAVIGATION—*see* River Waveney.

---

(16)—RIVER BURE, *alias* THE NORTH RIVER.

(a) *Short Description.*

The River Bure commences to be navigable at Aylsham, and proceeds by Coltishall and Wroxham to Great Yarmouth, where it forms a junction with the River Yare at the eastern extremity of Breydon Water, all in the county of Norfolk.   The upper portion of the river from Aylsham to Coltishall is known as the Aylsham Navigation.   The principal branches are the River Thurne, or Hundred Stream, and the River Ant.   There are also numerous dikes and broads communicating with the river.

(b) *Proprietors, Officers, and Offices.*

From Aylsham to a quarter of a mile below Coltishall Lock the river is under the jurisdiction of the Aylsham Navigation Commissioners.

Clerk : Henry G. Wright.

Office : Aylsham, Norfolk.

From a quarter of a mile below Coltishall Lock to the mouth, the river, including all the branches, is under the jurisdiction of the Great Yarmouth Port and Haven Commissioners.

Clerk : John Tolver Waters.

Office : 2, South Quay, Yarmouth.

Harbour Master : Captain Day.

Office : Gorleston-on-Sea.

(16)—RIVER BURE, *alias* THE NORTH RIVER—*continued.*

(c) Distance Table.

Main Line of River (No. 16a1).

	Miles.	Fur.
Aylsham Bridge and Staiths to—		
Aylsham Lock	1	0
Burgh Bridge	2	3
Burgh Lock	3	0
Oxnead Lock	3	6
Lamas Church	5	3
Buxton Lamas Lock	5	7
Coltishall Bridge	9	$0\frac{1}{2}$
Coltishall Lock	9	2
Boundary of Aylsham Navigation	9	4
Coltishall Staith	10	0
Coltishall Anchor Inn	10	4
Belaugh Village	11	3
Wroxham Railway Bridge	14	$5\frac{1}{2}$
Wroxham Bridge	14	7
Junction with north entrance to Wroxham Broad (No. 16a2)	16	0
Junction with south entrance to Wroxham Broad (No. 16a2)	16	4
Junction with entrance to Little Salhouse Broad (No. 16a3)	17	$0\frac{1}{2}$
Junction with western entrance to Great Salhouse Broad (No. 16a4)	17	2
Junction with eastern entrance to Great Salhouse Broad (No. 16a4)	17	4
Entrance to Hoveton Great Broad, private, not navigable	18	0
Entrance to Hoveton Little Broad, private, not navigable	19	1
Lower Street, Horning	19	6
Horning Ferry	20	4
Cockshoot Dike, not navigable, leading to Cockshoot Broad	20	7
Junction with Ranworth Dike (No. 16a5) ..	22	2
Junction with River Ant (No. 16b1) ..	23	4
Junction with Fleet Dike (No. 16a6) ..	24	1
St. Benedict's Abbey	24	$6\frac{1}{2}$
Thurne Mouth, junction with River Thurne (No. 16c1)	26	$2\frac{1}{2}$
Junction with Upton Dike (No. 16a7) ..	27	7
Acle Bridge	29	1
Junction with Acle Dike (No. 16a8)	29	7
Muck Fleet Dike, not navigable, communicates with Filby, Rollesby, and Ormesby Broads	30	4
Stokesby Ferry and Staith	31	2
Tunstall Dike, not navigable	31	$6\frac{1}{2}$
Stracey Arms Inn and Staith	32	3
Herringby Staith	33	5
Six Mile House	34	2
Runham Staith	34	6

(16)—RIVER BURE, *alias* THE NORTH RIVER—*continued*.

	Miles.	Fur.
Aylsham Bridge and Straiths to (*continued*)—		
Runham Swim Ferry and Five Mile House ..	35	3
Mautby Swim Ferry	36	2½
Three Mile House	37	6
Two Mile House..	38	7
Yarmouth Yacht Station	40	2
Yarmouth Public Staith and Suspension Bridge	40	3
Yarmouth, junction with River Yare (No. 128a) and eastern extremity of Breydon Water	40	5

Wroxham Broad (No. 16a2).

Adjoining the river. There is a public staith in the south-western corner of the Broad, distant about ⅜ of a mile from the south entrance.

Little Salhouse Broad (No. 16a3).

Adjoining the river. There is one staith on the Broad, distant from the river about ¾ of a furlong.

Great Salhouse Broad (No. 16a4).

Adjoining the river. There is one staith on the Broad, distant about one furlong from the river.

Ranworth Dike (No. 16a5).

⅜ of a mile in length, leading to Ranworth Broad, on which there are two staiths at Ranworth, both being distant about one furlong from the entrance of Ranworth Dike to the Broad.

Fleet Dike (No. 16a6).

⅝ of a mile in length, leading to South Walsham Broad, on the eastern shore of which there are two staiths—Jones' Staith and Debbage's Staith—situated respectively about 1 furlong and 1½ furlongs from the entrance of Fleet Dike to the Broad. Opening out of the western extremity of South Walsham Broad is Common Broad, private, on which is Ranworth Staith, distant about 5½ furlongs from the entrance of Fleet Dike to South Walsham Broad.

Upton Dike (No. 16a7).

⅜ of a mile in length to a point about ⅔ of a mile from Upton Village.

(16)—RIVER BURE, *alias* THE NORTH RIVER—*continued.*

Acle Dike (No. 16a8).

¼ of a mile in length to Acle Parish Staith.

River Ant (No. 16b1).

	Miles.	Fur.
Junction with River Bure (No. 16a1) to—		
Ludham Bridge	–	7
Irstead Church	4	1
Southern entrance of river to Barton Broad ..	4	4

There are four staiths on Barton Broad—

Irstead Staith, at the end of the western arm of the Broad, and distant about one mile from the southern entrance of the river to the Broad.

Callow Green Staith, private, on the north shore of the western arm of the Broad, not far from Irstead Staith, and distant about ¾ of a mile from the southern entrance of the river to the broad.

Catfield Staith, on the eastern shore of the Broad, and distant about ⅜ of a mile from the southern entrance of the river to the Broad, and 2 miles from Catfield Station by road.

Barton Turf Staith, in the north-west corner of the Broad, and distant about a ¼ of a mile from the northern entrance of the river to the Broad. The navigation channels on Barton Broad, except those to Irstead and Callow Green Staiths, are marked by posts.

Northern entrance of River to Barton Broad..	5	6
Junction with Stalham Dike (No. 16b2) ..	6	2½
Wayford Bridge and Staiths	7	7
Junction with North Walsham and Dilham Canal (No. 77)	8	0½

Stalham Dike (No. 16b2).

Junction with River Ant to—		
Junction with Sutton Dike (No. 16b3) ..	–	4
Stalham Staiths	1	1

Sutton Dike (No. 16b3).

Length from junction with Stalham Dike (No. 16b2) to Sutton Staith	–	7

River Thurne (No. 16c1).

Thurne Mouth, junction with River Bure (No. 16a1), to—		
Junction with Thurne Dike (No. 16c2) ..	–	3
Junction with Womack Water (No. 16c3) ..	1	2½
Pug Street Staith	2	2
Potter Heigham Bridge	3	0
Junction with Candle Dike (No. 16c4 and 16c5)	4	4
Martham Staith and Ferry	4	6½

(16)—River Bure, *alias* the North River—*continued*.

	Miles.	Fur.
Thurne Mouth, junction with River Bure (No. 16a1), to (*continued*)—		
Kelfleet Dike, not navigable	5	3
Head of the navigation of the river, and junction with navigation across Martham Broad to West Somerton (No. 16c6) ..	5	5½

Thurne Dike (No. 16c2).

Length to Thurne Village	–	1

Womack Water (No. 16c3).

Length to Ludham Village	–	7

Navigation through Candle Dike, Heigham Sound, and Whitesley Mere to Hickling Broad (No. 16c4).

	Miles.	Fur.
South end of Candle Dike, and junction with River Thurne (No. 16c1), to—		
North end of Candle Dike, and southern extremity of Heigham Sound	–	3
North-western extremity of Heigham Sound, and junction of Dike leading to Whitesley Mere	1	1½
Southern extremity of Whitesley Mere ..	1	2½
North-western extremity of Whitesley Mere, and junction of Dike leading to Hickling Broad	1	4½
South-eastern extremity of Hickling Broad ..	1	5

Hickling Broad is the largest fresh-water Broad in Norfolk. There are three staiths on Hickling Broad: Hickling Staith, at the northern extremity of the Broad, distant two miles by road from Catfield Station; a private staith a short distance to the east of Hickling Staith, now but little used—distance from these two staiths to the south-eastern extremity of the Broad about 1¾ miles; Catfield Staith, at the top end of a dike leading out of the west side of the Broad, distant one mile by road from Catfield Village, is about 1¼ miles from the south-eastern extremity of the Broad.

Lines of posts mark the navigation channel across the Broad to the staiths.

Navigation through Candle Dike, Heigham Sound, Meadow Dike, and Horsey Mere to Lown Bridge, Palling, on Waxham New Cut (No. 16c5).

	Miles.	Fur.
South end of Candle Dike, and junction with River Thurne (No. 16c1), to—		
North end of Candle Dike, and southern extremity of Heigham Sound	–	3
North-eastern extremity of Heigham Sound and junction with Meadow Dike	1	1½

(16)—River Bure, *alias* the North River—*continued.*

	Miles.	Fur.
South end of Candle Dike, and junction with River Thune (No. 16c1), to (continued)—		
Southern extremity of Horsey Mere	2	1

There is one staith on Horsey Mere, situated at its eastern end, distant about 7 furlongs from the southern extremity of the Mere, and ½ a mile by road from Horsey Village.

	Miles.	Fur.
Northern extremity of Horsey Mere, and junction with Waxham New Cut.. ..	2	6
Waxham Bridge	4	0
Lown Bridge, one mile from Palling Village	6	2

Navigation across Martham Broad to West Somerton (No. 16c6).

	Miles.	Fur.
Junction with River Thurne (No. 16c1) to—		
Western extremity of Martham Broad ..	–	1
Eastern extremity of Martham Broad, and junction of Dike leading to West Somerton	–	4
West Somerton Staiths, two miles from Martham Station	–	7

(d) Locks.

There are only five locks on the River Bure and branches, all of which are situated on that part of the river known as the Aylsham Navigation.

1. Aylsham.   4. Buxton Lamas.
2. Burgh.   5. Coltishall.
3. Oxnead.

Fall from Aylsham.

(e) *Maximum size of vessels that can use the navigation.*

Main Line of River (No. 16a1).

	Ft.	In.
From the junction with the River Yare at Yarmouth to Coltishall Staith—		
Length.—Not limited.		
Width.—Not limited.		
Draught .. .. about	4	0
From Coltishall Staith to the tail of Buxton Lamas Lock—		
Length	54	0
Width	13	9
Draught	3	6
From the tail of Buxton Lamas Lock to Aylsham—		
Length	54	0
Width	12	8
Draught	3	6
Headroom.—Burgh Bridge on the Aylsham Navigation is the lowest bridge on the river, the height above the usual water level being	6	4

All the bridges on the river are fixed.

(16)—River Bure, *alias* the North River—*continued.*

Wroxham Broad (No. 16a2).

	Ft.	In.
Length.—Not limited.		
Width.—Not limited.		
Draught	4	0

Little Salhouse Broad (No. 16a3).

Length.—Not limited.		
Width.—Not limited.		
Draught	3	6 to 4ft.

Great Salhouse Broad (No. 16a4).

Length.—Not limited.		
Width.—Not limited.		
Draught	4	0

Ranworth Dike and Broad (No. 16a5).

Length.—Not limited.		
Width.—Not limited.		
Draught	3ft. to 3	6

Fleet Dike, South Walsham Broad, and Common Broad (No. 16a6).

	Ft.	In.
Length.—Not limited.		
Width.—Not limited.		
Draught	4	0

Upton Dike (No. 16a7).

Length.—Not limited.		
Width.—Not limited.		
Draught	3ft. to 3	6

Acle Dike (No. 16a8).

Length.—Not limited.		
Width.—Not limited.		
Draught	3	6 to 4ft.

River Ant (No. 16b1).

Length.—Not limited.		
Width.—Vessels to pass Wayford Bridge should not exceed	12	4
Vessels to pass Ludham Bridge should not exceed	14	4
Draught	4	0
To Irstead and Callow Green Staiths on Barton Broad, maximum ..	3	6
To Barton Turf Staith, on Barton Broad	4	0
To Catfield Staith, on Barton Broad	3ft. to 3	6

(16)---RIVER BURE, *alias* THE NORTH RIVER—*continued*.

	Ft.	In.
Headroom.—Ludham Bridge is the lowest point on the river, the height of the arch in centre from the high-water level at ordinary times is	6	0

The arch rounds up sharply, and its headroom consequently diminishes rapidly towards either side from the centre.

Stalham Dike (No. 16b2) and Sutton Dike (No. 16b3).

	Ft.	In.
Length.—Not limited.		
Width.—Not limited.		
Draught ..	4	0

River Thurne (No. 16c1).

	Ft.	In.
Length.—Not limited.		
Width.—Not limited.		
Draught.—From the junction with the River Bure to the junction with Candle Dike ..	4	0
From the junction with Candle Dike to the head of the Navigation .. in winter	4	0
in summer	3	0

Thurne Dike (No. 16c2).

	Ft.	In.
Length.—Not limited.		
Width.—Not limited.		
Draught ..	4	0

Womack Water (No. 16c3).

Length.—Not limited.		
Width.—Not limited.		
Draught	3	6 to 4ft.

Navigation through Candle Dike, Heigham Sound, and Whitesley Mere to Hickling Broad (No. 16c4).

	Ft.	In.
Length.—Not limited.		
Width.—Not limited.		
Draught.—To Hickling and Catfield Staiths on Hickling Broad	3	0

Navigation through Candle Dike, Heigham Sound, Meadow Dike and Horsey Mere, to Lown Bridge, Palling, or Waxham New Cut (No. 16c5).

	Ft.	In.
Length.—Not limited.		
Width.—Not limited.		
Draught.—To Horsey Staith on Horsey Mere	3	9
To within 200yds. of Waxham Bridge	4	0

F

(16)—RIVER BURE, *alias* THE NORTH RIVER—*continued*.

	Ft.	In.
Draught.—To the end of the Cut at Lown Bridge, not over	3	0

Maximum loads to Lown Bridge are reckoned to be 15 tons in winter and 10 tons in summer.

Navigation from the River Thurne across Martham Broad to West Somerton (No. 16c6).

	Ft.	In.
Length.—Not limited.		
Width.—Not limited.		
Draught.—Variable	2	6 to 4ft.

(g) *Towing-path.*

There is no horse towing-path on any part of the river or its branches.

(h) *Tidal Information.*

The tide usually flows up the river to Horning, and backs up the water in the river to Wroxham Bridge, where the average rise and fall is about 3 inches. On very high tides the salt water has been known to flow up the river as far as Little Salhouse Broad.

The level of the water in the whole of the navigable dikes and broads leading out of the river below Wroxham Bridge is affected by the tide.

For the tide at Yarmouth, *see* River Yare.

High water at Acle Bridge about 3hrs. 30min. after Yarmouth.

High water at Horning about 4hrs. after Yarmouth.

RIVER ANT and branches :—

The tide flows up the River Ant only a short distance above Ludham Bridge, where the rise and fall is about 6in.

The level of the water throughout the River and branches is affected by the tide.

RIVER THURNE and branches :—

The tide flows up the River Thurne to the head of the navigation, where the average rise and fall is about 3in.

The level of the water throughout the river and branches is affected by the tide.

The salt water occasionally flows up to Potter Heigham.

(i) *Types of vessels using the navigation.*

Norfolk wherries.

As a rule, the maximum load carried on any part of the River Bure and branches does not exceed 23 tons on a draught of about 4ft.

BURSLEM BRANCH CANAL—*see* North Staffordshire Railway, Trent and Mersey Canal.

BURWELL LODE—*see* River Cam.

BUTE, MARQUIS OF—*see* Glamorganshire and Aberdare Canals.

---

(17)—CALDER AND HEBBLE NAVIGATION.

(a) *Short Description.*

The navigation commences by a junction with the Aire and Calder Navigation at the tail of Fall Ing Lock, Wakefield, and proceeds by Horbury, Thornhill, Ravensthorpe, Mirfield, Cooper Bridge, Brighouse, and Elland to Sowerby Bridge, where it joins the Rochdale Canal, all in the West Riding of the county of Yorkshire. There are sundry branches and portions of old navigation, the chief among which are—the Weir Stream at Wakefield; a branch leading through Horbury Branch Lock to the Old River Calder and Horbury Old Cut, the latter on the opposite side of the Old River; the Weir Stream from Thornhill Flood Lock to Fearnley Cut and Dewsbury Cut; Tag Cut, approached from a portion of the Old River branching off at the tail of Brookfoot Lock; and the Halifax Branch Canal, which forms a junction with the navigation at Salterhebble Top Lock.

The mileage of the branches leading out of the main line is 5½ miles.

(b) *Proprietors, Officers, and Offices.*

The Company of Proprietors of the Calder and Hebble Navigation.

General Manager: H. P. Swindells.

Office: Southgate, Halifax. Telegrams: " Canal, Halifax." Telephone No. 256.

(c) *Distance Table.*

Main Line (No. 17a).

	Miles.	Fur.
Fall Ing Lock, junction with Aire and Calder Navigation—Main Line—(No. 3a2), to—		
Hanson's Sewage Works	–	2
Smith's Wharf	–	2
Fernandes' Malt Kiln	–	4
Webb and Yates' Warehouse	–	4
Wakefield Wharf	–	4
Dunn's Grain Warehouse	–	6
Speight and Tunnicliffe's Mill	–	6
Railway Hoist	–	6
Reynolds and Haslegrave's No. 1 Mill	–	6
„ „ No. 2 Mill	1	C
Dam Head	1	0
Hurst's Malt Kiln	–	6
Wade's Mill	–	6

(The Weir Stream, Wakefield)

(17)—CALDER AND HEBBLE NAVIGATION—*continued.*

Fall Ing Lock, junction with Aire and Calder Navigation—Main Line—(No. 3a2), to (*continued*)—

	Miles.	Fur
Belle Isle Dyeworks	–	6
Booth's Mill	–	6
Stubley's Mill	1	0
Barker's Mill	1	4
Hodgson and Simpson's Works	1	4
Thornes Flood Lock	2	0
Wards Mill	3	4
Broad Cut	3	4
Waller's Wharf	3	6
Crigglestone Coal Staith	3	6
Calder Grove Colliery	3	6
Hartley Bank Colliery	4	2
Horbury Bridge	5	2
Horbury Bridge, Milnes Stansfield's Staiths	5	2
Horbury Branch, Basin End	5	2
Matthewman's Wharf (Horbury Old Cut)	5	4
Navigation Mill (Horbury Old Cut)	5	4
Pickard's Mill	5	2
Marsden Bros.' Old Mill	5	4
Healey Bridge Mill	6	0
Fawcet, Firth, and Jessops Mill	6	0
Healey New Mill	6	2
Sykes' Bridge	5	6
New Millbank Colliery (Ingham's)	6	0
Figure of Three Locks	6	2
Thornhill Combs Colliery (Ingham's)	7	0
Brown's Chemical Works	7	2
Tail of Double Locks, and junction with Dewsbury Cut of Aire and Calder Navigation (No. 3e)	7	2
Charlesworth's Malt Kiln	7	6
Slaithwaite Bridge	7	6
Kilner's Glass Works	8	0
Brewery Bridge	8	2
Thornhill Forge	8	4
Thornhill Coal Staith (Ingham's)	8	4
Calder Wharf	9	0
Weir stream leading to Fearnley Cut and Dewsbury Cut { Raven's Wharf	9	2
Haigh's Coal Staith	9	2
Fearnley Cut (No. 32), Howroyd and Oldroyd Works	9	6
Dewsbury Cut, Squire's Wharf	9	6
Thackrah's Newtown Mill	9	0
Howgate's Mill	9	0
Tharkrah's Netherfield Mill	9	2
Greenwood Lock	9	4
Calder Colliery	9	4
Mirfield Low Mill	9	6
Shepley Bridge Lock	10	0
Crowther's Malt Kiln	10	4

(17)—CALDER AND HEBBLE NAVIGATION—*continued.*

	Miles.	Fur.
Fall Ing Lock, Junction with Aire and Calder Navigation—Main Line—(No. 3a2), to (*continued*)—		
Radcliffe's Grease Works	10	4
Sheard's Malt Kiln	10	6
Bull Bridge	10	6
Crowther Bros.' Malt Kilns	10	6
Ledgard Cut End	11	0
Ledgard Steel Bridge	11	0
Hurst's Malt Kilns	11	2
Cardwell's Mill	11	2
Ledger's Oil Mill	11	4
Wellington Mill	11	6
Howarth's Mill	11	6
Battye Lock	11	6
Battye Cut End	12	2
West Mills	12	6
Cooper Bridge Low Lock	12	6
Cooper Bridge Wharf	13	0
Cooper Bridge Cut End	13	0
Junction with Huddersfield Broad Canal (No. 61a)	13	0
Robin Hood Malt Kiln	13	4
Kirklees Middle Lock	13	6
Kirklees Cut End	14	2
Shoesmith's Landing Wharf	14	4
Rastrick Gas Works Landing	14	6
Brighouse Gas Works Landing	15	0
Brighouse Wharf	15	4
Aspinall's Stone Wharf	15	4
Anchor Bridge	15	4
Sugden's Flour Mill	15	4
Brookfoot Stone Wharves	16	0
Freeman's Mill	16	2
Tag Cut Low Lock	16	6
Binns Bottom	17	4
Spencer's Wharf	17	6
Waterloo Mill	18	0
Kershaw's Malt Kiln	18	2
Elland Gas Works	18	2
Elland Wharf	18	2
Woodside Flour Mills	18	6
Head of Salterhebble Top Lock, and junction with Halifax Branch Canal (No. 17b)	19	4
Salterhebble Wharf	19	6
Illingworth's Chemical Works	19	6
Copley Coal Shoot	20	2
Sterne Mill	20	6
Canal Mills	21	2
Mearclough Mill	21	4
Gas Works	21	4
Sowerby Bridge, junction with Rochdale Canal—Main Line—(No. 87a)	21	4

(17)—CALDER AND HEBBLE NAVIGATION—*continued.*

Halifax Branch Canal (No. 17b).

Salterhebble Junction, junction with Main Line (No. 17a), to—					Miles.	Fur.
Goodall's Landing	..	..	..	..	–	6
Siddall Wharf	..	..	..	..	–	6
Barraclough's Mill	..	..	..	..	–	6
Holdsworth's Mills, Nos. 1 and 2		..	..	1	0
Goux Works	..	..	..	..	1	2
Ordish's Timber Yard	..	..	..	..	1	4
Halifax Wharf	..	..	..	..	1	6

In calculating distances for rates and tolls, each quarter mile of the distance on the Halifax Branch Canal, and each quarter mile of the distance between Fall Ing Lock, Wakefield, and Thornes Flood Lock are to be taken as equal to half a mile, but the whole of the distance between Fall Ing Lock and Thornes Flood Lock shall only be taken as equal to four miles.

(d) Locks.

Main Line (No. 17a).

1
and } Fall Ing.
2.

3
and } Thornes.
4.

5.—Thornes Flood Lock.

6
and } Broad Cut Low.
7.

8.—Broad Cut Top.

9
and } Figure of Three.
10.

11.—Millbank.

12
and } Double Locks.
13.

14.—Thornhill Flood.
15.—Greenwood.

16
and } Shepley Bridge.
17.

18.—Shepley Bridge Flood Lock.
19.—Battye.
20.—Cooper Bridge.
21.—Kirklees Low.
22.—Kirklees Top.
23.—Kirklees Flood Lock.
24.—Brighouse Low.
25.—Brighouse.
26.—Ganny.
27.—Brookfoot.

(17)—Calder and Hebble Navigation—*continued.*

28.—Cromwell.
29.—Park Nook.
30.—Elland Low.
31.—Elland Top.
32.—Long Lee.
33.—Salterhebble Low.
34.—Salterhebble Middle.
35.—Salterhebble Top.

Rise from Fall Ing, Wakefield.

Halifax Branch (No. 17b).

1
to   Halifax.
14.

Rise from Salterhebble Junction.

Branch Navigation leading through Horbury Branch Lock.

1.—Horbury Branch Lock.

Fall from Main Line.

Tag Cut.

1.—Tag Lock.

Rise from Main Line.

(e) *Maximum size of vessels that can use the navigation.*

Main Line and Branches.

			Ft.	In.
Length ..	.. ..		57	6
Width ..	.. ..		14	1
Draught ..	minimum 5ft. 0in., maximum		6	6
Headroom	.. ..		9	6

(g) *Towing-path.*

There is a towing-path throughout the main line of the navigation, on the Dewsbury Cut, and on the Halifax Branch Canal.

(i) *Types of vessels using the navigation.*

Yorkshire keels and boats.

Caldon Branch Canal—*see* North Staffordshire Railway, Trent and Mersey Canal.

———

(18)—River Cam.

(a) *Short Description.*

The river commences to be navigable at Kings Mill, Cambridge, and proceeds by Chesterton, Fen Ditton, Horningsea, Clayhithe, Bottisham, and Upware to Popes Corner, where it forms a junction with the River Ouse (Bedford), all in the county of Cambridgeshire. Leading out of the river at Upware, a portion of Reach Lode and the Burwell Lode forms a branch navigation to the village of Burwell. Reach Lode is not navigable beyond the point of its junction with Burwell Lode.

(18)—RIVER CAM—*continued.*

(b) Proprietors, Officers, and Offices.

From Kings Mill, Cambridge, to Clayhithe Bridge the river is under the jurisdiction of the Conservators of the River Cam.

Clerk : T. M. Francis (Messrs. Francis, Francis, and Collin, Solicitors).

Office : 18, Emmanuel Street, Cambridge.

Engineer : George Carmichael.

Office : Ely.

From Clayhithe Bridge to Popes Corner the river is under the jurisdiction of the South Level Drainage and Navigation Commissioners.

Clerk : Harold Archer.

Office : Ely.

Engineer : George Carmichael.

Office : Ely.

As regards Reach Lode and Burwell Lode, the South Level Drainage and Navigation Commissioners are obliged to keep these Lodes in navigable condition as far as the navigation of them extends.

The South Level Drainage and Navigation Commissioners jointly with the Bedford Level Corporation maintain Reach Lode Sluice.

Registrar to the Bedford Level Corporation : Harold Archer.

Engineer : George Carmichael.

Offices : Fen Office, Ely.

Reach Lode is also a drainage, and as such is under the jurisdiction of the Swaffham and Bottisham Drainage Commissioners, who receive the navigation tolls.

Clerk : T. M. Francis (Messrs. Francis, Francis, and Collin, Solicitors).

Office : 18, Emmanuel Street, Cambridge.

Burwell Lode is also a drainage, and as such is under the jurisdiction of the Burwell Fen Drainage Commissioners, who receive the navigation tolls.

Clerk : R. C. Giblin.

Office : Burwell, Cambridgeshire.

(c) Distance Table.

Main Line of River (No. 18a).

	Miles.	Fur
Kings Mill, Cambridge, to—		
Magdalen Bridge, Cambridge	–	6
Jesus Green Sluice (Lock), Cambridge ..	1	0
Chesterton Ferry	2	4
Fen Ditton	3	4

(18)—RIVER CAM—*continued.*

	Miles.	Fur.
Kings Mill, Cambridge, to (*continued*)—		
Baitsbite Sluice (Lock)	4	5
Horningsea	5	2
Claybithe Bridge—Waterbeach Station and Village distant ½ mile	6	5
Bottisham Sluice (Lock)	7	5
Mouth of Bottisham Lode	7	6
Mouth of Swaffham Lode	9	0
Upware, junction with Reach Lode (No. 18b)..	11	2
Popes Corner, junction with River Ouse, Bedford (No. 79b) ..	14	3

Reach Lode and Burwell Lode (No. 18b).

	Miles.	Fur.
Upware, junction of Reach Lode with River Cam (No. 18a), and Reach Lode Sluice (Lock), to—		
Pout Hall, termination of navigable portion of Reach Lode, and commencement of Burwell Lode	–	7
Burwell, Colchester, and Ball's Patent Manure Works	2	6
Burwell Village ..	3	6

(d) *Locks.*
Main Line of River (No. 18a).

1.—Jesus Green.
2.—Baitsbite.
3.—Bottisham.

Fall from Cambridge.

Reach Lode and Burwell Lode (No. 18b).

1.—Reach Lode Sluice, Upware.

Rise from River Cam to Reach Lode.

(e) *Maximum size of vessels that can use the navigation*

Main Line of River (No. 18a).

	Ft.	In.
Length	98	0
Width	15	0
Draught ..	3	9
Headroom	10	0

Reach Lode and Burwell Lode (No. 18b).

	Ft.	In.
Length	50	0
Width	10	0
Draught ..	4	0
Headroom	9	0

(g) *Towing-path.*

The haling-way (towing-path) on the main line of the river extends from a few yards above Jesus Green Sluice to Popes Corner. There is also a haling-way on Reach and Burwell Lodes from Upware to Burwell.

(18)—RIVER CAM—*continued.*

(i) *Types of vessels using the navigation.*

Fen lighters principally use the navigation, and are the only vessels which can use Reach and Burwell Lodes. A few barges measuring 70ft. in length by 14ft. beam, and drawing 3ft. 6in. of water, navigate between Cambridge and Kings Lynn. Two or three steam tugs are in use on the main line of the river, and also on Reach and Burwell Lodes.

CANDLE DIKE—*see* River Bure, River Thurne.

CANNOCK EXTENSION CANAL—*see* Birmingham Canal Navigations.

CHANNELSEA RIVER—*see* River Lee.

---

(19)—CHELMER AND BLACKWATER NAVIGATION.

(a) *Short Description.*

The navigation commences at Chelmsford and proceeds by Little Baddow to Heybridge, where it joins the River Blackwater Estuary, all in the county of Essex. The navigation is remarkable as being that on which trade is habitually conducted on the smallest draught of water of any river in the country.

(b) *Proprietors, Officers, and Offices.*

The Company of Proprietors of the Chelmer and Blackwater Navigation.

Clerk : Andrew Meggy.

Office : 71, Duke Street, Chelmsford.

(c) *Distance Table.*

	Miles.	Fur.
Chelmsford Basin to—		
Springfield Lock ..	–	3
Barnes Mill Lock	1	1
Sandford Lock ..	2	1
Cuton Lock	3	1
Stonehams Lock	4	0
Little Baddow Lock and Wharf	4	7
Paper Mill Lock	6	1
Rushes Lock	7	4
Hoe Mill Lock ..	8	6
Ricketts Lock ..	10	1
Beeleigh Lock ..	11	0
Heybridge Village	12	2
Heybridge Sea Lock	13	7

(19)—Chelmer and Blackwater Navigation—*continued.*

(d) Locks.

1.—Springfield.
2.—Barnes Mill.
3.—Sandford.
4.—Cuton.
5.—Stonehams.
6.—Little Baddow.
7.—Paper Mill.
8.—Rushes.
9.—Hoe Mill.
10.—Ricketts.
11.—Beeleigh.
12.—Beeleigh Flood Lock.
13.—Sea Lock, Heybridge.
Fall from Chelmsford.

(e) Maximum size of vessels that can use the navigation.

	Ft.	In.
Length	60	0
Width	16	0
Draught, average	2	0
„ maximum in winter..	2	3

Vessels 107ft. in length by 26ft. beam, and drawing 12ft. of water on Spring tides, and 8ft. on Neap tides can enter Heybridge Basin above Sea Lock, Heybridge.

(g) Towing-path.

There is a towing-path throughout the navigation.

(h) Tidal Information.

The tide in the River Blackwater flows to the tail of Sea Lock, Heybridge.

High water at the tail of Sea Lock, Heybridge, 1hr. 35min. before London Bridge.

Spring tides rise .. .. 12ft.
Neap „ „ .. .. 8ft.

(i) Types of vessels using the navigation.

Barges having a carrying capacity of about 25 tons, nearly all of which are open vessels without cabins.

Chelsea Creek, another name for the Kensington Canal—*see* West London Extension Railway Company.

Chester Canal Navigation—*see* Shropshire Union Canals.

Chesterfield Canal—*see* Great Central Railway.

(20)—RIVER CHET.

(a) Short Description.

The river commences to be navigable at Loddon Bridge, in the town of Loddon, and flows in a north-easterly direction for a distance of three and a half miles to Hardley Cross, where it forms a junction with the River Yare (No. 128a), all in the county of Norfolk.

(b) Proprietors, Officers, and Offices.

The river, as a drainage, is under the jurisdiction of the Chet Valley Drainage Commissioners.

Clerk : Edward Cadge.

Office : Messrs. Copeman and Cadge, Solicitors, Loddon, near Norwich.

(e) Maximum size of vessels that can use the navigation.

	Ft.	In.
Length.—Not limited.		
Width.—Not limited.		
Draught, average	3	0
,, maximum on good tides	4	0

(g) Towing-path.

There is no towing-path.

(h) Tidal Information.

The level of the water throughout the navigation is affected by the tide in the River Yare, the average rise and fall at Loddon being about 1ft. 6in.

(i) Types of vessels using the navigation.

Norfolk wherries.

---

(21)—CHICHESTER CANAL.

(a) Short Description.

The canal commences in the south of the city of Chichester, and proceeding by Hunston and Donnington joins the low water channel in Chichester Harbour near Birdham, all in the county of Sussex.

There is not much trade done on the canal.

(b) Proprietors, Officers, and Offices.

The Corporation of the City of Chichester.
Town Clerk : J. W. Loader Cooper.
Office : East Street, Chichester.

(c) Distance Table.

	Miles.	Fur.
Chichester Basin to—		
Hunston, junction of Old Portsmouth and Arundel Canal (derelict)	1	3
Donnington	2	1
Birdham Lock	3	2
Salterns Lock (entrance lock to canal) ..	4	0
Low-water Channel, Chichester Harbour ..	4	4

(21)—CHICHESTER CANAL—*continued*.

(d) Locks.

1.—Birdham.
2.—Salterns.

Fall from Chichester.

(e) Maximum size of vessels that can use the navigation.

		Ft.	In.
Length	..	70	0
Width	..	17	0
Draught, Winter..		5	3
„ Summer	..	4	0

Headroom.—Not limited, all bridges being opening bridges.

(g) Towing-path.

There is a towing-path from Chichester to Salterns Lock.

(h) Tidal Information.

The tide in Chichester Harbour flows to the tail of Salterns Lock.

High water at the tail of Salterns Lock is about the same time as that at Littlehampton, namely, 2hrs. 38min. before London Bridge.

Spring tides rise .. .. 14ft.
Neap   „   „ .. .. 11ft.

(i) Types of vessels using the navigation.

Barges.

CHICHESTER, CORPORATION OF THE CITY OF—*see* Chichester Canal.

CHURCHBRIDGE BRANCH CANAL—*see* Birmingham Canal Navigations.

CIRENCESTER BRANCH CANAL—*see* Thames and Severn Canal.

CITY MILLS RIVER—*see* River Lee.

CITY ROAD BASIN BRANCH CANAL—*see* Regents Canal.

---

(22)—CLIFTON AND KEARSLEY COAL CO.'S (LTD.) CANAL.

(a) Short Description.

The canal commences at the Clifton and Kearsley Coal Co.'s (Ltd.) Wharf near Dixon Fold Station on the Manchester and Bolton Line of the Lancashire and Yorkshire Railway, and proceeds in a south-easterly direction for a distance of one and a half miles to near Clifton Junction Station, where it forms a junction with the Manchester, Bolton, and Bury Canal (No. 55a), all in the county of Lancashire.

The canal is entirely used for coal traffic.

(b) Proprietors, Officers, and Offices.

The Clifton and Kearsley Coal Co. Ltd.
Office : Clifton, near Manchester.

(22)—CLIFTON AND KEARSLEY COAL CO.'S (LTD.) CANAL—*continued.*

(d) Locks.

1.—Entrance Lock at junction with Manchester, Bolton, and Bury Canal.

Fall to Manchester, Bolton, and Bury Canal.

(e) Maximum size of vessels that can use the navigation.

	Ft.	In.
Length	60	0
Width	14	0
Draught, maximum	2	9

(g) Towing-path.

There is a towing-path throughout the navigation.

(i) Types of vessels using the navigation.

Only narrow boats use the canal. The lock chamber is wide enough to take three narrow coal boats at a time.

COLCHESTER, CORPORATION OF THE TOWN OF—*see* River Colne.

---

(23)—RIVER COLNE.

(a) Short Description.

The river commences to be navigable at East Mill, Colchester, and proceeds by Wivenhoe to the North Sea at Colne Point, all in the county of Essex. The river below Wivenhoe forms an estuary of considerable width.

(b) Proprietors, Officers, and Offices.

The Corporation of the Town of Colchester.

Town Clerk : Henry Charles Wanklyn.

Engineer and Surveyor : Herbert Goodyear.

Offices : Town Hall, Colchester.

Harbour Master : William Crosby.

Office : The Hythe, Colchester.

(c) Distance Table.

	Miles.	Fur.
East Mill, Colchester, to—		
The Hythe, Colchester, wharves and warehouses	1	0
Rowhedge	3	2
Wivenhoe	3	6
Alresford Creek	5	5
Westmarsh Point, Brightlingsea	8	4
Mersea Point	8	6
Colne Point, limit of jurisdiction of the Corporation of Colchester	11	2

(23)—RIVER COLNE—*continued.*

    (e) *Maximum size of vessels that can use the navigation.*

	Ft.	In.

      Length.—Not limited.
      Width.—Not limited.
      Draught, maximum, to The Hythe, Colchester,
        on Spring tides   9   6
      Draught, maximum, to The Hythe, Colchester,
        on Neap tides   5   6

    The river is practically dry at low water above Wivenhoe; vessels at Colchester, consequently, have to take the ground.

(g) *Towing-path*

    There is a towing-path on both sides of the river from Colchester to just above Wivenhoe.

(h) *Tidal Information.*

    The navigation is tidal throughout, the tide flowing as far as East Mill, Colchester.

    High water at Wivenhoe 1hr. 48min. before London Bridge.
      Spring tides rise about   .. .. 15ft.
      Neap   ,,   ,,   ,, ... 10ft.
    High water at Colchester 10min. after Wivenhoe.
      Spring tides rise ..   ..   .. 10ft.
      Neap   ,,   ,, ... 6ft.

(i) *Types of vessels using the navigation.*

    Medway sailing barges, drawing about 6ft. of water loaded; coasting vessels up to 150 tons, drawing about 9ft. 6in. loaded; and small cargo steamers, drawing 6ft. to 8ft. loaded. The largest vessel that has been to Wivenhoe is one of 300 tons burden, and to Colchester one of 160 tons burden. Lighters are in use on the river for lightening cargoes at Wivenhoe to enable vessels to reach Colchester.

COMMON BROAD—*see* River Bure.

CORPS LANDING BRANCH NAVIGATION—*see* Driffield Navigation.

COUNTER WASH DRAIN—*see* Middle Level Navigations.

———

(24)—COVENTRY CANAL.

(a) *Short Description.*

    The canal commences at Coventry, and proceeds by Hawkesbury, Bedworth, Marston, Nuneaton, Atherstone, Polesworth, and Tamworth to Fazeley, where it forms a junction with the Birmingham and Fazeley Canal. There is also a detached portion leading from the Birmingham and Fazeley Canal at Whittington Brook and proceeding by Huddlesford to the Trent and Mersey Canal at Fradley.

(24)—COVENTRY CANAL—*continued*.

From Coventry to Tamworth the course of the canal is in the county of Warwickshire, the remaining portion being in the county of Staffordshire.

The Coventry Canal as originally designed was intended to have an unbroken course from Coventry to Fradley, but the capital became exhausted by the time the work of construction had proceeded from Coventry as far as Fazeley. Owing to difficulties having arisen with regard to the further raising of money by the Coventry Canal Company, the Birmingham and Fazeley Canal Company constructed the first portion and the Trent and Mersey Canal Company the second portion of the 11 miles of route between Fazeley and Fradley. The second portion between Whittington Brook and Fradley was subsequently acquired by the Coventry Canal Company, but the first portion between Fazeley and Whittington Brook remained as portion of the Birmingham and Fazeley Canal, and passed with that property to the Birmingham Canal Navigations, of which system it is still a part.

(b) Proprietors, Officers, and Offices.

Coventry Canal Company.

Clerk, and Superintendent in the Engineer's Department: J. Y. Greenwood.

Office : Canal Office, Bishop Street, Coventry.

(c) Distance Table.

	Miles.	Fur.
Coventry Basin to—		
Hill's Wharf	1	2
Stoke Basin	2	0
Navigation Wharf	2	6
New Inn Wharf	4	0
Longford Wharf..	4	4
Hawkesbury Junction, junction with Oxford Canal—Main Line—(No. 82a)	5	4
Newdigate Colliery Dock	6	4
Bulkington Lane	7	2
Charity Basin	8	0
Marston Junction, junction with Ashby Canal (No. 70a)	8	2
Griff, junction with Griff Colliery Co.'s Canal (No. 44)	9	2
Coton Old Wharf	10	0
Coton Boot Wharf	10	2
Wash Lane Wharf	11	0
Midland Quarry	11	6
Nuneaton Wharf	11	6
Judkin's Quarry..	11	6
Boon's Quarry	12	6
The Anchor	13	6
Hartshill Wharf	14	2
Wide Hole Wharf	14	6
Mancetter Wharf	15	6

(24)—COVENTRY CANAL—*continued.*

	Miles.	Fur.
Coventry Basin to (*continued*)—		
Atherstone, top of locks..	16	4
Baddesley Basin..	17	4
Polesworth	21	4
Pooley ..	22	2
Alvecote ..	23	2
Amington	23	4
Glascote ..	25	4
Fazeley Junction, junction with Birmingham and Fazeley Canal (No. 10p1)	27	0

Detached Portion.

	Miles.	Fur.
Whittington Brook, junction with Birmingham and Fazeley Canal (No. 11p1), to—		
Huddlesford Junction, junction with Wyrley and Essington Canal (No. 10q1)	1	4
Fradley Junction, junction with Trent and Mersey Canal—Main Line—(No. 76a) ..	5	4

In calculating distances for rates and tolls, each quarter of a mile of the distance between Hawkesbury Junction and Marston Junction is to be taken as half a mile.

(d) *Locks.*

1.—Hawkesbury Stop Lock.

Level.

2
to } Atherstone.
12.

13
and } Glascote.
14.

Fall from Coventry.

(e) *Maximum size of vessels that can use the navigation.*

	Ft.	In.
Length ..	72	0
Width ..	6	10
Draught, Coventry to Glascote .. about	4	0
,, Glascote to Fazeley, and on the detached portion from Whittington Brook to Fradley .. .. about	3	6
Headroom ..	9	0

(g) *Towing-path.*

There is a towing-path throughout the navigation.

(i) *Types of vessels using the navigation.*

Narrow Boats.

COWBRIDGE DRAIN—*see* Witham Drainage General Commissioners.

CRAY, RIVER—*see* Dartford and Crayford Navigation.

G

CROMFORD CANAL—*see* Midland Railway.

CUMBERLAND MARKET BRANCH CANAL—*see* Regents Canal.

DANKS BRANCH CANAL—*see* Birmingham Canal Navigations, Walsall Canal.

DARENTH RIVER—*see* Dartford and Crayford Navigation.

---

(25)—DARTFORD AND CRAYFORD NAVIGATION.

(a) *Short Description.*

The navigation consists of portions of the rivers Darenth and Cray made navigable. The navigation of the River Darenth extends from Dartford to the River Thames, near Crayford Ness, and the navigation of the River Cray forms a short branch from the River Darenth to Crayford Mill, all in the county of Kent. There is a good trade done to Dartford.

(b) *Proprietors, Officers, and Offices.*

The Dartford and Crayford Navigation Commissioners.

Clerk : J. C. Hayward.

Office : Sessions House, Lowfield Street, Dartford.

(c) *Distance Table.*

River Darenth (No. 25a).

	Miles.	Fur.
Head of the navigation at Dartford to—		
Dartford Lock	–	1
Junction with River Cray (No. 25b)	1	2
Junction with River Thames (No. 107a) ..	2	6

River Cray (No. 25b).

	Miles.	Fur.
Length from junction with River Darenth (No. 25a) to Crayford Mill	–	6

(d) *Locks.*

1. Dartford.

This lock was constructed in 1895 to hold up the tidal water, and so enables craft at Dartford to move from wharf to wharf independently of the tide.

(e) *Maximum size of vessels that can use the navigation.*

Length.—Not limited, except through Dartford Lock, which is 150ft. in length.

Width.—Not limited, except through Dartford Lock, which is 23ft. clear width.

(25)—DARTFORD AND CRAYFORD NAVIGATION—*continued.*

Draught.—From River Thames to the wharves immediately above Dartford Lock, average about 7ft.; maximum on Spring tides, 8ft. 4in.

From thence to the head of the navigation, average about 6ft.

River Cray. average about 5ft. 6in. to 6ft.

(g) Towing Path.

There is no towing-path, navigation being conducted on the ebb and flow of the tide.

(h) Tidal Information.

The navigation is tidal throughout.

High water at the junction with the River Thames about 37min. before London Bridge.

Spring tides rise about	18ft. 6in.
Neap ,, ,, ,,	15ft.

High water at Dartford Lock about 40min. before London Bridge.

(i) Types of vessels using the navigation.

Principally Medway sailing barges; some steamers trade to Dartford.

DARTMOUTH BRANCH CANAL—*see* Birmingham Canal Navigations, Wednesbury Old Canal.

DAW END BRANCH CANAL—*see* Birmingham Canal Navigations, Wyrley and Essington Canal.

DEARNE AND DOVE CANAL—*see* Sheffield and South Yorkshire Navigation.

---

(26)—RIVER DEE.

(a) Short Description.

The river commences to be navigable at the Dee Bridge, Chester, and proceeds by Saltney, Sandycroft, and Queensferry to Connah's Quay, where it becomes a wide estuary. The limit of the Dee Conservancy jurisdiction extends to an imaginary line drawn across the mouth of the estuary from the Old Lighthouse, Point of Air (Flintshire), to Hilbre Point (Cheshire). The upper portion of the navigation between Chester and Connah's Quay is situated in the counties of Cheshire and Flint. Below Connah's Quay the estuary divides these counties.

There is practically no trade done on the river above the gas works, Chester. The navigation to Chester is only used on the best of the Spring tides.

(26)—RIVER DEE—*continued.*

(b) Proprietors, Officers, and Offices.

The Dee Conservancy Board.

Acting Conservator and Harbour Master : Henry Enfield Taylor.

Office : 15, Newgate Street, Chester.

(c) Distance Table.

Chester, Dee Bridge, to—	Miles.	Fur.
Chester Gas Works	1	0
Chester, Crane Wharf, and junction with Shropshire Union Canal (No. 92c2) ..	1	2
Saltney	2	6
Sandycroft	5	5
Queensferry	6	7
Connah's Quay	8	6
Point of Air .. .. about	23	0

(e) Maximum size of vessels that can use the navigation.

Length.—Not limited. The length of the longest vessel that can turn in the river is from 180 to 200ft.

Width.—Not limited.

	Ft.	In.
Draught.—Maximum to Chester on Spring tides	12	0
To Connah's Quay on Spring tides, about	13	0
To Connah's Quay on Neap tides, about	8	0

(g) Towing-path.

There is no towing-path.

(h) Tidal Information.

The navigation is tidal throughout.

High water at Point of Air about 3hrs. before London Bridge.

Spring tides rise .. .. 25ft.
Neap ,, ,, ... 19ft.

High water at Connah's Quay on Spring tides 2hrs. 35min. before London Bridge, being about the same time as high water at Liverpool.

High water at Crane Wharf, Chester, about 1hr. 42min. before London Bridge.

Spring tides rise about 10ft.

The tidal wave or "bore" is encountered in the river between Connah's Quay and Chester at Spring tides,—*see* Section 8 (Tides).

(i) Types of vessels using the navigation.

Coasting vessels.

DEEPING FEN GENERAL WORKS OF DRAINAGE TRUSTEES—*see* River Glen and River Welland.

DENVER SLUICE COMMISSIONERS, THE, are the controlling authority in respect of the portion of the River Ouse (Bedford) from a point a quarter of a mile above Denver Sluice to the top of the Eau Brink Cut. They also maintain the fabric of Denver Sluice and all its sea doors, that is, all doors pointing down river.

DEPTFORD CREEK—*see* River Thames.

(27)—DERBY CANAL.

(a) *Short Description.*

The canal commences at Sandiacre by a junction with the Erewash Canal, and proceeds by Borrowash and Spondon to Derby, where there are junctions with the Little Eaton branch and a short branch to the upper portion of the River Derwent in the town. At Derby the canal crosses the River Derwent on the level between White Bear Lock and Pegg's Flood Lock, and continues by Osmaston and near Chellaston to Swarkeston, where it forms a junction with the Trent and Mersey Canal.

The branch to Little Eaton communicates at Little Eaton with a tramway four miles in length leading to Kilbourne and Denby.

The whole course of the canal is in the county of Derbyshire.

(b) *Proprietors, Officers, and Offices.*

The Derby Canal Company.
Manager : Sidney Burton.
Office : Cockpit Hill Wharf, Derby.

(c) *Distance Table.*

Main Line (No. 27a).

	Miles.	Fur.
Sandiacre Junction, junction with Erewash Canal (No. 30), to—		
Breaston	1	7
Borrowash Top Lock and Railway Station ..	4	7
Spondon Railway Station	6	1
Derby, junction with Little Eaton Branch (No. 27b)	8	6
Derby, junction with branch to upper portion of River Derwent (No. 27c)	9	0
Derby, White Bear Lock	9	1
Derby, Peggs Flood Lock	9	1½
Derby, Gandy's Wharf..	9	2
Derby, Gas Works	10	2
Osmaston	11	0
Shelton Top Lock	13	0
Baltimore Bridge, Chellaston	13	4
Swarkeston Junction, junction with Trent and Mersey Canal, Main Line (No. 76a) ..	14	4

(27)—DERBY CANAL—*continued.*

Little Eaton Branch (No. 27b).

	Miles.	Fur.
Derby, junction with Main Line (No. 27a), to—		
Depot Lock	–	5
Little Chester	–	6
Eaton Top Lock..	1	2
Ford Farm	2	3
Little Eaton, termination of Canal and Railway Station	3	1

Branch to upper portion of River Derwent, Derby (No. 27c).

	Miles.	Fur.
Junction with Main Line (No. 27a) to —		
Phœnix Lock	–	0½
Junction with River Derwent	–	1
G. N. Railway Bridge, River Derwent, termination of the navigation	–	2

(d) *Locks.*

Main Line (No. 27a).

1
and ⎫ Sandiacre.
2. ⎭

3
and ⎫ Borrowash.
4. ⎭

Rise to Derby.
5.—White Bear.

Fall to River Derwent, Derby.
6.—Pegg's Flood Lock.
7.—Day's.

Rise from River Derwent to Gandy's Wharf, Derby.

8
and ⎫ Shelton.
9. ⎭

Fall to Swarkeston.

Little Eaton Branch (No. 27b).

1.—Pasture.	3.—Sharon.
2.—Depot.	4.—Eaton Top.

Rise to Little Eaton.

Branch to upper portion of River Derwent, Derby (No. 27c).
1.—Phœnix.

Rise to upper portion of River Derwent.

(e) *Maximum size of vessels that can use the navigation.*

		Ft.	In.
Length		72	0
Width		14	0
Draught	3ft. to	3	8
Headroom		7	0

(27)—DERBY CANAL—*continued.*

(g) *Towing path.*

There is a towing-path throughout the navigation with the exception of the branch to the upper portion of the River Derwent, Derby.

(i) *Types of vessels using the navigation.*

Narrow boats and Upper Trent boats.

DERWENT, RIVER (Derby)—*see* Derby Canal.

DERWENT, RIVER (Durham)—*see* River Tyne.

DERWENT, RIVER (York)—*see* North Eastern Railway.

DEWSBURY CUT—*see* Calder and Hebble Navigation.

DEWSBURY OLD CUT—*see* Aire and Calder Navigation.

DIGBETH BRANCH CANAL—*see* Birmingham Canal Navigations, Birmingham and Fazeley Canal.

DIXON'S BRANCH CANAL—*see* Birmingham Canal Navigations, Main Line.

DON, RIVER (Durham)—*see* River Tyne.

---

(28)—RIVER DON (Yorkshire).

(a) *Short Description.*

The portion of the River Don dealt with in this section is that navigable portion which is not included in the jurisdiction of the Sheffield and South Yorkshire Navigation Company. It extends from Fishlake Old Ferry to the mouth of the river at Goole, all in the West Riding of the county of Yorkshire. The section between New Bridge and Goole is known as the Dutch River, and is an artificial channel, cut in 1625 by Cornelius Vermuyden as a diversion of the old river course for the improvement of the drainage of the neighbouring land.

(b) *Proprietors, Officers, and Offices.*

From Fishlake Old Ferry to New Bridge the river is an open navigation, having no controlling authority ; from New Bridge to Goole the river is under the jurisdiction of the Hatfield Chase Corporation.

Clerks : Messrs. Baxter & Co.

Office : Doncaster.

Expenditor : A. Wattee.

Office : Epworth, near Doncaster.

(28)—RIVER DON (Yorkshire)—*continued*.

(c) Distance Table.

	Miles.	Fur.
Fishlake Old Ferry, junction with River Don under the jurisdiction of the Sheffield and South Yorkshire Navigation (No. 91b1), to—		
New Bridge, commencement of Dutch River.	3	6
Rawcliffe Bridge	5	7
Goole, junction with River Ouse (No. 81) ..	9	2

(e) Maximum size of vessels that can use the navigation.

Length.—Not limited.
Width.—Not limited.
Draught .. .. about 6ft. 6in.

(g) Towing-path.

There is no towing-path, navigation being conducted on the ebb and flow of the tide.

(h) Tidal Information.

The river is tidal throughout—*see* Tidal Information, Goole, River Ouse (No. 81), and also Stainforth, Sheffield and South Yorkshire Navigation (No. 91g1).

(i) Types of vessels using the navigation.

Yorkshire keels ; some keels are towed between Stainforth and Goole by steam tug.

DOUGLAS, LOWER NAVIGATION, OR RUFFORD BRANCH CANAL.—*see* Leeds and Liverpool Canal.

---

(29)—DRIFFIELD NAVIGATION.

(a) Short Description.

The navigation commences at Great Driffield, and proceeds by Wansford and Brigham to a junction with the River Hull at the tail of Struncheon Hill Lock.

There are two short branches: one, called Frodingham Beck, to Frodingham Bridge and Foston Mills, and the other to Corps Landing.

The whole of the navigation is situated in the East Riding of the county of Yorkshire.

(b) Proprietors, Officers, and Offices.

The Commissioners of the Driffield Navigation.

Clerk : W. H. Jennings.

Office : Exchange Street, Great Driffield.

(29)—DRIFFIELD NAVIGATION—*continued.*

Inspector and Collector of Dues : T. H. Harrison.

Office : Exchange Street, Great Driffield.

Engineer : W. S. Lackland.

Office : St. Giles' Croft, Beverley.

The portion of Frodingham Beck between Frodingham Bridge and Foston Mills is the property of W. H. St. Quintin, Esq., of Lowthorpe, Hull, but the Commissioners of the Driffield Navigation have power to take certain tolls.

(c) *Distance Table.*
Main Line (No. 29a).

	Miles.	Fur.
Driffield Wharves to—		
Driffield Lock	–	3
Whin Hill Lock	1	5
Wansford Lock and Village	2	4
Snakeholme Lock	3	0
Junction with Frodingham Beck (No. 29b) ..	5	0
Junction with Branch to Corps Landing (No. 29c)	5	6
Struncheon Hill Lock, junction with River Hull (No. 48a)	7	0

Frodingham Beck (No. 29b).

Junction with Main Line (No. 29a) to—		
Frodingham Bridge	1	0
Foston Mills	1	6

Branch to Corps Landing (No. 29c).

Junction with Main Line (No. 29a), to—		
Corps Landing	1	6

(d) *Locks.*
Main Line (No. 29a).

1.—Driffield.
2.—Whin Hill.
3.—Wansford.
4 and 5. } Snakeholme (Staircase).
6 and 7. } Struncheon Hill ((Staircase).

Fall from Driffield.

(e) *Maximum size of vessels that can use the navigation.*

	Ft.	In.
Length	61	0
Width	14	6
Draught, main line	5	9 to 6ft.

(29)—DRIFFIELD NAVIGATION—*continued.*

	Ft.	In.
Draught.—Frodingham Beck, from junction with Main Line to Frodingham Bridge	5	9 to 6ft.
From Frodingham Bridge to Foston Mills	3	6 to 4ft.
Branch to Corps Landing 3ft. to	3	6
Headroom	11	0

(g) Towing-path.

There is a towing-path throughout the navigation, except on Frodingham Beck.

(i) Types of vessels using the navigation.

Yorkshire keels.

DROITWICH CANAL—*see* Sharpness New Docks and Gloucester and Birmingham Navigation Company.

DROITWICH JUNCTION CANAL—*see* Sharpness New Docks and Gloucester and Birmingham Navigation Company.

DUCKETT'S CANAL (an old name for the Hertford Union Canal)—*see* Regents Canal.

DUDLEY CANAL—*see* Birmingham Canal Navigations.

DUDLEY, EARL OF—*see* Pensnett Canal, alias Lord Ward's Canal.

DUKE'S CUT—*see* Oxford Canal.

RIVER DUN NAVIGATION—*see* Sheffield and South Yorkshire Navigation.

DUNKIRK BRANCH CANAL—*see* Birmingham Canal Navigations, Main Line.

DUTCH RIVER—*see* River Don (Yorkshire).

EASTERN COUNTIES NAVIGATION AND TRANSPORT COMPANY LIMITED—*see* River Larke.

EAU BRINK CUT—*see* River Ouse (Bedford).

ELLESMERE CANAL—*see* Shropshire Union Canals.

ELLESMERE BRANCH CANAL—*see* Shropshire Union Canals, Ellesmere Canal.

ELSECAR BRANCH CANAL—*see* Sheffield and South Yorkshire Navigation, Dearne and Dove Canal.

ENGINE BRANCH CANAL, SMETHWICK—*see* Birmingham Canal Navigations, Old Main Loop Line Smethwick Junction to Dudley Junction, Tipton.

(30)—ᴇʀᴇᴡᴀꜱʜ Cᴀɴᴀʟ.

(a) *Short Description.*

The canal commences at Langley Mill, where it joins the Cromford Canal, and proceeds by the outskirts of Ilkeston, Sandiacre, and Long Eaton to Trent Lock, where it forms a junction with the River Trent at the head of Cranfleet Cut.

For nearly a mile and a half from its commencement at Langley Mill the course of the canal is situated in the county of Nottinghamshire, the remainder being in the county of Derbyshire.

(b) *Proprietors, Officers, and Offices.*

The Company of Proprietors of the Erewash Canal.

Clerk : G. H. Woolley.

Office : Loughborough.

(c) *Distance Table.*

	Miles.	Fur.
Langley Mill, junction with Cromford Canal—Main Line—(No. 70b1), to—		
Shipley Colliery Wharf, and Shipley Gate Station, Midland Railway..	1	3
Road Bridge, from Ilkeston Junction Station to Ilkeston	3	5
Hallam Field Lock	5	6
The White House, junction with Nutbrook Canal (No. 78) and Stanton Iron Works ..	6	1
Junction Lock and Toll Office	6	2
Sandiacre Village	7	4
Sandiacre Junction, junction with Derby Canal (No. 27a) between Sandiacre Pasture and Sandiacre Locks	8	3
Sandiacre Lock	8	4
Long Eaton	10	0
Trent Lock and Toll Office, junction with River Trent (No. 112a)	11	6

(d) *Locks.*

1.—Eastwood.
2.—Shipley.
3.—Ilkeston Common Top.
4.—Ilkeston Common Bottom.
5.—Ilkeston Mill.
6.—Sough Close.
7.—Gallows Inn.
8.—Hallam Field.
9.—Junction.
10.—Sandiacre Pasture.
11.—Sandiacre.
12.—Dock Holme.
13.—Long Eaton.
14.—Trent.

Fall from Langley Mill.

(30)—EREWASH CANAL—*continued*.

(e) *Maximum size of vessels that can use the navigation.*

	Ft.	In.
Length	78	0
Width	14	6
Draught	3	6
Headroom, standard	7	4

Liable to reduction on account of subsidences due to mining.

(g) *Towing-path.*

There is a towing-path throughout the navigation.

(i) *Types of vessels using the navigation.*

Narrow boats and Upper Trent boats.

ESSEX SEWERS COMMISSION—*see* River Roding.

EXETER, CORPORATION OF THE CITY OF—*see* Exeter Ship Canal.

---

(31)—EXETER SHIP CANAL.

(a) *Short Description.*

The canal commences at the basin in the south of the city of Exeter, and proceeds by Topsham to Turf, where it joins the estuary of the River Exe, all in the county of Devonshire.

The River Exe in Exeter is also navigable from the junction with the canal through Kings Arms Flood Gates up to Exe Bridge.

There is a second entrance from the estuary of the River Exe to the canal at Topsham through Topsham Lock.

(b) *Proprietors, Officers, and Offices.*

The Corporation of the City of Exeter.

Town Clerk : G. R. Shorto.

Office : Town Hall, Exeter.

Wharfinger and Harbour Master : A. Clements.

Lock Master at Turf : Thomas Dixon.

(c) *Distance Table.*

	Miles.	Fur.
Head of Canal Basin, Exeter, to—		
Junction with River Exe through Kings Arms Flood Gates..	–	1½
Double Locks	1	4
Topsham, junction with River Exe estuary through Topsham Lock	4	0
Turf Lock, entrance lock to canal from River Exe estuary..	5	4

(31)—EXETER SHIP CANAL—*continued.*

River Exe.

	Miles.	Fur.
From junction with the canal through Kings Arms Flood Gates to—		
Exe Bridge, Exeter		5

(d) Locks.

Main Line.

1.—Double Locks (one lock).
2.—Turf.

Fall from Exeter.

River Exe Branch.

1.—Kings Arms Flood Gates (flood gates only).

Second Entrance to Canal.

1.—Topsham.

Fall from canal to River Exe estuary.

(e) Maximum size of vessels that can use the navigation.

	Ft.	In.
Length, Main Line of Canal	125	0
Width ,, ,, ,, ...	26	0
Draught ,, ,, ,, ...	12	6
Headroom ,, ,, ,, —Not limited..		
Width, through Kings Arms Flood Gates ..	26	0
Length, through Topsham Lock	90	0
Width ,, ,, ,, ...	24	0

(g) Towing-path.

There is a towing-path throughout the main line of the canal.

(h) Tidal Information.

The tide flows in the estuary of the River Exe to the tail of Turf Lock.

High water at Turf Lock 20min. after Exmouth, or 4hrs. 50min. after London Bridge.

Spring tides rise	15ft.
Neap ,, ,, ...	10ft.

(i) Types of vessels using the navigation.

Sea-going vessels up to 400 tons burden.

Steamers are allowed on the canal, but few use it.

The Corporation keep three horses and drivers for towing on the canal, and horse haulage has to be paid by all vessels using the canal, whether required or not. The Corporation also keep one tug for towing vessels to and from Turf and Topsham and the sea.

FAIRBOTTOM BRANCH CANAL—*see* Great Central Railway, Ashton Canal, Hollinwood Branch.

FARCET RIVER—*see* Middle Level Navigations.

---

(32)—FEARNLEY CUT.

(a) Short Description.

The canal, which is a little over one furlong in length, leads out of the Thornhill Flood Lock Weir Stream of the Calder and Hebble Navigation, and gives access to the works of the Calder and Mersey Extract Company Ltd., Dewsbury (formerly Messrs. Howroyd and Oldroyd).

(b) Proprietors, Officers, and Offices.

The ownership of the canal is not clearly defined.

(e) Maximum size of vessels that can use the navigation.

							Ft.	In.
Length	..	..	..	..	..	..	57	6
Width	..	..	..	..	..	..	14	1
Draught	..	..	..	..	..	..	5	0

(g) Towing-path.

There is no towing-path.

(i) Types of vessels using the navigation.

Yorkshire keels and boats.

FITZWILLIAM, EARL OF—*see* Park Gate Branch Canal.

FLEET DIKE—*see* River Bure.

FORTY FOOT RIVER, *alias* VERMUYDEN'S EAU—*see* Middle Level Navigations.

---

(33)—RIVER FOSS.

(a) Short Description.

The river commences to be navigable at Yearsley Baths, in the city of York, a short distance above the York Union Workhouse, and proceeds through the eastern portion of the city to Blue Bridge, where it forms a junction with the River Ouse.

(33)—RIVER FOSS—*continued.*

(b) *Proprietors, Officers, and Offices.*

The Corporation of the City of York.

Town Clerk : R. Percy Dale.

Deputy Town Clerk : William Giles.

Engineer : Alfred Creer.

Offices : The Guildhall, York.

Collector of Dues : Henry Stephenson, Bridge Street, York.

(c) *Distance Table.*

	Miles.	Fur.
Yearsley Baths to—		
Monk Bridge	–	5
Laverthorpe Bridge	–	7½
Leetham's Mills	1	2
Foss Bridge	1	3
Castle Mills Bridge and Lock	1	5
Blue Bridge, junction with River Ouse (No. 81)	1	7

(d) *Locks.*

1.—Castle Mills.

Fall to River Ouse.

(e) *Maximum size of vessels that can use the navigation.*

	Ft.	In.
Length	97	0
Width	18	6
Draught from River Ouse to Leetham's Mills	7	6
„ from Leetham's Mills to Yearsley Baths .. .. ..about	6	6
Headroom—at summer level	10	0

(g) *Towing-path.*

There is no towing-path ; vessels are propelled by poles or shafts.

(i) *Types of vessels using the navigation.*

Yorkshire keels and lighters.

The largest lighters in use are those engaged in Messrs. Leetham's grain traffic : they carry a maximum load of 230 tons.

FOSSDYKE CANAL--*see* Great Northern and Great Eastern Joint Railways.

(34)—FOXLEY BRANCH CANAL.

(a) Short Description.

The canal, which is five furlongs in length, leads out of the Caldon Branch of the Trent and Mersey Canal (No. 76c1) near Milton, and proceeds to Ford Green Iron Works, all in the county of Staffordshire.

(b) Proprietors, Officers, and Offices.

Proprietor : Robert Heath, Esq., Ford Green Ironworks, Milton, near Burslem.

(e) Maximum size of vessels that can use the navigation.

						Ft.	In.
Length	..	..	..	..	..	72	0
Width	..	..	..	..	..	7	0
Draught	..	..	..	..	..	3	8

(g) Towing-path.

There is a towing-path throughout the navigation.

(i) Types of vessels using the navigation.

Narrow boats.

FRITH BANK DRAIN, *alias* JUNCTION DRAIN—*see* Witham Drainage General Commissioners.

FRODINGHAM BECK BRANCH NAVIGATION—*see* Driffield Navigation.

———

(35)—FURNESS RAILWAY.

(a) Short Description.

The Furness Railway Company are the proprietors of the Ulverston Canal. The canal commences at the foot of Hoad Hill, Ulverston, which is about a quarter of a mile outside the town to the eastward, and proceeds in a south-easterly direction for a distance of one mile three furlongs to Morecambe Bay, all in the county of Lancashire.

The speed of vessels on the canal is limited to three knots per hour.

(b) Proprietors, Officers, and Offices.

The Furness Railway Company.

Secretary and General Manager : Alfred Aslett.

Engineer : W. S. Whitworth.

Goods Manager : Clement Mossop.

Offices : Barrow-in-Furness.

(35)—FURNESS RAILWAY—*continued.*

(d) *Locks.*

1.—Entrance Lock.
Fall from canal to Morecambe Bay.

(e) *Maximum size of vessels that can use the navigation.*

	Ft.	In.
Length	104	0
Width	27	0
Draught on Spring tides	12	6
„ on Neap tides	7	6

(g) *Towing-path.*

There is no towing-path.

A road runs along the northern bank of the canal almost entirely throughout its length, but it is not used for towing purposes.

(h) *Tidal Information.*

High water in Morecambe Bay at the entrance lock is about 15min. after that at Liverpool, or about 2hrs. 20min. before London Bridge.

Spring tides rise about .. .. 28ft.
Neap „ „ „ .. .. 21ft.

The tide sometimes makes a level with the water in the canal at high water of Spring tides.

(i) *Types of vessels using the navigation.*

Coasting vessels up to 120 tons burden, and a few steamers.

GERARD'S BRIDGE BRANCH CANAL—*see* London and North Western Railway, St. Helens Canal.

GIANTS GRAVE AND BRITON FERRY CANAL—*see* The Earl of Jersey's Canals.

GILBEY, SIR WALTER, BART.—*see* River Stort.

GIPPING, RIVER—*see* Ipswich and Stowmarket Navigation.

---

(36)—GLAMORGANSHIRE AND ABERDARE CANALS.

(a) *Short Description.*

The Glamorganshire Canal commences ot Cyfarthfa, near Merthyr Tydfil, and proceeds by Abercanaid, Abercynon, Pontypridd, Treforest, Nantgarw, Melin Griffith, and Llandaff Yard to Cardiff, where it joins the estuary of the River Taff at Sea Lock, all in the county of Glamorganshire.

H

(36)—GLAMORGANSHIRE AND ABERDARE CANALS—*continued.*

Owing to many serious subsidences caused by colliery workings, the section of the canal between Merthyr Tydfil and Abercynon has been closed since 6th December, 1898, and up to the present time has not been re-opened.   The canal between Cyfarthfa and Merthyr Tydfil Warehouse has been disused since 1865.

The Aberdare Canal commences at a point about half a mile to the south-east of the town of Aberdare, and proceeds by Mountain Ash to Abercynon, where it forms a junction with the Glamorganshire Canal, all in the county of Glamorganshire.   A tramroad used to connect the town of Aberdare with the basin at the canal head.

(b) *Proprietors, Officers, and Offices.*

Proprietor : The Marquis of Bute.

Traffic Manager : Lewis Llewellyn.

Office : West Canal Wharf, Cardiff.   Telephone No. 12.

Engineer : W. T. Lewis.

Office : West Canal Wharf, Cardiff.

The Proprietor acts as a carrier on the canal.

(c) *Distance Table.*

Glamorganshire Canal (No. 36a).

	Miles.	Fur.
Cyfartha Iron Works to—		
Merthyr Tydfil Warehouse	–	4
Abercanaid .. ..:	2	3
Ynys-y-gored	4	6
Aberfan	5	3
Abercynon, junction with Aberdare Canal		
(No. 36b) and head of lock No. 17 ..	8	6
Ynyscaedudwg	10	5
Cilfynydd	11	2
Coedpenmain	11	7
Pontypridd	12	2
Treforest	13	2
Denia, junction with Dr. Thomas's Canal		
(No. 109) and tail of lock (No. 34) ..	14	2
Upper Boat	15	1
Nantgarw	16	4
Tongwynlais	18	6
Mellin Griffith Basin	20	0
Llandaff Yard, and tail of Llandaff Lock, No. 45	21	4
Tunnel under Queen Street, Cardiff	24	0
Canal Warehouse and Offices, Cardiff	24	3½
Junction with Cut, one furlong in length, lead-		
ing to top end of the Bute West Dock,		
Cardiff, between locks Nos. 50 and 51 ..	24	4½
New Lock, Cardiff, No. 51	24	5
Sea Lock, Cardiff, No. 52, and entrance to canal	25	4

(36)—GLAMORGANSHIRE AND ABERDARE CANALS—*continued.*

Aberdare Canal (No. 36b).

	Miles.	Fur.
Canal Head, Aberdare, Wharf and Warehouse, to—		
Cwmbach Lock	1	0
Duffryn Lock	3	0
Mountain Ash, Nixon's Navigation Colliery, Pitwood Wharf	3	2
Mountain Ash, Nixon's Upper Limekiln, and Canal Wharf and Warehouse	3	4
Watson's Timber Yard and Nixon's Lower Limekiln	4	0
Abercynon, junction with Glamorganshire Canal (No. 36a)	6	6

(d) *Locks.*

Glamorganshire Canal (No. 36a).

1
to } Flight.
3

4
and } Glyndyris (Staircase).
5.

6
and } Aberfan (Staircase).
7.

8.—Pontygwaith.
9.—Cefnglas.

10
and } (Staircase).
11.

12
and } (Staircase).
13.

14
and } (Staircase).
15.

16
and } (Staircase).
17.

18
and } (Staircase).
19.

20
and } (Staircase).
21.

22
and } (Staircase).
23.

24.
25.—Ynyscaedudwg.
26.
27.—Road.

(36)—GLAMORGANSHIRE AND ABERDARE CANALS—*continued*

28
and } (Staircase).
29.

30.

31
and } (Staircase).
32.

33.—Duffryn.
34.—Denia.

35
to } Treble (Staircase).
37

38.—Taff's Well.
39.—Caeglas.
40.—Portobello.
41.—Ton.
42.—Llwynmellt.
43.—Forest.
44.
45.—Llandaff.
46.—College.
47.—Gabalva.
48.—Monachty.
49.—North Road.
50.—Crockherbtown.
51.—New.
52.—Sea.

Fall from Merthyr Tydfil.

Aberdare Canal (No. 36b).

1.—Cwmbach.
2.—Duffryn.

Fall from Aberdare.

(e) *Maximum size of vessels that can use the navigation.*

Glamorganshire Canal (No. 36a).

	Ft.	In.
Length.—From Canal Entrance to Canal Warehouses, Cardiff	90	0
From Canal Warehouses, Cardiff, to Cyfarthfa	60	0
Width.— From Canal Entrance to Canal Warehouses, Cardiff	24	0
From Canal Warehouses, Cardiff to Cyfarthfa	8	9
Draught.—From Sea Lock to New Lock	8	6
From New Lock to Canal Warehouses, Cardiff	7	0
From Canal Warehouses, Cardiff, to Melin Griffith	3	6
From Melin Griffith to Cyfarthfa	3	0
Headroom.—Standard (but liable to reduction owing to subsidences due to mining)	6	6

(36)—Glamorganshire and Aberdare Canals—*continued.*

Aberdare Canal (No. 36b).

	Ft.	In.
Length	60	0
Width	8	9
Draught	3	0
Headroom.—Standard (but liable to reduction owing to subsidences due to mining)	6	6

(f) Tunnels.

Glamorganshire Canal (No. 36a).

The Tunnel, Cardiff.

Length	115yds.	
Minimum height above water level	7	6
Minimum width at water level	10	8

Towing-path runs for 70ft. The remaining 276ft. is worked by the boatmen by chains fastened on the side wall.

(g) Towing-path.

There is a towing-path throughout the navigation.

(h) Tidal Information.

Glamorganshire Canal (No. 36a).

The tide flows to the tail of Sea Lock, Cardiff. The entrance channel from Sea Lock to the sea runs out dry at low water.

High water at Cardiff 5hrs. after London Bridge.

Spring tides rise	36ft. 6in.
Neap ,, ,, ...	27ft.

The average tide gives a depth of from 12ft. to 14ft. over the sill of Sea Lock, but at Neap tides the depth is as low as 5ft.

(i) Types of vessels using the navigation.

Boats of a type shorter and wider than the ordinary narrow boats ; the majority not having cabins.—*See* Glamorganshire and Aberdare Canal Boats, Section 9, Types of Vessels, (a) Non-sailing vessels.

Glan-y-wern Canal—*see* the Earl of Jersey's Canals.

Glasson Dock Branch Canal—*see* London and North Western Railway, Lancaster Canal (North end).

---

(37)—River Glen.

(a) Short Description.

The river commences to be navigable at Surfleet Railway Station, on the Spalding and Boston Line of the Great Northern Railway, and proceeds for a distance of one and a quarter miles to its junction with the River Welland (No. 119), all in the county of Lincolnshire.

(37)—RIVER GLEN—*continued*.

Very little trade is done on the river, the navigation of the River Welland having much declined. Although there is a fair depth of water for some distance above Surfleet Station, no trade has been conducted above that point for many years.

(b) Proprietors, Officers, and Offices.

The Deeping Fen General Works of Drainage Trustees have control of the water, and keep the bed of the river clear.

Clerks : Calthorp and Bonner, Solicitors.

Office : Spalding.

Superintendent : A. Harrison.

Office : Little London, Spalding.

The River Glen Bank Trustees control the banks of the river.

Clerk : C. E. Bonner, of Calthorp and Bonner, Solicitors, Spalding.

Superintendent : A. Harrison.

Office : Little London, Spalding.

(d) Locks.

There is a sluice at the mouth of the river, just above the junction with the River Welland, which serves to shut out the tide and hold back the land water. The sluice has two navigation openings, each 15ft. wide, and closed with vertical shutters or cloughs ; each opening is also provided with sea doors.

Vessels can pass the sluice either on the first level or back level of the tide.

(e) Maximum size of vessels that can use the navigation.

	Ft.	In.
Length.—Not limited	—	—
Width	14	6
Draught .. .. about	6	0

(g) Towing-path.

There is no towing-path.

(h) Tidal Information.

See Tidal Information, River Welland (No. 119).

(i) Types of vessels using the navigation.

Lighters, with a maximum carrying capacity of about 60 tons.

GLOUCESTER AND BERKELEY SHIP CANAL—*see* Sharpness New Docks and Gloucester and Birmingham Navigation Company.

GLOUCESTERSHIRE COUNTY COUNCIL—*see* Thames and Severn Canal.

GOSPEL OAK BRANCH CANAL—*see* Birmingham Canal Navigations, Walsall Canal.

GOWER BRANCH CANAL—*see* Birmingham Canal Navigations.

———

(38)—GRAND JUNCTION CANAL.

(a) *Short Description.*

The main line of the canal commences by a junction with the Oxford Canal at Braunston, in the county of Northamptonshire, and proceeds by Long Buckby, Weedon, Blisworth, Stoke Bruerne, and Cosgrove, in the same county; Wolverton, Fenny Stratford, Leighton Buzzard, and Cheddington, in the county of Buckinghamshire; Tring, Berkhampstead, and Rickmansworth, in the county of Hertfordshire; and Uxbridge to the River Thames at Brentford, in the county of Middlesex.

There are branches leading out of the main line as follows:—

At Weedon in Northamptonshire to Weedon Barracks, known as the Weedon Military Dock, which is the property of H. M. War Department.

From Gayton to Northampton, all in the county of Northamptonshire.

From Cosgrove to Old Stratford and Deanshanger, in the county of Northamptonshire, and to Leckhampstead and Buckingham, in the county of Buckinghamshire.

From Marsworth to Aylesbury, commencing and terminating in the county of Buckinghamshire, and traversing a portion of the county of Hertfordshire.

From Bulbourne to Wendover, in the counties of Hertfordshire and Buckinghamshire.

From Cowley Peachey, in the county of Middlesex, to Iver, Langley, and Slough, in the county of Buckinghamshire; and

From Bull's Bridge to Southall, Greenford, Alperton, Willesden, and Paddington, where there is a junction with the Regents Canal, all in the county of Middlesex.

The Leicester section of the canal commences at Norton, 4¼ miles south of Braunston, and proceeds by Welton, Crick, and Yelvertoft, in the county of Northamptonshire, and Husband's Bosworth, Foxton, Kilby Bridge, and Aylestone to Leicester, in the county of Leicestershire.

There are two branches leading out of the Leicester section, one from near North Kilworth to Welford, and the other from Foxton to Market Harborough, both in the county of Leicestershire.

The Wendover branch is not now navigable between the Stop Lock at Tring Ford and Wendover.

(38)—GRAND JUNCTION CANAL—*continued.*

The Old Stratford and Buckingham branch between Maids Moreton Mill and Buckingham is barely navigable.

The course of the Grand Junction Canal is for the most part through an agricultural country. A considerable through general trade passes from Birmingham, Leicester, Nottingham, and the Derbyshire Coal Fields to London.

On the portions of the canal and branches forming the route between Paddington and Slough, there is a large traffic in bricks, gravel, and manure.

The trade done on the Wendover, Old Stratford, and Buckingham, Welford, and Market Harborough branches is very small.

The canal is in fair condition as a whole, the worst portions of it as regards navigation being the Wendover, Old Stratford and Buckingham, Welford, and Market Harborough branches.

By an arrangement made in 1897 with the other canal companies forming the route between London and Birmingham, and London, Leicester, and the Derbyshire coal fields, the Grand Junction Canal Company have power to quote through tolls for traffic between these places.

(b) *Proprietors, Officers, and Offices.*

The Company of Proprietors of the Grand Junction Canal.

Clerk to the Company and General Manager : Hubert Thomas.

Office : 21, Surrey Street, Strand, London, W.C.

Telegrams : " Waterway," London. Telephone : 1899, Gerrard. Engineer : Gordon Thomas.

Office : 21, Surrey Street, Strand, London, W.C.

Telegrams : " Engineer Waterway," London.

Telephone : 1899, Gerrard.

(c) *Distance Table.*

Main Line (No. 38a1).

	Miles.	Fur.
Braunston Junction, junction with Oxford Canal, Braunston Branch (No. 82f), to—		
Braunston Tunnel, North-end, and head of Lock No. 6	1	2
Braunston Tunnel, South-end	2	4
Welton Wharf	2	6
Norton Junction and Wharf, junction with Leicester Section, Main Line (No. 38b1), and head of Lock No. 7	4	2
Buckby Wharves	4	6
Buckby Toll Office	5	2
Whilton Wharf	5	6
Muscot Mill	6	4

(38)—GRAND JUNCTION CANAL—*continued.*

	Miles.	Fur.
Braunston Junction, junction with Oxford Canal, Braunston Branch (No. 82f), to (*continued*)—		
Brockhall Bridge	7	0
Thornton's Wharf	7	6
Weedon Wharves, and junction with Weedon Military Dock (No. 38a2), between locks Nos. 13 and 14	9	0
Stowe Hill Wharf	10	0
Floore Lane Wharves	10	2
Heyford Furnaces	11	6
Bugbrook Wharves	13	0
Banbury Lane Wharf	15	0
Gayton Brick Field	16	2
Gayton Junction and Toll Office, junction with Northampton Branch (No. 38a3), between Locks Nos. 13 and 14	16	6
Blisworth Wharves	17	0
Blisworth Mill	17	6
Blisworth Tunnel Wharf	18	0
Blisworth Tunnel, North-end	18	2
Blisworth Tunnel, South-end	20	0
Stoke Bruerne, Lock No. 20	21	2
Grafton Bridge	22	6
Yardley Wharf	24	0
Castlethorpe Wharf	26	0
Head of Cosgrove Lock, and junction with Old Stratford and Buckingham Branch (No. 38a4)	27	0
Old Wolverton	28	0
Wolverton Station, L. & N. W. Railway	29	0
Bradwell	29	6
Statonbury	31	4
Linford Dock and Wharf	32	0
Willen	33	6
Woolston Mill	34	6
Simpson Wharf	37	0
Simpson Dock	37	4
Fenny Stratford Wharves and Lock	38	6
Water Eaton	39	4
Stoke Hammond	41	6
Soulbury Three Locks	42	6
Linslade	44	2
Leighton Buzzard—Fellows, Morton, & Clayton Ltd., Canal Carriers, Wharf	46	2
Grove Lock	47	6
Slapton	50	0
Horton Wharf	50	4
Ivinghoe Pumping Engine	51	2
Seabrook	52	2
Cheddington Wharf	52	6
Marsworth Junction, junction with Aylesbury Branch (No. 38a5) and tail of Lock No. 40	54	2
Stanhopesend	54	4

(38)—GRAND JUNCTION CANAL—*continued.*

	Miles.	Fur.
Braunston Junction, junction with Oxford Canal, Braunston Branch (No. 82f), to (*continued*)—		
Bulbourne Junction and Toll Office, junction with Wendover Branch (No. 38a6) and head of Lock No. 45	55	2
Bulbourne Stores	55	4
Pendley Wharf and Tring Station, L. & N. W. Railway	56	6
New Ground	57	6
Cowroast Lock	58	2
Dudswell Wharf	58	6
Northchurch	59	6
Berkhamsted Station and Wharf	61	0
Berkhamsted Mill	61	4
Bourne End Mill	63	2
Winkwell Wharf	63	4
Boxmoor Wharves	64	4
Two Waters Mill and Wharves	65	2
Frogmore Mill	66	0
Apsley Mill	66	0
Nash Mill	66	4
King's Langley Mill	67	6
Home Park Mill	68	2
Hunton Bridge Wharf	69	2
Hunton Bridge Mill	69	4
Watford, Lady Capel's Wharf	70	2
Watford, Grove Mill	70	6
Watford, Cassio Bridge Wharves	72	4
Croxley Mill, and head of Lock No. 79.. ..	73	0
Rickmansworth Lock, and Batchworth Mill and Wharves	74	6
Frogmore Wharf	75	0
Springwell	76	2
Harefield Lime Works	77	0
Copper Mill	77	2
Troy Mill	77	4
Harefield Brick and Cement Works	78	2
Harefield Moor Wharf	79	0
King's Mill	81	4
Uxbridge Wharves	81	6
Uxbridge Moor Wharves—Fellows, Morton, & Clayton Ltd., Canal Carriers	82	0
Uxbridge Gas Works	82	4
Cowley Lock and Toll Office	83	2
Cowley Peachy Junction, junction with Slough Branch (No. 38a7)	84	0
Cowley Brickfield	84	0
Yiewsley Dock	84	2
West Drayton Wharves and Railway Station, G. W. Railway	84	6
Horton	85	0
Rutter's and Eastwood's Docks	85	0
Dawley	86	0

(38)—Grand Junction Canal—*continued.*

	Miles.	Fur.
Braunston Junction, junction with Oxford Canal, Braunston Branch (No. 82f), to (*continued*)—		
Botwell	87	0
Bull's Bridge Junction and Toll Office, junction with Paddington Branch (No. 38a8) ..	87	6
North Hyde	88	0
Heston	88	4
Passenham Dock	88	6
Norwood Mill and Wharf	89	0
Pasmore Dock	89	4
Norwood Lock No. 90, and Toll Office ..	89	6
Windmill Lane	90	2
Hanwell Dock	90	4
River Brent	90	6
Brentford Locks, No. 100, Toll Office, and Fellows, Morton, & Clayton, Ltd., Canal Carriers, Wharves and Warehouses ..	93	0
Thames Lock, Brentford, junction with River Thames (No. 107a)	93	6

Weedon Military Dock (No. 38a2).

	Miles.	Fur.
Length from Weedon Wharves to Weedon Barracks	–	2

Northampton Branch (No. 38a3).

	Miles.	Fur.
Gayton Junction, junction with Main Line (No. 38a1), to—		
Blisworth Brickyard	–	2
Milton Road Bridge	1	0
Rothersthorpe Road Bridge	2	2
Hunsbury Hill Iron Works	3	2
Duston Mill Bridge	3	4
Cotton End Wharf	4	6
Northampton, junction with River Nene (No.74a)	5	0

Old Stratford and Buckingham Branch (No. 38a4).

	Miles.	Fur.
Cosgrove Junction, junction with Main Line (No. 38a1), to—		
Old Stratford Cut End	1	2
Towcester Road Bridge and Old Stratford Wharf	1	4
Passenham Road Bridge and Wharf	2	2
Deanshanger Wharves	3	0
Buckingham Road Bridge	4	0
Mount Hill Bridge	5	0
Little Hill Bridge	5	6
Thornton Road Bridge and Wharf	6	2
Leckhampstead Bridge and Wharf	7	2
Hyde Lane Lock	7	7
Maids Moreton Mill	9	0
Buckingham Lock	9	4
Bourton	9	6
Buckingham Wharf	10	6

(38)—GRAND JUNCTION CANAL.—*continued.*

Aylesbury Branch (No. 38a5).

	Miles.	Fur.
Marsworth Junction, junction with Main Line (No. 38a1), to—		
Long Marston Bridge	–	4
Wilstone Bridge and Wharf	1	0
Puttenham Road Bridge	2	0
Buckland Road Bridge	2	4
Broughton Road Bridge	4	6
Walton Mill	5	6
Walton Bridge	6	0
Aylesbury Wharf	6	2

Wendover Branch (No. 38a6).

	Miles.	Fur.
Bulbourne Junction, junction with Main Line (No. 38a1), to—		
Tring Wharf	–	6
Tring Ford Stop Lock and Little Tring Bridge	1	2
Wilstone Swing Bridge	2	0
Drayton Bridge	2	6
Buckland Bridge and Wharf	3	2
Aston Clinton Bridge	4	0
Halton	5	0
Weston Turville Road Bridge	5	6
Wendover Wharf	6	6

Slough Branch (No. 38a7).

	Miles.	Fur.
Cowley Peachy Junction, junction with Main Line (No. 38a1), to—		
Fray's Aqueduct	–	2
Colne Aqueduct and Wharf	–	4
Colne Brook Aqueduct and Studd's Wharf ..	–	6
Thorney Lane Wharf	1	0
Iver, Reed's Brickfields..	1	2
Mead's Wharves	1	6
Meeking's Bridge	2	0
Hollow Hill Wharf	2	2
Langley Station Wharf and Peek's Brickfield	2	6
Langley Brickfield	3	0
Langley Schools Bridge, and Williams' and Wallington's Brickfield	3	4
Middle Green Wharf	3	6
Uxbridge Road Wharf	4	2
Nash's Wharves	4	4
Slough Basin	5	0

Paddington Branch (No. 38a8).

	Miles.	Fur.
Bull's Bridge, junction with Main Line (No. 38a1), to—		
Stroud's Dock and Great Western Railway Sleepers Depot	–	2
Stroud's Dock	–	4
Southall Gas Works Dock	–	6

(38)—GRAND JUNCTION CANAL—*continued.*

Bull's Bridge, junction with Main Line
(No. 38a1), to—*continued.*

	Miles.	Fur.
Hayes Road Bridge	1	2
Hewitt's Dock	2	0
Odell's Dock	2	2
Odell's Yeading Dock	2	4
West End Wharf	2	6
Northolt Bridge	3	0
Greenford Wharf	4	6
Horsendon Road Bridge	5	6
Alperton Wharf	7	2
Alperton Valley	7	6
Twyford	8	2
Lower Place	9	2
Willesden Old Oak Wharf	9	6
Mitre Wharves	10	4
Kensal Green Bridge	11	2
Kensington Vestry Wharf	11	4
Harrow Road Wharves	11	6
Carlton Bridge	12	0
Amberley Road Wharves	12	4
Paddington Stop and Toll Office	12	6
Harrow Road Bridge, and junction with Regents Canal, Main Line (No. 86a)	13	0
Bishop's Road Bridge	13	2
Paddington Basin	13	6

Leicester Section, Main Line (No. 38b1).

Norton Junction, junction with Main Line
(No. 38a1), to—

	Miles.	Fur.
Welton Wharves and Railway Station, L. & N. W. Railway	1	6
Watford Locks	2	2
Crick Tunnel, South end	3	6
Crick Wharf	5	0
Yelvertoft Wharf	7	2
Junction with Welford Branch (No. 38b2)	15	4
North Kilworth Wharf	16	2
Husbands Bosworth Tunnel, North end	17	6
Lubenham Wharf (Morton's)	21	6
Foxton, junction with Market Harborough Branch (No. 38b3), and bottom of Foxton Lift and Locks	23	2
Debdale Wharf	24	2
Saddington Tunnel, South end	26	6
Lock No. 18	28	1
Kilby Bridge Wharf	33	0
Blaby Wharf	36	0
Aylestone Mill (Navigation enters River Soar)	39	2
St. Mary's Mills and Aylestone Gas Works	40	0
Leicester Corporation Wharves	40	4
Leicester, West Bridge, junction with Leicester Navigation (No. 59)	41	2

(38)—GRAND JUNCTION CANAL—*continued.*

Leicester Section, Welford Branch (No. 38b2).

	Miles.	Fur.
Junction with Leicester Section, Main Line (No. 38b1), to—		
Welford Lock	1	2
Welford Basin	1	6

Leicester Section, Market Harborough Branch (No. 38b3).

	Miles.	Fur.
Foxton, junction with Leicester Section, Main Line (No. 38b1), to—		
Foxton (Roadstone Landing)	–	4
Foxton Wharf	–	6
Foxton (Roadstone Landing)	2	2
Gallow Hill	2	2
Market Harborough Basin	5	6

(d) *Locks.*

Main Line (No. 38a1).

1
to } Braunston.
6.

Rise from Braunston.

7.—Buckby.
8.—Buckby.
9.—Buckby.
10
to } Buckby.
13.
14
and } Stoke Bruerne.
15.
16
to } Stoke Bruerne.
20.
21.—Cosgrove.

Fall from Braunston.

22.—Fenny Stratford.
23.
24
to } Soulbury.
26.
27.—Leighton Buzzard.
28.—Grove.
29.
30.
31.—Horton.
32
and } Ivinghoe.
33.
34.—Pitstowe.
35
and } Marsworth.
36.

(38)—GRAND JUNCTION CANAL.—*continued.*

37
and } Marsworth.
38.

39.—Marsworth.

40
to } Marsworth.
45.

            Rise from Braunston.

46.—Cowroast.

47
and } Dudswell.
48.

49.

50.—Northchurch.

51
and } Northchurch.
52.

53.—Berkhamsted.

54
and } Berkhamsted.
55.

56.

57
and } Bourne End.
58.

59.

60
and } Winkwell.
61.

62.

63.

64.—Boxmoor.

65
to } Apsley.
67.

68
and } Nash Mill.
69.

69a.—Kings Langley.

70.

71.

72
and } Hunton Bridge.
73.

74.—Lady Capel's.

75
and } Cassiobury.
76.

77.

78.—Watford.

79.

80.—Lot Mead.

81.—Rickmansworth.

82.

(38)—GRAND JUNCTION CANAL—*continued*

83.
84.
85.
86.
87.—Denham.
88.—Uxbridge.
89.—Cowley.
90
and } Norwood.
91.
92
to } Hanwell.
97.
98.—Osterley.
99.
100.—Brentford (Duplicate locks, side by side).
101.—Thames.

Fall from Braunston.
Total, 102 Locks, including No. 69a.

Northampton Branch (No. 38a3).

1
to } Rothersthorpe.
13.
14.—Wootton.
15.—Hardingstone.
16.—Northampton.
17.—Northampton.

Fall from Gayton Junction.

Old Stratford and Buckingham Branch (No. 38a4).

1.—Hyde Lane.
2.—Buckingham.

Rise from Cosgrove Junction.

Aylesbury Branch (No. 38a5).

1
to } Marsworth.
8.
9.—Wilstone.
10
and } Puttenham.
11.
12.—Buckland.
13.—Aston Clinton.
14.—Aylesbury.
15.—Aylesbury.
16.—Aylesbury.

Fall from Marsworth Junction.

Wendover Branch (No. 38a6).

1.—Tring Ford Stop Lock.
Fall from Bulbourne Junction.

(38)—GRAND JUNCTION CANAL—*continued.*

Leicester Section, Main Line (No. 38b1).

1.
2
to ⎰ (Staircase) ⎱ Watford.
5. ⎰
6.
7.

Rise from Norton Junction.

8 ⎰
to ⎱ (Staircase) ⎰ Foxton.
12. ⎱
13 ⎰
to ⎱ (Staircase)
17. ⎰
18 ⎰
to ⎱ Kibworth.
21. ⎰
22.—Cranes.
23.—Newton Top.
24.—Newton Middle.
25.—Newton Bottom.
26 ⎰
to ⎱ Wigston.
29. ⎰
30.—Kilby Bridge.
31.—Double Rail.
32.—Erving's.
33.—Bush.
34.—Little Glen.
35.—Whetstone Lane.
36.—Gee's.
37.—Blue Bank.
38.—King's.
39.—Aylestone Mill.
40.—St. Mary's Mill.
41.—Toll House, Leicester.

Fall from Norton Junction.

NOTE.—The Foxton Inclined Plane Lift now gives an alternative route to the Foxton flight of ten locks—*see* Section 4, (c) Lifts.

Welford Branch (No. 38b2).

1.—Welford.
Rise from the junction with the Leicester Section—Main Line—to Welford.

(e) *Maximum size of vessels that can use the navigation.*

Main Line (No. 38a1).

						Ft.	In.
Length	..	..	..	..	..	72	0
Width	..	..	..	..	..	14	3

I

(38)—GRAND JUNCTION CANAL—*continued.*

	Ft.	In.
Draught.—Brentford to Berkhampstead— maximum for narrow boats ..	4	3
Brentford to Berkhampstead— maximum for wide boats and barges	4	0
Berkhampstead to Braunston— maximum for narrow boats ..	3	8

Weedon Military Dock (No. 38a2).

	Ft.	In.
Length	72	0
Width	7	0
Draught .. .. maximum	3	8

Northampton Branch (No. 38a3).

	Ft.	In.
Length	72	0
Width	7	0
Draught. .. .. maximum	4	3

Old Stratford and Buckingham Branch (No. 38a4).

	Ft.	In.
Length	72	0
Width	7	0
Draught, maximum, from Cosgrove Junction to Maids Moreton Mill	3	0
,, maximum, from Maids Moreton Mill to Buckingham	1	8

Aylesbury Branch (No. 38a5).

	Ft.	In.
Length	72	0
Width	7	0
Draught	2	6

Wendover Branch (No. 38a6).

	Ft.	In.
Length	72	0
Width	7	0
Draught—maximum, from Bulbourne Junction to Tring Ford Stop Lock ..	2	6
Not navigable beyond.		

Slough Branch (No. 38a7).

	Ft.	In.
Length	72	0
Width	14	2
Draught—maximum, narrow boats	4	0
,, ,, wide boats and barges	3	9

Paddington Branch (No. 38a8).

	Ft.	In.
Length	72	0
Width	14	3
Draught—maximum, narrow boats	4	3
,, ,, wide boats and barges	4	0

(38)—GRAND JUNCTION CANAL—*continued.*

Leicester Section, Main Line (No. 38b1).

From Norton Junction to bottom of Watford Locks,
and from top of Watford Locks to Leicester.

		Ft.	In.
Length		72	0
Width		14	0
Draught	maximum	4	0

From bottom of Watford Locks to top of Watford Locks.

		Ft.	In.
Length		72	0
Width		7	0
Draught	maximum	4	0

Leicester Section, Welford Branch (No. 38b2).

		Ft.	In.
Length		72	0
Width		7	0
Draught	maximum	3	8

Leicester Section, Market Harborough Branch (No. 38b3).

		Ft.	In.
Length		72	0
Width		14	0
Draught		4	0
Headroom, throughout the whole of the Company's system of canals		8	0

(f) *Tunnels.*
Main Line (No. 38a1).

Braunston—
Length .. .. .. 2,042 yards.
Minimum height above water level 12 4
Minimum width at water level 15 10
No towing-path.

Blisworth—
Length .. .. .. 3,056 yards.
Minimum height above water level 10 9
Minimum width at water level 15 0
No towing-path.

The ordinary traffic through both Braunston and Blisworth tunnels is worked by the Canal Company's tugs. Gunpowder boats have to "leg" through. Independent steamers, if narrow boats, can enter at any time unless specially prohibited, and pass vessels in the case of Braunston tunnel on the right side of the tunnel, and in the case of Blisworth tunnel on the left side of the tunnel.

The Company's tugs leave the North end of Braunston Tunnel and the South end of Blisworth Tunnel at 5 a.m., 7 a.m., 9 a.m., 11 a.m., 1 p.m., 3 p.m., 5 p.m., and 7 p.m., and the South end of Braunston Tunnel and the North end of Blisworth Tunnel at 6 a.m., 8 a.m., 10 a.m., 12 noon, 2 p.m., 4 p.m., 6 p.m., and 8 p.m. Tickets are issued on production of Canal permit for Braunston Tunnel at Braunston and Buckby Toll Offices, and for Blisworth Tunnel at Gayton and Stoke Bruerne Toll Offices.

(38)—GRAND JUNCTION CANAL—*continued.*

Leicester Section, Main Line (No. 38b1).

		Ft.	In.
Crick—			
Length .. .. .. 1,528 yards.			
Minimum height above water level		10	6
Minimum width at water level		17	0

No towing-path.

Boats " shafted " or " legged " through.

Narrow boats enter from either end at any time.

		Ft.	In.
Husbands Bosworth—			
Length .. .. .. 1,166 yards.			
Minimum height above water level		9	6
Minimum width at water level		17	0

No towing-path.

Boats " shafted " or " legged " through.

Narrow boats enter from either end at any time.

		Ft.	In.
Saddington—			
Length .. .. .. 880 yards.			
Minimum height above water level		8	4
Minimum width at water level		16	0

No towing-path.

Boats " shafted " or " legged " through.

Narrow boats enter from either end at any time.

Unless obscured by fog or vapour, a clear view can be obtained from end to end through these three last-named tunnels.

(g) *Towing path.*

There is a towing-path throughout the whole of the Company's system of canals, with the exception of those portions of canal through the five tunnels above described.

(h) *Tidal Information.*

Main Line (No. 38a1).

High Spring tides flow into the canal at the Brentford end from the River Thames for the first three-quarters of a mile to the tail of Brentford Lock.

High water at Brentford is about one hour after London Bridge.

(i) *Types of vessels using the navigation.*

Barges navigate the Paddington and Slough branches and the main line between Brentford, Uxbridge, and Rickmansworth, and occasionally some go as far as Boxmoor and Berkhampstead. Wide boats navigate the London end of the canal principally for local trade. Narrow boats

(38)—GRAND JUNCTION CANAL——*continued.*

navigate the whole of the canal and branches, and are the only class of vessel which can use the Weedon Military Dock, the Northampton, Old Stratford and Buckingham, Aylesbury, and Wendover branches, and the portion of the Leicester Section, Main Line, covered by the Watford Locks, and also the Welford Branch. Steam narrow boats navigate the main line of the canal between Brentford, Paddington, and Braunston for Birmingham, and between Brentford, Paddington, and Leicester for Nottingham and neighbourhood.

GRAND SURREY CANAL, the old name for the Surrey Canal.

GRAND TRUNK CANAL, an old name for the Trent and Mersey Canal.

GRAND UNION CANAL, extends from Norton Junction to Foxton. In 1894, having previously been owned by an independent Company, it was purchased, together with the Old Union Canal (*alias* the Leicestershire and Northamptonshire Union Canal), by the Grand Junction Canal Company. The two together now form the Leicester section of that Company's system.

GRAND WESTERN CANAL—*see* Great Western Railway.

GRANTHAM CANAL—*see* Great Northern Railway.

GRAVESEND AND ROCHESTER CANAL—*see* South Eastern and Chatham Railway Company's Managing Committee.

---

(39)—GREAT CENTRAL RAILWAY.

(a) Short Description.

The canals belonging to the Great Central Railway Company consist of the Ashton, Peak Forest, and Macclesfield Canals, known as the Company's Western Canals, situated in the counties of Lancashire, Cheshire, and Derbyshire; and the Chesterfield Canal, situated in the counties of Derbyshire, West Riding of Yorkshire, and Nottinghamshire.

The Ashton Canal commences by a junction with the Rochdale Canal at Ducie Street, Manchester, and proceeds by Ancoats, Beswick, Bradford, Clayton, and Audenshaw to Ashton-under-Lyne, where it forms a junction with the Huddersfield Narrow Canal of the London and North Western Railway.

There are branches leading out of the main line as follows:—At Ancoats, a short branch known as the Islington Branch; the Stockport Branch from Clayton Junction, through Openshaw, Gorton, Reddish, and Heaton Norris to Stockport: the Hollinwood Branch from Fairfield Junction, passing through Droylsden and Audenshaw to Hollinwood; and the Fairbottom Branch from the Hollinwood Branch at Waterhouses to Bardsley Bridge. This latter branch is not now navigable beyond Bardsley Bridge.

(39)—GREAT CENTRAL RAILWAY—*continued.*

The Peak Forest Canal commences by a junction with the Ashton Canal at Dukinfield, and proceeds by Hyde, Woodley, Romiley, Marple, Disley, and New Mills to Bugsworth. There is a short branch from near Bugsworth to Whaley Bridge, and the canal is connected by a tramway 5¾ miles in length from Bugsworth, with Chapel-en-le-Frith and Dove-holes, by means of which stone is brought from Doveholes for loading into boats at Bugsworth.

The Macclesfield Canal commences by a junction with the Peak Forest Canal at Marple, and proceeds through Poynton, Adlington, Bollington, Macclesfield, Sutton, Bosley, and Congleton to Hall Green, where it joins a short branch from the main line of the Trent and Mersey Canal of the North Staffordshire Railway.

There is a short branch from the main line at a point about 2¼ miles south-west of Marple to High Lane Wharf.

The Chesterfield Canal commences at Chesterfield, and proceeds by Wheeldon Mill, Staveley, Renishaw, Killamarsh, Norwood, Kiveton Park, Shireoaks, Worksop, Retford, Hayton, Gringley, Walkeringham, and Misterton to Stockwith, where it forms a junction with the River Trent.

The canal does not appear to be in a navigable condition between Chesterfield and the tail of Dixon's Lock No. 4.

The trade done on any part of the canal is very small.

(b) Proprietors, Officers, and Offices.

Great Central Railway.

General Manager : S. Fay.

Secretary : Oliver S. Holt.

Goods Manager : Charles T. Smith.

Engineer : C. A. Rowlandson.

Canal District Agent : Henry Fish.

Head Offices : London Road Station, Manchester.

Ashton Canal.

(c) Distance Table.

Main Line (No. 39a1).

	Miles.	Fur.
Manchester, Ducie Street, junction with Rochdale Canal, Main Line (No. 87a), to—		
Store Street Aqueduct	–	1
Lock No. 1, Ancoats	–	2½
Ancoats Junction, junction with Islington Branch (No. 39a2)	–	3
Lock No. 3, Ancoats	–	4
Carruthers Street Bridge	–	5
Holt Town or Beswick Street Bridge	–	6
Gibbon Street or Quaker's Bridge	–	7
Manchester Corporation Gas Works	1	0½
Aqueduct over River Medlock and L. & Y. Ry. Bridge (Ardwick and Miles Platting Branch)	1	1½

(39)—GREAT CENTRAL RAILWAY—*continued.*

	Miles.	Fur.
Manchester, Ducie Street, junction with Rochdale Canal, Main Line (No. 87a), to (*continued*)—		
Lock No. 4, Beswick	1	2
Lock No. 6, Bradford	1	4
Clayton, Ashton New Road Bridge	1	7½
Lock No. 8, Clayton	2	0
Clayton Street Bridge	2	1½
Lock No. 10, Clayton	2	3
Clayton Junction, junction with Stockport Branch (No. 39a3)	2	3½
Lock No. 13, Clayton, and Crab Tree Swivel Bridge over lock	2	5½
Lock No. 14, Edge Lane	2	7
Lock No. 16, Edge Lane	3	0
Copperas House Swivel and Foot Bridges ..	3	3
Lock No. 17, Fairfield	3	4
Head of Lock No. 18, Fairfield and Fairfield Junction, junction with Hollinwood Branch (No. 39a4)	3	5½
Fairfield Road Bridge	3	6
Ashton Hill Lane Bridge	3	7½
Audenshaw, Ashton Old Road Bridge.. ..	4	1½
Kershaw Lane Bridge	4	2½
L. & N. W. Railway Bridge (Denton and Lumm Branch)	4	6
L. & N. W. Railway Bridge (Denton and Oldham Branch)	4	7
Hanover Street or China Bridge, and Ashton Moss Colliery Loading Stage	5	0
Guide Bridge Railway Station	5	3
Prince's Dock, for transhipping traffic from and to railway	5	6
Ashton-under-Lyne, Walk Mill Bridge ..	6	0½
Dukinfield Junction, junction with Peak Forest Canal, Main Line (No. 39b1)	6	1½
Ashton-under-Lyne, G. C. Rly. (Stalybridge Branch), Viaduct over canal	6	4
Ashton-under-Lyne, G. C. Rly., Ashton Station and Goods Warehouse	6	5
Ashton-under-Lyne, junction with Huddersfield Narrow Canal (No. 61b)	6	5½

Islington Branch (No. 39a2).

	Miles.	Fur.
Length, from junction with Main Line (No. 39a1)	--	2

Stockport Branch (No. 39a3).

	Miles.	Fur.
Clayton Junction, junction with Main Line (No. 39a1), to—		
Openshaw Local Board of Health Works ..	-	2
Openshaw, Pack Horse or Ashton Old Road Bridge	-	4½

	Miles.	Fur.
Clayton Junction, junction with Main Line (No. 39a1), to (*continued*)—		
Crab Croft or Ogden Lane Bridge	–	6
Gorton, Company's Boat Dock and Canal Works	–	$6\frac{1}{2}$
Canal Aqueduct over G. C. Rly. (Main Line) ..	–	7
Abbey Hey Bridge	1	2
Hyde Road Bridge	1	6
Canal Aqueduct over Sheffield and Midland Railway (Romiley and Ashbury's Branch)	2	$1\frac{1}{2}$
Reddish, Sandfold Bridge	2	$2\frac{1}{2}$
Woolfenden's Bridge	2	5
Davenport's Swivel Bridge	3	$1\frac{1}{2}$
Grey Horse Bridge	3	3
L. & N. W. Rly. Bridge (Heaton Norris and Guide Bridge Branch)	3	5
Bowlas Bridge	3	$6\frac{1}{2}$
Whitehills Bridge	4	$1\frac{1}{2}$
Stockport, Company's Wharf	4	6
Stockport, Termination of Canal	4	7

Hollinwood Branch (No. 39a4).

	Miles.	Fur.
Fairfield Junction, junction with Main Line (No. 39a2), to—		
Droylsden, Christy's, or Ashton New Road Bridge	–	1
Harrison's or Greenside Lane Bridge	–	3
Droylsden Gas Works and Wharves	–	$3\frac{1}{2}$
Clifford's Swivel Bridge	–	5
Bowden's Swivel Bridge	–	$6\frac{1}{2}$
Aqueduct over Lancashire and Yorkshire Rly. (Manchester and Stalybridge Branch) ..	1	$0\frac{1}{2}$
Cinderland Bridge	1	4
Waterhouses Bridge	2	$1\frac{1}{2}$
South end of Waterhouses Tunnel	2	$2\frac{1}{2}$
North end of Waterhouses Tunnel	2	3
Waterhouses Aqueduct over River Medlock ..	2	$3\frac{1}{2}$
Lock No. 1, Waterhouses	2	4
Head of Lock No. 4, Waterhouses, and Waterhouses Junction, junction with Fairbottom Branch (No. 39a5)	2	5
Crime Bridge	2	$7\frac{1}{2}$
Cutler Hill Bridge	3	$3\frac{1}{2}$
Street Bridge	3	7
Oldham Corporation Gas Works	4	$0\frac{1}{2}$
Bradley Bent Bridge	4	$1\frac{1}{2}$
Lock No. 5, Hollinwood	4	2
Lock No. 6, Hollinwood	4	3
Manchester and Oldham Road Bridge, and Lock No. 7, Hollinwood	4	$4\frac{1}{2}$
Hollinwood Top Wharf	4	5

(39)—GREAT CENTRAL RAILWAY—*continued.*

Fairbottom Branch (No. 39a5).

	Miles.	Fur.
Waterhouses Junction, junction with Hollinwood Branch (No. 39a4), to—		
Valley Aqueduct over road	–	3½
Bardsley Bridge and Wharves	–	5½
Old Termination of Canal	1	1

(d) Locks.
Main Line (No. 39a1).

1 to 3. } Ancoats.

4 to 7. } Beswick.

8 to 16. } Clayton.

17 and 18. } Fairfield.

Rise from Manchester.

Hollinwood Branch (No. 39a4).

1 to 4. } Waterhouses.

5 to 7. } Hollinwood.

Rise from Fairfield Junction.

(e) *Maximum size of vessels that can use the navigation.*
Main Line (No. 39a1) and Branches.

	Ft.	In.
Length	70	0
Width	7	0
Draught	3	3
Headroom	6	0

(f) *Tunnels.*
Hollinwood Branch (No. 39a4).

Waterhouses—

Length .. .. .. 66 yards.		
Minimum height above water level	9	1
Minimum width at water level	8	1

Towing-path through the tunnel.

(g) *Towing-path.*

There is a towing-path throughout the canal and branches with the exception of the Islington Branch.

(39)—Great Central Railway—*continued*.

(i) *Types of vessels using the navigation.*

Narrow boats. Steam haulage is not allowed.

Peak Forest Canal.

(c) *Distance Table.*

Main Line (No. 39b1).

	Miles.	Fur.
Dukinfield Junction, junction with Ashton Canal (No. 39a1), to—		
G. C. Railway Bridge (Stalybridge Branch)..	–	0½
Dukinfield Gas Works ..	–	2½
G. C. Railway Bridge (Main Line)	–	5
Dog Lane Bridge	–	6½
Dukinfield Hall or Well Bridge	1	0½
Newton Hall Bridge	1	5½
Hyde, Bowler's or Throstle Bank Bridge	2	1
Hyde, Company's Warehouse and Wharves ..	2	2
Hyde Gas Works	2	4
Apethorne Aqueduct over road	3	1½
Woodley Bridge	4	2
Cheshire Lines Railway Bridge (Woodley and Stockport Line) and North end of Woodley Tunnel	4	3
Sheffield and Midland Railway Bridge (Romiley and Stockport Line)	5	0
Hatherlow, Holehouse Fold Bridge	5	2½
Hatherlow Aqueduct over road	5	4
Chadkirk Aqueduct over road ..	5	5½
North end of Hyde Bank Tunnel	6	1½
South end of Hyde Bank Tunnel	6	3
Occupation Bridge	6	4
Marple, Aqueduct over River Etherow	6	6½
Marple, Sheffield and Midland Railway Bridge (Marple and Romiley Line), and Company's Wharf and Workshops	6	7
Lock No. 1, Marple	7	0
Marple, Sheffield and Midland Railway Tunnel under canal (Marple and Romiley Line) ..	7	2
Marple, Company's Warehouse and Wharf ..	7	5½
Marple, Head of Lock No. 16, and junction with Macclesfield Canal, Main Line (No. 39c1)	8	0½
Rawton Walls Bridge ..	9	1
Moore's or Turf Swivel Bridge ..	9	5
Stanley Hall, or Kicker's Bridge	9	7½
Woodend Swivel Bridge	10	2½
Higgins Clough or Shaly Knowl Swivel Bridge	10	4½
Disley, Dryhurst Bridge	10	7½
Greens Hall Bridge	11	2
Wirksmoor, Company's Warehouse and Wharf	12	0½
Bankend Bridge	12	3
Carr or Mellor's Swivel Bridge ..	12	6
Aqueduct over Furness Brook	13	1

(39)—GREAT CENTRAL RAILWAY—*continued.*

	Miles.	Fur.
Dukinfield Junction, junction with Ashton Canal (No. 39a1), to *(continued)*—		
Bong's or Yeardsley Bank Swivel and Foot Bridges	13	3½
Greensdeep or Bugsworth new Road Bridge ..	13	5
Junction with Whaley Bridge Branch (No 39b2)	14	0
Aqueduct over River Goyt	14	1
Bugsworth, Chinley Road Bridge	14	5½
Bugsworth, Termination of Canal	14	6

Whaley Bridge Branch (No. 39b2).

	Miles.	Fur.
Junction with Main Line (No. 39b1) to—		
Roots Wharf	–	1½
Whaley Bridge, Company's Warehouse and Wharf	–	3½

(d) Locks.

Main Line (No. 39b1).

1
to } Marple.
16.

Rise from Dukinfield.

(e) Maximum size of vessels that can use the navigation.

Main Line (No. 39b1) and Whaley Bridge Branch (No. 39b2).

	Ft.	In.
Length	70	0
Width	7	0
Draught	3	3
Headroom	5	10

(f) Tunnels.

Main Line (No. 39b1).

Woodley—			
Length	176 yards.		
Minimum height above water level		9	0½
Minimum width at water level		9	3½

Towing-path through the tunnel.

Hyde Bank—			
Length	308 yards.		
Minimum height above water level		6	8
Minimum width at water level		16	0

No towing-path boats " legged " or " shafted " through.

(g) Towing-path.

There is a towing-path throughout the canal and Whaley Bridge Branch, with the exception of Hyde Bank Tunnel.

(i) Types of vessels using the navigation.

Narrow boats. Steam haulage is not allowed.

(39)—Great Central Railway—*continued.*

Macclesfield Canal.

(c) *Distance Table.*

Main Line (No. 39c1).

	Miles.	Fur.
Marple Junction, junction with Peak Forest Canal, Main line (No. 39b1), to—		
Eccles Bridge	—	$4\frac{1}{2}$
Hyde's Bridge	1	$2\frac{1}{2}$
Windlehurst or Back Lane Bridge	1	6
Marriott's Bridge	2	0
Manchester and Buxton Road Bridge.. ..	2	$1\frac{1}{2}$
Junction with High Lane Branch (No. 39c2) ..	2	$2\frac{1}{2}$
Aqueduct over Stockport, Disley, and Whaley Bridge Railway	2	5
Poynton Colliery Wharves (Lord Vernon's) ..	3	$5\frac{1}{2}$
Red Acre Aqueduct	4	$3\frac{1}{2}$
Red Acre Colliery Wharf (J. Needham) ..	4	4
Adlington Colliery Wharves	5	0
Stypherson Wharf	5	$7\frac{1}{2}$
Hibbert's Brow or Corner Bridge	6	$1\frac{1}{2}$
Barton's Bridge	6	$3\frac{1}{2}$
Whiteley Green Wharf and Bridge	7	0
Sugar Lane Bridge	7	3
Bollington, Lord Vernon's Coal Wharf, and Bollington Aqueduct	7	6
Bollington, Company's Warehouses & Wharves	8	2
Wood's Bridge	9	2
Hurdsfield, Macclesfield, and Chapel-en-le-Frith Road Bridge	10	2
Macclesfield, Company's Wharf, Buxton Road	10	7
Macclesfield, Macclesfield and Buxton Road Bridge	10	$7\frac{1}{2}$
Macclesfield, Company's Warehouse & Wharves	11	$0\frac{1}{2}$
Macclesfield, Holland's Bridge	11	2
Macclesfield, Leek Old Road Bridge	12	$2\frac{1}{2}$
Leek New Road Bridge	12	$6\frac{1}{2}$
Fool's Nook Wharf	14	$2\frac{1}{2}$
Gee's or Cowley Farm Bridge	15	2
Crow Hole Bridge .. ..,	15	4
Lockett's Bridge	16	0
Bosley, Lock No. 1, and Daintry's Wharf ..	16	1
Bosley, Lock No. 5, Congleton and Buxton Road Bridge, and Company's Wharf	16	5
Bosley, Lock No. 11, and North Staffordshire Railway Bridge (Churnet Valley Line) ..	17	1
Bosley, Lock No. 12	17	$1\frac{1}{2}$
Aqueduct over River Dane	17	3
Wallworth's Bridge	17	5
North Staffordshire Railway Bridge (Main Line)	18	$1\frac{1}{2}$
Congleton and Buxton Road Bridge at Crossley Hall	18	$3\frac{1}{2}$
Congleton and Buxton Road Bridge at Tall Ash	19	$7\frac{1}{2}$

(39)—GREAT CENTRAL RAILWAY—*continued.*

	Miles.	Fur.
Marple Junction, junction with Peak Forest Canal, Main Line (No. 39b1), to (*continued*)—		
North Staffordshire Railway Bridge (Main Line)	20	3½
Biddulph Valley Railway Aqueduct	20	6½
North Staffordshire Railway Bridge (Main Line)	21	3½
Dog Lane or Canal Road Aqueduct	21	6
Congleton Warehouse and Wharf	21	6½
Watery Lane Aqueduct	23	2
Simpson's Bridge	24	1
Littler's Wharf	25	1
Hall Green, junction with Trent and Mersey Canal, Hall Green Branch (No. 76e), (half-way between the two stop locks) ..	26	1

High Lane Branch (No. 39c2).

	Miles.	Fur.
Length from junction from Main Line (No. 39c1) to the Company's Wharf, High Lane ..	–	1½

(d) *Locks.*

Main Line (No. 39c1).

1
to } Bosley.
12.

Fall from Marple.

13.—Hall Green Stop Lock.

(e) *Maximum size of vessels that can use the navigation.*

Main Line (No. 39c1) and High Lane Branch (No. 39c2).

	Ft.	In.
Length	70	0
Width	7	0
Draught	3	3
Headroom	6	0

(g) *Towing-path.*

There is a towing-path throughout the canal and High Lane Branch.

(i) *Types of vessels using the navigation.*

Narrow boats. Steam haulage is not allowed.

Chesterfield Canal (No. 39d).

(c) *Distance Table.*

	Miles.	Fur.
Chesterfield, Basin End, to—		
Tapton Mill Bridge	–	4
Ford Lane Lock	–	7
Chesterfield and Sheffield Midland Railway Bridge and Sheepbridge Wharf	1	0½
Wheeldon Mill, Top Bridge	1	4½

(39)—GREAT CENTRAL RAILWAY—*continued.*

	Miles.	Fur.
Chesterfield, Basin End, to (*continued*)—		
New Bridge Lane Lock (Wheeldon Mill) ..	1	$5\frac{1}{2}$
Blue Bank Lock	2	3
Dixon's Lock	2	7
Steel's Bridge	3	$0\frac{1}{2}$
Staveley Works, Station Bridge, and Lock ..	3	4
Staveley Gas Works	4	$3\frac{1}{2}$
Hartington Colliery	4	$7\frac{1}{2}$
G. C. Railway Bridge, Beighton to Chesterfield	5	1
Norbrigg's Foot Bridge	5	$7\frac{1}{2}$
Staveley, Red Bridge	6	$0\frac{1}{2}$
Hague's Bridge	6	$5\frac{1}{2}$
Renishaw Bridge and Wharf	7	2
Spinkhill Bridge and Wharf	7	7
Eckington New Bridge	8	$5\frac{1}{2}$
Killamarsh Forge Bridge	9	3
Killamarsh Bridge	9	6
Killamarsh Wharf	10	1
Belk Lane Bridge, Lock, and Wharf	10	5
Derbyshire Chemical Works	11	$0\frac{1}{2}$
Sheepbridge Company's Colliery and Brick Yard	11	$3\frac{1}{2}$
Gannow Lane Bridge	11	4
Norwood Bridge and Wharf	11	5
Norwood Low Treble Locks, Nos. 7, 8, and 9..	11	6
Norwood Top Treble Locks, Nos. 13, 14, and 15	11	7
West Kiveton Colliery	11	$7\frac{1}{2}$
Norwood Four Locks, Nos. 16, 17, 18, and 19, Top Pier	11	$7\frac{1}{2}$
Norwood Tunnel, West end	12	$0\frac{1}{2}$
Norwood Tunnel, East end	13	7
Kiveton Park, Chambers' Coal Wharf.. ..	14	3
Peck Mill Wharf	14	5
Canal Siding and Wharf	14	7
Anston Bridge	14	$7\frac{1}{2}$
Dule Hole Bridge	15	$2\frac{1}{2}$
Pudding Dyke Bridge	15	$6\frac{1}{2}$
Chambers' Brick Yard and Wharf	16	0
Top Treble or Summit Locks, Nos. 20, 21, and 22	16	1
Low Treble Locks, Nos. 26, 27, and 28.. ..	16	3
Brown's Lock, No. 32	16	$4\frac{1}{2}$
Quarry Lock, No. 35, and Wharf	16	$6\frac{1}{2}$
Stone Lock, No. 39	17	$0\frac{1}{2}$
Turner Wood Low Lock, No. 41, and Duke's Bridge	17	$1\frac{1}{2}$
Shireoaks Aqueduct	17	2
Shireoaks Top Lock, No. 42, and Lock House ..	17	6
Shireoaks Bottom Lock, No. 44, and Low Bridge and Wharf	17	7
Doefield Dunn Lock and Midland Railway Mansfield to Worksop	18	$2\frac{1}{2}$
Haggonfield Lock	18	$4\frac{1}{2}$
Deep Lock, High Ground, and High Ground Bridge	18	$7\frac{1}{2}$
Morse Lock	19	4

(39)—GREAT CENTRAL RAILWAY—*continued.*

	Miles.	Fur.
Chesterfield, Basin End, to (*continued*)—		
Shireoaks Colliery Company's Coal Wharf ..	19	7
Worksop Lock and Bridge	20	0
Worksop Gas Works and Wharf	20	1
Worksop Board of Health Yard	20	1½
Kilton Top Lock, No. 51	20	5
Worksop Aqueduct	20	6½
Kilton Low Lock, No. 52	20	7½
Manton Bridge, Wharf, and Viaduct, G. C. Rly.	21	5½
Osberton Hall Bridge	22	7½
Osberton Lock	23	2½
Wilkinson's Bridge and Wharf	23	7½
Chequer House, Warehouse and Wharf ..	25	0
Chequer House Bridge	25	1½
Green Mile Bridge and Wharf	26	4½
Forest Top Lock, No. 54	26	6
Turner's Old Wharf	26	7
Barnby Wharf and Bridge (London Old Road)	27	0
Forest Top Middle Lock, No. 55	27	1½
Forest Low Middle Lock, No. 56	27	4½
Forest Low Lock, No. 57	27	7
Simpson's Wharf and Bridge	28	3½
Girder Bridge, G. C. Railway	29	2
West Retford, Wharf, Bridge, and Lock ..	29	7
New Canal Warehouse, Retford Lock, and Toll Office	30	2½
New Gate, Green Bridge and Wharf ..	30	5½
Swathe Dyke Bridge	31	1
Welham Wharf and Bridge	31	4
Whitsunday Pye Lock	31	6
Clarboro' Bridge, St. John's	32	2
Clarboro', Clifton's Wharf	32	7½
Clarboro' Bridge..	32	0
Hayton Church Bridge	33	2
Hayton Middle Bridge	33	4½
Hayton Castle Brick Yard	34	7
Clayworth Wharf and Top Bridge ..	35	7
Wiseton Hall Bridge	37	6
Drakeholes Wharf and West end of Drakeholes Tunnel	39	0
Drakeholes Low Wharf	39	2½
Gringley Top Wharf and Top Lock	40	6
Gringley Top Lock and Low Lock Bridge ..	41	4
Walkeringham Bridge and Wharf	42	5
Misterton, Cooper's Bridge	43	6½
Misterton, Wharf and Bridge	44	3
Misterton Top Lock	44	5½
G. N. Railway Bridge	44	7
Stockwith Bridge	45	3½
West Stockwith, Trent Lock, and junction with River Trent (No. 112a)	45	4

In calculating distances for all purposes of tolls and charges, each quarter of a mile of the Summit Pool at Norwood is to be taken as equal to a distance of half a mile.

(39)—GREAT CENTRAL RAILWAY—*continued.*

(d) *Locks.*

1.—Ford Lane.
2.—New Bridge Lane.
3.—Blue Bank.
4.—Dixon's.
5.—Staveley Works.

Fall from Chesterfield.

6.—Belk Lane.

7
to } Norwood.
19.

Rise from Chesterfield.

20
to } Thorpe.
34.

35
to } Turner Wood.
41.

42
to } Shireoaks.
44.

45.—Doefield Dunn.
46.—Haggonfield.
47.—Deep.
48.—Stret.
49.—Morse.
50.—Worksop.
51.—Kilton.
52.—Kilton Low.
53.—Osberton.

54
to } Forest.
57.

58.—West Retford.
59.—Retford.
60.—Whitsunday Pyc.
61.—Gringley Top.
62.—Gringley Low.
63.—Misterton Top.
64.—Misterton Low.
65.—Trent.

Fall from Chesterfield.

(e) *Maximum size of vessels that can use the navigation.*

	Ft.	In.
Length	72	0
Width from Stockwith to Retford	14	10
,, from Retford to Chesterfield	6	10½
Draught	3	3
Headroom	4	10

(39)—Great Central Railway—*continued.*

(f) *Tunnels.*

	Ft.	In.
Norwood—		
Length .. .. .. 3,102 yards.		
Minimum height above water level	4	10
Minimum width at water level	8	10

No towing-path, boats " legged " through.

Boats enter from the Chesterfield end at 9 a.m., 3 p.m., and 9 p.m. ; and from the Kiveton Park end at 6 a.m., 12 noon, and 6 p.m.

The hours of working the tunnel are not strictly adhered to, as on account of the small traffic boatmen generally know the whereabouts of boats travelling in the opposite direction.

Some years ago, about 80 yards of Norwood Tunnel towards the Kiveton Park end collapsed, and this portion is now an open cutting.

	Ft.	In.
Drakeholes—		
Length .. .. .. 154 yards.		
Minimum height above water level	10	0
Minimum width at water level	15	6

No towing-path, boats " legged " or " shafted " through.

(g) *Towing-path.*

There is a towing-path throughout the canal except through Norwood and Drakeholes tunnels.

(i) *Types of vessels using the navigation.*

Narrow boats. Steam haulage is not allowed.

---

(40)—Great Eastern Railway.

(a) *Short Description.*

The Great Eastern Railway Company, as the successors of the Norwich and Lowestoft Navigation Company, incorporated 1827, are the proprietors of certain artificially constructed and adapted portions of waterway forming links in the direct line of navigation between Norwich and Lowestoft, such links not being portions of the natural channels of the Rivers Yare and Waveney.

These waterways above referred to consist of the New Cut from the River Yare at Reedham to the River Waveney at Haddiscoe, all in the county of Norfolk ; and the line of navigation from the River Waveney about one mile below Burgh St. Peter, through Oulton Dike, Oulton Broad, Lake Lothing, and Lowestoft Harbour to Lowestoft, all in the county of Suffolk.

The Great Eastern Railway Company are also joint proprietors with the Great Northern Railway Company of the Fossdyke Canal— *see* Great Northern and Great Eastern Joint Railways.

J

(40)—GREAT EASTERN RAILWAY——*continued.*

(b) *Proprietors, Officers, and Offices.*

Great Eastern Railway Company.

General Manager : J. F. S. Gooday.

Secretary : W. H. Peppercorne.

Engineer : John Wilson.

Goods Manager : W. Gardner.

Head Offices : Liverpool Street Station, London, E.C.

Harbour Master, Lowestoft : H. J. Henderson.

New Cut (No. 40a).

(c) *Distance Table.*

	Miles.	Fur.
Reedham, junction with River Yare (No. 128a), to—		
Haddiscoe Bridge and Railway Station ..	2	1½
Haddiscoe, junction with River Waveney (No. 117a)	2	3

(e) *Maximum size of vessels that can use the navigation.*

	Ft.	In.
Length.—Not limited.		
Width.—Not limited.		
Draught	7	0

(g) *Towing-path.*

There is no towing-path.

(h) *Tidal Information.*

The tide in the New Cut ebbs and flows from the Yare end at Reedham.

High water at Reedham about 2hrs. 30min. after Yarmouth. *See* Tidal Information, River Yare (No. 128).

(i) *Types of vessels using the navigation.*

Norfolk wherries.

Navigation from the River Waveney to Lowestoft (No. 40b).

(c) *Distance Table.*

	Miles.	Fur.
Junction with River Waveney (No. 117a) at North end of Oulton Dike to—		
Oulton Dike Staith	1	2
West end of Oulton Broad	1	4
Mutford Bridge Lock, Staith, East end of Oulton Broad, and entrance to Lake Lothing	2	2
Lowestoft Bridge	4	1
Mouth of Lowestoft Harbour	4	3½

(40)—G REAT E ASTERN R AILWAY—*continued.*

(d) Locks.

1.—Mutford Bridge.

Mutford Bridge Lock has four pairs of gates, the fall being sometimes from Oulton Broad to Lake Lothing, and sometimes from Lake Lothing to Oulton Broad, according to the tide.

(e) Maximum size of vessels that can use the navigation.

	Ft.	In.
The length and width are the dimensions available through Mutford Bridge Lock.		
Length	85	0
Width	20	0
Draught	7	0

(g) Towing-path.

There is no towing-path.

(h) Tidal Information.

The tide flows from Lowestoft to the east end of Mutford Bridge Lock.

High water at Lowestoft 42min. after Yarmouth, or about 4hrs. before London Bridge.

Spring tides rise	6ft. 6in.
Neap „ „	5ft. 3in.

Mutford Bridge Lock, East end, has high water practically at the same time as Lowestoft.

Spring tides rise	6ft.
Neap „ „	5ft.

The tide also ebbs and flows from the River Waveney through Oulton Dike, and effects the level of Oulton Broad up to the West end of Mutford Bridge Lock.

Mutford Bridge Lock, West end, has high water about 3hrs. later than high water at East end.

Average rise and fall of the tide about 2ft.

The water at both ends of the lock makes a level about 2hrs. after high water, and 2hrs. after low water at Lowestoft.

(i) Types of vessels using the navigation.

Norfolk wherries.

(41)—GREAT NORTHERN RAILWAY.

(a) *Short Description.*

The navigations belonging to the Great Northern Railway Company consist of the Grantham Canal and the Nottingham Canal, and also the River Witham Navigation from the High Bridge, Lincoln, to the Grand Sluice, Boston, which is separately described under the head of the River Witham.

The Great Northern Railway Company are also joint proprietors with the Great Eastern Railway Company of the Fossdyke Canal—*see* Great Northern and Great Eastern Joint Railways.

The Grantham Canal commences by a junction with the River Trent at Nottingham, and proceeds by Cropwell, Kinoulton, and Hickling, in the county of Nottinghamshire ; Harby, Plungar, and Redmile, in the county of Leicestershire ; and Woolsthorpe, to Grantham, in the county of Lincolnshire.

There is not much trade done on the canal, and it passes through a purely agricultural country.

The Nottingham Canal commences by a junction with the River Trent at Nottingham, and proceeds through the city of Nottingham, and the villages of Wollaton, Trowell, and Cossall to Langley Mill, where it forms a junction with the Cromford Canal of the Midland Railway, all in the county of Nottinghamshire.

There are two short branches in Nottingham known as the Poplar Arm and the Brewery Cut.

(b) *Proprietors, Officers, and Offices.*

Great Northern Railway Company.

General Manager : O. Bury.

Secretary : E. H. Burrows.

Chief Engineer : A. Ross.

Goods Manager : G. Shaw.

Head Offices : King's Cross Station, London, N.

Grantham Canal (No. 41a).

(c) *Distance Table.*

	Miles.	Fur.
Nottingham, junction with River Trent (No. 112a), to—		
Between Locks Nos. 4 and 5	4	0
Cropwell Top Lock, No. 11	6	7
Kinoulton Bridge	11	6
Hickling Wharf ..	13	1
Harby	18	0
Redmile ..	22	7
Woolsthorpe Bottom Lock	26	$5\frac{1}{2}$
Woolsthorpe Top Lock	28	0
Grantham	33	0

(41)—GREAT NORTHERN RAILWAY—*continued.*

(d) *Locks.*

1.—Trent.
2.—Bridgford.
3.—Gamston.
4) Skinner's.
and
5.) Sanders.
6.—Cotgrave Bridge.
7.—Hollygate Lane.
8.—Joss's.
9)
to ⎰ Cropwell.
11.)
12.—Woolsthorpe Bottom.
13) Stainwith.
and
14.) Kingston's.
15.—Bottom of Half Mile Pond.
16) Carpenters Shop.
17 ⎰ Willis's.
18.) Woolsthorpe Top.

Rise from Nottingham.

(e) *Maximum size of vessels that can use the navigation.*

						Ft.	In.
Length	..	..	..	..	..	75	0
Width	..	..	..	..	..	14	0
Draught	..	..	..	..	..	3	3

(g) *Towing-path.*

There is a towing-path throughout the navigation.

(i) *Types of vessels using the navigation.*

Narrow boats, and Upper Trent boats. Steam haulage is not allowed.

Nottingham Canal.

(c) *Distance Table.*

Main Line (No. 41b1).

	Miles.	Fur.
Nottingham, Trent Lock, and junction with River Trent (No. 112a), to—		
Nottingham, Trent Navigation Company's Wharves and Warehouses, and junction with Poplar Arm (No. 41b2)	–	6
Nottingham—Fellows, Morton, & Clayton Ltd. Canal Carriers, Wharves and Warehouses, Canal Street	1	1
Castle Lock	1	2
Leather Mill Lock	1	4

(41)—GREAT NORTHERN RAILWAY—*continued*.

	Miles.	Fur.
Nottingham, Trent Lock, and junction with River Trent (No. 112a), to (*continued*)—		
Lenton Chain, junction with Beeston Cut of River Trent Navigation (No. 112a) and Toll Office, between Locks Nos. 3 and 4 ..	2	3½
Radford	3	4
Wollaton, and head of Lock No. 19	5	2
Trowell	8	2
Cossall	10	2
Digby Colliery	11	0
Awsworth Railway Station	11	4
Newthorpe Railway Station	13	2
Langley Mill, junction with Cromford Canal—Main Line—(No. 70b1)	14	6

Poplar Arm (No. 41b2).

	Miles.	Fur.
Junction with Main Line (No. 41b1) to :—		
Junction with Brewery Cut (No. 41b3) ..	–	1
Junction with Earl Manvers Canal (No. 65) ..	–	1½

Brewery Cut (No. 41b3).

	Miles.	Fur.
Length from junction with Poplar Arm (No. 41b2)	–	1

(d) *Locks.*

Main Line (No. 41b1).

1.—Trent.
2.—Castle.
3.—Leather Mill.
4) Hickling's.
and
5.) Simpson's.
6.—Radford Bridge.
7.—Limekiln.
8.—Black.
9.—Bottom of first three.
10.—Middle of first three.
11.—Top of first three.
12.
13.—Blacksmith's.
14.—Bottom of top three.
15.—Middle of top three
16.—Coach Road Bridge.
17.—Bottom of Wood End Pond.
18.—Second of Wood End Pond.
19.—Wollaton.

Rise from Nottingham.

20.—Langley Mill Stop Lock.

(41)—GREAT NORTHERN RAILWAY—*continued*.

(e) Maximum size of vessels that can use the navigation.

Main Line (No. 41b1).

	Ft.	In.
Length from Trent Lock, Nottingham, to Lenton Chain	82	0
Length from Lenton Chain to Langley Mill	75	0
Width	14	0
Draught from Trent Lock, Nottingham, to Lenton Chain maximum	3	9
average	3	6
Draught from Lenton Chain to Langley Mill	3	3

Poplar Arm (No. 41b2) and Brewery Cut (No. 41b3).

Length	75	0
Width	14	0
Draught .. maximum	3	6

(g) Towing-path.

There is a towing-path throughout the canal and branches.

(i) Types of vessels using the navigation.

Narrow boats and Upper Trent boats. Steam haulage is allowed between Trent Lock, Nottingham, and Lenton Chain, but not on the remainder of the canal.

---

(42)—GREAT NORTHERN AND GREAT EASTERN JOINT RAILWAYS.

(a) Short Description.

The Great Northern and Great Eastern Joint Railway Companies are the proprietors of the Fossdyke Canal. It commences by a junction with the River Trent at Torksey, and proceeds by Saxilby and Skellingthorpe to the West end of Brayford Mere, Lincoln, where it forms a junction with the head of the River Witham Navigation, all in the county of Lincolnshire.

The Fossdyke Canal was originally constructed by the Romans, and is the oldest artificially constructed waterway in the country which is navigable at the present time.

(b) Proprietors, Officers, and Offices.

Great Northern and Great Eastern Joint Railway Companies.

Secretary : E. H. Burrows.

Office : King's Cross Station, London, N.

Manager : John Crabtree.

Office : Lincoln.

Local Canal Agent : H. Cunnington.

Office : Torksey Lock, near Lincoln.

(42)—GREAT NORTHERN AND GREAT EASTERN JOINT
    RAILWAYS—*continued.*

(c) Distance Table.

	Miles.	Fur.
Torksey Lock, junction with River Trent (No. 112a), to—		
Torksey Wharf ..	1	0
Hardwick Ferry	3	2
Drinsey Nook ..	3	6
Saxilby ..	5	4
Mill Lane..	5	6
Chemical Works..	6	4
Broxholme Lane	6	6
Odder Engine ..	7	0
Burton Lane	8	2
Skellingthorpe ..	9	0
Lincoln, West end of Brayford Mere, junction with River Witham (No. 124) ..	11	0

(d) Locks.

1.—Torksey.

Rise from River Trent.

(e) Maximum size of vessels that can use the navigation.

	Ft.	In.
Length ..	78	0
Width ..	15	2
Draught ..	5	0
Headroom	8	10

(g) Towing-path.

There is a towing-path throughout the navigation.

(i) Types of vessels using the navigation.

Principally Yorkshire keels. Steam haulage for the purposes of trade is not allowed, but pleasure steamers are admitted.

---

(43)—GREAT WESTERN RAILWAY.

(a) Short Description.

The canals belonging to the Great Western Railway Company consist of the Kennet and Avon Navigation, the Stratford-on-Avon Canal, the Stourbridge Extension Canal, a portion of the River Tone Navigation at Taunton, the Bridgwater and Taunton Canal, the Grand Western Canal, the Stover Canal, the Brecon and Abergavenny Canal, the Monmouthshire Canal, and the Swansea Canal, including the Trewyddfa Canal. The Great Western Railway Company are also joint proprietors with the Midland Railway Company of the Lydney Harbour and Canal, which forms part of the undertaking of the Severn and Wye and Severn Bridge Railway.

(43)—GREAT WESTERN RAILWAY—*continued.*

The Kennet and Avon Navigation commences at High Bridge, Reading, where it joins that portion of the River Kennet under the jurisdiction of the Thames Conservancy, and proceeds by Aldermaston, Woolhampton, Thatcham, Newbury, Kintbury, and Hungerford, in the county of Berkshire ; Froxfield, Little Bedwyn, Great Bedwyn, Wootton Rivers, Wilcot, Honeystreet, Bishops Cannings, Devizes, Seend, Semington, and Bradford-on-Avon, in the county of Wiltshire ; Claverton, Bathampton, Bath, Twerton, Kelston, Saltford, and Swinford, in the County of Somersetshire, and Keynsham to Hanham Lock, where it joins that portion of the River Avon under the jurisdiction of the Bristol Corporation, forming below Swinford the boundary between the counties of Somersetshire and Gloucestershire. The navigation may be divided into three sections: No. 1, the Kennet River Section, from High Bridge, Reading, to Newbury Wharf ; No. 2, the Kennet and Avon Canal Section, from Newbury Wharf to the Old Town Bridge on the River Avon at Bath ; and No. 3, the River Avon Section, from the Old Town Bridge at Bath to Hanham Lock.

The Stratford-on-Avon Canal commences at Kings Norton, in the county of Worcestershire, by a junction with the Worcester and Birmingham Canal of the Sharpness New Docks and Gloucester and Birmingham Navigation Company, and proceeds by Yardley Wood in the same county, Hockley Heath, Lapworth, Kingswood, Preston Bagot, Wootton Wawen, Wilmcote, and Bishopton to Stratford-on-Avon, in the county of Warwickshire, where it joins the Upper Avon Navigation, which since 1873 has been unnavigable and derelict, but in former years extended from Stratford-on-Avon to the Lower Avon Navigation at Evesham. There is a short branch at Kingswood forming a connection with the Warwick and Birmingham Canal.

The Stourbridge Extension Canal commences by a junction with the Stourbridge Canal at Brockmoor, Kingswinford, and terminates at Oak Farm, Kingswinford, all in the county of Staffordshire. There are two short branches, known as the Bromley Branch and the Sandhills Branch.

The portion of the River Tone Navigation at Taunton commences at the Gas Works, and terminates at Firepool, where it forms a junction with the Bridgwater and Taunton Canal. [NOTE.—The River Tone from the point of its junction with the Bridgwater and Taunton Canal at Firepool Lock, Taunton, to Ham Mill, the head of the navigation on that portion of the river controlled by the Somersetshire Drainage Commissioners, is unnavigable.]

The Bridgwater and Taunton Canal commences at Firepool Lock, Taunton, by a junction with the portion of the River Tone Navigation at Taunton, and proceeds by Creech, St. Michael, and Durston to the west end of Bridgwater Dock at Bridgwater, all in the county of Somersetshire. The Dock at Bridgwater communicates at its east end through a pair of gates with a tidal basin, which again communicates by means of a large pair of tidal gates for shipping and a barge lock for smaller craft, with the River Parrett.

(43)—GREAT WESTERN RAILWAY—*continued.*

The Grand Western Canal commences at Loudwell, and proceeds by Burlescombe, Sampford Peverell, and Halberton to Tiverton, all in the County of Devonshire. The canal as originally constructed formed a waterway from Taunton to Tiverton, but the section between Taunton and Loudwell has been closed since 1867. The canal is only used for a very small roadstone traffic from Whipcott and Burlescombe to various places up to and including Tiverton. The portion between Loudwell and Whipcott Wharf is practically unnavigable.

The Stover Canal commences by a junction with the River Teign at Jetty Marsh, Newton Abbot, and passing under the Moretonhampstead Branch of the Great Western Railway follows the course of that branch on its eastern side to Ventiford, a short distance to the north of Teigngrace Station, all in the county of Devonshire. The canal is not used for public traffic, but is leased to Messrs. Watts, Blake, Bearne, & Co., clay merchants, Newton Abbot, and at the present time is not used for traffic above their wharves at Teignbridge.

The Brecon and Abergavenny Canal commences at Brecon, and proceeds by Llanhamlach, Penkelly, Talybont, Llangynider, Llangattock, and Gilwern, in the county of Brecon ; Govilon, Llanfoist, Llanelen, and Mamhilad to Pontymoyle near Pontypool, in the county of Monmouthshire, where it joins the Monmouthshire Canal.

The Monmouthshire Canal commences at Pontymoyle near Pontypool by a junction with the Brecon and Abergavenny Canal, and proceeds by Panteg, Pontnewydd, Cwmbran, and Malpas to its termination near Llanarth Street, in the town of Newport. The canal at Newport as originally constructed communicated with the Newport Docks, but the portion between Llanarth Street and the Newport Docks was closed and filled in by Act of Parliament of 1879. The Crumlin Branch commences by a junction with the main line at Malpas, and proceeds by Cefn, Risca, Crosskeys, Abercarn, and New Bridge to Crumlin.

The whole course of the canal is situated in the county of Monmouthshire.

The Swansea Canal commences at Hen-hoydd in the parish of Ystradgynlais, and proceeds by Ystradgynlais in the county of Brecon, Ystalfera, Pontardawe, Clydach, Morriston, and Landore to Swansea, in the county of Glamorganshire, where it forms a junction with the North Dock Tidal Basin. There is a short branch in Swansea parallel to the North Dock. Only the lower six miles of the Swansea Canal are now used for traffic, the remainder being in bad condition. Above Ystalfera some of the pounds are dry, and no trade has been done to the head of the canal for over 20 years. The portion called the Trewyddfa Canal forms a link in the main line of the Swansea Canal 1¾ miles in length, situated between Landore and Morriston. This section was originally constructed at the expense of the Duke of Beaufort, and was purchased by the Great Western Railway Company at the same time as the Swansea Canal in 1872.

There is not much trade done on any of the Company's Canals.

(43)—GREAT WESTERN RAILWAY—*continued.*

(b) *Proprietors, Officers, and Offices.*

Great Western Railway Company.

General Manger : J. C. Inglis.

Secretary : G. K. Mills.

Chief Goods Manager : Thomas Henry Rendell.

Engineer : W. W. Grierson.

Marine and Dock Superintendent : J. Dunster.

Head Offices : Paddington Station, London, W.

Dock Master, Bridgwater : J. W. Sharman.

Kennet and Avon Navigation (No. 43a).

(c) *Distance Table.*

	Miles.	Fur.
High Bridge, Reading, commencement of River Kennet Section, and junction with portion of River Kennet under jurisdiction of Thames Conservancy (No. 107c), to—		
Southcote	2	4
Burghfield Village	3	4
Burghfield Mill	4	4
Sheffield	6	4
Tile Mill	8	0
Aldermaston Wharf	10	0
Aldermaston Mill	11	0
Woolhampton Mill	12	0
Hale's Lock	13	2
Brimpton	13	4
Midgham	13	6
Colthorpe	14	4
Longbridge	15	0
Widmead Lock	16	0
Ham Wharf	17	4
Newbury Wharf, commencement of Kennet and Avon Canal Section	18	4
Westfield	19	4
Hampstead	22	0
Kintbury	24	4
Dunn Mill	27	0
Hungerford	27	4
Picketfield	29	4
Froxfield	30	0
Little Bedwyn	31	4
Great Bedwyn Wharf	32	4
Freewarrens	34	4
Crofton Top Lock, No. 52	35	1
Savernake Tunnel, East end	36	0

(43)—GREAT WESTERN RAILWAY—*continued.*

	Miles.	Fur.
High Bridge, Reading, commencement of River Kennet Section, and junction with portion of River Kennet under jurisdiction of Thames Conservancy (No. 107c), to (*continued*)—		
Burbage Wharf	37	0
Wootton Rivers Top Lock, No. 53	37	1
Brimslade	38	0
Wootton Rivers	38	4
New Mill	39	4
Pewsey Wharf	41	4
Wilcot	43	0
Honeystreet Wharf	45	4
Horton Bridge	49	4
Devizes Top Lock of 29 Locks, No. 57 ..	53	4
Foxhangers	56	0
Wragg's Wharf	56	4
Scott's Wharf	56	6
Seend Wharf	58	0
Tail of Semington Bottom Lock, junction with Wilts and Berks Canal—not navigable (*see* Wilts and Berks Canal)—and Semington Wharf	60	4
Hilperton Wharf	63	0
Bradford-on-Avon, and Lock No. 93.. ..	65	4
Avoncliffe Wharf	67	0
Murhill Quarry	68	0
Limpley Stoke	69	0
Dundas, junction with Somersetshire Coal Canal (No. 93), between Locks Nos. 93 & 94	70	0
Hampton Quarry	72	4
Bathampton Mill	73	0
Darlington Old Wharf	74	0
Sydney Wharf, and Pinche's Wharf	74	4
Clapham's Wharf, and Widcombe Wharf ..	75	0
Bath, Bottom Lock, No. 100, and junction with River Avon	75	2
Bath, River Avon, centre of Bath Old Bridge, and commencement of River Avon Section	75	4
Weston Lock	77	6
Midland Railway Bridge	78	2
Midland Railway Bridge	79	4
Kelston Lock	80	6
Saltford Lock	81	4
Opposite Golden Valley Wharf	82	0
Swinford Lock	82	2
Centre of Avon and Gloucester Railway Wharf	84	0
Opposite Shellard's Lime Quarry	84	2
Keynsham Lock..	84	4
Londonderry Wharf	85	0
Tail of Hanham Lock, and junction with River Avon under jurisdiction of Bristol Corporation (No. 7)	86	4

(43)—GREAT WESTERN RAILWAY—*continued.*

(d) Locks.

Kennet River Section.

1.—County.
2.—Fobney.
3.—Southcot.
4.—Burghfield.
5.—Garston.
6.—Sheffield.
7.—Sulhampstead.
8.—Tide Mill.
9.—Upton.
10.—Towney.
11.—Padworth.
12.—Aldermaston.
13.—Woolhampton.
14.—Hale's.
15.—Midgham.
16.—Colthrope.
17.—Monkey Marsh.
18.—Widmead.
19.—Bulls.
20.—Ham Mills.
21.—Greenham.

Kennet and Avon Canal Section.

22.—Newbury.
23.—Gwyer's.
24.—Higg's.
25.—Beenham.
26.—Hamstead.
27.—Coppice.
28.—Drewell's.
29.—Kintbury.
30.—Fowles.
31.—Brunsdon's.
32.—Dunn's Mill.
33.—Hungerford.
34.—Hungerford Marsh.
35.—Cobbler's.
36.—Picklefield.
37.—Froxfield Bottom.
38.—Froxfield Middle.
39.—Oakhill.
40.—Little Bedwyn.
41.—Little Bedwyn Field.
42.—Knight's Mill.
43.—Great Bedwyn.
44 to 52. } Crofton.

Rise from Reading.

53 to 56. } Wootton Rivers.

(43)—GREAT WESTERN RAILWAY—*continued*.

57
to } Devizes.
85.

86
to } Seend.
90.

91.—Semington Top.
92.—Semington Bottom.
93.—Bradford-on-Avon.

94
to } Bath.
100.

River Avon Section

101.—Weston.
102.—Kelston.
103.—Saltford.
104.—Swinford.
105.—Keynsham.
106.—Hanham.

Fall to Hanham.

(e) *Maximum size of vessels that can use the navigation.*

Kennet River Section.

		Ft.	In.
Length		74	0
Width		14	0
Draught	average	3	6
Headroom		10	0

Kennet and Avon Canal Section.

		Ft.	In.
Length		73	0
Width		13	10
Draught	average	3	6
Headroom		8	10

River Avon Section.

		Ft.	In.
Length		75	0
Width		16	0
Draught	average	3	6
Headroom		9	0

Swinford Shoal, just below Swinford Lock, is the shallowest place in the navigation between Bath and Bristol; in very dry seasons the depth of water over this shoal is sometimes as low as 2ft. 9in.

(f) *Tunnels.*

Kennet and Avon Canal Section.

Savernake—

	Ft.	In.
Length .. ..502 yards ..		
Minimum height above water level	13	2
Minimum width at water level	17	4

No towing-path.

(43)—GREAT WESTERN RAILWAY—*continued.*

Boats hauled through by means of chains fixed to side wall.

A clear view can generally be obtained through the tunnel.

		Ft.	In.
No. 1.—Bath—			
Length	66 yards		
Minimum height above water level		13	4
Minimum width at water level		17	6
Towing-path through the tunnel.			
No. 2.—Bath—			
Length	64 yards		
Minimum height above water level		13	4
Minimum width at water level		17	8
Towing-path through the tunnel.			

(g) *Towing-path.*

There is a towing-path throughout the navigation, except through Savernake Tunnel.

(h) *Tidal Information.*

Spring tides in the River Avon sometimes flow up to Keynsham, but generally the tide does not flow beyond the tail of Hanham Lock, the termination of the navigation. *See* Tidal Information, River Avon (Bristol). No. 7.

(i) *Types of vessels using the navigation.*

Narrow boats and barges. On the River Kennet Section and the Kennet and Avon Canal Section steam haulage for the purposes of trade is not allowed, but pleasure steamers are admitted.

Stratford-on-Avon Canal.

(c) *Distance Table.*

Main Line (No. 43b1).

	Miles.	Fur.
Kings Norton, junction with Worcester and Birmingham Canal (No. 90b), to—		
Kings Norton Stop Lock	–	1
Kings Norton Tunnel	1	0
Yardley Wood	3	0
Warings Green	7	5
Hockley Heath	9	6
Lapworth Top Lock	11	0
Kingswood, head of Lock No. 20, and junction with branch to Warwick and Birmingham Canal (No. 43b2)	12	4
Lowsonford	14	2
Preston Bagot Locks	16	2
Wootton Wawen	18	4
Bearley Aqueduct	19	7
Wilmcote Railway Station	21	7
Bishopton	23	6
Stratford-on-Avon, Lock No. 55, and junction with Upper Avon Navigation, now derelict	25	4

(43)—GREAT WESTERN RAILWAY—*continued.*

Branch at Kingswood to Warwick and Birmingham Canal (No. 43b2).

	Miles.	Fur.
Length from Main Line to junction with Warwick and Birmingham Canal (No. 115)	–	1

(d) *Locks.*

Main Line (No. 43b1).

1.—Kings Norton Stop Lock.
Level.

2
to } Lapworth.
19.

20
to } Lapworth.
23.

24
to } Lapworth.
26.

27.

28.

29
and } Rowington.
30.

31.

32.

33
and } Claverton.
34.

35
to } Preston Bagot.
37.

38.—Wootton Wawen.

39
to } Old Stratford.
49.

50.—Bishopton.

51
to } Old Stratford.
54.

55.—River Avon Barge Lock.
Fall from Kings Norton.

Branch at Kingswood to Warwick and Birmingham Canal (No. 43b2).

1.—Lapworth.
Fall to Warwick and Birmingham Canal.

The level of the Warwick and Birmingham Canal at Kingswood is the same as that of the Stratford-on-Avon Canal between Locks 20 and 21. The arrangement of the Branch Canal descending one lock from the Stratford Canal between Locks 19 and 20 to the Warwick and Birmingham Canal ensures the latter Company a lock of water with all boats interchanged, to which they have a right.

(43)—GREAT WESTERN RAILWAY—*continued.*

(*e*) *Maximum size of vessels that can use the navigation.*

Main Line (No. 43b1).

	Ft.	In.
Length from Kings Norton to Kingswood ..	72	0
,, from Kingswood to Stratford.. ..	71	8
Width	7	0
Draught from Kings Norton to Kingswood ..	3	6
,, from Kingswood to Stratford ..	3	3
Headroom	6	0

Branch at Kingswood to Warwick and Birmingham Canal (No. 43b2).

	Ft.	In.
Length	72	0
Width	7	0
Draught	3	6
Headroom	6	0

(*f*) *Tunnels.*

Main Line (No. 43b1).

		Ft.	In.
Kings Norton—			
Length	352 yards		
Minimum height above water level		9	10
Minimum width at water level..		16	0

No towing-path.
Boats hauled through by means of handrail fixed to side wall.

(*g*) *Towing-path.*

There is a towing-path throughout the navigation except through Kings Norton Tunnel.

(*i*) *Types of vessels using the navigation.*

Narrow Boats.

Stourbridge Extension Canal.

(*c*) *Distance Table.*

Main Line (No. 43c1).

	Miles.	Fur.
Brockmoor Junction, junction with Stourbridge Canal (No. 99c), to—		
Stop Lock, and junction with Bromley Branch (No. 43c2)	–	1½
Junction with Sandhills Branch (No. 43c3) ..	–	5
Oak Farm	2	0

Bromley Branch (No. 43c2).

	Miles.	Fur.
Length from junction with Main Line (No. 43c1)	–	2½

K

(43)—GREAT WESTERN RAILWAY—*continued.*

Sandhills Branch (No. 43c3).

	Miles.	Fur.
Length from junction with Main Line (No. 43c1)	–	5

(d) *Locks.*

Main Line (No. 43c1).

1.—Stop Lock.

Level.

(e) *Maximum size of vessels that can use the navigation.*

Main Line (No. 43c1) and Branches.

						Ft.	In.
Length ..	..	..	..	..	..	72	0
Width ..	..	..	..	..	..	7	0
Draught ..	..	..	..	..	..	4	0
Headroom	..	..	..	..	..	6	6

(g) *Towing-path.*

There is a towing-path throughout the canal and branches.

(i) *Types of vessels using the navigation.*

Narrow boats.

River Tone Navigation (No. 43d).

(c) *Distance Table.*

	Miles.	Fur.
Length from Gas Works, Taunton, to Firepool, Taunton, the junction with Bridgwater and Taunton Canal (No. 43e)	–	6

(e) *Maximum size of vessels that can use the navigation.*

						Ft.	In.
Length ..	..	..	..	..	..	54	0
Width ..	..	..	..	..	..	13	0
Draught ..	..	..	..	..	..	3	0

(g) *Towing-path.*

There is no towing-path.

(i) *Types of vessels using the navigation.*

Barges carrying up to about 22 tons.

Bridgwater and Taunton Canal (No. 43e).

(c) *Distance Table.*

	Miles.	Fur.
Firepool Lock, Taunton, junction with River Tone Navigation (No. 43d), to—		
Bathpool	1	6
Creech St. Michael	3	0
Durston	6	0

(43)—GREAT WESTERN RAILWAY—*continued.*

	Miles.	Fur.
Firepool Lock, Taunton, junction with River Tone Navigation (No. 43d), to (*continued*)—		
Mansell Top Lock	6	6
Mansell Bottom Lock	7	0
North Newton	7	1
Kings Lock	8	2
Standard Lock	9	0
Ford Gate	9	6
Entrance Lock to Bridgwater Dock, and termination of Canal	14	0
Outlet from Bridgwater Dock to River Parrett (No. 84)	14	1½

(d) *Locks.*

1.—Firepool.
2.—Mansell Top.
3.—Mansell Bottom.
4.—Kings.
5.—Standard.
6.—Bridgwater.

Fall from Taunton.

There is one pair of tidal gates from Bridgwater Dock to Bridgwater Tidal Basin, and one pair of tidal gates and one barge lock from Bridgwater Tidal Basin to the River Parrett.

(e) *Maximum size of vessels that can use the navigation.*

	Ft.	In.
Length	54	0
Width	13	0
Draught	3	0
Depth of water in Bridgwater Dock 15ft. to	16	0
,, ,, in Tidal Basin at Spring tides..	15	0
,, ,, ,, ,, Neap tides ..	6	0
Available length for vessels in tidal basin ..	175	0
Available length for vessels in tidal basin if Drawbridge at top end is raised	195	0
Width of opening of gates from Dock to Tidal Basin	32	0
Width of opening of gates from Tidal Basin to River Parrett	42	0

Barge Lock from Tidal Basin to River Parrett for vessels 54ft. long by 13ft. wide.

(g) *Towing-path.*

There is a towing-path throughout the navigation.

(i) *Types of vessels using the navigation.*

Barges.

(43)—GREAT WESTERN RAILWAY—*continued.*

Grand Western Canal (No. 43f).

(c) *Distance Table.*

	Miles.	Fur.
Loudwell to—		
Whipcott Wharf	–	7
Burlescombe Wharf	1	6
Ayshford	2	7
Sampford Peverell	5	2
Rock House Wharf	6	4
Halberton	7	1
Main Road Bridge between Halberton and Tiverton	8	6
Tiverton	10	6

(e) *Maximum size of vessels that can use the navigation.*

	Ft.	In.
Length.—Not limited.		
Width	7	0
Draught	3	6
Headroom	7	3

(g) *Towing-path.*

There is a towing-path throughout the navigation.

(i) *Types of vessels using the navigation.*

At the present time there are apparently only two boats on the canal, which are engaged in the roadstone traffic. They work chained together fore and aft—the foremost one, which has a pointed bow, carrying about 8 tons, and the after one, which is a box boat, carrying about 10 tons ; each draws, when loaded, about 1ft. 8in. of water.

Stover Canal (No. 43g).

(c) *Distance Table.*

	Miles.	Fur.
Jetty Marsh, junction with River Teign (No. 105a), to—		
Jetty Marsh Lock	–	0½
Messrs. Watts, Blake, Bearne, & Co.'s Teignbridge Wharves, and Teignbridge Lock	–	7
Graving Dock Lock	1	2
Teigngrace Lock	1	3
Teigngrace Railway Station	1	4½
Termination of Canal	1	7

(d) *Locks.*

1.—Jetty Marsh.
2.—Teignbridge.
3.—Graving Dock.
4.—Teigngrace.

Rise from River Teign.

(43)—GREAT WESTERN RAILWAY—*continued.*

(e) *Maximum size of vessels that can use the navigation.*

						Ft.	In.
Length	..	..	..	..	..	54	0
Width	..	..	..	..	..	14	0
Draught	..	..	..	..	..	3	6

(g) *Towing-path.*

There is no horse towing-path, only a bow hauling-path for men.

(h) *Tidal Information.*

The water from the commencement of the navigation to the tail of Jetty Marsh Lock rises and falls with the tide in the River Teign. *See* Tidal Information, River Teign (No. 105).

(i) *Types of vessels using the navigation.*

River Teign. Stover Canal, and Hackney Canal barges—*see* Section 9, Types of Vessels, (*b*) Sailing Vessels.

Brecon and Abergavenny Canal (No. 43h).

(c) *Distance Table.*

Brecon, Davis's and Gas Works Wharves, to—					Miles.	Fur.
Walton Wharf	..	..	..	..	–	2
Brynich Bridge	..	..	..	..	1	4
Brynich Lock	..	..	..	..	2	0
Tynewydd Bridge	..	..	..	..	3	2
Stonehouse Bridge	..	..	..	..	3	4
Llanbrynean Bridge	..	..	..	..	3	6
Penkelly Wharf	..	..	..	..	4	4
Crosskeys Bridge	..	..	..	..	4	6
Cross Oak Draw Bridge	..	..	..	5	6
Gillstone Bridge	..	..	..	..	6	4
Talybont	..	..	..	..	6	6
Craiglas Bridge	..	..	..	..	7	2
Ashford Tunnel	..	..	..	..	7	3
Wenallt Bridge	..	..	..	..	8	2
Llanddetty Wharf	..	..	..	..	8	4
The Workhouse Bridge	..	..	..	9	2
Cwm Crawnon Lock No. 2	..	..	..	10	0
Llanguinider Lock No. 6	..	..	..	10	2
Llanguinider Wharf	..	..	..	..	10	4
Panteg Bridge	..	..	..	..	11	2
Aberhowye Bridge	..	..	..	..	12	0
Dwffrant Bridge	..	..	..	..	12	2
Vro Bridge	..	..	..	..	13	0
Llwyncelyn Bridge	..	..	..	..	13	4
Folly Bridge	..	..	..	..	14	2
Union Bridge	..	..	..	..	14	4
Ffawyddog Bridge	..	..	..	..	15	0

(43)—GREAT WESTERN RAILWAY—*continued.*

	Miles.	Fur.
Brecon, Davis's and Gas Works Wharves, to (*continued*)—		
Llangattock Wharf (Crickhowell distant one mile)..	15	2
Park Bridge	16	0
Pen-pedair-heol Bridge..	16	2
Dan-y-park Bridge	16	4
Graig-yr-glas-llwyd Bridge	17	0
Dany-graig Bridge	17	6
Llanelly Wharf ..	18	2
Clydach Wharf ..	18	4
Gilwern ..	18	6
Llanwenarth Draw Bridge	19	6
Govilon Wharf ..	20	4
Govilon Quarry ..	20	6
Llanfoist, Incline Bridge (Abergavenny distant one mile)..	21	6
Castle Bridge	22	4
Richards Bridge..	23	0
Llanelen Bridge ..	23	6
Twynglas Bridge	24	2
Roberts Bridge ..	24	4
Saddlers and Red House Bridges	25	0
Halls and Llanover Wharves ..	25	6
Mount Pleasant Bridge..	26	0
Cottage and Lapstone Bridges	26	6
Goytre Bridge ..	27	2
Parkybrain Wharf	28	2
Croesynypant and Peutre Bridges	29	2
Summerfield Bridge	29	6
Mamhilad Bridge	30	4
Keepers Bridge ..	31	0
Werne Bridge ..	31	4
Typoeth and Llanvihangel Bridges ..	32	2
Road Bridge ..	33	0
Pontymoyle, junction with Monmouthshire Canal (No. 43i1) (Pontypool distant half-a-mile) ..	33	2

(d) Locks.

1.—Brynich.

2
to } Llanguinider.
6.

Fall from Brecon.

(e) Maximum size of vessels that can use the navigation.

	Ft.	In.
Length ..	64	9
Width ..	9	2
Draught ..	3	0
Headroom	5	10

(43)—GREAT WESTERN RAILWAY—*continued.*

(f) *Tunnels.*

Ashford—

		Ft.	In.
Length	375 yards		
Minimum height above water level		8	4
Minimum width at water level		10	9

No towing-path.

Boats "shafted" or "legged" through.

(g) *Towing-path.*

There is a towing-path throughout the navigation, except through Ashford Tunnel.

(i) *Types of vessels using the navigation.*

Glamorganshire, Aberdare, Brecon and Abergavenny, and Monmouthshire Canal boats—*see* Section 9, Types of Vessels, (a) Non-sailing Vessels.

Monmouthshire Canal.

(c) *Distance Table.*

Main Line (No. 43i1).

	Miles.	Fur.
Pontymoyle, junction with Brecon and Abergavenny Canal (No. 43h) (Pont-y pool distant half-a-mile), to—		
Coedygric Wharf	–	4
Panteg Bridge	–	6
Sebastopol	1	0
Pontrhydyyn Wharf	1	2
Cwmbran Tunnel	1	6
Pontnewydd Locks, Nos. 1 to 5..	2	2
Pontnewydd Wharf and Four Locks Wharf ..	2	6
Woodside Brick Yard	3	0
Cwmbran Furnaces	3	2
Cwmbran Siding	3	4
Half Way	3	6
Oakfield Wharf	4	0
Two Locks, Nos. 16 and 17, Hanson's Wharf and Jones Brick Yard	4	2
Tycock Wharf, and Sketch Brick Yard ..	5	4
Llantarnan Wharf, and Parfitts Brick Yard	5	4
Tynyffynon Wharf	6	0
Malpas Wharf	7	0
Lock No. 30	7	2
Malpas junction, junction with Crumlin Branch (No. 43i2), below Lock No. 31	7	4
Crindau Bridge	7	6
Tunnel Wharf	8	0
Tunnel Yard	8	2
Newport, Dos Works	8	4
Newport, Corporation Wharf	8	6
Newport, Llanarth Street	9	0

(43)—GREAT WESTERN RAILWAY—*continued.*

Crumlin Branch (No. 43i2).

Malpas Junction, junction with Main Line (No. 43i1), to—

	Miles.	Fur.
Alteryn Bottom Lock, No. 1 ..	–	4
Alteryn Brick Works ..	1	0
Pensarn Bridge ..	1	4
Cefn Wharf ..	1	6
Meeting House Bridge ..	2	4
Pont-y-mason Bridge ..	3	0
Roberts Wharf ..	3	4
Tynycwm Quarry ..	3	6
Gile Aqueduct ..	4	2
Low Bridge ..	4	4
Moriah Bridge ..	4	6
Risca, Pen-y-rhiw Quarry ..	5	0
Risca, Navigation Bridge ..	5	2
Cromwell's Quarry, Phillips' Quarry, and Jones' Brick Yard ..	5	4
Nicholas and Johnson's Brick Works ..	5	6
Crosskeys ..	6	6
Pont-y-waun ..	7	0
Chapel Bridge ..	7	4
Abercarn Colliery ..	8	2
Abercarn Lime Mills ..	8	4
Celynen Colliery..	9	2
Newbridge ..	9	4
Crumlin ..	10	6

(d) Locks.

Main Line (No. 43i1),

1 to 5. } Pontnewydd.

6 to 15. } Cwmbran.

16 and 17. } Two Locks.

18 to 27. } Tycock.

28.—Tynyffynon.
29.—Malpas.
30.—Gwastad.
31.—Town.

Fall from Pontymoyle.

Crumlin Branch (No. 43i2).

1 to 5 } Alteryn.

(43)—GREAT WESTERN RAILWAY—*continued.*

6
to ⎬ Cefn.
20

21.—Cwmcarn.

22
to ⎬ Abercarn.
28

29.—Cwmdows.

30
to ⎬ Newbridge.
32

Rise from Malpas Junction.

(e) *Maximum size of vessels that can use the navigation.*

Main Line (No. 43i1), and Crumlin Branch (No. 43i2).

						Ft.	In.
Length	..	..	..	..	..	64	9
Width	..	..	..	..	..	9	2
Draught	..	..	..	..	..	3	0
Headroom	..	..	..	..	..	5	10

(f) *Tunnels.*

Main Line (No. 43i1).

				Ft.	In.
Cwmbran—					
Length	87 yards				
Minimum height above water level	..	..		7	9
Minimum width at water level ..	..	..		10	4

No towing-path.
Boats " shafted " or " legged " through.

(g) *Towing-path.*

Main Line (No. 43i1).

There is a towing-path throughout the navigation, except through Cwmbran Tunnel.

Crumlin Branch (No. 43i2).

There is a towing-path throughout the navigation.

(i) *Types of vessels using the navigation.*

Glamorganshire, Aberdare, Brecon and Abergavenny, and Monmouthshire Canal boats—*see* Section 9, Types of Vessels, (a) Non-sailing Vessels.

Swansea Canal.

(c) *Distance Table.*

Main Line (No. 43j1).

						Miles.	Fur.
Hen-hoydd to—							
Penrhos	..	..	..	..	..	1	0
Ystradgynlais	..	..	..	..	..	2	2
Gyrnos	..	..	..	..	..	3	2

(43)—GREAT WESTERN RAILWAY—*continued.*

	Miles.	Fur.
Hen-hoydd to (*continued*)—		
Ystalfera Railway Station	3	6
Ystalfera ..	4	4
Pontardawe	8	0
Lock No. 30	10	2
Clydach ..	11	0
Cwm Clydach Station and Lock No. 32	11	1
Morriston Bridge	13	3
Craig Trewddfa ..	13	7
Plas Marl..	14	4
Landore Railway Station, Low Level	15	0
Swansea, Lock No. 33 ..	15	6½
Swansea, head of Lock No. 36, and junction with short branch running parallel with North Dock (No. 43j2)	16	1½
Swansea, junction with North Dock and termination of canal ..	16	2

Short branch in Swansea running parallel with North Dock (No. 43j2)

	Miles.	Fur.
Length from junction with Main Line ..	-	1½

(*d*) *Locks.*

Main Line (No. 43j1).

1
and } 1st Flight.
2.

3
to } 2nd Flight.
7.

8.

9
to } 3rd Flight.
12.

13
and } 4th Flight.
14.

15
to } 5th Flight.
21.

22.
23.

24
and } 6th Flight.
25.

26
and } 7th Flight.
27.

28
and } 8th Flight.
29.

(43)—Great Western Railway—*continued.*

30
and } 9th Flight.
31.

32.

33
to } 10th Flight.
36.

Fall to Swansea.

(e) *Maximum size of vessels that can use the navigation.*

Main Line (No. 43j1), and short branch in Swansea (No. 43j2).

						Ft.	In.
Length	..	..	..	..	..	69	2
Width	..	..	..	..	..	7	6
Draught	..	..	..	..	..	3	0
Headroom	..	..	..	..	..	7	0

(g) *Towing-path.*

There is a towing-path throughout the navigation.

(i) *Types of vessels using the navigation.*

Swansea Canal Boats—*see* Section 9, Types of Vessels, (a) Non-sailing Vessels.

Great Yarmouth Port and Haven Commissioners, The, are the Controlling Authority in respect of—the River Wensum from New Mills, Norwich, to the end of Carrow Works, Norwich ; the River Yare from the end of Carrow Works, Norwich, to its mouth at Gorleston, including Rockland Dike and Broad ; the River Waveney from the termination of the Bungay Navigation, shortly below Shipmeadow Lock, to its junction with the River Yare at the west end of Breydon Water ; the River Bure from the termination of the Aylsham Navigation shortly below Coltishall Lock to its junction with the River Yare at the east end of Breydon Water including all navigable Dikes and Broads communicating with the River, except Common Broad, which is private property ; also the River Ant and all navigable branches except the North Walsham and Dilham Canal, and the River Thurne and all navigable branches.

---

(44)—Griff Colliery Company's Canal.

(a) *Short Description.*

The canal commences by a junction with the main line of the Coventry Canal two-and-a-half miles south of Nuneaton, in the county of Warwickshire, and proceeds westward for a distance of six furlongs to a wharf to which coal is brought from the collieries by means of a tramway for loading into boats.

(44)—GRIFF COLLIERY COMPANY'S CANAL—*continued*.

The canal is of very narrow section throughout the greater part of its length, and boats cannot pass each other.

(b) *Proprietors, Officers, and Offices.*

The Griff Colliery Company.

Office : Griff Colliery, near Nuneaton.

(e) *Maximum size of vessels that can use the navigation.*

						Ft.	In.
Length	..	..	..	..	..	72	0
Width	..	..	..	..	..	6	10
Draught	..	..	..	..	..	3	6

(g) *Towing-path.*

There is a towing-path throughout the navigation.

(i) *Types of vessels using the navigation.*

Narrow boats.

---

(45)—GROSVENOR CANAL.

(a) *Short Description.*

The canal commences by a junction with the tidal portion of the River Thames in London just below Chelsea Bridge, and proceeds in a northerly direction for a distance of three furlongs to its termination at Ebury Bridge, Buckingham Palace Road. The canal as originally constructed extended to a dock on the present site of the Victoria Station of the London, Brighton, and South Coast Railway; the dock was closed to form the station in 1860, making the head of the canal at Eccleston Bridge. In 1902, in consequence of further land being required for extensions of the London, Brighton, and South Coast Railway, the portion of the canal between Eccleston Bridge and Ebury Bridge was closed.

(b) *Proprietors, Officers, and Offices*

The Duke of Westminster.

Office : Grosvenor Estate Office, 52, Davies Street, Berkeley Square, London, W.

For traffic enquiries, address The Lockmaster, Grosvenor Canal, Pimlico, London, S.W.

(d) *Locks.*

1.—Entrance Lock.

Rise from River Thames.

The lock is provided with a pair of flood gates at the top end to shut out abnormally high tides from the canal.

(45)—Grosvenor Canal.—*continued*

(e) *Maximum size of vessels that can use the navigation.*

	Ft.	In.
Length	90	0
Width	18	6
Draught, maximum on Spring tides	10	0
„ on Neap tides.. .. .. about	7	6

(g) *Towing-path.*

There is a towing-path throughout the navigation.

(h) *Tidal Information.*

High water at Entrance Lock about 20min. after London Bridge.

(i) *Types of vessels using the navigation.*

Barges and lighters.

Guildsfield Branch Canal—*see* Shropshire Union Canals—Montgomeryshire Canal.

---

(46)—Hackney Canal.

(a) *Short Description.*

The canal commences by a junction with the estuary of the River Teign at Hackney, about four miles west of Teignmouth, and, passing under the main line of the Great Western Railway between Teignmouth and Newton Abbot, proceeds in a north-westerly direction to its termination at a point adjoining the main road between Newton Abbot and Kingsteignton, all in the county of Devonshire. The trade on the canal is confined to china and pottery clay, which is sent to Teignmouth for shipment.

(b) *Proprietors, Officers, and Offices.*

Henry Barnes Knight, Esq., Hilary House, Axminster, Devonshire.

(c) *Distance Table.*

	Miles.	Fur.
Hackney, junction with estuary of the River Teign (No. 105a), to—		
Hackney Lock	–	1
Termination of canal	–	5

(d) *Locks.*

1.—Hackney.

Rise from River Teign.

(46)—HACKNEY CANAL—*continued.*

    (e) Maximum size of vessels that can use the navigation.

	Ft.	In.
Length : Hackney Lock will accommodate two of the local barges each 54ft. in length		
Width	14	0
Draught	3	9

(g) Towing-path.

There is no horse towing-path, only a bow hauling-path for men.

(h) Tidal Information.

The tide from the estuary of the River Teign flows to the tail of Hackney Lock.

High water at the tail of Hackney Lock about 6min. after Teignmouth.

Spring tides rise	10ft.
Neap ,, ,, ...	6ft.

High water at Teignmouth 4hrs. after London Bridge.

(i) Types of vessels using the navigation.

River Teign, Stover Canal, and Hackney Canal Barges—*see* Section 9, Types of Vessels, (*b*) Sailing Vessels.

HAINES BRANCH CANAL — *see* Birmingham Canal Navigations, Walsall Canal.

HALFORD BRANCH CANAL — *see* Birmingham Canal Navigations, Wednesbury Old Canal.

HALIFAX BRANCH CANAL—*see* Calder and Hebble Navigation.

HALL GREEN BRANCH CANAL — *see* North Staffordshire Railway, Trent and Mersey Canal.

HARDLEY DIKE—*see* River Yare.

HATFIELD CHASE COMMISSIONERS—*see* River Idle and River Don.

HATHERTON BRANCH CANAL—*see* Staffordshire and Worcestershire Canal.

LORD HAY'S BRANCH CANAL — *see* Birmingham Canal Navigations, Wyrley and Essington Canal.

HEATH, ROBERT, ESQ.—*see* Foxley Branch Canal.

HEIGHAM SOUND—*see* River Bure, River Thurne.

HERTFORD UNION CANAL—*see* Regents Canal.

HEYWOOD BRANCH CANAL—*see* Rochdale Canal.

HICKLING BROAD—*see* River Bure, River Thurne.

HIGH LANE BRANCH CANAL—*see* Great Central Railway, Macclesfield Canal.

HOBHOLE DRAIN — *see* Witham Drainage General Commissioners' Navigable Drains.

HOLLINWOOD BRANCH CANAL—*see* Great Central Railway, Ashton Canal.

HORBURY OLD CUT—*see* Calder and Hebble Navigation.

HORSEY MERE—*see* River Bure, River Thurne.

---

(47)—HOUGHTON BRANCH CANAL.

(a) *Short Description.*

The canal commences by a junction with the Old Main Loop Line from Smethwick Junction to Tipton Factory Junction of the Birmingham Canal Navigations (No. 10c1), and proceeds in a southerly direction for a distance of 2½ furlongs, giving access to various works and waterside premises.

(b) *Proprietors, Officers, and Offices,*

Messrs. Chance and Hunt, Messrs. Albright and Wilson, and the London Works Iron Company, Oldbury, jointly pay the cost of maintaining the canal, and the Birmingham Canal Company provide the water.

(e) *Maximum size of vessels that can use the navigation.*

						Ft.	In.
Length	..	..	..	..	..	71	6
Width	..	..	..	..	..	7	1½
Draught	..	..	..	..	..	3	6

(g) *Towing-path.*

There is no towing-path.

(i) *Types of vessels using the navigation.*

Narrow boats.

HUDDERSFIELD BROAD CANAL—*see* London and North Western Railway.

HUDDERSFIELD NARROW CANAL—*see* London and North Western Railway.

---

(48)—RIVER HULL.

(a) *Short Description.*

The navigation commences by a junction with the Driffield Navigation at the tail of Struncheon Hill Lock on that navigation, and proceeds by Aike, Hull Bridge, Grove Hill, and Stone Ferry to the City of Hull, where it forms a junction with the River Humber, all in the East Riding of the county of Yorkshire.

There is one short branch leading out of the main line of the river known as Arram Beck, which has been practically disused for traffic for the past ten years.

(b) *Proprietors, Officers, and Offices.*

The river from the tail of Struncheon Hill Lock to Sculcoates Goate in the City of Hull, including Arram Beck, is a free navigation, but as a drainage is under the jurisdiction of the Commissioners of Sewers for the east parts of the East Riding of Yorkshire, who enforce the repair of the banks by the occupiers or owners of the adjoining lands.

Clerk : Henry Broomhead Broomhead.

Office : Beverley, Yorkshire.

The river in the City of Hull from Sculcoates Goate to its junction with the River Humber is under the jurisdiction of the Hull Corporation.

Town Clerk : E. Laverack.

Borough Engineer : A. E. White.

Office : Town Hall, Hull.

(c) *Distance Table.*

Main Line of River (No. 48a).

Tail of Struncheon Hill Lock, and junction with Driffield Navigation (No. 29), to—

	Miles.	Fur.
Tophill Low Landing	1	2
Baswick Landing	1	4
Aike	4	0
Junction with Leven Canal (No. 60)	4	4
Junction with Arram Beck (No. 48b)	5	5
Hull Bridge	7	2

(48)—RIVER HULL—*continued.*

	Miles.	Fur.
Tail of Struncheon Hill Lock, and junction with Driffield Navigation (No. 29), to (*continued*)—		
J. Scarr & Sons' Ship Yard	8	7
Grove Hill, junction with Beverley Beck (No. 9)	9	0
Stone Ferry	17	4
Hull, Sculcoates Goate	19	1
Hull, junction with Queen's Dock	19	1½
Hull, junction with Drypool Basin, leading to Victoria Dock	19	4
Hull, junction with River Humber (No. 49) ..	20	0

Arram Beck (No. 48b).

Length from junction with main line of river ..	–	2½

(e) Maximum size of vessels that can use the navigation.

Main Line (No. 48a) and Arram Beck (No. 48b).

	Ft.	In.
Length.—Not limited.		
Width.—Not limited.		
Draught from Hull to Grove Hill	6	6
,, from Grove Hill to the tail of Struncheon Hill Lock	6	0
,, Arram Beck .. .. .. about	3	0

(g) Towing-path.

There is a towing-path between Hull Bridge and the tail of Struncheon Hill Lock but it is not much used, navigation being only conducted on the ebb and flow of the tide.

(h) Tidal Information.

The river is tidal throughout, the tide flowing strongly at the lower end.

High water at Hull about 4hrs. 30min. after London bridge.

Spring tides rise	20ft. 9in.
Neap ,, ,, ...	16ft. 3in.

High water at Stone Ferry about 20min. after Hull.   The first of the flood tide reaches here about 3hrs. after the first of the flood tide at the mouth of the river, there being a considerable difference of level between these places.

High water at Grove Hill about 2hrs. after Hull.

High water at the junction with the Leven Canal about 2hrs. 15min. after Hull.   The first of the flood tide reaches here about the time of high water at Hull.

L

(48)—River Hull—*continued*.

High water at the tail of Struncheon Hill Lock of the Driffield Navigation about 3hrs. after Hull.

Tides rise .. .. 1ft. 3in. to 2ft.

(i) Types of vessels using the navigation.

Yorkshire keels and lighters.

Hull, Corporation of the City of—*see* River Hull.

Hulme Locks Branch Canal—*see* Manchester Ship Canal, Bridgewater Canal.

---

(49)—River Humber.

(a) Short Description.

The River Humber is an estuary formed by the junction of the Rivers Ouse and Trent at Trent Falls, and scarcely comes within the category of an inland navigation, but it serves to connect the Rivers Ouse and Trent with the Market Weighton Canal, the River Ancholme Drainage and Navigation, and the River Hull. The estuary divides the county of Lincolnshire from the East Riding of the county of Yorkshire.

The navigation of the River Humber is very dangerous, except to those who are fully acquainted with it, on account of the great strength of the tide and the numerous shifting sandbanks.

(b) Proprietors, Officers, and Offices.

The estuary is under the jurisdiction of the River Humber Conservancy Commissioners.

Clerk : E. S. Wilson.

Conservator : D. E. Hume.

Office : Conservancy Buildings, Whitefriargate, Hull.

(c) Distance Table.

Left Bank. Miles.	Fur.		Right Bank. Miles.	Fur.
		Trent Falls, junction with River Ouse (No. 81) and River Trent (No. 112a), to—		
2	0	Junction with Market Weighton Canal (No. 66)		
3	4	Broomfleet		
		Whitton	3	4
6	0	Brough		
		Winteringham Haven	7	0
		Ferriby Sluice, junction with River Ancholme Drainage and Navigation (No. 5) ..	8	0

(49)—RIVER HUMBER—*continued.*

Left Bank. Miles. Fur.			Right Bank. Miles. Fur.	
		Trent Falls, junction with River Ouse (No. 81) and River Trent (No. 112a), to (*continued*)—		
		South Ferriby	9	0
9	0	North Ferriby		
		Chowder Ness	11	0
		Barton-upon-Humber	13	0
13	0	Hessle		
		New Holland	16	0
18	0	Hull, junction with River Hull (No. 48a)		

(e) *Maximum size of vessels that can use the navigation.*

Ft.   In.

Length.—Not limited.
Width.—Not limited.
Draught .. .. 14ft. to 18   0

(g) *Towing-path.*

There is no towing-path.

(h) *Tidal Information.*

The river is tidal throughout.
High water at Hull about 4hrs. 30min. after London Bridge.
    Spring tides rise .. .. 20ft. 9in.
    Neap   ,,   ,, ... 16ft. 3in.
High water at Ferriby Sluice about 12min. after Hull.
    Spring tides rise .. .. 20ft. 3in.
High water at Trent Falls about 30min. after Hull.
    Spring tides rise .. .. 16ft.

(i) *Types of vessels using the navigation.*

Sea-going vessels, Yorkshire keels, billy-boys, and lighters.

HUMBER ARM BRANCH CANAL—*see* Shropshire Union Canals.

HUNDRED FOOT RIVER, *alias* NEW BEDFORD RIVER—*see* River Ouse (Bedford).

HUNDRED STREAM, another name for the River Thurne—*see* River Bure.

ICKNIELD PORT WHARF BRANCH CANAL—*see* Birmingham Canal Navigations, Main Line.

(50)—River Idle.

(a) Short Description.

The river commences to be navigable at Misson, near Bawtry, and proceeds by Idle Stop and Misterton to Stockwith, where it forms a junction with the River Trent a short distance below the entrance to the Chesterfield Canal.

The whole course of the river from Misson to Stockwith is in the county of Nottinghamshire.

There is very little trade done on the river.

(b) Proprietors, Officers, and Offices.

From Misson to Idle Stop, and from above Misson to Retford, the river is under the jurisdiction of the River Idle Commissioners.

Clerk : J. D. Dimock (Messrs. Mee & Co., Solicitors, Retford).

From Idle Stop to Stockwith, which is an artificial channel originally constructed by Vermuyden, is under the jurisdiction of the Hatfield Chase Commissioners.

Clerks : Messrs. Baxter & Co., Solicitors.

Office : Doncaster.

Expenditor : A. Wattee.

Office : Epworth, near Doncaster.

Sluice keeper at Misterton Soss : R. Threadgold, Misterton Soss, Gainsborough.

(c) Distance Table.

	Miles.	Fur.
Misson to—		
Idle Stop	3	0
Misterton and Haxey Road Bridge	6	0
Misterton Soss	7	1
Stockwith, junction with River Trent (No.		
112a)	8	0

(d) Locks.

1.—Misterton Soss.

Misterton Soss is a sluice having one pair of tidal gates and one pair of sea doors, the former serve to hold up the water in the upper portion of the river at low tide, and the latter to keep out the tide at high water. Vessels can only pass Misterton Soss when the tide makes a level.

(e) Maximum size of vessels that can use the navigation.

	Ft.	In.
Length.—Not limited.		
Width, being the width through the gates of		
Misterton Soss	18	0
Draught .. .. 3ft. to 3		6

(50)—RIVER IDLE – *continued*.

(g) *Towing-path*.

There is a towing-path throughout the navigation, which is, however, not always continuous.

(h) *Tidal Information*.

High water at Stockwith about 5hrs. after Hull.

Spring tides rise	15ft. 6in.
Neap „ „	5ft.

(i) *Types of vessels using the navigation*.

Upper and Lower River Trent boats and narrow boats.

---

(51)—IPSWICH AND STOWMARKET NAVIGATION.

(a) *Short Description*.

The navigation commences at Stowupland Bridge, Stowmarket, and following the course of the River Gipping proceeds by Needham Market, Baylham, Great Blakenham, Claydon, Bramford, and Sproughton to Stoke Bridge, Ipswich, where it joins the River Orwell above Ipswich Dock, all in the county of Suffolk.

The navigation is very narrow and tortuous. Not much trade is done above the Patent Manure Works at Bramford.

(b) *Proprietors, Officers, and Offices*.

The Trustees of the Ipswich and Stowmarket Navigation.

Clerk : P. C. G. Hayward.

Office : Messrs. Hayward & Peecock, Solicitors, Stowmarket.

Engineer : Henry Miller.

Office : Museum Street, Ipswich.

(c) *Distance Table*.

Stowmarket, Stowupland Bridge, to—	Miles.	Fur.
Stowupland Lock	–	6
Badley Lock	2	2
Needham Market and Needham Lock ..	3	7
Barking Lock	4	5
Bosmere Lock	5	3
Pips Lock	5	6
Baylham and Baylham Lock	6	4
Chamford Lock	7	3
Great Blakenham and Blakenham Lock ..	8	1

(51)—Ipswich and Stowmarket Navigation—*continued.*

	Miles.	Fur.
Stowmarket, Stowupland Bridge, to (*continued*)—		
Claydon and Claydon Lock	8	7
Paper Mill Lock..	10	3
Bramford and Bramford Lock	11	5
Sproughton and Sproughton Lock	12	6
Chantry Lock	13	6
Ipswich, Tide Lock	15	1
Ipswich, Stoke Bridge	15	7

(*d*) *Locks.*

1.—Stowupland.
2.—Badley.
3.—Needham.
4.—Barking.
5.—Bosmere.
6.—Pips.
7.—Baylham.
8.—Chamford.
9.—Blakenham.
10.—Claydon.
11.—Paper Mill.
12.—Bramford.
13.—Sproughton.
14.—Chantry.
15.—Ipswich Tide Lock.

Fall from Stowmarket.

(*e*) *Maximum size of vessels that can use the navigation.*

	Ft.	In.
Length	55	0
Width	14	0
Draught from Stowmarket to Bramford about	3	0
„ from Bramford to Ipswich	3	6
Headroom	7	0

(*g*) *Towing-path.*

There is a towing-path throughout the navigation.

(*h*) *Tidal Information.*

The tide flows to the tail of the tide lock at Ipswich.

High water at Ipswich about 1hr. 23min. before London Bridge. Spring tides rise .. .. 13ft. 6in.

(*i*) *Types of vessels using the navigation.*

Barges. Steam barges habitually trade to the Patent Manure Works at Bramford.

Irwell Upper Reach—*see* Manchester Ship Canal.

ISLINGTON BRANCH CANAL—*see* Great Central Railway, Ashton Canal.

IVEL RIVER, another name for the River Yeo.

---

(52)—EARL OF JERSEY'S CANALS.

(a) *Short Description.*

These canals consist of the Giants Grave and Briton Ferry Canal, the Glan-y-wern Canal, and the Tir-isaf Branch Canal.

The Giants Grave and Briton Ferry Canal (No. 52a) is a continuation of the Neath Canal (No. 72) from its termination at Giants Grave to the Iron Works at Briton Ferry. The canal is half-a-mile in length, and is on a level with the bottom pound of the Neath Canal. At the present time it is not used for navigation, but only as a source of water supply to the Iron Works at Briton Ferry.

The Glan-y-wern Canal (No. 52b) leads out of the Tennant Canal (No. 106a) about two miles from Swansea, and proceeds for a distance of one mile three furlongs to a wharf at the head of the canal, which is connected by means of a tramway with the Glan-y-wern Colliery.

The Tir-isaf Branch Canal (No. 52c) leads out of the Tennant Canal (No. 106a) about half-a-mile from Swansea, and proceeds for a distance of one mile to Tir-isaf Colliery.

(b) *Proprietors, Officers, and Offices.*

The Earl of Jersey.

Agent : Thomas Williams.

Office : Tennant Canal and Estate Office, Neath, South Wales.

Glan-y-wern Canal.

(e) *Maximum size of vessels that can use the navigation.*

	Ft.	In.
Length	60	0
Width	9	0
Draught	1	9

(g) *Towing-path.*

The towing-path is not continuous throughout the navigation.

(i) *Types of vessels using the navigation.*

Neath and Tennant Canal boats, carrying about 12 tons—*see* Section 9, Types of Vessels, (a) Non-sailing Vessels.

(52)—EARL OF JERSEY'S CANALS—*continued*.

Tir-isaf Branch Canal.

(e) *Maximum size of vessels that can use the navigation.*

	Ft.	In.
Length	60	0
Width	9	0
Draught	2	5

(g) *Towing-path.*

There is a towing-path throughout the navigation.

(i) *Types of vessels using the navigation.*

Neath and Tennant Canal boats, carrying about 20 tons—*see* Section 9, Types of Vessels, (a) Non-sailing Vessels.

JUNCTION DRAIN, *alias* FRITH BANK DRAIN—*see* Witham Drainage General Commissioners.

KENNET, RIVER—*see* Great Western Railway, Kennet and Avon Navigation, and River Thames.

KENNET AND AVON NAVIGATION—*see* Great Western Railway.

KENSINGTON CANAL—*see* West London Extension Railway.

KENT, EAST, COMMISSIONERS OF SEWERS FOR—*see* River Stour (Kent).

KINGS DIKE—*see* Middle Level Navigations.

KINGS LYNN CONSERVANCY BOARD—*see* River Ouse (Bedford).

KNIGHT, HENRY BARNES, ESQ.—*see* Hackney Canal.

KNOTTINGLEY AND GOOLE CANAL—*see* Aire and Calder Navigation, Main Line.

---

(53)—KYME EAU.

(a) *Short Description.*

The portion of Kyme Eau now remaining navigable extends from Ewerby Waithe Common, near South Kyme, to Chapel Hill, near Dogdyke, all in the county of Lincolnshire, forming at the latter place a junction with the River Witham. Kyme Eau was formerly the lower portion of the Sleaford Navigation, which extended from the town of Sleaford to Chapel Hill, and which was abandoned by Act of Parliament of 1878.

There is very little trade done on the navigation.

(53)—KYME EAU—*continued.*

(b) Proprietors, Officers, and Offices.

The question of the jurisdiction in respect of Kyme Eau and its banks has been the subject of some litigation and controversy since the date of the Sleaford Navigation Abandonment Act, and the rights are not at all clearly defined. The duty of " roding," or cutting the weeds in the Eau, and of keeping Lower Kyme Lock in repair belongs to the riparian owners, for whom (under an arrangement) the Witham Drainage General Commissioners perform the work.

Clerk to the Witham Drainage General Commissioners : R. W. Millington.

Engineer : T. Healey Johnson.

Offices : Witham Office, Boston, Lincolnshire.

(c) Distance Table.

Ewerby Waithe Common to—	Miles.	Fur.
Halfpenny Hatch	0	4
South Kyme	2	2
Lower Kyme Lock	4	7
Chapel Hill, junction with River Witham (No. 124)	6	4

(d) Locks.

1.—Lower Kyme.
Fall to Chapel Hill.

(e) Maximum size of vessels that can use the navigation.

	Ft.	In.
Length	74	0
Width	14	3
Draught very uncertain, but in winter time a depth can often be found of	3	0

(g) Towing-path.

There is a towing-path throughout the navigation.

(i) Types of vessels using the navigation.

Barges.

---

(54)—LAKENHEATH LODE.

(a) Short Description.

The Lode commences to be navigable at Lakenheath village in the county of Suffolk, and proceeds in a north-westerly direction to a junction with the Brandon River half-a-mile below Crosswater Staunch.

(54)—Lakenheath Lode—*continued.*

(b) *Proprietors, Officers, and Offices.*

The navigation of the Lode is under no controlling authority. The staunch at the High Bridge appears to have been repaired on various occasions by different private individuals for the purpose of passing their own traffic.

The trade done on the Lode is confined to gravel, which is brought down from Lakenheath.

(c) *Distance Table.*

	Miles.	Fur.
Lakenheath Wharf to—		
High Bridge and Staunch	–	6
Great Eastern Railway Bridge (Main Cambridge Line)	2	7
Junction with Brandon River (No. 14) ..	3	2

(d) *Locks.*

1.—High Bridge Staunch (Navigation Weir).

(e) *Maximum size of vessels that can use the navigation.*

	Ft.	In.
Length.—Not limited.		
Width	12	6
Draught	2	6

(g) *Towing-path.*

There is a towing-path throughout the navigation.

(i) *Types of vessels using the navigation.*

Fen lighters.

---

(55)—Lancashire and Yorkshire Railway.

(a) *Short Description.*

The Lancashire and Yorkshire Railway Company are the proprietors of the Manchester, Bolton, and Bury Canal. The canal commences at Salford, Manchester, by a junction with the River Irwell Upper Reach of the Manchester Ship Canal Company's Mersey and Irwell Navigation, and proceeds in a north-westerly direction to Pendleton, Clifton, Ringley, Prestolee, Radcliffe, and Bury.

The Bolton Branch forms a junction with the main line at the top of Prestolee Locks and proceeds by Darcy Lever to Bolton. The canal between Bury, Radcliffe, the top of Prestolee Locks, and Bolton is all on one level.

The whole course of the canal is situated in the county of Lancashire.

(55)—LANCASHIRE AND YORKSHIRE RAILWAY—*continued.*

There is fair trade between Salford and Bury, but only a small amount of trade to Bolton, as the wharves at that place being so much below the main level of the town heavy cartage expenses are incurred in delivery.

(b) *Proprietors, Officers, and Offices.*

Lancashire and Yorkshire Railway Company.

General Manager : J. A. F. Aspinall.

Secretary : R. C. Irwin.

Goods Manager : Josiah Wharton.

Head Offices : Hunts Bank.

Superintendent of Canal : R. Unsworth.

Office : Oldfield Road Locks, Salford, Manchester.

Engineer : Thomas Barratt.

Office : Prestolee, near Bolton.

(c) *Distance Table.*

Main Line (No. 55a).

Salford (Manchester), junction with River Irwell Upper Reach (No. 64d4) and Salford Lock No. 1, to—

	Miles.	Fur.
Ordsall Lane Lock	–	1
Oldfield Road Top Lock	–	3
Windsor Bridge	1	0
Pendleton, Strawberry Hill Bridge	1	2
Pendleton, Frederick Street Bridge	1	4
Pendleton Bridge	1	6
Cock Robin Bridge	2	0
Park House Bridge, Brindle Heath	2	6
Agecroft Bridge	3	0
Clifton, Hogg's Bridge	4	4
Junction with Clifton and Kearsley Coal Company's (Ltd.) Canal (No. 22)	4	5
Rhodes Bridge	5	2
Rhodes Lock	5	4
Kilcobie Bridge	6	0
Giants Seat Locks	6	2
Ringley Fold Old Bridge	6	4
Ringley Locks	7	0
Dickie Bridge	7	4
Prestolee Bridge	7	6
Head of Prestolee Top Lock No. 17, and junction with Bolton Branch (No. 55b)	8	0
Bailey Bridge	8	2
Ladyshore Bridge	8	6
Whittaker's Shoot	9	0
Mount Sion Bridge	9	2

(55)—LANCASHIRE AND YORKSHIRE RAILWAY—*continued.*

	Miles.	Fur.
Salford (Manchester), junction with River Irwell Upper Reach (No. 64d4) and Salford Lock No. 1, to (*continued*)—		
Nickerhole Bridge	9	4
Radcliffe, Water Lane Bridge	10	2
Whittaker's Bridge	10	4
Hampson's Bridge (Within's Lane, Public Wharf, Radcliffe)	11	0
Rothwell Bridge..	11	2
Bank Top Bridge	11	6
Daiseyfield Bridge	12	2
Barlow Bridge	12	4
Bury Wharves	12	6

Bolton Branch (No. 55b).

Junction with Main Line (No. 55a) and Nob End Bridge to—		
Farnworth Bridge	–	6
Fogg's Bridge	1	0
Darcy Lever, Smithy Bridge	1	6
Bentley Bridge	2	0
Burnden Viaduct	2	2
Springfield Bridge	2	4
Haulgh Hall Bridge	2	6
Bolton Wharves..	3	0

(d) Locks.

Main Line (No. 55a).

1
and } Salford (Staircase).
2.

3.—Ordsall Lane.

4
and } Oldfield Road (Staircase).
5.

6.—Oldfield Road Top.
7.—Rhodes.

8
and } Giants Seat (Staircase).
9.

10
and } Ringley (Staircase).
11.

12
to } Prestolee (Staircase).
14

15
to } Prestolee (Staircase).
17

Rise from River Irwell at Salford.

(55)—LANCASHIRE AND YORKSHIRE RAILWAY—*continued.*

(e) *Maximum size of vessels that can use the navigation.*

Main Line (No. 55a) and Bolton Branch (No. 55b).

						Ft.	In.
Length	..	..	..	..	..	68	0
Width	..	..	..	..	..	14	2
Draught	..	..	..	..	..	3	6
Headroom	..	..	..	..	..	9	0

(f) *Tunnels.*

Main Line (No. 55a).

No. 1 Salford—

Length	..	..	..	..	34 yards	
Minimum height above water level		..	..	9	2
Minimum width at water level ..		..	..	14	10

No towing-path.
Boats " shafted " through.

No. 2 Salford—

Length	..	..	..	..	49 yards	
Minimum height above water level		..	..	9	0
Minimum width at water level ..		..	..	17	10

No towing-path.
Boats " shafted " through.

Bury—

Length	..	..	..	..	141 yards	
Minimum height above water level		..	..	9	4
Minimum width at water level ..		..	..	9	6

No towing-path.
Boats " shafted " through.

(g) *Towing-path.*

There is a towing-path throughout the navigation, except through the three tunnels enumerated above.

(i) *Types of vessels using the navigation.*

Flats, boats, short narrow boats, and narrow coal boats without cabins.

There are some coal boats in use on the canal for short-distance traffic carrying coal in boxes which are lifted in and out by cranes ; each box contains a bare two tons, and about ten boxes go to a boat load, the total load carried being about 18 tons.

LANCASTER CANAL—*see* London and North Western Railway.

LANGLEY DIKE—*see* River Yare.

---

(56)—RIVER LARKE.

(a) *Short Description.*

The river commences to be navigable at Icklingham, in the county of Suffolk, and proceeds by Barton Mills, Mildenhall, Worlington, and West Row, in the same county, Isleham, and Prickwillow to a junction with the River Ouse, about four miles below Ely, in the county of Cambridgeshire.

(56)—RIVER LARKE——*continued.*

There is a short branch from near Barton Mills to Tuddenham Mill, which is the Tuddenham Mill Stream made navigable.

(b) *Proprietors, Officers, and Offices.*

From Icklingham to Lee Brook, and from above Icklingham to Bury St. Edmunds, the river is under the jurisdiction of the Eastern Counties Navigation and Transport Company, Ltd., which was formed in 1889 to improve the navigation from Lee Brook to Mildenhall, and to restore it from Mildenhall to Bury St. Edmunds. The work was completed in September, 1894. The restoration, however, proved a failure, and the works speedily began to fall into decay. At the present time the portion of the river between Icklingham and Bury St. Edmunds, eight-and-a-half miles in length, is unnavigable. In December, 1894, a Receiver was appointed by the Court of Chancery to take over the management of the Company on behalf of the debenture holders, and he is still in office at the present time.

Receiver and Manager : H. A. Deal.

Office : 1, Gresham Buildings, London, E.C.

From Lee Brook to a point about half-a-mile above Prickwillow, being a portion of the natural channel of the river, is an open navigation under no controlling authority, and is toll free. The Bedford Level Corporation cut the weeds over this length, and the South Level Drainage and Navigation Commissioners maintain Isleham Sluice. From half-a-mile above Prickwillow to the junction with the River Ouse, being an artificial cut, is under the jurisdiction of the South Level Drainage and Navigation Commissioners, who take tolls over this length.

(c) *Distance Table.*

Main Line of River (No. 56a).

Icklingham, and Icklingham Sluice (Lock), to—	Miles.	Fur.
Temple Bridge Staunch	–	6
Jack Tree Staunch	1	0
Junction with Tuddenham Mill Stream (No. 55b)	2	4
Barton Mills Sluice (Lock)	3	0
Barton Mills Staunch	3	4
Mildenhall, Gas Works Lock	4	1
Mildenhall, New Lock	4	2
Worlington, and Kings Staunch	5	6
Judes Ferry (West Row, distant half-a-mile)..	6	6
West Row Staunch	7	2
Lee Brook	7	6
Isleham Sluice (Lock) .. .:	8	4
Prickwillow	17	0
Junction with River Ouse (No. 79b)	19	0

Tuddenham Mill Stream (No. 56b).

Length from junction with Main Line of River (No. 55a) to Tuddenham Mill ..	1	2

(56)—RIVER LARKE—*continued.*

(d) Locks.

Main Line of River (No. 56a).

1.—Icklingham.
2.—Temple Bridge   (Navigation Weir).
3.—Jack Tree   do.
4.—Barton Mills.
5.—Barton Mills   (Navigation Weir).
6.—Mildenhall Gas Works.
7.—Mildenhall New.
8.—Kings   (Navigation Weir).
9.—West Row   do.
10.—Isleham.

Fall from Icklingham.

(e) Maximum size of vessels that can use the navigation.

Main Line of River (No. 56a) and Tuddenham Mill Stream (No. 56b).

	Ft.	In.
Length	48	0
Width	10	0
Draught	3	6
Headroom	8	0

(g) Towing-path.

There is a towing-path throughout the navigation.

(i) Types of vessels using the navigation.

Fen lighters.

LEA WOOD BRANCH CANAL—*see* Midland Railway, Cromford Canal.

---

(57)—RIVER LEE.

(a) Short Description.

The river commences to be navigable at the Town Mill, Hertford, and proceeds by Ware, Stanstead Abbots, Broxbourne, Waltham, Enfield Lock, Ponders End, Edmonton, Tottenham, Lee Bridge, Homerton, Hackney, Old Ford, Bow, and Bromley to Limehouse, where it joins the River Thames a short distance below the entrance to the Limehouse Basin of the Regents Canal and Dock Company.

There are sundry portions of tidal navigation leading out of the lower part of the Main River, and which consist of :—

The navigation through Old Ford Tide Gates, at the tail of Old Ford Locks, along the course of the Old River Lee to St. Thomas's Mill Stream, the City Mills River, and the Waterworks River ;

(57)—RIVER LEE—*continued.*

St. Thomas's Creek from just above Bow Bridge through Marsh Gate Lock to the tail of City Mill ;

The navigation of the upper portion of Bow Creek commencing at the tail of Three Mills, connecting a short distance below with the main line of the River Lee Navigation through Bow Tidal Lock, and terminating at Barking Road Bridge between Poplar and Canning Town by a junction with the lower portion of Bow Creek, which enters the River Thames at Blackwall, and which is under the jurisdiction of the Thames Conservancy ; and

The navigation of Abbey Creek from shortly below the head of Bow Creek to Abbey Mills, there joining the Channelsea River, which is navigable to Stratford Wharf.

The navigation is situated in the counties of Hertfordshire, Essex, and Middlesex.

(b) Proprietors, Officers, and Offices.

River Lee Conservancy.

Clerk : George Corble.

Office : 12, Finsbury Circus, London, E.C. Telegraphic Address : " Riverbank," London.

Engineer : C. N. Tween.

Office : Lee House, Enfield Lock.

On the main line of the river from Hertford Town Mill to the tail of Old Ford Lock (24¾ miles) tolls are charged ; from the tail of Old Ford Lock to Bromley Stop Lock (1½ miles), and known as the Bow River, is toll free ; and on Limehouse Cut, being from Bromley Stop Lock to the junction with the River Thames at Limehouse Lock (1½ miles), tolls are charged. The Branch Tidal Navigations, consisting of the Old River Lee through Old Ford Tide Gates, St. Thomas's Creek, Bow Creek from Three Mills down to Barking Road Bridge, Abbey Creek, and the Channelsea River, are all toll free, and are under the jurisdiction of the Lee Conservancy.

(c) Distance Table.

Main Line of River (No, 57a).

	Miles.	Fur.
Hertford Town Mill to—		
Hertford, Dicker Mill Bridge	–	4
Hertford Lock	–	6
Balance Engine House, New River Water Company's Intake	1	2
Ware Lock	2	2
Ware Bridge	2	7
Amwell, Hard Mead Lock	3	6
Amwell, Marsh Bridge	4	2
Stanstead Lock	4	6
Stanstead Bridge	5	1
Rye House Bridge	6	5
Junction with River Stort (No. 96)	7	1

(57)—RIVER LEE—*continued.*

	Miles.	Fur.
Hertford Town Mill to (*continued*)—		
Fieldes' Weir Lock	7	2
Dobbs' Weir Lock	8	0
Carthagena Lock	8	6
Broxbourne Bridge	9	2
Wormley, Aqueduct Lock	10	6
Holy Field Marsh Bridge	11	2
Cheshunt Lock	11	6
Cheshunt Dock	12	4
Waltham Common Lock	12	6
Waltham, Town Bridge and Lock	13	6
Rammey Marsh Lock	14	0
Enfield Lock, Toll Office, and Lee Conservancy Workshops	14	6
Ponder's End Lock	16	6
Picketts Lock	17	6
Bleak Hall Bridge	18	6
Stonebridge Lock	20	0
Tottenham Lock	20	6
Lee Bridge	23	0
Pond Lane Flood Lock..	23	2
Junction with Hertford Union Canal (No. 86d)	24	7
Old Ford Locks and Toll Office	25	0
Junction with Old River Lee through Old Ford Tide Gates (No. 57b)	25	0
Junction with St. Thomas's Creek (No. 57c) ..	25	6
Bow Bridge	25	6
Bow Toll Office, and junction with Bow Creek (No. 57d) through Bow Tidal Lock ..	26	2
Bromley Stop Lock	26	1
Britannia Stop Lock	27	4
Limehouse Lock and Toll Office, junction with River Thames (No. 107a)	27	6

Navigation of Old River Lee through Old Ford Tide Gates (No. 57b).

	Miles.	Fur.
Old Ford Tide Gates, junction with Main Line of River (No. 57a), to—		
Junction with St. Thomas's Mill Stream ..	–	1
Junction with City Mills River	–	2
Junction with Waterworks River	–	3
St. Thomas's Mill Stream is navigable, and is in length	–	4
City Mills River is navigable to the head of City Mill, and is in length	–	5
Waterworks River is navigable to West Ham Waterworks, and is in length	–	5

St. Thomas's Creek (No. 57c).

	Miles.	Fur.
Bow Bridge, junction with Main Line of River (No. 57a), to—		
Marsh Gate Lock	–	1
Tail of City Mill	–	2

M

(57)—RIVER LEE—*continued*.

Bow Creek (No. 57d).

	Miles.	Fur.
Head of Bow Creek at tail of Three Mills to—		
Junction with Abbey Creek (No. 57e)	–	0½
Junction with Main Line of River (No. 57a) through Bow Tidal Lock	–	2½
Barking Road Bridge, limit of jurisdiction of Lee Conservancy, and junction with portion of Bow Creek under jurisdiction of Thames Conservancy (No. 107f)	1	2½

Abbey Creek (No. 57e).

	Miles.	Fur.
From junction with Bow Creek (No. 57d) to—		
Abbey Mills, junction with Channelsea River (No. 57f)	–	4

Channelsea River (No. 57f).

	Miles.	Fur.
Abbey Mills, junction with Abbey Creek (No. 57e), to—		
Stratford Wharves, High Street, Stratford, termination of navigation..	–	4

(d) Locks.

Main Line of River (No. 57a).

1.—Hertford.
2.—Ware.
3.—Hard Mead.
4.—Stanstead.
5.—Fieldes' Weir.
6.—Dobbs' Weir.
7.—Carthagena.
8.—Aqueduct.
9.—Cheshunt.
10.—Waltham Common.
11.—Waltham.
12.—Ramney Marsh.
13.—Enfield.
14.—Ponders End.
15.—Picketts.
16.—Stonebridge.
17.—Tottenham.
> Fall from Hertford.
18.—Pond Lane Flood Lock.
> Level.
19.—Old Ford—duplicate locks side by side.
> Fall from Hertford.
20.—Bromley Stop Lock.
> Level.
21.—Britannia Stop Lock.
> Level.
22.—Limehouse.
> Fall from Hertford.

(57)—RIVER LEE—*continued.*

Navigation of Old River Lee through Old Ford Tide Gates (No. 57b).

1.—Old Ford Tide Gates.

This tidal sluice consists of two pairs of single gates side by side ; vessels can only pass on the levels of the tide.

St. Thomas's Creek (No. 57c).

1.—Marsh Gate.
Fall to City Mill, level at High Water.

Bow Creek (No. 57d).

1.—Bow Tidal Lock.
Fall to Bow Creek, level at High Water.

Bow Tidal Lock consists of one lock and three tidal openings each fitted with a pair of gates. Barges are charged one shilling each to lock through, but are free on the levels of the tide through the tidal openings.

Abbey Creek (No. 57e).

1.—Abbey Mills Tide Gates.

This tidal sluice consists of a single pair of gates. Vessels can only pass on the levels of the tide.

(e) *Maximum size of vessels that can use the navigation.*

Main Line of River (No. 57a).

	Ft.	In.
Length	88	0
Width from Limehouse to the tail of Old Ford Lock	19	0
Width from the tail of Old Ford Lock to the tail of Ponders End Lock	18	0
Width from the tail of Ponders End Lock to the tail of Enfield Lock	15	6
Width from the tail of Enfield Lock to Hertford	13	3
Draught from Limehouse to Enfield Lock ..	5	0
Do. from Enfield Lock to Hertford ..	4	4
Headroom, Lee Bridge	7	6
Do. Waltham Bridge	6	10

Navigation of Old River Lee through Old Ford Tide Gates (No. 57b).

	Ft.	In.
Length	88	0
Width through both openings of Old Ford Tide Gates	19	0
Draught at high water of average tides.. 6ft. to 7		0

St. Thomas's Creek (No. 57c).

	Ft.	In.
Length	88	0
Width	19	0
Draught at high water of average tides.. 6ft. to 7		0

(57)—RIVER LEE—*continued.*

Bow Creek (No. 57d).

	Ft.	In.
Length, if not passing through Bow Tidal Lock, not limited		
Length through Bow Tidal Lock	90	0
Width, if not passing through Bow Tidal Lock or Tidal Gates, not limited		
Width through Bow Tidal Lock or Tidal Gates	19	6
Draught, minimum on any tide	6	0

Abbey Creek (No. 57e) and Channelsea River (No. 57f).

	Ft.	In.
Length.—Not limited.		
Width through Abbey Mills Tide Gates ..	17	6
Draught, minimum on any tide	6	0

(g) *Towing-path.*

Main Line of River (No. 57a).

There is a towing-path throughout the navigation.

Navigation of Old River Lee through Old Ford Tide Gates (No. 57b), St. Thomas's Creek (No. 57c), Bow Creek (No. 57d), Abbey Creek (No. 57e), and Channelsea River (No. 57f).

There is no towing-path, navigation being only conducted on the ebb and flow of the tide.

(h) *Tidal Information.*

The tide flows from Limehouse to the tail of Old Ford Lock, and also flows up Bow Creek into the main line of the river at Bow Lock, and meets the tide from Limehouse in Limehouse Cut. The navigation of the Old River Lee through Old Ford Tide Gates, St. Thomas's, Creek, Bow Creek, Abbey Creek, and the Channelsea River are all tidal.

High water at Limehouse 10min. before London Bridge.

Spring tides rise .. .. 20ft.
Neap ,, ,, ... 16ft.

High water at the tail of Old Ford Lock 3min. after London Bridge.

High water at Bow Lock of tide flowing up Bow Creek, same time as high water at London Bridge.

High water at Stratford Wharf on Channelsea River about 3min. after London Bridge.

(i) *Types of vessels using the navigation.*

Barges and lighters.

(58)—LEEDS AND LIVERPOOL CANAL.

(a) *Short Description.*

The canal commences by a junction with the Aire and Calder Navigation just above Victoria Bridge, Leeds, and proceeds by Armley, Kirkstall, Newlay, Rodley, Calverley, Apperley Bridge, Shipley, Bingley, Morton, Silsden, Kildwick, Skipton, Gargrave, Marton, and Barnoldswick in the West Riding of the county of Yorkshire, Foulridge, Barrowford, Burnley, Hapton, Clayton-le-Moors, Rishton, Blackburn, Cherry Tree, Wheelton, Botany Bay, Cowling, Adlington, Wigan, Appley Bridge, Parbold, Burscough, Lydiate, Maghull, Melling, Aintree, Netherton, Litherland, and Bootle to Liverpool in the county of Lancashire, where it terminates at Pall Mall, near the Exchange Station of the Lancashire and Yorkshire Railway.

There are branches leading out of the main line as follows :—

> The Springs Branch from Skipton to Skipton Rock Stone Staith ;
>
> The Walton Summit Branch from the bottom lock at Johnson's Hillock to Walton Summit ;
>
> The Leigh Branch, from the bottom of the 21st lock at Wigan to Leigh, there joining the Stretford and Leigh Branch of the Manchester Ship Canal Company's Bridgewater Canal ;
>
> The Rufford Branch, or the Lower Douglas Navigation, from Burscough to Tarleton Lock, where it joins the tidal estuary of the River Douglas ; and
>
> The Stanley Dock Cut Branch in Liverpool, which connects the main line of the canal through the Stanley, Collingwood, and Salisbury Docks with the tidal River Mersey.

The portion of the main line of the canal between the top lock at Wigan and Johnson's Hillock and also the Walton Summit Branch, constitute the Lancaster Canal (south end), which, together with the Lancaster Canal (north end) from Preston to Kendal, is the property of the London and North Western Railway Company, who lease the south end to the Leeds and Liverpool Canal Company at an annual rental. For further information, *see* London and North Western Railway, Lancaster Canal.

The Leeds and Liverpool Canal Company are also joint proprietors with the Undertakers of the Aire and Calder Navigation of the Bradford Canal.

The length of the main line of the canal situated in Lancashire carries a far larger portion of traffic than that situated in Yorkshire.

(b) *Proprietors, Officers, and Offices.*

.Leeds and Liverpool Canal Company.

Secretary : Robert Davies.

Traffic Manager : Alfred Peploe.

Engineer : Robert H. White.

Law Clerk : F. H. Hill.

Offices : Pall Mall, Liverpool.   Telegrams : " Canal, Liverpool." Telephone No. 836.

The Proprietors act as carriers.

(58)—Leeds and Liverpool Canal——*continued.*

(c) *Distance Table.*

Main Line (No. 58a).

	Miles.	Fur.
Leeds, River Lock, and junction with Aire and Calder Navigation (No. 3a1), to—		
Leeds Wharf and Office Lock	–	2
St. Anne's Ing Lock	–	4
Oddy Locks	–	6
Spring Garden's Locks	1	0
Armley Wharf	1	4
Kirkstall Wharf	3	0
Kirkstall Lock	3	4
Kirkstall Forge Locks	4	0
Newlay Locks	4	4
Rodley Wharf	6	2
Apperley Bridge, Wharf, and Dobson Locks..	9	0
Field Locks	10	2
Junction with Bradford Canal (No. 13) ..	12	4
Shipley Wharf	12	6
Hirst Lock	14	0
Dowley Gap Locks	14	3
Bingley, Dubb Wharf	15	2
Bingley Lower Locks	15	3
Bingley Upper Locks	16	2
Morton Wharf	17	2
Stock Bridge Wharf	18	'3
Silsden Wharf	22	4
Kildwick Wharf..	24	2
Snaygill Bridge	27	6
Skipton Wharf, and junction with Springs Branch (No. 58b)	29	0
Bottom Lock, Gargrave, and Holme Bridge ..	33	2
Gargrave Wharf..	33	6
Top Lock, Gargrave	35	0
Bottom Lock, Banknewton	35	2
Top Lock, Banknewton	35	6
Bottom Lock, Greenberfield	40	4
Top Lock, Greenberfield	40	6
Coates Wharf (Barnoldswick distant half-a-mile)..	41	4
Salterforth Wharves	43	4
Foulridge Wharf	45	0
North-east end of Foulridge Tunnel	45	1
Top Lock, Barrowford	46	6
Barrowford Wharf	47	2
Bottom Lock, Barrowford	47	4
Nelson Wharf	48	6
Brierfield Wharf (Lob Lane)	50	2
Reedley Colliery..	51	6
Bankhall Colliery	53	0
Burnley Wharf, and Walker Hey Wharf, Burnley	54	4
Gannow Bridge Coal Tips	56	0

(58)—Leeds and Liverpool Canal—*continued.*

	Miles.	Fur.
Leeds, River Lock, and junction with Aire and Calder Navigation (No. 3a1), to (*continued*)—		
Rose Grove Wharf	56	4
Hapton Bridge	58	2
Enfield Wharf	62	2
Church New Wharf (Accrington distant one mile)..	63	6
Church Wharf	64	0
Aspen Collieries	64	2
Rishton Bridge	66	0
Whitebirk Bridge	68	6
Blackburn, Dry Dock Wharf	70	0
Blackburn, Eanam Wharf, and Grimshaw Park Coal Wharves	70	2
Blackburn Top Lock	71	0
Blackburn, Nova Scotia Wharf and bottom lock	71	4
Cherry Tree Wharf	73	0
Stanworth Bridge and Quarries	75	0
Blackburn Corporation, Finnington Depot	75	4
Riley Green Bridge	76	0
Wheelton Wharves	78	6
Top Lock, Johnson's Hillock	79	2
Tail of Bottom Lock, Johnson's Hillock, and junction with Walton Summit Branch (No. 58c)	79	6
Botany Wharf (Chorley distant one mile)	81	0
Cowling Bridge	82	2
Adlington Wharf	85	0
Aberdeen Coal Tip	86	0
Red Rock Bridge	87	4
Wigan Top Lock	90	0
Rose Bridge	91	0
Branch to Ince Hall Collieries	91	4
Junction with Leigh Branch (No. 58d), between Locks Nos. 85 and 86	92	0
Wigan Bottom Lock	92	2
Wigan Wharf and Winstanley Coal Tip	92	4
Wigan Corporation Wharf	93	0
Newton and Meadows Coal Tip	93	2
Pagefield New Lock	93	3
Douglas Bank Coal Tip	93	6
Ell Meadow Lock	94	0
Crook Lock	94	4
Orrel Coal Tip	94	6
Norley Coal Tip	95	0
Dean Lock	96	0
Appley Bridge	97	4
Appley Lock	98	0
Parbold Quarry Wharf	98	4
Parbold Bridge	99	4
Junction with Rufford Branch (No. 58e)	102	4
Burscough Bridge Wharf	103	2
Burscough, New Lane Bridge	104	2

(58)—LEEDS AND LIVERPOOL CANAL—*continued.*

	Miles.	Fur.
Leeds, River Lock, and junction with Aire and Calder Navigation (No. 3a1), to (*continued*)—		
Scarisbrick, Heaton's Bridge	106	0
Scarisbrick Bridge (Southport distant 4 miles)	107	0
Halsall Bridge	108	4
Down Holland Cross Bridge	110	6
Lydiate, Holme's Bridge	112	6
Maghull, Red Lion Bridge	114	2
Maghull Hall Bridge	114	6
Pye's Bridge, Melling	116	6
Blue Anchor Bridge	118	0
Old Roan Bridge	118	6
Netherton Bridge	119	6
Gorsey Lane Bridge	121	0
Litherland Bridge	122	6
Linacre Gas Works	123	6
Bootle Corporation Wharf	124	0
Bootle Wharf and Coffee House Bridge ..	124	4
Bankhall Wharf..	125	4
Sandhills, Liverpool Corporation Wharf ..	125	6
Sandhills, Commercial Road Wharves ..	126	0
Liverpool, junction with Stanley Dock Cut Branch (No. 58f)	126	4
Liverpool, Pall Mall, Leeds and Liverpool Canal Company's Wharves and Warehouses	127	2

In calculating distances for all purposes of rates, tolls, and charges, the summit pools at Barrowford and Wigan shall be taken as equal respectively to a distance of nine miles; the summit pool at Leeds shall be taken as equal to a distance of four miles; and each mile of the distance between the Liverpool termini at Pall Mall and Stanley Dock and Litherland Bridge, and between the terminus of the Canal at Leeds and Newlay, shall be taken as two miles.

A boat shall be deemed to pass through the summit pool at Leeds only when it passes between the lower and the upper reaches of the River Aire; a boat shall be deemed to pass through the summit pool at Wigan only when it passes through the Dover Locks on the Leigh Branch and the twenty-second lock at Wigan.

Springs Branch (No. 58b).

	Miles.	Fur.
Junction with Main Line (No. 58a) to—		
Mill Bridge	--	2
Skipton Rock Stone Staiths	–	4

Walton Summit Branch (No. 58c).

	Miles.	Fur.
Junction with Main Line (No. 58a) to—		
Johnson's Hillock Bridge Wharf	–	2
Moss Bridge Wharves	1	2
Radburn Bridge Wharf	2	0
Walton Summit	3	0

(58)—LEEDS AND LIVERPOOL CANAL—*continued.*

A tramroad formerly ran from Walton Summit to the termination of the Lancaster Canal (north end) at Preston, a distance of about five miles, forming a connection between the Lancaster Canal (south end and north end). It was abandoned in the year 1857.

Leigh Branch (No. 58d).

	Miles	Fur
Junction with Main Line (No. 58a) to—		
Poolstock New Lock	–	3
Pearson and Knowles' Coal Tip	1	2
Park Lane Coal Tip	1	6
Cripping's Coal Tip	2	0
Cross, Tetley and Company's Coal Tip	2	4
Dover Locks	3	6
Edge Green Basin (R. Evans & Co.)	4	4
Abram Coal Tip and Plank Lane Lock	5	4
Bickershaw Colliery Basin	5	6
West Leigh Coal Tip	6	2
Wigan Coal and Iron Company's Basin	6	6
Leigh Wharf	7	0
Junction with Stretford and Leigh Branch of Manchester Ship Canal Company's Bridgewater Canal (No. 64b3)	7	2

Rufford Branch, or Lower Douglas Navigation (No. 58e).

	Miles.	Fur.
Junction with Main Line (No. 58a) to—		
Moss Lock	–	6
Baldwin's Lock	1	4
Marsh Moss Bridge and Wharves	2	4
Rufford Lock	3	0
Sollom	5	2
Bank Bridge and Wharves	6	2
Town End Bridge and Wharf	6	6
West Lancashire Railway Sidings	7	0
Tarleton Lock, junction with tidal River Douglas	7	2

From the junction with the River Douglas at Tarleton Lock to the estuary of the River Ribble is a further distance of four miles. A small trade is carried on down the River Douglas on Spring tides to Freckleton Mill, on the north shore of the River Ribble estuary.

Stanley Dock Cut Branch (No. 58f).

	Miles.	Fur.
Liverpool, junction with Main Line (No. 58a), to—		
Junction with Stanley Dock	–	2

From the junction of the canal with the north end of Stanley Dock, through Collingwood and Salisbury Docks, to the tidal River Mersey, is a further distance of three furlongs.

(58)—LEEDS AND LIVERPOOL CANAL—*continued.*

(*d*) *Locks.*

Main Line (No. 58a).

1.—River.
2.—Office.
3.—St. Anne's Ing.

4
and } Oddy (Staircase).
5.

6.—Spring Gardens.
7.—Kirkstall.

8
to } Forge (Staircase).
10.

11
to } Newlay (Staircase).
13.

14
and } Dobson (Staircase).
15.

16
to } Field (Staircase).
18.

19.—Hurst.

20
and } Dowley Gap (Staircase).
21.

22
to } Bingley Lower (Staircase).
24.

25
to } Bingley Upper (Staircase).
29.

30.—Holme Bridge.
31.—Eshton Road.
32.—Ireland.
33.—Anchor.
34.—Scarland.
35.—Stegneck.

36
to } Bank Newton.
41.

42
to } Greenberfield.
44.

Rise from Leeds.

45
to } Barrowford.
51.

52
to } Blackburn.
57.

(58)—LEEDS AND LIVERPOOL CANAL—*continued.*

58
to } Johnson's Hillock.
64.

65
to } Wigan.
85.

85a.—Pagefield.
86.—Wigan (22nd lock).
87.—Wigan (23rd lock).
88.—Ell Meadow (two locks side by side).
89.—Crook.
90.—Dean (two locks side by side).
91.—Appley (two locks side by side).

Fall to Liverpool.

Leigh Branch (No. 58d).

1.—Poolstock.
2.—Dover Top.
3.—Dover Low.
4.—Plank Lane.

Fall from Wigan.

Rufford Branch (No. 58c).

1.—Latham Top.
2.—Latham Bottom.
3.—Runnel Brow.
4.—Moss.
5.—Germans.
6.—Baldwins.
7.—Rufford.
8.—Tarleton.

Fall from junction with Main Line.

Stanley Dock Cut Branch (No. 58f).

1
to } Stanley Dock Cut.
4.

Fall from junction with Main Line.

(e) *Maximum size of vessels that can use the navigation.*

Main Line (No. 58a).

	Ft.	In.
Length from Leeds to the tail of the 21st Lock at Wigan	62	0
Length from the tail of the 21st Lock at Wigan to Liverpool	72	0
Width	14	3
Draught from Leeds to Skipton	3	11
,, from Skipton to Blackburn	3	9
,, from Blackburn to Liverpool	4	3
Headroom	7	6

(58)—LEEDS AND LIVERPOOL CANAL—*continued.*

Springs Branch (No. 58b).

		Ft.	In.
Length		62	0
Width		14	3
Draught		3	9

Walton Summit Branch (No. 58c).

Length		62	0
Width		14	3
Draught		3	3

Leigh Branch (No. 58d).

Length		72	0
Width		14	3
Draught		4	3

Rufford Branch (No. 58e).

Length		62	0
Width		14	3
Draught		3	6

Stanley Dock Cut Branch (No. 58f).

Length		72	0
Width		14	6

Width.—Vessels exceeding 14ft. 3in. in width
entering the Main Line from the Stanley
Dock Cut Branch can only navigate
between Litherland and the termination
of the Canal at Liverpool.

Draught		4	9

(f) *Tunnels.*

Main Line (No. 58a).

Foulridge—

Length .. .. 1640 yards		
Minimum height above water level	8	0
Minimum width at water level	17	0

No towing-path.

The ordinary traffic is worked by the Canal Company's steam tug
leaving the Foulridge end at 6-0 a.m., 8-0 a.m., 10-0 a.m., 12 noon, 2-0 p.m.,
4-0 p.m., and 6-0 p.m. on Mondays, Tuesdays, Wednesdays, Thursdays,
and Fridays ; at 6-0 a.m., 8-0 a.m., 10-0 a.m., 12 noon, and 2-0 p.m. on
Saturdays ; and at 8-0 a.m. and 4-0 p.m. on Sundays ; and leaving the
Barrowford end at 7-0 a.m., 9-0 a.m., 11-0 a.m., 1-0 p.m., 3-0 p.m., 5-0 p.m.,
and 7-0 p.m. on Mondays, Tuesdays, Wednesdays, Thursdays, and
Fridays ; at 7-0 a.m., 9-0 a.m., 11-0 a.m., 1-0 p.m., and 3-0 p.m. on
Saturdays ; and at 9-0 a.m. and 5-0 p.m. on Sundays.

Gannow—

		Ft.	In.
Length .. .. 559 yards			
Minimum height above water level		10	6
Minimum width at water level		16	5

No towing-path.

(58)—LEEDS AND LIVERPOOL CANAL—*continued.*

The ordinary traffic is worked by the Canal Company's steam tug leaving the Burnley end at 7-0 a.m. and at each hour to 7-0 p.m. on Mondays, Tuesdays, Wednesdays, Thursdays, and Fridays ; at 7-0 a.m. and at each hour to 3-0 p.m. on Saturdays ; and from the west end at 7-30 a.m. and at 30 min. past each hour to 7-30 p.m. on Mondays, Tuesdays, Wednesdays, Thursdays, and Fridays ; at 7-30 a.m. and 30 min. past each hour to 3-30 p.m. on Saturdays.

The tug does not run on Sundays.

(g) *Towing-path.*
Main Line (No. 58a) and Branches.

There is a towing-path throughout the navigation, except through Foulridge and Gannow Tunnels on the main line.

(h) *Tidal Information.*
Rufford Branch (No. 58e).

The tide flows to the tail of Tarleton Lock, where high water is about 2 hrs. after high water at Liverpool.

Spring Tides rise, maximum	..	13ft. 6in.
Neap „ „ minimum ..	..	1ft. 0in.

(i) *Types of vessels using the navigation.*

Leeds and Liverpool Canal short boats navigate the whole of the main line and branches, and there are also several of these vessels in use fitted up as steamers for the main line traffic—*see* Section 9, Types of Vessels, (*a*) Non-sailing Vessels.

Between Liverpool and the bottom of the 21st lock at Wigan, and also on the Leigh Branch, craft of greater length than the above are in use.

LEEK BRANCH CANAL—*see* North Staffordshire Railway, Trent and Mersey Canal.

---

(59)—LEICESTER NAVIGATION.

(a) *Short Description.*

The navigation commences at West Bridge, Leicester, by a junction with the Leicester Section of the Grand Junction Canal, which at this point is the channel of the River Soar, and proceeds by Belgrave, Birstall, Thurmaston, Cossington, Sileby, Mountsorrel, and Barrow-on-Soar to Loughborough, where it forms a junction with the Loughborough Navigation, all in the county of Leicestershire.

The navigation for the most part passes along the course of the River Soar, and is liable to floods in wet weather.

(59)—Leicester Navigation—*continued.*

(b) Proprietors, Officers, and Offices.

The Company of Proprietors of the Leicester Navigation.

Manager : Charles James Dawes.

Office : Public Wharf, Leicester.

(c) Distance Table.

	Miles.	Fur.
Leicester, West Bridge, junction with Leicester Section, Grand Junction Canal (No. 38b1), to—		
Leicester, North Dock	0	6
Leicester, Fellows, Morton, & Clayton Ltd., Canal Carriers, Wharves and Warehouses, and Public Wharf	1	2
Belgrave	2	4
Birstall	4	0
Thurmaston	5	0
Barkby Wharf	6	0
Junction Lock	6	6
Cossington	7	6
Sileby	9	2
Mountsorrel	10	2
Barrow-on-Soar	12	0
Loughborough Wharf	15	0
Junction with Loughborough Navigation (No. 62)	15	6

(d) Locks.

1.—North.
2.—Limekiln.
3.—Belgrave.
4.—Birstall.
5.—Thurmaston.
6.—Junction.
7.—Cossington.
8.—Sileby.
9.—Mountsorrel.
10.—Barrow-on-Soar.

Fall from Leicester.

11.—Flood Lock.

(e) Maximum size of vessels that can use the navigation.

	Ft.	In.
Length	70	0
Width	14	6
Draught	3	6
Headroom	7	6

(g) Towing-path.

There is a towing-path throughout the navigation.

(i) Types of vessels using the navigation.

Narrow boats and Upper Trent boats.

LEICESTER SECTION, GRAND JUNCTION CANAL—*see* Grand Junction Canal.

LEICESTERSHIRE AND NORTHAMPTONSHIRE UNION CANAL—*see* Old Union Canal.

LEIGH BRANCH CANAL—*see* Leeds and Liverpool Canal.

LEMINGTON GUT—*see* River Tyne.

---

(60)—LEVEN CANAL.

(a) *Short Description.*

The canal commences by a junction with the tidal River Hull (No. 48a) about half-a-mile to the south of Aike in the East Riding of the county of Yorkshire, and proceeds in an easterly direction for a distance of three-and-a-quarter miles to the village of Leven. The course of the canal is through an agricultural country, and is entirely in the parish of Leven. There are no wharves except at Leven.

(b) *Proprietors, Officers, and Offices.*

William Bethell, Esq., Rise Park, Hull.

Agent : Ralph Hollis, Esq., Rise Estate Office, Skirlaugh, Hull.

(d) *Locks.*

1.—Entrance Lock.

The lock has two pairs of sea gates as well as two pairs of navigation gates, the fall being sometimes from the River Hull to the canal and sometimes from the canal to the river, according to the state of the tide in the river.

(e) *Maximum size of vessels that can use the navigation.*

	Ft.	In.
Length	64	0
Width	14	10
Draught	6	0

Headroom.—Not limited.

(g) *Towing-path.*

There is a towing-path throughout the navigation.

(h) *Tidal Information.*

See Tidal Information, River Hull.

(i) *Types of vessels using the navigation.*

Yorkshire keels.

LILLESHALL COMPANY LTD.—*see* Duke of Sutherland's Tub Boat Canal.

LIMEHOUSE CUT, the portion of the River Lee Navigation extending from Bromley Stop Lock to the junction with the River Thames at Lime-house—*see* River Lee.

LINTON LOCK NAVIGATION—*see* River Ouse (York).

LITTLE EATON BRANCH CANAL—*see* Derby Canal.

LONDON AND HAMPSHIRE CANAL, OR BASINGSTOKE CANAL—old names for the Woking, Aldershot, and Basingstoke Canal.

---

(61)—LONDON AND NORTH WESTERN RAILWAY.

(a) Short Description.

The canals belonging to the London and North Western Railway Company consist of the Huddersfield Broad Canal, or Sir John Ramsden's Canal, the Huddersfield Narrow Canal, the Lancaster Canal (North end and South end), the St. Helens Canal, and the Shropshire (Coalport) Canal.

The London and North Western Railway Company also control the Birmingham Canal Company, and the Shropshire Union Railways and Canal Company, guaranteeing to the former a minimum dividend of 4 per cent on their capital, and to the latter half of the current rate of dividend on the London and North Western Railway Company's ordinary stock.

The Huddersfield Broad Canal commences at Cooper Bridge, where it forms a junction with the Calder and Hebble Navigation, and proceeds in a south-westerly direction to the town of Huddersfield, where it forms a junction with the Huddersfield Narrow Canal, all in the West Riding of the county of Yorkshire.

The Huddersfield Narrow Canal commences in the town of Hudders-field by a junction with the Huddersfield Broad Canal, and proceeds by Golcar, Linthwaite, and Slaithwaite to the summit level at Marsden in the West Riding of the county of Yorkshire, thence passing under Standedge through Standedge Tunnel, it enters the county of Lancashire, and continues by Diggle, Saddleworth, and Mossley in the same county, Stalybridge in the county of Cheshire, to Ashton-under-Lyne in the county of Lancashire, where it forms a junction with the Ashton Canal.

The Lancaster Canal (North end) commences at Kendal, in the county of Westmorland, and proceeds by Holme and Burton-in-Kendal in the same county, Carnforth, Bolton-le-Sands, Lancaster, Calgate, and Garstang to Preston in the county of Lancashire, where it terminates in a basin adjoining Corporation Street. It must be noted that there is no connection between the Lancaster Canal in Preston and the River Ribble or Preston Docks. A branch leaves the main line of the canal at Lodge Hill, near Calgate, and runs in a westerly direction to Glasson Dock, on the estuary of the River Lune.

(61)—London and North Western Railway—*continued.*

The Lancaster Canal (South end) extends from Walton Summit to Wigan Top Lock on the Leeds and Liverpool Canal, all in the county of Lancashire. The canal forms the Walton Summit Branch and a link in the main line of the Leeds and Liverpool Canal, being leased to that Company at an annual rental, and is described under the heading of the Leeds and Liverpool Canal.

The main line of the St. Helens Canal commences at Blackbrook, near St. Helens, and proceeds by Earlestown, Winwick, Sankey Bridges near Warrington, and Fiddler's Ferry where there is an entrance from the tidal River Mersey, to Widnes, where it terminates by a junction with the tidal River Mersey. The canal has three branches, the Blackbrook Branch at Blackbrook, the Gerrards Bridge Branch (from Blackbrook to near Gerrards Bridge in the northern part of the town of St. Helens), and the Boardmans Bridge Branch, leading out of the Gerrards Bridge Branch in St. Helens, and terminating in the southern part of the town.

The whole course of the canal is in the county of Lancashire.

The Shropshire (Coalport) Canal, which is a tub-boat canal, commences at Tweedale, and proceeds by Madeley to Blisser's Hill Blast Furnaces, all in the county of Shropshire. At the present time the canal is not in use below this point, but its course continues a further distance of one mile two furlongs to Coalport, to which place it descends 213ft. by means of the Coalport Inclined Plane, situated half-a-mile below Blisser's Hill Blast Furnaces. The canal at Coalport has never had any connection with the River Severn at that place, its lowest pound was constructed so as to be above the flood level of the river.

With the exception of the Lancaster Canal, there is not much traffic on any of the Company's canals.

(b) Proprietors, Officers, and Offices.

London and North Western Railway Company.

General Manager : Sir Frederick Harrison.

Secretary : James Bishop.

Chief Engineer : E. B. Thornhill.

Chief Goods Manager : F. Ree.

Offices : Euston Station, London, N.W.

Huddersfield Broad Canal (No. 61a).

(c) Distance Table.

	Miles.	Fur.
Cooper Bridge, junction with Calder and Hebble Navigation (No. 17a), to—		
Bradley	–	4
Deighton	1	2
Fartown Green	2	2
Huddersfield, junction with Huddersfield Narrow Canal (No. 61b)	3	6

N

(61)—London and North Western Railway—*continued.*

(d) Locks.

1.
2.
3.
4.
5 ⎫
to ⎬ Flight.
8. ⎭
'9.

Rise from Cooper Bridge.

(e) *Maximum size of vessels that can use the navigation.*

						Ft.	In.
Length ..	..	..	..	..	..	58	0
Width ..	..	..	..	..	..	14	2
Draught ..	..	..	..	..	..	4	6
Headroom	..	..	..	..	..	9	2

(g) Towing-path.

There is a towing-path throughout the navigation.

(i) Types of vessels using the navigation.

Yorkshire keels and boats.

Huddersfield Narrow Canal (No. 61b).

(c) Distance Table.

	Miles.	Fur.
Huddersfield, junction with Huddersfield Broad Canal (No. 61a), to—		
Milnsbridge	2	5
Golcar	3	2
Linthwaite	3	7
Slaithwaite	5	0
Head of Lock No. 42, Marsden, and north-east end of summit level	7	2
Marsden Railway Station	7	6
North-east end of Standedge Tunnel	8	2
South-west end of Standedge Tunnel, and Diggle Railway Station	11	3
Head of Lock No. 43, Diggle, and south-west end of summit level	11	4
Saddleworth	13	6
Upper Mill	14	0
Greenfield	14	7
Mossley	16	0
Scout Mill	16	5
Millbrook..	17	3
Stalybridge	18	6
Ashton-under-Lyne, junction with Ashton Canal (No. 39a1)	20	0

(61)—LONDON AND NORTH WESTERN RAILWAY—*continued.*

(d) *Locks.*

1
to } Flight.
3.

4
and } Flight.
5.

6.

7
to } Flight
11.

12.

13
and } Flight.
14.

15
to } Flight.
17.

18
and } Flight.
19.

20
to } Flight.
24.

25.

26
to } Flight.
31.

32
to } Flight.
42.

Rise from Huddersfield.

43
to } Flight.
51.

52
and } Flight
53.

54.

55
to } Flight.
57.

58
to } Flight.
60.

61.

62.

63.

64.

65
and } Flight.
66.

67.

(61) – LONDON AND NORTH WESTERN RAILWAY—*continued.*

68 ⎫
to ⎬ Flight.
71. ⎭

72 ⎫
and ⎬ Flight.
73. ⎭
74.

Fall to Ashton-under-Lyne.

(e) *Maximum size of vessels that can use the navigation.*

						Ft.	In.
Length	..	..	..	..	..	70	0
Width	..	..	..	..	..	7	0
Draught ..	..	..	..	..	..	3	6
Headroom	..	..	..	..	..	6	8

(f) *Tunnels.*

Standedge—

Length	..	..	..	..	5456 yards	
Minimum height above water level	..	..	6	8		
Minimum width at water level ..	..	..	7	8		

No towing-path; boats " legged " through.

Boats enter from the Marsden end at 6-0 a.m., 2-0 p.m., and 10-0 p.m., and from the Diggle end at 2-0 a.m., 10-0 a.m., and 6-0 p.m.

There is telephonic communication between the tunnel-keepers at either end of the tunnel. Should a boat require to pass at a time not corresponding with the above hours, it can do so if the tunnel is clear on obtaining permission from the tunnel-keeper.

(g) *Towing-path.*

There is a towing-path throughout the navigation, except through Standedge Tunnel.

(i) *Types of vessels using the navigation.*

Narrow boats.

Lancaster Canal—North End.

(c) *Distance Table.*

Main Line (No. 61c1).

					Miles.	Fur.
Kendal, Canal Head, to—						
Natland Millbeck	..	..	..	..	1	1
Larkrigg ..	..	..	..	..	3	0
Hincaster Tunnel, West End ..	..	..	5	1		
Crooklands	..	..	..	..	7	6
Farleton ..	..	..	..	..	9	3
Holme	..	..	..	..	..	10	6
Burton and Holme Station (Burton-in-Kendal distant one mile) ..	..	..	..	12	1	

(61)—LONDON AND NORTH WESTERN RAILWAY—*continued.*

	Miles.	Fur.
Kendal, Canal Head, to (*continued*)—		
Tewitfield Top Lock	13	7
Tewitfield Bottom Lock and Tewitfield Bridge	14	5
Borwick	15	3
Kellet Bridge	17	2
Carnforth..	18	5
Bolton-le-Sands	21	0
Hest Bank Station	22	4
Lancaster Aqueduct over River Lune ..	25	3
Lancaster..	26	6
Calgate Railway Station	31	6
Lodge Hill, junction with Glasson Dock Branch (No. 61c2)	32	1
Goose Green	35	0
Bells Bridge	38	0
Garstang	39	6
Stubbing's Bridge	42	2
Bamford's Bridge	43	3
Hankinson Bridge	46	7
Kellet's Bridge	50	1
Salwick Hall	51	6
Westleigh..	53	5
Preston	57	0

Glasson Dock Branch (No. 61c2).

Lodge Hill, junction with Main Line (No. 61c1), to—		
Thurnham Mill	1	4
Conder Bridge	1	6
East end of Glasson Basin	2	4
West end of Glasson Basin, Glasson Basin Lock, and junction with Glasson Dock, belonging to Lancaster Port Commissioners.. ..	2	5½

The outlet from Glasson Dock to the estuary of the River Lune is through a pair of tidal gates.

(d) Locks.
Main Line (No. 61c1).

1.—Tewitfield.
2.— ,,
3.— ,,
4.— ,,
5.— ,,
6.— ,,
7.— ,,
8.— ,,

Fall from Kendal.

Glasson Dock Branch (No. 61c2).

1.
2 }
and
3. }

(61)—LONDON AND NORTH WESTERN RAILWAY—*continued.*

4.

5
and
6.

7.—Glasson Basin.

Fall from junction with Main Line.

(e) *Maximum size of vessels that can use the navigation.*

Main Line (No. 61c1).

	Ft.	In.
Length	72	0
Width	14	6
Draught	3	10
Headroom to key of arch at Preston	5	8
„ north of Preston	9	4

Glasson Dock Branch (No. 61c2).

	Ft.	In.
Length from estuary of River Lune to West end of Glasson Basin through Glasson Basin Lock	86	0
„ from east end of Glasson Basin to junction with Main Line ..	72	0
Width through tidal gates of Glasson Dock ..	35	0
„ through Glasson Basin Lock	25	0
„ from east end of Glasson Basin to junction with Main Line ..	14	6
Draught in Glasson Dock, Spring tides ..	20	0
„ in Glasson Dock, Neap tides.. ..	12	0
„ in Glasson Basin	13	6
„ from east end of Glasson Basin to Thurnham Mill	7	0
„ from Thurnham Mill to junction with Main Line	3	10
Headroom	9	4

(f) *Tunnels.*

Main Line (No. 61c1).

Hincaster—

Length .. .. 380 yards		
Minimum height above water level	10	3
Minimum width at water level	10	6

No towing-path; boats hauled through by means of rope fixed on side wall, or " legged."

(g) *Towing-path.*

There is a towing-path throughout the navigation, except through Hincaster Tunnel.

(61)—LONDON AND NORTH WESTERN RAILWAY—*continued.*

(h) *Tidal Information.*

Glasson Dock Branch (No. 61c2).

The tide flows to the tail of Glasson Basin Lock.

High water at Glasson Dock 2 hrs. 42 min. before London Bridge.

Spring tides rise	.. ..	20ft.
Neap ,. .,	.. ..	14ft.

(i) *Types of vessels using the navigation.*

Sea-going vessels use Glasson Dock and Basin, and barges the remainder of the canal.

The barges working on the canal are nearly all built of iron, and carry from 48 to 50 tons. Some wooden barges are still in use which carry from 40 to 42 tons.

St. Helens Canal.

(c) *Distance Table.*

Main Line (No. 61d1).

	Miles.	Fur.
Head of Old Double Lock, Blackbrook, and junction with Blackbrook Branch (No. 61d2) and Gerrards Bridge Branch (No. 61d3), to—		
Engine Lock	–	5
Earlestown, Newton Common Lock	2	2
Bradley Lock	2	6
Hey Lock	3	4
Winwick Lock	5	0
Winwick Wharf and Canal Workshops ..	5	1
Hulme Lock	5	3
Bewsey Lock	6	5
Cheshire Lines Railway Viaduct	7	0
Sankey Bridges (Warrington distant one mile)	8	1
Fiddler's Ferry, junction through Fiddler's Ferry Lock with River Mersey (No. 68) ..	9	6
Widnes Locks, junction with River Mersey (No. 68)	13	1

Blackbrook Branch (No. 61d2).

Length from junction with Main Line (No. 61d1) at head of Old Double Lock ..	–	5

Gerrards Bridge Branch (No. 61d3).

Junction with Main Line (No. 61d1) at head of Old Double Lock, to—		
Junction with Boardmans Bridge Branch (No. 61d4)	1	1
Termination of canal near Gerrards Bridge, St. Helens	1	3½

(61)—London and North Western Railway—*continued*.

Boardmans Bridge Branch (No. 61d4).

	Miles.	Fur.
Length from junction with Gerrards Bridge Branch (No. 61d3) and New Double Lock, to—		
Termination of canal in the southern part of St. Helens	1	5

(d) Locks.

Main Line (No. 61d1).

1
and } Old Double Lock.
2.

3.—Engine.
4.—Newton Common.
5.—Bradley.
6.—Hey.
7.—Winwick.
8.—Hulme.
9.—Bewsey.
10.—Widnes (two locks side by side).

Fall to River Mersey at Widnes.

Entrance from River Mersey at Fiddler's Ferry.

1.—Fiddler's Ferry.

Fall to River Mersey.

Boardmans Bridge Branch (No. 61d4).

1
and } New Double Lock
2.

Rise from junction with Gerrards Bridge Branch.

(e) Maximum size of vessels that can use the navigation.

St. Helens Canal (No. 61d1) and Branches.

	Ft.	In.
Length through Widnes Locks	75	0
Length remainder of canal and branches ..	68	0
Width through Widnes Locks	20	0
Width remainder of canal and branches ..	16	9
Draught	6	3
Headroom	11	0

(g) Towing-path.

There is a towing-path throughout the navigation.

(h) Tidal Information.

See Tidal Information, River Mersey (No. 69).

(i) Types of vessels using the navigation

Mersey flats.

(61)—LONDON AND NORTH WESTERN RAILWAY—*continued.*

Shropshire (Coalport) Canal (No. 61e).

(c) *Distance Table.*

	Miles.	Fur.
Length from Tweedale to Blissers Hill Blast Furnaces.	1	2

(e) *Maximum size of vessels that can use the navigation.*

	Ft.	In.
Length	19	9
Width	6	2
Draught	2	0
Headroom	3	7

(g) *Towing-path.*

There is a towing-path throughout the navigation.

(i) *Types of vessels using the navigation.*

Tub boats—*see* Section 9, Types of Vessels, (a) Non-Sailing Vessels.

The boats work in trains of about 18 or 20 towed by two horses. The steering is done by a man walking along the towing-path pushing against the head of the first boat with a long shaft. The boats carry coal and iron ore from the head of the canal to Blissers Hill Blast Furnaces ; much of the cargo carried is loaded in shallow boxes, which are lifted into the boat by a hand crane and taken out at destination in a similar manner, four of these boxes being a load for one boat.

LOTHING, LAKE—*see* Great Eastern Railway, Navigation from the River Waveney to Lowestoft.

----

(62)—LOUGHBOROUGH NAVIGATION.

(a) *Short Description.*

The navigation commences at Loughborough Wharf, shortly below which it forms a junction with the Leicester Navigation, and proceeds by Normanton-on-Soar, Zouch, Kegworth, Kingston-on-Soar, and Ratcliffe-on-Soar, and terminates at the junction of the River Soar with the River Trent near Thrumpton Weir. From Loughborough to Bishops Meadow Lock the course of the navigation is situated in the county of Leicestershire, the remainder of the navigation forms approximately the boundary between the counties of Leicestershire and Nottingham-shire. The navigation. with the exception of a few artificial cuts, follows the course of the River Soar, and is liable to floods in wet weather.

(62)—LOUGHBOROUGH NAVIGATION—*continued.*

(b) *Proprietors, Officers, and Offices.*

The Company of Proprietors of the Loughborough Navigation.

Clerk : G. H. Woolley.

Office : Loughborough.

(c) *Distance Table.*

Loughborough Wharf to—	Miles.	Fur.
Loughborough, junction with Leicester Navigation (No. 59)	–	1
Loughborough Lock	–	3
Bishops Meadow Lock	1	4
Normanton-on-Soar	2	3
Zouch Mills	3	1
Zouch Lock	3	5
Kegworth	6	0
Kingston-on-Soar	7	1
Ratcliffe-on-Soar	7	7
Red Hill Lock	8	7
Junction with River Trent (No. 112b).. ..	9	2

NOTE.—The Loughborough Navigation joins the River Trent in the Soar Mouth or Red Hill branch of the navigation. On leaving the Loughborough Navigation all boats must turn up stream to the left until the head of Cranfleet Cut is reached. Down stream leads to Thrumpton Weir only.

(d) *Locks.*

1.—Loughborough.
2.—Bishops Meadow.
3.—Zouch.
4.—Kegworth Old.
5.—Kegworth New, Flood Lock.
6.—Ratcliffe.
7.—Red Hill.

Fall from Loughborough.

(e) *Maximum size of vessels that can use the navigation.*

	Ft.	In.
Length	72	3
Width	14	3
Draught	3	6
Headroom	9	0

(g) *Towing-path.*

There is a towing-path throughout the navigation.

(i) *Types of vessels using the navigation.*

Narrow boats and Upper Trent boats.

(63)—LOUTH NAVIGATION.

(a) Short Description.

The navigation commences at River Head in the town of Louth, and proceeds by Keddington and Alvingham to Tetney Haven, there joining the River Humber immediately opposite Spurn Head, all in the county of Lincolnshire. The navigation can only be entered by a loaded keel (drawing five feet six inches of water) during about one week on Spring tides. Vessels usually wait at Hull until the tides have become big enough for them to make the entrance.

(b) Proprietors, Officers, and Offices.

The Commissioners of the Louth Navigation.

Clerk : Porter Wilson.

Office: Messrs. Wilson & Son, Solicitors, Westgate, Louth, Lincolnshire.

Collector of Tolls : W. H. Smith.

Office : River Head, Louth.

(c) Distance Table.

	Miles.	Fur.
Louth, River Head, to—		
Louth Top Lock	–	2
Keddington Lock	–	5
Ticklepenny Lock	1	0
Willows Lock	1	3
Salter Fen Lock	2	1
Alvingham and Alvingham Lock	2	4
High Bridge	3	4
Out Fen Lock	4	0
Austen Fen	5	0
Beargate Bridge	6	0
Firebeacon First Wharf	6	6
Firebeacon Second Wharf	7	0
Fulstow Bridge	7	6
Thoresby Bridge	8	6
Tetney Lock	10	6
Tetney Warehouse	11	0
Sea Bank or White Gate, end of canal	11	6

From this point to the Humber at low water, immediately opposite Spurn Head, is a further distance of three-and-a-half miles by a channel leading through sand flats. The channel is marked by beacons, as the sand flats are covered at high water.

(d) Locks.

1.—Louth.
2.—Keddington.
3.—Ticklepenny.
4.—Willows.
5.—Salter Fen.
6.—Alvingham.
7.—Out Fen.
8.—Tetney.

Tetney Lock has two pairs of sea doors and two pairs of navigation doors.

Fall from Louth.

(63)—LOUTH NAVIGATION—*continued*.

(e) *Maximum size of vessels that can use the navigation.*

	Ft.	In.
Length	72	0
Width	15	1
Draught	5	6

When the tide gives a depth of 23ft. 6in. on the sill of Albert Dock, Hull, there is a navigable draught into the Louth Navigation of   5   6

Headroom.—Not limited.

(g) *Towing-path.*

There is a towing-path throughout the navigation.

(h) *Tidal Information.*

The tide flows to Tetney Lock.

High water at Tetney Lock 10min. after Grimsby, or 3hrs. 48min. after London Bridge.

Spring tides rise   ..   ..   14ft.
Neap   ,,   ,, ...   3ft.

(i) *Types of vessels using the navigation.*

Yorkshire keels and billy-boys.

LOWESTOFT HARBOUR—*see* Great Eastern Railway, Navigation from the River Waveney to Lowestoft.

LYDNEY HARBOUR AND CANAL—*see* Midland and Great Western Joint Railways.

MACCLESFIELD CANAL—*see* Great Central Railway.

MANCHESTER, BOLTON, AND BURY CANAL—*see* Lancashire and Yorkshire Railway.

MANCHESTER AND SALFORD JUNCTION CANAL—*see* Manchester Ship Canal Company.

---

(64)—MANCHESTER SHIP CANAL COMPANY.

(a) *Short Description.*

The canals belonging to the Manchester Ship Canal Company consist of the Manchester Ship Canal, the Bridgewater Canal, the Runcorn and Weston Canal, portions of the Mersey and Irwell Navigation—being such portions as are not absorbed in the Manchester Ship Canal—and the Manchester and Salford Junction Canal.

(64)—MANCHESTER SHIP CANAL COMPANY—*continued*.

The Company are also the proprietors of Runcorn Docks.

The Manchester Ship Canal commences at Woden Street foot-bridge in the City of Manchester, there joining the Irwell Upper Reach of the Mersey and Irwell Navigation, and proceeds by Manchester Docks, Salford Docks, Eccles, and Barton-upon-Irwell, in the county of Lancashire ; Irlam, Partington, Warburton, Thelwall, Latchford (near Warrington), Runcorn, Weston Point, Weston Marsh, Ince, and Ellesmere Port to Eastham, in the county of Cheshire, where it forms a junction with the tidal River Mersey.

The Port of Manchester is constituted by section 3 of the Manchester Ship Canal Act, 1885 (48 and 49 Vic.), and by the same section the Manchester Ship Canal Company is constituted the Harbour Authority of the Port.

The Customs Port of Manchester commences at the eastern termination of the Port of Liverpool, that is to say, at an imaginary straight line across the River Mersey from Dungeon Point on the Lancashire shore to Ince Ferry on the Cheshire shore, and includes the River Mersey above the said line and the River Irwell, so far as the same are navigable, the River Weaver to Frodsham Bridge, and also the Manchester Ship Canal from the entrance at Eastham (where it touches the Port of Liverpool) to Hunts Bank in the City of Manchester, with all channels, havens, streams, creeks, cuts, and docks within the limits aforesaid.

The canal was opened for traffic on 1st January, 1894, and officially opened by Her late Majesty Queen Victoria on 21st May, 1894.

The maximum speed in the canal must not exceed six miles an hour unless a special permit has been obtained from the Company's Manager.

The Manchester Dock railways are 40 miles in extent, and completely intersect the dock estate. The total length of railways already completed at the docks, and at many points alongside the Ship Canal, is upwards of 95 miles. The following railways connect with the docks :—London and North Western, Lancashire and Yorkshire, Great Northern, Midland, Great Central, and Cheshire Lines.

The Canal Company's railways alongside the Ship Canal between Manchester and Eastham are connected with the railways of other companies as follows :—With the Cheshire Lines at Irlam and Glazebrook ; with the London and North Western at Latchford and Runcorn Docks ; with the joint line of the London and North Western and Great Western at Walton Old Junction (near Warrington), and Ellesmere Port.

Traffic can be conveyed in railway wagons between the various loading and discharging berths at the docks and other places on the canal, and over the above lines, to every railway station in Great Britain.

The Manchester Ship Canal Company supplies lists of exceptional through rates (inclusive of railway carriage and Ship Canal toll) for the conveyance of traffic between inland towns and the Manchester Docks which will compare favourably with the rates in operation between those towns and other ports in competition with Manchester.

(64)—MANCHESTER SHIP CANAL COMPANY—*continued.*

The Bridgewater Canal commences at Castle Field in the city of Manchester, where it forms a junction with the main line of the Rochdale Canal, and proceeds by Old Trafford, Stretford, and Sale, in the county of Lancashire ; Altrincham, Lymm, Thelwall, Grappenhall, Stockton Quay, and Preston Brook to Runcorn, in the county of Cheshire, where it terminates by a junction with the Manchester Ship Canal at Runcorn Docks. Access can be obtained at Runcorn to the tidal River Mersey by crossing the Ship Canal and going out into the river through the Bridgewater Side Lock.

The canal has three branches :—

(1) The Hulme Locks Branch, from Castlefield to the River Irwell Upper Reach of the Mersey and Irwell Navigation, all in the city of Manchester.

(2) The Stretford and Leigh Branch, from the Waters Meeting, Stretford, to Barton-upon Irwell, Patricroft, Worsley, and Leigh, there joining the Leigh Branch of the Leeds and Liverpool Canal, all in the county of Lancashire.

(3) The Preston Brook Branch, from the Waters Meeting at Preston Brook to a junction with the Trent and Mersey Canal, all in the county of Cheshire.

The Runcorn and Weston Canal commences at Runcorn Docks by a junction with the Runcorn new line of locks of the Bridgewater Canal, and terminates at Weston Point by a junction with the River Weaver Canal of the main line of navigation of the River Weaver, all in the county of Cheshire.

The portions of the Mersey and Irwell Navigation still navigable consist of :—

(1) The navigation from Rixton Junction on the Manchester Ship Canal to Bank Quay, Warrington, following the course of the River Mersey with the exception of two artificial cuts known as the Butchersfield Canal and the Woolston Canal. At Bank Quay, Warrington, the navigation joins that portion of the tidal River Mersey which is under the jurisdiction of the Upper Mersey Navigation Commissioners. The navigation forms the boundary between the counties of Lancashire and Cheshire.

(2) A branch from the last-named navigation at Arpley, Warrington, through Walton Lock to the Manchester Ship Canal and the Warrington Timber Float.

(3) A portion of the Runcorn and Latchford Canal, extending from a point about half-a-mile above Howley Quay, Warrington, on the navigation between Rixton Junction and Bank Quay, to a junction with the Manchester Ship Canal near Twenty Steps Lock, Stockton Heath.

(4) The River Irwell Upper Reach, from a junction with the Manchester Ship Canal at Woden Street footbridge to Hunts Bank, all in the city of Manchester.

(64)—MANCHESTER SHIP CANAL COMPANY—*continued.*

The Manchester and Salford Junction Canal commences by a junction with the River Irwell Upper Reach of the Mersey and Irwell Navigation, and terminates at the Great Northern Railway Company's new Goods Station in Deansgate, all in the city of Manchester. The canal used formerly to run through and connect with the main line of the Rochdale Canal, but the upper portion has been closed for some years.

(b) *Proprietors, Officers, and Offices.*

Directors appointed by Shareholders :

Chairman : John K. Bythell, Esq., 41, Spring Gardens, Manchester, and Sedgley Park, Prestwich.

The Right Hon. Earl Egerton, 7, St. James' Square, S.W., and Tatton Park, Knutsford.

Sir E. G. Jenkinson, K.C.B., Thurlow, Holloway Hill, Godalming, Surrey.

Sir W. H. Bailey, Albion Works, Salford, and Sale Hall, Cheshire.

Sir Joseph Leigh, M.P., The Towers, Didsbury, Manchester.

W. J. Crossley, Esq., Openshaw, and Glenfield, Altrincham.

C. J. Galloway, Esq., Knot Mill Iron Works, Manchester, and Thorney-holme, Knutsford, Cheshire.

W. C. Bacon, Esq., Shawbrook Lodge, Burnage Lane, Levenshulme.

C. H. Scott, Esq., West Bank, Heaton Mersey, Manchester.

H. C. Pingstone, Esq., Yew Bank, Heaton Chapel, near Manchester.

Appointed by the Manchester Corporation :

Deputy-Chairman : Alderman J. W. Southern, Store Street Saw Mills, Manchester.

Alderman Sir Bosdin Leech, Oak Mount, Timperley, Cheshire.

Alderman Joseph Thompson, Riversdale, Wilmslow, Cheshire.

Alderman Walton Smith, Granville House, Heaton Chapel, near Manchester.

Councillor William Henry Vaudrey, 84, Eccles Old Road, Pendleton, Manchester.

Alderman John Richards, Hornsey Villa, High Lane, Chorlton-cum-Hardy.

Alderman Robert Gibson, Montague House, Old Trafford, Stretford.

Alderman Alexander MacDougall, Willow Bank, Moss Lane East, Manchester.

Councillor Henry Samson, 28, Oxford Street, Manchester.

Alderman Thomas Briggs, The Cedars, Langham Road, Bowdon.

Councillor Wm. Thos. Rothwell, 800, Oldham Road, Newton Heath.

(64)—MANCHESTER SHIP CANAL COMPANY—*continued.*

Officers :

Auditors (elected by Shareholders) : George Hicks and Edwin Guthrie.

Bankers : Glyn, Mills, Currie, and Co., London ; Williams Deacon's Bank Limited, Manchester, and Dock Office.

Land Agents : Dunlop, Wallis, & Co., 57, King Street, Manchester.

Solicitors : Grundy, Kershaw, Samson, & Co., 31, Booth Street, Manchester.

Chief Engineer : W. Henry Hunter, M. Inst. C.E.

Consulting Engineer : Sir E. Leader Williams, M. Inst. C.E.

General Superintendent : Ernest Latimer.

Chief Traffic Superintendent : Herbert M. Gibson.

Dock Traffic Superintendent : William Browning.

Dock Railways Superintendent : John Hamilton.

Railway Traffic Indoor Superintendent : E. C. Cowen.

Grain Elevator Superintendent : G. H. Milsom.

Stores Department : C. E. Mitchell.

Indoor Superintendent : A. E. O. Secchi.

Coal Superintendent (Partington) : M. Pickwick.

Dock Master and Canal Superintendent (Manchester Section) : Capt. Williams.

Canal Superintendents : Irlam and Barton Section, Capt. Dudley ; Latchford Section, Cap. Waring ; Eastham Section, Capt. Heasley.

Secretary and Accountant : F. A. Eyre.

Head Office : 41, Spring Gardens, Manchester.

Dock Office : Trafford Road, Old Trafford, Manchester.

Exchange Enquiry Office : 11, Bank Street, Manchester.

Liverpool Representative : W. Walkden, 18a, Chapel Street, and Exchange Newsroom.

London Representative : James S. McConechy, 140, Leadenhall Street, E.C., and Shipping Exchange.

Canadian Representative : R. Dawson Harling, 26, Wellington Street East, Toronto.

	Telegraphic Addresses.	Nat. Tel. No.
Head Office—		
Secretary	" Canal, Manchester."	688 and 1077
Chief Engineer ..	" Navigation, Manchester."	688 and 1077

(64)—MANCHESTER SHIP CANAL COMPANY—*continued.*

	Telegraphic Addresses.	Nat. Tel. No.
Dock Office—		
General and other Supts.	"Waterway, Manchester."	2402, 2401, 2786, and 5186.
Dock Traffic Supt. (Stock Department)	"Outdoor, Manchester."	841 and 3829
Railway Department..		4102 and 4440
Indoor Superintendent Tolls Department, &c.	"Indoor, Manchester."	4118
Grain Elevator		4117 and 4940
Partington Coal Office	"Coal, Cadishead."	4-Irlam
Liverpool Office	"Waterway, Liverpool."	5517
London Office	"Chiusa, London."	2824-Avenue.

The locks and swing bridges are all connected by private telephone with each other, and with the head and dock offices.

Bridgewater Department:

Superintendent : John Oldfield, Chester Road, Manchester.

Manchester Agent (Water Street) : Frederick Holt.

Warrington Agent (Howley Quay) : Joseph Bridgwater.

Runcorn Agent : James Evans.

Liverpool Agent (Duke's Dock) : Joseph Broome.

Engineer : Francis Wiswall, Runcorn.

Office	Telegraphic Addresses.	Nat. Tel. No.
Superintendent	"Bridgewater Canal, Manchester."	788
Manchester Agent ..	"Quay, Manchester."	1397
Warrington Agent ..	"Quay, Warrington."	17
Runcorn Agent	"Docks, Runcorn."	43
Liverpool Agent	{ "Navigation, Liverpool." { "18, Chapel Street, Liverpool."	1043 7592

H. M. Customs (Custom House, Trafford Road, Salford) :

Collector, Registrar of Shipping, and Receiver of Wrecks : W. H. Bignold.

Board of Trade and Mercantile Marine :

(Offices, Custom House).

Superintendent : J. C. Hill.

Lloyds' Agents :

George Simpson & Co., Guildhall Chambers, Lloyd Street, Manchester.

o

(64)—MANCHESTER SHIP CANAL COMPANY—*continued.*

Lloyds' Registry :

Surveyors : F. W. Pitt and G. C. Vaux, 162, Trafford Road, Salford.

Port Sanitary Authority :

Medical Officer : A. M. N. Pringle, M.B., D.P.H. (Camb.), 29, Howard Street, Salford.

Clerk : Arthur Holmes, 40, Brazennose Street, Manchester, and Bexley Square, Salford.

Nautical Assessors :

Captain George Smith, Captain Turner, and Captain Woodhill.

Manchester Ship Canal (No. 64a).

(*c*) *Distance Table.*

	Miles.	Fur.
Manchester, Woden Street Footbridge, Head of Ship Canal, and junction with River Irwell Upper Reach (No. 64d4), to—		
Cornbrook Wharf	–	2
Manchester Docks Nos. 1, 2, 3, 4, and 5	–	4
Trafford Road Swing Bridge	1	0
Railway Swing Bridge	1	1
Trafford Wharf, and Manchester Docks Nos. 6, 7, and 8	1	2
Dry Dock Company's Dock and Pontoon	2	0
Mode Wheel Locks, and Manchester Corporation Storm Overflow Sewer	2	1
Cattle Wharves	2	2
Salford Sewage Works and Wharf	2	4
Trafford Hall Wharf	2	5
Eccles Stage, Salters Lane	3	3
Barton Swing Aqueduct and Barton Swing Bridge	4	2
Eccles Wharf	4	4
Bromyhurst Wharf	5	0
Stickens Wharf	5	3
Barton Locks and Manchester Corporation Main Outfall Sewer	5	5
Hulmes Bridge Ferry	6	3
Irlam Ferry and Flixton Wharf	7	4
Irlam Locks	7	6
Co-operative Wholesale Society's Wharf and Soapworks	7	7
Deviation Railway No. 5, and Mersey Weir	8	0
Manchester and Salford Corporation Wharf	8	1
Manchester Corporation Carrington Wharf	8	2
Peaksnook Wharf	8	6
Partington Coal Basin and Hoists	8	7
Deviation Railway No. 4	9	1
Cadishead Wharf	9	3
Millbank Wharf	10	0
Glazebrook Outfall	10	1

(64)—MANCHESTER SHIP CANAL COMPANY—*continued.*

	Miles.	Fur.
Manchester, Woden Street Footbridge, Head of Ship Canal, and junction with River Irwell Upper Reach (No. 64d4), to (*continued*)—		
Hollin's Ferry	10	4
Warburton High Level Bridge	10	7
Warburton Wharf	11	0
Rixton New Hall	11	3
Rixton Junction, junction with Mersey and Irwell Navigation, Rixton Junction to Bank Quay, Warrington (No. 64d1) ..	12	1
Statham Wharf	13	1
Footbridge at Wilgrave	14	0
Thelwall Ferry	14	2
Latchford Locks	15	1
Deviation Railway No. 3	15	3
Knutsford Road Swing Bridge	15	5
Latchford High Level Bridge	16	0
Twenty Steps Swing Bridge, and junction with Runcorn and Latchford Canal (No. 64d3)	16	5
Junction with Walton Lock Branch of Mersey and Irwell Navigation (No. 64d2).. ..	17	1
Stag Inn Swing Bridge	17	2
Walton Wharf	17	3
Acton Grange Viaduct, Deviation Railways Nos. 1 and 2	18	2
Haydock Colliery Company's Wharf	18	4
Moore Lane Swing Bridge	19	0
Moss Lane Wharf	19	4
Pumping Station	19	7
Randall's Sluices and Vyrnwy Syphon ..	20	6
Stonedelph Dock and Turning Basin.. ..	21	0
Point Turnbridge Ferry	22	0
Wigg's Wharves and Lay-bye	22	5
Runcorn Swing Bridge and Tidal Opening..	22	6
Junction with tidal River Mersey (No. 68), through Runcorn (Old Quay) Lock ..	23	1
Runcorn High Level Bridge	23	4
Junction with Bridgewater Canal (No. 64b1)..	23	7
Entrance to Runcorn Docks	24	1
Junction with tidal River Mersey (No. 68) through Bridgewater Lock	24	2
Bridgewater Wharf and Lay-bye	24	5
Bridgewater Coal Tip	24	6
Entrance to Weston Point Docks and Main Line of Navigation of River Weaver (No. 118a)	25	1
Junction with tidal River Mersey (No. 68) through Weston Mersey Lock	25	2
Weaver Sluices	26	0
Weston Marsh, River Weaver Tidal Openings, and junctions with River Weaver Old Line of Navigation (No. 118c), and River Weaver—Main Line of Navigation— (No. 118a), through Weston Marsh Side Lock	26	1

(64)—MANCHESTER SHIP CANAL COMPANY—*continued.*

	Miles.	Fur.
Manchester, Woden Street Footbridge, Head of Ship Canal, and junction with River Irwell Upper Reach (No. 64d4), to (*continued*)—		
Saltport Jetties and Frodsham Ferry ..	26	5
Powder Magazines and Holpool Gutter ..	28	3
Ince Wharf	29	3
Ince Ferry	29	7
Ince Hall	30	2
River Gowy and Syphons	31	2
Stanlow Point	31	3
Stanlow Ferry	31	4
Bass and Smith's Wharf	31	7
Coal Tip and Wharf	32	0
Dry Dock Company's Pontoon	32	3
Stuart's Wharf	32	4
Tidal Opening	32	5
Slipway to Ellesmere Port Docks	32	6
Junction with Shropshire Union Canal (No.92c1), and Ellesmere Port Docks	32	6
Shropshire Union Wharf	33	0
Pool Hall Wharf	33	5
Pool Hall	33	6
Mount Manisty	34	1
Hooton Wharf	34	6
Bankfield Wharf	35	3
Eastham Locks and junction with tidal River Mersey (No. 68)	36	0

(d) Locks.

1.—Mode Wheel (two locks side by side).
2.—Barton   do.
3.—Irlam   do.
4.—Latchford.   do.
5.—Eastham   (three locks side by side).
       Fall from Manchester.

Side locks giving access from Ship Canal to the tidal River Mersey :

     Runcorn, Old Quay.
     Runcorn, Bridgewater Lock.
     Weston Mersey.

Fall from Ship Canal to tidal River Mersey at low water, level with tidal River Mersey at high water.

(e) Maximum size of vessels that can use the navigation.

	Ft.	In.
The dimensions of the locks on the Ship Canal are as follows :—		
Mode Wheel, Barton, Irlam, and Latchford, large locks .. .. .. Length	600	0
These locks are further divided by an intermediate pair of gates so as two locks of 150ft. and 450ft. in length, respectively, can be made.		
Width	65	0

(64)—Manchester Ship Canal Company—*continued.*

	Ft.	In.
Mode Wheel, Barton, Irlam, and Latchford, small locks .. .. .. Length	350	0

These locks are further divided by an intermediate pair of gates so as two locks of 120ft. and 230ft. in length, respectively, can be made.

| Width .. .. | 45 | 0 |

Eastham Large Lock.

| Length .. .. | 600 | 0 |
| Width .. .. | 80 | 0 |

Eastham Medium Lock.

| Length .. .. | 350 | 0 |
| Width .. .. | 50 | 0 |

Eastham Small Lock.

| Length .. .. | 150 | 0 |
| Width .. .. | 30 | 0 |

The total fall from the level of the water in Manchester Docks to the level of the tide rising 14ft. 2in. above Old Dock sill, Liverpool, which is the ordinary water level in the canal between Eastham and Latchford, is 60ft. 6in. The falls at the various locks being as follows :—

Mode Wheel	13	0
Barton	15	0
Irlam	16	0
Latchford	16	6

Side locks giving access from Ship Canal to the tidal River Mersey :

Runcorn Old Quay.

	Ft.	In.
Length	250	0
Width	45	0

Runcorn, Bridgewater Lock.

| Length .. .. | 400 | 0 |
| Width .. .. | 45 | 0 |

Weston Mersey.

| Length .. .. | 600 | 0 |
| Width .. .. | 45 | 0 |

The bottom width of the canal at the full depth is 120ft. with the following exceptions :—(*a*) At the curve at the River Weaver outfall the width at the full depth is 180ft. ; at the bend at Runcorn, approaching the Runcorn railway bridge, the width is 150ft. (*b*) For a distance of about one mile between Latchford Locks and Partington Coal Basin the bottom width is at present only 80ft. to 90ft., and large vessels are not allowed to pass each other on that portion of the canal. (*c*) From Barton Aqueduct to the Manchester Docks the bottom width is 170ft.

(64)—Manchester Ship Canal Company—*continued.*

The minimum available draught of water between the entrance of the canal at Eastham and the docks at Manchester is 26ft., but in the tidal portion of the canal between Eastham and Latchford the available depth varies from 26ft. to 33ft., according to the state of the tide. The level of the water in this section of the canal is maintained at not less than 14ft. 2in. above Old Dock sill, Liverpool (or 9ft. 6in. above Ordnance Datum, *i.e.*, mean sea level), which gives a depth of 26ft. of water in this portion of the canal.

The height from the normal water level in the canal to the under side of the girders of the seven fixed bridges over the canal leaves a clear headroom of 75ft. ; as, however, the headroom is necessarily a few feet less when high tides or floods occur, masts should clear the bridges at 70ft. above the water level.

The depth of water on the upper sills of all the locks is 28ft., which will enable the depth of water in the canal to be eventually increased to 28ft. if found requisite.

(g) Towing-path.

There is a towing-path only from Dock No. 5, Manchester, to Woden Street footbridge, the head of the canal.

(h) Tidal Information.

When the tide in the River Mersey rises to a level of 14ft. 2in. above the Old Dock sill, Liverpool, which takes place on about nine or ten days in a fortnight, it enters the Ship Canal at Eastham and affects the level of the water in the bottom pound of the canal to the tail of Latchford Locks.

High water at Eastham 10min. after Liverpool, or 2hrs. 25min. before London Bridge.

Spring tides rise	..	..	..	27ft. 6in.
Neap ,, ,,	..	..	..	20ft. 3in.

High water at Runcorn (inside Ship Canal, not in River Mersey) one hour after Liverpool.

High water at the tail of Latchford Locks about 1hr. 15min. after Liverpool.

Ordinary Spring tides rise	..	..	4ft. 8in.
High Spring tides rise	..	..	6ft. 10in.

Tidal levels above level of Old Dock sill, Liverpool :

	Ft.	In.
High water at Equinoctial Spring tides ..	21	0
Average high water at ordinary Spring tides ..	18	10
Ordinary water level of Ship Canal between Eastham and Latchford	14	2
Average high water at ordinary Neap tides ..	11	7
Lowest high water at Neap tides	8	7
Mean tide level	4	9

(64)—Manchester Ship Canal Company—*continued.*

Tidal levels below Old Dock sill, Liverpool :

	Ft.	In.
Average low water of ordinary Neap tides ..	1	5
Average low water of ordinary Spring tides..	8	8
Lowest low water of Equinoctial Spring tides	10	4
Liverpool new dock sills, bottom of Ship Canal, and present depth of approach channel at Eastham	12	0
	12	0
Ultimate depth of approach channel at Eastham to be	20	0
Eastham Lock sills	23	0

(*i*) *Types of vessels using the navigation.*

The largest vessel which has navigated to Manchester is the "Moyune," length 410ft., breadth 48ft., gross tonnage 4,640, net tonnage 3,000.

Bridgewater Canal.

(*c*) *Distance Table.*

Main Line (No. 64b1).

	Miles.	Fur.
Manchester, Castle Field, junction with Rochdale Canal—Main Line—(No. 87a), to—		
Manchester, Egerton Street Bridge, and junction with Hulme Locks Branch (No. 64b2)	–	2
Manchester Corporation Stone Wharf ..	–	4
Hulme Hall Boat Dock	–	5
Bennett's or Harrop's Timber Yards, and Cornbrook Bridge and Wharf	–	6
Manchester Docks, Cornbrook..	1	0
Bridgewater Trustees' Coal Wharf	1	2
Throstle Nest Bridge	1	3
Trafford Park Bridge	1	4
Stretford—Waters Meeting, junction with Stretford and Leigh Branch (No. 64b3) ..	2	6
Stretford Gas Works	3	0
Stretford Stone Wharf and Longford Bridge ..	3	2
Stretford Wharf, Edge Lane Bridge, and Rathbone's Boat Yard	3	6
Inman's Works	3	7
Stretford Watch House	4	0
River Mersey Aqueduct (Barfoot)	4	3
Dane Road Manure Wharf and Dr. White's Bridge	4	6
Sale Warehouse and Wharf	5	1
Bridgewater Trust Coal Wharf and Sale Moor Bridge	5	2
Roebuck Lane Wharf	5	5
Marsland's Bridge	5	7
Timperley Bridge	6	7
Railway Bridge (Stockport Line)	7	1
Railway Bridge (L. & N. W. Rly.)	7	3

(64)—MANCHESTER SHIP CANAL COMPANY—*continued.*

	Miles.	Fur.
Manchester, Castle Field, junction with Rochdale Canal—Main Line—(No. 87a), to (*continued*)—		
Broadheath Stone Wharves	7	4
Broadheath Warehouse, Bridge, and Bridgewater Trust Coal Wharf	7	5
Seamon's Moss Bridge	8	4
Brickfield Basin	8	5
Dunham School Bridge	9	3
Dunham Town Bridge	9	6
Dunham Underbridge (Woodhouse Lane Aqueduct)	10	1
River Bollin Aqueduct	10	2
Bollington Warehouse and Wharf	10	5
Agden Bridge and Wharf	11	3
Burford Lane Warehouse and Wharf ..	12	1
Burford Lane Underbridge	12	2
Grantham's Bridge	12	3
Oughtrington Bridge	12	6
Lymm Stables	13	0
Lymm Gas Works	13	2
Lymm Warehouse	13	4
Lymm Bridge	13	5
Whitborough Aqueduct	13	6
Iron Road Bridge	13	7
Barsbank Aqueduct	14	2
Ditchfield Bridge and Wharf	14	5
Massey Brook Canal Arm	15	0
Thelwall Under Bridge	15	4
Pickering's Bridge	15	6
Cliff Lane Wharf and Under Bridge	16	2
Grappenhall Bridge	16	5
Stanny Lunt Bridge	17	0
Lumb Brook Under Bridge	18	0
Stockton Quay, Warehouse, Wharf, and Bridge	18	4
Red Lane Bridge	18	7
Hough's Bridge, Walton	19	3
Walton Lea Bridge	19	5
Walton Wharf	19	6
Walton Bridge	19	7
Chester Road Under Bridge and Wharf ..	20	1
Thomason's Bridge	20	2
Acton Grange Bridge	20	4
Moore Bridge	21	0
Moorefield Bridge	21	4
Keckwick Bridge	21	6
Keckwick Hill Bridge	22	2
George Cleave's Bridge	22	3
Red Brow Under Bridge	23	0
Preston Brook, Waters Meeting, junction with Preston Brook Branch (No. 64b4) ..	23	3
Norton Warehouse, Canal Arm, and Railway Aqueduct	23	4
Cawley's Bridge	23	6

(64)—MANCHESTER SHIP CANAL COMPANY—*continued.*

	Miles.	Fur.
Manchester, Castle Field, junction with Rochdale Canal—Main Line—(No. 87a), to (*continued*)—		
Borrow's Bridge	23	7
Railway Bridge	24	0
Norton Town Bridge	24	2
Norton Bridge	24	5
Norton Townfield Bridge	25	0
Green Bridge	25	4
Astmoor Bridge	26	1
Astmoor Tannery	26	2
Bates' Bridge	26	8
Highfield Tanning Company, Astmoor Wharf and Basin, and Royal Oak Tannery	26	7
Gas Works, Halton Road	26	7
Earp's Tannery and Halton Road Wharf	27	1
Runcorn Delph Bridge and Bridgewater Foundry	27	4
Runcorn Dock Yard (The Sprinch)	27	5
Runcorn Soap and Alkali Company's Works, and Camden Soap Works	27	6
Runcorn Bridge and Top Locks Warehouse	28	0
Runcorn, Top of Locks, Waterloo Bridge, and Railway Arches	28	1
Runcorn, junction with Manchester Ship Canal (No. 64a)	28	4

In calculating distances for all purposes of rates and tolls, the distance between the top lock and the bottom lock at Runcorn, or any part thereof, is to be taken as equal to a distance of five miles.

Hulme Locks Branch (No. 64b2).

	Miles.	Fur.
Length from junction with Main Line (No.64b1) to junction with River Irwell Upper Reach (No. 64d4)	–	1

Stretford and Leigh Branch (No. 64b3).

	Miles.	Fur.
Stretford, Waters Meeting, junction with Main Line (No. 64b1), to—		
Taylor's Bridge	–	1
Stretford Moss Turn Bridge	–	6
Barton Swing Aqueduct over Manchester Ship Canal	2	2
Patricroft Basin and Warehouse	2	5
Patricroft Bridge	2	6
Patricroft Railway Bridge	3	1
Monton Green Bridge	3	5
Worsley Coke Ovens	4	2
Worsley Warehouse and Wharf	4	4
Worsley Bridge	4	6
Keeper's Turn	5	6

(64)—MANCHESTER SHIP CANAL COMPANY—*continued.*

	Miles.	Fur.
Stretford, Waters Meeting, junction with Main Line (No. 64b1), to (*continued*)—		
Bridgewater Trust Colliery Tips and Boothstown Bridge	6	4
Vicar's Hall Bridge	7	0
Whitehead Hall Bridge	7	4
Astley Bridge	7	6
Lingard's Bridge	8	0
Morley's Bridge	8	4
Marsland Green Bridge	8	7
Great Fold Bridge	9	1
Hall House Bridge	9	3
Butts' Basin and Wharf	9	6
Butts' Bridge	9	7
Dick Mather's Bridge	10	2
Railway Bridge	10	4
Leigh Warehouse, Toll Office, and junction with Leigh Branch of Leeds and Liverpool Canal (No. 58d)	10	6

Preston Brook Branch (No. 64b4).

Preston Brook, Waters Meeting, junction with Main Line (No. 64b1), to—		
Preston Brook Warehouse	–	1
Preston Brook Bridge	–	2
Cotton's Bridge	–	4
Preston Brook, junction with Trent and Mersey Canal—Main Line—(No. 76a)	–	6

(d) *Locks.*

Main Line (No. 64b1).

1
to } Runcorn.
11.

The old line of locks forming a junction with the Manchester Ship Canal.

Fall to Ship Canal.

1
to } Runcorn.
10.

The new line of locks, alternative and parallel to the old line of locks, forming a junction with the Runcorn and Weston Canal, the tidal dock of Runcorn Docks, and through tidal dock to Manchester Ship Canal.

Fall to Ship Canal.

Hulme Locks Branch (No. 64b2).

1
to } Hulme.
3.

Fall from Main Line.

(64)—Manchester Ship Canal Company—*continued.*

(e) *Maximum size of vessels that can use the navigation.*

Main Line (No. 64b1) and Preston Brook Branch (No. 64b4).

	Ft.	In.
Length	71	11
Width	15	0
Draught from Castle Field, Manchester, to		
Cornbrook Bridge	5	0
,, from Cornbrook Bridge to Preston		
Brook, Waters Meeting, and		
Preston Brook Branch	4	4
,, from Preston Brook, Waters Meeting,		
to Runcorn Chemical Works ..	4	6
,, from Runcorn Chemical Works to		
Manchester Ship Canal	5	3
Headroom	10	6

Hulme Locks Branch (No. 64b2).

	Ft.	In.
Length	75	2
Width	14	9
Draught	5	0
Headroom	10	6

Stretford and Leigh Branch (No. 64b3).

Length.—Not limited.
Width.—Not limited.

	Ft.	In.
Draught	4	4
Headroom	10	0

(g) *Towing-path.*

There is a towing-path throughout the navigation and branches.

(i) *Types of vessels using the navigation.*

Mersey flats and Bridgewater Canal lighters. There are also small open coal boats without cabins, which mostly work between Worsley, on the Stretford and Leigh Branch, and Manchester.

Runcorn and Weston Canal (No. 64c).

(c) *Distance Table.*

	Miles.	Fur.
Runcorn, junction with new line of locks of Bridgewater Canal (No. 64b1) and entrance to Runcorn Docks, to—		
Parr's Lock, between Francis Dock and Arnold Dock	–	$2\frac{1}{2}$
Railway Lock, termination of Runcorn Docks	–	6
Weston Point, junction with River Weaver— Main Line of Navigation—(No. 118a) ..	1	$2\frac{1}{2}$

(d) *Locks.*

1.—Parr's.
2.—Railway.

Fall from new line of locks Runcorn, Bridgewater Canal.

(64)—MANCHESTER SHIP CANAL COMPANY—*continued*.

(e) *Maximum size of vessels that can use the navigation.*

						Ft.	In.
Length	..	..	..	..	..	73	0
Width	..	..	..	..	..	18	5
Draught ..	..	..	..	..	..	8	0
Headroom	..	..	..	..	..	18	0

(g) *Towing-path.*

There is a towing-path from Railway Lock to Weston Point.

(i) *Types of vessels using the navigation.*

Mersey flats.

Mersey and Irwell Navigation.

(c) *Distance Table.*

Main Line, Rixton Junction to Bank Quay, Warrington (No. 64d1).

	Miles.	Fur.
Rixton Junction, junction with Manchester Ship Canal (No. 64a), to—		
Commencement of Butchersfield Canal ..	–	$2\frac{1}{2}$
Termination of Butchersfield Canal	–	4
Statham Lane River Bridge	1	2
Woolston Lock and Bridge, commencement of Woolston Canal	2	0
Paddington Soap Works	3	0
Paddington Lock, termination of Woolston Canal	3	5
Junction with Runcorn and Latchford Canal (No. 64d3)	4	2
Warrington, Howley Quay and Warehouse ..	4	5
Warrington Lock and Weir	5	0
Warrington, Mersey Mills	5	1
L. & N. W. Railway Bridge, Arpley	5	5
Junction with Walton Lock Branch to Manchester Ship Canal (No. 64d2), and Warrington Timber Float	6	4
Deviation Railway Bridge	6	6
Warrington, Bank Quay, junction with River Mersey under jurisdiction of Upper Mersey Navigation Commissioners (No. 68) ..	7	6

Walton Lock Branch (No. 64d2).

	Miles.	Fur.
Junction with Mersey and Irwell Navigation— Main Line—(No. 64d1), to—		
Walton Lock	–	$2\frac{1}{2}$
Junction with Warrington Timber Float (a timber pond seven furlongs in length) ..	–	3
Junction with Manchester Ship Canal (No. 64a)	–	$3\frac{1}{2}$

(64)—MANCHESTER SHIP CANAL COMPANY—*continued.*

Runcorn and Latchford Canal (No. 64d3).

	Miles.	Fur.
Junction with Mersey and Irwell Navigation—Main Line—(No. 64d1) and head of Manor Lock, to—		
Black Bear Wharf and Latchford Road Bridge	–	4
Deviation Railway Bridge	–	6
Wilderspool Turnbridge	–	7
Twenty Steps Swing Bridge and Lock	1	1
Junction with Manchester Ship Canal (No. 64a)	1	2

River Irwell Upper Reach (No. 64d4).

	Miles.	Fur.
Manchester, Woden Street Footbridge, and junction with Manchester Ship Canal (No. 64a), to—		
Junction with Hulme Locks Branch of Bridgewater Canal (No. 64b2)	–	1
Regent Road Bridge	–	2
Prince's Bridge, and junction with Manchester, Bolton, and Bury Canal (No. 55a)	–	4
Junction with Manchester and Salford Junction Canal (No. 64e)	–	5
Manchester Ship Canal Company's Bridgewater Warehouses, Water Street, and Irwell Street Bridge	–	6
Albert Bridge	–	7
Bonded Warehouse	1	0
Blackfriars Bridge	1	1
Victoria Bridge and Station Approach	1	2
Hunt's Bank	1	3

(d) Locks.

Main Line, Rixton Junction to Bank Quay, Warrington (No. 64d1).

1.—Woolston.
2.—Paddington, or Dobbie's.
3.—Warrington.

Fall to tidal River Mersey at Warrington.

Walton Lock Branch (No. 64d2).

1.—Walton.

Walton Lock has two pairs of gates, as the fall may be in either direction, according to the tide.

Runcorn and Latchford Canal (No. 64d3).

1.—Manor.
2.—Twenty Steps.

Fall to Manchester Ship Canal.

Manor Lock has a pair of flood gates at its upper end to keep out the Mersey floods. Before the Manchester Ship Canal was constructed the name of this lock was Latchford Lock.

(64)—MANCHESTER SHIP CANAL COMPANY—*continued.*

(*e*) *Maximum size of vessels that can use the navigation.*

Main Line, Rixton Junction to Bank Quay, Warrington (No. 64d1).

	Ft.	In.
Length from Rixton Junction to Warrington Lock	72	8
,, through Warrington Lock {	69	7
,, from Warrington Lock to Bank Quay, Warrington—not limited.		
Width from Rixton Junction to Warrington Lock	16	4
,, through Warrington Lock	17	9
,, from Warrington Lock to Bank Quay, Warrington—not limited.		
Draught	5	6
Headroom from Rixton Junction to Warrington Lock	11	6
,, from Warrington Lock to Bank Quay, Warrington, at High Water	8	0

Walton Lock Branch (No. 64d2).

	Ft.	In.
Length } dimensions of Walton Lock { ..	150	0
Width } ..	30	0
Draught	6	0
Headroom at High Water	14	0

Runcorn and Latchford Canal (No. 64d3).

	Ft.	In.
Length	72	3
Width	18	4
Draught	5	6
Headroom	10	6

River Irwell Upper Reach (No. 64d4).

	Ft.	In.
Length.—Not limited.		
Width	25	0
Draught from Woden Street Footbridge to Water Street Warehouse ..	5	6
,, from Water Street Warehouse to Bonded Warehouse	4	6
,, from Bonded Warehouse to Hunt's Bank	3	6
Headroom	15	0

When the River Irwell is in flood the above draughts may be increased by any amount up to an additional five feet.

(*g*) *Towing-path.*

Main Line, Rixton Junction to Bank Quay, Warrington (No. 64d1).

There is a towing-path throughout the navigation, with the exception of a distance of about 100 yards to the East of Warrington Bridge, for which length towing-horses are taken through the street.

(64)—MANCHESTER SHIP CANAL COMPANY—*continued.*

Walton Lock Branch (No. 64d2).

There is no towing-path.

Runcorn and Latchford Canal (No. 64d3).

There is a towing-path throughout the navigation.

River Irwell Upper Reach (No. 64d4).

There is a towing-path from Woden Street Footbridge to Albert Bridge only.

(h) *Tidal Information.*

Main Line, Rixton Junction to Bank Quay, Warrington (No. 64d1).

High Spring tides will flow to Woolston Weir on the Weir Stream of the river just below Woolston Lock.

High water at Bank Quay, Warrington, on Spring tides, about 1hr. 15min. after Liverpool.

Spring tides rise .. .. 8ft. to 9ft.

High water at Warrington Lock on Spring tides about 1hr. 20min. after Liverpool.

Walton Lock Branch (No. 64d2).

Spring tides flow from the River Mersey to the West end of Walton Lock.

High water at Walton Lock about 1hr. 20min. after Liverpool.

Spring tides rise .. .. 8ft. to 9ft.

(i) *Types of vessels using the navigation.*

Mersey Flats.

Manchester and Salford Junction Canal (No. 64e).

(c) *Distance Table.*

	Miles.	Fur.
Junction with River Irwell Upper Reach (No. 64d4) to—		
Head of Lock No. 2	–	0½
Commencement of Tunnel	–	1
Lifts from tunnel communicating with Great Northern Railway Company's Goods .. Station, Deansgate, and termination of canal	–	3

(d) *Locks.*

1.—Manchester.
2.—Manchester.

Rise from junction with River Irwell Upper Reach.

(64)—MANCHESTER SHIP CANAL COMPANY—*continued.*

(e) *Maximum size of vessels that can use the navigation.*

						Ft.	In.
Length	..	..	..	..	..	71	11
Width	..	..	..	..	..	14	4
Draught	..	..	..	..	..	4	0
Headroom	..	..	..	..	..	10	0

(f) *Tunnels.*

The last two furlongs of the canal are in tunnel, extending under portion of Charles Street, Camp Street, and Alport Town.

(g) *Towing-path.*

There is a towing-path from the junction with the River Irwell Upper Reach to the head of Lock No. 2.   There is a footpath only along the side of the portion of the canal in tunnel.

(i) *Types of vessels using the navigation.*

Mersey flats.

------

(65)—EARL MANVERS' CANAL.

(a) *Short Description.*

The canal commences by a junction with the Poplar Arm of the Nottingham Canal (No. 41b2), in the city of Nottingham, and proceeds in an easterly direction for a distance of about half a furlong to Manvers Street, Nottingham.   There are no locks on the canal, and the maximum dimensions of vessels that can use the navigation are identical with those relating to the Poplar Arm of the Nottingham Canal, namely, length 75ft., width 14ft., draught (maximum) 3ft. 6in.

A portion of the canal at the Manvers Street end has lately been closed, and absorbed by the new line of the Great Central and Great Northern Railways.

MARKET HARBOROUGH BRANCH CANAL—*see* Grand Junction Canal, Leicester Section.

------

(66)—MARKET WEIGHTON DRAINAGE AND NAVIGATION.

(a) *Short Description.*

The portion of the Market Weighton Drainage which is navigable at the present time commences at the tail of the Old Lock at Sod House, about two-and-a-half miles to the north of the village of Newport, and proceeds in a southerly direction through the village of Newport and Walling Fen to a junction with the River Humber at Weighton (or Humber) Lock, all in the East Riding of the county of Yorkshire.

(66)—MARKET WEIGHTON DRAINAGE AND NAVIGATION—*continued.*

The drainage was formerly navigable throughout from the Humber to Weighton River Head, a total distance of a little over nine miles, but the portion between Sod House Lock and Weighton River Head was closed for navigation by Act of Parliament of 1900.

The traffic on the navigation is almost entirely from the Brick and Tile Works in Walling Fen.

(b) Proprietors, Officers, and Offices.

Market Weighton Drainage and Navigation Trustees.

Clerk : S. Powell.

Office : Market Weighton.

The North Eastern Railway Company are the proprietors of any profits which may be derived from the Navigation Tolls—*see* North Eastern Railway.

(c) Distance Table.

	Miles.	Fur.
Tail of Old Sod House Lock, and head of the navigation, to—		
Sandholme Landing	2	0
Newport Bridge	2	6
Weighton (or Humber) Lock, junction with River Humber (No. 49)	6	0

(d) Locks.

1.—Weighton, or Humber.

Weighton Lock has two pairs of sea gates and two pairs of navigation gates.

(e) Maximum size of vessels that can use the navigation.

	Ft.	In.
Length	66	0
Width	14	10
Draught	5	6 to 6ft.

(g) Towing-path.

There is a towing-path throughout the navigation.

(i) Types of vessels using the navigation.

Yorkshire Keels.

MARTHAM BROAD—*see* River Bure, River Thurne.

MAUD FOSTER DRAIN—*see* Witham Drainage General Commissioners.

P

McMURRAYS LTD. ROYAL PAPER MILLS, WANDSWORTH—*see* Wandsworth Cut.

MEADOW DIKE—*see* River Bure, River Thurne.

MEDLAM DRAIN—*see* Witham Drainage General Commissioners.

---

(67)—RIVER MEDWAY.

(a) *Short Description.*

The river commences to be navigable at the town of Tonbridge, and proceeds by Yalding, Wateringbury, Teston, East Farleigh, Maidstone, Allington, Aylesford, Ditton, New Hythe, Snodland, Halling, Wouldham, Cuxton, Rochester, Strood, Chatham, Brompton, Gillingham, and Port Victoria to Sheerness, all in the county of Kent, where it forms a junction with the Estuary of the River Thames. The course of the river from Tonbridge to Maidstone is through some of the best agricultural districts in Kent. Between Maidstone and Rochester there are numerous cement works on the banks of the river. Below Gillingham the river gradually becomes considerably wider to Sheerness.

(b) *Proprietors, Officers, and Offices.*

From Tonbridge to Messrs. Edmunds' Wharf, Maidstone, opposite All Saints' Church, and from above Tonbridge up to Forest Row in Sussex, which is not navigable, the river is under the jurisdiction of the Medway Upper Navigation Company.

Secretary : Walter J. Hodge.

Engineer : H. F. Stephens.

Office : Tonbridge. Telegrams : " Medway, Tonbridge."

Telephone No. 202.

The Company act as carriers, and carry nearly the whole of the traffic on the Upper Navigation between Tonbridge and Maidstone.

Wharves and Warehouses, London : West Kent Wharf, London Bridge, S.E. ; and at Tonbridge, Branbridge's and Yalding.

Agent, London : W. A. Fisher, Lighterman, Water Lane, E.C.

Agents, Rochester : Watson and Gill, Shipbrokers.

From Messrs. Edmunds' Wharf, Maidstone, to Hawkwood the river is under the jurisdiction of the Medway Lower Navigation Company.

Clerk : Richard T. Tatham (Messrs. Hoar, Howlett, and Tatham, Solicitors, 9, King Street, Maidstone).
The navigation between Hawkwood and New Hythe is toll free.

(67)—RIVER MEDWAY—*continued.*

From Hawkwood to Sheerness the navigation is under the jurisdiction of the Medway Conservancy.

Clerk : Frederick F. Smith.

Office : 42, High Street, Rochester.

Harbour Master : Captain Godfrey T. Richards.

Office : Rochester.

(c) *Distance Table.*

	Miles.	Fur.
Tonbridge Wharf and Bridge to—		
Tonbridge Town Lock and Gas Works..	–	2
Hartlake Wharf ..	3	0
East Lock	3	6
Foord Green Bridge	4	2
Norwood Bridge	5	0
Arnold's Mill Head	6	0
Branbridge's Wharf and Arnold's Mills	6	4
Railway Bridge and Stoneham Lock ..	7	0
Hutson's Yard ..	7	2
Mouse Bay	7	4
Yalding Wharf ..	8	0
Hampstead Lock	8	4
Wateringbury, Hutson's Wharf	10	0
Wateringbury, Liney's Wharf..	10	2
Teston Lock	11	2
Teston Bridge ..	11	4
Barming Bridge..	12	6
Lewis's Wharf and Farleigh Wate Works ..	13	2
Ellis's Wharf	13	4
Point Shoot	14	2
Tovil Paper Mills and Benstead's and Constable's Wharves	15	0
Maidstone, Messrs. Edmunds' Wharf, boundary of Medway Upper and Lower Navigations	16	0
Medway Mill	16	6
Allington Lock ..	18	0
Forstal	18	6
Preston ..	19	0
Aylesford	19	2
Mill Hall ..	20	0
New Hythe	21	0
Hawkwood, boundary of Medway Lower Navigation and Medway Conservancy ..	22	0
Snodland	23	0
Halling ..	24	2
Wouldham	25	0
Cuxton ..	26	6
Rochester Bridge	29	2
Strood ..	29	2
Chatham ..	30	4
Brompton and Gillingham	34	0
Port Victoria	41	0
Mouth of the Swale and Queenborough Pier ..	42	2
Sheerness, junction with estuary of River Thames (No. 107a)	43	0

(67)—RIVER MEDWAY—*continued*.

(d) *Locks.*

Medway Upper Navigation.
1.—Tonbridge Town.
2.—Child's.
3.—Eldridge's.
4.—Porters.
5.—East.
6.—Oak Weir.
7.—New Lock.
8.—Sluice Weir.
9.—Branbridge's.
10.—Stoneham.
11.—Hampstead.
12.—Teston.
13.—Farleigh.
Medway Lower Navigation.
14.—Allington.

This lock is divided into two sections by an intermediate pair of gates.

Fall from Tonbridge.

(e) *Maximum size of vessels that can use the navigation.*

	Ft.	In.
Length from Sheerness to the tail of Allington Lock—not limited.		
„ from the tail of Allington Lock to the tail of Farleigh Lock	160	0
„ from the tail of Farleigh Lock to Tonbridge	65	0
Width from Sheerness to the tail of Allington Lock—not limited.		
„ from the tail of Allington Lock to the tail of Farleigh Lock	20	0
„ from the tail of Farleigh Lock to Tonbridge	15	6
Draught—Vessels drawing 24ft. can navigate from Sheerness to just below Rochester Bridge, where they can be berthed to lie afloat at low water of Spring tides.		
„ from Rochester Bridge to Maidstone	7	0
„ from Maidstone to Yalding	4	6
„ from Yalding to Tonbridge	4	3
Headroom from Sheerness to Rochester Bridge—not limited.		
„ from Rochester Bridge to Maidstone at high water, about	12	0
„ from Maidstone to Tonbridge	6	0

(g) *Towing-path.*

There is a horse towing-path from Tonbridge to New Hythe, and a bow hauling path for men from New Hythe to Hawkwood.

(67)—RIVER MEDWAY—*continued.*

(h) Tidal Information.

The tide usually flows to Allington Lock. High Spring tides sometimes flow beyond.

High water at Sheerness 1hr. 21min. before London Bridge.
Spring tides rise	.. ..	16ft.
Neap ,, ,,	.. ..	13ft. 3in.

High water at Chatham 1hr. 15min. before London Bridge.
Spring tides rise	.. ..	18ft. 3in.
Neap ,, ,,	.. ..	14ft. 6in.

High water at Allington Lock 30min. before London Bridge.
Spring tides rise	.. ..	13ft. 6in.
Neap ,, ,,	.. ..	10ft. 6in.

The flood tide flows here for about 3hrs.

(i) Types of vessels using the navigation.

Sea-going vessels navigate from Sheerness to just below Rochester Bridge. Medway sailing barges and small vessels with lowering masts navigate to Maidstone, and the smallest size of Medway sailing barges carrying about 60 tons, navigate to Tonbridge,

---

(68)—RIVER MERSEY.

(a) Short Description.

The portion of the River Mersey dealt with in this section is that part which lies between Bank Quay, Warrington, and Liverpool, and does not include the portion of the river comprised in the Mersey and Irwell Navigation of the Manchester Ship Canal, for which see Manchester Ship Canal Company.

The whole course of the navigation forms the boundary between the counties of Lancashire and Cheshire.

There is a regular trade from Liverpool to Eastham, Runcorn, and Widnes on all tides, but the navigation between Runcorn and Widnes to Warrington is only used on Spring tides. Vessels bound from Liverpool to Warrington on Neap tides enter the Ship Canal at Eastham, and rejoin the River Mersey at Warrington by means of the Walton Lock Branch.

The navigation channel of the river between Bank Quay, Warrington, and Dingle Point is through shifting sand-banks.

(b) Proprietors, Officers, and Offices.

From Bank Quay, Warrington, to an imaginary line drawn across the river from Eastham to Garston the river is under the jurisdiction of the Upper Mersey Navigation Commissioners.

Clerk : John Meadowcroft.

Office : Runcorn.

(68)—River Mersey—*continued.*

Below an imaginary line drawn across the river from Eastham to Garston the river is under the jurisdiction of the Mersey Docks and Harbour Board.

General Manager and Secretary : Miles Kirk Burton.

Engineer : A. G. Lyster.

Harbour Master : H. M. Liardet.

Offices : Liverpool.

(c) *Distance Table.*

Left Bank. Miles.	Fur.		Right Bank. Miles.	Fur.
		Bank Quay, Warrington, junction with Mersey and Irwell Navigation of Manchester Ship Canal Company (No. 64d1), to—		
		Fiddler's Ferry, junction with St. Helens Canal (No. 61d1) through Fiddler's Ferry Lock	3	0
		Widnes, junction with main entrance to St. Helens Canal (No. 61d1)	7	4
7	4	Runcorn, junction with Manchester Ship Canal (No.64a) through Runcorn Old Quay Lock.		
7	6	Runcorn Bridge	7	6
		Widnes, West Bank Dock ..	7	7
8	6	Runcorn, junction with Manchester Ship Canal (No. 64a) through Bridgewater Lock.		
9	6	Weston Point, junction with Manchester Ship Canal (No. 64a) through Weston Mersey Lock.		
18	0	Eastham, junction with main entrance to Manchester Ship Canal (No. 64a).		
		Garston	18	4
		Dingle Point	21	0
23	4	Birkenhead.		
		Liverpool, Prince's Landing Stage	24	0
		Liverpool, Salisbury Dock, giving access through Collingwood and Stanley Docks to the Stanley Dock Cut Branch of the Leeds and Liverpool Canal (No. 58f)	25	0
37	0	Mersey Bar Light Ship	37	0

(68)—River Mersey—*continued*.

(e) *Maximum size of vessels that can use the navigation.*

	Ft.	In.

Length.—Not limited.

Width.—Not limited.

Draught—When the tide in the river rises to a level of 14ft. 2in. above the level of the Old Dock sill, Liverpool, there is a draught of 26ft. 2in. from Liverpool to the entrance of the Manchester Ship Canal at Eastham.

	Ft.	In.
,, from Liverpool to Garston on Spring tides	28	0
,, from Liverpool to Garston on Neap tides	17	0
,, from Liverpool to Runcorn on Spring tides	16	0to17ft.
,, from Liverpool to Runcorn on Neap tides	8	0
,, from Liverpool to Bank Quay, Warrington, maximum on Spring tides	11	6

On Neap tides the available depth of water between Liverpool and Warrington would be as low as 1ft. 6in.

Headroom practically unlimited. When the river rises to a level of 14ft. 2in. above the Old Dock sill, Liverpool, which is the normal level of the water in the Manchester Ship Canal between Eastham and Latchford, there is a headroom under Runcorn Bridge of 75 0

(g) *Towing-path.*

There is no towing-path.

(h) *Tidal Informattion.*

The river is tidal throughout.

High water at Liverpool 2hrs. 35min. before London Bridge.

| Spring tides rise | .. | .. | 27ft. 6in. |
| Neap ,, ,, | .. | .. | 20ft. 3in. |

High water at Garston 14min. after Liverpool.

| Spring tides rise | .. | .. | 22ft. 6in. |
| Neap ,, ,, | .. | .. | 15ft. 3in. |

(68)—River Mersey—*continued*.

High water at Eastham 7min. after Liverpool.

Spring tides rise	.. ..	27ft. 6in.
Neap ,, ,,	.. ..	20ft. 3in.

High water at Weston Point 30min. after Liverpool.

High water at Runcorn, Bridgewater Lock, 40min. after Liverpool.

Spring tides rise	.. ..	17ft.
Neap ,, ,, ..	.. ..	8ft.

High water at Widnes 50min. after Liverpool.

Spring tides rise ..	.. ..	14ft.
Neap ,, ,,	.. ..	5ft.

High water at Fiddler's Ferry on Spring tides about 1hr. 5min. after Liverpool.

High water at Bank Quay, Warrington, on Spring tides about 1hr. 15min. after Liverpool.

Spring tides rise	.. ..	8ft. to 9ft.

(*i*) *Types of vessels using the navigation.*

Sea-going vessels and Mersey flats.

Mersey and Irwell Navigation—*see* Manchester Ship Canal Company.

Middle Level Drain—*see* Middle Level Navigations.

———

(69)—Middle Level Navigations.

(*a*) *Short Description.*

The following are the rivers and drains, or portions of them, under the jurisdiction of the Middle Level Commissioners which are navigable, being situated in the counties of Huntingdonshire, Cambridgeshire, and Norfolk :—Kings Dike, the Farcet River, Whittlesey Dike, Bevils Leam, Black Ham Drain, the Old River Nene, New Dike, Ramsey High Lode, Well Creek, the Twenty Foot River, Popham's Eau or Sea, the Middle Level Drain, the Sixteen Foot River, the Forty Foot River or Vermuyden's Drain, the Old Bedford River, and the Counter Wash Drain.

Kings Dike commences at the head of Stanground Sluice, Peterborough, by a junction with the Stanground Branch of the River Nene (third division) known as the Broadwater, and terminates at Whittlesey, where it forms a junction with Whittlesey Dike.

(69)—Middle Level Navigations—*continued.*

The Farcet River leads out of King's Dike at Horsey Sluice, and proceeding by Farcet Village is navigable to the Great Northern Railway Main Line Bridge, three-quarters of a mile west of Yaxley Village.

Whittlesey Dike commences at Whittlesey by a junction with King's Dike, and proceeds by Angle Corner, where it forms junctions with Bevils Leam and the Twenty Foot River, to Floods Ferry, where it forms a junction with the Old River Nene.

Bevils Leam commences at Angle Corner, where it forms a junction with Whittlesey Dike and the Twenty Foot River, and proceeds to Mere Mouth, where it forms junctions with the Old River Nene and Black Ham Drain.

Black Ham Drain commences at Mere Mouth, where it forms junctions with Bevils Leam and the Old River Nene, and proceeding along the northern boundary of Old Whittlesey Mere, which was drained in 1853, is navigable to the Great Northern Railway Main Line Bridge, three-quarters of a mile south-west of Yaxley Village.

The Old River Nene commences at Mere Mouth, where it forms junctions with Bevils Leam and Black Ham Drain, and proceeds by Nightingale's Corner, where it forms a junction with New Dike, Stancers Bridge, where it forms a junction with Ramsey High Lode, Wells Bridge, where it forms a junction with the Forty Foot River, Benwick, Floods Ferry, where it forms a junction with Whittlesey Dike, March, Twenty Foot End, where it forms a junction with the Twenty Foot River, and Popham's Sea End, where it forms a junction with Popham's Eau, to Outwell, where it forms junctions with Well Creek and the Wisbech Canal.

New Dike commences at Nightingale's Corner by a junction with the Old River Nene, and is navigable to Holme Railway Station on the Great Northern Railway Main Line.

Ramsey High Lode commences at Stancers Bridge by a junction with the Old River Nene, and is navigable to the town of Ramsey.

Well Creek commences at Outwell by junctions with the Old River Nene and the Wisbech Canal, and, crossing the Middle Level Drain by an aqueduct, proceeds by Nordelph to Salters Lode, where it forms a junction with the tidal River Ouse.

The Twenty Foot River commences at Angle Corner by junctions with Whittlesey Dike and Bevils Leam, and terminates by a junction with the Old River Nene at Twenty Foot End.

Popham's Eau or Sea commences at Popham's Sea End by a junction with the Old River Nene, and proceeding by Three Holes Bridge, where it forms a junction with the Sixteen Foot River, is navigable to its junction with the Middle Level Drain. The portion of Popham's Eau between the junction with the Middle Level Drain and Nordelph is not navigable.

The Middle Level Drain commences by a junction with Popham's Eau, and is navigable to the aqueduct carrying Well Creek over the drain, but not beyond.

(69)—MIDDLE LEVEL NAVIGATIONS—*continued.*

The Sixteen Foot River commences at Three Holes Bridge by a junction with Popham's Eau, and proceeding by Stonea Railway Station terminates by a junction with the Forty Foot River near Horseway.

The Forty Foot River, or Vermuyden's Drain, commences at Wells Bridge by a junction with the Old River Nene, and proceeds by Chatteris Dock and Horseway, near to which latter place it forms a junction with the Sixteen Foot River, to Welches Dam, where it forms junctions with the Old Bedford River and the Counter Wash Drain.

The Old Bedford River commences to be navigable at Welches Dam, where it forms junctions with the Forty Foot River and the Counter Wash Drain, and proceeds by Welney to Old Bedford Sluice, Salters Lode, where it forms a junction with the tidal River Ouse. The Old Bedford River is now unnavigable south-west of Welches Dam, as the Old Bedford barrier bank has been placed across the river at this place, cutting it in two, and diverting the navigation into the Counter Wash Drain, which runs parallel with the Old Bedford River. The upper portion of the Old Bedford River from the River Ouse at Earith to Welches Dam is solely used for the purpose of filling the Hundred Foot Wash Lands in times of flood ; the Old Bedford barrier bank thus runs from Earith to Welches Dam on the north-west side of the Old Bedford River, and from Welches Dam to Old Bedford Sluice, Salters Lode, on the south-east side.

The Counter Wash Drain commences at Welches Dam by junctions with the Old Bedford River and the Forty Foot River, and is navigable to Mepal Pumping Engine.

The trade on the Middle Level Navigations is principally the carrying of agricultural produce from the Fen farms to the various railway centres for transhipment on to rail, and the supply of coal to the various pumping engines for draining the land.

No vessel is allowed to navigate through any sluice between the hours of 10 a.m. and 4 p.m. on a Sunday or Christmas Day.

Lighters bound from the River Nene at Stranground to the River Ouse at Salters Lode, or vice versa, prefer travelling via the Twenty Foot River between Angle Corner and Twenty Foot End instead of by the Old River Nene through March, as the haling-way (towing-path) is more convenient by the former route.

The artificial waterways of the Fen Country having been constructed for the purposes of drainage, navigation is looked upon as a secondary matter.

(b) *Proprietors, Officers, and Offices.*

Middle Level Commissioners.

Clerk : Robert Dawbarn.

Engineer : Alfred Lunn.

Office : March.

(69)—MIDDLE LEVEL NAVIGATIONS—*continued.*

(c) Distance Table.

King's Dike (No. 69a).

	Miles.	Fur.
Head of Stanground Sluice (Lock), and junction with Stanground Branch of River Nene, Third Division (No. 74c), known as the " Broadwater," to—		
Junction with Farcet River (No. 69b).. ..	1	1
Fields End Bridge	2	2
Whittlesey Village, junction with Whittlesey Dike (No. 69c)	4	2

Farcet River (No. 69b).

Junction with King's Dike (No. 69a) and Horsey Sluice (Lock) to—		
Farcet Village	1	7
G. N. Railway Main Line Bridge, three-quarter mile west of Yaxley Village ..	3	3

Whittlesey Dike (No. 69c).

Whittlesey Village, junction with King's Dike (No. 69a) to—		
Whittlesey or Ashline Sluice (Lock)	–	$3\frac{1}{2}$
Angle Corner, junction with Twenty Foot River (No. 69j) and Bevils Leam (No. 69d)	2	6
Floods Ferry, junction with Old River Nene (No. 69f)	6	1

Bevils Leam (No, 69d).

Angle Corner, junction with Whittlesey Dike (No. 69c) and Twenty Foot River (No. 69j), to—		
Chapelbridge	1	$4\frac{1}{2}$
Pondersbridge	3	5
Tebbit's Bridge	4	4
Mere Mouth, junction with Old River Nene (No. 69f) and Black Ham Drain (No. 69e)	5	0

Black Ham Drain (No. 69e).

Mere Mouth, junction with Bevils Leam (No. 69d), and Old River Nene (No. 69f), to—		
G. N. Railway Main Line Bridge, three-quarter mile south-west of Yaxley Village	3	5

Old River Nene (No. 69f).

Mere Mouth, junction with Bevils Leam (No. 69d) and Black Ham Drain (No. 69e), to—		
Stoke's Bridge	2	4
Nightingale's Corner, junction with New Dike (No. 69g)	2	6
St. Mary's Village and Bridge	3	4

(69)—Middle Level Navigations—*continued.*

	Miles.	Fur.
Mere Mouth, junction with Bevils Leam (No. 69d) and Black Ham Drain (No. 69e), to (*continued*)—		
Stancers Bridge, junction with Ramsey High Lode (No. 69h)	5	6
Wells Bridge, junction with Forty Foot River (No. 69n)	6	5
Benwick Village and Bridge	10	5
Floods Ferry, junction with Whittlesey Dike (No. 69c)	13	2
Blackfriars Bridge	14	2
March	18	2
Twenty Foot End, junction with Twenty Foot River (No. 69j)	20	$3\frac{1}{2}$
Popham's Sea End, junction with Popham's Eau (No. 69k)	22	3
Marmont Priory Sluice (Lock)	24	1
Upwell	25	3
Outwell, junction with Well Creek (No. 69i) and Wisbech Canal (No. 123)	26	1

New Dike (No. 69g).

	Miles.	Fur.
Nightingale's Corner, junction with Old River Nene (No. 69f), to—		
Holme Station, G. N. Railway Main Line ..	3	2

Ramsey High Lode (No. 69h).

	Miles.	Fur.
Stancers Bridge, junction with Old River Nene (No. 69f), to—		
Ramsey	1	1

Well Creek (No. 69i).

	Miles.	Fur.
Outwell, junction with Old River Nene (No. 69f) and Wisbech Canal (No. 123), to—		
Aqueduct over Middle Level Drain	1	2
Nordelph	3	3
Salters Lode Sluice (Lock) and junction with River Ouse (No. 79)	5	3

Twenty Foot River (No. 69j).

	Miles.	Fur.
Angle Corner, junction with Whittlesey Dike (No. 69c) and Bevils Leam (No. 69d), to—		
Poplar Tree Bridge	–	5
Beggars Bridge	1	2
Infields Bridge	4	2
Goosetree Farm	5	6
Hobbs Bridge	6	6
Twenty Foot End. junction with Old River Nene (No. 69f)	10	3

(69)—MIDDLE LEVEL NAVIGATIONS—*continued.*

Popham's Eau or Sea (No. 69k).

	Miles.	Fur.
Popham's Sea End, junction with Old River Nene (No. 69f), to—		
Three Holes Bridge, junction with Sixteen Foot River (No. 69m)	2	2
Junction with Middle Level Drain (No. 69l)	2	4

Middle Level Drain (No. 69l).

Junction with Popham's Eau (No. 69k) to—		
Pingle Bridge	1	3
Aqueduct carrying Well Creek over the Middle Level Drain	2	0

Sixteen Foot River (No. 69m).

Three Holes Bridge, junction with Popham's Eau (No. 69k), to—		
Cottons Corner	–	6
Bedlam Bridge	4	1
Stonea Railway Station	5	1
Boots Bridge	6	6
Junction with Forty Foot River (No. 69n))	9	5

Forty Foot River, or Vermuyden's Drain (No. 69n).

	Miles.	Fur.
Wells Bridge, junction with Old River Nene (No. 69f), to—		
Forty Foot Bridge	–	4
Puttocks Bridge	3	2
Carter's Bridge	5	2
Chatteris Dock (Chatteris distant one mile)	6	0
Junction with Sixteen Foot River (No. 69m)	7	6
Horseway Village	8	1
Horseway Sluice (Lock)	8	4
Welches Dam Sluice (Lock), and junction with Old Bedford River (No. 69o) and Counter Wash Drain (No. 69p)	10	7

Old Bedford River (No. 69o).

Welches Dam, junction with Forty Foot River (No. 69n), and Counter Wash Drain (No. 69p), to—		
Purls Bridge	–	6
G. E. Railway Bridge (Ely and Peterborough Line)	2	5
Welney Village and Bridge	6	0
Old Bedford Sluice, Salters Lode, and junction with River Ouse (No. 79)	12	2

(69)—MIDDLE LEVEL NAVIGATIONS—*continued*.

Counter Wash Drain (No. 69p).

	Miles.	Fur.
Welches Dam, junction with Forty Foot River (No.69n) and Old Bedford River (No.69o), to—		
Mepal Pumping Engine	3	0

(*d*) *Locks.*

King's Dike (No. 69a).

1.—Stanground.

Fall to Whittlesey.

In dry seasons, when the water in the River Nene is very low, a level can sometimes be made through Stanground Sluice. In times of flood, when the water in the River Nene has reached the 18ft. mark on the Nene Valley datum gauge at Stanground Sluice, the sluice is closed for the passage of lighters, the lower wing walls of the sluice not being considered strong enough to bear this extra pressure.

Farcet River (No. 69b).

1.—Horsey.

Fall to Farcet Village.

Whittlesey Dike (No. 69c).

1.—Whittlesey, or Ashline.

Fall to Floods Ferry.

Old River Nene (No. 69f).

1.—Marmont Priory.

Fall to Outwell.

Well Creek (No. 69i).

1.—Salters Lode.

Salters Lode Sluice has two pairs of sea doors and two pairs of navigation doors, as the fall is sometimes from Well Creek to the River Ouse and sometimes from the River Ouse to Well Creek, according to the state of the tide in the River Ouse.

Forty Foot River (No. 69n).

1.—Horseway.

Rise to Welches Dam.

2.—Welches Dam.

Usually level, in times of full water rise to the Old Bedford River.

Old Bedford River (No. 69o).

1.—Old Bedford Sluice, Salters Lode.

Old Bedford Sluice consists of a single pair of navigation doors and a single pair of sea doors only. The fall is sometimes from the Old Bedford River to the River Ouse, and sometimes from the River Ouse to the Old Bedford River, according to the state of the tide in the River Ouse. Lighters are only allowed to pass the sluice on the back level, that is, on the level of the ebb tide.

(69)—MIDDLE LEVEL NAVIGATIONS—*continued.*

    (*e*) *Maximum size of vessels that can use the navigation.*

	Ft.	In.
Length	46	0
Width	11	0

The above dimensions are those at which a lighter can pass Stanground Sluice (Lock), which is the smallest of all the sluices on the Middle Level Navigations.

Draught.—The whole of the Middle Level Navigations are navigable by Fen lighters loaded with the approximate maximum load of 25 tons, and drawing about 3ft. 6in. of water, with the exception of the following :—

Draught—The Farcet River (No. 69)c, about	2	3
Draught—Black Ham Drain (No. 69e), for the first 1¾ miles .. .. .. about	3	0
and for the remainder of the distance about	2	0
Draught—Counter Wash Drain (No. 69p) ..	2	9 to 3ft.
Headroom	6	0

    (*g*) *Towing-path.*

There is a haling-way (towing-path) throughout the navigations, with the exception of gaps for a few yards here and there. In no case is the towing-path carried under bridges, the towing line having always to be cast-off and reattached on the far side. In many cases the bridges are rather remote from the point where the towing-path changes from one side of the navigation to the other, which necessitates the horse being taken a long way round to cross over. To obviate this, a horse boat is often taken with a gang of lighters to ferry the horse over.

    (*i*) *Types of vessels using the navigation.*

Fen lighters. Steam vessels of all kinds are strictly prohibited from using any of the navigations.

MIDDLEWICH BRANCH CANAL—*see* Shropshire Union Canals, Chester Canal Navigation.

---

(70)—MIDLAND RAILWAY.

    (*a*) *Short Description.*

The canals belonging to the Midland Railway Company consist of the Ashby Canal and the Cromford Canal.

The Company are also joint proprietors with the Great Western Railway Company of Lydney Harbour and Canal, which form part of the undertaking of the Severn and Wye and Severn Bridge Railway.

(70)—MIDLAND RAILWAY—*continued.*

The Ashby Canal commences by a junction with the Coventry Canal at Marston near Bedworth, and proceeds by Burton Hastings in the county of Warwickshire, Higham-on-the-Hill, Stoke Golding, Dadlington, Shenton, Market Bosworth, Congerstone, Shackerstone, and Snarestone in the county of Leicestershire, Measham and Donisthorpe in the county of Derbyshire, to Moira in the county of Leicestershire.

The principal trade done on the canal is the carrying of coal from the collieries at Moira and Measham.

The Cromford Canal commences at Langley Mill in the county of Nottinghamshire by a junction with the Erewash Canal, forming also at the same place a short distance from its termination a junction with the Nottingham Canal, and proceeds by Codnor Park, Butterley, Ambergate, and Whatstandwell to Cromford.

The course of the canal for the first one-and-a-quarter miles is situated in the county of Nottinghamshire, the remainder being in the county of Derbyshire.

The canal has two short branches, one from Codnor Park to Pye-bridge and Pinxton, and the Lea Wood Branch from a point about one-and-a-half miles below Cromford to Lea Wood Wharves. The canal is not much used, and as a whole is in indifferent condition ; the portion between the west end of Butterley Tunnel and Cromford is almost entirely worked as a separate navigation. Butterley Tunnel requires constant repairs, owing to subsidences due to mining operations. At the present time (1904) it is impassible.

(b) *Proprietors, Officers, and Offices.*

Midland Railway Company.

General Manager : John Mathieson.

Secretary : Alexis L. Charles.

Chief Engineer : J. A. McDonald.

Goods Manager : W. E. Adie.

Head Office : Derby.

Ashby Canal (No. 70a).

(c) *Distance Table.*

	Miles.	Fur.
Marston Junction, junction with Coventry Canal (No. 24) and Marston Stop Lock, to—		
L. & N. W. Railway Bridge (Trent Valley Line)	–	6
Bramcote Wharf	2	2
Burton Hastings	3	0
Watling Street Bridge, boundary between Warwickshire and Leicestershire	5	0

(70)—MIDLAND RAILWAY—*continued.*

	Miles.	Fur.
Marston Junction, junction with Coventry Canal (No. 24) and Marston Stop Lock, to (*continued*)—		
Hinckley Brick Yard	5	5
Hinckley Wharf (Hinckley distant 1¼ miles) ..	5	7
Higham-on-the-Hill	7	4
Stoke Golding Wharf	8	6
Dadlington	9	7
Sutton Wharf Bridge	11	2
Shenton	13	0
Market Bosworth Station (Market Bosworth distant one mile)	14	7
Carlton Bridge	15	6
Congerstone	17	1
Shackerstone	18	2
Snarestone Village and Tunnel	21	0
Boundary between Leicestershire and Derby- shire	22	4
Measham	24	1
Donisthorpe	27	4
Boundary between Derbyshire and Leicester- shire	27	6
Moira, Rawdon Colliery Wharf	29	0
Moira, Church Gresley Colliery Wharves ..	30	0

(d) Locks.

1.—Marston Junction Stop Lock.

The fall varies from level to a fall of about one inch from the Ashby Canal to the Coventry Canal.

(e) Maximum size of vessels that can use the navigation.

	Ft.	In.
Length	72	0
Width	7	0
Draught	3	6
Headroom	8	0

(f) Tunnels.

Snarestone.

Length	250 yards.		
Minimum height above water level		9	3
Minimum width at water level		16	4

No towing-path; boats "legged" or "shafted" through.

Narrow boats can pass each other in the tunnel, and enter from either end at any time.

(g) Towing-path.

There is a towing-path throughout the navigation.

(i) Types of vessels using the navigation.

Narrow boats.

Q

(70)—MIDLAND RAILWAY—*continued.*

Cromford Canal.

(c) *Distance Table.*

Main Line (No. 70b1).

	Miles.	Fur.
Langley Mill, junction with Erewash Canal (No. 30), to—		
Langley Bridge Lock	–	0½
Langley Mill, junction with Nottingham Canal (No. 41b1)	–	1
Strutts Lock	–	3
Vickers Lock	–	6
Stoneyford and Stoneyford Lock	1	4
Lock No. 8	2	5
Head of Lock No. 14, and junction with Pinxton Branch (No. 70b2)	3	3
Butterley Tunnel, East end	4	4
Butterley Tunnel, West end	6	2
Buckland Hollow	7	6
Ambergate	9	3
Whatstandwell	11	5
Junction with Lea Wood Branch (No. 70b3) ..	13	3
Cromford Wharves	14	5

Pinxton Branch (No. 70b2).

	Miles.	Fur.
Junction with Main Line (No. 70b1) to—		
Pyebridge	1	0
Pinxton and Pinxton Colliery	2	2

Lea Wood Branch (No. 70b3).

	Miles.	Fur.
Length from junction with Main Line (No.70b1) to—		
Lea Wood Wharves	–	2½

(d) *Locks.*

Main Line (No. 70b1).

1.—Langley Bridge.
2.—Strutts.
3.—Vickers.
4.—Stoneyford shallow.
5.—Stoneyford deep.
6.—Stoneyford.
7.—Butterley Company's.
8.—Bottom of Flight.
9.—Marshall's.
10.—Gas House.
11.—Smith's.
12.—Pottery.
13.—Boat Dock.
14.—Top of Flight.

Rise from Langley Mill.

(70)—MIDLAND RAILWAY—*continued.*

(e) *Maximum size of vessels that can use the navigation.*

Main Line (No. 70b1).

	Ft.	In.
Length	78	0
Width from Langley Mill to Butterley Tunnel East end	14	0
Width from Butterley Tunnel East end to Cromford	7	0
Draught	3	0
Headroom	8	0

Pinxton Branch (No. 70b2).

Length	78	0
Width	14	0
Draught	2	6
Headroom	8	0

Lea Wood Branch (No. 70b3).

Length	78	0
Width	7	0
Draught	3	0
Headroom	8	0

(f) Tunnels.
Main Line (No. 70b1).

Butterley—

Length .. .. 3,063 yards.		
Minimum height above water level	8	3
Minimum width at water level	9	0

No towing path; boats "legged" through.

Boats enter from the east end from 5 a.m. to 6 a.m., from 1 p.m. to 2 p.m., and from 9 p.m. to 10 p.m., and from the west end from 1 a.m. to 2 a.m., from 9 a.m. to 10 a.m., and from 5 p.m. to 6 p.m. The time taken to pass through the tunnel must not exceed three hours. The figures of the minimum height of the tunnel above water level are not to be depended on, as subsidences in the tunnel are continually taking place, and the brick lining of the tunnel is in a very indifferent condition.

Buckland—

Length .. .. 32 yards.		
Minimum height above water level	8	6
Minimum width at water level	13	2

Towing-path through the tunnel.

Hay—

Length .. .. 92 yards.		
Minimum height above water level	8	9
Minimum width at water level	13	4

Towing-path through the tunnel.

(70)—Midland Rilway—*continued.*

<table>
<tr><td></td><td></td><td>Ft.</td><td>In.</td></tr>
</table>

Gregory—
    Length   ..   ..   42 yards.
    Minimum height above water level   9   6
    Minimum width at water level   13   4
           Towing-path through the tunnel.

(g) *Towing-path.*

There is a towing-path throughout the navigation, except through Butterley Tunnel.

(i) *Types of vessels using the navigation.*

Narrow boats.

---

(71)—Midland and Great Western Joint Railways.

(a) *Short Description.*

The Midland and Great Western Joint Railway Companies, as owners of the Severn and Wye and Severn Bridge Railway, are the proprietors of Lydney Harbour and Canal.

The navigation consists of a tidal basin entered from the estuary of the River Severn a short distance below and on the opposite side to Sharpness, and a short canal running from the head of the tidal basin westwards to near Lydney Junction Station, all in the county of Gloucestershire.

There is a good trade done in the harbour and canal.

(b) *Proprietors, Officers, and Offices.*

The harbour and canal are the joint property of the Midland Railway Company and of the Great Western Railway Company, as owners of the Severn and Wye and Severn Bridge Railway.

Traffic Manager : J. A. Carter.

Office : Lydney.

Harbour Master : Samuel Lewis.

(c) *Distance Table.*

<table>
<tr><td></td><td>Miles.</td><td>Fur.</td></tr>
<tr><td>Head of canal near Lydney Junction Station to—</td><td></td><td></td></tr>
<tr><td>Lock at west end of tidal basin   ..   ..</td><td>–</td><td>5</td></tr>
<tr><td>Tidal gates at east end of tidal basin and
    junction with River Severn estuary (No. 89a)</td><td>–</td><td>5½</td></tr>
</table>

(71)—Midland and Great Western Joint Railways—*continued.*

(d) Locks.

There is one lock between the tidal basin and canal, and one pair of tidal gates from tidal basin to River Severn estuary.

The lock is not much worked, as vessels are generally passed through it on the levels of the tide.

(e) Maximum size of vessels that can use the navigation.

	Ft.	In.
Length into tidal basin should not exceed ..	180	0
Length into canal locking through lock between tidal basin and canal	100	0
Width into tidal basin through tidal gates	33	0
Width into canal through lock between tidal basin and canal	24	6
Draught into tidal basin average on Spring tides	25	0
Draught into tidal basin average on Neap tides	12	0
Draught into canal	12	0
The canal is in width	72	0

(g) Towing-path.

There is a towing-path alongside the canal.

(h) Tidal Information.

See Tidal Information, River Severn (No. 89).

(i) Types of vessels using the navigation.

Sea-going vessels use the tidal basin. The canal is mostly frequented by Severn trows.

Monmouthhshire Canal—*see* Great Western Railway.

Montgomeryshire Canal—*see* Shropshire Union Canals.

Monway Branch Canal—*see* Birmingham Canal Navigations, Walsall Canal.

---

(72)—Neath Canal.

(a) Short Description.

The canal commences at Glyn Neath, and proceeds down the Vale of Neath by Resolven to Aber-dulais, where, after passing the junction with the Tennant Canal, it bends sharply to the southward for a quarter of a mile, and continues its course on the south-east side of the valley

(72)—NEATH CANAL—*continued*.

through the town of Neath to its termination at Giant's Grave, near Briton Ferry. Here it joins the Giant's Grave and Briton Ferry Canal, belonging to the Earl of Jersey. The whole course of the canal is in the county of Glamorganshire.

The principal trade is coal and silica. The portion of the canal between the town of Neath and Giant's Grave is not much used.

(b) *Proprietors, Officers, and Offices.*

The Company of Proprietors of the Neath Canal Navigation.

Clerk : Thomas Williams.

Office : Victoria Chambers, Neath, South Wales.

(c) *Distance Table.*

Glyn Neath, head of canal, to—	Miles.	Fur.
Lock No. 1	–	2½
Aber-pergwm	–	3
Aber-clwyd and Lock No. 9	2	4
Resolven and Lock No. 12	4	2
Lock No. 15	5	2
Lock No. 18	7	4
Aber-dulais, junction with Tennant Canal, Main Line (No. 106a)	8	5
Lock No. 19	9	1
Neath, Main Road Bridge over Canal	10	5
Giant's Grave, termination of canal, and junction with the Earl of Jersey's Giant's Grave and Briton Ferry Canal (No. 52a)	13	0

(d) *Locks.*

1.
2.
3.
4.
5.
6.
7.
8.
9.
10.
11.
12.
13.
14.
15.
16.
17.
18.
19.

Fall from Glyn Neath.

72)—NEATH CANAL—*continued.*

(e) Maximum size of vessels that can use the navigation.

						Ft.	In.
Length	..	..	..	..	..	60	0
Width	..	..	..	..	..	9	0
Draught	..	..	..	..	maximum	2	9
Headroom	..	..	..	..	..	6	0

The lowest bridge on the canal is that carrying the main road over he canal in the town of Neath.

(g) Towing-path.

There is a towing-path throughout the navigation.

(i) Types of vessels using the navigation.

Neath and Tennant Canal boats—*see* Section 9, Types of Vessels, ι) Non-Sailing Vessels.

The average load carried on the canal is 20 tons on a draught of ft. 6in.

---

73)—RIVER NEATH.

(a) Short Description.

The River Neath is navigable from the main road bridge in the own of Neath to Briton Ferry and Swansea Bay, all in the county of Ilamorganshire. The channel of the river from Briton Ferry Dock to w water of Swansea Bay runs through sand flats. A branch of the ver known as Red Jacket Pill, on which are situated Red Jacket Pill harves, affords communication with the Tennant Canal at a point bout three miles below the town of Neath.

(b) Proprietors, Officers, and Offices.

Neath Harbour Commissioners.

Clerk and Solicitor : C. Valentine Pegge.

Harbour Master and Collector of Dues : Lieutenant Gwyn Lewis.

Office : 22, Villiers Street, Briton Ferry, South Wales.

(c) Distance Table.

Main Line (No. 73a).

			Miles.	Fur.
Neath, Main Road Bridge, to—				
Junction with Red Jacket Pill (No. 73b)	..	..	3	0
Entrance to Briton Ferry Docks	..	..	4	0
Swansea Bay, low water	..	..	6	4

(73)—RIVER NEATH—*continued.*

Red Jacket Pill (No. 73b).

	Miles.	Fur.
Length from junction with Main Line (No. 73a) to—		
Red Jacket Wharves, and junction with Red Jacket Pill Branch of Tennant Canal (No. 106b)	–	2

(e) Maximum size of vessels that can use the navigation.

Main Line (No. 73a) and Red Jacket Pill (No. 73b).

	Ft.	In.
Length.—Not limited.		
Width.—Not limited.		
Draught to Red Jacket Wharves and Neath Wharf, on Spring tides	12	0

(g) Towing-path.

There is no towing-path, navigation being conducted on the ebb and flow of the tide.

(h) Tidal Information.

The river is tidal throughout.
High water at Neath 4hrs. 18min. after London Bridge.
Spring tides rise .. .. 13ft. 6in.

(i) Types of vessels using the navigation.

Sea-going vessels.

NECHELLS BRANCH CANAL—*see* Birmingham Canal Navigations, Bentley Canal.

---

(74)—RIVER NENE.

(a) Short Description.

The western source of the River Nene commences to be navigable at a point in the town of Northampton where it is joined by the Northampton Branch of the Grand Junction Canal, being one furlong above Northampton South Bridge.

The northern source of the River Nene commences to be navigable just below West Bridge, Northampton, and forms a junction with the western source of the river a few yards above Northampton South Bridge. Leaving Northampton the river proceeds by Abington, Houghton, Billing, Cogenhoe, Castle Ashby, Doddington, Wellingborough, Ditchford, Higham Ferrers, Irthlingborough, Stanwick, Ringstead, Woodford, Denford, Thrapston, Islip, Titchmarsh, Thorpe, Wadenhoe, Lilford, Barnwell, Oundle, Ashton, Cotterstock, Tansor, Fotheringay, Warmington, Elton, Nassington, Yarwell, Wansford, Waternewton, Alwalton, Woodstone, Peterborough, Guyhirne, Bevis Hall, Wisbech, and Sutton Bridge, to The Wash at Crabs Hole.

The course of the river is situated in the counties of Northamptonshire, Huntingdonshire, Cambridgeshire, Norfolk, and Lincolnshire.

74)—River Nene—*continued.*

There is very little trade done on the river between Northampton and Peterborough. A small amount of traffic exists between Northampton and Wellingborough. Between Wellingborough and Wansford practically nothing is done. Fen lighters trade up to Wansford for stone.

The channel of the river between Northampton and Peterborough is very tortuous, and the navigation is in indifferent condition, and very liable to interruption caused by drought and flood. The numerous staunches on the portion of the river below Wellingborough are also a great hindrance to navigation.

Between Peterborough and Wisbech the navigation is also in poor condition, the principle obstruction being the Northey gravel shoal between Peterborough and Dog-in-a-Doublet. In 1864 a contract was let for the dredging of this shoal by the River Nene Navigation Commissioners—Third Division—but the work was never commenced, as in the following year a perpetual injunction was obtained by the Duke of Bedford which prohibited the removal of the shoal. The object of this was to prevent the supply of fresh water to the Duke's Thorney Estate, by means of the Thorney River leaving the Nene at Dog-in-a-Doublet, being interfered with by reason of any increase in the section of the channel between Dog-in-a-Doublet and Peterborough, causing the salt-water to flow further up the river than before.

As a rule, the tide only gives a depth of water in the river between Peterborough and Wisbech sufficient for the passage of loaded lighters on about five days in a fortnight, gangs of lighters being often assisted over the Northey gravel shoal by flushes of water drawn from Woodstone and Orton staunches, above Peterborough.

The main channel of the river, from the point where it leaves the junction of the Stanground Branch to Guyhirne, is an artificial channel, cut in 1726–8, and known as Smith's Leam.

From Wisbech to The Wash the river is used by sea-going vessels.

The Sutton Bridge Dock below Sutton Bridge, which was opened in 1881, and collapsed at the same time, has not yet been restored.

(b) *Proprietors, Officers, and Offices.*

The western source of the River Nene from the junction with the Grand Junction Canal in Northampton to South Bridge, Northampton, and from above the junction with the Grand Junction Canal to Bugbrooke Parish, which latter portion is not navigable, and the northern source of the River Nene from West Bridge, Northampton, to the junction with the western source shortly above South Bridge, Northampton, and from above West Bridge, Northampton, to Brampton Parish, which latter portion is not navigable, are all under the jurisdiction of the Nene Valley Drainage and Navigation Improvement Commissioners—First District.

Clerk : James Botterell.

Office : Grove Villa, Pellatt Grove, Wood Green, London, N.

Surveyor : John M. Siddons.

Office : West Street, Oundle.

(74)—RIVER NENE—*continued*

The river from South Bridge, Northampton, to Peterborough Bridge is under the jurisdiction of the Nene Valley Drainage and Navigation Improvement Commissioners—Second District.

Clerk : James Botterell.

Office : Grove Villa, Pellatt Grove, Wood Green, London, N.

Surveyor : John M. Siddons.

Office : West Street, Oundle.

From Peterborough Bridge to Bevis Hall, including the Stanground Branch known as the " Broadwater," the river is under the jurisdiction of the Nene Navigation Commissioners—Third Division.

Clerk : Edward McD. C. Jackson.

Office : Wisbech.

From Bevis Hall to Osborne House, near Wisbech, the river is under the jurisdiction of the Wisbech Corporation.

Town Clerk : George Carrick.

Harbour Master : J. D. Wiseman.

Office : Wisbech.

From Osborne House to The Wash at Crabs Hole the river is under the jurisdiction of the Nene Outfall Commissioners.

Clerk : Edward H. Jackson.

Office : Wisbech.

(c) *Distance Table.*

Main Line (No. 74a).

	Miles.	Fur.
Northampton, junction with Northampton branch of Grand Junction Canal (No. 38a3), to—		
Junction with Branch to West Bridge, Northampton (No. 74b)	–	0½
Northampton, South Bridge	–	1
Northampton Lock	–	3
Rush Mill Lock	1	7
Abington Mill Lock	2	7
Weston Lock	3	5
Houghton Lock	4	3
Billing Lock	4	7
Cogenhoe Lock	6	2
Whiston Lock	7	4
Castle Ashby, or White Mills, Lock	8	3
Barton Lock	9	1
Hardwater Lock	9	7
Doddington Lock	11	0

(74)—River Nene—*continued.*

	Miles.	Fur.
Northampton, junction with Northampton branch of Grand Junction Canal (No. 38a3), to (*continued*)—		
Wellingborough Lock and Whitworth's Mill (Wellingborough distant one mile)	12	5
Wellingborough Staunch	13	4½
Ditchford Lock	15	3
Higham Ferrers Lock	17	5
Irthlingborough Lock	18	3
Stanwick Staunch	19	2
Ringstead Lock	21	0
Ringstead Bottom Lock	21	5
Woodford Lock	23	7
Denford Lock	24	7
Thrapston, L. & N. W. Railway Bridge	25	7
Islip Lock	26	3
Titchmarsh Lock	28	6
Thorpe Staunch	29	3
Wadenhoe Lock	31	3
Lilford Lock	32	4
Barnwell Lock	34	5
Barnwell Staunch	35	1
Ashton Lock	37	1
Oundle, South side Oundle Bridge	38	1
Cotterstock Lock	39	1
Tansor	40	1
Perio Lock	40	7
Perio Staunch	41	2
Fotheringay Bridge	42	1
Warmington Lock	43	3
Elton Lock	45	1
Elton Staunch (Nassington Wharves)	45	7
Yarwell Lock	48	1
Wansford Lock	49	3
Wansford Staunch	50	1
Waternewton Lock	53	1
Alwalton Lock	54	7
Alwalton Staunch	55	5
Orton Staunch	58	5
Woodstone Staunch	60	1
Peterborough Bridge	60	5
Peterborough, junction with Branch to Stanground (No. 74c), known as the " Broadwater "	61	1
Commencement of Northey Gravel Shoal	63	2
Termination of Northey Gravel Shoal	63	7
Dog-in-a-Doublet, junction with Thorney River (No. 210)	65	7
Popeley's Gull	67	4
Cross Guns	70	4
Guyhirne	73	7
Bevis Hall	77	2
Wisbech Town Bridge	79	6
Wisbech, junction with Wisbech Canal (No. 123)	79	7

(74)—RIVER NENE—*continued.*

	Miles.	Fur.
Northampton, junction with Northampton branch of Grand Junction Canal (No. 38a3) to (*continued*)—		
Horse Shoe Bend	80	4
Osborne House	80	7
West Walton Ferry	82	6
Sutton Bridge	87	3
The Wash at Crabs Hole, mouth of River ..	91	6

Branch to West Bridge, Northampton (No. 74b).

Northampton, junction with Main Line (No. 74a), to—		
Fellows, Morton, and Clayton Ltd. (Canal Carriers) Wharves and Warehouses ..	–	$1\frac{1}{2}$
Gas Works	–	3
Watkin Bros. Ltd. Timber Yard, and West Bridge	–	$5\frac{1}{2}$

Branch to Stanground, known as the " Broadwater " (No. 74c).

	Miles.	Fur.
Peterborough, junction with Main Line (No. 74a), to—		
Head of Stanground Sluice (Lock), and junction with King's Dike (No. 69a)—Middle Level Navigations	–	5

(d) *Locks.*

Main Line (No. 74a).

Second District :—

1.—Northampton.
2.—Rush Mill.
3.—Abington.
4.—Houghton.
5.—Billing.
6.—Cogenhoe.
7.—Whiston.
8.—Castle Ashby.
9.—Barton.
10.—Hardwater.
11.—Doddington.
12.—Wellingborough.
13.—Wellingborough Staunch (Navigation Weir).
14.—Ditchford.
15.—Higham Ferrers.
16.—Irthlingborough.
17.—Stanwick Staunch (Navigation Weir).
18.—Ringstead.
19.—Ringstead Bottom.
20.—Woodford.
21.—Denford.
22.—Islip.
23.—Titchmarsh.

(74)—River Nene—*continued.*

24.—Thorpe Staunch (Navigation Weir).
25.—Wadenhoe
26.—Lilford.
27.—Barnwell.
28.—Barnwell Staunch (Navigation Weir).
29.—Ashton.
30.—Cotterstock.
31.—Perio.
32.—Perio Staunch (Navigation Weir).
33.—Warmington.
34.—Elton.
35.—Elton Staunch (Navigation Weir).
36.—Yarwell.
37.—Wanstord.
38.—Wansford Staunch (Navigation Weir).
39.—Waternewton.
40.—Alwalton.
41.—Alwalton Staunch (Navigation Weir).
42.—Orton Staunch   do.
43.—Woodstone Staunch   do.

Fall from Northampton.

(e) *Maximum size of vessels that can use the navigation.*

Main Line (No. 74a).

	Ft.	In.
Length from The Wash at Crabs Hole to the tail of Alwalton Lock—not limited.		
Length from the tail of Alwalton Lock to Northampton	84	0
Width from The Wash at Crabs Hole to Wisbech—not limited.		
Width from Wisbech to Northampton	10	0
Draught from The Wash at Crabs Hole to Wisbech, on Spring Tides	20	0
on Neap Tides	12	0
Draught from Wisbech to junction with Stanground Branch, Peterborough, on Spring Tides .. about	3	1
Draught from junction with Stanground Branch, Peterborough, to Northampton—maximum	3	9
Headroom from The Wash at Crabs Hole to Wisbech—not limited.		
Headroom from Wisbech to Northampton	6	0

Branch to West Bridge, Northampton (No. 74b).

	Ft.	In.
Length	84	0
Width	10	0
Draught from junction with Main Line to Northampton Gas Works	3	9
Draught from Gas Works to Watkin Bros. Ltd. Timber Yard	2	6

(74)—RIVER NENE—*continued.*

Branch to Stanground, known as the " Broadwater " (No. 74c).

						Ft.	In.
Length.—Not limited.							
Width	..	..	..	..	..	..	10	0
Draught ..	..	..	..	..	..	3	6

(g) *Towing-path.*
Main Line (No. 74a).

There is a towing-path throughout the navigation, but bridges are often remote from the points where the path changes from one side of the river to the other.

Branch to West Bridge, Northampton (No. 74b).
There is no towing-path.

Branch to Stanground, known as the " Broadwater " (No. 74c).
There is no towing-path.

(h) *Tidal Information.*

Spring tides flow to Dog-in-a-Doublet or a little beyond, and affect the level of the water in the river up to Peterborough. The salt-water does not flow beyond Dog-in-a-Doublet. Neap tides do not affect the level of the water in the river beyond Dog-in-a-Doublet.

Spring tides rise, Sutton Bridge .. 20ft. 6in.

High water at Wisbech 5hrs. 30min. after London Bridge.

Spring tides rise .. .. 15ft. 3in.
,,　　,,　　,, Dog-in-a-Doublet 2ft. 10in.
,,　　,,　　,, Peterborough 2in. to 3in.

(i) *Types of vessels using the navigation.*

Sea-going vessels navigate to Wisbech. Fen lighters use the navigation between Wisbech and Wansford. There is practically no trade between Wansford and Wellingborough. Narrow boats use the navigation between Wellingborough and Northampton.

NENE, OLD RIVER—*see* Middle Level Navigations.

NETHERTON TUNNEL BRANCH CANAL—*see* Birmingham Canal Navigations.

NEW BEDFORD RIVER, *alias* HUNDRED FOOT RIVER—*see* River Ouse (Bedford).

NEW CUT—*see* Great Eastern Railway.

NEW DIKE—*see* Middle Level Navigations.

NEWARK DIKE, or NEWARK NAVIGATION—*see* River Trent.

NEWCASTLE-UNDER-LYME BRANCH CANAL—*see* North Staffordshire Railway Trent and Mersey Canal.

NEWHALL BRANCH CANAL—*see* Birmingham Canal Navigations, Birmingham and Fazeley Canal.

NEWHAVEN HARBOUR COMPANY—*see* River Ouse (Sussex).

NEWHAVEN HARBOUR AND OUSE LOWER NAVIGATION, TRUSTEES OF—*see* River Ouse (Sussex).

NEWPORT BRANCH CANAL—*see* Shropshire Union Canals.

---

(75)—NORTH EASTERN RAILWAY.

(a) *Short Description.*

The navigations belonging to the North Eastern Railway Company consist of the River Derwent, the Pocklington Canal, and the River Ure Navigation, otherwise known as the Ripon and Boroughbridge, or Boroughbridge and Ripon Canal.

The North Eastern Railway Company are also the proprietors of any profits which may be derived from the working of the navigation of the Market Weighton Drainage and Navigation.

The River Derwent commences to be navigable at Malton, and proceeds by Castle Howard, Kirkham, Scrayingham, Buttercrambe, Stamford Bridge, Kexby, Elvington, Sutton-upon-Derwent, Cottingwith, Bubwith, and Wressell to Barmby-on-the-Marsh, where it forms a junction with the tidal River Ouse.

From Malton to Stamford Bridge the navigation forms the boundary between the East and North Ridings of the county of Yorkshire; below Stamford Bridge the course of the navigation is situated in the East Riding.

The trade done on the river is very small, what there is being almost exclusively confined to the tidal portion below Sutton Lock.

The Pocklington Canal commences by a junction with the River Derwent at Cottingwith Ferry, and proceeds by Melbourne and Beilby to a point on the main road between Market Weighton and York situated about one mile to the south of Pocklington, all in the East Riding of the county of Yorkshire.

There is very little trade done on the Canal the upper portion of which appears to be practically derelict.

The River Ure Navigation commences at Ripon and proceeds for two-and-a-quarter miles by a canal to the tail of Ox Close Lock, where it joins the River Ure, whence it proceeds by Boroughbridge, following the course of the river to Swale Nab, where the confluence of the Rivers Ure and Swale form together the River Ouse, by which the navigation is continued. The River Swale is not navigable.

(75)—NORTH EASTERN RAILWAY—*continued.*

The course of the navigation is situated in the West Riding of the county of Yorkshire, with the exception of a small portion at the lower end, which forms the boundary between the West and North Ridings.

There is a small trade done from the Ouse up as far as Boroughbridge. There is practically no trade between Boroughbridge and Ripon ; the canal between the latter place and Ox Close is in indifferent condition.

(b) *Proprietors, Officers, and Offices.*

North Eastern Railway Company.

General Manager : Sir G. S. Gibb.

Secretary : R. L. Wedgwood.

Chief Goods Manager : William Robinson.

Offices : York.

Collector of Dues for River Derwent : Matthew Robinson, Barmby-on-the-Marsh.

River Derwent (No. 75a).

(c) *Distance Table.*

	Miles.	Fur.
Malton to—		
Cherry Islands ..	2	5
Huttons Ambo Station	3	1
Castle Howard Station	5	7
Kirkham Abbey Lock ..	6	6
Howsham Lock ..	9	4
Scrayingham ..	12	0
Buttercrambe Lock	13	0
Buttercrambe Bridge ..	13	2
Stamford Bridge Lock ..	16	1
Kexby Bridge ..	19	5
Bridge between Elvington (right bank) and Sutton-upon-Derwent (left bank)..	22	3
Sutton Lock ..	22	4
Ings Bridge ..	25	0
Cottingwith Ferry and junction with Pocklington Canal (No. 75b) ..	26	4
Thorganby ..	27	4
Ellerton Landing ..	28	1
Bubwith, Derwent Bridge ..	31	1
Menthorpe ..	32	6
Breighton ..	33	1
Wressell ..	35	0
Loftsome Bridge ..	35	7
Barmby-on-the-Marsh Village ..	37	4
Barmby-on-the-Marsh, junction with River Ouse (No. 81) ..	38	0

(75)—Nᴏʀᴛʜ Eᴀsᴛᴇʀɴ Rᴀɪʟᴡᴀʏ—*continued.*

(d) Locks.

1.—Kirkham Abbey.
2.—Howsham.
3.—Buttercrambe.
4.—Stamford Bridge.
5.—Sutton.

Fall from Malton.

(e) Maximum size of vessels that can use the navigation.

	Ft.	In.
Length from Barmby-on-the-Marsh to the tail of Sutton Lock—not limited.		
Length from the tail of Sutton Lock to Malton	55	0
Width from Barmby-on-the-Marsh to the tail of Sutton Lock—not limited.		
Width from the tail of Sutton Lock to Malton	14	0
Draught from Barmby-on-the-Marsh to the tail of Sutton Lock	4	9
Draught from the tail of Sutton Lock to Malton	4	6
Headroom	10	6

(g) Towing-path.

There is a towing-path throughout the navigation.

(h) Tidal Information.

The river is tidal from Barmby-on-the-Marsh to the tail of Sutton Lock.

High water at Barmby-on-the-Marsh about 1hr. 40min. after Hull.

Spring tides rise	about	11ft.
Neap ,, ,,	about	6ft. 9in.

The first of the flood tide in the River Ouse reaches here about 1hr. before high water at Hull.

Spring tides affect the level of the water in the river up to the tail of Sutton Lock, where high water is about 5hrs. after Hull, and the rise from 1ft. 6in. to 2ft. Neap tides are not felt above Cottingwith.

(i) Types of vessels using the navigation.

Yorkshire keels.

Pocklington Canal (No. 75b).

(c) Distance Table.

	Miles.	Fur.
Cottingwith Ferry, junction with River Derwent (No. 75a), to—		
Cottingwith Lock	–	2
East Cottingwith	–	4
Storthwaite	1	5
Gardham Lock	1	7
Hagg Bridge	2	2

(75)—North Eastern Railway—*continued.*

	Miles.	Fur.
Cottingwith Ferry, junction with River Derwent (No. 75a), to (*continued*)—		
Melbourne	4	7
Thornton Lock	5	2
Warbutt Lock	6	1
Beilby	7	0
Coates Lock	7	6
Fourth Lock	8	1
Third Lock	8	6
Canal Head (Pocklington distant one mile) ..	9	4

(d) *Locks.*

1.—Cottingwith.
2.—Gardham.
3.—Thornton.
4.—Warbutt.
5.—Coates.
6.
7.
8.
9.

Rise from Cottingwith.

(e) *Maximum size of vessels that can use the navigation.*

	Ft.	In.
Length	58	0
Width	14	3
Draught	4	9
Headroom	9	0

(g) *Towing-path.*

There is a towing-path throughout the navigation.

(i) *Types of vessels using the navigation.*

Yorkshire keels.

River Ure Navigation (No. 75c).

(c) *Distance Table.*

	Miles.	Fur.
Ripon to—		
Lock No. 1	–	5
Lock No. 2	–	7
Littlethorpe	1	2
Ox Close Lock	2	2
Westwick Lock	4	1
Boroughbridge	7	4
Milby Lock	7	7
Swale Nab, junction with River Ouse (No. 81), and junction with River Swale, not navigable	10	2

(75)—NORTH EASTERN RAILWAY—*continued.*

(d) *Locks.*

1.
2.
3.—Ox Close.
4.—Westwick.
5.—Milby.

Fall from Ripon.

(e) *Maximum size of vessels that can use the navigation.*

	Ft.	In.
Length	58	0
Width	14	6
Draught from Swale Nab to Boroughbridge ..	5	0
Draught from Boroughbridge to Ripon ..	4	9
Headroom	8	6

(g) *Towing-path.*

There is a towing-path throughout the navigation.

(i) *Types of vessels using the navigation.*

Yorkshire keels.

NORTH RIVER, THE—another name for the River Bure.

NORTH STAFFORD CANAL—another name for the Trent and Mersey Canal— *see* North Staffordshire Railway.

---

(76)—NORTH STAFFORDSHIRE RAILWAY.

(a) *Short Description.*

The North Staffordshire Railway Company are the proprietors of the Trent and Mersey Canal, also formerly known by the name of the Grand Trunk Canal.

The canal commences by a junction with the River Trent at Derwent Mouth, and proceeds by Shardlow, Aston-upon-Trent, Weston-upon-Trent, Swarkestone, and Willington, in the county of Derbyshire; Horninglow Wharf (from which place Burton-upon-Trent is distant half-a-mile), Barton-under-Needwood, Alrewas, Fradley, Armitage, Rugeley, Colwich, Little Haywood, Great Haywood, Ingestre, Weston-upon-Trent, Sandon, Stone, Barlaston, Trentham, Stoke-upon-Trent, Etruria, Tunstall, Chatterley, and Harecastle, in the county of Staffordshire; Lawton, Wheelock, Middlewich, Wincham, Anderton, and Barnton to Preston Brook, in the county of Cheshire, where it forms a junction with the Preston Brook Branch of the Manchester Ship Canal Company's Bridgewater Canal.

(76)—North Staffordshire Railway—*continued.*

There is a very good trade done on the northern part of the canal in coal potters' materials, earthenware, and salt. The portion of the canal which is least used is that between Derwent Mouth and Fradley Junction.

The Newcastle Branch leaves the main line at Stoke-upon-Trent and proceeds to Newcastle-under-Lyme, all in the county of Staffordshire. The bulk of the trade done on this branch is to the wharves in Stoke-upon-Trent.

The Caldon Branch leaves the main line at Etruria and proceeds by Hauley, Milton, Heakley, Stanley, Hazlehurst, Cheddleton, and Consall to Froghall Basin, all in the county of Staffordshire. Limestone is brought to Froghall Basin for shipment into boats from the North Staffordshire Railway Company's quarries at Caldon Low by means of a Tramway three-and-a-half miles in length.

The Leek Branch leaves the Caldon Branch at Hazlehurst and proceeds to the town of Leek, all in the county of Staffordshire. There is not much traffic on this branch.

The Burslem Branch is a short arm from the main line near Burslem to the town of Burslem, all in the county of Staffordshire.

The Hall Green Branch leaves the main line at Harding's Wood Junction, near Harecastle, in the county of Staffordshire, and proceeds to Hall Green, in the county of Cheshire, where it forms a junction with the Macclesfield Canal of the Great Central Railway.

The Wardle Lock Branch forms part of the cross canal between Middlewich and Barbridge, in the county of Cheshire, which belongs to the Shropshire Union Railways and Canal Company. The portion belonging to the North Staffordshire Railway Company is Wardle Lock only, which is the entrance lock from the main line at Middlewich.

(b) *Proprietors, Officers, and Offices.*

North Staffordshire Railway Company.

General Manager : W. D. Phillipps.

Secretary : R. E. Pearce.

Offices : Stoke-upon-Trent, Staffordshire.   Telephone No. 2002.

Engineer for Canal Department : E. B. Smith.

Office : Etruria, Staffordshire.

(c) *Distance Table.*

Main Line (No. 76a).

	Miles.	Fur.
Derwent Mouth, Derwent Mouth Lock, and junction with River Trent (No. 112a), to—		
Shardlow	1	0
Dickenson's Wharf	1	6
Aston, Pegg and Harper's Wharf	2	2
Weston Cliffe	5	0

(76)—North Staffordshire Railway—*continued.*

	Miles.	Fur.
Derwent Mouth, Derwent Mouth Lock, and junction with River Trent (No. 112a), to (*continued*)—		
Cuttle Wharf	6	4
Swarkestone Junction, junction with Derby Canal (No. 27a), and head of Swarkestone Lock..	7	0
Swarkestone Brick Wharf	7	2
Swarkestone Tile Wharf	8	0
Stenson Lock	10	0
Findarn Common	11	0
Willington Wharf	12	2
Clay Mills Wharf	14	6
Horninglow Wharf (Burton-upon-Trent distant half-a-mile)	16	4
Shobnall, Staton and Co.'s Wharf	17	4
Barton Turn Coal Wharf	21	2
Barton Turn Brick Wharf	21	4
Wichnor Lock Wharf	23	0
Alrewas Public Wharf	24	4
Fradley Junction, junction with Coventry Canal (No. 24), and head of Fradley Junction Lock	26	2
Wood End Lock	27	2
King's Bromley	28	4
Hansacre, Brereton's Co.'s Wharf	30	4
Armitage	30	6
Armitage Sanitary Works	31	0
Armitage Stone Wharf	32	0
Brereton Wharf and Basin	32	6
Brereton Foundry	33	6
Rugeley Wharf	34	0
Rugeley Plaster Wharf	34	2
Brindley's Bank	35	0
Little Haywood, Sproston's Wharf	37	6
Haywood Lock	38	7
Haywood Junction, junction with Staffordshire and Worcestershire Canal—Main Line (No. 95a)	39	0
Hoo Mill	39	6
Ingestre and Shirleywich	41	2
Shirleywich Salt Works	42	0
Weston	42	4
Sandon, Lord Harrowby's Wharf	43	6
Sandon Lock Coal Wharf, Sproston's	44	4
Stone	48	6
Barlaston, Turner's Boat Yard	52	0
Trentham and Kirby's Wharf	53	2
Hem Heath	53	6
Sideway Flint Mills	55	6
Stoke Basin	56	2
Stoke Wharf	56	4
Stoke, junction with Newcastle Branch (No. 76b), between Locks Nos. 35 and 36	56	6

(76)—North Staffordshire Railway—*continued*.

	Miles.	Fur.
Derwent Mouth, Derwent Mouth Lock, and junction with River Trent (No. 112a), to (*continued*)—		
Stoke, Shelton Wharf	57	0
Cockshute Wharf	57	4
Cliffe Vale	57	6
Etruria Summit Lock and Toll Office ..	57	7
Etruria, junction with Caldon Branch (No. 76c1)	58	0
Etruria, Wedgwood's Works	58	2
Etruria, Shelton Iron, Steel, and Coal Co.'s Works	58	4
Burslem Junction, junction with Burslem Branch (No. 76d)	59	2
Newport	59	4
Middleport, Anderton Co.'s Boat Dock ..	59	6
Middleport, Anderton Co.'s Wharf	60	0
Longport Wharf..	60	2
Longport, Fox's Boat Yard	60	4
Tunstall	60	6
Chatterley Basin	61	2
Chatterley, South end of Harecastle Tunnels..	61	6
Harecastle, North end of Harecastle Tunnels..	63	3
Harding's Wood Junction, junction with Hall Green Branch (No. 76e)	63	5
Red Bull Top Lock	63	6
Harding's Wood..	63	7
Red Bull Wharf..	64	1
Lawton Basin and Wharf	64	5
Lawton, Bibbey's Sand Pits	65	7
Lawton, Bibbey's Wharf	66	3
Rode Heath Wharf	66	5
Chells Hill Wharf	67	3
Hassall Green Wharf	68	1
Hassall Green	69	1
Malkin's Bank	69	4
Wheelock Wharf	70	3
Rookery Bridge Wharf..	71	7
Rookery Bridge Bone and Manure Works ..	72	1
Moss Wharf	72	5
Crow Nest Wharf	73	3
Stud Green	73	5
King's Lock	76	2
Middlewich, junction with Wardle Lock Branch (No. 76f) leading to Shropshire Union Canal (No. 92b2)	76	3
Middlewich Top Lock	76	4
Middlewich Public Wharf	76	5
Middlewich Barge Lock	77	1
Croxton Mill	77	5
Billinge Green	81	3
Broken Cross	82	3
Lostock	83	1
Lostock Gralam and Wincham Wharf ..	83	3

(76)—North Staffordshire Railway—*continued.*

	Miles.	Fur.
Derwent Mouth, Derwent Mouth Lock, and junction with River Trent (No. 112a), to (*continued*)—		
Wincham	84	3
Marbury Wharf	85	7
Anderton Public Wharf	86	3
Anderton, junction with Anderton Lift Branch of River Weaver Navigation (No. 118b)..	86	5
Soot Hill Wharf..	86	7
Barnton Coal Wharf, and South end of Barnton Tunnel	87	3
North end of Barnton Tunnel..	87	7
South end of Saltersford Tunnel	88	1
North end of Saltersford Tunnel	88	3
Saltersford Wharf	88	5
Little Leigh	89	5
Acton Bridge Wharf	90	1
Dutton, Kinsey's Wharf	91	3
Dutton Stop Lock and Toll Office, and South end of Preston Brook Tunnel	92	5
North end of Preston Brook Tunnel, and junction with Preston Brook Branch of Manchester Ship Canal Co.'s Bridgewater Canal (No. 64b4)	93	3

In calculating distances for all purposes of tolls and charges, the distance through either of the Harecastle Tunnels is to be taken as four miles instead of the actual distance of 1 mile 5 furlongs.

Newcastle Branch (No. 76b).

Stoke, junction with Main Line (No. 76a), to—

	Miles.	Fur.
Stoke, Wolfe Street Wharf	—	2
Stoke, Kirby's Mill	—	4
Stoke, Premevese and Son	—	6
Trent Vale, Stoke Corporation Wharf ..	1	6
Trent Vale Coal Yard	2	0
Newcastle-under-Lyme Sewage Works ..	3	4
Newcastle-under-Lyme, Pool Dam Wharf ..	4	0

Caldon Branch (No. 76c1).

Etruria, junction with Main Line (No. 76a), to—

	Miles.	Fur.
Etruria Wharf	—	2
Shelton	—	4
Caldon Place	—	6
Joiner's Square, Hanley Corporation Wharf..	1	4
Joiner's Square	1	6
Hanley	2	0
Ivy House Wharf	2	2
Ivy House, Hanley and Bucknall Colliery ..	2	4
Prime's Pit	3	0
The Abbey, Gas Lime Wharf	3	6
Milton, junction with Foxley Branch Canal (No. 34), between Locks Nos. 2 and 3 ..	4	4

(76)—NORTH STAFFORDSHIRE RAILWAY—*continued.*

	Miles.	Fur.
Etruria, junction with Main Line (No. 76a), to (*continued*)—		
Milton, Jackson's Boat Dock	5	4
Heakley Wharf	5	6
Stockton Brook Waterworks Basin	6	4
Stockton Brook Wharf	6	6
Summit Lock	6	7
Stockton Brook, Harrison's Wharf	7	2
Stanley	7	4
Park Lane Wharf	8	4
Hazlehurst Junction, junction with Leek Branch (No. 76c2) and head of Hazlehurst Top Lock	9	4
Wall Grange Public Wharf	10	2
Cheddleton Wharf	11	2
Cheddleton, Heaton's Wharf	12	2
Canal enters River Churnet	13	4
Consall Quarry	14	2
Canal leaves River Churnet	14	6
Consall, Goodwin's Wharf No. 1, and Consall Lock	15	0
Froghall Brick Works	16	6
Froghall Tunnel	16	7
Froghall Basin, and terminus of the North Staffordshire Railway Co.'s Tramway to Caldon Low Limestone Quarries (distant 3½ miles)	17	4

Leek Branch (No. 76c2).

	Miles.	Fur.
Hazlehurst Junction, junction with Caldon Branch (No. 76c1), to—		
Leek Tunnel	2	0
Leek Wharves	3	2

Burslem Branch (No. 76d).

	Miles.	Fur.
Length from Burslem Junction, junction with Main Line (No. 76a), to—		
Burslem	–	3

Hall Green Branch (No. 76e).

	Miles.	Fur.
Length from Harding's Wood Junction, junction with Main Line (No. 76a), to—		
Hall Green, junction with Macclesfield Canal (No. 39c1) (half-way between the two stop locks)	1	4

Wardle Lock Branch (No. 76f).

Extends from a junction with the Main Line (No. 76a) at the tail of Wardle Lock, Middlewich, to the head of Wardle Lock only, where it joins the Middlewich Branch of the Shropshire Union Canal (No. 92b2).

(76)—North Staffordshire Railway—*continued.*

(d) *Locks.*

Main Line (No. 76a).

1.—Derwent Mouth.
2.—Shardlow.
3.—Aston.
4.—Weston.
5.—Swarkestone.
6.—Stenson.
7.—Dallow Lane.
8.—Branstone.
9.—Tatenhill.
10.—Barton Turn.
11.—Wichnor.
12.—Alrewas.
13.—Bagnall.
14.) Fradley bottom.
15.) Fradley middle.
16.) Fradley top.
17.) Fradley Junction.
18.—Shade House.
19.—Wood End.
20.—Bromley Common.
21.—Colwich.
22.—Haywood.
23.—Hoo Mill.
24.—Weston.
25.—Sandon
26.—Aston.
27)
to } Stone.
30.)
31)
to } Meaford.
34.)
35.—Trentham.
36.) Stoke Bottom.
37.) Fenton's.
38.) Twyford's.
39.) Johnson's.
40) Etruria Summit Lock.

Rise from Derwent Mouth.

41)
to } Red Bull.
46.)
47)
to } Lawton.
52.)
53)
and } Thurlwood.
54.)
55)
and } Pierpoints.
56.)

(76)—NORTH STAFFORDSHIRE RAILWAY—*continued.*

57
and } Hassall Green.
58.

59
to } Malkin's Bank.
64.

65
and } Wheelock.
66.

67
to } Booth Lane.
69.

70.—Rumps.
71.— Kings.

72
to } Middlewich.
74.

75.—Middlewich Barge Lock.

Fall to Middlewich.

76.—Dutton Stop Lock.

Level.

Locks 41 to 54, and 57 to 66, are in duplicate side by side.

Caldon Branch (No. 76c1).

1
and } Etruria (Staircase).
2.

3.—Engine.

4
to } Stockton Brook.
8.

Rise from Etruria.

9
to } Hazlehurst.
11.

12
and } Cheddleton.
13.

14.—Woods.
15.—Oak Meadow.
16.—Consall.

Fall from Hazlehurst.

Hall Green Branch (No. 76e).

1.—Hall Green Stop Lock.

Level.

Wardle Lock Branch (No. 76f).

1.—Wardle.

Rise from junction with main line at Middlewich to Middlewich branch of Shropshire Union Canal.

(76)—NORTH STAFFORDSHIRE RAILWAY—*continued.*

(e) *Maximum size of vessels that can use the navigation.*

Main Line (No. 76a).

	Ft.	In.
Length	72	0
Width from Derwent Mouth to Horninglow Wharf	13	6
Width from Horninglow Wharf to tail of Lock No. 74, Middlewich	7	0
Width from tail of Lock No. 74, Middlewich, to Anderton, junction with Anderton Lift Branch of River Weaver Navigation	14	6
Width from Anderton to Preston Brook	7	0
Draught from Derwent Mouth to Horninglow Wharf	3	6
Draught from Horninglow Wharf to Middlewich	4	0
Draught from Middlewich to Anderton	5	0
Draught from Anderton to Preston Brook	4	0
Headroom	7	0

Newcastle Branch (No. 76b).

	Ft.	In.
Length	72	0
Width	7	0
Draught	3	6
Headroom	6	8

Caldon Branch (No. 76c1).

	Ft.	In.
Length	72	0
Width	7	0
Draught from Etruria to Ivy House	3	6
Draught from Ivy House to Consall Lock	3	3
Draught from Consall Lock to Froghall	3	6
Headroom, being the height of Froghall Tunnel	6	8

Leek Branch (No. 76c2).

	Ft.	In.
Length	72	0
Width	7	0
Draught	3	0
Headroom	7	0

Burslem Branch (No. 76d).

	Ft.	In.
Length	72	0
Width	7	0
Draught	4	0
Headroom	7	0

Hall Green Branch (No. 76e).

	Ft.	In.
Length	72	0
Width	7	0
Draught	4	0
Headroom	7	0

(76)—North Staffordshire Railway—*continued.*

Wardle Lock Branch (No. 76f).

						Ft.	In.
Length	..	..	..	..	..	72	0
Width	..	..	..	..	..	6	10
Draught ..	..	..	..	..	..	3	3
Headroom	..	..	..	..	..	7	0

(f) *Tunnels.*

Main Line (No. 76a).

Armitage—
Length	..	..	..	..	130 yards		
Minimum height above water level	..		..	13	0
Minimum width at water level		..	..	10	5

Towing-path through the tunnel.

Harecastle Old—
Length	..	..	..	..	2,897 yards		
Minimum height above water level	..		..	5	10
Minimum width at water level		..	..	8	6

No towing-path ; boats " legged " through.

Harecastle New—
Length	..	..	..	..	2,926 yards		
Minimum height above water level	..		..	8	10
Minimum width at water level		..	..	9	3

Towing-path through the tunnel.

The two Harecastle tunnels run parallel to each other, the old tunnel takes the traffic passing from north to south, and the new tunnel the traffic from south to north. Boats in ordinary working enter their proper tunnels at any time.

There is telephonic communication between the tunnel-keepers at both ends of the tunnels.

Barnton—
						Ft.	In.
Length	..	..	..	..	572 yards		
Minimum height above water level	..		..	9	2
Minimum width at water level		..	..	13	6

No towing-path.

Saltersford—
Length	..	..	..	..	424 yards		
Minimum height above water level	..		..	10	1
Minimum width at water level		..	..	13	6

No towing-path.

Boats are worked in trains by the Company's steam tugs between the south end of Barnton Tunnel and the north end of Saltersford Tunnel.

(76)—North Staffordshire Railway—*continued.*

The tug leaves Barnton Tunnel (south end) at 6-0 a.m., 7-40 a.m., 9-20 a.m., 11-10 a.m., 12-50 p.m., 2-25 p.m., 4-0 p.m., 5-40 p.m., and 7-35 p.m. ; and Saltersford Tunnel (north end) at 6-50 a.m., 8-30 a.m., 10-10 a.m., 12-0 noon, 1-40 p.m., 3-10 p.m., 4-50 p.m., 6-40 p.m., and 8-30 p.m.

	Ft.	In.
Preston Brook—		
Length .. .. 1,239 yards		
Minimum height above water level	10	5
Minimum width at water level	13	7

No towing-path.

Boats are worked in trains by the Company's steam tugs, leaving the south end of the tunnel at 6-50 a.m., 8-30 a.m., 10-10 a.m., 11-50 a.m., 1-40 p.m., 3-20 p.m., 5-0 p.m., 6-45 p.m., and 8-30 p.m. ; and the north end of the tunnel at 6-0 a.m., 7-40 a.m., 9-20 a.m., 11-0 a.m., 12-40 p.m., 2-30 p.m., 4-10 p.m., 5-50 p.m., and 7-35 p.m.

Caldon Branch (No. 76c1).

	Ft.	In.
Froghall—		
Length .. .. 76 yards		
Minimum height above water level	6	8
Minimum width at water level	8	8

No towing-path ; boats " legged " or " shafted " through.

Leek Branch (No. 76c2).

	Ft.	In.
Leek—		
Length .. .. 130 yards		
Minimum height above water level	9	2
Minimum width at water level	9	0

No towing-path ; boats " legged " or " shafted " through.

(g) *Towing-path.*

There is a towing-path throughout the navigation, except through certain of the tunnels enumerated above.

(i) *Types of vessels using the navigation.*

Narrow boats use the whole of the main line and branches. Barges can use the main line from Derwent Mouth to Horninglow Wharf, and from the tail of Lock No. 74, Middlewich, to Anderton, the junction with the Anderton Lift Branch of the River Weaver Navigation.

---

(77)—North Walsham and Dilham Canal.

(a) *Short Description.*

The canal commences by a junction with the River Ant near Dilham, and proceeds by Honing, Briggate, and Spa Common, near North Walsham, to Swafield Bridge, all in the county of Norfolk. There is not much trade done on the canal.

(77)—North Walsham and Dilham Canal—*continued.*

(b) *Proprietors, Officers, and Offices.*

Proprietor : Edward Press, Esq., Muckle Hill Farm, North Walsham, Norfolk.

(c) *Distance Table.*

	Miles.	Fur.
Junction with River Ant (No. 16b1) to—		
Honing Lock	2	2
Honing Common Bridge	2	4
Briggate Lock and Mill	3	3
E Bridge Lock and Mill	5	1
Spa Common Bridge (North Walsham distant one mile)	6	$0\frac{1}{2}$
Bacton Wood Lock	6	1
Austin Bridge	6	$4\frac{1}{2}$
Swafield Bridge and Mills	7	$3\frac{1}{2}$

The canal was formerly navigable for a further distance of 1 mile 3 furlongs through two locks (Swafield) to Antingham Ponds, but this portion has been disused since 1893, and the locks are decayed.

(d) *Locks.*

1.—Honing.
2.—Briggate.
3.—E Bridge.
4.—Bacton Wood.

Rise from junction with River Ant.

(e) *Maximum size of vessels that can use the navigation.*

	Ft.	In.
Length	50	0
Width	12	4
Draught	3	6
Headroom	7	6

(g) *Towing-path.*

There is no horse towing-path. When the wind is unfavourable for vessels sailing, bow-hauling from the banks by the wherrymen is often resorted to.

(i) *Types of vessels using the navigation.*

Norfolk wherries.

North Wilts Branch Canal—*see* Wilts and Berks Canal.

Northampton Branch Canal—*see* Grand Junction Canal.

Norwich River, The—another name for the River Yare.

Norwich and Lowestoft Navigation—*see* Great Eastern Railway.

Nottingham Canal—*see* Great Northern Railway.

(78)—NUTBROOK CANAL.

(a) *Short Description.*

Although at the present time the Nutbrook Canal is quite unnavigable, and has been so since 1895, it has been thought advisable to give a description of its leading features, as schemes for its restoration have several times been mooted.

The canal commences at the White House, near Sandiacre, by a junction with the Erewash Canal, and passing Stanton Iron Works proceeds by New Stanton, Kirk Hallam, West Hallam, and Shipley Collieries to Shipley Wharf, all in the county of Derbyshire.

(b) *Proprietors, Officers, and Offices.*

Nutbrook Canal Company.

Clerk and Surveyor : John Shaw.

Office : Messrs. John Shaw and Son, Land Agents and Surveyors, The College, All Saints, Derby.

(c) *Distance Table.*

	Miles.	Fur.
The White House, junction with Erewash Canal (No. 30) and Stanton Iron Works, to—		
Back Saddle Lock	–	1
New Stanton	1	0
Old Furnace Lock	1	1
Kirk Hallam	1	7
Bottom of Three Lock and Manners Colliery..	2	2
Straws Lock	2	5
Peewit Lock	3	0
Mapperley Lock and West Hallam Collieries	3	5
Nutbrook Lock	3	6
Top Lock, Shipley	4	2
Shipley Wharf, head of Canal	4	4

(d) *Locks.*

1.—Back Saddle.
2.—Stanton.
3.—Old Furnace.
4.—Birches.
5.—Bottom of Three.
6.—Sharb Pond.
7.—Straws.
8.—Peewit.
9.—Lime Kiln.
10.—Mapperley.
11.—Nutbrook.
12.—Top Side, Nutbrook.
13.—Top Lock, Shipley.

Rise from junction with Erewash Canal.

(78)—NUTBROOK CANAL—*continued.*

 (*e*) *Maximum size of vessels that can use the navigation.*

						Ft.	In.
Length ..	..	..	..	..	..	72	0
Width ..	..	..	..	..	..	14	3
Headroom	..	..	..	..	..	8	0

(*g*) *Towing-path.*

There is a towing-path throughout the navigation.

OCKER HILL BRANCH CANAL—*see* Birmingham Canal Navigations, Wednesbury Oak Loop Line.

OCKER HILL LOWER BRANCH CANAL—*see* Birmingham Canal Navigations, Walsall Canal.

OLD BEDFORD RIVER—*see* Middle Level Navigations.

OLD SHROPSHIRE CANAL—*see* Shropshire Union Canals.

OLD STRATFORD AND BUCKINGHAM BRANCH CANAL—*see* Grand Junction Canal.

OLD UNION CANAL (*alias* THE LEICESTERSHIRE AND NORTHAMPTON-SHIRE UNION CANAL) extends from Market Harborough to West Bridge, Leicester. In 1894, having previously been an independent company, it was purchased, together with the Grand Union Canal, by the Grand Junction Canal Company. The two together now form the Leicester Section of that Company's system.

OLD WEST RIVER—*see* River Ouse (Bedford).

OLDBURY LOOP LINE CANAL—*see* Birmingham Canal Navigations.

OOZELLS STREET BRANCH CANAL—*see* Birmingham Canal Navigations, Main Line.

OULTON DIKE AND BROAD—*see* Great Eastern Railway, Navigation from the River Waveney to Lowestoft.

---

(79)—RIVER OUSE (BEDFORD).

(*a*) *Short Description.*

 The river commences to be navigable at Bedford, and proceeds by Cardington, Willington, Great Barford, Roxton, Tempsford, Little Barford, Eaton Socon, St. Neots, Great Paxton, Offord Darcy, Offord Cluney, Brampton, Godmanchester, Huntingdon, Hartford, Houghton, Hemingford, St. Ives, Holywell, Earith, Sutton, Mepal, Oxlode, Salters Lode, Downham Market, Wiggenhall, and Kings Lynn to The Wash.

(79)—RIVER OUSE (BEDFORD)—*continued.*

The course of the river is situated in the counties of Bedfordshire, Huntingdonshire, Cambridgeshire, and Norfolk.

From Earith to three furlongs above Salters Lode the main channel of the river is through an artificial cut, constructed about 1650, called the Hundred Foot, or New Bedford River.

The old course of the river from Earith to three furlongs above Salters Lode leaves the main channel by the Hermitage Sluice at Earith, and proceeds by Popes Corner, Ely, Littleport, and Southery to Denver Sluice, immediately below which it rejoins the main channel.

The portion of the old course of the river between the Hermitage Sluice at Earith and Popes Corner—the junction with the River Cam—is known by the name of the Old West River, and the portion between Littleport Bridge and Denver Sluice is known by the name of the Ten Mile River.

The navigation rights between Bedford and Holywell have for some time past been the subject of much litigation between the proprietor and neighbouring public bodies.

The proprietor acquired these rights in 1893, and spent a large sum of money in putting the navigation between Bedford and Holywell in good order, but, as the result of differences with local authorities, announced the closing of the navigation from and after the 1st October, 1897. At the present time, however, the navigation is open from Holywell to St. Neots, and remains closed between St. Neots and Bedford.

The portion of the old course of the river between Earith and Popes Corner, known as the Old West River, is very little used for traffic, and is, except in times of full water, a narrow and restricted waterway.

(b) *Proprietors, Officers, and Offices.*

The navigation rights of the river between Bedford and Holywell are private property.

Proprietor : L. T. Simpson, Esq., Sevenoaks, Kent.

Manager and Engineer : W. Thornber.

Office : Navigation Wharf, Bedford.

From Holywell to Earith the river is an open navigation, having no controlling authority, but Brownshill or Over Staunch is maintained by the South Level Drainage and Navigation Commissioners.

Clerk : Harold Archer.

Engineer : George Carmichael.

Offices : Ely.

From Earith to three furlongs above Salters Lode the artificial cut known as the Hundred Foot River is under the jurisdiction of the Bedford Level Corporation.

Registrar : Harold Archer.

Engineer : George Carmichael.

Offices : Fen Office, Ely.

s

(79)—RIVER OUSE (BEDFORD)—*continued.*

The old course of the river from Earith to Popes Corner, known as the Old West River, is dredged and kept open by the South Level Drainage and Navigation Commissioners, but the Bedford Level Corporation cut the weeds and are the owners of Hermitage Sluice.

From Popes Corner to Littleport Bridge the river is under the jurisdiction of the South Level Drainage and Navigation Commissioners.

From Littleport Bridge to a quarter-of-a-mile above Denver Sluice the river is an open navigation, having no controlling authority.

From a quarter-of-a-mile above Denver Sluice to the commencement of the Eau Brink Cut the river is under the jurisdiction of the Denver Sluice Commissioners.

Clerk : Harold Archer.

Office : Ely.

The Bedford Level Corporation built Denver Sluice, own the site, and also appoint the sluice keeper. The Denver Sluice Commissioners maintain the fabric of the sluice and all the sea doors, and the South Level Drainage and Navigation Commissioners maintain the Navigation doors.

From the commencement of the Eau Brink Cut to its termination at the Free Bridge the river is under the jurisdiction of the Conservators of the Ouse Outfall, which body is composed of an equal number of representatives of the Middle Level and South Level Drainage and Navigation Commissioners.

Clerk : Harold Archer.

Office : Ely.

From the termination of the Eau Brink Cut at the Free Bridge to the Mouth the river is under the jurisdiction of the Kings Lynn Conservators.

Clerk : W. D. Ward.

Harbour Master : A. H. Brown.

Offices : Kings Lynn.

The haling-ways (towing-paths) between Denver Sluice and Kings Lynn are under the jurisdiction of the Ouse Haling-Ways Commissioners.

Clerk : W. D. Ward.

Office : Kings Lynn.

The banks of the river between Denver Sluice and the commencement of the Eau Brink Cut are under the jurisdiction of the Ouse Banks Commissioners, and are divided into six districts.

Clerk : Harry Wayman.

Office : Kings Lynn.

(79)—RIVER OUSE (BEDFORD)—*continued.*

(c) *Distance Table.*

Main Line of River (No. 79a).

	Miles.	Fur.
Bedford to—		
Bedford, Duck Mill Lock	–	2
Cardington Lock	2	0
Castle Lock	3	5
Castle Staunch	3	7
Willington Lock	5	6
Old Mills Lock	6	4
Great Barford and Great Barford Lock	7	2
Roxton Lock	9	5
Tempsford Staunch	10	1
Little Barford	12	5
Eaton Socon and Eaton Socon Lock	13	7
St. Neots	15	0
St. Neots Lock	16	2
Belford Staunch	16	5
Great Paxton	18	0
Offord Darcy	20	1
Offord Cluney and Offord Lock	20	6
Brampton and Brampton Lock	23	1
Godmanchester and Godmanchester Lock	24	3
Huntingdon	25	1
Hartford	26	2
Houghton Lock	27	7
Hemingford Lock	29	3
St. Ives Bridge	30	6
St. Ives Staunch	31	1
Holywell	33	4
Brownshill or Over Staunch	36	2
Earith Village	38	0
Earith, commencement of Hundred Foot River and junction with old course of river—Earith to Denver—(No. 79b) and Earith Bridge	38	4
Sutton Bridge	42	1
Mepal Bridge	43	3
Oxlode	47	4
Welney Suspension Bridge	52	6
Termination of Hundred Foot River, and junction with old course of river—Earith to Denver—(No. 79b) at the tail of Denver Sluice.	58	6
Salter's Lode, junction with Old Bedford River (No. 69o), and junction with Well Creek (No. 69i)	59	1
Downham Bridge (Downham Market distant one mile)	60	1
Stow Bridge	62	7
Magdalen Bridge	66	0
Wiggenhall Bridge	68	0
Commencement of Eau Brink Cut	68	3

(79)—River Ouse (Bedford)—*continued.*

	Miles.	Fur.
Bedford to (*continued*)—		
The Free Bridge, and termination of Eau Brink Cut	71	3
Kings Lynn, entrance to Kings Lynn Docks ..	72	6
The Wash, mouth of river	74	6

Old Course of River—Earith to Denver—(No. 79b).

	Miles.	Fur.
Earith, junction with Main Line of River (No. 79a) and Hermitage Sluice, to—		
Aldreth Bridge	3	3
Twenty Pence Ferry	7	1
Streatham Ferry	8	6
Popes Corner, junction with River Cam (No. 18a)	11	5
Ely Station Dock	14	3
Ely Bridge	14	6
Junction with River Larke (No. 56a)	18	6
Littleport Bridge	20	7
Brandon Creek, junction with Brandon River (No. 14)	24	2
Southery Ferry	25	3
Hilgay Bridge	28	0
Denver Sluice, and junction with Main Line of River (No. 79a)	31	1

(d) Locks.

Main Line of River (No. 79a).

1.—Duck Mill, Bedford.
2.—Cardington.
3.—Castle.
4.—Castle Staunch (Navigation Weir).
5.—Willington.
6.—Old Mills.
7.—Great Barford.
8.—Roxton.
9.—Tempsford Staunch (Navigation Weir).
10.—Eaton Socon.
11.—St. Neots.
12.—Belford Staunch (Navigation Weir).
13.—Offord.
14.—Brampton.
15.—Godmanchester.
16.—Houghton.
17.—Hemingford.
18.—St. Ives (commonly known by the name of St. Ives Staunch, but now a lock).
19.—Brownshill or Over (commonly known by the name of Brownshill or Over Staunch, but now a lock).

Fall from Bedford.

(79)—RIVER OUSE (BEDFORD)—*continued.*

Old Course of River—Earith to Denver—(No. 79b).

1.—Hermitage.

Rise from junction with Main Line (No. 79a) at Earith.

2.—Denver.

Fall in either direction according to the state of the tide.

Denver Sluice consists of a lock for navigation purposes fitted with a pair of sea doors, and three drainage openings each 18ft. wide, also fitted with sea doors.

(e) *Maximum size of vessels that can use the navigation.*

Main Line of River (No. 79a).

	Ft.	In.
Length from the mouth of the river to Brownshill Staunch—not limited.		
Length from Brownshill Staunch to Bedford: all the locks are capable of taking two Fen Lighters, the minimum length being	101	0
Width from the mouth of the river to Brownshill Staunch—not limited.		
Width from Brownshill Staunch to Bedford ..	10	8
Draught from the mouth of the river to Kings Lynn Docks, on Spring tides ..	24	0
on Neap tides	17	0
Draught from Kings Lynn Docks to the junction with the Old Course of River (No. 79b) at the tail of Denver Sluice. ..	9	0
Draught from the junction with the Old Course of the River (No. 79b) at the tail of Denver Sluice to Bedford, the maximum draught in times of fair water is 3ft. 6in., but unless land water is flowing down the river freely lighters will only find this draught over the shallows at Oxlode, at the upper end of the Hundred Foot River, on about three or four days on each Spring tide.		

Old Course of River—Earith to Denver (No. 79b).

	Ft.	In.
Length if locking through the lock at Denver Sluice	70	0
Length if passing Denver Sluice on the levels of the tides—not limited.		
Length through Hermitage Sluice	90	0
Width through Denver Sluice	16	6
Width through Hermitage Sluice	12	6
Draught from the tail of Denver Sluice to Ely	9	0
Draught from Ely to Popes Corner	3	9
Draught from Popes Corner to the junction with the Main Line at Earith maximum	3	6

(79)—River Ouse (Bedford)—*continued.*

(g) *Towing-path.*

Main Line of River (No. 79a) and Old Course of River—Earith to Denver — (No. 79b).

There is a towing-path throughout the navigation, with the exception of the portion between the mouth of the river and Kings Lynn.

(h) *Tidal Information.*

Main Line of River (No. 79a).

Spring tides flow to the upper portion of the Hundred Foot River and affect the level of the water in the river to the tail of Brownshill or Over Staunch.

High water at Kings Lynn about 4hrs. 50min. after London Bridge.

Spring tides rise	..	..	about	22ft. 6in.
Neap ,,	,,	.. ..	about	15ft. 9in.

High water at Salters Lode about 5hrs. 45min. after London Bridge.

Spring tides rise	..	..	about	14ft. 6in.
Neap ,,	,,	.. ..	,,	7ft. 6in.
Earith Spring ,,	,,	.. ..	,,	1ft. 6in.

Old Course of River—Earith to Denver—(No. 79b).

The tide flows to the tail of Denver Sluice, and rises above the level of the water in the river on the upper side of the Sluice, being kept out by the sea doors, which are capable of holding a 24ft. rise of tidal water. The water in the river on the upper side of Denver Sluice is maintained at a height of 13ft. 6in. above the sills of the Sluice.

High water at Denver Sluice about 5hrs. 45min. after London Bridge.

Spring tides rise	..	..	about	14ft. 6in.
Neap ,,	,,	.. ..	,,	7ft. 6in.

The flood tide flows here for about 3hrs. on Spring tides and 3½hrs. on Neap tides.

(i) *Types of vessels using the navigation.*

Sea-going vessels use the river from its mouth to King's Lynn. Fen lighters navigate the whole of the river above King's Lynn. There are a few lighters, measuring 70ft. by 14ft. and drawing 3ft. 6in. of water and carrying 70 tons, using the navigation between Kings Lynn and Popes Corner for Cambridge.

Yorkshire keels used to trade to the river and navigate as far as Ely, principally carrying coal, but they are now seldom seen.

Ouse River, Little—another name for the Brandon River.

(80)—River Ouse (Sussex).

(a) Short Description.

The river commences to be navigable at the ruins of Hamsey Lock, between Barcombe and Lewes, and proceeds by Lewes, Southease, and Piddinghoe to Newhaven, where it enters Newhaven Harbour, all in the County of Sussex.

The navigation between Lewes and Newhaven follows the course of the river, with the exception of six cuts made to take off curves many years ago.

From the ruins of Hamsey Lock to a quarter-of-a-mile above Lewes Bridge there is no trade on the navigation, but below this there is a trade principally in corn, coal, timber, and pig iron to Lewes from Newhaven.

(b) Proprietors, Officers, and Offices.

From Lewes Bridge to a point about half-a-mile north of Newhaven Bridge, where the Horseshoe Sluice discharges itself, the river is under the jurisdiction of the Trustees of Newhaven Harbour and Ouse Lower Navigation.

Clerk : Frederick Holman.

Expenditor : Thomas Colgate.

Offices : 86, High Street, Lewes, Sussex.

Above Lewes Bridge to the ruins of Hamsey Lock, and beyond that to Barcombe, which latter portion of the river is not navigable, the Trustees have a drainage jurisdiction, and cut the weeds in the river.

From a point about half-a-mile north of Newhaven Bridge to the mouth of Newhaven Harbour the river is under the jurisdiction of the Newhaven Harbour Company.

General Manager : W. Forbes.

Secretary : J. J. Brewer.

Engineer : C. L. Morgan.

Offices : London Bridge Station, L. B. & S. C. Rly., London, S.E.

Harbour Master : Captain Morris.

Office : Newhaven.

(c) Distance Table.

Ruins of Hamsey Lock to—	Miles.	Fur.
Lewes Corporation Wharf and Phœnix Foundry	1	2
Lewes Bridge	1	4
Hillman, Hillman and Weller's Lime Works ..	2	0
Southerham Swing Bridge, L. B. & S. C. Rly...	2	2
Sound Bridge (not a bridge over the navigation)	3	6
Southease Bridge (Swing Bridge)	5	2
Piddinghoe	6	7
Termination of Trustees boundary, and commencement of Newhaven Harbour ..	8	0
Newhaven Bridge (Swing Bridge)	8	4
Newhaven Harbour Mouth	9	4

(80)—RIVER OUSE (SUSSEX)—*continued.*

(e) *Maximum size of vessels that can use the navigation.*

Length.—Not limited.

The river at Lewes is narrow, but vessels from 130ft. to 140ft. can swing at Sound Bridge.

	Ft.	In.
Width.—Not limited.		
Draught.—Vessels can enter Newhaven Harbour drawing on Spring tides	20	0
on Neap tides	15	0
Draught.—From Newhaven to Lewes the shallowest part of the navigation is at Lewes Bridge, where there is a depth of water on Spring tides of	10	0
on Neap tides	5	0

Headroom,—Lewes Bridge is the lowest bridge on the navigation, the crown of the arch being 7ft. above the level of the water on Spring tides.

(g) *Towing-path.*

A portion of the old towing-path is still in existence from about one mile below Southease Bridge to the entrance of Lewes Town, but is seldom used. Navigation is conducted on the ebb and flow of the tide, vessels being assisted by sails or quanting (shafting).

(h) *Tidal Information.*

The river is tidal throughout.

High water at Newhaven Harbour 2hrs. 45min. before London Bridge.

Spring tides rise .. .. 19ft.
Neap   ,,   ,, ... 14ft.

High water at Lewes about 1hr. after Newhaven.

Spring tides rise ..   .. .. 9ft. to 10ft.

(i) *Types of vessels using the navigation.*

Coasting vessels, small steamers, and Medway sailing barges trade to the river and navigate to Lewes. Small sailing barges, loading about 20 tons, work locally between Lewes and Newhaven.

---

(81)—RIVER OUSE (YORK).

(a) *Short Description.*

The river is formed by the confluence of the Rivers Ure and Swale at Swale Nab, near Myton-on-Swale, and is navigable from its commencement. Leaving Swale Nab the river proceeds by Aldwark, Linton, Newton-on-Ouse, Beningbrough, Overton, Nether Poppleton, Clifton, York, Bishopthorpe, Naburn, Acaster Malbis, Acaster Selby, Cawood, Kelfield, Barlby, Selby, Hemingbrough, Barmby-on-the-Marsh, Long

(81)—RIVER OUSE (YORK)—*continued.*

Drax, Asselby, Howden, Hook, Skelton, Goole, Swinefleet, Saltmarshe, Whitgift, and Blacktoft to Trent Falls, where, together with the River Trent, it forms the Humber Estuary.

From Swale Nab to York the course of the navigation forms almost entirely the boundary between the North and West Ridings of the county of Yorkshire, and below York the boundary between the East and West Ridings.

The portion of the river above York is not much used for traffic. Below York there is a fair trade done from Hull to Goole and intermediate places up to York.

In dry seasons the upper portion of the tideway between Barmby-on-the-Marsh and Naburn Locks is very liable to a reduction of the navigable depth by reason of the deposit of " warp " or silt brought up by the tide from the Humber estuary, which remains until scoured out by a flood. A single tide will sometimes deposit as much as six inches of warp.

The non-tidal portion of the river above Naburn Locks is liable to floods, which at York often reach a height of 12ft., and have been known to attain to a height of 16ft. 6in., above summer level.

(b) *Proprietors, Officers, and Offices.*

The river from Swale Nab to Widdington Ings, near Newton-on-Ouse, is known as the Linton Lock Navigation, and is under the jurisdiction of the Linton Lock Navigation Commissioners.

Secretary : J. E. Jones.

Office : Messrs. Jones and Piercey, Solicitors, 1, Market Street, York.

From Widdington Ings to a point 100 yards below Hook Railway Bridge the river is under the jurisdiction of the Corporation of the City of York.

Town Clerk : R. Percy Dale.

Deputy Town Clerk : William Giles.

Engineer : Alfred Creer.

Offices : The Guildhall, York.

Collector of Dues at York : Henry Stephenson, Bridge Street, York.

Lock Master at Naburn, Collector of Dues, and River Bailiff : Thomas Leetham, Naburn Locks, near York.

Agent at Hull : J. Goodare, 6, Spyvee Street, Hull.

From 100 yards below Skelton Railway Bridge to the mouth of the river at Trent Falls the river is under the jurisdiction of the Undertakers of the Aire and Calder Navigation.

Manager : Thomas Marston.

Secretary : Samuel Barraclough.

Offices : Dock Street, Leeds. Telegrams : " Navigation, Leeds." Telephone No. 530.

The Corporation of York are the proprietors of two steam tugs engaged in towing vessels from Hull to York.

(81)—River Ouse (York)—*continued.*

(c) *Distance Table.*

	Miles.	Fur.
Swale Nab, junction with River Ure Navigation (No. 75c), and junction with River Swale (not navigable), to—		
Aldwark Bridge ..	4	2
Linton Lock	7	6
Newton-on-Ouse..	8	6
Widdington Ings	9	6
Junction with River Nidd (not navigable)	10	0
Beningbrough	11	2
Overton ..	13	2
Nether Poppleton	13	6
Rawcliffe Ings ..	14	6
Clifton Ings	15	6
York, Lendal Bridge	17	4
York, Ouse Bridge	17	6
York, Skeldergate Bridge	18	0
York, junction with River Foss (No. 33)	18	2
Bishopthorpe	20	6
Naburn Village and Ferry	22	2
Acaster Malbis ..	22	6
Naburn Locks ..	23	4
Acaster Selby	26	2
Junction with River Wharfe (No.122)..	28	0
Cawood ..	29	0
Kelfield ..	30	2
Riccall Landing ..	31	4
Barlby	35	2
Selby	36	6
Selby, junction with Selby Branch Canal of Aire and Calder Navigation (No. 3c)	37	0
Hemingbrough ..	42	2
Barmby-on-the-Marsh, junction with River Derwent (No. 75a) ..	43	4
Long Drax Railway Bridge (Hull and Barnsley Line).. ..	44	1
Asselby Island, junction with River Aire (No. 2)	47	2
Airmyn Ferry ..	47	6
Howden Dike, Ferry, and J. Scarr & Son's Ship Yard ..	50	0
Hook Village (right bank), Skelton Village (left bank) ..	50	6
Boundary of jurisdiction of the York Corporation, 100 yards below Hook Railway Bridge	51	2
Goole, entrance to Docks, and junction with Aire and Calder Navigation Main Line— (No. 3a3)	52	6
Goole, junction with the portion of the River Don (No. 28) known as the Dutch River..	52	7
Swinefleet	54	6
Saltmarshe	56	6

(81)—RIVER OUSE (YORK)—*continued.*

	Miles.	Fur.
Swale Nab, junction with River Ure Navigation (No. 75c), and junction with River Swale (not navigable), to (*continued*)—		
Whitgift	57	6
Blacktoft..	59	6
Trent Falls, junction with River Humber (No. 49) and River Trent (No. 112a) ..	60	6

(d) Locks.

1.—Linton.
2.—Naburn (two locks side by side).

Fall from Swale Nab.

(e) Maximum size of vessels that can use the navigation.

	Ft.	In.
Length from Trent Falls to the tail of Naburn Locks—not limited.		
Length from the tail of Naburn Locks to York	134	0
Length from York to Swale Nab	60	0
Width from Trent Falls to the tail of Naburn Locks—not limited.		
Width from the tail of Naburn Locks to York	25	0
Width from York to Swale Nab	15	4
Draught from Trent Falls to Goole –		
On Spring tides about	18	0
On Neap tides ,,	12	6
Draught from Goole to Selby—		
On Spring tides ,,	13	0
On Neap tides ,,	8	6
Draught from Selby to Naburn Locks—		
On Spring tides ,,	9ft. 6in. to 10 ft.	
On Neap tides ,,	7ft. to 8ft.	
	Ft.	In.
Draught from Naburn Locks to York	9	6
Draught from York to Swale Nab	6	0
Headroom from Trent Falls to Ouse Bridge, York, not limited, as all the bridges up to this point are opening bridges.		
Headroom from Ouse Bridge, York, to Swale Nab	6	4

(g) Towing-path.

There is a towing-path from Swale Nab to the junction with the River Wharfe one mile above Cawood, with the exception of a short distance through the City of York. The portion, however, below Naburn Locks is not now used.

(h) Tidal Information.

The tide flows to the tail of Naburn Locks.

High water at Goole 1hr. after Hull, or 5hrs. 30min. after London Bridge.

Spring tides rise..	13ft.	
Neap ,, ,, ...	9ft.	

(81)—River Ouse (York)—*continued.*

High water at Barmby-on-the-Marsh about 1hr. 40min. after Hull. The first of the flood tide reaches here about 1hr. before high water at Hull.

High water at Selby about 2hrs. 30min. after Hull .

<table>
<tr><td>Spring tides rise..</td><td>..</td><td>..</td><td>8ft.</td></tr>
<tr><td>Neap   ,,</td><td>,, ..</td><td>..</td><td>..</td><td>4ft. 3in.</td></tr>
</table>

The first of the flood tide reaches here about the same time as high water at Hull.

High water at Naburn Locks about 4hrs. after Hull.

<table>
<tr><td>Spring tides rise..</td><td>..</td><td>..</td><td>8ft.</td></tr>
<tr><td>Neap   ,,</td><td>,, ..</td><td>..</td><td>..</td><td>3ft.</td></tr>
</table>

The first of the flood tides reaches here on Spring tides about 1hr. 30min., and on Neap tides about 1hr. 50min. after high water at Hull.

Below Selby the tide in the river runs with considerable strength.

(*i*) *Types of vessels using the navigation.*

Sea-going vessels navigate up to Goole from Hull.

Lighters of 230 tons carrying capacity, engaged in Messrs. Leetham's grain traffic, navigate to the River Foss in York.

Steamers up to 120 tons burden navigate to York.

Yorkshire keels are in use throughout the whole of the navigation.

Ouse Burn—*see* River Tyne.

Ouse Outfall, Conservators of the—*see* River Ouse (Bedford).

---

(82)—Oxford Canal.

(*a*) *Short Description.*

The canal commences by a junction with the main line of the Coventry Canal at Hawkesbury, near Coventry, and proceeds by Wyken Colliery, Ansty, Stretton-under-Fosse, Brinklow, Easenhall, Newbold-on-Avon, Brownsover near Rugby, and Hillmorton, in the county of Warwickshire ; Barby in the county of Northamptonshire ; Willoughby in the county of Warwickshire ; Braunston in the county of Northamptonshire ; Wolfhamcote, Lower Shuckburgh, Napton Junction, Napton-on-the-Hill, Marston Doles, Wormleighton, and Fenny Compton, in the county of Warwickshire ; Claydon, Cropredy, Banbury, Kings Sutton, and Adderbury, in the county of Oxfordshire ; Aynho Wharf in the county of Northamptonshire ; Somerton, Heyford, North Brook, Kirtlington, Enslow, Thrupp, Kidlington, and Wolvercote, to Oxford, in the county of Oxfordshire, where, shortly before its termination in the city, it forms a junction with the River Thames.

(82)—OXFORD CANAL—*continued.*

The main line of the canal as originally constructed from Hawkesbury to Oxford was 91 miles in length, but the distance has been reduced by improvements made between Hawkesbury and Napton Junction—between the years 1829 and 1834—to its present length of 77½ miles.

There are sundry branches leading out of the main line between Hawkesbury and Napton Junction which almost entirely consist of portions of the ancient course of the canal, the most important of these being the Braunston Branch, which connects the main line of the canal with the main line of the Grand Junction Canal at Braunston.

There is a good trade on the canal between Hawkesbury and Braunston and Napton Junction, the portion between Braunston and Napton Junction forming a link in the through route between London and Birmingham. From Napton Junction to Oxford there is not so much trade done as on the northern portion of the canal, and the section of the waterway is more restricted.

Between the Summit Lock at Claydon and Oxford the majority of the bridges over the canal are wooden drawbridges.

(b) *Proprietors, Officers, and Offices.*

The Company of Proprietors of the Oxford Canal Navigation.

Secretary : Henry Robinson.

Office : Oxford. Telegraphic Address : " Canal, Oxford."

Superintendent of Works : F. Chamberlain.

Office : Hillmorton, near Rugby.

The Dukes Cut Branch, which gives access from the main line of the canal near Oxford to the upper reaches of the Thames, is the property of the Duke of Marlborough, and is held by the Oxford Canal Company under a long lease.

(c) *Distance Table.*

Main Line (No. 82a).

	Miles.	Fur.
Hawkesbury Junction and Stop Lock, junction with Coventry Canal (No. 24), to—		
Tushes Bridge	1	0
Junction with branch to Wyken Old Colliery (not navigable)	1	4
Northern junction of Wyken New Colliery Loop Line Branch (No. 82b)	1	6
Southern junction of Wyken New Colliery Loop Line Branch (No. 82b)	2	2
Ansty Bridge	3	6
Hopsford Valley Aqueduct	5	0
Lord Craven's	5	2
Grime's Bridge, Combe	6	4
Stretton Stop Lock and Toll Office, junction with Stretton Wharf Branch (No. 82c)	7	2

(82)—OXFORD CANAL—*continued*.

	Miles.	Fur.
Hawkesbury Junction and Stop Lock, junction with Coventry Canal (No. 24), to (*continued*)—		
North end of Brinklow Hill, junction with Brinklow Wharf Branch (No. 82d) ..	7	6
Easenhall Lane Bridge	8	0
Hall Oaks Corner	8	2
Hungerfield	9	0
North end of Walton's Hill, junction with branch to Fennis Field Lime Works (not navigable)	9	4
Cathian Lane Bridge	10	2
Newbold and Harborough Road Bridge, junction with branch to Norman's and Walker's Lime Works (not navigable) ..	11	0
Newbold Wharf	11	4
Junction with Rugby Wharf Branch (No. 82e)	12	4
Brownsover Wharf	13	0
Brownsover Mill..	13	4
Clifton New Wharf, junction with branch to Clifton Mill (not navigable)	14	0
Hillmorton Bottom Lock	15	2
Hillmorton	15	4
Kilsby Road Bridge	16	6
Barby Road Bridge, Norman's Wharf.. ..	17	4
Barby Wood Bridge	18	4
Willoughby Wharf	21	0
Braunston Turn, junction with Braunston Branch (No. 82f)	22	6
Wolfhamcote	23	4
Nethercote	24	6
Flecknoe	25	0
Shuckburgh Wharf	26	2
Napton Junction, junction with Warwick and Napton Canal (No. 116)	27	6
Coventry Road Bridge	28	2
Napton Wharf	28	6
Napton Brickyard	29	0
Napton Bottom Lock	30	0
Marston Doles and top of Napton Locks ..	31	6
Griffin's Bridge, Wormleighton	37	0
Sherne Hill Bridge	39	0
Fenny Compton	39	2
Claydon Top Lock	42	6
Broadmoor Bridge	44	4
Cropredy	45	4
Grimsbury Mill	49	2
Banbury, Toll Office, Lock, and Wharves ..	50	0
Twyford Wharf (Kings Sutton distant one mile)..	52	6
Adderbury	55	0
Nell Bridge Wharf	55	4
Aynho Wharf (Aynho distant one mile) ..	56	6

(82)—Oxford Canal—*continued.*

	Miles.	Fur.
Hawkesbury Junction and Stop Lock, junction with Coventry Canal (No. 24), to (*continued*)—		
Souldern Wharf	57	2
Somerton Wharf	59	0
Somerton Mill	60	0
Upper Heyford Mill	61	2
Lower Heyford Mill	62	2
Lower Heyford	62	6
North Brook	64	6
Washford Hill Stone Quarries	66	2
Kirtlington, Enser's Mill Lock	66	6
Enslow	68	0
Canal enters River Cherwell	68	4
Weir Lock, canal leaves River Cherwell ..	69	3
Thrupp	70	4
Langford Lane Wharf	71	0
Kidlington Bridge and Round Ham Lock ..	71	6
Yarnton Lane Bridge	72	2
King's Bridge Wharf	73	4
Tail of Shuttleworth's Lock, and junction with Dukes Cut Branch (No. 82g), leading to River Thames	74	0
Wolvercote Bridge and Lock	74	6
Summertown	75	6
Heyfield Road Wharf	76	0
Oxford, Walton Well Bridge	76	4
Oxford, junction with branch to River Thames through Isis Lock (No. 82h)	77	0
Oxford, Wharves and Warehouses	77	4

Wyken New Colliery Loop Line Branch (No. 82b).

	Miles.	Fur.
Northern junction with Main Line (No. 82a) to—		
Junction with Wyken Colliery Co.'s Canal to Wyken New Colliery, quarter-of-a-mile in length	–	3
Southern junction with Main Line (No. 82a) ..	–	6

Stretton Wharf Branch (No. 82c).

Length from junction with Main Line (No.82a) to Stretton Wharf	–	2

Brinklow Wharf Branch (No. 82d).

Length from junction with Main Line (No. 82a) to Brinklow Wharf..	–	2

Rugby Wharf Branch (No. 82e).

Length from junction with Main Line (No. 82a) to Rugby Wharf	–	2

(82)—OXFORD CANAL—*continued.*

Miles.   Fur.

Braunston Branch (No. 82f).

Length from junction with Main Line (No. 82a)
to—

Braunston Stop Lock, Toll Office, Fellows,
   Morton, & Clayton Ltd. (Canal Carriers)
   Wharf, and Braunston Junction, junction
   with Main Line of Grand Junction Canal
   (No. 38a1) ..   ..   –   4

Dukes Cut Branch (No. 82g).

Length from junction with Main Line (No.82a)
   and Dukes Lock to—

Junction with River Thames (No. 107a), half-
   a-furlong above Kings Weir   ..   ..   –   6

Branch to River Thames through Isis Lock, Oxford (No. 82h).

The branch consists solely of the lock, which
   connects the main line of the canal at the
   head of the lock with a backwater of the
   River Thames at the lock tail. This
   backwater forms the Oxford Canal Branch
   of the River Thames (No. 107b)

(d) *Locks.*

Main Line (No. 82a).

1.—Hawkesbury Stop Lock.

> Rise about 6in. from the Coventry Canal.

2
to } Hillmorton (duplicate locks, side by side).
4.

5.
to } Napton.
10.

11.—Green's.

12
and } Napton Top.
13.

> Rise from Hawkesbury.

14
to } Claydon.
18.

19.—Elkington's.
20.—Varney's.
21.—Broadmoor.
22.—Cropredy.
23.—Slat Mill.
24.—Jobson's.
25.—Salmon's.
26.—Banbury.
27.—Grant's.

(82)—Oxford Canal—*continued.*

28.—Kings Sutton.
29.—Nell Bridge.
30.—Weir.
31.—Somerton.
32.—Heyford Common.
33.—Heyford Mill.
34.—Dashwood's.
35.—North Brook.
36.—Enser's Mill, or Pigeon's.
37.—Baker's, or Gibraltar.
38.—Weir, or Cherwell.
39.—Round Ham.
40.—Kidlington Green.
41.—Shuttleworth's.
42.—Wolvercote.

Fall to Oxford.

Dukes Cut Branch (No. 82g).

1.—Dukes.

Dukes Lock is fitted with gates to work in either direction, the fall being normally from the canal to the River Thames, but when the river is in flood in the reverse direction.

Branch to River Thames through Isis Lock, Oxford (No. 82h).

1.—Isis, or Louse.

Fall from Main Line of the canal to backwater leading to River Thames.

(e) *Maximum size of vessels that can use the navigation.*

Main Line (No. 82a) and Branches.

	Ft.	In.
Length	72	0
Width	7	0
Draught	3	8

With the exception of that portion of the Wyken New Collery Loop Line Branch (No. 82b) situated between the northern junction with the Main Line (No. 82a), and the junction with the Wyken Colliery Company's Canal leading to the Colliery, which is only navigable by empty boats.

| Headroom .. .. | 7 | 0 |

(f) *Tunnels.*

Main Line (No. 82a).

Newbold—

Length	250 yards	
Minimum height above water level	14	0
Minimum width at water level	15	0

Towing-path both sides, boats enter from either end at any time.

T

(82)—OXFORD CANAL—*continued*

(g) Towing-path.

There is a towing-path throughout the canal and branches.

(i) Types of vessels using the navigation.

Narrow boats. Steamers engaged in the London and Birmingham traffic regularly trade over the portion of the canal between Braunston and Napton Junction.

PADDINGTON BRANCH CANAL—*see* Grand Junction Canal.

---

(83)—PARK GATE BRANCH CANAL.

(a) Short Description.

The canal forms a branch from the main line of the Sheffield and South Yorkshire Navigation (No. 91b1) near Rotherham Road Station of the Great Central Railway, and proceeds northwards for a distance of five furlongs to Park Gate Iron Works, all in the West Riding of the county of Yorkshire.

(b) Proprietors, Officers, and Offices.

Proprietor : The Earl of Fitzwilliam.

Estate Office : Wentworth House, Wentworth.

(e) Maximum size of vessels that can use the navigation.

	Ft.	In.
Length	61	6
Width	15	3
Draught	6	6

(g) Towing-path.

There is a towing-path throughout the navigation.

(i) Types of vessels using the navigation.

Yorkshire keels.

PARKER BRANCH CANAL—*see* Birmingham Canal Navigations, Main Line.

---

(84)—RIVER PARRETT.

(a) Short Description.

The river commences to be navigable at the bridge which carries the main road between Langport and South Petherton over the river at Thorney Mills, near Langport, and proceeds by Langport, Borough Bridge, Bridgwater, Dunball, Combwich, Stert Point, and Burnham to Bridgwater Bar, where it enters Bridgwater Bay at low water, all in the county of Somersetshire.

(84)—River Parrett—*continued.*

The course of the river from Stert Point to Bridgwater Bar is through Stert Sand Flats, which are covered at high tide.

There is a good trade from the mouth of the river up to Bridgwater, the principal imports being coal and timber ; and exports, bricks and bath scouring bricks, which latter are made from the mud deposited on the river banks in the neighbourhood of Bridgwater.

Above Bridgwater there is a good trade at all times to the various brick works situated within the first two miles of the river beyond the town, but beyond this the trade is extremely small. Barges can only navigate to Langport on Spring tides, and between Langport and Thorney Mills when there is a fair amount of land water coming down the river.

The River Brue, which enters the River Parrett about a mile above Burnham, and is navigable to Highbridge, is included under the Port of Bridgwater.

Information as to the Great Western Railway Company's Bridgwater Dock will be found under Bridgwater and Taunton Canal (No. 43e).

(b) Proprietors, Officers, and Offices.

From the mouth of the river at Bridgwater Bar to a point 100 yards above Bridgwater Town Bridge, including Burnham, and also Highbridge on the River Brue, the river, as the Port of Bridgwater, is under the jurisdiction of the Corporation of the town of Bridgwater.

Town Clerk : W. T. Baker.

Office : Town Clerk's Office, Bridgwater, Somersetshire.

Borough Surveyor : Francis Parr.

Harbour Master : Captain Jobson.

Office : West Quay, Bridgwater.

The whole of the navigable portion of the river from its mouth to Thorney Mills Bridge, including the River Brue to Highbridge, is also a drainage under the jurisdiction of the Somersetshire Drainage Commissioners, who are the only authority in respect of the portion of the river above Bridgwater.

Clerk : J. Lovibond.

Office : Bridgwater.

Engineer : W. Lunn.

Office : Taunton Road, Bridgwater.

(c) Distance Table.

	Miles.	Fur.
Thorney Mills Bridge to—		
Junction of Old Westport Canal (not navigable)	–	6
Junction with River Yeo (No. 129)	3	0
Langport Bridge	3	6
Langport Flood Gates	3	$7\frac{1}{2}$

(84)—River Parrett—*continued.*

Thorney Mills Bridge to (*continued*)—

	Miles.	Fur.
Oath Flood Gates	6	4
Stathe	7	4
Borough Bridge, junction with River Tone		
(No. 111.)	9	0
Dunwear Brick Works	13	6
Bridgwater, Town Bridge	15	2
Bridgwater, entrance to Great Western Railway Company's Dock, and Bridgwater and Taunton Canal (No. 43e)	15	5
Dunball	18	6
Combwich	23	6
Stert Point	27	7
Junction with River Brue, forming branch to Highbridge	28	3
Burnham	29	2
Bridgwater Bar, Mouth of River	34	2

River Brue.

	Miles.	Fur.
Length from junction with River Parrett to Highbridge	1	4

(*d*) *Locks.*

There are no locks on the river, but there are two pair of flood gates above Bridgwater—one pair at Oath, and one pair shortly below Langport Bridge. These gates are used to maintain the level of the river in summer time for irrigation purposes, and they can only be passed by barges when the tide makes a level.

(*e*) *Maximum size of vessels that can use the navigation.*

	Ft.	In.
Length.—Not limited.		
Width.—Not limited, except through Oath and Langport Flood Gates, where the width is	14	0
Draught from Bridgwater Bar to Combwich—		
on Spring tides	27	0
on Neap tides..	17	6
Draught from Combwich to Bridgwater—		
on Spring tides	17ft. to 18ft.	
on Neap tides..	8ft. to 9ft.	

	Ft.	In.
Draught above Bridgwater on Spring tides about	3	0
Draught from the junction with the River Parrett to Highbridge on the River Brue—		
on Spring tides	20	0
on Neap tides	9	0

Headroom.—From Bridgwater Bar to Bridgwater Town Bridge, not limited.

Headroom.—Above Bridgwater the bridge at Borough Bridge is the lowest bridge on the navigation, forming a considerable obstruction to the passage of barges.

(84)—River Parrett—*continued.*

(g) *Towing-path.*

There is a towing-path from Thorney Mills Bridge to Bridgwater. There is no towing-path below Bridgwater, vessels being towed by tugs on the tide.

(h) *Tidal Information.*

High Spring tides will at times flow to Langport and affect the level of the water in the river up to the head of the navigation at Thorney Mills Bridge. Neap tides usually flow to about Borough Bridge.

The influence of the tide in the upper portion of the river depends very much on the amount of land water coming down. In summer, a high Spring tide will cause a rise of from 4ft. to 5ft. in the level of the water at Langport, when there is no land water coming down.

Below Bridgwater the tide runs strongly, and except at the lowest tides, forms a " bore " just below Combwich, which has an average height of 2ft., and a maximum height of from 3ft. to 4ft.

High water at Bridgwater Bar 4hrs. 52min. after London Bridge.

Spring tides rise	35ft.
Neap ,, ,,	26ft. 6in.

High water at Bridgwater Town 1hr. 10min. after Bridgwater Bar.

Spring tides rise	15ft.
Neap ,, ,,	6ft.

(i) *Types of vessels using the navigation.*

Sea-going vessels and coasting vessels navigate up to Bridgwater. Barges carrying about 35 tons navigate to the Brick Works within a distance of two miles above Bridgwater ; smaller barges of about 16 to 20 tons burden carry on what little trade there is on the upper portion of the river.

Peak Forest Canal—*see* Great Central Railway.

Peckham Branch Canal—*see* Surrey Canal.

---

(85)—Pensnett Canal, *alias* Lord Ward's Branch Canal.

(a) *Short Description.*

The canal commences by a junction with the Dudley Canal of the Birmingham Canal Navigations at the south end of Dudley Tunnel, and proceeds in a south-westerly direction to its termination near Round Oak Railway Station on the Oxford, Worcester, and Wolverhampton Line of the Great Western Railway, all in the county of Worcestershire.

The canal affords communication to several large and important iron works.

(85)—Pensnett Canal, *alias* Lord Ward's Branch Canal—*continued.*

(*b*) *Proprietors, Officers, and Offices.*

Proprietor : The Earl of Dudley.

Agent : G. H. Claughton, The Priory, Dudley.

(*c*) *Distance Table.*

	Miles.	Fur.
Length from junction with Dudley Canal, Line No. 1 (No. 10f1), to Round Oak	1	2

(*e*) *Maximum size of vessels that can use the navigation.*

	Ft.	In.
Length	71	6
Width	7	1½
Draught	3	6

(*g*) *Towing-path.*

There is a towing-path throughout the navigation.

(*i*) *Types of vessels using the navigation.*

Narrow boats.

Pensnett Chase Branch Canal—*see* Stourbridge Canal.

Pinxton Branch Canal—*see* Midland Railway—Cromford Canal.

Pocklington Canal—*see* North Eastern Railway.

Pontcysyllte Branch Canal—*see* Shropshire Union Canals, Ellesmere Canal.

Popham's Sea, *alias* Popham's Eau—*see* Middle Level Navigations.

Poplar Arm Branch Canal—*see* Great Northern Railway, Nottingham Canal.

Prees Branch Canal—*see* Shropshire Union Canals, Ellesmere Canal.

Press, Edward, Esq.—*see* North Walsham and Dilham Canal.

Preston Brook Branch Canal—*see* Manchester Ship Canal Company, Bridgewater Canal.

Rainham Creek—*see* River Thames.

Sir John Ramsden's Canal, *alias* The Huddersfield Broad Canal—*see* London and North Western Railway.

Ramsey High Lode—*see* Middle Level Navigations.

Ranworth Dike and Broad—*see* River Bure.

REACH LODE—*see* River Cam.

RED JACKET PILL BRANCH CANAL—*see* Tennant Canal.

---

(86)—REGENTS CANAL.

(a) Short Description.

The canal commences by a junction with the Grand Junction Canal Company's Paddington Branch Canal at Paddington, and proceeds by Marylebone, St. Johns Wood, Camden Town, St. Pancras, Islington, St. Lukes, Shoreditch, Hackney, Bethnal Green, Mile End, and Stepney to Limehouse Basin. through which it forms a junction with the River Thames.

There are short branches leading out of the main line of the canal to Cumberland Market and City Basin, and just below Old Ford Locks the Hertford Union Branch Canal leaves the main line, forming a communication with the River Lee at Old Ford.

There is a considerable traffic on the canal, especially at the Limehouse end.

The numerous wharves, business premises, and warehouses lining the banks cause the canal to partake more of the nature of an extended dock than of a waterway for through traffic.

Limehouse Basin has an acreage of ten acres, and is provided with large warehouse accommodation and extensive wharf area for the storage of goods.

(b) Proprietors, Officers, and Offices.

The Regents Canal and Dock Company.

Manager : John Glass.

Secretary : Elkanah Clarkson.

Offices : 5, Lloyd's Avenue, London, E.C.   Telegrams : " Towing, London."   Telephone No. 4007, Avenue.

(c) Distance Table.

Main Line (No. 86a).

	Miles.	Fur.
Paddington, junction with Paddington Branch of Grand Junction Canal (No. 38a8), to—		
Maida Hill Tunnel	--	3
Finchley Road Bridge	--	7
Avenue Road Bridge	1	2
Junction with Cumberland Market Branch (No. 86b)	1	7
Hampstead Road Locks and Chalk Farm Road Bridge	2	2

(86)—REGENTS CANAL—*continued*.

	Miles.	Fur.
Paddington, junction with Paddington Branch of Grand Junction Canal (No. 38a8), to (*continued*)—		
Kentish Town Locks and Kentish Town Road Bridge	2	$3\frac{1}{2}$
St. Pancras Locks	3	1
York Road Bridge	3	3
Caledonian Road Bridge	3	5
West end of Islington Tunnel	3	6
East end of Islington Tunnel	4	2
City Road Locks	4	$2\frac{1}{2}$
Junction with City Basin Branch (No. 86c) ..	4	3
Sturts Locks	4	7
Kingsland Road Bridge	5	$3\frac{1}{2}$
Acton's Locks	5	7
Cambridge Road Bridge	6	2
Old Ford Locks	6	$5\frac{1}{2}$
Junction with Hertford Union Canal (No. 86d)	6	7
Devonshire Street Goods Station, G. E. Rly...	7	1
Mile End Locks	7	3
Mile End Road Bridge	7	$3\frac{1}{2}$
Johnson's Locks..	7	6
Salmon's Lane Locks	8	$0\frac{1}{2}$
Commercial Road Locks and entrance to Limehouse Basin	8	3
Limehouse Basin Locks and junction with River Thames (No. 107a)	8	5

Cumberland Market Branch (No. 86b).

Length from junction with Main Line (No. 86a) to Cumberland Market Basin. ..	–	$5\frac{1}{2}$

City Basin Branch (No. 86c).

Junction with Main Line (No. 86a) to—		
Fellows, Morton, and Clayton Ltd. (Canal Carriers) Wharves and Warehouses ..	–	1
End of City Basin	–	$2\frac{1}{2}$

Hertford Union Canal (No. 86d).

Junction with Main Line (No. 86a) to—		
Top of Old Ford Three Locks..	–	$7\frac{1}{2}$
Junction with River Lee—Main Line—(No. 57a)	1	$1\frac{1}{2}$

(d) Locks.

Main Line (No. 86a).

1.) Hampstead Road.
2. } Hawley.
3.) Kentish Town.
4.—St. Pancras.

(86)—REGENTS CANAL—*continued.*

    5.—City Road.
    6.—Sturts.
    7.—Acton's.
    8.—Old Ford.
    9.—Mile End.
  10.—Johnson's.
  11.—Salmon's Lane.
  12.—Commercial Road.

Fall to Limehouse Basin.

All the above locks on the main line are in duplicate, side by side.

Locks giving access to River Thames from Limehouse Basin.

One Ship Lock 350ft. in length by 60ft. in width.

One Barge Lock 79ft. in length by 14ft. 6in. in width.

Fall from Limehouse Basin to River Thames at low water, level at high water.

Hertford Union Canal (No. 86d).

  1. ⎫ Upper.
  2. ⎬ Middle.
  3. ⎭ Lower.

Fall to junction with River Lee at Old Ford.

(e) Maximum size of vessels that can use the navigation.

Main Line (No. 86a), Cumberland Market Branch (No. 86b), and City Basin Branch (No. 86c).

	Ft.	In.
Length	80	0
Width	14	6
Draught	4	6
Headroom	9	9

Vessels in length and width within the dimensions of the Ship Lock given above can enter Limehouse Basin from the River Thames drawing on Spring tides 20   0

Hertford Union Canal (No. 86d).

	Ft.	In.
Length	84	0
Width	14	5
Draught	4	6

(f) Tunnels.

Main Line (No. 86a).

Maida Hill—
  Length .. .. 272 yards
  Minimum height above water level 9   11
  Minimum width at water level 16   9

No towing-path; barges and boats " legged " or " shafted " through.

(86)—Regents Canal—*continued.*

<table>
<tr><td></td><td>Ft.</td><td>In.</td></tr>
</table>

Islington—
    Length   ..   ..   960 yards
    Minimum height above water level   9   9
    Minimum width at water level   17   0

No towing-path; barges and boats worked through by the Company's tug, leaving the East end of the tunnel at 4-0 a.m., 6-0 a.m., 8-0 a.m., 10-0 a.m., 12 noon, 2-0 p.m., 4-0 p.m., 6-0 p.m., and 8-0 p.m., and the West end at 5-0 a.m., 7-0 a.m., 9-0 a.m., 11-0 a.m., 1-0 p.m., 3-0 p.m., 5-0 p.m., 7-0 p.m., and 9-0 p.m.

(g) Towing-path.

There is a towing-path throughout the navigation, except through the two tunnels on the main line enumerated above.

(i) Types of vessels using the navigation.

Barges, wide boats, and narrow boats. Sea-going and coasting vessels use Limehouse Basin.

Ridgacre Branch Canal—*see* Birmingham Canal Navigations, Wednesbury Old Canal.

Ripon and Boroughbridge Canal—*see* North Eastern Railway, River Ure Navigation.

---

(87)—Rochdale Canal.

(a) Short Description.

The canal commences at Sowerby Bridge by a junction with the Calder and Hebble Navigation, and proceeds by Mytholmroyd, Hebden Bridge, Todmorden, and Walsden to the summit level at Warland, all in the West Riding of the county of Yorkshire. It then enters the county of Lancashire, and proceeds by Littleborough, Rochdale, Castleton, Failsworth, Newton Heath, and Miles Platting to Castle Field, in the City of Manchester, where it forms a junction with the Manchester Ship Canal Company's Bridgewater Canal.

There are two branches: one from near Rochdale to Rochdale Wharves, and the other from Maden Fold, near Castleton, to Heywood.

The bulk of the trade on the canal is carried on for a few miles from both extremities. There is very little through traffic from end to end, the large number of locks to be worked making progress very slow.

(b) Proprietors, Officers, and Offices.

Rochdale Canal Company.

Secretary and General Manager :   C. R. Dykes.

Office : 75, Dale Street, Manchester.   Telegrams : " Rochcan."

Engineer : H. Brooke.

Office : Canal Yard, Rochdale.

The Proprietors act as carriers.

(87)—ROCHDALE CANAL—*continued.*

(c) *Distance Table.*

Main Line (No. 87a).

	Miles.	Fur.
Sowerby Bridge, junction with Calder and Hebble Navigation (No. 17a), to—		
Sowerby Bridge Wharf and Wharf Mill ..	–	2
Fourth Lock, Bates' Foundry, and Smith's Yard..	–	4
Morris's Mill, Firth's Foundry, and Greenwood's Mill	–	6
Hollin's Mill	1	0
High Royd	1	4
Longbottom Bridge	1	6
Crowther's Mill and Copper House Mill ..	2	0
Denholme	2	2
Luddenden Foot Wharf	2	4
Luddenden Upper Foot	2	6
Brearley Bridge and Mill	3	2
Ewood Holmes	3	4
Mytholmroyd Wharf	4	2
Broadbottom and Hawksclough	4	4
Pothouse and Fallingroyd Bridge	4	6
End Mayroyd Estate	5	0
Mayroyd Mill	5	4
Hebden Bridge Wharf	5	6
Hebble End Crane	6	0
Mytholm and Stubbings	6	2
Horsehold Wood or Whiteley's Mill	6	4
Rawden Mill Lock, No. 12	7	0
Callis Bridge	7	2
Burnt-acres Bridge, and Eastwood, or Wood Mill	7	6
Holmcoat Lock, No. 14..	8	0
Stoodley Bridge and Hinchcliffe's Mill ..	8	2
Shaw Bridge	8	4
Lob Mill, Ingham's Mill, and Woodhouse Bridge	9	0
Millwood	9	2
Kilnhurst Bridge, Sandholme Wharf, and Derdale Mill	9	4
Baltimore Bridge	9	6
Todmorden Wharf and Waterside	10	0
Dobroyd	10	2
Shade	10	4
Gauxholme Wharf	10	6
Copperas House Mill and Smithy Holme ..	11	0
Holling's Clough and Lacy's Mill	11	4
Inchfield Mill, Travis Mill, Birk's Wharf, and Walsden	11	6
Nip Square and Winterbutlee	12	0
Light Bank Lock, No 31	12	2
Deanroyd Bridge and Lane Bottom	12	4
Stonehouse	12	6
Warland Wharf and East Summit Lock, No. 36 ..	13	0

(87)—Rochdale Canal—*continued.*

	Miles.	Fur.
Sowerby Bridge, junction with Calder and Hebble Navigation (No. 17a), to (*continued*)—		
Steanorbottom	13	2
Longlees	13	4
West Summit Lock, No. 37	13	6
Chelburn, Sladen Wood, Tetlow's Wharf, Punchbowl Wharf, and Rock Nook ..	14	0
Tappit Mill, Green Vale Mill, and Sladen Mill Bridge	14	4
Benthouse and Windy Bank	15	0
Durn Wharf and Littleborough Bridge ..	15	4
Littleborough Wharf	15	6
Cleggswood Collery Staith	16	0
Bank Bridge	16	2
Brown Lodge and Smithy Bridge	16	6
Little Clegg	17	0
Clegg Hall Bridge	17	4
Belfield Mill	17	6
Belfield Hall, Fir Grove, and Wallhead ..	18	0
Moss Swivel Bridge	18	6
Walker Bridge	19	0
King's Mills	19	4
Royd's Branch, Moss Lock Bridge, and junction with Rochdale Branch (No. 87b), between Locks Nos. 50 and 51	19	6
Lower Place Bridge	20	0
Dicken Green Mill	20	2
Lower Hey	20	4
Hartley Bridge	20	6
Gorrell's Bridge	21	0
March Barn Bridge	21	2
Castleton and Marland	21	4
Blue Pits Lower Lock, No. 53..	21	6
Maden Fold, Trub Smithy, and junction with Heywood Branch (No. 87c), between Locks Nos. 53 and 54	22	0
Hopwood Moss	22	6
Slattock's and Laneside	23	2
Touchet Hall	23	6
Andrew's Coal Pit	24	0
Boarshaw Lane	24	2
Scowcroft Lane	24	4
Walk Mill, M'Dougall's Works..	24	6
Chadderton Bridge, Mill's Hill Wharf, and Irishman's Bridge	25	0
Boundary Mill	25	2
Firwood Mill, Kay Lane Lock No. 64, Linnet Wharf, and Slack's Valley..	26	0
Whitegate Bridge	27	0
Earnshaw Lane	27	2
Bower Collery Coal Staith and Wrigley Head Bridge	27	4
Tail of Failsworth Lock, No. 65	28	0

(87)—ROCHDALE CANAL—*continued.*

	Miles.	Fur.
Sowerby Bridge, junction with Calder and Hebble Navigation (No. 17a), to (*continued*)—		
Back Lane Bridge	28	4
Tanner's Field	28	6
Newton Heath	29	0
Newton Heath Swivel Bridge	29	2
Ten-acres Mill	29	6
Grimshaw Wharf	30	0
Anthony Lock, No. 77	30	2
Miles Platting, Coal Pit Lock No. 80	30	4
Miles Platting, Cobler Lock No. 81	30	6
Butler Lane and Bengal Arm	31	0
Pott Street Arm	31	2
Brownsfield Arm, north and south	31	4
Manchester, Brownsfield Lock No. 83, Dale Street Wharves and Warehouses, and Ducie Street, junction with Ashton Canal (No. 39a1), between Locks No. 83 and 84	31	6
Manchester, Chorlton Street, and Dickinson Street Arms	32	2
Manchester, Tib Lock, No. 89	32	4
Manchester, Deansgate Coal Wharves	32	6
Manchester, Castle Field, junction with Bridgewater Canal (No. 64b1)	33	0

In calculating the distances for all purposes of rates, tolls, and charges, each quarter-of-a-mile of the distance between the junction of the canal with the Bridgewater Canal and Brownsfield Lock shall be taken as equal to a distance of three-quarters-of-a-mile, and each quarter-of-a-mile of the distance between Brownsfield Lock and Failsworth Lock shall be taken as equal to a distance of half-a-mile ; and the distance at the Summit Pool (situated between Littleborough and Todmorden) for traffic which passes through the Locks at each end of the Summit Pool shall be taken as equal to five miles.

Rochdale Branch (No. 87b).

	Miles.	Fur.
Length from junction with Main Line (No. 87a) to Rochdale Wharves and Warehouses	–	4

Heywood Branch (No. 87c).

	Miles.	Fur.
Length from junction with Main Line (No. 87a) to Heywood	1	4

(d) *Locks.*

Main Line (No. 87a).

1 to 4. } Sowerby Bridge.

5 and 6. } Brearley.

(87)—Rochdale Canal—*continued.*

    7.—Broadbottom.
    8.—Mayroyd Mill.
    9.—Black Pit.

10
and } Stubbing.
11.

12
and } Rawdon Mill.
13.   Callis.

  14.—Holmcoat.
  15.—Shawplains.
  16.—Lob Mill.
  17.—Old Royd.

18
and } Todmorden.
19.

20
to } Gauxholme.
24.

25
to } Walsden.
30.

31. } Light Bank.
32.   Sands.
33. } Bottomley.

34
to } Warland.
36.

Rise from Sowerby Bridge.

37
to } West Summit.
45.

  46.—Benthouse.

47
and } Littleborough.
48.

49
and } Rochdale.
50.

51
to } Blue Pits, Castleton.
53.

54
to } Laneside.
59.

  60—Boarshaw.

61
to } Walk Mill.
63.

  64.—Kay Lane.
  65.—Failsworth.

66
to } Tanners Field
68.

(87)—ROCHDALE CANAL—*continued*.

69.—Newton Heath.

70
to } Ten-acres.
76.

77.—Anthony.

78
to } Miles Platting.
81.

82.—Ancoats Lane,
83.—Brownsfield,
84.—Dale Street,
85.—Piccadilly,
86.—Chorlton Street,
87.—Princess Street, } Manchester.
88.—Oxford Street,
89.—Tib,
90.—Albion Mills,
91.—Tunnel,
92.—Castle Field,

Fall to Manchester.

(e) *Maximum size of vessels that can use the navigation*

Main Line (No. 87a) and Branches

	Ft.	In.
Length	72	0
Width	14	2
Draught from Sowerby Bridge to Ducie Street, Manchester, the junction with the Ashton Canal; and Rochdale and Heywood Branches .. .. .. maximum	4	0
Draught from Ducie Street, Manchester, the junction with the Ashton Canal, to Castle Field, Manchester .. .. maximum	4	2
Headroom	8	11

(f) *Tunnels.*

Main Line (No. 87a).

Sowerby Long Bridge—

Length	43 yards	
Minimum height above water level	11	7
Minimum width at water level	16	6

Towing-path through the tunnel.

Knott Mill, Manchester—

Length	78 yards	
Minimum height above water level	10	2
Minimum width at water level	15	6

No towing-path ; boats " shafted " through.

(g) *Towing-path.*

There is a towing-path throughout the navigation, except through Knott Mill Tunnel in Manchester.

(87)—ROCHDALE CANAL—*continued.*

(*i*) *Types of vessels using the navigation.*

Mersey flats and narrow boats. The Rochdale Canal Company are the proprietors of several steamboats engaged in their carrying trade.

ROCHDALE BRANCH CANAL—*see* Rochdale Canal.

ROCKLAND DIKE AND BROAD—*see* River Yare.

---

(88)—RIVER RODING.

(*a*) *Short Description.*

The river is navigable on Spring tides from Ilford Bridge, Great Ilford, to Barking, where, through Barking Sluice, it enters the head of Barking Creek, which is under the jurisdiction of the Thames Conservancy, all in the county of Essex.

There is a small trade to Ilford in bricks, lime, coal, and building materials.

(*b*) *Proprietors, Officers, and Offices.*

The river is under the jurisdiction of the Essex Sewers Commission as a drainage.

Clerk : W. C. Clifton.

Office : Romford, Essex.

Marsh Bailiff : A. Carter, 8, Cambridge Road, Barking.

(*c*) *Distance Table.*

	Miles.	Fur.
Ilford Bridge to—		
Barking Bridge	1	4
Tail of Barking Sluice and junction with head of Barking Creek—River Thames (No. 107g)	1	6

(*d*) *Locks.*

1.—Barking Sluice.

This sluice has a single pair of gates only, and vessels can only pass when the tide makes a level.

Fall to Barking Creek except at high water.

(*e*) *Maximum size of vessels that can use the navigation.*

	Ft.	In.
Length.—Not limited.		
Width through Barking Sluice must not exceed	16	4
Draught on Spring tides .. maximum	5	6
Headroom.—There is a low bridge at Barking Sluice.		

(88)—River Roding—*continued.*

(*g*) *Towing-path.*

There is no towing-path.

(*h*) *Tidal Information.*

The tide flows to Ilford.

High water at Barking 25min. before London Bridge.

High water at Ilford the same time as at London Bridge.

(*i*) *Types of vessels using the navigation.*

Barges carrying about 100 tons. Steamers come up to the head of Barking Creek from the Thames, but do not navigate this river on account of the low bridge at Barking Sluice.

Rother River Branch Navigation—*see* Sheffield and South Yorkshire Navigation, River Dun Navigation.

Royal Military Canal, or Shorncliffe and Rye Canal.

The canal extends from Shorncliffe, in the county of Kent, to Rye, in the county of Sussex, and is nearly 30 miles in length. The canal is not now navigable, and was originally constructed as a work of defence. The *Edinburgh Encyclopædia*, 1830, says :—
" Mr. Pitt was a great promoter of the canal, which was commenced in 1804 under the direction of the Quartermaster-General his assistant (Colonel Browne) having the management of the practical operations."

The canal is kept filled with fresh water, and is the property of the War Department of His Majesty's Government, who let the fishing and pleasure-boating to the South Eastern and Chatham Railway Company. There are dams of timber across the canal in different places so as to divide it off into sections for the purpose of cleaning, etc.

Rufford Branch Canal, or Lower Douglas Navigation—*see* Leeds and Liverpool Canal.

Rugby Wharf Branch Canal—*see* Oxford Canal.

Runcorn and Latchford Canal—*see* Manchester Ship Canal Company, Mersey and Irwell Navigation.

Runcorn and Weston Canal—*see* Manchester Ship Canal Company.

Rushall Canal—*see* Birmingham Canal Navigations.

U

ST. HELENS CANAL—*see* London and North Western Railway.

ST. QUINTIN, W. H., ESQ.—*see* Driffield Navigation, Frodingham Beck.

ST. THOMAS'S CREEK—*see* River Lee.

ST. THOMAS'S MILL STREAM—*see* River Lee.

SALHOUSE BROAD, GREAT—*see* River Bure.

SALHOUSE BROAD, LITTLE—*see* River Bure.

SANDHILLS BRANCH CANAL—*see* Great Western Railway, Stourbridge Extension Canal.

SANDWICH, CORPORATION OF THE TOWN OF—*see* River Stour (Kent).

SANKEY CANAL, an old name for the St. Helens Canal—*see* London and North Western Railway.

SELBY BRANCH CANAL—*see* Aire and Calder Navigation.

---

(89)—RIVER SEVERN.

(a) Short Description.

The navigation of the River Severn may be said to commence at Arley Quarry Landing, between Upper Arley and Highley, in the county of Shropshire. Regular trade on the river is, however, only carried on between the junction with the Staffordshire and Worcestershire Canal at Stourport and the junction with the Gloucester and Berkeley Ship Canal in Gloucester.

In times of full water a few boats navigate from Stourport up to Bewdley and Arley, but the trade is very small.

Leaving Arley, the river proceeds by Bewdley, Stourport, Hampstall, Holt, Grimley, Hawford, Hallow, Worcester, Diglis, Kempsey, Pixham, Clevelode, Rhydd, Severn Stoke, and Upton-on-Severn, in the county of Worcestershire ; Tewkesbury, Chaceley, Deerhurst, The Haw, Ashleworth, Gloucester, Elmore, Minsterworth, Framilode, Newnham, and Fretherne to Sharpness, in the county of Gloucestershire, and thence to Aust, Beachley, Avonmouth, etc.

The portion of the river between Sharpness and Gloucester, to avoid which the Gloucester and Berkeley Ship Canal was constructed, is hardly used at all for navigation on account of the dangerous shifting sands and great strength of the tide. Occasionally, however, it is used by trows desirous of saving the tolls incurred on the Gloucester and Berkeley Ship Canal.

(89)—RIVER SEVERN—*continued.*

After leaving Gloucester the river soon widens out into an estuary, which, between Fretherne and the Severn Tunnel, varies between five furlongs and 2¼ miles in width. Below the Severn Tunnel the estuary again increases in width, and finally becomes merged into the Bristol Channel.

The whole course of the river above Gloucester is very liable to floods.

In a paper read before the Institution of Civil Engineers in 1860, Mr. Edward Leader Williams stated that the floods in the river had been known to rise eighteen feet in five hours, and not unfrequently to attain to a height of twenty-five feet above the level of low water.

The western channel of the river from the Upper Parting via Maisemore to the Lower Parting in Gloucester is not a through route, but is only used by vessels going to local wharves.

(b) *Proprietors, Officers, and Offices.*

Above the point where Gladder or Whitehouse Brook enters the river near Stourport, the river is an open navigation, having no controlling authority.

From Gladder or Whitehouse Brook to the Lower Parting, Gloucester, including the Maisemore Channel from the Upper Parting to the point of junction with the old Herefordshire and Gloucestershire Canal, the river is under the jurisdiction of the Severn Commissioners.

Clerk : Thomas Southall.

Office : Bank Buildings, Cross, Worcester.

Engineer : E. D. Marten, The Birches, Codsall, near Wolverhampton.

Telegrams :—" Marten, Birches, Codsall," and 13, Victoria Street, Westminster, London, S.W.

Superintendent : John Bradley.

Office : Diglis Locks, Worcester.

Below the Lower Parting, Gloucester, the river is an open navigation, having no controlling authority.

(c) *Distance Table.*

Main Line of River (No. 89a).

	Miles.	Fur.
Arley Quarry Landing to—		
Upper Arley Ferry	1	4
Bewdley Bridge	5	2
Gladder or Whitehouse Brook enters River ..	8	3
Stourport Bridge	9	0
Stourport, junction with Staffordshire and Worcestershire Canal (No. 95a) ..	9	1
Lincomb Lock ..	10	3
Hampstall Ferry	11	4
Lenchford Ferry	13	6
Holt Lock	14	5

(89)—RIVER SEVERN—*continued.*

	Miles.	Fur.
Arley Quarry Landing to (*continued*)—		
Holt Village	15	4
Grimley	17	0
Hawford, junction with Droitwich Canal (No. 90d)	17	5
Bevere Lock	18	1
Hallow	19	0
Pope Iron	20	3
Worcester Quay	21	4
Diglis, junction with Worcester and Birmingham Canal (No. 90b)	22	0
Diglis Locks	22	3
Kempsey	25	1
Pixham	25	5
Clevelode	27	2
Rhydd	28	3
Severn Stoke	29	2
Hanley	31	0
Upton-on-Severn	32	0
Sextons Lode	33	4
Barley House	34	4
Dowdeswell's Elms	36	4
Tewkesbury Bridge (Bushley distant 1½ miles)	37	5
Tewkesbury, junction with River Avon (No. 8)	38	0
Tewkesbury Lock	38	4
Tewkesbury, Lower Lode and Ferry ..	39	3
Chaceley (right bank), Deerhurst (left bank)..	40	7
Apperley	42	0
Haw Bridge	42	6
Coombe Hill	43	7
Wainlode	44	1
Ashleworth	46	1
Upper Parting, junction with Maisemore Channel from Upper Parting to Lower Parting (No. 89b)	48	4
Gloucester, Westgate Bridge	50	5
Gloucester, junction with Gloucester and Berkeley Ship Canal (No. 90a)	51	0
Gloucester, Llanthony Lock	51	3
Gloucester, Lower Parting, junction with Maisemore Channel from Upper Parting to Lower Parting (No. 89b)	52	0

Left Bank			Right Bank	
Miles.	Fur.		Miles.	Fur.
55	3	Stone Bench.		
55	6	Elmore.		
		Minsterworth	57	6
63	6	Framilode, junction with Stroudwater Canal (No. 100).		
		Newnham	68	4
		Bullo Pill	69	4
72	2	Fretherne		
78	4	Severn Bridge	78	4

(89)—RIVER SEVERN—*continued.*

Left Bank			Right Bank	
Miles.	Fur.		Miles.	Fur.
		Arley Quarry Landing to (*continued*)—		
79	1	Sharpness Point, junction with old entrance to Gloucester and Berkeley Ship Canal (No. 90a).		
79	6	Sharpness, junction with entrance to Sharpness Docks and Gloucester and Berkeley Ship Canal (No. 90a).		
		Junction with Lydney Harbour and Canal (No. 64)	81	0
91	0	Aust Cliff.		
		Beachley Point, and junction with River Wye (No. 127)	92	0
94	4	Severn Tunnel	94	4
100	4	Avonmouth, junction with River Avon, Bristol (No. 7).		

Maisemore Channel from Upper Parting to Lower Parting (No. 89b).

		Miles.	Fur.
Upper Parting, junction with Main Line of River (No. 89a), to—			
Maisemore Lock		–	2
Maisemore Bridge		–	4
Junction of Old Herefordshire and Gloucestershire Canal—now closed		1	3
Gloucester, Lower Parting, junction with Main Line of River (No. 89a)		1	7

(d) *Locks.*

Main Line of River (No. 89a).

1.—Lincomb.
2.—Holt.
3.—Bevere, or Camp.
4.—Diglis (two locks side by side).
5.—Upper Lode, Tewkesbury.
6.—Llanthony.

Fall from Stourport.

Maisemore Channel from Upper Parting to Lower Parting (No. 89b).

1.—Maisemore.

Fall from Upper Parting.

(e) *Maximum size of vessels that can use the navigation.*

Main Line of River (No. 89a).

	Ft.	In.
Length up to the tail of Llanthony Lock, Gloucester—not limited.		
Length from the tail of Llanthony Lock to the junction with the Gloucester and Berkeley Ship Canal, Gloucester	90	0

(89)—River Severn—*continued*.

	Ft.	In.
Length from the junction with the Gloucester and Berkeley Ship Canal, Gloucester, to Worcester Quay	135	0
Length above Worcester Quay..	87	0
Width up to the tail of Llanthony Lock, Gloucester—not limited.		
Width from the tail of Llanthony Lock to the junction with the Gloucester and Berkeley Ship Canal, Gloucester	17	6
Width from the junction with the Gloucester and Berkeley Ship Canal, Gloucester, to Worcester Quay	22	0
Width above Worcester Quay	15	6
Draught up to Sharpness Docks, on Spring tides	24	0
Draught through Llanthony Lock, Gloucester	7	0
Draught from the junction with the Gloucester and Berkeley Ship Canal, Gloucester, to Worcester Quay	8	0 to 9ft.
Draught from Worcester Quay to Stourport ..	6	0
Draught above Stourport, entirely dependent on the amount of land water coming down the river.		
Headroom up to the junction with the Gloucester and Berkeley Ship Canal, Gloucester, not limited, except for Severn Bridge Railway Bridge, just above Sharpness, which is not low.		
Headroom from the junction with the Gloucester and Berkeley Ship Canal, Gloucester, to Stourport, being the headroom under Westgate Bridge, Gloucester, at low summer level	17	0

Maisemore Channel from Upper Parting to Lower Parting (No. 89b).

	Ft.	In.
Length through Maisemore Lock	73	0
Width through Maisemore Lock	7	3
Draught	4	2
Headroom	24	9

(g) *Towing-path.*

Main Line of River (No. 89a).

There is a towing-path throughout the upper portion of the navigation from Arley Quarry Landing to Gloucester. From Arley to Bewdley the towing-path and river bank is much overgrown with bushes. From Stourport to Gloucester the towing-path is not the property of the Severn Commissioners, but is in the hands of two separate companies, one extending from Stourport to Worcester, and the other from Worcester to Gloucester. The towing-path between Stourport and Gloucester is very little used, as steam tugs haul practically the whole of the traffic.

(89)—RIVER SEVERN—*continued.*

Maisemore Channel from Upper Parting to Lower Parting (No. 89b).

There is no towing-path.

(*h*) *Tidal Information.*

High Spring tides flow to Upton-on-Severn, and effect the level of the water in the river up to the tail of Diglis Locks.

Neap tides flow to between Framilode and Gloucester.

On Spring tides the first of the flood tide runs up the lower part of the river to Gloucester with a " bore " or tidal wave, which attains its greatest height about Stone Bench. A tide giving from 15ft. to 16ft. of water on the sill of Bathurst Basin Lock, Bristol, which is about midway between the highest and lowest tides, will set up a " bore " in the river.

The tide in the river below Gloucester runs with great velocity, which is stated on Spring tides to be as much as 12 knots an hour past Sharpness Point.

High water at Avonmouth about 15min. before Bristol or 5hrs. after London Bridge.

Spring tides rise about	..	36ft. 6in.
Neap ,, ,, ,, ..	..	25ft.

High water at Sharpness about 1hr. after Avonmouth.

Spring tides rise about	..	28ft.
Neap ,, ,, ,, ..	..	15ft.

High water at Framilode about 1hr. 45min. after Avonmouth.

Spring tides rise about	..	10ft.

High water at Gloucester on Spring tides about 2hrs. 45min. after Avonmouth.

Spring tides rise	.. ..	4ft. to 7ft.

A tide giving 17ft. of water on the sill of Bathurst Basin Lock at Bristol will flow above the weir of Llanthony Lock, Gloucester.

High water at Tewkesbury on Spring tides about 3hrs. 45min. after Avonmouth.

High water at Upton-on-Severn on Spring tides about 4hrs. 30min. after Avonmouth.

High water at the tail of Diglis Locks, on Spring tides about 5hrs. 10min. after Avonmouth.

Spring tides rise up to ..	..	1ft.

(*i*) *Types of vessels using the navigation.*

Sea-going vessels navigate the river up to Sharpness Docks. Vessels of 200 tons burden can navigate up to Diglis, Worcester. Severn trows navigate the whole of the river. Narrow boats navigate the river above

(89)—RIVER SEVERN—*continued.*

the entrance of the Gloucester and Berkeley Ship Canal at Gloucester. Steam tugs belonging to the Severn and Canal Carrying Company tow vessels regularly between Gloucester and Diglis, and between Diglis and Stourport.

---

(90)—SHARPNESS NEW DOCKS AND GLOUCESTER AND BIRMINGHAM NAVIGATION COMPANY.

(a) *Short Description.*

The canals belonging to the Company are the Gloucester and Berkeley Ship Canal and the Worcester and Birmingham Canal. The Company are also the Lessees of the Droitwich Canal and the Droitwich Junction Canal.

The Gloucester and Berkeley Ship Canal commences by a junction with the River Severn at Gloucester, and after passing numerous wharves and warehouses in the city proceeds to Sharpness, where it forms a junction with the estuary of the River Severn through Sharpness Docks, all in the county of Gloucestershire. Eight miles from Gloucester, near Saul, the canal crosses the Stroudwater Canal on the level.

The canal was constructed to avoid the navigation of the dangerous reaches of the River Severn between Sharpness and Gloucester. Practically the whole of the traffic above Sharpness to Gloucester, and places beyond, passes over the canal.

The Worcester and Birmingham Canal commences by a junction with the main line of the Birmingham Canal Navigations at Worcester Bar, Birmingham, and proceeds by Edgbaston, in the county of Warwickshire, Selly Oak, Bournville, Lifford, King's Norton, Hopwood, Alvechurch, Tardebigge, Stoke Prior, Hanbury Wharf, Hadzor, Oddingley, Tibberton, and Hindlip to Worcester, in the county of Worcestershire, where it forms a junction with the River Severn shortly above the Diglis Locks. The canal is remarkable as having no less than fifty-eight locks, in which are included the famous flight of thirty at Tardebigge ; the whole of the locks are within the last fifteen-and-a-half miles of the canal nearest Worcester.

The Droitwich Junction Canal forms a link between the Worcester and Birmingham Canal at Hanbury Wharf and the Droitwich Canal in the town of Droitwich, all in the county of Worcestershire.

The Droitwich Canal commences by a junction with the Droitwich Junction Canal in the town of Droitwich, and proceeds by Salwarpe and Ladywood to Hawford, where it forms a junction with the River Severn, all in the county of Worcestershire.

(b) *Proprietors, Officers, and Offices.*

Sharpness New Docks and Gloucester and Birmingham Navigation Company.

General Manager and Secretary : Hubert Waddy.

Office : Gloucester. Telegrams : " Waddy, Docks, Gloucester."

Telephone No. 62.

Engineer : F. A. Jones.

(90)—Sharpness New Docks and Gloucester and Birmingham Navigation Company—*continued.*

District Superintendent of Worcester and Birmingham Canal Section, including Droitwich Junction and Droitwich Canals : W. D. George.

Office : 4, Gas Street, Birmingham. Telegrams: " George, Gas Street, Birmingham."

Engineer of Worcester and Birmingham Canal Section : W. F. Hobrough.

Office : Stoke Prior, near Bromsgrove.

The Droitwich Junction Canal Company was incorporated in 1852, and leased at the same date to the Sharpness New Docks and Gloucester and Birmingham Navigation Company for 99 years.

Secretary : W. D. George.

Office : 4, Gas Street, Birmingham.

The Droitwich Canal was leased in 1874 to the Sharpness New Docks and Gloucester and Birmingham Navigation Company for 999 years.

Proprietors : The Droitwich Canal Company.

Clerk : Frank Holyoke.

Office : Droitwich.

Gloucester and Berkeley Ship Canal (No. 90a).

(c) *Distance Table.*

	Miles.	Fur.
Gloucester, Entrance Lock, and junction with River Severn (No. 89a), to—		
Hempsted	1	3
Hardwicke	4	6
Parkend Bridge	6	2
Saul, junction with Stroudwater Canal (No.100) right and left	8	0
Splatt Bridge	10	0
Purton	14	4
Sharpness, junction with old line of canal three furlongs in length to River Severn (No.89a) at Sharpness Point	16	0
Sharpness, lock giving access to Tidal Basin	16	4
Sharpness, Tidal Basin Gates, and junction with River Severn (No. 89a)	16	6

For all purposes of tolls and charges in respect of any merchandise which is conveyed in a boat through the Severn Locks at Gloucester, and is loaded or unloaded at any place on the canal situate within two miles from the said locks, the distance traversed by such boat on the canal shall be taken as equal to four miles.

(d) *Locks.*

1.—Gloucester.
Rise from River Severn.
2.—Sharpness, giving access from canal to Sharpness Tidal Basin.
Fall to Tidal Basin.

(90)—Sharpness New Docks and Gloucester and Birmingham Navigation Company—*continued.*

Old Line of Canal at Sharpness to River Severn at Sharpness Point.

One barge lock and one ship lock, being alternative outlets to River Severn.

Fall to River Severn.

(e) *Maximum size of vessels that can use the navigation.*

The dimensions of the locks on the Canal are as follows :—

	Ft.	In.
Gloucester—		
Length	144	0
Width	22	9
Depth of water on sill	10	0
Sharpness Lock from canal to Tidal Basin—		
Length	320	0
Width	60	0
Depth of water on sill	24	0

Old Line of Canal at Sharpness to River Severn at Sharpness Point.

	Ft.	In.
Ship Lock—		
Length	163	0
Width	38	0
Depth of water on sill	18	0
Barge Lock—		
Length	31	6
Width	19	6
Depth of water on sill	18	0
Depth of water in Sharpness Docks	25	0
Width of entrance from Tidal Basin to River Severn	60	0

Sailing vessels may navigate the canal when the water is at its full height—

If not exceeding 180ft. in length and 33ft. 6in. in breadth, and not exceeding :

	Aft.		Forward.	
	Ft.	In.	Ft.	In.
500 tons register ..	15	0	15	0
501 to 550　　,, ..	14	9	14	6
551 to 600　　,, ..	14	6	14	3
601 to 650　　,, ..	14	3	14	0
651 and upwards ,, ..	14	0	13	6

If from 181ft. to 200ft. in length they must not exceed 33ft. beam, and must be lightened to 13ft. 9in. aft and 13ft. 6in. forward.

(90)—SHARPNESS NEW DOCKS AND GLOUCESTER AND BIRMINGHAM
NAVIGATION COMPANY—*continued.*

	Aft.			Forward.	
	Ft.	In.		Ft.	In.

Steamers not exceeding 32ft. beam
may navigate the canal when
the water is at its full height
at the following draughts—

				Aft. Ft.	In.		Forward. Ft.	In.
If under 160ft. long	..	..		14	6	..	14	3
,, 180ft. ,,	..	..		14	3	..	14	0
,, 225ft. ,,	..	..		14	0	..	13	6

Any steamer exceeding 32ft. beam or 225ft. in length can only pass
up the canal by special permission, and at such draught as the Harbour
Master may direct.

(g) Towing-path.

There is a towing-path throughout the navigation.

(h) Tidal Information.

The tide from the River Severn at Sharpness does not flow beyond
Sharpness Tidal Basin—*see* Tidal Information, River Severn.

(i) Types of vessels using the navigation.

Sea-going vessels, Severn trows, barges, and narrow boats.

Worcester and Birmingham Canal (No. 90b).

(c) Distance Table.

	Miles.	Fur.
Birmingham, Worcester Bar, junction with Birmingham Canal Navigations, Main Line (No. 10a1), to—		
Birmingham, Granville Street Bridge	–	2
Birmingham, Davenport's Brewery	–	3
Birmingham, Sturge's and Bloxham's Wharves	–	4
Edgbaston Brewery	–	6
Islington and Wheeley's Road Wharves ..	–	7
Stop Gates, Worcester end of Edgbaston Valley	1	6
Prichett's Wharf	2	2
Metchley Park Tip	2	4
Kirby's Pool Tip	2	6
Selly Oak Wharves, and junction with Birmingham Canal Navigations, Dudley Canal, Line No. 2 (No. 10f2)	3	0
Elliott's, Hudson's, and Enamel Works ..	3	2
Stirchley Street Tip	4	0
Cadbury's, Sparrey's, and Prescott's Wharves	4	2
Endurance Tube, etc., Company's Works ..	4	3
Nettlefold's, Breedon Cross Wharf, Vale's Timber Yard, and Lifford Goods Station	4	6
King's Norton Sanitary Authority's Wharf ..	5	0
King's Norton Metal Company's Works and Baldwin's Wharf	5	3
King's Norton Junction, junction with Stratford-on-Avon Canal (No. 43b1)	5	4
King's Norton Wharves	5	6
King's Norton Tunnel Tug Coal Shed	6	2
Hopwood Wharf	8	6

(90)—Sharpness New Docks and Gloucester and Birmingham Navigation Company—*continued.*

	Miles.	Fur.
Birmingham, Worcester Bar, junction with Birmingham Canal Navigations, Main Line (No. 10a1), to (*continued*)—		
Junction with Bittall Arm (four furlongs in length)	9	4
Bittall Arm Wharf	10	0
Bittall Wharf	9	6
Lane House Wharf	10	0
Cooper's Hill Wharf	10	4
Withybed Green	10	6
Wynn's Brick Works and Scarfield's Wharf ..	11	0
Grange Wharf	11	6
Shortwood Tunnel Wharf	12	2
Harris' Bridge	12	6
Tardebigge Old Wharf	13	2
Tardebigge Crane	13	4
Tardebigge New Wharf	14	0
London Lane, Engine House, and Tardebigge Top Lock	14	4
Round Pond	15	0
Half-way House Bridge	15	2
Bate's Wharf (between Locks Nos. 30 and 31)	16	2
Thompson's House	16	4
Stoke Prior Wharf (Lock No. 36)	17	2
Stoke Prior Salt Works Central	18	0
Gittus Mill	18	2
Lock No. 42	19	2
Groves' Brick Works	20	4
Hanbury Wharf, and junction with Droitwich Junction Canal (No. 90c)	20	6
Hadzor Wharf	21	2
Dunhampstead Old Tramway Wharf ..	22	2
Dunhampstead Wharf	22	4
Oddingley Brick Works	23	2
Tibberton Wharf	24	2
Lock No. 43	24	6
Hindlip Wharf	25	2
Tolladine Private Wharf	26	0
Blackpole Wharf	26	6
Bilford Bridge	27	6
Worcester, Gregory's Mill and Lock No. 53 ..	28	0
Worcester, Barker's Brick Works and Wharves	28	2
Worcester, Lansdown and Horn Lane Bridge	28	4
Worcester, Lowesmoor Wharves	29	0
Worcester, Tallow Hill, Blockhouse and Sidbury	29	2
Worcester, Porcelain Works and Lucy and Townshend's Mill	29	6
Worcester, Diglis Basin, Diglis Locks, and junction with River Severn (No. 89a) ..	30	0

In calculating the distances for all purposes of tolls and charges, each quarter of a mile of the first six miles of the canal at the Birmingham end shall be taken as equal to a distance of three-eighths of a mile.

(90)—Sharpness New Docks and Gloucester and Birmingham Navigation Company—*continued.*

(d) Locks.

1 to 30. } Tardebigge.

31 to 36. } Stoke Prior.

37 to 42. } Dodder Hill.

43 to 48. } Tibberton or Offerton.

49.—Hindlip.
50.—Hindlip.

51 and 52. } Gilbert's or Bilford.

53.—Gregory's Mill.
54.—Gregory's Mill.
55.—Blockhouse.
56.—Sidbury.

57 and 58. } Diglis.

Fall to River Severn at Diglis, Worcester.

(e) Maximum size of vessels that can use the navigation.

From Birmingham, Worcester Bar, to Diglis Basin.

	Ft.	In.
Length	71	6
Width	7	0
Draught	4	0
Headroom	9	0

From Diglis Basin, through the two Diglis Locks, to the junction with the River Severn.

	Ft.	In.
Length	76	0
Width	18	6
Draught	6	0

(f) Tunnels.

Edgbaston—

Length .. .. 103 yards.		
Minimum height above water level	13	3
Minimum width at water level	15	8

Towing-path through the tunnel.

(90)—SHARPNESS NEW DOCKS AND GLOUCESTER AND BIRMINGHAM
NAVIGATION COMPANY—*continued.*

	Ft.	In.
West Hill, commonly called King's Norton—		
Length .. .. 2,750 yards.		
Minimum height above water level	12	6
Minimum width at water level	16	0

No towing-path; boats towed through by the Company's tug, leaving
the north end of the tunnel at 4-0 a.m., 6-0 a.m., 8-0 a.m., 10-0 a.m.,
12 noon, 2-0 p.m., 4-0 p.m., 6-0 p.m., and 8-0 p.m., and the south end of
the tunnel at 5-0 a.m., 7-0 a.m., 9-0 a.m., 11-0 a.m., 1-0 p.m., 3-0 p.m.,
5-0 p.m., 7-0 p.m., and 9-0 p.m. on week days; and the north end of the
tunnel at 6-0 a.m., 8-0 a.m., 10-0 a.m., and 12 noon, and the south end
of the tunnel at 7-0 a.m., 9-0 a.m., 11-0 a.m., and 1-0 p.m. on Sundays.

	Ft.	In.
Shortwood—		
Length .. .. 608 yards.		
Minimum height above water level	10	6
Minimum width at water level	16	6

No towing-path.

	Ft.	In.
Tardebigge—		
Length .. .. 568 yards.		
Minimum height above water level	11	0
Minimum width at water level	16	0

No towing-path; boats are towed by the Company's tug between the
north end of Shortwood Tunnel and the south end of Tardebigge Tunnel,
leaving the north end of Shortwood Tunnel at 5-0 a.m., 7-0 a.m., 9-0 a.m.,
11-0 a.m., 1-0 p.m., 3-0 p.m., 5-0 p.m., 7-0 p.m., and 9-0 p.m., and the
south end of Tardegigge Tunnel at 4-0 a.m., 6-0 a.m., 8-0 a.m , 10-0 a.m.,
12 noon, 2-0 p.m., 4-0 p.m., 6-0 p.m., and 8-0 p.m. on week days; and
the north end of Shortwood Tunnel at 7-0 a.m., 9-0 a.m., 11-0 a.m., and
1-0 p.m., and the south end of Tardebigge Tunnel at 6-0 a.m., 8-0 a.m.,
10-0 a.m., and 12 noon on Sundays.

	Ft.	In.
Dunhampstead—		
Length .. .. 326 yards.		
Minimum height above water level	9	0
Minimum width at water level	16	0

No towing-path; boats worked through the tunnel by means of handrail fixed on side wall.

(g) *Towing-path.*

There is a towing-path throughout the navigation, except through
certain of the tunnels enumerated above.

(i) *Types of vessels using the navigation.*

Narrow boats. Severn trows can pass from the River Severn at
Diglis, Worcester, through the two Diglis Locks to Diglis Basin, but
not beyond.

(90)—Sharpness New Docks and Gloucester and Birmingham Navigation Company—*continued.*

Droitwich Junction Canal (No. 90c).

(c) *Distance Table.*

	Miles.	Fur.
Hanbury Wharf, junction with Worcester and Birmingham Canal (No. 90b), to—		
Droitwich, Hanbury Road Wharves	1	2
Droitwich, junction with Droitwich Canal (No. 90d)	1	4

(d) *Locks.*

1
to
5.

6.

7.—Droitwich. This lock regulates the supply of water from the River Salwarpe to the Droitwich Canal.

Fall to Droitwich.

(e) *Maximum size of vessels that can use the navigation.*

	Ft.	In.
Length	71	6
Width	7	1
Draught	4	0
Headroom	8	0

(g) *Towing-path.*

There is a towing-path throughout the navigation.

(i) *Types of vessels using the navigation.*

Narrow boats.

Droitwich Canal (No. 90d).

(c) *Distance Table.*

	Miles.	Fur.
Droitwich, junction with Droitwich Junction Canal (No. 90c) and Central Wharf, to—		
Droitwich Canal Basin, Corbett's Wharf, Gas Works Wharf, and Town Bridge or Lower Wharf	–	2
Siding Lane Wharf	1	0
Salwarpe Bridge	2	2
Ladywood Lock	3	0
Porter's Mill Lock	3	4
Mildenham Mill Bridge	4	4
Hawford Bridge	5	4
Hawford, Lock No. 8, and junction with River Severn (No. 89a)	5	6

(90)—SHARPNESS NEW DOCKS AND GLOUCESTER AND BIRMINGHAM NAVIGATION COMPANY—*continued.*

(d) Locks.

1.) Ladywood.
2.| ,,
3.}   ,,
4.| ,,
5.) Porter's Mill.
6.—Ladywood.
7.—Hawford.
8.—Hawford.

Fall to River Severn at Hawford.

(e) Maximum size of vessels that can use the navigation.

						Ft.	In.
Length	..	..	..	..	..	71	6
Width	..	..	..	..	..	14	6
Draught	..	..	..	..	..	5	9
Headroom	..	..	..	..	..	8	0

(g) Towing-path.

There is a towing path throughout the navigation.

(i) Types of vessels using the navigation.

Narrow boats and trows.

SEVERN AND WYE AND SEVERN BRIDGE RAILWAY—*see* Lydney Harbour and Canal.

SHEFFIELD CANAL—*see* Sheffield and South Yorkshire Navigation.

---

(91)—SHEFFIELD AND SOUTH YORKSHIRE NAVIGATION.

(a) Short Description.

The navigations belonging to the Company consist of the Sheffield Canal, the River Dun Navigation, the Stainforth and Keadby Canal, and the Dearne and Dove Canal.

The Company are also joint proprietors with the Aire and Calder Navigation of the Aire and Calder and Sheffield and South Yorkshire Junction Canal.

The Sheffield Canal commences at Sheffield and proceeds by Attercliffe and Broughton Lane to Tinsley, where it joins the River Dun Navigation.

(91)—SHEFFIELD AND SOUTH YORKSHIRE NAVIGATION—*continued.*

The River Dun Navigation commences at Tinsley and proceeds by Holmes, Rotherham, Aldwarke, Kilnhurst, Swinton, Mexborough, Conisbrough, Sprotbrough, Doncaster, Sandall, Barnby Dun, Bramwith, and Stainforth to Fishlake Old Ferry, where it joins that portion of the River Don which is an open navigation, having no controlling authority.

The River Rother forms a short branch in Rotherham, being navigable for about one furlong from its point of junction with the River Dun Navigation.

The Stainforth and Keadby Canal commences by a junction with the River Dun Navigation at Stainforth, and proceeds by Thorne, Medge Hall, and Crowle Wharf to Keadby, where it forms a junction with the tidal River Trent.

As the Sheffield Canal, the River Dun Navigation, and the Stainforth and Keadby Canal forms practically the Main Line of the Navigation the distances throughout are given from Sheffield.

The Dearne and Dove Canal commences by a junction with the River Dun Navigation at Swinton, and proceeds by Wath, Wombwell, and Stairfoot to Barnsley Junction, near Barnsley, where it forms a junction with the Barnsley Canal of the Aire and Calder Navigation.

There are two short branches leading out of the canal known as the Elsecar and Worsborough Branches, and which afford communication to Elsecar and Worsborough respectively.

The whole of the navigations are situated in the West Riding of the county of Yorkshire, with the exception of the portion of the Stainforth and Keadby Canal between Crowle and Keadby, which is in the county of Lincolnshire.

There is a good trade on the navigation, especially between Sheffield and Keadby.

The portion of the River Dun Navigation between Stainforth and Fishlake Old Ferry giving access to Goole, via the River Don, is that which is least used for traffic.

(b) *Proprietors, Officers, and Offices.*

The Sheffield and South Yorkshire Navigation Company.

General Manager : George Welch.

Office : Corn Exchange Buildings, Sheffield.

Telegrams : " Traffic, Sheffield."   Telephone No. 530.

Secretary : Arthur Wightman.

Office : Messrs. Broomhead, Wightman, and Moore, Solicitors, 14, George Street, Sheffield.   Telegrams : " Waterway, Sheffield."

Engineer : C. A. Rowlandson.

Office : London Road Station, G. C. Railway, Manchester.

v

(91)—SHEFFIELD AND SOUTH YORKSHIRE NAVIGATION—*continued.*

(c) *Distance Table.*

Sheffield Canal (No. 91a).

	Miles.	Fur.
Sheffield, Basin and Warehouses, to—		
Great Central Railway Main Line Bridge ..	–	2
Midland Railway Bridge	–	3½
Corporation Wharf	–	6½
Blagden Bridge	1	0
Pinfold Lane Bridge	1	2½
Shirland Lane Bridge	1	4
Coleridge Road Bridge	2	0½
Broughton Lane Bridge	2	2
Top Lock of Tinsley Top Locks	2	5½
Tinsley Top Wharf	2	7
Bottom Lock of Tinsley Top Locks	3	1½
Turnpike Bridge Lock, and Road Bridge ..	3	3½
Tinsley Low Wharf	3	4
Top Lock of Tinsley Low Locks	3	5½
Bottom Lock of Tinsley Low Locks, and junction with River Dun Navigation (No. 91b1)	3	7

In calculating distances for all purposes of tolls and charges, each quarter of a mile of the distance between the terminus of the canal at Sheffield and the bottom lock at Tinsley is to be taken as equal to half a mile.

River Dun Navigation (No. 91b1)—Distances from Sheffield.

	Miles.	Fur.
Tinsley, junction with Sheffield Canal (No. 91a)	3	7
Jordan Lock	4	4
Holmes Wharf	4	7
Holmes Lock and Bridge	5	0
Holmes Colliery	5	2½
Ickles Wharf	5	4
Rotherham, junction with River Rother (No. 91b2)	5	7½
Rotherham, Flood Lock and Top Wharf ..	6	2
Rotherham Wharf	6	3
Parkgate Railway Station, and junction with Parkgate Branch Canal (No. 83)	7	1
Eastwood Top Lock	7	5
Aldwarke Wharf	8	2
Aldwarke Lock	8	3
Roundwood Colliery	9	5
Kilnhurst Flood Lock	10	3
Thrybergh Colliery	10	4
Kilnhurst Pottery and Colliery	10	5
Kilnhurst Road Bridge..	10	7
Kilnhurst Lock	11	3
Burton Ings Bridge	11	5
Swinton Wharf, and junction with Dearne and Dove Canal (No. 91d1), between Locks Nos. 9 and 10	11	7

(91)—Sheffield and South Yorkshire Navigation—*continued.*

	Miles.	Fur.
Distances from Sheffield (*continued*)—		
Swinton Road Bridge	12	1
Mexborough Railway Station and Road Bridge	12	5½
Mexborough Top Lock	13	2
Mexborough Local Board Wharf	13	6½
Mexborough Low Lock	14	5
Denaby Main Colliery	14	6½
River Dearne Bridge and Road to Cadeby ..	15	1
Conisbrough Wharf	15	6
Warmsworth Lime Kilns	17	4
Warmsworth Wharf	17	7½
Sprotbrough Lock	18	1½
Hexthorpe Sand Wharf	19	7
Doncaster, Great Northern Railway Company's Works	20	7½
Doncaster Lock	21	2¾
Doncaster Corporation Wharf	21	5
Arksey Landing	24	3
Sandall Wharf	24	7
Kirk Sandall Wharf	25	7½
Barnby Dun Wharf	26	6½
Bramwith, junction with Aire and Calder and Sheffield and South Yorkshire Junction Canal (No. 4)	28	0½
Bramwith Lock	28	1
Stainforth Wharf	30	0
Head of Stainforth Lock, and junction with Stainforth and Keadby Canal (No. 91c) ..	30	1
Fishlake Wharf	30	7½
Thorne Waterside Wharf	32	4
Fishlake Old Ferry, junction with River Don (No. 28)	32	7

River Rother (No. 91b2).

Length from junction with River Dun Navigation (No. 91b1) at Rotherham to—		
Messrs. Robinson Bros. Mill	–	1

Stainforth and Keadby Canal (No. 91c)—Distances from Sheffield.

	Miles.	Fur.
Head of Stainforth Lock and junction with River Dun Navigation (No. 91b1) ..	30	1
Dunston Hill Swing Bridge	30	3½
Thorne Lock	32	5
Thorne Wharf	33	0
Thorne Low Wharf	33	1
Wike Well Wharf	33	6½
Medge Hall Wharf	37	1
Godnow Bridge Wharf	38	1½
Crowle Wharf	39	5
Keadby Railway Station	42	2
Keadby Lock, and junction with River Trent, Main Line (No. 112a)	42	7

(91)—Sheffield and South Yorkshire Navigation—*continued.*

Dearne and Dove Canal (No. 91d1).

	Miles.	Fur.
Swinton, junction with River Dun Navigation (No. 91b1), to—		
Swinton Top Lock	–	4
Ardwick Siding	1	0
Manvers Main Colliery Wharf	1	2
Adwick Wharf	1	4½
Wath Flour Mill	1	6
Wath Gas Works	2	2
Wath Wharf	2	3
Wetmoor Bridge, West Melton	2	7½
Elsecar Junction Bottom Lock	4	0½
Brampton Wharf	4	1½
Head of Elsecar Junction Top Lock, and junction with Elsecar Branch (No. 91d2)	4	3½
Wombwell Junction Road Bridge	4	4
Wombwell Gas Works	5	1½
Mitchell Main Colliery	6	1
Aldham Bridge, Lock, and Wharf	6	4
Worsborough Junction Bottom Lock ..	6	6½
Head of Worsborough Junction Top Lock, and junction with Worsborough Branch (No. 91d3)	7	1
Stairfoot Wharf	7	6
Stairfoot Bridge	8	0
Spink Hill Wharf	8	3½
Old Oaks Basin	8	6
Micklethwaite's Basin	9	0
Beever Mill Wharf	9	2
Barnsley Junction Lock and Barnsley Junction, junction with Barnsley Canal, Aire and Calder Navigation (No. 3b)	9	5

Elsecar Branch (No. 92d2).

	Miles.	Fur.
Junction with Dearne and Dove Canal (No. 91d1) to—		
Lundhill Bridge and Basin	–	4½
Hemingfield Bottom Lock	–	7½
Birks Bridge and Wharf	1	0
Hemingfield Top Lock	1	3
Elsecar Low Colliery Basin	1	4
Hoyland and Elsecar Colliery Basin	1	6
Elsecar Bridge	1	7½
Elsecar Top Lock	2	0
Elsecar Basin	2	1½

Worsborough Branch (No. 91d3).

	Miles.	Fur.
Junction with Dearne and Dove Canal (No. 91d1) to—		
Swaithe Colliery	–	4½
Lewden Bridge Wharf	1	1½

(91)—Sheffield and South Yorkshire Navigation—*continued.*

Junction with Dearne and Dove Canal (No. 91d1) to (*continued*)—	Miles.	Fur.
Worsborough Dale Gas Works	1	$4\frac{1}{2}$
Darley Main Wharf	1	5
Worsborough Dale Foundry	2	0
Worsborough Basin	2	$1\frac{1}{2}$

(*d*) *Locks.*

Sheffield Canal (No. 91a).

1
to } Tinsley Top.
8.

9.—Turnpike Bridge.

10
to } Tinsley Low.
12.

Fall from Sheffield.

River Dun Navigation (No. 91b1).

1.—Jordan.
2.—Holmes.
3.—Ickles.
4.—Rotherham Flood Lock.
5.—Eastwood Top.
6.—Eastwood Low.
7.—Aldwarke.
8.—Kilnhurst Flood Lock.
9.—Kilnhurst Forge.
10.—Swinton.
11.—Mexborough Top.
12.—Mexborough Low.
13.—Conisbrough.
14.—Sprotbrough.
15.—Doncaster.
16.—Sandall.
17.—Bramwith.
18.—Stainforth.

Fall from Tinsley.

The lock at Stainforth has a pair of flood gates in the centre to keep back the water in the lower river in times of flood. There being only one pair of flood gates, traffic is stopped when they are in use.

Stainforth and Keadby Canal (No. 91c).

1.—Thorne.
2.—Keadby.

Fall from Stainforth.

Keadby Lock has two pair of sea gates and two pair of navigation gates, as a high tide in the Trent will sometimes rise above the level of the water in the canal.

(91)—Sheffield and South Yorkshire Navigation—*continued.*

Dearne and Dove Canal (No. 91d1).

1
to } Swinton.
6.

7
to } Elsecar Junction.
10.

11.—Aldam.

12
to } Worsborough Junction.
18.

19.—Barnsley Junction.

Rise from Swinton.

Elsecar Branch (No. 91d2).

1
to } Hemingfield.
3.

4
to } Elsecar.
6.

Rise to Elsecar.

(e) *Maximum size of vessels that can use the navigation.*

Sheffield Canal (No. 91a).

						Ft.	In.
Length	..	..	..	..	..	61	6
Width	..	..	..	..	..	15	3
Draught	..	..	..	..	..	6	0
Headroom	..	..	..	..	..	10	0

River Dun Navigation (No. 91b1) and River Rother (No. 91b2).

						Ft.	In.
Length	..	..	..	..	..	61	3
Width	..	..	..	..	..	15	3
Draught	..	..	..	..	..	6	6
Headroom	..	..	..	..	..	10	0

Stainforth and Keadby Canal (No. 91c).

						Ft.	In.
Length	..	..	..	..	..	65	0
Width	..	..	..	..	..	17	0
Draught	..	..	..	..	..	6	6
Headroom	..	..	..	..	..	10	0

Dearne and Dove Canal (No. 91d1) and Branches.

						Ft.	In.
Length	..	..	..	..	..	58	0
Width	..	..	..	..	..	14	10
Draught	..	..	..	..	..	5	6
Headroom	..	..	..	..	..	10	0

(91)—Sheffield and South Yorkshire Navigation—*continued.*

(g) Towing-path.

There is a towing-path throughout the whole of the navigation, with the exception of the small branch formed by the River Rother in Rotherham and that portion of the River Dun Navigation situated between Stainforth Lock and Fishlake Old Ferry.

(h) Tidal Information.

River Dun Navigation (No. 91b1).

The tide from Goole up the River Don flows past Fishlake Old Ferry to the tail of Stainforth Lock.

High water at Stainforth Lock 1hr. 20min. after Goole.

Spring tides rise   ..   ..   7ft. 6in.

For Goole Tidal Information—*see* River Ouse, York (No. 81).

(i) Types of vessels using the navigation.

Yorkshire keels use the whole of the navigation and branches.

Shoreham Harbour Trustees—*see* River Adur.

Shorncliffe and Rye Canal—*see* Royal Military Canal.

Shrewsbury Canal—*see* Shropshire Union Canals.

Shropshire (Coalport) Canal—*see* London and North Western Railway.

Shropshire, Old, Canal—*see* Shropshire Union Canals

---

(92)—Shropshire Union Railways and Canal Company

(a) Short Description.

The canals forming the Company's system consist of the Birmingham and Liverpool Junction Canal, the Chester Canal Navigation, the Wirral Line (Ellesmere Canal), the Newport Branch, the Humber Arm, the Middlewich Branch, the Branch to the River Dee (Chester), the Ellesmere Canal (Hurleston Junction to Carreghofa), the Montgomeryshire Canal (Eastern Branch), the Montgomeryshire Canal (Western Branch), the Whitchurch Branch, the Prees Branch, the Ellesmere Branch, the Pontcysyllte Branch, the Weston Branch, the Guildsfield Branch, the Shrewsbury Canal (Wappenshall Junction to Shrewsbury), and the Shrewsbury Canal (Old Shropshire Canal Section)

(92)—SHROPSHIRE UNION RAILWAYS AND CANAL COMPANY—*continued.*

The Birmingham and Liverpool Junction Canal commences by a junction with the Staffordshire and Worcestershire Canal at Autherley, near Wolverhampton, and proceeds by Brewood, Wheaton Aston, Church Eaton, Gnosall, Norbury Junction, and Shebdon, in the county of Staffordshire ; Market Drayton Wharf and Adderley, in the county of Shropshire ; Audlem and Hack Green to Nantwich Basin, in the county of Cheshire, where it forms a junction with the Chester Canal Navigation.

The Chester Canal Navigation commences at Nantwich Basin by a junction with the Birmingham and Liverpool Junction Canal, and proceeds by Hurleston Junction, Barbridge Junction, Wardle, Calveley, Bunbury, Tilston, Beeston, and Christleton to Tower Wharf, Chester, all in the county of Cheshire, where it forms a junction with the Wirral Line (Ellesmere Canal).

The Wirral Line (Ellesmere Canal), commences at Tower Wharf, Chester, by a junction with the Chester Canal Navigation, and proceeds by Mollington, Backford, Stoak, and Stanney to Ellesmere Port Docks, all in the county of Cheshire, where it forms a junction with the semi-tidal portion of the Manchester Ship Canal.

The three above-named canals, extending from Autherley Junction to Ellesmere Port, may be said to form the main line of the navigation.

There are branches leading out of the main line as follows :—

The Newport Branch, from the Birmingham and Liverpool Junction Canal at Norbury Junction, in the county of Staffordshire, to Newport and Wappenshall Junction, in the county of Shropshire, at which latter place it joins both sections of the Shrewsbury Canal—one from Wappenshall Junction to Shrewsbury, and the other from Wappenshall Junction to Trench and Donnington, known as the Old Shropshire Canal.

The Humber Arm, which forms a junction with the Newport Branch two miles above Wappenshall Junction, and proceeds to Lubstree Wharf, all in the county of Shropshire.

The Middlewich Branch, from the Chester Canal Navigation at Barbridge Junction to Cholmondeston, Minshull, and Middlewich, where it forms a junction with the main line of the North Staffordshire Railway Company's Trent and Mersey Canal through that Company's Wardle Lock, all in the county of Cheshire.

The branch to the River Dee in Chester, from the Wirral Line (Ellesmere Canal) to the River Dee in that city.

The Ellesmere Canal commences by a junction with the Chester Canal Navigation at Hurleston Junction, and proceeds by Swanley, Baddiley, Wrenbury, and Marbury, in the county of Cheshire ; Grindley Brook and Whixall Moss, in the county of Shropshire; Bettisfield in the county of Flintshire ; Hampton Bank, Ellesmere, Frankton, Rednal, Maesbury, and Llanymynech, in the county of Shropshire, to Carreghofa, in the county of Montgomeryshire, where it joins the Eastern Branch of the Montgomeryshire Canal.

(92)—SHROPSHIRE UNION RAILWAYS AND CANAL COMPANY—*continued.*

The Eastern Branch of the Montgomeryshire Canal commences at Carreghofa by a junction with the Ellesmere Canal, and proceeds by Arleen, Burgedden, Pool Quay, Buttington, Welshpool, Belan, and Berriew to Garthmyl, where it forms a junction with the Western Branch of the Montgomeryshire Canal.

The Western Branch of the Montgomeryshire Canal commences at Garthmyl by a junction with the Eastern Branch of the Montgomeryshire Canal, and proceeds by Pennant Dingle, Brynderwyn, and Aberbechan to its termination at Newtown.

The three above-named canals form the through route of the navigation between Hurleston Junction and Newtown. The navigation between Welshpool and Newtown is not so good as that on the other portion of the Montgomeryshire Canal.

There are branches leading out of the Ellesmere Canal as follows :—

The Whitchurch Branch, from near Grindley Brook to Whitchurch, in the county of Shropshire.

The Prees Branch, from Whixall Moss to Waterloo and Edstaston, in the county of Shropshire.

The Ellesmere Branch to the town of Ellesmere, in the county of Shropshire.

The Pontcysyllte Branch, from Frankton to Hindford and St. Martin's, in the county of Shropshire ; Chirk, Vron, Pontcysyllte, Llangollen, and Llantisilio, in the county of Denbighshire, where it terminates at stop gates, through which water for feeding the canal is admitted from the River Dee. The Pontcysyllte Branch from Pontcysyllte to Llantisilio is narrow, and may be said to be a navigable feeder only. There is no turning place for boats at Llantisilio, the nearest being at Llangollen.

The Weston Branch, from Lockgate Bridge to Hordley, and Weston Wharf, in the county of Shropshire.

The Guildsfield Branch leaves the Eastern Branch of the Montgomeryshire Canal at Burgedden, and proceeds to Varchoel and Tyddyn, in the county of Montgomeryshire.

The Shrewsbury Canal (Wappenshall Junction to Shrewsbury) commences at Wappenshall Junction, where it joins the Newport Branch and the Old Shropshire Canal section of the Shrewsbury Canal, and proceeds by Eyton, Roddington, and Berwick to its termination in the town of Shrewsbury at Castle Foregate, all in the county of Shropshire.

The Shrewsbury Canal (Old Shropshire Canal section) commences at Wappenshall Junction, where it joins the Newport Branch and the Shrewsbury Canal (Wappenshall Junction to Shrewsbury), and proceeds to Trench, where there is an inclined plane rising to Wombridge. Leaving Wombridge Wharf the canal proceeds to Donnington, where it forms a junction with the Duke of Sutherland's Tub Boat Canal, all in the county of Shropshire. The canal between Wappenshall Junction and the foot

(92)—SHROPSHIRE UNION RAILWAYS AND CANAL COMPANY—*continued.*

of Trench Inclined Plane can only be used by a special type of narrow boat, smaller than those in general use (*see* " Narrow Boats," Section 9, Types of Vessels, (*a*) Non-Sailing Vessels). From the foot of Trench Inclined Plane to Donnington the canal is only navigable by tub boats (*see* Section 9, Types of Vessels, (*a*) Non-Sailing Vessels).

A considerable amount of traffic which used to come off the Duke of Sutherland's Tub Boat Canal and down the Trench Inclined Plane to Wappenshall Junction is now sent by means of a tramroad to Lubstree Wharf, at the end of the Humber Arm.

The Shropshire Union Railways and Canal Company is an amalgamation of railways and canals, with a view originally of converting the latter into the former. This object it was found impracticable to carry out, especially after an arrangement had been entered into with the London and North Western Railway Company, which was itself invalid until sanctioned by Parliament. The supervening difficulties were overcome by Act of 1854, which may be regarded as the incorporating of the Company.

The Company own 23½ miles of railways. By lease to the London and North Western Railway Company under the powers of the Shropshire Union Leasing Act 1847, the proprietors of Shropshire Union stock are secured half the amount of the dividend on the London and North Western Railway Company's ordinary stock in perpetuity.

There is a fair trade done on the main line of the navigation from Autherley Junction to Ellesmere Port. The general trade on the remainder of the system is not great, with the exception of the limestone traffic from Llanymynech on the Ellesmere Canal, and from Trevor on the Pontcysyllte Branch.

The available draught of water throughout the Company's system of canals is somewhat less than that prevailing generally on narrow boat canals, but the works are well maintained.

(*b*) *Proprietors, Officers, and Offices.*

Shropshire Union Railways and Canal Company.

Secretary : James Bishop.

Office : Euston Station, L. & N. W. Railway, London, N.W.

General Manager : Thomas Hales.

Office : Chester.

Engineer : G. R. Jebb.

Office : New Street Station, Birmingham.

The Proprietors act as carriers.

(92)—SHROPSHIRE UNION RAILWAYS AND CANAL COMPANY—*continued.*

(c) Distance Table.

Birmingham and Liverpool Junction Canal (No. 92a1).

	Miles.	Fur.
Autherley Junction, junction with Staffordshire and Worcestershire Canal (No. 95a), to—		
Chillington	3	5
Dean's Hall	4	4
Brewood	5	0
Watling Street Road	6	2
Wheaton Aston	7	6
Church Eaton	10	6
Gnosall	13	0
Norbury Junction, junction with Newport Branch (No. 92a2)	15	4
Shebdon	19	0
Park Heath	21	0
Goldstone	23	0
Tyrley Top Lock	25	2
Tyrley Bottom Lock	25	5
Market Drayton Wharf (Market Drayton distant half a mile)	26	5
Victoria Wharf	27	1
Adderley Wharf and Adderley Top Lock	29	7
Adderley Bottom Lock	30	1
Audlem Top Lock	31	4
Audlem Wharf and Warehouse	32	6
Hack Green	36	5
Nantwich Basin (Nantwich distant half mile)	38	7

Chester Canal Navigation (No. 92b1)—Distances from Autherley Junction.

	Miles.	Fur.
Nantwich Basin (Nantwich distant half mile)	38	7
Hurleston Junction, junction with Ellesmere Canal (No. 92d1)	40	6
Barbridge Junction, junction with Middlewich Branch (No. 92b2)	42	1
Wardle	43	3
Calveley	43	7
Bunbury	44	7
Tilston Mill	45	5
Beeston	46	5
Wharton's Lock	47	4
Bate's Mill	47	7
Crow Nest	50	2
Egg Bridge	53	6
Christleton	55	3
Tarvin Lock	56	2
Cow Lane	57	3
Chester, Tower Wharf	57	7

(92)—Shropshire Union Railways and Canal Company--*continued.*

Wirral Line Ellesmere Canal (No. 92c1)—Distances from Autherley Junction.

	Miles.	Fur.
Chester, Tower Wharf	57	7
Chester, junction with branch to River Dee (No. 92c2)	58	0
Mollington	59	7
Backford	61	7
Caughall	62	7
Stoak	63	3
Stanney	64	3
Ellesmere Port Docks, and junction with Manchester Ship Canal (No. 64a)	66	4

Newport Branch (No. 92a2).

	Miles.	Fur.
Norbury Junction, junction with Birmingham and Liverpool Junction Canal (No. 92a1), to —		
Newport Bottom Lock	1	4
Newport, between Haycock's and Newport Wharf Locks	4	0
Edgmond Lock	5	5
Junction with Humber Arm (No. 92a3) ..	8	4
Wappenshall Junction, junctions with Shrewsbury Canal—Wappenshall Junction to Shrewsbury (No. 92g), and Shrewsbury Canal—Old Shropshire Canal Section— (No. 92h)	10	4

Humber Arm (No. 92a3).

	Miles.	Fur.
Length from junction with Newport Branch (No. 92a2) to—		
Lubstree Wharf	–	6

Middlewich Branch (No. 92b2).

	Miles.	Fur.
Barbridge Junction, junction with Chester Canal Navigation (No. 92b1), to—		
Cholmondeston	1	3
Egerton's Bridge	2	7
Minshull	4	7
Middlewich, junction with Wardle Lock Branch—Trent and Mersey Canal (No. 76f)	10	0

Branch to River Dee, Chester (No. 92c2).

	Miles.	Fur.
Length from junction with Wirral Line— Ellesmere Canal (No. 92c1) to—		
Junction with River Dee (No. 26) at Crane Wharf, Chester	–	1

(92)—SHROPSHIRE UNION RAILWAYS AND CANAL COMPANY—*continued.*

Ellesmere Canal—Hurleston Junction to Carreghofa (No. 92d1).

	Miles.	Fur.
Hurleston Junction, junction with Chester Canal Navigation (No. 92b1), to—		
Ravensmoor	1	5
Swanley ..	2	2
Baddiley ..	4	3
Wrenbury	6	2
Marbury ..	8	2
Steer Brook	8	7
Quoisley ..	9	7
Grindley Brook ..	12	1
Junction with Whitchurch Branch (No. 92d2)	13	3
New Mill ..	13	5
Tilstock ..	16	7
Platt Lane	17	3
Whixall Moss Roving Bridge, junction with Prees Branch (No. 92d3) ..	19	0
Bettisfield	20	7
Hampton Bank ..	21	7
Little Mill	23	5
Junction with Ellesmere Branch (No. 92d4) ..	25	5
Tetchill ..	27	1
Frankton, top of Frankton Locks, and junction with Pontcysyllte Branch (No. 92d5) ..	29	0
Lockgate Bridge, junction with Weston Branch (No. 92d6), at bottom of Frankton Locks	29	4
Rednal ..	32	1
Queenshead	33	0
Maesbury	35	1
Redwith ..	36	3
Crickheath	37	1
Waen Wen	38	0
Pant ..	38	3
Old Railway	38	6
Llanymynech ..	39	4
Wall's Bridge, Wharf and Warehouse..	39	7
Carreghofa, junction with Montgomeryshire Canal—Eastern Branch (No. 92e)	40	4

Montgomeryshire Canal—Eastern Branch (No. 92e1)—Distances from Hurleston Junction.

	Miles.	Fur.
Carreghofa, junction with Ellesmere Canal— Hurleston Junction to Carreghofa (No. 92d1) ..	40	4
Newbridge	41	0
Clopton's Wharf	42	0
Mardu ..	43	1
Arleen	44	2
Burgedden, top of Burgedden Locks, and junction with Guildsfield Branch (No.92e2)	44	6
Gwernfelen	45	2

(92)—Shropshire Union Railways and Canal Company—*continued.*

Distances from Hurleston Junction (*continued*)—

	Miles.	Fur.
Bank Lock	46	2
Pool Quay	47	2
Buttington	49	1
Welshpool	50	5
Whitehouse	51	4
Belan	52	0
Brithdir	54	2
Berriew	55	2
Evelvach	55	3
Redgate	56	3
Garthmyl, junction with Montgomeryshire Canal—Western Branch (No. 92f) ..	56	6

Montgomeryshire Canal—Western Branch (No. 92f).

Distances from Hurleston Junction.

	Miles.	Fur.
Garthmyl, junction with Montgomeryshire Canal—Eastern Branch (No. 92e1) ..	56	6
Bunker's Hill	58	1
Pennant Dingle	58	7
Brynderwyn	59	6
Newhouse	60	6
Aberbechan	61	5
Newtown Basin	64	1

Whitchurch Branch (No. 92d2).

Length from junction with Ellesmere Canal (No. 92d1) to—

	Miles.	Fur.
Whitchurch	1	0

Prees Branch (No. 92d3).

Whixall Moss Roving Bridge, junction with Ellesmere Canal (No. 92d1), to—

	Miles.	Fur.
Minshull or Rodenhurst's Bridge	–	5
Boodle's Bridge or Waterloo	1	5
Sydney Bridge or Edstaston	3	0
Quina Brook	3	6

Ellesmere Branch (No. 92d4).

Length from junction with Ellesmere Canal (No. 92d1) to—

	Miles.	Fur.
Ellesmere	–	2

Pontcysyllte Branch (No. 92d5).

Frankton, junction with Ellesmere Canal (No. 92d1), to—

	Miles.	Fur.
Maesterfyn	1	2
Hindford	2	4
New Martin Top Lock	3	5

(92)—Shropshire Union Railways and Canal Company—*continued.*

Frankton, junction with Ellesmere Canal
   (No. 92d1), to (*continued*)—

	Miles.	Fur.
St. Martin's	4	6
Lovett's Wharf	5	3
Rhoswell	6	0
Gledryd	6	2
Chirk Bank	7	0
Chirk Aqueduct	7	1
Chirk Basin, north end of Chirk Tunnel	7	4
Black Park	8	4
Irish Bridge	9	5
Vron	10	5
Pontcysyllte Aqueduct	11	1
Pontcysyllte	11	2
Plas Isaf	12	5
Trevor	13	5
Llangollen	15	3
Pentrevelin	16	3
Llantisilio	17	0

Weston Branch (No. 92d6).

Lockgate Bridge, junction with Ellesmere
   Canal (No. 92d1), to—

	Miles.	Fur.
Hordley Bridge	–	7
Shade Oak Bridge	4	2
Weston	6	0

Guildsfield Branch (No. 92e2).

Burgedden, junction with Montgomeryshire
   Canal—Eastern Branch (No. 92e1), to—

	Miles.	Fur.
Varchoel	2	0
Tyddyn	2	2

Shrewsbury Canal—Wappenshall Junction to Shrewsbury (No. 92g).

Wappenshall Junction, junction with Newport
   Branch (No. 92a2) and Shrewsbury Canal
   —Old Shropshire Canal Section (No. 92h),
   to—

	Miles.	Fur.
Long Lane, or Eyton's Wharf	2	0
Long Wharf, or Hazledine's Wharf	3	2
Long Wharf, Young's	3	4
Roddington Wharf	5	6
Upton Forge Wharf	8	2
Berwick Wharf	9	2
South east end of Berwick Tunnel	9	6
Sundorn Wharf	12	0
Old Factory	14	0
Shrewsbury Basin	14	4

(92)—SHROPSHIRE UNION RAILWAYS AND CANAL COMPANY—*continued.*

Shrewsbury Canal—Old Shropshire Canal Section (No. 92h).

	Miles.	Fur.
Wappenshall Junction, junction with Newport Branch (No. 92a2) and Shrewsbury Canal—Wappenshall Junction to Shrewsbury (No. 92g), to—		
Trench Wharf and bottom of Trench Inclined Plane	2	0
Wombridge Wharf and top of Trench Inclined Plane	2	4
Steam Mills	3	2
Donnington, junction with Duke of Sutherland's Tub Boat Canal (No. 102)	3	6

(d) Locks.

Birmingham and Liverpool Junction Canal (No. 92a1).

1.—Autherley.
2.—Wheaton Aston.
3)
to } Tyrley.
7.)
8)
to } Adderley.
12.)
13)
and } Audlem 1st flight.
14.)
15)
to } Audlem 2nd flight.
27.)
28)
and } Hack Green.
29.)

Fall from Autherley.

Chester Canal Navigation (No. 92b1).

1)
and } Bunbury (staircase).
2.)
3.—Tilston.
4)
and } Beeston.
5.)
6.—Wharton.
7) Christleton.
and {
8.) Greenfield.
9.—Tarvin.
10) Chemistry.
and {
11.) Hoole Lane.
12)
to } North Gate, Chester (staircase).
14.)

Fall from Nantwich

(92)—SHROPSHIRE UNION RAILWAYS AND CANAL COMPANY—*continued.*

Wirral Line—Ellesmere Canal (No. 92c1).

1
and } Ellesmere Port, Locks for Flats, or
2.

1
and } Ellesmere Port, Locks for Boats.
2.

These locks give access from the canal at Ellesmere Port to Ellesmere Port Docks.

3.—Ellesmere Port, Ship Lock, or
3.—Ellesmere Port, Flat Lock.

These locks give access from the Ellesmere Port Docks to the Manchester Ship Canal.

Fall to Manchester Ship Canal at Ellesmere Port.

Newport Branch (No. 92a2).

1
to } Newport.
17.
18.—Meretown.
19.—Haycock's.
20.—Newport Wharf.
21.—Ticket House.
22.—Polly's.
23.—Edgmond.

Fall from Norbury Junction.

Middlewich Branch (No. 92b2).

1.—Cholmondeston.
2.—Minshull.
3.—Stanthorne.

Fall from Barbridge Junction.

Branch to River Dee, Chester (No. 92c2).

1
to } Dee.
3.

Fall to River Dee.

(d) Locks.

Ellesmere Canal—Hurleston Junction to Carreghofa (No. 92d1).

1
to } Hurleston.
4.
5
and } Swanley.
6.
7
to } Baddiley.
9.
10.—Marbury.

W

(92)—Shropshire Union Railways and Canal Company—*continued.*

11.—Quoisley.
12.—Willymoor.
13.—Povey's.
14.
15.
16. } Grindley Brook.
17.
18. } (staircase).
19.

Rise from Hurleston.

20.
21. } Frankton.   } (staircase).
22.
23.

24
to } Aston.
26.

Fall to Carreghofa.

Montgomeryshire Canal—Eastern Branch (No. 92e1).

1
and } Carreghofa.
2.

3
and } Burgedden.
4.

Fall from Carreghofa.

5.—Bank.
6 } Cabin.
and }
7. } Crowther.
8.—Pool Quay.
9.—Welshpool.
10
and } Belan.
11.
12.—Brithdir.
13.—Berriew.

Rise to Garthmyl.

Montgomeryshire Canal—Western Branch (No. 92f).

1.—Brynderwyn.
2.—Byles.
3.—Newhouse.
4.—Freestone.
5.—Dolfer.
6.—Rock.

Rise to Newtown.

Pontcysyllte Branch (No. 92d5).

1
and } New Martin.
2.

Rise from Frankton Junction.

(92)—SHROPSHIRE UNION RAILWAYS AND CANAL COMPANY—*continued.*

Shrewsbury Canal—Wappenshall Junction to Shrewsbury (No. 92g).

1
and ⎬ Eyton.
2.

Fall from Wappenshall Junction.

The bottom gates of these locks are of the " Guillotine " pattern.

The locks can pass four tub-boats at a time.

Shrewsbury Canal—Old Shropshire Canal Section (No. 92h).

1
to ⎬ Trench.
7.
8.—Bakers.
9.—Trench Wharf.

Rise from Wappenshall Junction.

The bottom gates of these locks are of the " Guillotine " pattern.

The locks can pass three tub-boats at a time.

The Trench Inclined Plane Lift rises from Trench to Wombridge Wharf—*see* Section 4, (*c*) Lifts.

The Inclined Plane is closed on Saturday afternoons and Sundays.

(*e*) *Maximum size of vessels that can use the navigation.*

Birmingham and Liverpool Junction Canal (No. 92a1).

		Ft.	In.
Length	.. ..	71	6
Width	.. ..	6	10
Draught	.. ..	3	3
Headroom	.. ..	8	9

Chester Canal Navigation (No. 92b1).

Length	.. ..	74	5
Width	.. ..	13	3
Draught	.. ..	3	3
Headroom	.. ..	8	6

Wirral Line—Ellesmere Canal (No. 92c1).

Length	.. ..	74	0
Width	.. ..	14	6
Draught	.. ..	3	3
Headroom	.. ..	8	8

Newport Branch (No. 92a2) and Humber Arm (No. 92a3).

		Ft.	In.
Length	.. ..	72	0
Width	.. ..	6	10
Draught	.. ..	3	3
Headroom	.. ..	7	11

(92)—SHROPSHIRE UNION RAILWAYS AND CANAL COMPANY—*continued.*

Middlewich Branch (No. 92b2).

						Ft.	In.
Length	..	..	..	..	..	72	0
Width	..	..	..	..	..	6	10
Draught	..	..	..	..	..	3	3
Headroom	..		..	..	..	8	0

Branch to River Dee, Chester (No. 92c2).

						Ft.	In.
Length	..	..	..	..	..	74	0
Width	..	..	..	..	..	14	6
Draught	..	..	..	..	..	3	3
Headroom	..	..	..	..	..	8	8

Ellesmere Canal—Hurleston Junction to Carreghofa (No. 92d1).

						Ft.	In.
Length	..	..	..	..	..	72	0
Width	..	..	..	..	..	6	9
Draught	..	..	..	..	..	2	6
Headroom	..	..	..	..	..	7	7

Montgomeryshire Canal—Eastern Branch (No. 92e1) and Western Branch (No. 92f).

						Ft.	In.
Length	..	..	..	..	..	72	0
Width	..	..	..	..	..	6	10
Draught	..	..	..	..	..	2	6
Headroom	..	..	..	..	..	5	11

Whitchurch Branch (No. 92d2), Prees Branch (No. 92d3), Ellesmere Branch (No. 92d4), and Pontcysyllte Branch (No. 92d5).

						Ft.	In.
Length	..	..	..	..	..	72	0
Width	..	..	..	..	..	6	9
Draught	..	..	..	..	..	2	6
Headroom	..	..	..	..	..	7	7

Weston Branch (No. 92d6).

						Ft.	In.
Length	..	..	..	..	..	72	0
Width	..	..	..	..	..	6	9
Draught	..	..	..	..	..	2	6
Headroom	..	..	..	..	..	6	7

Guildsfield Branch (No. 92c2).

						Ft.	In.
Length	..	..	..	..	..	72	0
Width	..	..	..	..	..	6	10
Draught	..	..	..	..	..	2	6
Headroom	..	..	..	..	..	5	11

(92)—Shropshire Union Railways and Canal Company—*continued.*

Shrewsbury Canal—Wappenshall Junction to Shrewsbury (No. 92g).

	Ft.	In.
Length	81	0
Width	6	9
Draught	2	6
Headroom	6	10

The length of the locks (81ft.) permits of the passage of four tub-boats at one time.

Shrewsbury Canal—Old Shropshire Canal Section (No. 92h)

				Ft.	In.
Length from Wappenshall Junction to Trench				71	0
Width	do.	do.	do.	6	2
Draught	do.	do.	do.	2	6
Headroom				5	5

Between the foot of Trench Inclined Plane and Donnington the canal is only navigable by tub-boats 19ft. 9in. in length and 6ft. 2in. in width, and drawing 2ft. of water with a load of 5 tons (*see* Section 9, Types of Vessels, (*a*) Non-Sailing Vessels), but as the Duke of Sutherland's canal, on which the loading arises, can only pass these boats carrying 3 tons on a draught of about 1ft. 3in., this is the ordinary load carried.

(f) Tunnels.

Birmingham and Liverpool Junction Canal (No. 92a1).

Cowley—
	Ft.	In.
Length 81 yards.		
Minimum height above water level	12	7
Minimum width at water level	17	4
Towing-path through the tunnel.		

Ellesmere Canal—Hurleston Junction to Carreghofa (No. 92d1).

Ellesmere—
	Ft.	In.
Length 87 yards.		
Minimum height above water level	10	0
Minimum width at water level	9	9
Towing-path through the tunnel.		

Pontcysyllte Branch (No. 92d5).

Whitehouses—
	Ft.	In.
Length 191 yards.		
Minimum height above water level	10	0
Minimum width at water level	9	6
Towing-path through the tunnel.		

Chirk—
	Ft.	In.
Length 459 yards.		
Minimum height above water level	12	7
Minimum width at water level	12	9
Towing-path through the tunnel.		

(92)—SHROPSHIRE UNION RAILWAYS AND CANAL COMPANY—*continued.*

Shrewsbury Canal—Wappenshall Junction to Shrewsbury (No. 92g).

				Ft.	In.
Berwick—					
Length			970 yards.		
Minimum height above water level ..		..		6	10
Minimum width at water level	..	..		7	0

No towing-path ; boats " legged " through.

There are no fixed hours for boats to pass through this tunnel.   There is a white mark in the middle of the tunnel, and should two boats meet, the one who has reached the middle of the tunnel first has the right of way.

(g) Towing-path.

There is a towing-path throughout the whole of the navigation, except through Berwick Tunnel.

(i) Types of vessels using the navigation.

Narrow boats use the whole of the navigation with the exception of the Old Shropshire Canal Section of the Shrewsbury Canal.

On the Old Shropshire Canal Section of the Shrewsbury Canal narrow boats of a smaller type, of which the Shropshire Union Railways and Canal Company possess about 24 (*see* Section 9, Types of Vessels, (*a*) Non-Sailing Vessels), navigate from Wappenshall Junction to Trench Wharf.   Tub-boats (*see* Section 9, Types of vessels, (*a*) Non-Sailing Vessels) are the only boats which can use the canal between Trench Wharf and Donnington.   They also navigate to Newport and Shrewsbury.

Mersey flats habitually navigate the Wirral Line—Ellesmere Canal— between Ellesmere Port and Chester, and also the Chester Canal Navigation between Chester and Egg Bridge, but they do not as a rule travel further south than the latter place.

SIMPSON, L. T. ESQ.—*see* River Ouse (Bedford).

SIXTEEN FOOT RIVER—*see* Middle Level Navigations.

SLOUGH BRANCH CANAL—*see* Grand Junction Canal.

SMITH'S LEAM, the name given to that portion of the River Nene extending between "The Cuts Mouth," Peterborough, and Guyhirne.

SNEYD AND WYRLEY BANK BRANCH CANAL—*see* Birmingham Canal Navigations, Wyrley and Essington Canal.

SOAR RIVER, navigable portions of, are comprised in the Grand Junction Canal (Leicester Section), the Leicester Navigation, and the Loughborough Navigation.

SOHO BRANCH CANAL—*see* Birmingham Canal Navigations, Main Line.

SOMERLEYTON DIKE—*see* River Waveney.

---

(93)—SOMERSETSHIRE COAL CANAL NAVIGATION.

(a) *Short Description.*

The canal commences by a junction with the Kennet and Avon Navigation of the Great Western Railway Company at the west end of Dundas Aqueduct, and proceeds by Monkton Combe, Midford, Combe Hay, Dunkerton, and Camerton to Timsbury Colliery Landing, half-a-mile to the west of Camerton, all in the county of Somersetshire.

The Company is in the hands of a liquidator.

Since November, 1898, in consequence of the expenses having exceeded the income, the pumping engine situated between Camerton and Dunkerton for supplying the Summit Level with water has not been worked, traffic on the canal has practically ceased, and it is reported that negotiations have been entered into with the Great Western Railway Company with a view to their acquiring the site for the purpose of constructing a new line of railway.

The traffic which used to be carried on the canal was almost entirely coal from three collieries—one at Timsbury, situated about a quarter-of-a-mile from the canal, and communicating with it by means of a tramroad from the landing, and the other two close to the canal at Camerton.

(b) *Proprietors, Officers, and Offices.*

The Company of Proprietors of the Somersetshire Coal Canal Navigation.

Liquidator : W. Jeffrey.

Office : 2, Cumberland Buildings, Bath.

(c) *Distance Table.*

Dundas, junction with Kennet and Avon Navigation (No. 43a), to—	Miles	Fur.
Monkton Combe Church	–	6
Midford	2	0
Combe Hay Bottom Lock	2	7
Combe Hay Top Lock	4	2
Combe Hay Village	4	4
Dunkerton	6	6
Camerton	9	0
Timsbury Colliery Landing	9	4

The canal as originally constructed extended westwards towards Timsbury for a further distance of one mile, but this latter portion has been disused for many years.

(93)—Somersetshire Coal Canal Navigation—*continued.*

(d) Locks.

1.—Dundas.

2
to } Combe Hay.
28.

Rise from Dundas.

(e) Maximum size of vessels that can use the navigation.

	Ft.	In.
Length	72	0
Width	7	2
Draught prior to November, 1898, when the pumping engine for the supply of water to the Summit Level ceased work, boats could navigate the canal drawing from	2	6 to 3ft.
Headroom	8	0

(f) Tunnels.

Combe Hay—

Length	65 yards.	
Minimum height above water level	7	7
Minimum width at water level	11	9
Towing-path through the tunnel.		

(g) Towing-path.

There is a towing-path throughout the navigation.

(i) Types of vessels using the navigation.

Narrow boats.

Somersetshire Drainage Commissioners, The, are the Drainage Authority in respect of the portions of the following rivers which are navigable, namely :—The River Parrett from Thorney Mill to Bridgwater Bay, and the River Brue below Highbridge, the River Tone from Ham Mill to Borough Bridge, and the River Yeo from Ilchester to Langport.

---

(94)—South Eastern and Chatham Railway Companies Managing Committee.

(a) Short Description.

The Committee are the proprietors of the Gravesend and Rochester Canal. The canal, originally known as the Thames and Medway Canal, was constructed under an Act of Parliament of 1800. It was purchased by the Gravesend and Rochester Railway and Canal Company in 1845, who took a portion of the canal between Higham Station and Rochester for their railway, and changed the name of the remaining portion of the canal to the Gravesend and Rochester Canal. In 1846 the Gravesend and Rochester Railway and Canal Company was absorbed by the South

Eastern Railway Company, and in 1899 the South Eastern Railway
Company fromed an amalgamation with the London, Chatham, and
Dover Railway Company under an Act of Parliament which provided
that the two companies should be managed and maintained as one undertaking.

The entrance to the canal from the River Thames at Gravesend
is through a lock giving access to a tidal basin, from this tidal basin
another lock communicates with the canal. Leaving Gravesend, the
canal proceeds by Chalk and Shorne to its termination at Higham
Station on the railway between Gravesend and Rochester.

The whole course of the canal is situated in the county of Kent.

The canal is in fair order, but there is not much trade done on it.

(b) Proprietors, Officers, and Offices.

South Eastern and Chatham Railway Companies Managing
Committee.

General Manager : Vincent W. Hill.

Secretary : Charles Sheath.

Engineer : Percy C. Tempest.

Offices : London Bridge Station, London S.E.

Goods Manager : G. Wallis.

Office : Imperial Buildings, Holborn Viaduct, London, E.C.

(c) Distance Table.

	Miles.	Fur.
Gravesend, entrance lock to tidal basin, and junction with River Thames (No. 107a), to—		
Gravesend, lock from tidal basin to canal	–	1
Chalk	1	2
Shorne Landing	1	5
Higham Station, termination of canal	4	0

(d) Locks.

1.—Gravesend, from River Thames to Tidal Basin.
2.—Gravesend, from Tidal Basin to canal.

This latter lock has also a pair of sea gates above the navigation top
gates, to keep the tide from the River Thames out of the canal.

Rise from River Thames at low water.

(e) Maximum size of vessels that can use the navigation.

	Ft.	In.
Length	80	0
Width	19	0
Draught	4	3
Headroom	about 16	0

(94)—SOUTH EASTERN AND CHATHAM RAILWAY COMPANIES MANAGING COMMITTEE—*continued.*

(g) *Towing-path.*

There is a towing-path throughout the navigation.

(h) *Tidal Information.*

See Tidal Information, River Thames (No. 107).

(i) *Types of vessels using the navigation.*

Barges, and Medway sailing barges.

SOUTH FORTY FOOT RIVER, another name for the Black Sluice Drainage and Navigation.

SOUTH LEVEL DRAINAGE AND NAVIGATION COMMISSIONERS, THE, are the Controlling Authority in respect of :—

Brandon River.

> The Staunch, known as Crosswater Staunch, situated between Wilton Bridge and the junction with the River Ouse (Bedford) at Brandon Creek, which is an open navigation, having no controlling authority.

River Cam.

> The portion of the river extending from Clayhithe to Pope's Corner, and the navigation of Reach Lode and Burwell Lode so far as the navigation of them extends. The Commissioners also maintain Reach Lode Sluice jointly with the Bedford Level Corporation.

River Larke.

> The Sluice or Lock known as Isleham Sluice, situated on the portion of the river between Lee Brook and a point about half-a-mile above Prickwillow, which is an open navigation, having no controlling authority ; and the portion of the river between the last-named point and its junction with the River Ouse (Bedford).

River Ouse (Bedford).

> The Sluice or Lock known as Over Staunch, situated on the portion of the river between Holywell and Earith, which is an open navigation, having no controlling authority; the portion of the river between Earith and Popes Corner known as the Old West River; the portion of the river between Pope's Corner and Littleport Bridge ; and the navigation doors of Denver Sluice, that is, all the doors pointing up river.

SOUTH WALSHAM BROAD—*see* River Bure.

SOW, RIVER—*see* Staffordshire and Worcestershire Canal, Stafford Branch.

---

(95)—STAFFORDSHIRE AND WORCESTERSHIRE CANAL.

(a) *Short Description.*

The canal commences by a junction with the River Severn at Stourport, and proceeds by Kidderminster and Wolverley, in the county of Worcestershire ; Kinver, Stourton, Swindon, Wombourne, Tettenhall, Aldersley, Autherley, Gailey, Penkridge, and Tixall, to Great Haywood, in the county of Staffordshire, where it forms a junction with the North Staffordshire Railway Company's Trent and Mersey Canal.

There are branches leading out of the Main Line as follows :—

A connection with a short piece of the River Stour near Oldington, through Pratt's Wharf Lock, giving access to Pratt's Wharf and Wilden Iron Works, all in the county of Worcestershire.

The Hatherton Branch, which leaves the main line near Saredon, and forms a junction with the Churchbridge Branch of the Birmingham Canal Navigations at Churchbridge, all in the county of Staffordshire.

The Stafford Branch, which leaves the main line near Baswich, and passing through Baswich Lock, descends to the River Sow, the course of which it follows to Stafford.

There is a fair trade on the navigation, and the works are well maintained.

(b) *Proprietors, Officers, and Offices.*

Staffordshire and Worcestershire Canal Company.

Clerk : J. Neve.

Traffic Manager : A. G. Butler.

Offices : 87, Darlington Street, Wolverhampton.

On the portion of the River Stour forming the branch to Pratt's Wharf and Wilden Iron Works, Pratt's Wharf Lock is the property of the Staffordshire and Worcestershire Canal Company, but the river is an open navigation, having no controlling authority.

The portion of the River Sow forming the Stafford Branch is leased from Lord Stafford by the Staffordshire and Worcestershire Canal Company.

(95)—Staffordshire and Worcestershire Canal—*continued.*

(c) *Distance Table.*

Main Line (No. 95a).

	Miles.	Fur.
Stourport, junction with River Severn—Main Line—(No. 89a), and entrance locks to Stourport Basin, to—		
Lower Mitton Bridge	–	3
Gilgal Bridge and Wharf	–	5
Mitton Chapel Bridge	–	6
Upper Mitton Bridge and Wharf	1	0
Bullock's Lane Wharf	1	4
Oldington Bridge	2	0
Junction with River Stour (No. 95b), through Pratt's Wharf Lock, between Locks No. 3 and 4	2	3
Falling Sands Lock	2	6
Falling Sands Bridge and Iron Works ..	3	1
Caldwall Bridge and Lock	3	4
Round Hill Bridge	3	6
Caldwall Mill Bridge	3	6
Caldwall Hall Bridge and Public Wharf ..	4	0
Kidderminster Lock, Wharf, and Warehouse	4	3
Limekiln Bridge and Wharf	4	5
Stour Vale Iron Works..	5	4
Wolverley Court Bridge and Lock	5	5
Wolverley Mill Wharf	5	7
Wolverley Bridge, Lock and Wharf	6	1
Wolverley Forge Bridge and Lock ..	6	3
Debdale Bridge and Lock	7	2
Cookley Tunnel and Iron Works, ...	7	4
Austcliffe Bridge and Wharf	8	0
Clay House Bridge	8	2
Whittington Bridge, Lock, and Iron Works..	9	4
Whittington Horse Bridge	9	6
Kinver Bridge, Lock, and Wharf	10	3
Hyde Bridge, Lock, and Iron Works ..	11	0
Dunsley Tunnel	11	5
Stewponey Wharf, Lock, and Warehouse ..	12	0
Stourton Bridge and Junction, junction with Stourbridge Canal—Main Line—(No. 99a), between Locks Nos. 13 and 14	12	2
Round House Wharf and Iron Works ..	13	5
Gothersley Bridge and Lock	14	0
Gothersley, or Hockley, Lock	14	3
Green's Forge Bridge, Lock, and Wharf ..	15	1
Hincksford Bridge and Lock	16	2
Swindon Forge Bridge, Wharf, Lock, and Iron Works	16	5
Marsh Lock	16	7
Botterham Bridge and Two Locks	17	2
Wombourne Common Bridge and Wharf ..	17	5
Heath Forge Wharf	17	7
Bumble Hole Bridge and Lock	18	4

(95)—STAFFORDSHIRE AND WORCESTERSHIRE CANAL—*continued.*

Stourport, junction with River Severn—Main
Line—(No. 89a), and entrance locks to
Stourport Basin, to (*continued*)—

	Miles.	Fur.
Bratch Bridge and Three Locks	18	7
Aw Bridge and Lock	19	6
Ebstree Lock	20	2
Dimmingsdale Lock and Reservoir	20	4
Dimmingsdale Bridge, Wharf, and Warehouse	20	6
Mops Farm Bridge	21	3
Castle Croft Bridge	21	6
Whightwick Bridge and Lock	22	4
Whightwick Mill Bridge and Lock	22	5
Compton Wharf, Lock, and Bridge	23	2
Tettenhall Bridge and Wharf	24	0
Dunstall Water Bridge..	24	5
Aldersley Junction, junction with Birmingham Canal Navigations—Main Line—No. 10a1)	25	1
Autherley Junction, junction with Shropshire Union Canals—Birmingham and Liverpool Junction Canal—(No. 92a1)	25	5
Marsh Lane Bridge	26	3
Coven Heath Bridge, First Wharf	27	4
Coven Heath Bridge, Second Wharf	27	7
Cross Green Bridge and Wharf	28	3
Slade Heath Bridge and L. & N. W. Rly. Bridge	29	0
Laches Bridge	29	6
Moat House Bridge	30	2
Deepmore Bridge and Wharf	30	6
The Cross Bridge, Hatherton Junction, junction with Hatherton Branch (No. 95c)..	31	1
Calf Heath Bridge and Wharf	32	0
Gravelley Way Bridge ..	32	1
Gailey Wharf, Bridge, Lock, and Warehouse	33	3
Brick-kiln Lock ..	33	4
Boggs Lock	33	6
Rodbaston Bridge and Lock	34	4
Otherton Lane Bridge ..	34	6
Otherton Lock ..	35	0
Line Hill Bridge..	35	1
Filance Lock	35	2
Penkridge Bridge, Wharf, Lock, and Warehouse	36	1
Longford Bridge and Lock	36	5
Longford Bridge..	36	7
Teddesley Bridge	37	1
Park Gate Bridge, Wharf, and Lock ..	37	4
Shutt Hill Bridge and Lock	38	2
Acton Bridge and Wharf	38	6
Roseford Bridge	39	5
Deptmore Lock ..	40	0
Hazlestrine Bridge	40	3

(95)—STAFFORDSHIRE AND WORCESTERSHIRE CANAL—*continued.*

	Miles.	Fur.
Stourport, junction with River Severn—Main Line—(No. 89a), and entrance locks to Stourport Basin, to (*continued*)—		
Radford Bridge, Wharf, and Warehouse ..	41	2
Baswich Bridge and Salt Works	41	6
Junction with Stafford Branch (No. 95d) ..	42	0
Lodgfield Bridge..	42	4
Stoneford Bridge	43	0
Millford Bridge	43	6
Tixall Bridge	44	4
Old Hill Bridge, Wharf, and Lock	44	6
Haywood Wharf and Junction, junction with Trent and Mersey Canal (No. 76a) ..	46	1

River Stour (No. 95b).

Length from junction with Main Line (No. 95a), Pratt's Wharf Lock, and Pratt's Wharf, to—		
Wilden Iron Works	1	2

Hatherton Branch (No. 95c).

Hatherton Junction, junction with Main Line (No. 85a), to—		
Saredon Mill Bridge	–	6
Four Crosses Bridge	1	2
Wedges Mills	2	0
Walk Mill, Old Coppice, and Great Wyrley Collieries	2	6
Churchbridge Junction, junction with Birmingham Canal Navigations—Churchbridge Branch Canal—(No. 10s.)	3	4

Stafford Branch (No. 95d).

Junction with Main Line (No. 95a), and Baswich Lock to—		
Stafford Wharf	1	0

(d) Locks.

Main Line (No. 95a).

$$\left.\begin{matrix}1\\ \text{and}\\ 2.\end{matrix}\right\} \text{Stourport Barge Locks or} \left\{\begin{matrix}1\\ 1a\\ 2\\ 2a\end{matrix}\right. \begin{matrix}\left.\right\}\text{(staircase).}\\ \text{Stourport Boat Locks.}\\ \left.\right\}\text{(staircase).}\end{matrix}$$

Giving access from River Severn to Stourport Basin.

3.—Stourport.
4.—Falling Sands, or Oldington.
5.—Caldwall.
6.—Kidderminster.

(95)—STAFFORDSHIRE AND WORCESTERSHIRE CANAL—*continued.*

7.—Wolverley Court.
8.—Wolverley.
9.—Cookley, or Debdale.
10.—Whittington.
11.—Kinver.
12.—Hyde.
13.—Stewponey.
14.—Gothersley.
15.—Hockley.
16.—Green's Forge.
17.—Hincksford.
18.—Swindon.
19.—Marsh.
20 }
and } Botterham (staircase).
21. }
22.—Bumble Hole.
23 }
to } Bratch.
25. }
26.—Aw Bridge.
27.—Ebstree.
28.—Dimmingsdale.
29.—Whightwick.
30.—Whightwick Mill.
31.—Compton.
      Rise from River Severn at Stourport.
32.—Gailey.
33.—Brick-kiln.
34.—Boggs.
35.—Rodbaston.
36.—Otherton.
37.—Filance.
38.—Penkridge.
39.—Longford.
40.—Park Gate.
41.—Shutt Hill.
42.—Deptmore.
43.—Old Hill, or Tixall.
      Fall to Great Haywood.

      River Stour (No. 95b).
1.—Pratt's Wharf.
      Fall from Main Line.

      Hatherton Branch (No. 95c).

1.
2.
3.
4.
5.
6.
7.
8.
      Rise to Churchbridge.

(95)—STAFFORDSHIRE AND WORCESTERSHIRE CANAL—*continued.*

Stafford Branch (No. 95d).

1.—Baswich.

Fall from Main Line.

(e) *Maximum size of vessels that can use the navigation.*

Main Line (No. 95a), River Stour (No. 95b), and Hatherton Branch (No. 95c).

	Ft.	In.
Length	72	0
Width	6	9
Width from River Severn at Stourport to Stourport Basin, through Barge Locks ..	15	0
Draught	4	0
Headroom	8	8

Stafford Branch (No. 95d).

		Ft.	In.
Length		72	0
Width		6	9
Draught .. .. ..from 3ft. 10in. up to		5	0
according to the amount of water in the River Sow.			
Headroom		8	8

(f) *Tunnels.*

Main Line (No. 95a).

Cookley—

Length	65 yards		
Minimum height above water level		8	8
Minimum width at water level		8	2
Towing-path through the tunnel.			

(g) *Towing-path.*

There is a towing-path throughout the navigation.

(i) *Types of vessels using the navigation.*

Narrow boats. Severn trows can pass from the River Severn at Stourport through the Barge Locks to Stourport Basin, but not beyond.

STAINFORTH AND KEADBY CANAL—*see* Sheffield and South Yorkshire Navigation.

STALHAM DIKE—*see* River Bure, River Ant.

STANLEY DOCK CUT BRANCH CANAL—*see* Leeds and Liverpool Canal.

STOCKPORT BRANCH CANAL—*see* Great Central Railway, Ashton Canal.

STONEBRIDGE DRAIN—*see* Witham Drainage General Commissioners.

(96)—RIVER STORT.

(a) Short Description.

The river commences to be navigable at Bishop's Stortford, in the county of Hertfordshire, and proceeds by Sawbridgeworth, Harlow, Parndon, and Roydon to Fieldes Weir on the River Lee, where it forms a junction with that river shortly above Fieldes Weir Lock.

The course of the navigation forms for the most part the boundary between the counties of Hertfordshire and Essex, and is somewhat narrow and tortuous.

The lock gates are mostly of the old pattern, without balance beams, hung on hooks and rides.

The principal trade is malt.

(b) Proprietors, Officers, and Offices.

Proprietor : Sir Walter Gilbey, Bart.

Agents : Messrs. William Gee & Sons.

Office : Bishop's Stortford.

(c) Distance Table.

	Miles.	Fur.
Bishop's Stortford to—		
Twyford ..	2	0
Spelbrook	3	0
Tednambury	4	6
Sawbridgeworth ..	5	0
Harlow ..	7	0
Latton ..	8	0
Burnt Mill	9	2
Parndon ..	9	6
Hunsdon ..	11	0
Roydon ..	12	6
Junction with River Lee (No. 57a)	13	6

(d) Locks.

1.—South Mill.
2.—Twyford.
3.—Spelbrook.
4.—Tednambury.
5.—Sawbridgeworth.
6.—Sheering.
7.—Feakes.
8.—Harlow.
9.—Latton.
10.—Burnt Mill.
11.—Parndon.
12.—Hunsdon.
13.—Roydon.
14.—Roydon Brick.
15.—Roydon Lower.

Fall from Bishop's Stortford.

x

(96)—RIVER STORT—*continued.*

(e) *Maximum size of vessels that can use the navigation.*

	Ft.	In.
Length	78	6
Width	13	0
Draught from Bishop's Stortford to Sawbridgeworth	3	0
Draught from Sawbridgeworth to the junction with the River Lee..	3	3
Headroom	6	0

(g) *Towing-path.*

There is a towing-path throughout the navigation.

(i) *Types of vessels using the navigation.*

Barges carrying from 50 to 60 tons.

---

(97)—RIVER STOUR (KENT).

(a) *Short Description.*

The river commences to be navigable at Fordwich Bridge, two miles north-east of Canterbury, and proceeds by Grove Ferry, Sarre, Minster Ferry, and Sandwich to Pegwell Bay, where it enters the North Sea, all in the county of Kent.

There is a fair trade done from the mouth of the river up to Sandwich, although the course of the river is very tortuous. Above Sandwich there is practically no trade, but the river is not at all in bad condition.

From the west to the east end of Stonar Cut, which is scarcely one furlong in length, and is situated at North Stonar on the main road between Sandwich and Margate, the river makes a detour of over five miles by the town of Sandwich. Stonar Cut is not navigable, being only used as a relief channel in flood time.

(b) *Proprietors, Officers, and Offices.*

From the mouth ot the river to North Poulder's Sluice, three-quarters-of-a-mile above Sandwich Bridge, the river is under the jurisdiction of the Corporation of the Town of Sandwich as sole authority.

From North Poulder's Sluice to Fordwich the Corporation of Sandwich are the Navigation Authority, and the Commissioners of Sewers for East Kent are the Drainage Authority.

Corporation of Sandwich.

Town Clerk : Dick Baker.

Office : Town Hall, Sandwich.

Commissioners of Sewers for East Kent.

Clerk : Montague Kingsford.

Office : Canterbury.

The Corporation of Sandwich are the proprietors of a steam tug employed in towing vessels from the mouth of the river to Sandwich.

(97)—River Stour (Kent)—*continued.*

(c) Distance Table.

	Miles.	Fur.
Fordwich Bridge to—		
Grove Ferry	4	7
Sarre Pen	7	6
Pluck's Gutter	8	1
Minster Ferry	10	5
Stonar Cut, top entrance (not navigable) ..	12	7
Richborough	13	6
North Poulder's Sluice	14	4
Sandwich Bridge	15	2
Stonar Cut, bottom entrance (not navigable) ..	18	4
Pegwell Bay, high water mark	19	5

From this point to the North Sea at low water of Spring tides is a further distance of two miles by a channel leading through Sandwich sand flats.

The channel is marked by beacons, the sand flats being covered at high water.

(e) Maximum size of vessels that can use the navigation.

	Ft.	In.
Length.—Not limited.		
Width.—Not limited.		
Draught from the mouth of the river to Sandwich	11	0
Draught from Sandwich to Fordwich about	7	0
Headroom from Pegwell Bay to any part of Sandwich, not limited, Sandwich Town Bridge being an opening bridge		

(g) Towing-path.

There never was a horse towing-path alongside the navigation, but there is a bow-hauling path throughout the whole, which is still used occasionally.

(h) Tidal Information.

Spring tides flow to Grove Ferry. Neap tides generally flow to Pluck's Gutter.

High water at Pegwell Bay 2hrs. 14min. before London Bridge, being the same time as at Ramsgate.

Spring tides rise	15ft.
Neap ,, ,, ...	12ft.

High water at Sandwich 25min. after Pegwell Bay.

Spring tides rise	8ft.
Neap ,, ,, ...	7ft.

(i) Types of vessels using the navigation.

Small coasting vessels, Medway sailing barges, and barges.

(98)—RIVER STOUR (SUFFOLK).

(a) Short Description.

The river commences to be navigable at the town of Sudbury, in the county of Suffolk, and proceeds by Bures, Nayland, Stratford St. Mary, Dedham, and Brantham Lock to Cattawade Bridge, shortly below which it widens out into an estuary of about one mile in width, and, passing Manningtree and Mistley, finally enters the North Sea at Harwich.

Excepting for the first three-quarters-of-a-mile below Sudbury, the river forms the boundary between the counties of Suffolk and Essex.

There is very little trade done on the navigation.

The locks and other works on the navigation are of the old-fashioned type, and not in very good repair.

(b) Proprietors, Officers, and Offices.

The River Stour Navigation Company Ltd.

Secretary : Frank Boggis.

Office : Station Road, Sudbury, Suffolk.

(c) Distance Table.

Sudbury to—		Miles.	Fur.
Cornard Lock		1	0
Henny Lock		2	3
Pitmore Lock		3	6
Bures Bridge and Wharf		6	6
Bures Lock		7	3
Wormingford Lock		9	1
Swan Lock		9	3
Wiston Lock		11	3
Nayland Lock and Village		12	5
Horkesley Lock		13	1
Boxted Lock		16	1
Langham Lock		17	1
Stratford Lock		18	7
Stratford Bridge		19	5
Dedham Lock and Village		20	4
Flatford Lock		22	1
Brantham Lock		23	5
Cattawade Bridge		24	3
Manningtree	about	25	0
Mistley	about	26	0
Wrabness	about	30	0
Parkeston	about	34	0
Harwich	about	35	4

(d) Locks.

1.—Cornard.
2.—Henny.
3.—Pitmore.
4.—Bures.

(98)—RIVER STOUR (SUFFOLK)—*continued.*

    5.—Wormingford.
    6.—Swan.
    7.—Wiston.
    8.—Nayland.
    9.—Horkesley.
  10.—Boxted.
  11.—Langham.
  12.—Stratford.
  13.—Dedham.
  14.—Flatford.
  15.—Brantham.

Fall from Sudbury.

(e) *Maximum size of vessels that can use the navigation.*

	Ft.	In.
Length.—All the locks have an available length of 95ft. so as to accommodate two lighters at a time, each measuring in length ..	47	0
Width	10	9
Draught .. .. 2ft. 6in. to 2		8
Headroom	5	3

(g) *Towing-path.*

There is a towing-path from Sudbury to a point half-a-mile below Brantham Lock. Below this, navigation is only conducted on the ebb and flow of the tide.

(h) *Tidal Information.*

Spring tides flow to the tail of Flatford Lock, Neap tides flow to Brantham Lock.

High water at Harwich 1hr. 52min. before London Bridge.
      Spring tides rise   ..   ..   ..   11ft. 6in.
      Neap   ,,   ,, ...   9ft. 9in.

High water at Wrabness 23min. after Harwich.
      Spring tides rise   ..   ..   ..   12ft.

High water at Mistley 42 min. after Harwich.
      Spring tides rise   ..   ..   ..   11ft. 9in.

High water at Cattawade Bridge 1hr. 2min. after Harwich.
      Spring tides rise   ..   ..   ..   4ft. 3in.

(i) *Types of vessels using the navigation.*

River Stour (Suffolk) lighters navigate the river between Sudbury and Mistley, and are the only type of vessel using the river above Cattawade Bridge—*see* Section 9, Types of Vessels, (*a*) Non-Sailing Vessels.

STOUR, RIVER (WORCESTERSHIRE)—*see* Staffordshire and Worcestershire Canal.

(99)—STOURBRIDGE CANAL.

(a) Short Description.

The canal commences at Stourton Junction by a junction with the Staffordshire and Worcestershire Canal, and proceeds by Wordsley Junction, Buckpool, The Lays Junction, and Brettell Lane to Black Delph, where it forms a junction with the Dudley Canal of the Birmingham Canal Navigations.

There are two short branches leading out of the main line, one from Wordsley Junction to the town of Stourbridge, and the other from The Lays Junction to The Fens on Pensnett Chase, which latter also gives access to the Great Western Railway Company's Stourbridge Extension Canal.

The whole course of the canal is situated in the county of Staffordshire.

There is a fair trade done on the canal to the town of Stourbridge.

(b) Proprietors, Officers, and Offices.

The Company of Proprietors of the Stourbridge Navigation.

Secretary : G. Harward.

Office : 118, High Street, Stourbridge.

Manager :

Office : 87, Darlington Street, Wolverhampton.

(c) Distance Table.

Main Line (No. 99a).

	Miles.	Fur.
Stourton Junction, junction with Staffordshire and Worcestershire Canal—Main Line—(No. 95a), and tail of Stourton Bottom Lock, to—		
Head of Stourton Top Lock	–	2
Wordsley Junction, junction with Stourbridge Branch (No. 99b), and bottom of The Sixteen Locks	2	0
Buckpool..	2	7
Lays Junction, junction with Branch to The Fens on Pensnett Chase (No. 99c), and top of The Sixteen Locks	3	2
Brettell Lane	4	3
Black Delph, junction with Birmingham Canal Navigations—Dudley Canal—Line No. 1 (No. 10f1)	5	1

Stourbridge Branch (No. 99b).

Wordsley Junction, junction with Main Line (No. 99a), to—		
Holloway End	–	7
Stourbridge	1	2

(99)—STOURBRIDGE CANAL—*continued*.

Branch to The Fens on Pensnett Chase (No. 99c).

	Miles.	Fur.
Lays Junction, junction with Main Line (No. 99a), to—		
Brockmoor Junction, junction with Stourbridge Extension Canal (No. 43c1) ..	–	2
The Fens, Pensnett Chase	–	6½

(*d*) *Locks.*

Main Line (No. 99a).

1 to 4. } Stourton.

5 to 20. } The Sixteen Locks.

Rise from Stourton Junction.

(*e*) *Maximum size of vessels that can use the navigation.*

Main Line (No. 99a) and Branches

	Ft.	In.
Length	70	0
Width	7	0
Draught	4	0
Headroom	9	0

(*g*) *Towing-path.*

There is a towing-path throughout the navigation.

(*i*) *Types of vessels using the navigation.*

Narrow boats.

STOURBRIDGE BRANCH CANAL—*see* Stourbridge Canal.

STOURBRIDGE EXTENSION CANAL—*see* Great Western Railway

---

(100)—STROUDWATER CANAL.

(*a*) *Short Description.*

The canal commences at Wallbridge, Stroud, by a junction with the Thames and Severn Canal, and proceeds by Dudbridge, Stonehouse, Eastington, and Saul to Framilode, where it joins the estuary of the River Severn, all in the county of Gloucestershire. One mile from Framilode the canal crosses the Gloucester and Berkeley Ship Canal on the level

(100)—STROUDWATER CANAL—*continued.*

(b) *Proprietors, Officers, and Offices.*

The Company of Proprietors of the Stroudwater Navigation.

Clerk and Surveyor : W. J. Snape.

Office : 13, Wallbridge, Stroud, Gloucestershire.

(c) *Distance Table.*

	Miles.	Fur.
Wallbridge, Stroud, junction with Thames and Severn Canal—Main Line—(No. 108a), to—		
Dudbridge Top Lock	–	4
Double Locks	1	6
Stonehouse Bridge	2	5
Newtown Bridge	3	5
Newtown Lock	3	6
Pike Lock and Bridge	4	1
Westfield Lock and Bridge	4	4
Bristol Road Lock	5	3
Whitminster Lock	6	5
Saul, junction with Gloucester and Berkeley Ship Canal (No. 90a) right and left	7	0
Junction Lock	7	1
Tail of Framilode Lock and junction with River Severn estuary (No. 89a)	8	0

(d) *Locks.*

1 and 2. } Dudbridge Upper. Dudbridge Lower.

3 and 4. } Double Locks (staircase).

5.—Newtown.
6. } Blunder.
7. } Pike.
8. } Dock.
9. } Westfield.
10.—Bristol Road.
11.—Whitminster.
12.—Junction.
13.—Framilode.

Fall from Stroud.

(e) *Maximum size of vessels that can use the navigation.*

	Ft.	In.
Length	70	0
Width	15	6
Draught	maximum 5	0
Headroom	11	6

(100)—STROUDWATER CANAL—*continued*.

(g) *Towing-path*.

There is a towing-path throughout the navigation.

(i) *Types of vessels using the navigation*.

Severn trows and barges carrying up to 75 tons.

STOVER CANAL—*see* Great Western Railway.

STOWMARKET AND IPSWICH NAVIGATION—*see* Ipswich and Stowmarket Navigation.

STRATFORD-ON-AVON CANAL—*see* Great Western Railway.

STRETFORD AND LEIGH BRANCH CANAL—*see* Manchester Ship Canal, Bridgewater Canal.

STRETTON WHARF BRANCH—*see* Oxford Canal.

---

(101)—SURREY CANAL.

(a) *Short Description*.

The canal commences by a junction with the New Greenland Dock of the Surrey Commercial Docks, in the parish of Rotherhithe, in the county of Surrey, and proceeds through the parish of St. Paul, Deptford, in the county of Kent, to its termination at Camberwell Road, in the parish of St. Giles, Camberwell, also in the county of Kent.

There is a short branch leading out of the main line to Peckham.

Access to the canal from the River Thames is obtained through either the Surrey Entrance or the Lavender Entrance of the Surrey Commercial Docks, each being distant about one mile from the commencement of the canal at the South end of the New Greenland Dock.

The principal trade on the canal is coal and timber.

(b) *Proprietors, Officers, and Offices*.

The Surrey Commercial Dock Company.

Secretary : T. H. Cullis.

Office : 106, Fenchurch Street, London, E.C.

Superintendent : S. Brownfield.

Office : Surrey Commercial Docks, Rotherhithe, London, S.E.

(101)—Surrey Canal—*continued.*

(c) *Distance Table.*

Main Line (No. 101a).

	Miles.	Fur.
South end of New Greenland Dock, Canal Lock, and Toll Office, to—		
Lower Road Bridge, Deptford	–	5
South Metropolitan Company's Gas Works ..	1	5
Old Kent Road Bridge	2	0
Junction with Peckham Branch (No. 101b) ..	2	2½
Camberwell Wharf	3	1

Peckham Branch (No. 101b).

	Miles.	Fur.
Junction with Main Line (No. 101a) to—		
Commercial Road Bridge, Peckham	–	3
Peckham Wharf	–	5

(d) *Locks.*

Main Line (No. 101a).

1.—The Canal Lock.

This lock gives access to the canal from the New Greenland Dock.

The fall from the New Greenland Dock to the canal varies from nil to seven feet, according to the level of the water in the dock, which is ruled by the height of the tides in the River Thames.

(e) *Maximum size of vessels using the navigation.*

Main Line (No. 101a) and Peckham Branch (No. 101b).

	Ft.	In.
Length	105	0
Width	17	9
Draught	4	9
Headroom	8	0

(g) *Towing-path.*

There is a towing-path throughout the navigation.

(i) *Types of vessels using the navigation.*

Barges, lighters, and Medway sailing barges.

Surrey Commercial Dock Company—*see* Surrey Canal.

(102)—Duke of Sutherland's Tub Boat Canal.

(a) Short Description.

The canal commences at Donnington by a junction with the Shrewsbury Canal—Old Shropshire Canal Section—of the Shropshire Union Railways and Canal Company, and proceeds by Muxton Bridge and Lilleshall Abbey to its termination, about one mile to the westward of the main road between Wolverhampton and Newport, all in the county of Shropshire.

There is a small coal traffic on the canal from Muxton Bridge and intermediate places to the Shropshire Union Railways and Canal Company's system. Beyond Muxton Bridge the canal is only used in a very small degree for agricultural purposes.

The canal used formerly to extend a further distance of one mile through the estate of an adjoining landowner to Pave Lane, on the main road between Wolverhampton and Newport, but this latter portion has lately been closed.

(b) Proprietors, Officers, and Offices.

Proprietor : The Duke of Sutherland.

The portion of the canal between Donnington and Muxton Bridge is leased to the Lilleshall Company Ltd., the remainder being in the hands of the proprietor.

Lilleshall Company Ltd.

Head Office : Prior's Lee, near Shifnal, Shropshire.

(c) Distance Table.

	Miles.	Fur.
Donnington, junction with Shrewsbury Canal—Old Shropshire Canal Section (No. 92h), to—		
Muxton Bridge	1	4
Termination of Canal	4	2

(e) Maximum size of vessels that can use the navigation.

	Ft.	In.
Length	19	9
Width	6	2
Draught .. .. about	1	3

(g) Towing-path.

There is a towing-path throughout the navigation.

(i) Types of vessels using the navigation.

Tub boats—*see* Section 9, Types of Vessels, (a) Non-Sailing Vessels. The load for these boats is about three tons on any part of the canal.

Sutton Dike—*see* River Bure, River Ant.

Swansea Canal—*see* Great Western Railway.

Tag Cut—*see* Calder and Hebble Navigation.

---

(103)—River Tamar.

(a) Short Description.

The river commences to be navigable at New Bridge, Gunnislake, about three miles to the west of the town of Tavistock, and proceeds by Morwellham Quay, Calstock, Halton Quay, and Pentillie to Weirquay, below which place it becomes an estuary varying from a quarter-of-a-mile to three-quarters-of-a-mile in width, and after passing Cargreen, Saltash, and Devonport enters the English Channel at Plymouth.

The navigation throughout the whole of its course forms the boundary between the counties of Devonshire and Cornwall.

The principal trade is in bricks, stone, and vitriol to the upper portion of the navigation.

(b) Proprietors, Officers, and Offices.

From New Bridge, Gunnislake, to Morwellham Quay the river is under the jurisdiction of the Tamar Manure Navigation Company.

Clerk : Stephen Paul.

Office : Messrs. Fox, Fowler, & Co., Bankers, Calstock, Cornwall.

Agent : John Bridgman.

Office : Bealswood Terrace, Gunnislake, Tavistock.

Below Morwellham Quay the river is an open navigation, having no controlling authority.

(c) Distance Table.

New Bridge, Gunnislake, to—					Miles.	Fur.
Weir Head Lock	..	..	..	..	1	0
Morwellham Quay	..	..	..	..	2	6
New Quay..	..	..	..	..	3	4
Calstock ..	..	..	..	..	5	5
Halton Quay	..	..	..	..	8	7
Pentillie ..	..	..	..	..	9	4
Weirquay..	..	..	..	..	11	4
Cargreen ..	..	..	..	..	13	0
Saltash Railway Bridge		..	..	..	15	5
Devonport	..	..	..	..	18	4
Plymouth	..	..	..	..	20	0

(d) Locks.

1.—Weir Head.

Fall from Gunnislake.

(103)—River Tamar—*continued.*

(e) *Maximum size of vessels that can use the navigation.*

	Ft.	In.
Length.—Not limited ⎫ except through Weir		
⎬ Head Lock, the		
Width.—Not limited ⎭ dimensions of which are :		
Length	80	0
Width	20	0
Draught from the mouth of the river to·Morwellham Quay .. .. .. about	10	0
Draught from Morwellham Quay to Weir Head Lock—on Spring tides .. .. about	8	0
on Neap tides .. .. about	5	0
Draught from Weir Head Lock to New Bridge, Gunnislake	7	0
Headroom.—Practically not limited. Saltash Bridge above river at high water	100	0

(g) *Towing-path.*

There is a towing-path from New Bridge, Gunnislake, to Weir Head Lock.

(h) *Tidal Information.*

The tide flows to the tail of Weir Head Lock.

High water at Plymouth 3hrs. 39min. after London Bridge.
        Spring tides rise .. .. .. 15ft. 6in.
        Neap   ,,   ,, ... 12ft.

High water at Devonport 6min. after Plymouth.
        Spring tides rise .. .. .. 15ft. 6in.
        Neap   ,,   ,, ... 12ft.

High water at Saltash 8min. after Plymouth.
        Spring tides rise .. .. .. 15ft.
        Neap   ,,   ,, ... 11ft.

High water at Cargreen 10min. after Plymouth.
        Spring tides rise .. .. .. 14ft. 9in.
        Neap   ,,   ,, ... 10ft. 9in.

High water at Pentillie 18min. after Plymouth.
        Spring tides rise .. .. .. 13ft. 6in.
        Neap   ,,   ,, ... 9ft. 6in.

High water at Calstock 29min. after Plymouth.
        Spring tides rise .. .. .. 12ft. 6in.
        Neap   ,,   ,, ... 8ft. 6in.

High water at Morwellham Quay 35min. after Plymouth.
        Spring tides rise .. .. .. 10ft. 6in.
        Neap   ,,   ,, ... 6ft. 6in.

High water at Weir Head Lock 40min. after Plymouth.
        Spring tides rise .. .. .. 5ft. 3in.
        Neap   ,,   ,, ... 1ft. 3in.

(103)—River Tamar—*continued.*

(i) Types of vessels using the navigation.

Coasting vessels and sailing barges, the latter carrying from 52 to 80 tons.

Tamar Manure Navigation Co.—*see* River Tamar.

Tame Valley Canal—*see* Birmingham Canal Navigations.

Team, Rivulet—*see* River Tyne.

---

(104)—River Tees.

(a) Short Description.

The river commences to be navigable at High Worsall, and proceeds by Yarm, Stockton, Thornaby, Newport, Middlesbrough, and Port Clarence to the North Sea.

The navigation throughout the whole of its course forms the boundary between the county of Durham and the North Riding of the county of Yorkshire.

The channel of the river for about the last five miles from the mouth is through sand flats, which are covered at high water, the channel being marked by beacons.

The navigation is chiefly used by sea-going vessels, which can navigate up the river as far as Stockton Bridge. Above this point there is a moderate amount of barge traffic in coal, whinstone, lime, manure, etc., to Yarm and High Worsall. Navigation, however, between Yarm and High Worsall is only conducted on Spring tides.

(b) Proprietors, Officers, and Offices.

The river from High Worsall to an imaginary line drawn across Tees Bay from Redcar to Hartlepool. is under the jurisdiction of the Tees Conservancy Commissioners.

Clerk : John H. Amos.

Engineer : George J. Clarke.

Offices : Queen's Terrace, Middlesbrough.

Harbour Master : Captain Livett.

Office : Harbour Master's Office, Middlesbrough.

(c) Distance Table.

Left Bank Miles.	Fur.					Right Bank Miles.	Fur.
		High Worsall to—					
2	0	Aislaby ..	..	..	..		
3	2	Yarm Bridge ..	..	..	..	3	2

(104)—RIVER TEES—*continued.*

Left Bank.			Right Bank.	
Miles	Fur.		Miles	Fur.
		High Worsall to (*continued*)—		
		Victoria Bridge, connecting Stockton (left bank) with		
10	5	Thornaby (right bank)	10	5
10	7	Stockton, Corporation Wharf		
		Newport	13	2
15	7	Ferry between Middlesbrough (right bank) and Port Clarence (left bank)	15	7
		Entrance to Middlesbrough Dock	16	4
22	0	Mouth of river at low water about	22	0

(e) *Maximum size of vessels that can use the navigation.*

	Ft.	In.
Length.—Not limited.		
Width.—Not limited.		
Draught from the mouth of the river to Middlesbrough— on Spring tides	24	0
on Neap tides	21	0
Draught from Middlesbrough to Stockton—		
on Spring tides	21	0
on Neap tides	19	0
Draught from Stockton to Yarm—		
on Spring tides.. ..	7	0
on Neap tides	5	6
Draught from Yarm to High Worsall uncertain, navigation only conducted on Spring tides.		
Headroom, Victoria Bridge, Stockton ..	18	0
,, Yarm Bridge varies from 16ft. 3in. to above high water of Spring tides.	23	0

(g) *Towing-path.*

There is no towing-path.

(h) *Tidal Information.*

The river is tidal throughout.

High water at the mouth of the river 1hr. 47min. after London Bridge.

Spring tides rise	..	.. ..	15ft.
Neap ,, ,,	..	.. ..	12ft. 3in.

High water at Middlesbrough 1hr. 49min. after London Bridge

Spring tides rise	..	.. ..	15ft.
Neap ,, ,,	..	.. ..	12ft. 3in.

High water at Stockton 53min. after Middlesbrough.

Spring tides rise	..	.. ..	12ft.
Neap ,, ,,	..	.. ..	10ft.

High water at Yarm about 1hr. 38min. after Middlesbrough

Spring tides rise	..	.. ..	10ft.
Neap ,, ,,	..	.. ..	8ft.

(104)—RIVER TEES—*continued.*

(*i*) *Types of vessels using the navigation.*

Sea-going vessels navigate the river up to Stockton Bridge. Barges use the navigation between Middlesbrough and High Worsall.

---

(105)—RIVER TEIGN.

(*a*) *Short Description.*

The river commences to be navigable at a wharf near Newton Abbot, situated on the main road between Newton Abbot and Kingsteignton. Three furlongs below this point a backwater half-a-mile in length, giving access to the Stover Canal, leaves the main channel of the river. Passing Newton Abbot Wharves the river soon widens out into an estuary of an average width of about three-eighths-of-a-mile, which continues to the mouth of the river at Teignmouth.

The whole course of the navigation is situated in the county of Devonshire.

The Hackney Canal forms a junction with the river at the western extremity of its estuary near Newton Abbot.

The trade on the river is almost entirely confined to china and pottery clay brought from the Stover and Hackney Canals for shipment at Teignmouth.

(*b*) *Proprietors, Officers, and Offices.*

Teignmouth Harbour Commissioners.

Clerk : Edward J. Tozer.

Office : 2 and 3, Orchard Gardens, Teignmouth.

(*c*) *Distance Table.*

Main Line of River (No. 105a).

	Miles.	Fur.
Head of Navigation, near Newton Abbot, to— Newton Abbot, junction with backwater leading to Stover Canal (No. 105b)	–	3
Newton Abbot Wharves and Great Western Railway Bridge—Main Line	–	4
Western extremity of estuary and junction with Hackney Canal (No. 46)	1	2
Teignmouth, mouth of river	5	0

Backwater leading to Stover Canal (No. 105b).

	Miles.	Fur.
Length from junction with Main Line of River (No. 105a) to Jetty Marsh, junction with Stover Canal (No. 43g)	–	4

(105)—River Teign—*continued.*

(e) *Maximum size of vessels that can use the navigation.*

	Ft.	In.
Length.—Not limited.		
Width.—Not limited.		
Draught	3	9

Headroom from Great Western Railway Bridge at Newton Abbot to Teignmouth not limited, Teignmouth Bridge being an opening bridge.

(g) *Towing-path.*

There is no horse towing-path, navigation being conducted on the ebb and flow of the tide. A little bow-hauling is occasionally done from the river banks in the neighbourhood of Newton Abbot.

(h) *Tidal Information.*

The navigation is tidal throughout.

High water at Teignmouth 4hrs. 2min. after London Bridge.
> Spring tides rise .. .. .. 13ft.
> Neap ,, ,, ... 9ft. 3in.

High water at Newton Abbot 7min. after Teignmouth.
> Spring tides rise .. .. .. 9ft. to 10ft.
> Neap ,, ,, ... 6ft.

(i) *Types of vessels using the navigation.*

River Teign, Stover Canal, and Hackney Canal Barges—*see* Section 9, Types of Vessels, (b) Sailing Vessels.

Teignmouth Harbour Commissioners—*see* River Teign.

Ten Mile River, The—the name given to the portion of the River Ouse (Bedford) situated between Littleport Bridge and Denver Sluice.

---

(106)—Tennant Canal.

(a) *Short Description.*

The canal commences at Aber-dulais by a junction with the Neath Canal, and, after crossing the River Neath by an aqueduct, proceeds down the north-west side of the Vale of Neath, and through the town of Neath, to Swansea, where, shortly before its termination, it forms a junction through a side lock with the Prince of Wales Dock.

There is a short branch from a point about three miles below the town of Neath to Red Jacket Pill, a branch of the River Neath, on which are situated the Red Jacket Wharves.

The whole course of the canal is situated in the county of Glamorganshire.

Y

(106)—TENNANT CANAL—*continued.*

(b) *Proprietors, Officers, and Offices.*

Proprietor : Mrs. Tennant.

Agent : Thomas Williams.

Office : Victoria Chambers, Neath, South Wales.

(c) *Distance Table.*

Main Line (No. 106a).

	Miles.	Fur.
Aber-dulais, junction with Neath Canal (No. 72), to—		
Aber-dulais Lock, and south end of aqueduct over River Neath	–	1
Neath, Main Road Bridge over canal	1	6½
Neath Abbey Railway Station	3	0
Junction with Red Jacket Pill Branch (No. 106b)	4	7
Briton Ferry Road Railway Station	5	6
Junction with Glan-y-wern Canal (No. 52b) ..	6	3
Junction with Tir-isaf Branch Canal (No. 52c)	7	5
Swansea, junction with Prince of Wales Dock through side lock	8	3
Swansea, termination of canal	8	3½

Red Jacket Pill Branch (No. 106b).

Length from junction with Main Line (No. 106a) to—		
Red Jacket Lock and junction with Red Jacket Pill (No. 73b)	–	1

(d) *Locks.*

Main Line (No. 106a).

1.—Aber-dulais.

Fall from junction with Neath Canal.

One side lock at Swansea giving access to Prince of Wales Dock.

Fall to Prince of Wales Dock.

Red Jacket Pill Branch (No. 106b).

1.—Red Jacket.

Fall to Red Jacket Pill.

(e) *Maximum size of vessels that can use the navigation.*

Main Line (No. 106a) and Red Jacket Pill Branch (No. 106b).

	Ft.	In.
Length	60	0
Width, except through Red Jacket Lock ..	9	0
Width, through Red Jacket Lock	15	0
Draught .. .. maximum	2	9

(106)—TENNANT CANAL—*continued.*

(g) Towing-path.

There is a towing-path throughout the navigation.

(i) Types of vessels using the navigation.

Neath and Tennant Canal boats—*see* Section 9, Types of Vessels, (a) Non-Sailing Vessels. The average load carried on the canal is 20 tons on a draught of 2ft. 6in.

---

(107)—RIVER THAMES.

(a) Short Description.

Although there is no navigation on the river above the junction with the Thames and Severn Canal at Inglesham, yet the jurisdiction of the Thames Conservancy commences at Cricklade, and the Conservators have power to charge tolls from that place. The course of the river between Cricklade and Inglesham is in close proximity to the line of the Thames and Severn Canal, passing Eisey, Castle Eaton, and Kempsford. Leaving Inglesham the river proceeds by Lechlade, Buscot, Radcot Bridge, Tadpole Bridge, Shifford, New Bridge, Northmoor, Bablock-hithe Ferry, Eynsham, Godstow, Oxford, Iffley, Sandford, Abingdon, Culham, Clifton Hampden, Shillingford, Benson, Wallingford, Moulsford, Streatley, Goring, Whitchurch, Pangbourne, Mapledurham, Caversham, Reading, Sonning, Shiplake, Wargrave, Henley, Hambledon, Medmenham, Hurley, Marlow, Bourne End, Cookham, Maidenhead, Bray, Windsor, Eton, Datchet, Old Windsor, Staines, Laleham, Chertsey, Weybridge, Shepperton, Walton, Sunbury, Hampton, East Molesey, Hampton Court, Thames Ditton, Long Ditton, Kingston, Teddington, Twickenham, Richmond, Isleworth, Brentford, Kew, Mortlake, Barnes, Chiswick, Hammersmith, Putney, Fulham, Wandsworth, Battersea, Chelsea, Vauxhall, Lambeth, Westminster, Blackfriars, and Southwark to London Bridge. Leaving London Bridge the river continues its course by St. Katherine's Dock, London Docks, Wapping, Shadwell, Surrey Commercial Docks, Limehouse Docks, West India Docks (upper entrance), Millwall Docks, Deptford, Greenwich, Blackwall, West India Docks (lower entrance), East India Docks, Victoria Docks, Woolwich, Royal Albert Dock, Beckton, Cross Ness, Erith, Purfleet, Greenhithe, Grays Thurrock, Northfleet, Tilbury Docks, and Gravesend. Below Gravesend the river rapidly widens out into an estuary, and after passing Southend and The Nore, where it receives the River Medway, becomes merged into the North Sea.

From Cricklade to a point about half-a-mile below Castle Eaton Bridge, the course of the river is situated in the county of Wiltshire; for the remainder of its course the river forms almost entirely the boundary between various counties, which extend approximately as follows :—

On the left bank, from half-a-mile below Castle Eaton Bridge to near Eaton Weir, Gloucestershire; from near Eaton Weir to a point about three-quarters-of-a-mile below Henley Bridge, Oxfordshire; from about three-quarters-of-a-mile below Henley Bridge to Staines, Buckinghamshire; from Staines to Bow Creek, Middlesex; and from Bow Creek to the mouth of the river, Essex.

(107)—River Thames—*continued.*

On the right bank, from half-a-mile below Castle Eaton Bridge to St. John's Lock, Lechlade, Wiltshire ; from St. John's Lock, Lechlade, to about one furlong below the Bells of Ouseley, near Old Windsor, Berkshire ; from about one furlong below the Bells of Ouseley to near Crossness, Surrey ; and from near Crossness to the mouth of the river, Kent.

The upper or non-tidal portion of the river above Teddington Lock is principally a waterway for pleasure boats of all kinds, which frequent it in large numbers in summer time.   There is, however, a fair trade done up to Reading, and a little to Oxford, but above Oxford there is as yet practically nothing, the river having only of late years been restored to good navigable condition by the expenditure of large sums of money on dredging and providing new locks at Grafton, Radcot, Shifford, and Northmoor.   The river is liable to floods, but they have been reduced both in height and duration of late years by numerous works executed to assist the rapid discharge of the surplus land water.   During the flood of November, 1894, which was the maximum of any recent years, the river attained the following heights above ordinary summer level at the undermentioned places :—

		Ft.	In.
Oxford, below Osney Lock	about	6	6
Reading, below Caversham Lock	,,	9	3
Windsor, below Romney Lock	,,	13	6
Teddington, below Teddington Lock	,,	12	9

There are branches leading out of the Main Line of the river as follows :—

A short length of backwater from Four Streams, Oxford, giving access to the Main Line of the Oxford Canal through a side lock.

The last mile of the River Kennet from its junction with the Thames in Reading to the High Bridge, where it joins that portion of the River Kennet which forms the River Kennet Section of the Kennet and Avon Navigation belonging to the Great Western Railway Company.

Wandsworth Creek at Wandsworth, which, together with Wandsworth Cut immediately below the Creek, are both formed by the mouth of the River Wandle.

Deptford Creek, between Deptford and Greenwich, which is perhaps the busiest of all the branches out of the Main River.   The River Ravensbourne flows into the Creek at its upper end, but is not navigable.

Bow Creek is really the mouth of the River Lee.   The jurisdiction of the Thames Conservancy over the Creek only extends to Barking Road Bridge, above which point it is under the River Lee Conservancy. There is a good barge and lighter traffic up Bow Creek to the main line of the River Lee Navigation through Bow Tidal Lock and Sluices, which are situated nearly at the head of the Creek.

Barking Creek, from a junction with the Main River at about a mile below Albert Dock to Barking Town Wharves, at the head of the Creek, where there is a junction with the River Roding.

(107)—RIVER THAMES—*continued*.

Rainham Creek, from a junction with the river at about one-and-a-half miles above Erith to Rainham Wharf, adjoining Rainham Railway Station on the London, Tilbury, and Southend Railway.

(b) *Proprietors, Officers, and Offices.*

From Cricklade Town Bridge in the county of Wiltshire to an imaginary line drawn from the entrance to Yantlet Creek in the county of Kent to the Crow Stone, situated between Leigh and Southend, in the county of Essex, the river is under the jurisdiction of the Conservators of the River Thames.

Conservators:

Admiralty :
  Admiral G. S. Bosanquet.
  Admiral William H. Maxwell.

Board of Trade :
  Sir C. Cecil Trevor, C.B.
  Mr. W. H. Grenfell.

Trinity House :
  Rear-Admiral H. B. Stewart.
  Captain William Ladds.

Wilts and Gloucester County Councils :
  Mr. Wilfred J. Cripps, C.B.

Oxfordshire County Council :
  Mr. J. Darell Blount.

Oxford City and County Borough.
  Mr. Robert Buckell.

Berks County Council :
  Mr. Hugh W. Russell.

Reading County Borough :
  Mr. W. B. Monck.

Bucks County Council :
  Mr. Alfred Gilbey.

Herts County Council :
  Right Hon. T. F. Halsey, M.P.

Surrey County Council :
  Mr. Charles Burt.

Middlesex County Council :
  Sir F. D. Dixon Hartland, M.P., Chairman of the Board.

(107)—RIVER THAMES—*continued*.

Essex County Council :
  Mr. W. W. Glenny.

London County Council :
  Sir J. McDougall, Mr. W. C. Steadman, Mr. R. Strong, Mr. E. A.
    Cornwall, Mr. J. D. Gilbert, Mr. R. A. Robinson.

Common Council of Corporation of London :
  Alderman Sir R. Hanson, Alderman Sir Walter Wilkin, Mr. W.
    Cooper, Mr. E. E. Ashby, Mr. W. H. Pannell, Mr. A. C. Morton.

West Ham County Borough :
  Mr. J. Byford, Jun.

Kent County Council :
  Mr. F. J. Beadle.

Metropolitan Water Companies :
  Mr. Frederick Tendron.

Shipowners :
  Mr. G. Butler Paul, Mr. C. F. Cory-Wright, Mr. Thomas Lane
    Devitt.

Owners of Sailing Barges, Lighters, and Steam Tugs :
  Mr. W. V. Williams, Mr. T. W. Jacobs, Jun.

Dockowners :
  Mr. Sydney E. Bates.

Wharfingers :
  Mr. J. A. Humphrey.

  Secretary : Robert Philipson.

  Engineer : Charles J. More.

  Solicitor : James Hughes.

  Offices : Victoria Embankment, London, E.C.   Telegraphic Address :
    " Conservancy, London."   Telephone No. 205, Holborn.

  Harbour Master, Upper District : Captain R. S. Pasley.

  Office : Temple Pier, London, E.C.

  Harbour Master, Lower District : Captain A. W. Wilson.

  Office : Gravesend.

  Chief Inspector of Upper River : J. Laurie.

  Office : Reading.

(107)—RIVER THAMES—*continued.*

(c) *Distance Table.*

Main Line of River—Not Navigable.

Distances above London Bridge.

	Miles.	Fur.
Thames Head Bridge (over Thames and Severn Canal)	161	2½
Cricklade Bridge and River Churn	154	3
Bridge to Eisey	153	3½
Bridge to Water Eaton	152	5½
Castle Eaton Bridge	150	1½
St. Mary's Church, Kempsford	148	5½
Hannington Bridge	147	4
St. John's Church, Inglesham..	144	2½
Inglesham, junction with Thames and Severn Canal—Main Line—(No. 108a)	144	0

Main Line of River (No. 107a).

Distances above London Bridge.

	Miles.	Fur.
Inglesham, junction with Thames and Severn Canal—Main Line—(No. 108a), and junction with River Coln (not navigable)	144	0
Lechlade Bridge..	143	2½
St. John's Lock and Bridge	142	5½
Buscot Lock	141	4
Eaton Weir	140	1½
Kelmscot..	140	6
Grafton Lock	138	1½
Radcot Bridge	137	0
Radcot Lock	136	2½
Old Man's Footbridge	136	1
Rushey Lock	133	5½
Tadpole Bridge	133	0
Tenfoot Footbridge	131	1½
Shifford Weir	129	7½
Shifford Lock	129	3
Old Shifford	128	7½
Junction with River Windrush (not navigable)	126	7
New Bridge	126	6½
Hart's Footbridge	125	5½
Northmoor Lock	124	5½
Bablockhithe Ferry	123	1
Skinner's Footbridge	121	4
Pinkhill Lock	120	6½
Swinford Bridge, Eynsham	119	3½
Eynsham Weir	119	1½
Junction with River Evenlode (not navigable)	118	1
Wytham Mill Stream	117	1
Junction with Dukes Cut Branch—Oxford Canal—(No. 82g)	116	5
Kings Weir	116	4½
Godstow Bridge	115	4½
Godstow Lock	115	3

(107)—RIVER THAMES—*continued.*

	Miles.	Fur.
Distances above London Bridge (*continued*)—		
Medley Weir	114	0
Oxford, Four Streams, junction with Branch to Oxford Canal (No. 107b)	113	3
Oxford, Osney Bridge	113	1½
Oxford, Osney Lock	112	7½
Oxford, Folly Bridge	112	0½
Old mouth of River Cherwell (not navigable)	111	6½
New mouth of River Cherwell (not navigable)	111	5
Iffley Lock	110	5
Kennington Railway Bridge	110	0½
Sandford Lock	108	7½
Nuneham Railway Bridge	105	6
Towing-path Ferry	104	6½
Abingdon Lock	104	3
Abingdon Bridge	103	7
Abingdon, junction with River Ock (not navigable)	103	5
Abingdon, junction with Wilts and Berks Canal, not navigable (*see* Wilts and Berks Canal)	103	5
Culham Lock	101	6½
Sutton Bridge	101	5½
Appleford Railway Bridge	100	4
Clifton Weir	99	4½
Clifton Lock	99	0
Clifton Hampden Bridge	98	4
Burcot	97	5
Days Lock	96	0
Junction with River Thame (not navigable)	95	1½
Keen Edge Ferry	94	0½
Shillingford Bridge	93	2½
Benson Lock	92	0½
Wallingford Bridge	90	6½
Chalmore Ferry	90	2½
Little Stoke Ferry	88	1
Moulsford Railway Bridge	87	4
South Stoke Ferry	86	6½
Cleeve Lock	85	4½
Goring Lock	84	7½
Streatley Bridge	84	7
Gatehampton Railway Bridge	83	5
Gatehampton Ferry	83	3
Whitchurch Lock	80	7
Whitchurch, or Pangbourne Bridge	80	6
Mapledurham Lock	78	4½
Tilehurst Ferry	77	5½
Reading, Caversham Bridge	74	7
Reading, Caversham Lock	74	1½
Reading, junction with River Kennet (No. 107c)	73	3½
Sonning Lock	71	4½
Sonning Bridge	71	2
Shiplake Lock	68	5

(107)—River Thames—*continued.*

Distances above London Bridge (*continued*)—

	Miles.	Fur.
Junction with River Loddon (not navigable)..	68	4
Shiplake Railway Bridge	68	$3\frac{1}{2}$
Wargrave Ferry	68	1
Lashbrook Ferry	67	4
Harpsden Ferry ..	66	5
Marsh Lock	66	$0\frac{1}{2}$
Henley Bridge ..	65	$0\frac{1}{2}$
Regatta Island Temple..	63	$5\frac{1}{2}$
Hambledon Lock	62	$6\frac{1}{2}$
Aston Ferry	62	$2\frac{1}{2}$
Medmenham Abbey and Ferry	60	$5\frac{1}{2}$
Hurley Lock	59	1
Temple Lock	58	4
Marlow Suspension Bridge	57	0
Marlow Lock	56	$6\frac{1}{2}$
Spade Oak Ferry	54	6
Bourne End Railway Bridge ..	54	$0\frac{1}{2}$
Junction with Wycombe Stream (not navigable)	53	6
Cookham Bridge and Upper Ferry	53	$0\frac{1}{2}$
Cookham Lock and Lower Ferry	52	$4\frac{1}{2}$
My Lady Ferry ..	52	$0\frac{1}{2}$
Boulters Lock	50	$3\frac{1}{2}$
Maidenhead Bridge	49	$6\frac{1}{2}$
Maidenhead Railway Bridge ..	49	5
Bray Lock	48	$2\frac{1}{2}$
Surly Hall	45	$6\frac{1}{2}$
Boveney Lock	45	$1\frac{1}{2}$
G. W. Railway Bridge, Eton Wick	43	$5\frac{1}{2}$
Windsor Bridge ..	43	2
Romney Lock	42	$6\frac{1}{2}$
S. W. Railway Bridge ..	42	4
Victoria Bridge ..	42	$0\frac{1}{2}$
Datchet	41	4
Albert Bridge	40	5
Old Windsor Lock	39	$6\frac{1}{2}$
The Bells of Ouseley	39	0
Bell Weir, or Egham Lock	36	$7\frac{1}{2}$
Junction with Colne Brook (not navigable) ..	36	$6\frac{1}{2}$
London Stone	36	2
Staines Bridge	35	$7\frac{1}{2}$
Junction with River Colne (not navigable)	35	$6\frac{1}{2}$
S. W. Railway Bridge ..	35	5
Penton Hook Lock	34	$0\frac{1}{2}$
Laleham Ferry ..	33	2
Chertsey Lock	32	1
Chertsey Bridge ..	31	$7\frac{1}{2}$
Tail of Shepperton Lock and junction with River Wey (No. 121)	30	1
Shepperton	29	4
Lower Halliford ..	28	7
Walton Bridge ..	28	0
Sunbury Lock	26	$3\frac{1}{2}$

(107)—RIVER THAMES—*continued.*

	Miles.	Fur.
Distances above London Bridge (*continued*)—		
Hampton Ferry	24	2½
Molesey Lock	23	4
Hampton Court Bridge..	23	2½
Junction with River Mole (not navigable) ..	23	2
Junction with River Imber (not navigable) ..	23	0
Thames Ditton Ferry	22	2½
Long Ditton Ferry	22	1
Kingston Bridge..	20	3½
S. W. Railway.Bridge	20	2½
Teddington Lock	18	5½
Twickenham Ferry	17	2½
Richmond Bridge	16	0
S. W. Railway Bridge	15	5
Richmond Lock and Footbridge	15	3½
Church Ferry, Isleworth	14	6
Brentford, entrance to G. W. Rly. Co.'s Dock, and junction with Grand Junction Canal (No. 38a1)	13	5
Kew Bridge and Pier	12	7½
Kew Railway Bridge	12	4½
Mortlake, Ship Inn	11	4½
Barnes Pier	11	0½
Barnes Railway Bridge..	10	7½
Chiswick Church	10	0
Hammersmith Bridge and Pier	9	1
" Crab Tree," Fulham	8	5
Craven Cottage	8	0½
Putney Pier	7	3
Putney Bridge	7	2½
Fulham Pier and Fulham Railway Bridge ..	7	1
Junction with Wandsworth Creek (No. 107d)	6	5
Junction with Wandsworth Cut (No. 114) ..	6	5
Wandsworth Pier	6	2½
Wandsworth Bridge	6	2
Battersea Railway Bridge	5	4
Battersea Pier	5	2½
Counters Creek, junction with Kensington Canal (No. 120)	5	1½
Battersea Bridge and Carlyle Pier	4	7
Albert Suspension Bridge and Cadogan Pier	4	5
Battersea Park Pier	4	1
Victoria Pier	4	0
Chelsea Suspension Bridge, and junction with Grosvenor Canal (No. 45)	3	7
Victoria Railway Bridge	3	6½
Pimlico Pier	3	4
Nine Elms Pier	3	1
Vauxhall Bridge..	2	6½
Lambeth Suspension Bridge	2	2½
Lambeth Pier	2	2
Westminster Bridge and Pier	1	6½
Charing Cross Railway Bridge and Pier ..	1	4
Waterloo Pier and Bridge	1	2½

(107)—River Thames—*continued*.

Distances above London Bridge (*continued*)—	Miles	Fur.
Temple Pier	1	0½
Blackfriars Bridge and Pier	—	6
Blackfriars Railway Bridge	—	5½
Southwark Bridge	—	2⅓
Cannon Street Railway Bridge	—	1½
Old Swan Pier	—	0½
London Bridge	—	—

Main Line of River (No. 107a).

Distances below London Bridge.

Left Bank Miles	Left Bank Fur.		Right Bank Miles	Right Bank Fur.
		London Bridge, and Pier, to—		
—	4½	Tower Bridge	—	4½
—	5½	St. Katherine's Dock Entrance		
—	7	Hermitage Entrance, London Docks		
1	1	Wapping Entrance, London Docks		
		Cherry Garden Pier	1	1½
1	3½	Tunnel Pier		
1	4½	Thames Tunnel	1	4½
		Surrey Commercial Docks Entrance	1	6½
1	7	Shadwell Old Entrance, London Docks		
1	7½	Shadwell New Entrance, London Docks		
2	3	Entrance to Limehouse Basin and junction with Regents Canal (No. 86a)		
2	3½	Junction with Limehouse Cut—River Lee (No. 57a)		
		Surrey Commercial Docks, New Entrance	2	3½
2	5	Limehouse Pier		
2	6	West India Dock, Limehouse Entrance.		
2	7	South Dock, Limehouse Entrance.		
3	0	West India Docks Pier.		
		Surrey Commercial Dock Pier	3	2
		Surrey Commercial Docks Entrance	3	3
		Surrey Commercial Docks, South Entrance	3	4
3	4½	Millwall Dock Entrance.		
		Stairs, Royal Victualling Yard	3	6
		Junction with Deptford Creek (No. 107e)	4	3
4	5½	Greenwich Ferry	4	5½
		Greenwich Pier	4	6
		Greenwich Hospital (centre)	4	7

(107)—RIVER THAMES—*continued.*

Left Bank.			Right Bank.	
Miles	Fur.		Miles	Fur.
		London Bridge, and Pier, to (*continued*)—		
6	1	South Dock Entrance, Blackwall.		
6	2½	West India Dock Entrance, Blackwall, and Blackwall Tunnel.		
6	5	Blackwall Pier.		
6	5½	East India Dock Entrance		
6	6	East India Dock New Entrance.		
6	7	Junction with Bow Creek (No. 107f).		
7	0½	Victoria Dock Entrance.		
9	4½	Woolwich Ferry	9	4½
		Woolwich Town Pier	9	5
10	4	Albert Docks Entrance.		
10	5	Albert Docks New Entrance.		
11	1½	Beckton Gas Works Jetty.		
11	3½	Northern Outfall Metropolitan Main Drainage.		
11	6	Junction with Barking Creek (No. 107g).		
		Half-Way House, Crossness ..	13	1½
		Southern Outfall (chimney) Main Drainage	13	5
15	1	Junction with Rainham Creek (No. 107h).		
		Erith Pier	16	5½
		Crayfordness	17	6
		Dartford Creek, junction with Dartford and Crayford Navigation (No. 25)	18	1½
18	3½	Purfleet.		
		Long Reach Tavern	18	3½
		West Kent Drainage Outfall ..	19	3½
		Greenhithe Causeway	21	4½
21	5	Stoneness.		
		Broadness	23	2
23	4	Grays Thurrock Causeway.		
		Northfleet Lighthouse	25	0
25	1	Tilbury Ness.		
27	7½	Tilbury Docks.		
26	2	Tilbury Pier.		
		Gravesend Town Pier	26	3½
		Gravesend, junction with Gravesend and Rochester Canal (No. 94)	26	6½
		Gravesend, " Ship and Lobster " Inn	27	4½
		Shornmead Fort	29	2
29	6	Ovens Buoy.		
		Cliffe Fort	30	4
		Cliffe Creek	30	5

(107)—River Thames—*continued*.

Left Bank			Right Bank	
Miles	Fur.		Miles	Fur.
		London Bridge, and Pier, to (*continued*)—		
33	1	Mucking Lighthouse.		
		West Blyth Buoy	33	2
34	2	Thames Haven Pier.		
36	0	Hole Haven.		
		Middle Blyth Buoy	36	0
		East Blyth Buoy	38	4½
38	6½	Chapman Lighthouse.		
		Yantlet Buoy	44	1½
41	5	Crow Stone, Leigh, to London Stone Yantlet	41	5
		(Thames Conservancy Limits).		
43	4	Southend Pier.		
46	2	Shoebury Ness.		
		Nore Light Ship, and mouth of River Medway (No. 67) ..	47	5

Branch to Oxford Canal (No. 107b).

	Miles	Fur.
Length from junction with Main Line of River (No. 107a) at Four Streams, Oxford, to— Junction with Branch to River Thames through Isis Lock, Oxford, of Oxford Canal (No. 82h), and tail of Isis Lock ..	–	1

Portion of River Kennet, Reading (No. 107c).

	Miles	Fur.
Reading, junction with Main Line of River (No. 107b), to—		
Reading, Blakes Lock		4
Reading, High Bridge, junction with Kennet and Avon Navigation (No. 43a)	1	0

Wandsworth Creek (No. 107d).

	Miles	Fur.
Length from junction with Main Line of River (No. 107a) to upper end of Creek	–	2

Deptford Creek (No. 107e).

	Miles	Fur.
Length from junction with Main Line of River (No. 107a) to upper end of Creek	–	5

Bow Creek (No. 107f).

	Miles	Fur.
Length from junction with Main Line of River (No. 107a) to—		
Barking Road Bridge, limit of jurisdiction of Thames Conservancy, and junction with portion of Bow Creek under jurisdiction of River Lee Conservancy (No. 57d) ..	1	0

(107)—RIVER THAMES—*continued.*

Barking Creek (No. 107g).

	Miles	Fur.
Length from junction with Main Line of River (No. 107a) to—		
Barking Town Wharves at upper end of Creek, and junction with River Roding (No. 88)	2	0

Rainham Creek (No. 107h).

	Miles	Fur.
Length from junction with Main Line of River (No. 107a) to—		
Rainham Wharf, adjoining Rainham Railway Station	1	2

(d) *Locks.*

Main Line of River (No. 107a).

1.—St. John's.
2.—Buscot.
3.—Eaton Weir (Navigation Weir).
4.—Grafton.
5.—Radcot.
6.—Rushey.
7.—Shifford.
8.—Northmoor.
9.—Pinkhill.
10.—Eynsham Weir (Navigation Weir).
11.—King's Weir (Navigation Weir).
12.—Godstow.
13.—Medley Weir (Navigation Weir).
14.—Osney.
15.—Iffley.
16.—Sandford.
17.—Abingdon.
18.—Culham.
19.—Clifton.
20.—Days.
21.—Benson.
22.—Cleeve.
23.—Goring.
24.—Whitchurch.
25.—Mapledurham.
26.—Caversham.
27.—Sonning.
28.—Shiplake.
29.—Marsh.
30.—Hambledon.
31.—Hurley.
32.—Temple.
33.—Marlow.
34.—Cookham.
35.—Boulters.
36.—Bray.
37.—Boveney.
38.—Romney.

(107)—River Thames—*continued.*

39.—Old Windsor.
40.—Bell Weir, or Egham.
41.—Penton Hook.
42.—Chertsey.
43.—Shepperton.
44.—Sunbury.
45.—Molesey.
46.—Teddington.

There are three locks at Teddington alternative to each other, and measuring respectively 650ft. × 25ft., 177ft. 3in. × 24ft. 11in., and 50ft. × 6ft.

Fall to London.

47.—Richmond.

This lock is a half-tide lock, that is to say, it retains the water in the reach above at a level corresponding to about half that set up by the flood tide. The weir consists of three large Stoney's Patent Sluices, which are raised for the passage of traffic when the tide has run about half flood and made a level with the water in the reach above, and are closed correspondingly when the tide has half ebbed. The lock is consequently only used during the period between half ebb and half flood tide. In flood time it sometimes happens that these sluices are never closed for days together to permit of the free discharge of the land water.

Portion of the River Kennet, Reading (No. 107c).

1.—Blakes.

Fall to junction with River Thames at Reading.

(e) *Maximum size of vessels that can use the navigation.*

Main Line of River (No. 107a).

From the mouth of the river to London Bridge.

Length.—Not limited.

Width.—Not limited.

The following table gives the width of the channel, and the depth of the channel at low water of Spring tides, from The Nore to London Bridge :—

	Width of Channel.		Depth of Channel at Low Water of Spring Tides.	
	Ft.	In.	Ft.	In.
The Nore to Gravesend	1000	0	26	0
Gravesend to Crayfordness	1000	0	24	0
Crayfordness to Albert Dock	500	0	22	0
Albert Dock to Millwall Docks	300	0	18	0
Millwall Docks to Thames Tunnel	300	0	16	0
Thames Tunnel to London Bridge	200	0	14	0

The approximate available depth of water on the tide at various places can be ascertained by adding the difference between the height of high water (of Spring tides or Neap tides as required) and low water of Spring tides contained in the tide table under "Tides" to the figures of the depth of the channel at low water of Spring tides contained in the above table.

(107)—RIVER THAMES—*continued.*

Headroom not limited, except for the Tower Bridge, which has a headroom of 29ft. 6in. above Trinity High Water Mark through the centre opening when the bascules are lowered in position. When the bascules are raised there is a headroom of 141ft. above Trinity High Water Mark to the High Level Footways.

Trinity High Water Mark is 12ft. 6in. above Ordnance Datum.

Above London Bridge.

	Ft.	In.
Length from London Bridge to Abingdon ..	120	0
Length from Abingdon to Oxford	110	0
Length from Oxford to Inglesham	100	0
Width from London Bridge to Oxford.. ..	17	0
Width from Oxford to Inglesham	14	0
(See note below.)		
Draught, in Summer, from London to Reading	4	0
Draught, in Summer, from Reading to Inglesham	3	6

NOTE.—Between Four Streams, Oxford, and Kings Weir, the navigation of the river is narrow, tortuous, and of uncertain draught. The traffic above Oxford, which is almost exclusively confined to narrow boats, is habitually worked between Four Streams and Kings Weir by way of the Oxford Canal and the Dukes Cut Branch of the same.

The following table gives the headroom of bridges on the tidal portion of the river between London Bridge and Teddington, showing height above Trinity High Water Mark, which is 12ft. 6in. above Ordnance Datum :—

	Ft.	In.
London Bridge	28	6
Cannon Street Railway Bridge	24	10
Southwark Bridge	29	0
Blackfriars Railway Bridge	26	0
Blackfriars Bridge	24	8
Waterloo Bridge	26	8
Charing Cross Railway Bridge	25	0
Westminster Bridge	19	8
Lambeth Bridge	19	10
Vauxhall Bridge..	25	8
Victoria Railway Bridge	21	8
Chelsea Suspension Bridge	21	10
Albert Suspension Bridge	19	6
Battersea Bridge	20	0
Battersea Railway Bridge	22	1
Wandsworth Bridge	19	8
Fulham Railway Bridge	22	3
Putney Bridge	19	9
Hammersmith Bridge	15	1
Barnes Railway Bridge	20	0
Kew Railway Bridge	20	4
Kew Bridge	23	0
Richmond Footbridge	21	0
Richmond Railway Bridge	20	7
Richmond Bridge	20	5

(107) —RIVER THAMES—*continued.*

Headroom of Bridges from Teddington to Inglesham at Ordinary
Summer Level of River.

		Ft.	In.
From Teddington to Sunbury..		17	0
,, Sunbury to Old Windsor		14	0
,, Old Windsor to Cookham		12	6
,, Cookham to Abingdon ..		12	0
,, Abingdon to Oxford		10	0
,, Oxford to Inglesham		8	0

Branch to Oxford Canal (No. 107b).

Length	..	..	..	..	..	72	0
Width	..	..	..	..	..	7	0
Draught	..	..	..	..	..	3	6

Portion of River Kennet, Reading (No. 107c).

						Ft.	In.
Length	..	..	..	..	..	74	0
Width	..	..	..	..	..	14	0
Draught	..	..	..	..	..	3	6

The tidal creeks mentioned below are almost exclusively used by
sailing barges, barges, etc., except Barking Creek, up which, in addition,
coasting vessels navigate to Barking.

Wandsworth Creek (No. 107d).

	Ft.	In.
Draught on Spring tides.. .. .. about	8	0

No trade on Neap tides.

Deptford Creek (No. 107e).

Draught on high water .. .. average	8	0 to 9ft.

Bow Creek (No. 107f).

Draught on high water .. .. average	6	0 to 7ft.

Barking Creek (No. 107g).

Draught on Spring tides	..	..	16	0
Draught on Neap tides ..	..	..	12	0

Rainham Creek (No. 107h).

Draught for the first three-quarters-of-a-mile on Spring tides	10	0
Draught for the first three-quarters-of-a-mile on Neap tides	6	0
Draught for the last half-mile on Spring tides	5	0 to 6ft.
Draught for the last half-mile on Neap tides ..	2	0

(107)—RIVER THAMES—*continued*.

(g) Towing-path.

There is a towing-path from Inglesham to the point of junction of the Beverley Brook with the river about half-a-mile above Putney Bridge. The path is not quite continuous throughout, as there are some few breaks, the principal one being between the Victoria and Albert Bridges, Datchet.

There is no towing-path on any of the Branches or Creeks with the exception of the portion of the River Kennet, Reading (No. 107c).

(h) Tidal Information.

The tide flows to Teddington Lock ; high Spring tides occasionally flow to Kingston Bridge.

The following table shows the time of high water at various places compared with the time of high water at London Bridge, and the average rise and fall of the tides. The figures prefixed with the sign + give amounts above, and those prefixed with the sign − below, Trinity High Water Mark, which is 12ft. 6in. above Ordnance Datum.

Time of High Water before or after High Water at London Bridge.	Places.	High Water.		Low Water.	
		Spring Tides.	Neap Tides.	Neap Tides.	Spring Tides.
Hrs. min.		Ft. in.	Ft. in.	Ft. in.	Ft. in.
1 26 before	Southend Pier	− 1 10	− 5 10	− 15 9	− 19 9
1 0 ,,	Gravesend Town Pier	− 1 3	− 5 5	− 17 0	− 21 0
− 30 ,,	Woolwich Ferry	+ 0 4	− 4 2	− 17 2	− 21 4
− 6 ,,	Cherry Garden Pier	+ 0 11	− 3 9	− 17 0	− 21 0
− −	London Bridge	+ 1 0	− 3 9	− 16 9	− 20 8
− 10 after	Lambeth Pier	+ 1 1	− 3 8	− 16 2	− 19 1
− 20 ,,	Chelsea Pier	+ 1 1	− 3 8	− 15 7	− 17 7
− 31 ,.	Fulham Pier	+ 1 1	− 3 7	− 15 0	− 16 5
− 39½ ,,	Hammersmith Bridge	+ 1 2	− 3 6	− 14 7	− 15 6
− 50 ,,	Barnes				
− 55 ,,	Kew Railway Bridge	+ 1 3	− 3 3	− 13 9	− 14 3
1 0 ,,	Brentford				
1 11 ,,	Richmond Lock	+ 1 7	− 2 9	− 11 0	− 11 0
1 30 ,,	Teddington Lock				

The level of low water above Chelsea is affected by the amount of land water coming down the river at the time : the figures given relate to the ordinary summer flow.

Wandsworth Creek (No. 107d), Deptford Creek (No. 107e), Bow Creek (No. 107f), Barking Creek (No. 107g), and Rainham Creek (No. 107h) are all tidal, and their times of high water may be approximately ascertained by reference to the figures for the nearest place on the Main Line of the river.

(i) Types of vessels using the navigation.

Sea-going vessels navigate the Main Line of the river up to London Bridge ; practically any vessel except those of the largest class, such as Telegraph ships, can navigate up to Albert Dock on the tide. Vessels of between 2000 and 3000 tons burden navigate up to Fresh Wharf, immediately below London Bridge, but have to take the ground at low water and become only partially water-borne. A few colliers carrying gas coal, specially constructed to clear the bridges, navigate above London Bridge to Vauxhall. Medway sailing barges navigate up to Kingston

(107)—River Thames—*continued.*

and to all creeks below, but do not as a rule go beyond Kingston. Lighters are in use on the river mostly between Woolwich and Teddington and on all creeks between those places. Barges, like lighters, are not much used on the river below Woolwich, but navigate up to Oxford and all intermediate creeks and branches between Woolwich and Oxford. Narrow boats are in use on the river between Greenwich and Inglesham ; below Brentford they are generally fastened two together side by side. Steam tugs habitually tow barges to Reading, and at times to Oxford, but not beyond.

Thames and Medway Canal.—the old name for the Gravesend and Rochester Canal—*see* South Eastern and Chatham Railway Companies Managing Committee.

––––––––

(108)—Thames and Severn Canal.

(a) *Short Description.*

The canal commences at Wallbridge, Stroud, where it forms a junction with the Stroudwater Canal, and proceeds by Brimscombe, Chalford, Daneway, Siddington, South Cerney, Latton, Marston Meysey, and Kempsford to Inglesham, where it forms a junction with the River Thames, all in the county of Gloucestershire.

There is one short branch from Siddington to Cirencester.

In 1895, owing to the canal having become unnavigable between Chalford and Inglesham, a Trust consisting of representatives of the neighbouring Navigations and Local Authorities was formed to take over the navigation from the old Thames and Severn Canal Company, the shares in this company being held to the extent of about four-fifths of the whole by the Great Western Railway Company. The expenditure by the Thames and Severn Canal Trust proved insufficient to render the canal fit for navigation. Although the entire length of the canal was opened for traffic for about three months in 1899, certain serious leakages were found to exist in the summit level of the canal over a distance of about three miles eastwards from the east end of Sapperton Tunnel, and the section of the canal between Chalford and Inglesham had again to be closed in the autumn of that year. A further sum of money, which the Trust was unable to raise, being required to execute the necessary repairs, resulted in the canal being handed over to the Gloucestershire County Council under a Warrant of Abandonment by the former proprietors, which was confirmed by Act of Parliament on the 2nd July, 1901

It is confidently expected that the additional works which have been executed by the County Council will, in future, enable the traffic on the canal to be maintained without interruption.

(108)—THAMES AND SEVERN CANAL—*continued.*

(b) *Proprietors, Officers, and Offices.*

The Gloucestershire County Council.

Clerk : Edward T. Gardom.

Office : Shire Hall, Gloucester.

Manager : W. J. Snape.

Office : 13, Wallbridge, Stroud, Gloucestershire. Telephone No. 0275.

(c) *Distance Table.*

Main Line (No. 108a).

	Miles.	Fur.
Wallbridge, Stroud, junction with Stroudwater Canal (No. 100), to—		
Wallbridge Upper Lock	–	1½
Griffin's Lock	1	3
Gough's Orchard Lock	2	2
Brimscombe Basin	2	4
Bourne Lock	2	6
St. Mary's Lock	3	5
Chalford Wharf	4	0
Chalford Chapel Lock	4	0½
Golden Valley Lock	4	6½
Baker's Mill Wharf	5	5
Puck Mill Upper Lock	5	7
Whitehall Upper Lock	6	5
Daneway Summit Lock and Wharf	7	1
West end of Sapperton Tunnel	7	4
East end of Sapperton Tunnel	9	5
Thames Head Wharf	11	3
Thames Head Pumping Station	11	5
Smerril Aqueduct Stop Gates	12	4
Head of Siddington Top Lock, and junction with Cirencester Branch (No. 108b)	15	2
Siddington Bottom Lock	15	4
South Cerney Top Lock	16	6
Boxwell Lock	17	4
Wildmoorway Lock	18	3½
Cerney Wick Lock	19	3
Latton Junction, junction with Wilts and Berks Canal—North Wilts Branch, not navigable (*see* Wilts and Berks Canal)	20	1
Latton Lock	20	7
Latton Wharf, Cricklade	21	0
Eisey	22	0
Eisey Lock	22	5
Marston Meysey	23	4
Castle Eaton Bridge	24	0
Kempsford Wharf	25	4
Dudgrove Locks	28	1
Tail of Inglesham Lock, and junction with River Thames (No. 107a)	28	6

In calculating distances for all purposes of tolls and charges, the length of Sapperton Tunnel is to be taken as equal to a distance of six miles.

(108)—THAMES AND SEVERN CANAL—*continued.*

Cirencester Branch (No. 108b).

	Miles.	Fur.
Length from junction with Main Line (No. 108a) to Cirencester	1	3

(d) Locks.

Main Line (No. 108a).

1
and } Wallbridge.
2.

3.—Bowbridge.
4.—Griffin's.
5.—Ham Mill.

6 } Hope Mill.
and
7. } Gough's Orchard, or Lewis.

8.—Bourne.
9.—Beal's.
10.—St. Mary's.

11. } Grist Mill, or Iles Mill.
12. } Ballingers.
13. } Chalford Chapel.

14 } Bell.
and
15. } Clawes, or Red Lion.

16.—Golden Valley.

17 } Bolting.
and
18. } Baker's Mill.

19. } Puck Mill Lower.
20. } Puck Mill Upper.
21. } Whitehall Lower.

22. } Whitehall Upper.
23. } Bathurst Meadow Lower.
24. } Bathurst Meadow Upper.
25. } Sickeridge Wood Lower.
26. } Sickeridge Wood Upper.
27. } Daneway Lower.
28. } Daneway Upper, or Summit Lock.

Rise from Stroud.

29
to } Siddington.
32.

33
to } South Cerney.
35.

36.—Boxwell.

37 } Humpback.
and
38. } Wildmoorway.

(108)—THAMES AND SEVERN CANAL—*continued.*

    39.—Cerney Wick.
    40.—Latton.
    41.—Eisey.
    42)
  and } Dudgrove Double Locks.
    43.)
    44.—Inglesham.

Fall to Inglesham.

(*e*) *Maximum size of vessels that can use the navigation.*

Main Line (No. 108a).

	Ft.	In.
Length from Stroud to Brimscombe	70	0
Length from Brimscombe to Inglesham ..	71	0
Width from Stroud to Brimscombe	15	6
Width from Brimscombe to Inglesham ..	11	0
Draught from Stroud to Brimscombe	5	0
Draught from Brimscombe to Inglesham ..	3	6
Headroom from Stroud to Brimscombe ..	11	0
Headroom from Brimscombe to Inglesham ..	8	6

Cirencester Branch (No. 108b).

Length ..	..	..	..	..	..	71	0
Width ..	..	..	..	..	..	11	0
Draught ..	..	..	..	..	..	3	6
Headroom	..	..	..	..	..	7	6

(*f*) *Tunnels.*

Main Line (No. 108a).

Sapperton—
    Length   ..   ..   .. 3808 yards
    Minimum height above water level   10   0
    Minimum width at water level   11   4½

No towing-path ; boats " legged " or " shafted " through.

Boats enter the west end of the tunnel at 12 noon, and the east end of the tunnel at 7-0 a.m. and 6-0 p.m., except on Sundays.

(*g*) *Towing-path.*

There is a towing-path throughout the navigation, except through Sapperton Tunnel.

(*i*) *Types of vessels using the navigation.*

Barges navigate the canal between Stroud and Brimscombe. Narrow boats are in use on the whole of the Main Line and Cirencester Branch.

———

(109)—Doctor Thomas's Canal.

(a) Short Description.

The canal commences by a junction with the Glamorganshire Canal (No. 36a) at the tail of Lock No. 34, Denia, and proceeds in a north-westerly direction for a distance of one mile, almost parallel with the line of the Glamorganshire Canal, to its termination at Treforest without change of level.

The course of the canal is situated in the county of Glamorganshire.

There is a small trade done on the canal from a colliery communicating with Treforest Wharf by a tramroad.

(b) Proprietors, Officers, and Offices.

The Trustees of the Thomas Estate.

Agents : Messrs. Rickards & Blosse, Solicitors.

Office : Charles Street, Cardiff.

(e) Maximum size of vessels that can use the navigation.

	Ft.	In.
Length	60	0
Width	8	9
Draught	3	0

(g) Towing-path.

There is a towing-path throughout the navigation.

(i) Types of vessels using the navigation.

Glamorganshire and Aberdare Canal boats—*see* Section 9, Types of Vessels, (a) Non Sailing Vessels.

Thetford, Corporation of the Town of—*see* Brandon River.

---

(110)—Thorney River.

(a) Short Description.

The navigation commences by a junction with the River Nene Navigation—Third Division—at Dog-in-a-Doublet, near Peterborough, and proceeds in a northerly direction to the village of Thorney, all in the county of Cambridgeshire.

There is very little traffic on the river, its principal use being for the supply of fresh water to the Thorney Estate of the Duke of Bedford.

(b) Proprietors, Officers, and Offices.

Proprietor : The Duke of Bedford.

Steward of Thorney and Wansford Estates : Arthur J. Forrest.

Office : Thorney, near Peterborough.

(110)—THORNEY RIVER—*continued.*

(c) *Distance Table.*

	Miles.	Fur.
Dog-in-a-Doublet, junction with River Nene Navigation—Main Line—(No. 74a), to—		
Stone Bridge Corner	1	0
Thorney	3	1

(d) *Locks.*

1
and ⎰ Dog-in-a-Doublet.
2.

Fall to Thorney.

Lock No. 1 is the entrance Lock from the River Nene; Lock No. 2 is an old wooden Lock, fitted with Portcullis gates, immediately below No. 1.

(e) *Maximum size of vessels that can use the navigation.*

	Ft.	In.
The locks on the navigation are constructed to pass one Fen Lighter at a time, and have an available length of	50	0
Width	12	0
Draught .. .. about	2	6

(g) *Towing-path.*

There is a towing-path throughout the navigation.

(i) *Types of vessels using the navigation.*

Fen lighters.

THURNE DIKE—*see* River Bure, River Thurne.

THURNE, RIVER—*see* River Bure.

TIR-ISAF BRANCH CANAL—*see* The Earl of Jersey's Canals.

TITFORD BRANCH CANAL—*see* Birmingham Canal Navigations.

TOLL END COMMUNICATION—*see* Birmingham Canal Navigations.

———

(111)—RIVER TONE.

(a) *Short Description.*

The portion of the navigation of the River Tone dealt with in this section is that which commences at Ham Mill, Creech St. Michael, near Taunton, and terminates at the mouth of the river at Borough Bridge, where it forms a junction with the River Parrett, all in the county of Somersetshire.

(111)—RIVER TONE—*continued.*

There is only a small trade on the river, principally in corn and coal to Ham Mill.

Navigation is liable to interruption caused by floods and drought.

It is to be noted that the River Tone between Ham Mill and Fire-pool, Taunton, where the short piece of the River Tone Navigation belonging to the Great Western Railway Company commences, is un-navigable.

(b) Proprietors, Officers, and Offices.

The river, as a drainage, is under the jurisdiction of the Somersetshire Drainage Commissioners.

Clerk : J. Lovibond.

Office : Bridgwater.

Engineer : W. Lunn.

Office : Taunton Road, Bridgwater.

(c) Distance Table.

Ham Mill to—	Miles.	Fur.
Knapp Bridge	1	4
New Bridge	2	7
Hook Bridge	4	3
Athelney Railway Station	5	1
Borough Bridge, junction with River Parrett (No. 84)	6	4

(e) Maximum size of vessels that can use the navigation.

	Ft.	In.
Length.—Not limited.		
Width.—Not limited.		
Draught .. .. about	3	0

(g) Towing-path.

There is a towing-path throughout the navigation.

(h) Tidal Information.

Spring tides from the River Parrett will back up the water in the river at Ham Mill when the amount of land water coming down from the upper portion of the river is not great. Neap tides usually flow to about Borough Bridge.

(i) Types of vessels using the navigation.

Small barges carrying from about 16 to 20 tons.

TONE, RIVER, NAVIGATION (TAUNTON)—*see* Great Western Railway.

(112)—RIVER TRENT.

(a) Short Description.

The river commences to be navigable at Wilden Ferry, near Shardlow, in the county of Derbyshire, and proceeds by Derwentmouth, Sawley, Cranfleet, Thrumpton, and Barton to Beeston.   At Beeston the Main Line of the navigation leaves the main river and proceeds by Beeston Cut to Lenton Chain, where it forms a junction with the Nottingham Canal, and is continued by that canal through the city of Nottingham to the tail of Trent Lock, Nottingham, where it again joins the main river.

Leaving Trent Lock, Nottingham, the river proceeds by Holme, Radcliffe, Stoke Bardolph, Burton Joyce, Gunthorpe, East Bridgford, Hoveringham, Fiskerton, East Stoke, and Farndon to Averham Weir, where the Main Line of the navigation again leaves the main river, and passing Newark by means of Newark Dike rejoins the main river at Crankley Point.   There is a gap in the west end of Averham Weir through which in flood time vessels will occasionally pass, and travel by the main channel of the river down to Crankley Point, thus altogether avoiding Newark Dike and the town of Newark.

From Crankley Point the river continues its course by Muskham, Collingham, Carlton, Sutton, South Clifton, Dunham Bridge, Torksey, Marton, Littleborough, Knaith, Gainsborough, Morton, Walkerith, West Stockwith, Wildsworth, Owston, Butterwick, Burringham, Althorpe, Keadby, Amcotts, and Burton Stather to Trent Falls, where, together with the River Ouse, it forms the Humber Estuary.

The Soar Mouth or Red Hill Branch, which leaves the Main Line of the navigation at the head of Cranfleet Cut, forms a branch navigation as far as the junction with the Loughborough Navigation.

On the main channel of the river between Beeston and Trent Lock, Nottingham, the portion between Beeston and Clifton Colliery is quite unnavigable at ordinary times, and is difficult in times of flood owing to the channel being very intricate.

From Clifton Colliery to Trent Lock, Nottingham, the river has of late years been dredged, and is now navigable.

The course of the river lies through or between the counties of Derbyshire, Leicestershire, Nottinghamshire, and Lincolnshire.

The river is liable to floods, which on rare occasions cause interruption to traffic.

The stream at all times flows swiftly between Holme Lock and Fiskerton, and from Crankley Point down to the tidal portion of the river.   The seasons very much affect the draught of water throughout the whole of the tideway of the river ; during the summer, " warp " or silt is brought up by the tide from the Humber Estuary, and remains in the tideway until scoured out by a flood, and it, of course, depends upon the amount of rainfall to what extent this scouring takes place.

(b) Proprietors, Officers, and Offices.

The Main Line of the navigation from Wilden Ferry to Lenton Chain, Nottingham, and from the tail of Trent Lock, Nottingham, to Gainsborough, is under the jurisdiction of the Trent Navigation Company.

(112)—RIVER TRENT—*continued.*

The portion of the Main Line of the navigation from Lenton Chain, Nottingham, to the tail of Trent Lock, Nottingham, being portion of the Nottingham Canal, is the property of the Great Northern Railway Company.

From the commencement of Newark Dike at the east end of Averham Weir to the termination of Newark Dike at Crankley Point, also known by the name of the Newark Navigation, is the property of the Newark Navigation Commissioners, and is leased by them to the Trent Navigation Company.

From Gainsborough to the mouth of the river at Trent Falls is an open navigation, having no controlling authority.

The Soar Mouth or Red Hill Branch, and the portion of the main river from Beeston to Trent Lock, Nottingham, are also under the jurisdiction of the Trent Navigation Company.

Trent Navigation Company.

Secretary ⎫
⎬ and Joint Managers : ⎰ William H. Blundstone.
Engineer ⎭ ⎱ F. Rayner.

Traffic Superintendent : J. Goodchild.

Head Offices : Island Street, London Road, Nottingham. Telegrams : "Traffic, Nottingham." Telephone Nos. 377 and 1772.

The Company act as carriers between the Humber Ports and the towns on their own system, and Loughborough, Leicester, Derby, &c.

Branch Offices :

Hull: Humber Dock Basin. Telegrams : "Traffic, Hull." Telephone No. 366.

Newark : Millgate. Telephone No. 15.

Loughborough : Derby Road.

Leicester: Belgrave Gate. Telephone No. 120 Y.

Agencies :

Goole: J. H. Heworth, Messrs. Meek & Sons, Bank Chambers. Telegrams : "Meek, Goole." Telephone No. 27.

Derby: J. W. Gandy, Bridgewater Wharf. Telephone No. 159.

London: Joseph C. Mount & Co., 115, Leadenhall Street, E.C. Telegrams : "Anticlimax, London." Telephone No. 5512, Avenue.

(c) *Distance Table.*

Main Line of Navigation (No. 112a).

	Miles.	Fur.
Wilden Ferry, and Cavendish Bridge, to—		
Cavendish Bridge Brewery	–	1½
Derwent Mouth, junction with Trent and		
Mersey Canal (No. 76a)	1	3
Sawley Wharf	2	0½
Sawley Lock	2	3½

(112)—RIVER TRENT—*continued.*

	Miles.	Fur.
Wilden Ferry, and Cavendish Bridge, to (*continued*)—		
Head of Cranfleet Cut, junction with Erewash Canal (No. 30)—left, and junction with Soar Mouth or Red Hill Branch (No. 112b)—right	3	3
Cranfleet, or Old Sal's, Lock	4	1
Thrumpton Ferry	4	$5\frac{1}{2}$
Barton Plaster Wharf	6	$1\frac{1}{2}$
Barton Ferry	6	$3\frac{1}{2}$
Beeston Lock, and commencement of Beeston Cut	8	$3\frac{1}{2}$
Lenton Chain, termination of Beeston Cut, and junction with Nottingham Canal (No. 41b1)	11	0

For intermediate distances on Nottingham Canal between Lenton Chain and Trent Lock, Nottingham—*see* Great Northern Railway, Nottingham Canal (No. 41b1).

	Miles.	Fur.
Tail of Trent Lock, Nottingham, termination of Nottingham Canal (No. 41b1), and junction with main river—Beeston to Trent Lock, Nottingham—(No. 112c)	13	$3\frac{1}{2}$
Nottingham, junction with Grantham Canal (No. 41a)	13	5
Holme Flood Lock	15	$3\frac{1}{2}$
Holme Lock	15	6
Colwick Top Roving	16	6
Radcliffe Ferry	18	1
Stoke Bardolph Ferry	19	7
Burton Lane End	20	7
Gunthorpe Bridge (Notts.)	23	$2\frac{1}{2}$
East Bridgford Wharf	23	4
Hoveringham Ferry	25	4
Hazleford Ferry	27	$5\frac{1}{2}$
Fiskerton Ferry	29	$5\frac{1}{2}$
Fiskerton Wharf	30	$0\frac{1}{2}$
East Stoke Wharf	31	3
Farndon Ferry	33	$1\frac{1}{2}$
East end of Averham Weir, and commencement of Newark Dike	34	$3\frac{1}{2}$
Farndon Field Maltkiln	35	4
Newark, Plaster Wharf	36	1
Newark, Mill Bridge	36	$3\frac{1}{2}$
Newark, Town Lock	36	5
Newark, Town Wharf	36	$6\frac{1}{2}$
Newark, Cow Lane Wharf	37	$0\frac{1}{2}$
Newark, tail of Nether Lock	37	$4\frac{1}{2}$
Crankley Point, and termination of Newark Dike	38	$2\frac{1}{2}$
Muskham Ferry	40	$3\frac{1}{2}$
Collingham Wharf	43	5
Carlton Ferry	45	$1\frac{1}{2}$

(112)—River Trent—*continued.*

	Miles.	Fur.
Wilden Ferry, and Cavendish Bridge, to (*continued*)—		
Carlton Wharf	45	2
Besthorpe Staith	46	3½
Meering Ferry	46	7½
Sutton Wharf	47	1½
Girton Lane End	48	5
South Clifton Wharf	50	6
Marnham Ferry	51	2
North Clifton Lane End	52	4
Dunham Bridge	54	2
Laneham Ferry	56	0
Torksey, junction with Fossdyke Canal (No.42)	58	2
Torksey Railway Bridge, Great Central Railway	58	7
Trent Port, Marton	60	4
Littleborough Ferry	61	6
Knaith	63	4
Gainsborough Road Bridge	68	4
Morton	70	3
Walkerith Ferry..	71	7
West Stockwith, junction with Chesterfield Canal (No. 39d)	73	0
West Stockwith, junction with River Idle (No. 50)	73	1
Gunthorpe (Lincolnshire)	75	1
Wildsworth	75	6
Owston Ferry	76	3
Kelfield	78	5
Susworth	79	4
Butterwick Ferry	81	6
Burringham	84	2
Althorpe Ferry	84	4
Keadby Railway Bridge, Great Central Railway	85	1
Keadby, junction with Sheffield and South Yorkshire Navigation—Stainforth and Keadby Canal (No. 91c)	85	6
Amcotts Ferry	88	5
Burton Stather Ferry	91	6
Trent Falls, junction with River Humber (No. 49) and River Ouse (No. 81)	94	6

NOTE.—Distances at and below the tail of Trent Lock, Nottingham, include the distance of two miles three-and-a-half furlongs on the Nottingham Canal between Lenton Chain and Trent Lock.

Soar Mouth or Red Hill Branch (No. 112b).

	Miles.	Fur.
Junction with Main Line of navigation (No. 112a), at the head of Cranfleet Cut, to junction with Loughborough Navigation (No. 62)	–	1

Beyond the junction with the Loughborough Navigation the stream leads to Thrumpton Weir only.

(112)—RIVER TRENT—*continued.*

Main River—Beeston to Trent Lock, Nottingham—(No. 112c).

	Miles.	Fur.
Beeston Weir to—		
Clifton	–	4
Wilford	2	4
Clifton Colliery	2	7
Wilford Bridge	3	1
Nottingham, Trent Bridge	4	3
Nottingham, Junction with Main Line of navigation (No. 112a) at tail of Trent Lock of Nottingham Canal (No. 41b1)	4	5

(d) *Locks.*

Main Line of Navigation (No. 112a).

1.—Sawley Flood Lock.
2.—Sawley (two locks side by side).
3.—Cranfleet, or Old Sal's.
4.—Beeston.

For locks on the Nottingham Canal between Lenton Chain and the tail of Trent Lock, Nottingham—*see* Great Northern Railway, Nottingham Canal (No. 41b1).

5.—Holme Flood Lock.
6.—Holme.
7.—Newark Town.
8.—Newark Nether.

Fall from Wilden Ferry.

(e) *Maximum size of vessels that can use the navigation.*

Main Line of Navigation (No. 112a).

	Ft.	In.
Length from Trent Falls to the tail of Nether Lock, Newark, not limited.		
Length from the tail of Nether Lock, Newark, to Wilden Ferry	81	0
Width from Trent Falls to the tail of Nether Lock, Newark, not limited.		
Width from the tail of Nether Lock, Newark, to Wilden Ferry	14	6
Draught from Trent Falls to Gainsborough on Spring tides.. .. .. .. about	9	0 to 10ft.
Draught on Neap tides in Summer minimum	5	0 to 6ft.
Draught from Gainsborough to Torksey on Spring tides.. .. .. .. about	7	0 to 8ft.
Draught on Neap tides in Summer minimum	3	0
a fair average being	5	0 to 6ft.
Draught from Torksey to Nether Lock, Newark .. .. minimum	3	0
average .. .. about	5	0
Draught, Newark Dike, from Nether Lock, Newark, to Averham Weir minimum	3	0
average	3	6 to 4ft.

(112)—RIVER TRENT—*continued.*

	Ft.	In.
Draught from Averham Weir to Trent Lock, Nottingham .. .. minimum	2	0
average .. .. about	4	0
Draught from Trent Lock, Nottingham, to Lenton Chain on the Nottingham Canal, and from Lenton Chain to Beeston on Beeston Cut, average .. .. about	3	6
Draught from Beeston to Cranfleet Lock ..	3	6
Draught from Cranfleet Lock to Wilden Ferry .. .. 3ft. to 3		6
Headroom from Trent Falls to Gainsborough not limited, Keadby Railway Bridge being an opening bridge.		
Headroom from Gainsborough to Wilden Ferry	9	0

Soar Mouth or Red Hill Branch (No. 112b).

	Ft.	In.
Length.—Not limited.		
Width.—Not limited.		
Draught	3	6

Main River—Beeston to Trent Lock, Nottingham—(No. 112c).

	Ft.	In.
Length.—Not limited.		
Width.—Not limited.		
Draught from Clifton Colliery to Trent Lock, Nottingham.. .. .. .. about	4	0

(g) *Towing-path.*

Main Line of Navigation (No. 112a).

There is a towing-path from Wilden Ferry to Gainsborough.

Soar Mouth or Red Hill Branch (No. 112b).

There is a towing-path from the junction with the Loughborough Navigation to the junction with the Main Line of navigation at the head of the Weir Stream, where the horses have to be ferried across the river.

Main River—Beeston to Trent Lock, Nottingham—(No. 112c).

There is a towing-path from Beeston Weir to Trent Lock, Nottingham.

(h) *Tidal Information.*

Spring tides flow to about Dunham Bridge. Low Neap tides cause no appreciable rise at this place, but high Spring tides will back up the water in the river as far as Carlton Ferry.

High water at Keadby about 1hr. after Hull.

Spring tides rise	14ft.
Neap ,, ,, ...	9ft.

(112)—River Trent—*continued*.

High water at Gainsborough about 2hrs. 15min. to 2hrs. 45min. after Hull.

Spring tides rise	..	..	..	8ft.
Neap ,, ,,	..	..	..	4ft.

High water at Dunham Bridge about 4hrs. 30min. to 5hrs. after Hull.

The first of the flood tide reaches some point in the river between Susworth and Stockwith at the time of high water at Hull. Spring tides rise with great velocity, the rate at times being about nine miles an hour and averaging about six. On Spring tides the flood tide sets up the river with a tidal wave, or " Aegre," which rises almost instantly at Keadby to a height of about 3ft., and attains its maximum height of about 4ft. to 5ft. in the neighbourhood of Susworth. The " Aegre " is not formed on tides which give a less depth than 27ft. 6in. on the Albert Dock sill, Hull.

(i) *Types of vessels using the navigation*.

Yorkshire keels navigate from the mouth of the river usually as far as Torksey for the Fossdyke Canal. Lower Trent boats use the whole of the navigation. Upper Trent boats navigate down to Gainsborough, but do not usually go below, and in no case further than Keadby. Narrow boats use the navigation above Stockwith.

Trent and Mersey Canal—*see* North Staffordshire Railway.

Trewyddfa Canal—*see* Great Western Railway, Swansea Canal.

Tuddenham Mill Stream Branch Navigation—*see* River Larke.

Twenty Foot River—*see* Middle Level Navigations.

Two Lock Line Canal—*see* Birmingham Canal Navigations.

---

(113)—River Tyne.

(a) *Short Description*.

The river commences to be navigable at Hedwin Streams, near Heddon, which is the limit of the tidal flow, and proceeds by Ryton, Newburn, Blaydon, Scotswood, Elswick, Newcastle, Gateshead, Walker, Wallsend, Hebburn, Jarrow, Howdon, North Shields, and South Shields to Tynemouth, where it enters the North Sea.

The navigation throughout the whole of its course forms the boundary between the counties of Northumberland and Durham.

Below Blaydon, up to which point sea-going vessels can navigate, both banks of the river are lined with a succession of wharves, warehouses, factories, coal staiths, and other business premises.

(113)—RIVER TYNE—*continued.*

There are three docks in the port, namely : the Northumberland and Albert Edward Docks, on the north side of the river, belonging to the Tyne Improvement Commissioners ; and Tyne Dock, on the south side of the river, belonging to the North Eastern Railway Company.

There are branches leading out of the Main Line as follows, which are navigable at high water by barges :—

Lemington Gut, from a point about one mile above Scotswood to Lemington Staiths, which are distant about half-a-mile from the main river.

The River Derwent, which enters the main river about one mile above Elswick, and is navigable for a distance of about two miles up from its mouth.

The Team Rivulet, which enters the river about three-quarters of a mile below Elswick, and is navigable for a distance of about three-quarters of a mile up from its mouth.

The Ouse Burn, which enters the river about one and three-quarter miles below Newcastle, and is navigable for a distance of about three-quarters of a mile up from its mouth.

The River Don, which enters the south-west corner of Jarrow Slake at Jarrow, and is navigable for a distance of about one and a half miles up from its mouth.

(b) *Proprietors, Officers, and Offices.*

From Hedwin Streams to the mouth of the river, including such portions of all branches as are within the limit of the tidal flow, is under the jurisdiction of the Tyne Improvement Commissioners.

Secretary : Robert Urwin.

Office : Bewick Street, Newcastle-on-Tyne.   Telegrams : " Tynecom, Newcastle-on-Tyne."

Engineer : James Walker.

Office : Bewick Street, Newcastle-on-Tyne.

Harbour Master : John Bruce.

Office : New Quay, North Shields.

(c) *Distance Table.*

Main Line of River (No. 113a).

Left Bank.			Right Bank.	
Miles.	Fur.		Miles.	Fur.
		Hedwin Streams to—		
		Ryton	–	4
1	5	Newburn Bridge.		
		Stella	2	6
		Blaydon	3	4
4	0	Junction with Lemington Gut (No. 113b).		
4	4	Scotswood Suspension Bridge...	4	4
		Junction with River Derwent (No. 113c)	5	0

AA

(113)—RIVER TYNE—*continued*.

Left Bank.			Right Bank.	
Miles.	Fur.		Miles.	Fur.
		Hedwin Streams to (*continued*)—		
6	0	Elswick.		
		Junction with Team Rivulet (No. 113d)	6	6
7	4	Redheugh Bridge	7	4
8	0	Newcastle High Level Bridge, Newcastle—left; Gateshead—right	8	0
9	6	Junction with Ouse Burn (No. 113e).		
		Felling	10	3
		Heworth	11	2
12	0	Walker.		
13	0	Wallsend.		
		Hebburn	14	0
14	0	Willington.		
		Jarrow	15	0
15	0	Howdon.		
		West end of Jarrow Timber Pond	15	4
16	0	Entrance to Northumberland Dock.		
		East end of Jarrow Slake; the River Don (No. 113f) enters Jarrow Slake at the south-west corner	16	0
		Entrance to Tyne Dock.. ..	16	2
16	7	Entrance to Albert Edward Dock.		
17	4	North Shields.		
		South Shields	17	4
18	2	Tynemouth.		
19	2	Mouth of Harbour	19	2

(e) Maximum size of vessels that can use the navigation.

	Ft.	In.

Length.—Not limited.

Width.—Not limited.

Draught.—The following are the depths of water in the channel from the mouth of the river to Scotswood at low water of ordinary Spring tides. The approximate depth at high water of Spring tides may be found by adding about 15ft. to these figures.

From the mouth of the river to Northumberland Dock .. .. .. about   25   0

From Northumberland Dock to Newcastle Swing Bridge .. .. about   20   0

From Newcastle Swing Bridge to Scotswood .. .. about   18   0

Draught from Scotswood to Hedwin Streams—dredging operations are in progress for giving a depth at low water of ordinary Spring tides of .. .. .. about   12   0

(113)—River Tyne—*continued.*

	Ft.	In.
Draught on Lemington Gut (No. 113b)—there is a depth in the channel from the main river to Lemington Staiths at high water of ordinary Spring tides of . . . . about	10	0 to 12ft.

Draught.—With regard to the draught of water in the River Derwent (No. 113c), Team Rivulet (No. 113d), Ouse Burn (No. 113e), and River Don (No. 113f), no figures are available. There is a considerable variation owing to floods, which render their available depths from time to time very uncertain.

Headroom from the mouth of the river to Newcastle High Level Bridge, not limited.

	Ft.	In.
Headroom, Newcastle High Level Bridge at high water of ordinary Spring tides about	83	0
Headroom, Redheugh Bridge at high water of ordinary Spring tides . . . . about	87	0
Headroom, Scotswood Suspension Bridge at high water of ordinary Spring tides about	18	0
Headroom, Scotswood Railway Bridge at high water of ordinary Spring tides . . about	22	3
Headroom, Newburn Bridge at high water of ordinary Spring tides . . . . about	21	0

(g) Towing-path.

There is no towing-path on any portion of the river or branches.

(h) Tidal Information.

The tide flows to Hedwin Streams.

High water at Tynemouth, mouth of river, 1hr. 20min. after London Bridge.

Spring tides rise	15ft. 3in.
Neap ,, ,, ...	10ft. 9in.

High water at North Shields 3min. after Tynemouth.

Spring tides rise	14ft. 9in.
Neap ,, ,, ...	11ft.

High water at Howdon 5min. after Tynemouth.

Spring tides rise	15ft.
Neap ,, ,, ...	11ft. 3in.

High water at Walker 8min. after Tynemouth.

Spring tides rise	15ft. 3in.
Neap ,, ,, ...	11ft. 6in.

High water at Newcastle 14min. after Tynemouth.

Spring tides rise	15ft. 6in.
Neap ,, ,, ...	11ft. 9in.

(113)—RIVER TYNE—*continued*.

High water at Scotswood 18min. after Tynemouth.

Spring tides rise   ..   ..   ..   15ft.
Neap   ,,   ,, ...   11ft. 3in.

High water at Hedwin Streams 21min. after Tynemouth ; high water of ordinary Spring tides just reaches here.

(i) *Types of vessels using the navigation.*

Sea-going vessels navigate from the mouth of the river up to Blaydon. Barges navigate from Blaydon up to Hedwin Streams, and on all branches, at high water.

There are several steam wherries in use on the river.

ULVERSTON CANAL—*see* Furness Railway.

UPTON DIKE—*see* River Bure.

URE, RIVER—*see* North Eastern Railway.

VERMUYDEN'S EAU, *alias* FORTY FOOT RIVER—*see* Middle Level Navigations.

WALKER, W. D., ESQ.—*see* River Waveney, Bungay Navigation.

WALSALL CANAL—*see* Birmingham Canal Navigations.

WALSALL BRANCH CANAL—*see* Birmingham Canal Navigations.

WALTON SUMMIT BRANCH CANAL—*see* Leeds and Liverpool Canal.

WANDSWORTH CREEK—*see* River Thames.

---

(114)—WANDSWORTH CUT.

(a) *Short Description.*

The Cut is formed by one of the mouths of the River Wandle at Wandsworth, and commences by a junction with the River Thames (No. 107a) immediately below Wandsworth Creek, and proceeds for a distance of three furlongs to McMurrays Ltd. Royal Paper Mills, all in the county of Surrey.

(b) *Proprietors, Officers, and Offices.*

McMurrays Ltd. Royal Paper Mills, Wandsworth.

(114)—Wandsworth Cut—*continued.*

(d) *Locks.*

1.—Entrance Lock.

Rise from River Thames at low water.

The lock is provided with a pair of flood gates to keep out the tide from the river.

(e) *Maximum size of vessels that can use the navigation.*

	Ft.	In.
Length	77	0
Width	17	9
Draught on Spring tides	5	6
Draught on Neap tides	3	6

(g) *Towing-path.*

There is no towing-path.

(h) *Tidal Information*

For Tidal Information—*see* River Thames (No. 107a).

(i) *Types of vessels using the navigation.*

Barges, and Medway sailing barges.

Ward's, Lord, Canal—*see* Pensnett Canal.

Wardle Lock Branch Canal—*see* North Staffordshire Railway, Trent and Mersey Canal.

---

(115)—Warwick and Birmingham Canal.

(a) *Short Description.*

The canal commences in Birmingham by a junction with the Digbeth Branch Canal of the Birmingham Canal Navigations near Bordesley Wharf, Lower Fazeley Street, and proceeds by Bordesley and Sparkbrook, in the county of Warwickshire ; Hay Mills and Acock's Green, in the county of Worcestershire ; Solihull, Knowle, Kingswood, Rowington, Hatton, and Budbrooke, to its termination at Warwick, in the county of Warwickshire.

The length of the canal from Birmingham to Budbrooke is principally used as portion of the through route between London and Birmingham ; the short piece of the canal between Budbrooke and Warwick has very little trade on it.

(115)—WARWICK AND BIRMINGHAM CANAL—*continued.*

(b) Proprietors, Officers, and Offices.

The Company of Proprietors of the Warwick and Birmingham Canal Navigation.

Secretary : G. J. Blunn.

Engineer : William Salt.

Office : Fazeley Street, Birmingham.   Telegrams : "Canals, Birmingham."

(c) Distance Table.

	Miles.	Fur.
Birmingham, junction with Birmingham Canal Navigations — Digbeth Branch — (No. 10p3), Birmingham Bar Stop Lock and Toll Office, to—		
Birmingham, Fellows, Morton, & Clayton, Ltd.—Canal Carriers,—Lower Fazeley Street Wharves and Warehouses	–	1½
Birmingham, Great Barr Street Wharf ..	–	2
Tail of Bottom Lock, Bordesley, and junction with Birmingham and Warwick Junction Canal (No. 11)	–	4
Chunk Pond	–	5
Corporation Wharf and Sandy Lane Pond ..	–	6
Top Lock, Bordesley	1	0
South Road Wharf	1	1
National Ammunition Co.'s Wharf	1	3
Evans' Kingston Wharf	1	6
Sparkbrook Small Arms Factory Basin ..	2	1
Hay Mill Wharf	2	6
Yardley Old Wharf	3	1
Thornton's Bridge Wharf	3	3
Yardley Tunnel Wharf	3	5
Acock's Green Wharf	4	5
Olton Wharf	4	7
Alston's Manure Wharf	5	4
Solihull Wharf	6	5
Elmdon Heath Wharf	6	7
Catherine de Barnes Heath Wharf	8	1
Catherine de Barnes Heath, Boat Inn Wharf..	8	2
Henwood, Corporation Manure Wharf.. ..	9	0
Cop Heath Wharf	9	2
Waterfield Free Wharf	10	3
Kixley Wharf	10	6
Knowle Hall Wharf	11	0
Knowle Top Lock	11	2
Hernfield Wharf..	12	0
Bakers Lane Free Wharf	12	5
Rising Bridge Wharf	13	7
Kingswood Wharf	14	5
Kingswood Junction, junction with Stratford-on-Avon Canal (No. 43b2)	14	7
Rowington Green Wharves	15	5

(115)—Warwick and Birmingham Canal—*continued*.

	Miles.	Fur.
Birmingham, junction with Birmingham Canal Navigations — Digbeth Branch — (No. 10p3), Birmingham Bar Stop Lock and Toll Office, to (*continued*)—		
North-West end of Shrewley Tunnel	18	0
Hatton, Glebe Wharf	18	6
Hatton, John's Wharf and Arkwright's Upper Wharf	19	4
Hatton Top Lock	19	6
Hatton, Arkwright's Lower Wharf and Hatton Fourth Lock	20	0
Hatton, Asylum Wharf and Hatton Eleventh Lock	20	4
Hatton Bottom Lock	21	5
Budbrooke, junction with Warwick and Napton Canal (No. 116)	22	1
Saltisford Wharf	22	3
Warwick, Wharf and Basin	22	5

(d) *Locks.*

1.—Birmingham Bar Stop Lock.

Level.

2
to } Bordesley
7.

Rise from Birmingham.

8
to } Knowle.
13.

14
to } Hatton.
34.

Fall to Warwick.

(e) *Maximum size of vessels that can use the navigation.*

	Ft.	In.
Length	72	0
Width	7	0
Draught	3	8
Headroom	8	0

(f) *Tunnels.*

Shrewley—

		Ft.	In.
Length	433 yards		
Minimum height above water level		12	9
Minimum width at water level		16	2

No towing-path ; boats principally hauled through by means of handles fixed to side walls. Boats enter from either end at any time, the tunnel being of sufficient width to allow of two boats passing.

(115)—WARWICK AND BIRMINGHAM CANAL—*continued.*

(g) Towing-path.

There is a towing-path throughout the navigation, except through Shrewley Tunnel.

(i) Types of vessels using the navigation.

Narrow boats. Steamers engaged in the London and Birmingham traffic regularly trade over the canal between Birmingham and Budbrooke.

---

(116)—WARWICK AND NAPTON CANAL.

(a) Short Description.

The canal commences by a junction with the Warwick and Birmingham Canal at Budbrooke, near Warwick, and proceeds by Emscote, Leamington, Radford, Offchurch, Long Itchington, and Stockton to Napton-on-the-Hill, where it forms a junction with the Oxford Canal, all in the county of Warwickshire.

The canal throughout its entire length forms a portion of the through route between London and Birmingham.

(b) Proprietors, Officers, and Offices.

The Company of Proprietors of the Warwick and Napton Canal Navigation.

Secretary : A. O. Anderson.

Office : 3, Church Street, Warwick.

Engineer : William Salt.

Office : Fazeley Street, Birmingham.

(c) Distance Table.

	Miles.	Fur.
Budbrooke, junction with Warwick and Birmingham Canal (No. 115), to—		
Warwick, Cape Wharf	–	4
Warwick Top Lock	–	4½
Warwick, Guy's Cliff Wharf	1	3
Emscote, Nelson's Works	1	5
Emscote, Reynolds' Wharf	1	6
Emscote, Blaydon's Old Wharf and Buffery's Lime Wharf	1	7
Leamington Stone Wharf	3	2
Leamington, Nutter's Wharf	3	3
Leamington, Watkin's Oil Mill	3	4
Leamington, Flavel's Foundry	3	5
Leamington, Frost's Wharf	3	6
Radford, Gulliman's Wharf	4	4

(116)—Warwick and Napton Canal—*continued.*

	Miles.	Fur.
Budbrooke, junction with Warwick and Birmingham Canal (No. 115) to (*continued*)—		
Offchurch Wharf	5	4
Radford Bottom Lock	5	4½
Foss Road Wharf	6	4
Longhole Wharf..	7	4
Bascote, Buffery's Lime Stone Wharf	8	4
Bascote Wharf ..	9	1
Cuttle Wharf, Long Itchington	9	7
Stockton, Tatham and Witherington's Lime Works	10	3
Stockton, Greaves & Co.'s Lime Works	10	4
Stockton, Griffin's Lime Works	10	7
Stockton Top Lock	11	0
Birdingbury Wharf	11	2
Nelson's Lime Works ..	11	5
Gibralter Wharf	11	7
Calcutt Bottom Lock ..	13	5
Napton Junction, junction with Oxford Canal (No. 82a) ..	14	2

(d) Locks.

1
and } Warwick.
2.

Fall from Budbrooke.

3.—Radford Bottom.

4
and } Fosse.
5.

6.—Fosse Top.

7.—Wood.

8.—Welch Road.

9
to } Bascote.
12.

13.—Itchington Bottom.

14
to } Stockton.
22.

23
to } Calcutt.
25.

Rise to Napton Junction.

(e) *Maximum size of vessels that can use the navigation.*

	Ft.	In.
Length	72	0
Width	7	0
Draught ..	3	8
Headroom	8	0

(116)—WARWICK AND NAPTON CANAL—*continued*.

(g) Towing-path.

There is a towing-path throughout the navigation.

(i) Types of vessels using the navigation.

Narrow boats. Steamers engaged in the London and Birmingham traffic regularly trade over the canal.

WATERWORKS RIVER—*see* River Lee.

WATTS, BLAKE, BEARNE, AND CO., MESSRS.—*see* Great Western Railway, Stover Canal.

––––––––

(117)—RIVER WAVENEY.

(a) Short Description.

The river commences to be navigable at Bungay, in the county of Suffolk, and proceeds by Ellingham, Shipmeadow Lock near Geldeston, Beccles, Aldeby, Burgh St. Peter, Somerleyton, Haddiscoe, St. Olave's, and Burgh Castle to a junction with the River Yare at the west end of Breydon Water. The upper portion of the river from Bungay to a point about one furlong below Shipmeadow Lock, where the Weir Stream enters the navigation, is known as the Bungay Navigation.

The navigation throughout the whole of its course forms the boundary between the counties of Suffolk and Norfolk.

(b) Proprietors, Officers, and Offices.

From Bungay to about one furlong below Shipmeadow Lock, where the Weir Stream enters the navigation, the navigation is in private hands.

Proprietor : W. D. Walker, Esq. (Messrs. W. D. & A. E. Walker, Maltsters and Merchants).

Office : Bungay, Suffolk.

From one furlong below Shipmeadow Lock to the junction with the River Yare the river is under the jurisdiction of the Great Yarmouth Port and Haven Commissioners.

Clerk : John Tolver Waters.

Office : 2, South Quay, Yarmouth.

Harbour Master : Captain Day.

Office : Gorleston-on-Sea.

Somerleyton Dike is the property of Sir Savile Crossley, Bart.

(117)—RIVER WAVENEY—*continued.*

(c) Distance Table.

Main Line or River (No. 117a).

	Miles.	Fur.
Bungay Staiths to—		
Wainford Mill and Lock	–	5
Ellingham Mill and Lock	2	0
Shipmeadow Lock	4	1½
Nine Poplars	6	1½
Beccles Railway Bridge (Waveney Valley Line)	7	2½
Beccles Town Bridge	7	3½
Stanley Brickyard Staith	8	7½
Beccles Railway Bridge	9	2
Aldeby Staith	10	1
Norlingham Staith	10	4
Six Mile Corner	11	6
Seven Mile Corner	12	5
Carlton Share Mill	14	0½
Burgh St. Peter Staith and Ferry	14	3½
Junction with Oulton Dike, Great Eastern Railway Co.'s Navigation to Lowestoft (No. 40b)	15	2
Somerleyton Railway Bridge	18	1
Junction with Somerleyton Dike (No. 117b) ..	18	1½
Somerleyton Staith and Ferry	18	2
St. Olave's Railway Bridge	19	6
Haddiscoe, Bagshaw's Staith, and junction with Great Eastern Railway Co.'s New Cut (No. 40a)	20	1
St. Olave's Bridge and Staiths	20	3½
Burgh Staith and Brickyard	25	1
Burgh Castle	25	3
Junction with River Yare (No. 128a) at West end of Breydon Water	25	6

Somerleyton Dike (No. 117b).

Length from junction with Main Line of river (No. 117a) to Staith at upper end ..	–	0½

(d) Locks.

Main Line of River (No. 117a).

There are three locks on the river, all of which are situated on the portion of the river known as the Bungay Navigation—

1.—Wainford.
2.—Ellingham.
3.—Shipmeadow.

Fall from Bungay.

(117)—RIVER WAVENEY—*continued.*

(*e*) *Maximum size of vessels that can use the navigation.*

Main Line of River (No. 117a).

From the junction with the River Yare to Beccles.

	Ft.	In.
Length.—Not limited.		
Width.—Not limited.		
Draught .. .. about	7	0

From Beccles to Bungay.

	Ft.	In.
Length	70	0
Width	16	0
Draught	3	0 to 4ft.

Headroom from the mouth of the river to St. Olave's Bridge, not limited ; above St. Olave's Bridge, Beccles Town Bridge is the next fixed bridge, the three intermediate railway bridges being all opening bridges.

Somerleyton Dike (No. 117b).

	Ft.	In.
Length.—Not limited.		
Width.—Not limited.		
Draught	3	0 to 4ft.

(*g*) *Towing-path.*

There is no horse towing-path on any part of the river.

(*h*) *Tidal Information.*

The tide usually flows up the river to Beccles, where it rises to a height of from 2ft. to 3ft. ; above Beccles it backs up the water in the river to Shipmeadow Lock, making an average rise and fall of about 1ft. at that place.

High water at St. Olave's Bridge about 2hrs. after Yarmouth.

High water at Beccles about 4hrs. after Yarmouth.

For the tide at Yarmouth—*see* River Yare.

(*i*) *Types of vessels using the navigation.*

Norfolk wherries. The largest wherry trading to Bungay carries 34 tons.

WAXHAM NEW CUT—*see* River Bure, River Thurne.

(118)—RIVER WEAVER.

(a) Short Description.

The river commences to be navigable at Winsford Bridge, and proceeds by Vale Royal, Hartford Bridge, Northwich, Anderton, Barnton, Saltersford, Acton Bridge, and Dutton to Sutton Locks. Here the Main Line of the navigation is continued parallel to the Old Line of navigation by a canal known as the River Weaver, or Weston Canal, to Weston Marsh and Weston Point, where it terminates by a junction with the Manchester Ship Canal at Weston Point Docks.

Access to the tidal estuary of the River Mersey is obtained at Weston Point after crossing the Manchester Ship Canal by means of Weston Mersey Side Lock of the Ship Canal. There is also a side lock at Weston Marsh communicating with the Old Line of navigation and the Manchester Ship Canal.

There is a short branch at Anderton consisting of the Anderton Hydraulic Lift and its approach channels, giving access from the Main Line of navigation to the Main Line of the Trent and Mersey Canal.

The principal trade, on the navigation is salt which is carried in large quantities. There is also a considerable traffic in chemicals, and in china clay, flints, etc., for the Staffordshire Potteries via the Anderton Lift.

The Old Line of navigation—head of Frodsham Cut to Weston Marsh—commences at the head of Frodsham Cut half-a-mile above Sutton Locks, and proceeds a distance of half-a-mile to Frodsham Lock, where it forms a junction with the old tidal channel of the river, which continues to its mouth at Weston Marsh. Here it forms a junction with the Manchester Ship Canal, and also a junction through Weston Marsh Side Lock with the Weaver Canal, which forms the Main Line of the navigation at this point. This portion of the navigation is now only used for local traffic.

The whole course of the navigation is situated in the county of Cheshire.

The river is liable to floods; but of late years, owing to large expenditure on works of improvement, the average height to which they attain has been much reduced.

(b) Proprietors, Officers, and Offices.

The whole of the Main Line of the navigation from Winsford Bridge to Weston Point, including Weston Point Docks, the Anderton Lift Branch, and the portion of the Old Line of navigation—head of Frodsham Cut to Weston Marsh—from the head of Frodsham Cut to Frodsham Bridge is under the jurisdiction of the Weaver Navigation Trustees.

General Manager : E. S. Inman.

Office : Northwich, Cheshire. Telegrams : " Weaver, Northwich." Telephone No. 44.

Engineer : J. A. Saner.

Office : Northwich, Cheshire. Telegrams : " Saner, Northwich." Telephone No. 78.

The portion of the Old Line of navigation—head of Frodsham Cut to Weston Marsh—from Frodsham Bridge to Weston Marsh is an open navigation, having no controlling authority.

(118)—River Weaver—*continued.*

(c) Distance Table.

Main Line of Navigation (No. 118a).

	Miles.	Fur.
Winsford Bridge to—		
Garner's Works	–	1
Birkenhead, Liverpool, and Runcorn Alkali Works	–	2
Uploont and Wharton Meadow Works ..	–	4
Deakins, Over, and Cheshire Amalgamated Works	–	6
Hickson's, Stubbs', and Little Meadow Works	1	0
Meadow, Bostock, and National Works ..	1	2
Meadowbank Works	1	4
Falks Works	1	6
Newbridge Works and Bridge..	2	0
Lord Delamere's Quay	2	6
Vale Royal Locks	3	2
Hartford Bridge..	3	7
Hunt's Locks	5	1
Woodcock's Yard	5	2
Northwich, mouth of River Dane, and Navigation Yard of River Weaver Trustees ..	5	4
Northwich, Barons Quay	5	6
Witton Works and Witton Brook Works ..	6	0
Cheshire Amalgamated Works	6	2
Byeflat Works	6	4
Higgins' Works	6	6
Junction with Anderton Lift Branch (No. 118b)	7	0
Upper Chemical Works—Brunner, Mond, & Co.	7	0
Crystal Plant Works—Brunner, Mond, & Co...	7	2
Stott's Wharf	7	6
Barnton Island	8	4
Saltersford Locks	9	2
Gerrard's Stage	9	2
Wilbraham's Quay	10	2
Acton Bridge	11	1
Dutton Locks	12	3
Dutton Culvert	12	4
Pickering's Wharf and Bridge..	13	2
Aston Tickles Wharf	15	3
Junction with Old Line of navigation—head of Frodsham Cut to Weston Marsh (No. 118c)	16	0
Sutton Locks	16	4
Sutton Bridge	16	7
Runcorn Bone Works	17	1
Sutton Dock	17	1
Rock Savage	17	3
Hadfield's Works	18	2
Weston Works	18	3
Weston Marsh Side Lock, giving access to Manchester Ship Canal (No. 64a), and Old Line of navigation (No. 118c) ..	19	0

(118)—RIVER WEAVER—*continued.*

	Miles.	Fur.
Winsford Bridge to (*continued*)—		
Sand Quarry	19	2
Stone Quarry	19	6
Junction with Runcorn and Weston Canal (No. 64c)	19	6
Weston Point Docks, and junction with Manchester Ship Canal (No. 64a)	20	0

Anderton Lift Branch (No. 118b).

Junction with Main Line of navigation (No. 118a) to—		
Junction with Trent and Mersey Canal—Main Line—(No. 76a)	–	1

Old Line of Navigation—Head of Frodsham Cut to Weston Marsh—
(No. 118c).

	Miles.	Fur.
Junction with Main Line of navigation (No. 118a) and head of Frodsham Cut to—		
Frodsham Lock	–	4
Frodsham Bridge	1	0
Weston Marsh, junction with Manchester Ship Canal (No. 64a), and Main Line of navigation (No. 118a) through Weston Marsh Side Lock	2	2

(d) Locks.

Main Line of Navigation (No. 118a).

1.—Vale Royal (two locks side by side).
    One 229ft. by 42ft. 6in.
    One 100ft. by 22ft.

2.—Hunts (two locks side by side).
    One 229ft. by 42ft. 6in.
    One 100ft. by 22ft.

3.—Saltersford (two locks side by side).
    One 229ft. by 42ft. 6in.
    One 220ft. by 25ft.

4.—Dutton (two locks side by side).
    One 229ft. by 42ft. 6in.
    One 220ft. by 25ft.
Fall from Winsford.

5.—Sutton (two locks side by side).
    One 220ft. by 40ft.
    One 100ft. by 18ft.

The gates of Sutton Locks are nearly always open, being only required to be closed at high water of Spring tides, or in flood time.

6.—Weston Point Dock Locks.
    Width 40ft.
Normally level.

(118)—RIVER WEAVER—*continued.*

  7.—Weston Point Tidal gates.
      Width 40ft.

Fall to Manchester Ship Canal at ordinary times, level at high water of high Spring tides.

Weston Marsh Side Lock.
      One lock 229ft. by 42ft. 6in.

Fall from Main Line of Navigation to Manchester Ship Canal and Old Line of Navigation—Head of Frodsham Cut to Weston Marsh.

Anderton Lift Branch (No. 118b).

Anderton Lift—*see* Section 4, (c) Lifts.

Rise to Trent and Mersey Canal.

Old Line of Navigation—Head of Frodsham Cut to Weston Marsh—
(No. 118c).

  1.—Frodsham.
      Fall towards Weston Marsh at Low water.

(*e*) *Maximum size of vessels that can use the navigation.*

Main Line of Navigation (No. 118a).

	Ft.	In.

The locks on the Main Line of the navigation, measuring 229ft. by 42ft. 6in., are available for four vessels at one time of the ordinary type using the river ; these measure 90ft. in length by 21ft. in width, and carry about 250 tons each. Larger craft, measuring up to 120ft. in length by 25ft. in width, use the river at times.

	Ft.	In.
Draught	10	5

The sills of the locks are constructed for a draught of 15ft. to allow for the river being deepened in the future.

Vessels not drawing over 14ft. can enter Weston Point Docks from the Manchester Ship Canal at any time, and vessels not drawing over 16ft. can pass Weston Marsh Side Lock to Weston Marsh Wharf from the Manchester Ship Canal at any time.

Headroom.—The lowest fixed bridge is Hartford Bridge, which has a headroom of 16ft. Except for this bridge the headroom is 56ft.

(119)—RIVER WEAVER—*continued.*

Anderton Lift Branch (No. 118b).

						Ft.	In.
Length	..	..	..	..	..	72	0
Width	..	..	..	..	..	14	6
Draught	..	..	..	..	..	5	0
Headroom	..	..	..	..	..	9	0

Old Line of Navigation—Head of Frodsham Cut to Weston Marsh— (No. 118c).

Length	100	0
Width, being the length and width of Frodsham Lock..	18	0
Draught .. .. about	6	6
Headroom, being the approximate headroom under Frodsham Bridge at high water of Spring tides	18	0

(g) Towing path.

Main Line of Navigation (No. 118a).

There is a towing-path throughout the navigation.

Anderton Lift Branch (No. 118b).

There is no towing-path.

Old Line of Navigation—Head of Frodsham Cut to Weston Marsh— (No. 118c).

There is a towing-path from the head of Frodsham Cut to Frodsham Bridge.

(h) Tidal Information.

The tide flows up the Old Line of navigation (No. 118c) to the tail of Frodsham Lock ; high Spring tides flow past Frodsham Lock and into the Main Line of navigation between Sutton and Dutton Locks.

The time of high water at Frodsham Lock varies according to the tide in the Manchester Ship Canal, and is very irregular.

(i) Types of vessels using the navigation.

Weaver flats—*see* Section 9, Types of Vessels, (a) Non-Sailing Vessels.

The use of steam flats for carrying cargo and towing other flats has much increased of late years.

Small coasting vessels navigate up to Northwich.

WEAVER CANAL, OR WESTON CANAL—*see* River Weaver.

WEDNESBURY OAK LOOP LINE—*see* Birmingham Canal Navigations.

WEDNESBURY OLD CANAL—*see* Birmingham Canal Navigations.

WELFORD BRANCH CANAL—*see* Grand Junction Canal, Leicester Section.

WELL CREEK—*see* Middle Level Navigations.

———

(119)—RIVER WELLAND.

(a) Short Description.

There is very little trade done on any portion of the river.   In wet seasons the river is more or less navigable from Market Deeping, where there is a mill dam across the river, down to Spalding, but the navigation is very uncertain.   From Spalding to the junction with the River Glen the river is only navigable for paying loads on Spring tides.   From the junction with the River Glen to the mouth of the river at Fosdyke Bridge the river is navigable for paying loads at all times except on the very lowest tides.   Below Fosdyke Bridge the river rapidly widens out and enters The Wash.

From Market Deeping to near Crowland the river forms the boundary between the counties of Lincolnshire and Northamptonshire, the remainder of the river is situated in the county of Lincolnshire.

The seasons very much affect the available draught of water in the river below Spalding ; during the Summer " warp " or silt is brought up by the tide, and remains until scoured out by a flood, and it of course depends on the amount of rainfall to what extent this scouring takes place.

(b) Proprietors, Officers, and Offices.

The portion of the navigation above Spalding, as a drainage, is under the jurisdiction of the Deeping Fen General Works of Drainage Trustees.

Clerks : Calthorp and Bonner, Solicitors.

Office : Spalding.

Superintendent : A. Harrison.

Office : Little London, Spalding.

From Spalding to Fosdyke Bridge, and below Fosdyke Bridge in the open estuary of The Wash as far as the junction with the River Witham old channel, the river is under the jurisdiction of the Trustees of the River Welland Outfall Act, 1869.

Clerks : Calthorp and Bonner, Solicitors.

Office : Spalding.

Superintendent and Receiver of River Dues : John Kirkby.

Office : Fosdyke Bridge, near Spalding.

(c) Distance Table.

	Miles.	Fur.
Market Deeping Mill to—		
Deeping St. James	1	4
Crowland	7	0
Spalding Bridge..	16	0
Junction with River Glen (No. 37) ; this point		
is also called " The Reservoir "	20	6
Fosdyke Bridge	23	6

(119)—River Welland.—*continued.*

(e) *Maximum size of vessels that can use the navigation.*

	Ft.	In.
Length.—Not limited.		
Width.—Not limited.		
Draught from Fosdyke Bridge to the junction with the River Glen, except on the lowest tides	6	0
Draught from the junction with the River Glen to Spalding during only about 3 or 4 days in the fortnight	6	0
Headroom up to Spalding Bridge not limited, Fosdyke Bridge being an opening bridge.		

(g) *Towing-path.*

Vessels navigate the river on the ebb and flow of the tide, but the river bank between Fosdyke Bridge and Spalding would be quite suitable for horse haulage if required.

(h) *Tidal Information.*

Spring tides flow above Spalding, Neap tides scarcely flow beyond the junction with the River Glen. The river at Spalding runs out dry at low water of Spring tides when there is little land water coming down the river from above.

On Spring tides the flood tides sets up the river with a small tidal wave or " Aegre," but the height of the wave is not great.

High water at Fosdyke Bridge about 5hrs. after London Bridge.

Spring tides rise .. .. .. 12ft.

High water at the junction with the River Glen from about 15 to 20min. after high water at Fosdyke Bridge.

High water at Spalding about 1hr. after Fosdyke Bridge.

Spring tides rise .. .. about 8ft.

(i) *Types of vessels using the navigation.*

The few vessels in use on the river are of a miscellaneous type, and are principally open lighters, of which the maximum load is about 60 tons on a draught of 6ft.

Wendover Branch Canal—*see* Grand Junction Canal.

Wensum, River—*see* River Yare.

West Fen Drain—*see* Witham Drainage General Commissioners.

(120)—West London Extension Railway.

(a) Short Description.

The West London Extension Railway Company are the proprietors of the Kensington Canal. The canal, also known by the name of Chelsea Creek, commences by a junction with the River Thames at Counters Creek about a quarter-of-a-mile below Battersea Railway Bridge, and proceeds in a northerly direction, following the line of the West London Extension Railway, to its termination at Stanley Bridge Mills, Kings Road, Chelsea, adjoining Chelsea Station of the West London Extension Railway.

The canal used formerly to extend a further distance of one mile three furlongs northward to a dock or basin known as Warwick Basin, but this portion was closed under powers of an Act of Parliament of 1859, to enable the site to be occupied by the railway.

There is a good trade done to the wharves on the canal side, and to the Imperial Gas Works Tidal Basin.

(b) Proprietors, Officers, and Offices.

West London Extension Railway Company.

Secretary : Ernest C. Price.

Office : 57, Moorgate Street, London, E.C.

Superintendent : J. Groom.

Office : Kensington Station, Addison Road, London W.

(c) Distance Table.

	Miles.	Fur.
Counter's Creek, junction with River Thames (No. 107a), to—		
Junction with Imperial Gas Works Tidal Basin	–	1½
Head of Creek at Stanley Bridge Mills, adjoining Chelsea Railway Station of West London Extension Railway	–	3

(e) Maximum size of vessels that can use the navigation.

	Ft.	In.
Length.—Not limited.		
Width.—Not limited.		
Draught on Spring tides.. .. .. about	7	6
Draught on Neap tides.. .. .. ,,	5	6

Vessels to enter the Imperial Gas Works Company's Tidal Basin through the tidal gates should not exceed 18ft. in width. Barges carrying about 120 tons on Spring tides and 60 tons on Neap tides can navigate to the Gas Works.

| Headroom .. .. | 6 | 5 |

(120)—West London Extension Railway—*continued.*

(g) Towing-path.

There is no towing-path.

(h) Tidal Information.

The canal is tidal throughout ; the upper portion runs out dry at low water.

High water 25min. after London Bridge.

Spring tides rise	8ft.
Neap ,, ,, ...	6ft.

(i) Types of vessels using the navigation.

Barges, lighters, and Medway sailing barges.

Weston Canal, or Weaver Canal—*see* River Weaver.

Weston Branch Canal—*see* Shropshire Union Canals, Ellesmere Canal.

Westminster, Duke of—*see* Grosvenor Canal.

———

(121)—River Wey.

(a) Short Description.

The river commences to be navigable at Godalming, and proceeds by Shalford, Guildford, Send, Pyrford, and Woodham to Weybridge, where it forms a junction with the River Thames.

The whole course of the navigation is situated in the county of Surrey.

There is fair trade done on the river from the Thames to Guildford, but not much between Guildford and Godalming.

(b) Proprietors, Officers, and Offices.

The river from Godalming to Guildford Wharf, known as the Upper or Godalming Navigation, is under the jurisdiction of the Commissioners of the River Wey Godalming Navigation, the owners not being known.

Manager : William Stevens.

Office : Guildford Wharf, Guildford.

The river from Guildford Wharf to a short distance below Thames Lock, Weybridge, is the property of the Trustees of William Hussey, Esq.

Manager : William Stevens.

Office : Guildford Wharf, Guildford.

(121)—-River Wey—*continued.*

(c) *Distance Table.*

	Miles.	Fur.
Godalming Wharf to—		
Catteshall Lock	–	4
Unstead Lock	1	6
Junction with old Wey and Arun Canal (derelict)	2	2
St. Catherine's Lock, Shalford	3	0
Guildford Lock	4	1
Guildford Bridge	4	2
Guildford Wharf	4	3
Stoke Lock	6	6
Bower's Lock	8	0
Triggs Lock	10	0
Worsfold Flood Gates	10	5
Send Bridge	10	7
Paper Court Lock	12	2
Newark Lock	13	0½
Walsham Flood Gates	13	5
Pyrford, or Anchor Lock	14	5
Woodham, junction with Woking, Aldershot, and Basingstoke Canal (No. 126)	16	5
Newhaw Lock	17	2
Cox's Lock	18	1
Weybridge Lock	18	6
Thames Lock	19	3
Junction with River Thames (No. 107a) ..	19	5

(d) *Locks.*

1.—Catteshall.
2.—Unstead.
3.—St. Catherine's.
4.—Guildford.

The above are on the Godalming Navigation, and fall to Guildford.

5.—Stoke.
6.—Bower's.
7.—Triggs.
8.—Worsfold (flood gates).
9.—Paper Court.
10.—Newark.
11.—Walsham (flood gates).
12.—Pyrford, or Anchor.
13.—Newhaw.
14.—Cox's.
15.—Weybridge.
16.—Thames.

Fall from Guildford.

(121)—RIVER WEY—*continued.*

(e) *Maximum size of vessels that can use the navigation.*

	Ft.	In.
Length	72	0
Width	13	10½
Draught from the Thames to Guildford Wharf :		
In Summer .. .. average	3	7
In Winter .. .. ,,	3	10
Draught from Guildford Wharf to Catteshall :		
In Summer .. .. average	3	4
In Winter .. .. ,,	3	6
Draught from Catteshall to Godalming :		
In Summer .. .. average	2	8
In Winter .. .. ,,	2	11
Headroom from the Thames to Guildford Wharf	7	0
Headroom from Guildford Wharf to Godalming	6	6

(g) *Towing-path.*

There is a towing-path throughout the navigation.

(i) *Types of vessels using the navigation.*

Barges.

WHALEY BRIDGE BRANCH CANAL—*see* Great Central Railway, Peak Forest Canal.

———

(122)—RIVER WHARFE.

(a) *Short Description.*

The river is navigable at Spring tides from its junction with the River Ouse to Ulleskelf. Beyond Ulleskelf navigation is conducted up to Tadcaster at such times as the amount of land water coming down the river permits ; in dry seasons keels have to wait sometimes for weeks to reach Tadcaster.

The course of the navigation from its junction with the River Ouse to Tadcaster is situated in the West Riding of the county of Yorkshire.

There is very little trade done on the river, what there is being principally coal.

In 1890, a company obtained an Act of Parliament to make the river navigable from Tadcaster to the River Ouse for vessels carrying 50 tons, but the works undertaken not having proved successful the company was wound up in 1898, and the river remains at the present time practically in its natural condition.

(122)—River Wharfe—*continued.*

(b) *Proprietors, Officers, and Offices.*

The river is an open navigation, having no controlling authority.

(c) *Distance Table.*

						Miles.	Fur.
Tadcaster Bridge to—							
Kirkby Wharf	..	..	..	..	..	2	4
Ulleskelf	..	..	..	..	..	3	7
Ryther	..	..	..	..	..	6	5
Nun Appleton Park	..	..	..	..	7	0
Junction with River Ouse—York—(No. 81)..			9	2

(e) *Maximum size of vessels that can use the navigation.*

		Ft.	In.
Length.—Not limited.			
Width.—Not limited.			
Draught—Uncertain .. .. maximum		5	0 to 6ft.
Headroom, from the junction with the River Ouse to Ulleskelf, not limited.			

(g) *Towing-path.*

There is no towing-path.

(h) *Tidal Information.*

The navigation is tidal throughout. Spring tides flow to Ulleskelf and back up the water in the river to a height of about 10in. at Tadcaster. A tide giving a depth of 28ft. on the Albert Dock Sill, Hull, will raise the water at the mouth of the river 3ft.

See also Tidal Information, River Ouse—York.

(i) *Types of vessels using the navigation.*

Yorkshire keels.

Whitchurch Branch Canal—*see* Shropshire Union Canals, Ellesmere Canal.

Whitesley Mere—*see* River Bure, River Thurne.

Whittlesey Dike—*see* Middle Level Navigations.

Willenhall Branch Canal—*see* Birmingham Canal Navigations, Walsall Canal.

Wilts and Berks Canal.

Although the canal is not officially closed, navigation throughout the whole of the system has practically ceased owing to the income being insufficient to meet the cost of maintenance.

WILTS AND BERKS CANAL—*continued.*

The Main Line of the canal commences by a junction with the River Thames at Abingdon, and proceeds by Grove, Challow, Uffington, and Shrivenham, in the county of Berkshire ; Swindon, Wootton Bassett, Dauntsey, Lacock, and Melksham to Semington, in the county of Wiltshire, where it forms a junction with the Kennet and Avon Navigation, a total distance of 52 miles.

There are branches leading out of the Main Line, as follows :—

From near Grove to Wantage one mile in length, and

From near Shrivenham to Longcot Wharf, three-quarters of a mile in length, both in the county of Berkshire.

The North Wilts Branch nine miles in length, from Swindon to Purton, Cricklade, and Latton, where it forms a junction with the Thames and Severn Canal, all in the county of Wiltshire.

From Stanley to Calne three miles in length, and

From near Pewsham to Chippenham two miles in length, also in the county of Wiltshire.

Wilts and Berks Canal Company.

Secretary : W. J. Ainsworth.

Office : Central Chambers, Swindon.

WIRRAL LINE (ELLESMERE CANAL)—*see* Shropshire Union Canals.

———

(123)—WISBECH CANAL.

(a) Short Description.

The canal commences by a junction with the tidal portion of the River Nene at Wisbech, and proceeds by New Walsoken, Elm, and Emneth to Outwell, where it forms junctions with the Old River Nene and Well Creek of the Middle Level Navigations.

The course of the canal forms approximately the boundary between the counties of Cambridgeshire and Norfolk.

There is not much trade done on the canal, and the proprietors have lately unsuccessfully sought Parliamentary powers to enable them to close it.

The canal, being above the level of the River Nene at Wisbech, is supplied with water from that river at Spring tides only, and thus can only be filled up every fortnight, which operation is called " putting the tide in."   Often just before the tide is put in there is barely navigable water in the canal.

(123)—Wisbech Canal—*continued.*

(b) Proprietors, Officers, and Offices.

The Wisbech Canal Company.

Clerk : Edward McD. C. Jackson.

Office : Wisbech.

(c) Distance Table.

	Miles.	Fur.
Wisbech, junction with River Nene (No. 74a) and Wisbech Lock, to—		
New Walsoken	–	4
Elm	1	6
Emneth Bridge	2	6
Boyce's Bridge	3	7
Outwell, Outwell Lock, junction with Old River Nene (No. 69f), and Well Creek (No. 69i)	5	2

(d) Locks.

1.—Wisbech.

The lock has two pair of navigation gates and two pair of sea gates.

Fall to River Nene at low water, level at high water of Spring tides.

2.—Outwell.

Fall from Wisbech.

(e) Maximum size of vessels that can use the navigation.

	Ft.	In.
Length, being the available length of Wisbech Lock..	50	0
At such times as the tide in the River Nene makes a level with the water in the canal at Wisbech (*see* Tidal Information) longer vessels could pass through the canal, as then the only lock used would be Outwell, which has a length of	97	0
Width	10	10
Draught	3	6
Headroom	5	9½

(g) Towing-path.

There is a towing-path throughout the navigation.

(123)— WISBECH CANAL—*continued.*

(h) Tidal Information.

High water at Wisbech 5hrs. 30min. after London Bridge.
The tide in the River Nene makes a level with the water in the canal for about one week, or a little less, during the fortnight.

(i) Types of vessels using the navigation.

Fen lighters.

WISBECH, CORPORATION OF THE TOWN OF—*see* River Nene.

---

(124)—RIVER WITHAM.

(a) Short Description.

The River commences to be navigable at the east end of Brayford Mere, Lincoln, where it forms a junction with the Fossdyke Canal, and proceeds by Washingborough, Bardney, Stixwould, Kirkstead, Tattershall Bridge, Dogdyke, Chapel Hill, and Langrick to Boston, four miles below which town the mouth of the river is reached near the outlet of Hobhole Drain, the artificial channel being carried a further distance of three miles through sand flats to Clay Hole, in The Wash.

The whole course of the navigation is situated in the county of Lincolnshire. From Lincoln to Tattershall it skirts the Lincolnshire Wolds, and after leaving Tattershall passes entirely through Fen country.

There is very little trade done on the river between Lincoln and Boston. There is, however, a good trade by sea-going and coasting vessels from the mouth of the river to Boston Dock.

(b) Proprietors, Officers, and Offices.

From Brayford Mere, Lincoln, up to and including the Grand Sluice, Boston, the navigation of the river is the property of the Great Northern Railway Company.

Secretary : William Latta.

Office : King's Cross Station, London, N.

Engineer in charge of Canals : C. Kirby.

Office : District Engineer's Office, G. N. Railway, Boston.

Local Agent : H. Cunnington.

Office : Torksey Lock, near Lincoln.

From Brayford Mere, Lincoln, to the Grand Sluice, Boston, the river is also a drainage under the jurisdiction of the Witham Drainage General Commissioners.

Clerk : R. W. Millington.

Engineer : T. Healey Johnson.

Offices : Witham Office, Boston, Lincolnshire.

(124)—River Witham—*continued.*

Below the Grand Sluice, Boston, the river, as far as maintenance is concerned, is under the jurisdiction of the Witham Outfall Board, but the Boston Harbour and Dock Commissioners have power to dredge and deepen the channel for navigation purposes, and maintain the lights and beacons.

Witham Outfall Board.

Clerk : H. A. Peake.

Office : Sleaford, Lincolnshire.

Engineer : T. Healey Johnson.

Office : Witham Office, Boston, Lincolnshire.

Boston Harbour and Dock Commissioners.

Clerk : Benjamin B. Dyer.

Engineer : William Henry Wheeler.

Dock Manager : Andrew B. Anderson.

Harbour and Dock Master : Captain Hudson.

Offices : Boston, Lincolnshire.

(c) Distance Table.

	Miles.	Fur.
Lincoln, east end of Brayford Mere, junction with Fossdyke Canal (No. 42), to—		
Lincoln, High Bridge	–	1
Lincoln, Stamp End Lock	–	4
Washingborough	2	6
Five Mile House Station and Ferry	5	3
Horsley Deeps Lock, Bardney	8	6
Bardney Station....	9	4
Southrey Station and Ferry	12	2
Stixwould Station and Ferry	13	6
Kirkstead Station	15	6
Junction with Old Horncastle Navigation (not navigable)	19	2
Tattershall Bridge	19	6
Dogdyke Station and Ferry	20	7
Chapel Hill, junction with Kyme Eau (No. 53)	21	6
Langrick Station and Ferry	27	1
Anton's Gowt, junction with Frith Bank Drain (No. 125a)	29	2
Boston, Grand Sluice (Lock)	31	5
Boston Iron Bridge	32	0
Boston, junction with Black Sluice Drainage and Navigation (No. 12)	32	7
Entrance to Boston Dock	33	2½
Outlet of Maud Foster Drain (No. 125d) through Maud Foster Sluice (no navigation through Sluice)	33	3
Mouth of River and Outlet of Hobhole Drain (No. 125h) through Hobhole Sluice (no navigation through Sluice)	36	1

(124)—River Witham—*continued.*

(d) *Locks.*

1.—Stamp End, Lincoln.
2.—Horsley Deeps, Bardney.
    Fall from Lincoln.
3.—Grand Sluice, Boston.

The lock and all the sluice openings are provided with sea doors.
    Fall from Lincoln at low water, level at high water,

(e) *Maximum size of vessels that can use the navigation.*

From the Mouth of the River to the Tail of the Grand Sluice, Boston.

	Ft.	In.
Length.—Not limited.		
Width.—Not limited.		
Draught from the mouth of the river to Boston		
Dock average .. .. .. about	16	0
Maximum on Spring tides .. about	21	0
Draught from Boston Dock to the tail of the		
Grand Sluice Boston :		
On Spring tides .. .. about	16	0
On Neap tides.. .. .. ,,	10	6
Headroom, from the mouth of the river to the Iron Bridge, Boston, not limited, Boston Dock Railway Bridge being an opening bridge.		
Headroom, from the Iron Bridge to the Grand Sluice, Boston, being the headroom of the		
Iron Bridge: At high water of Spring tides	4	6
At high water of Neap tides	11	0

From the Tail of the Grand Sluice, Boston, to Brayford Mere, Lincoln.

Length	78	0
Width	15	2
Draught	5	0
Headroom	8	10

(g) *Towing-path.*

There is a towing-path from Brayford Mere, Lincoln, to the Grand Sluice, Boston.

(h) *Tidal Information.*

The tide flows to the tail of the Grand Sluice, Boston.

High water at Boston Deep, Clay Hole, 4hrs. after London Bridge.

Spring tides rise	22ft.
Neap ,, ,, ...	15ft. 4in.

High water at Boston Dock 30min. after Boston Deep, Clay Hole.

Spring tides rise	21ft.
Neap ,, ,, ...	14ft. 4in.

High water at the Grand Sluice, Boston, about the same time as at Boston Dock.

Spring tides rise	13ft. 3in.

(124)—River Witham—*continued.*

(*i*) *Types of vessels using the navigation.*

Sea-going vessels navigate from the mouth of the river to Boston Dock, and occasionally to Boston Iron Bridge. Barges and Yorkshire keels use the river between Boston Dock and Lincoln.

(125)—Witham Drainage General Commissioners Navigable Drains.

(*a*) *Short Description.*

The drains in question consist of a group situated to the north and east of the town of Boston, all in the county of Lincolnshire, access to the whole of which for navigation purposes is only obtained by means of the Frith Bank Drain, which forms a junction with the River Witham at Anton's Gowt, 2 miles 3 furlongs above the Grand Sluice, Boston.

There is a very limited amount of trade done on these drains. Navigation on them is very uncertain, and much depends on the wetness of the season.

The drains are as follows :—

Frith Bank Drain, *alias* Junction Drain (No. 125a), commencing by a junction with the River Witham (No. 124) at Anton's Gowt and proceeding to Cowbridge, a distance of 1 mile 7 furlongs, where it forms a junction with the West Fen Drain (No. 125b) and Maud Foster Drain (No. 125d).

West Fen Drain (No. 125b) from Cowbridge, where it forms a junction with Frith Bank Drain (No. 125a) and Maud Foster Drain (No. 125d), to Mount Pleasant Junction with Medlam Drain (No. 125c) 2 miles, Bunker's Hill 4 miles 1 furlong, New York 5 miles 2 furlongs.

The drain is not navigable beyond New York.

Medlam Drain (No. 125c), from a junction with the West Fen Drain (No. 125b), at Mount Pleasant, to Gilliat's Brick Works 6 furlongs, Revesby Bridge 6 miles 4 furlongs.

The drain is not in use for navigation above Gilliat's Brick Works.

Maud Foster Drain (No. 125d), from the tail of Cowbridge Stop Lock, where it forms a junction with Frith Bank Drain (No. 125a) and West Fen Drain (No. 125b) to the head of Cowbridge Stop Lock, where it forms a junction with Stone Bridge Drain (No. 125e) and Cowbridge Drain (No. 125g), and to Bargate Bridge, Boston, 1 mile 5 furlongs, and Maud Foster Sluice, Boston, 2 miles 5 furlongs, where it joins the River Witham (No. 124), but there is no navigation through Maud Foster Sluice.

(125)—Witham Drainage General Commissioners Navigable Drains—*continued.*

Stone Bridge Drain (No. 125e), from a junction with Cowbridge Drain (No. 125g) and Maud Foster Drain (No. 125d) at the head of Cowbridge Stop Lock to its termination at Northlands, 4 miles 2 furlongs, where it forms a junction with the West Fen Catchwater Drain (No. 125f) and the East Fen Catchwater Drain.

The East Fen Catchwater Drain is not navigable.

The West Fen Catchwater Drain (No. 125f), from a junction with Stone Bridge Drain (No. 125e) at Northlands to Revesby Bridge, 6 miles 4 furlongs. The drain is not in use for navigation.

Cowbridge Drain (No. 125g), from a junction with Stone Bridge Drain (No. 125e) and Maud Foster Drain (No. 125d) at the head of Cowbridge Stop Lock to East Fen Lock, 2 miles 2 furlongs, and to junction with Hobhole Drain (No. 125h) 2 miles 4 furlongs.

Hobhole Drain (No. 125h) from the upper side of Hobhole Sluice at its outlet to the River Witham (No. 124)—there being no navigation through Hobhole Sluice—to junction with Cowbridge Drain (No. 125g) 3 miles 6 furlongs, Old Leake Railway Station 4 miles 2 furlongs, Lade Bank Pumping Engines and Lock 5 miles 4 furlongs, upper end of drain 9 miles 6 furlongs.

(b) *Proprietors, Officers, and Offices.*

The drains are under the jurisdiction of the Witham Drainage General Commissioners.

Clerk : R. W. Millington.

Engineer : T. Healey Johnson.

Offices : Witham Office, Boston, Lincolnshire.

(d) *Locks.*

Frith Bank Drain (No. 125a).

1.—Anton's Gowt.

Fall from River Witham entrance to Drain.

Dimensions :—

Length..	..	..	..	..	90ft.
Width ..	..	..	..	..	18ft.

Maud Foster Drain (No. 125d).

1.—Cowbridge Stop Lock.

Rise from junction with Frith Bank Drain.

Dimensions :—

Length..	..	..	..	..	71ft.
Width ..	..	..	..	..	11ft. 10in.

Cowbridge Drain (No. 125g).

1.—East Fen.

Fall to junction with Hobhole Drain.

Dimensions :—

Length ..	..	..	..	..	61ft.
Width ..	..	..	..	..	15ft. 8in.

(125)—Witham Drainage General Commissioners Navigable Drains—*continued.*

Hobhole Drain (No. 125h).

1.—Lade Bank.

The lock is used when the Lade Bank engines are at work, the fall is then towards the upper end of the drain.

Dimensions :—

Length..	71ft. 6in.
Width	12ft.

(g) *Towing-path.*

There is a towing-path throughout all the drains.

(i) *Types of vessels using the navigation.*

Barges.

Witham Outfall Board—*see* River Witham.

Withymoor Branch Canal—*see* Birmingham Canal Navigations.

---

(126)—Woking, Aldershot, and Basingstoke Canal.

(a) *Short Description.*

The canal, formerly known by the name of the Basingstoke Canal, or the London and Hampshire Canal, commences by a junction with the River Wey at Woodham, near Byfleet, and proceeds by Woking, Brookwood, Pirbright, Frimley Green, and North Camp to Ash, in the county of Surrey.   Shortly after it enters the county of Hampshire, and continues its course by Aldershot, Fleet, Crookham, Winchfield, Odiham, North Warnborough, Greywell, Up Nateley, Maplederwell, and Basing to its termination at Basingstoke Wharf, also in the same county.

The canal was purchased in 1896 by its present proprietors, who have expended a considerable amount of money on its restoration and improvement, but apparently without success, as at the present time (1904) the navigation is again for sale.   Of late the towing-path has become much overgrown in places, thereby causing horse towing to be very difficult.

(b) *Proprietors, Officers, and Offices.*

Woking Aldershot and Basingstoke Canal Company Ltd.

Manager and Engineer : Melland Smith.

Chief Office : 32, Victoria Street, Westminster. London, S.W. Telephone No. 54, Westminster.

Local Office : Onslow Buildings, Woking.   Telegrams : " Navigation, Woking."

The Company act as Carriers.

(126)—W<small>OKING</small>, A<small>LDERSHOT</small>, <small>AND</small> B<small>ASINGSTOKE</small> C<small>ANAL</small>—*continued.*

(c) *Distance Table.*

	Miles.	Fur.
Woodham, junction with River Wey (No. 121), to—		
Woodham Bottom Lock	–	2
Woodham Top Lock	1	4
Sheerwater	2	2
Mayburyhill	3	0
Woking, Wheatsheaf Bridge	3	7
Goldsworth Bottom Lock	5	2
Goldsworth Top Lock	5	5
Brookwood Bottom Lock	7	3
Brookwood Top Lock	7	4
Pirbright, bottom of Frimley Locks	8	5
Frimley Top Lock	10	4
Frimley Green	11	7
Mitchet Lake	13	2
North Camp Railway Station	13	6
Ash Lock	16	0
Aldershot, Main Road Bridge, Aldershot, to Farnborough	17	6
Pondtail Bridge	20	5
Fleet	21	5
Crookham	23	5
Winchfield	27	0
Odiham	29	0
North Warnborough	30	1
Greywell, and east end of Greywell Tunnel	31	1
West end of Greywell Tunnel	31	7
Up Nateley	32	5
Maplederwell	33	3
Basing	35	4
Basingstoke Wharf	37	4

(d) *Locks.*

1.—Woodham.
2.— ,,
3.— ,,
4.— ,,
5.— ,,
6.— ,,

7
to } Goldsworth.
11.

12
to } Brookwood.
14.

15
to } Frimley.
28.

29.—Ash.

Rise from junction with River Wey.

(126)—WOKING, ALDERSHOT, AND BASINGSTOKE CANAL—*continued.*

(e) *Maximum size of vessels that can use the navigation.*

	Ft.	In.
Length	72	0
Width	13	9
Draught, ordinary	3	6
Draught.—In dry weather the draught at the Basingstoke end of the canal might be reduced to	2	6
Headroom	9	6

(f) *Tunnels.*

Greywell—

Length .. .. 1,200 yards		
Minimum height above water level	10	0
Minimum width at water level	13	10

No towing-path ; boats " legged " or shafted through.

(g) *Towing-path.*

There is a towing-path throughout the navigation, except through Greywell Tunnel.

(i) *Types of vessels using the navigation.*

Barges.

WOMACK WATER—*see* River Bure, River Thurne.

WORCESTER AND BIRMINGHAM CANAL—*see* Sharpness New Docks and Gloucester and Birmingham Navigation Company.

WORSBOROUGH BRANCH CANAL—*see* Sheffield and South Yorkshire Navigation, Dearne and Dove Canal.

WROXHAM BROAD—*see* River Bure.

------

(127)—RIVER WYE.

(a) *Short Description.*

The river commences to be navigable at Bigsweir Bridge, up to which place vessels can navigate on Spring tides, and proceeds by Llandogo, Brockweir, Tintern, Lancaut, and Chepstow to Beachley Point, where it forms a junction with the estuary of the River Severn.

The navigation throughout the whole of its course forms the boundary between the counties of Gloucestershire and Monmouthshire.

(127)—RIVER WYE—*continued.*

The river is navigable to Chepstow on all tides. The course of the river above Chepstow is very tortuous, and the numerous fishing weirs placed partially across the river cause rapids, which are very dangerous to navigation, unless conducted on the top of the tide.

There is a small general trade done up to Chepstow ; stone is brought down from Lancaut Quarries, and timber from Brockweir.

The opening of the Wye Valley Railway in 1876 caused the bulk of the trade on the river to cease.

(b) *Proprietors, Officers, and Offices.*

The river is an open navigation, having no controlling authority.

(c) *Distance Table.*

	Miles.	Fur.
Bigsweir Bridge to—		
Llandogo	1	2
Brockweir Ferry	3	1
Tintern Railway Bridge	3	7
Tintern Bridge	4	6
Lancaut Stone Quarries	9	6
Chepstow Bridge	12	0
Beachley Point, mouth of river, and junction with River Severn Estuary (No. 89a) ..	15	0

(e) *Maximum size of vessels that can use the navigation.*

	Ft.	In.
Length.—Not limited.		
Width.—Not limited.		
Draught from the mouth of the river to Chepstow on any tide	20	0
Draught from Chepstow to Bigsweir on Spring tides..	6	0
Draught.—A high Spring tide giving 20ft. of water on the sill of Bathurst Basin Lock at Bristol will give a depth between Chepstow and Brockweir of	12	0

(g) *Towing-path.*

There is no towing-path. The old towing-path extended from Monmouth to Brockweir. The portion between Brockweir and Bigsweir is not now used at all, and is much overgrown in places.

(h) *Tidal Information.*

The river is tidal throughout.

High water at Chepstow 5hrs. 32min. after London Bridge, or 20min. after Bristol.

Spring tides rise	..	..	38ft.
Neap „ „	..	..	28ft. 6in.

The height of the maximum recorded tide at Chepstow is 53ft.—*see* Section 8, Tides.

(127)—River Wye—*continued*.

High water at Brockweir 10min. after Chepstow.

There is, as a rule, no " bore " or tidal wave formed in the river by the first of the flood tide; but in summer, when there is very little land water coming down, a high Spring tide will sometimes cause one to rise above Chepstow.

(*i*) *Types of vessels using the navigation.*

Severn trows.

Wyken New Colliery Branch Canal—*see* Oxford Canal.

Wyrley and Essington Canal—*see* Birmingham Canal Navigations.

———

(128)—River Yare, *alias* The Norwich River.

(*a*) *Short Description.*

The navigation commences at New Mills in the city of Norwich, adjoining the City Station of the Midland and Great Northern Joint Railways, and, after a somewhat devious course of about two and three-quarter miles round the north-east part of the city, receives the Trowse Branch at the eastern extremity of Messrs. J. &. J. Colman's Works.

It must be noted that this upper portion of the navigation from New Mills to the junction of the Trowse Branch, although forming the Main Line, is actually over the course of the River Wensum. The River Yare, which commences by forming the Trowse Branch from Trowse Mills, does not constitute the Main Line of navigation until the junction with the River Wensum is reached.

Leaving Norwich the river proceeds by Thorpe, Postwick, Bramerton, Surlingham, Brundall, Buckenham Ferry, Cantley Ferry, Hardley Cross, Reedham, and Berney Arms, shortly below which it receives the River Waveney and enters Breydon Water, a large inland lake having an area of 1,218 acres.

For the next four miles the navigation is continued across Breydon Water, a double line of posts marking the channel, to the north part of the town of Yarmouth. Here, after receiving the River Bure, the river again enters a confined channel, and turning southward proceeds through Yarmouth to its mouth at Gorleston, where it enters the North Sea.

There are branches leading out of the Main Line as follows :—

A branch to Trowse Mills from the eastern border of the city of Norwich, formed by the River Yare. The trade on this branch is almost exclusively confined to that of Messrs. J. & J. Colman to and from Trowse Mills.

(128)—River Yare, *alias* The Norwich River—*continued.*

The Old Line of river forming a loop line round Thorpe Village, which the Main Line of navigation avoids by passing through an artificial cut.

Barnes' Dike, Rockland Dike and Broad, Langley Dike, and Hardley Dike.

The course of the navigation from Norwich to the west end of Breydon Water, together with all branches, is situated in the county of Norfolk, the remainder forming the boundary between the counties of Norfolk and Suffolk.

There is a substantial trade done between Norwich and Yarmouth, the navigation being in good order.

(b) *Proprietors, Officers, and Offices.*

From New Mills, Norwich, to the mouth of the river at Gorleston including the loop line of the Old River round Thorpe Village, and Rock land Dike and Broad, is under the jurisdiction of the Great Yarmouth Port and Haven Commissioners.

Clerk : John Tolver Waters.

Office : 2, South Quay, Yarmouth.

Harbour Master : Captain Day.

Office : Gorleston-on-Sea.

The branch to Trowse Mills formed by the River Yare is under the jurisdiction of the River Yare Commissioners.

Clerk (Town Clerk of Norwich) : Arnold H. Miller.

Office : Guildhall, Norwich.

Barnes' Dike, Langley Dike, and Hardley Dike are private properties.

(c) *Distance Table.*

Main Line of Navigation (No. 128a).

	Miles.	Fur.
Norwich, New Mills to—		
Norwich, Fye Bridge	–	4½
Norwich, Bishop Bridge	1	1½
Norwich, Foundry Bridge, and Thorpe Station, G. E. Rly.	1	4
Norwich, Carrow Bridge, and Great Yarmouth Port and Haven Commissioners Toll Office	2	1½

(128)—RIVER YARE, *alias* THE NORWICH RIVER—*continued*.

	Miles.	Fur.
Norwich, New Mills to (*continued*)—		
Norwich, east end of Colman's Works, and junction with branch to Trowse Mills (No. 128b)	2	6½
West end of Thorpe New Cut, and western junction of loop line of old river round Thorpe Village (No. 128c)	3	1
East end of Thorpe New Cut, and eastern junction of loop line of old river round Thorpe Village (No. 128c)	3	6
Whitlingham Staith	4	1
Thorpe Asylum	4	7
Postwick Hall	6	0
Bramerton Staith	6	4
Surlingham, Barnes' Brickyard Staith ..	7	3
Surlingham Ferry and Staith	8	2
Surlingham Ice House Staith	9	3
Brundall Station, G. E. Rly.	9	6
Coldham Hall Ferry and Staith	10	2½
Junction with Barnes' Dike (No. 128d) ..	10	3½
Junction with Strumpshaw Dike (not navigable)	10	5¼
Junction with Rockland Dike, leading to Rockland Broad (No. 128e)	11	4½
Buckenham Staith	12	5
Buckenham Ferry	12	7
Junction with Hasingham Dike (not navigable)	13	5
Junction with Langley Dike (No. 128f) ..	14	6½
Cantley Ferry and Railway Station, G. E. Rly	15	6½
Hardley Brickyard Staith	17	0½
Junction with Hardley Dike (No. 128g) ..	17	2½
Hardley Cross, junction with River Chet (No. 20)	18	3
Norton Staith	18	5
Reedham Ferry	18	7
Reedham, junction with Great Eastern Railway Co.'s New Cut (No. 40a)	20	2
Upper Seven Mile House	21	7
Six Mile House	22	7
Berney Arms Staith and Railway Station, G. E. Rly.	24	4
Western extremity of Breydon Water and junction with River Waveney (No. 117a)	24	6
Breydon Railway Bridge	28	4
Yarmouth, eastern extremity of Breydon Water, and junction with River Bure (No. 16a1)	28	5
Yarmouth Bridge	28	7
Gorleston Ferry	30	2
Gorleston, mouth of river	31	5

(128)—RIVER YARE, *alias* THE NORWICH RIVER—*continued.*

Branch to Trowse Mills (No. 128b).

	Miles.	Fur.
Junction with Main Line of navigation (No. 128a) to—		
Trowse Station, G. E. Rly.	–	$6\frac{1}{2}$
Trowse Mills	–	$7\frac{1}{2}$

Loop Line of Old River round Thorpe Village (No. 128c).

	Miles.	Fur.
Western junction with Main Line of navigation (No. 128a) to—		
Thorpe Staith	–	$4\frac{1}{2}$
Eastern junction with Main Line of navigation (No. 128a)	–	$5\frac{1}{2}$

Barnes' Dike (No. 128d).

	Miles.	Fur.
Length from junction with Main Line of navigation (No. 128a) to—		
Staith at upper end	–	3

Rockland Dike and Rockland Broad (No. 128e).

	Miles.	Fur.
Junction with Main Line of navigation (No. 128a) to—		
Commencement of Rockland Broad	–	5
Rockland Staith on Rockland Broad ..	–	7

A line of posts marks the navigation channel across the Broad.

Langley Dike (No. 128f).

	Miles.	Fur.
Length from junction with Main Line of navigation (No. 128a) to—		
Staith at upper end	–	$2\frac{1}{2}$

Hardley Dike (No. 128g).

	Miles.	Fur.
Length from junction with Main Line of navigation (No. 128a) to Hardley Staith at upper end	–	$2\frac{1}{2}$

(128)—River Yare, *alias* **The Norwich River**—*continued.*

(e) Maximum size of vessels that can use the navigation.

Main Line of Navigation (No. 128a).

	Ft.	In.
Length.—Not limited		

The longest vessel that has entered
Yarmouth was 315ft. in length, but this was
not on full draught. The sharp right angle
bend in the river just inside the mouth of
the harbour precludes the safe entrance of
longer vessels.

Width.—Not limited.

Draught.—The average maximum depth of
water from the mouth of the river at
Gorleston to Yarmouth Bridge is—

	Ft.	In.
On Spring tides	17	0
On Neap tides	15	6

Draught—From the mouth of the river at
Gorleston to Yarmouth Bridge there is a

	Ft.	In.
depth at low water in the channel of ..	12	0
It is hoped soon to increase this to ..	14	0
Draught from Yarmouth Bridge to Bishop Bridge, Norwich	7	0
Draught from Bishop Bridge, Norwich, to New Mills, Norwich	5	0 to 6ft.

There is a gauge on Bishop Bridge, and
no vessel must pass if drawing more water
than shown by the gauge at the time.

Headroom from Carrow Bridge, Norwich, to
the mouth of the river at Gorleston, not
limited, all bridges between these points
being opening bridges.

Branch to Trowse Mills (No. 128b).

Length.—Not limited.
Width.—Not limited.

	Ft.	In.
Draught	4	0

Loop Line of Old River round Thorpe Village (No. 128c).

	Ft.	In.
Length.—Not limited.		
Width.—Not limited.		
Draught	6	0 to 7ft.

Barnes' Dike (No. 128d), Rockland Dike and Rockland Broad (No. 128e), Langley Dike (No. 128f), and Hardley Dike (No. 128g).

	Ft.	In.
Length.—Not limited.		
Width.—Not limited.		
Draught	3	0

(g) Towing-path.

There is no horse towing-path on any part of the river or its branches.

(128)—RIVER YARE, *alias* THE NORWICH RIVER—*continued.*

(h) Tidal Information.

The tide usually flows up the river to Coldham Hall and backs up the water in the river to the head of the navigation at New Mills, Norwich, to an average height of about 6in. at that place. The level of the water in the whole of the navigable branches leading out of the river is affected by the tide.

High water at the mouth of the river 4hrs. 32min. before London Bridge.

Spring tides rise	6ft.
Neap ,, ,, ...	4ft. 6in.

Yarmouth Bridge—

Spring tides rise	5ft.
Neap ,, ,, ...	4ft.

High water at Reedham about 2hrs. 30min. after Yarmouth.

High water at Cantley about 3hrs. after Yarmouth.

High water at Buckenham about 3hrs. 30min. after Yarmouth.

High water at Coldham Hall about 4hrs. after Yarmouth.

(i) Types of vessels using the navigation.

Norfolk wherries.

YARE, RIVER, COMMISSIONERS—*see* River Yare.

---

(129)—RIVER YEO

(a) Short Description.

The navigation of the river may be said to commence at Ilchester, whence it proceeds by Little Load and Pidsbury to a junction with the River Parrett, about three-quarters-of-a-mile above Langport, all in the county of Somersetshire.

There is scarcely any trade done on the river ; a barge occasionally navigates from the River Parrett as far as Pidsbury or Little Load, but nothing has been beyond for some years.

(b) Proprietors, Officers, and Offices.

The river, as a drainage, is under the jurisdiction of the Somersetshire Drainage Commissioners.

Clerk : J. Lovibond.

Office : Bridgwater.

Engineer : W. Lunn.

Office : Taunton Road, Bridgwater.

(129)—RIVER YEO—*continued.*

(c) Distance Table.

	Miles.	Fur.
Junction with River Parrett (No. 84a) to—		
Pidsbury	1	0
Little Load Bridge	4	0
Ilchester	8	0

(e) Maximum size of vessels that can use the navigation.

	Ft.	In.
Length.—Not limited.		
Width.—Not limited.		
Draught—Uncertain .. .. .. about	2	6 to 3ft.

(g) Towing-path.

There is no towing-path.

(h) Tidal Information.

Spring tides affect the level of the water in the lower part of the river when there is but little land water coming down.

(i) Types of vessels using the navigation.

Small barges carrying from 10 to 15 tons are the only vessels which can use the river.

YORK, CORPORATION OF THE CITY OF, are the Controlling Authority in respect of the River Ouse (York) and the River Foss.

YORKSHIRE, COMMISSIONERS OF SEWERS FOR THE EAST PARTS OF THE EAST RIDING OF—*see* River Hull.

(12)—THE INLAND NAVIGATIONS OF ENGLAND
AND WALES, ARRANGED IN GROUPS, EACH
GROUP CONSISTING OF THOSE NAVIGATIONS
WHICH HAVE INLAND COMMUNICATION WITH
EACH OTHER.

GROUP No. 1 (The Main System of connected Waterways).

No. 2 River Aire.

No. 3 Aire and Calder Navigation.

No. 4 Aire and Calder and Sheffield and South Yorkshire Junction Canal.

No. 5 River Ancholme Drainage and Navigation.

No. 7 River Avon (Bristol).

No. 8 River Avon (Warwickshire).

No. 9 Beverley Beck.

No. 10 Birmingham Canal Navigations.

No. 11 Birmingham and Warwick Junction Canal.

No. 12 Black Sluice Drainage and Navigation, *alias* the South Forty Foot Drain.

No. 13 Bradford Canal.

No. 14 Brandon River, *alias* the Little Ouse River.

No. 17 Calder and Hebble Navigation.

No. 18 River Cam.

No. 22 Clifton and Kearsley Coal Co.'s (Ltd.) Canal.

No. 24 Coventry Canal.

No. 25 Dartford and Crayford Navigation.

No. 26 River Dee.

No. 27 Derby Canal.

No. 28 River Don.

No. 29 Driffield Navigation.

No. 30 Erewash Canal.

No. 32 Fearnley Cut.

No. 33 River Foss.

No. 34 Foxley Branch Canal.

No. 38 Grand Junction Canal.

No. 39 Great Central Railway Co.'s Canals.

No. 41 Great Northern Railway Co.'s Canals.

No. 42 Great Northern and Great Eastern Joint Railway Co.'s— Fossdyke Canal.

No. 43 Great Western Railway Co.'s—Kennet and Avon Navigation, Stratford-on-Avon Canal, and Stourbridge Extension Canal.

No. 44 Griff Colliery Co.'s Canal.

(12)—INLAND NAVIGATIONS OF ENGLAND AND WALES, ETC.—*continued.*

GROUP No. 1 (The Main System of connected Waterways)—*continued.*

No. 45 Grosvenor Canal.

No. 47 Houghton Branch Canal.

No. 48 River Hull.

No. 49 River Humber.

No. 50 River Idle.

No. 53 Kyme Eau.

No. 54 Lakenheath Lode.

No. 55 Lancashire and Yorkshire Railway Co.'s—Manchester Bolton and Bury Canal.

No. 56 River Larke.

No. 57 River Lee.

No. 58 Leeds and Liverpool Canal.

No. 59 Leicester Navigation.

No. 60 Leven Canal.

No. 61 London and North Western Railway Co.'s—Huddersfield Broad Canal, Huddersfield Narrow Canal, and St. Helens Canal.

No. 62 Loughborough Navigation.

No. 64 Manchester Ship Canal Co.'s Canals.

No. 65 Earl Manver's Canal.

No. 66 Market Weighton Drainage and Navigation.

No. 68 River Mersey.

No. 69 Middle Level Navigations.

No. 70 Midland Railway Co.'s Canals.

No. 71 Midland and Great Western Joint Railway Co.'s—Lydney Harbour and Canal.

No. 74 River Nene.

No. 75 North Eastern Railway Co.'s Canals.

No. 76 North Staffordshire Railway Co.'s —Trent and Mersey Canal.

No. 78 Nutbrook Canal.

No. 79 River Ouse (Bedford).

No. 81 River Ouse (York).

No. 82 Oxford Canal.

No. 83 Park Gate Branch Canal.

No. 85 Pensnett Canal, *alias* Lord Ward's Branch Canal.

No. 86 Regents Canal.

No. 87 Rochdale Canal.

No. 88 River Roding.

No. 89 River Severn.

(12)—Inland Navigations of England and Wales, etc.—*continued*.

Group No. 1 (The Main System of connected Waterways)—*continued*.

No. 90 Sharpness New Docks and Gloucester and Birmingham Navigation Co.'s Canals.

No. 91 Sheffield and South Yorkshire Navigation.

No. 92 Shropshire Union Railways and Canal Co.'s Canals.

No. 93 Somersetshire Coal Canal Navigation.

No. 94 South Eastern and Chatham Railway Companies Managing Committee's—Gravesend and Rochester Canal.

No. 95 Staffordshire and Worcestershire Canal.

No. 96 River Stort.

No. 99 Stourbridge Canal.

No. 100 Stroudwater Canal.

No. 101 Surrey Canal.

No. 102 Duke of Sutherland's Tub Boat Canal.

No. 107 River Thames.

No. 108 Thames and Severn Canal.

No. 110 Thorney River.

No. 112 River Trent.

No. 114 Wandsworth Cut.

No. 115 Warwick and Birmingham Canal.

No. 116 Warwick and Napton Canal.

No. 118 River Weaver.

No. 120 West London Extension Railway Co.'s—Kensington Canal.

No. 121 River Wey.

No. 122 River Wharfe.

No. 123 Wisbech Canal.

No. 124 River Witham.

No. 125 Witham Drainage General Commissioners Navigable Drains.

No. 126 Woking, Aldershot, and Basingstoke Canal.

No. 127 River Wye.

Group No. 2.

No. 113 River Tyne.

Group No. 3.

No. 104 River Tees.

Group No. 4.

No. 63 Louth Navigation.

(12)—INLAND NAVIGATIONS OF ENGLAND AND WALES, ETC.—*continued*.

GROUP No. 5.
No. 119 River Welland.
No.　37 River Glen.

GROUP No. 6.
No.　16 River Bure, *alias* the North River.
No.　20 River Chet.
No.　40 Great Eastern Railway Co.'s Navigations.
No.　77 North Walsham and Dilham Canal.
No. 117 River Waveney.
No. 128 River Yare, *alias* the Norwich River.

GROUP No. 7.
No.　51 Ipswich and Stowmarket Navigation.

GROUP No. 8.
No.　98 River Stour (Suffolk).

GROUP No. 9.
No.　23 River Colne.

GROUP No. 10.
No.　19 Chelmer and Blackwater Navigation.

GROUP No. 11.
No.　67 River Medway.

GROUP No. 12.
No.　97 River Stour (Kent).

GROUP No. 13.
No.　80 River Ouse (Sussex.)

GROUP No. 14.
No.　1 River Adur.

GROUP No. 15.
No.　6 River Arun.

GROUP No. 16.
No.　21 Chichester Canal.

GROUP No. 17.
No.　31 Exeter Ship Canal.

(12)—Inland Navigations of England and Wales, etc.—*continued.*

Group No. 18.

    No. 43 Great Western Railway Co.'s—Stover Canal.
    No. 46 Hackney Canal.
    No. 105 River Teign.

Group No. 19.
    No. 103 River Tamar.

Group No. 20.
    No. 15 Bude Canal.

Group No. 21.
    No. 43 Great Western Railway Co.'s—Grand Western Canal.

Group No. 22.
    No. 43 Great Western Railway Co.'s—River Tone Navigation
           and Bridgwater and Taunton Canal.
    No. 84 River Parrett (including River Brue).
    No. 111 River Tone.
    No. 129 River Yeo.

Group No. 23.
    No. 43 Great Western Railway Co.'s—Brecon and Abergavenny
           Canal, and Monmouthshire Canal.

Group No. 24.
    No. 36 Glamorganshire and Aberhare Canals.
    No. 109 Doctor Thomas's Canal.

Group No. 25.
    No. 43 Great Western Railway Co.'s—Swansea Canal.
    No. 52 Earl of Jersey's Canals.
    No. 72 Neath Canal.
    No. 73 River Neath.
    No. 106 Tennant Canal.

Group No. 26.
    No. 61 London and North Western Railway Co.'s—Lancaster
           Canal—North end.

Group No. 27.
    No. 35 Furness Railway Co.'s—Ulverston Canal.

Group No. 28.
    No. 61 London and North Western Railway Co.'s—Shropshire
           (Coalport) Canal.

(13)—INDEX OF PRINCIPAL PLACES AND TOWNS TO WHICH THERE IS WATER COMMUNICATION.

Place.	County.	Name and No. of Navigation.	No. of Group. Section 12.
Aberdare	Glamorganshire	Aberdare Canal (No. 36b)	24
Abergavenny	Monmouthshire	Brecon and Abergavenny Canal (No. 43h)	23
Abingdon	Berkshire	River Thames (No. 107a)	1
Accrington	Lancashire	Leeds and Liverpool Canal (No. 58a)	1
Adlington	Lancashire	Leeds and Liverpool Canal (No. 58a)	1
Aldershot	Hampshire	Woking, Aldershot, and Basingstoke Canal (No. 126)	1
Armley	Yorkshire, West Riding	Leeds and Liverpool Canal (No. 58a)	1
Arundel	Sussex	River Arun (No. 6)	15
Ashton-under-Lyne	Lancashire	Ashton Canal (No. 39a1), and	1
		Huddersfield Narrow Canal (No. 61b)	1
Aston	Warwickshire	Birmingham Canal Navigations (No. 10p1)	1
Atherstone	Warwickshire	Coventry Canal (No. 24)	1
Audenshaw	Lancashire	Ashton Canal (No. 39a4)	1
Avonmouth	Gloucestershire	River Avon (Bristol) No. 7), and	1
		River Severn (No. 89a)	1
Aylesbury	Buckinghamshire	Grand Junction Canal (No. 38a5)	1
Aylsham	Norfolk	River Bure (No. 16)	6
Banbury	Oxfordshire	Oxford Canal (No. 82a)	1
Barking	Essex	River Roding (No. 88), and	1
		River Thames (No. 107g)	1
Barnsley	Yorkshire, West Riding	Aire and Calder Navigation (No. 3b)	1
Barrow-on-Soar	Leicestershire	Leicester Navigation (No. 59)	1
Barton-upon-Humber	Lincolnshire	River Humber (No. 49)	1
Basingstoke	Hampshire	Woking, Aldershot, and Basingstoke Canal (No. 126)	1
Bath	Somersetshire	Kennet and Avon Navigation (No. 43a)	1
Beccles	Suffolk	River Waveney (No. 117a)	6
Bedford	Bedfordshire	River Ouse (Bedford) (No. 79a).	1
Bedworth	Warwickshire	Coventry Canal (No. 24)	1
Berkhamsted	Hertfordshire	Grand Junction Canal (No. 38a1)	1
Beverley	Yorkshire, East Riding	Beverley Beck (No. 9)	1
Bewdley	Worcestershire	River Severn (No. 89a)	1
Bingley	Yorkshire, West Riding	Leeds and Liverpool Canal (No. 58a)	1
Birkenhead	Cheshire	River Mersey (No. 68)	1
Birmingham	Warwickshire	Birmingham Canal Navigations (Nos. 10a1, 10a2, 10a3, 10a4, 10p1, 10p2, and 10p3)	1
		Birmingham and Warwick Junction Canal (No. 11)	1
		Worcester and Birmingham Canal (No. 90b), and	1
		Warwick and Birmingham Canal (No. 115)	1
Bishops Stortford	Hertfordshire	River Stort (No. 96)	1
Blackburn	Lancashire	Leeds and Liverpool Canal (No. 58a)	1
Blaydon	Durham	River Tyne (No. 113a)	2
Bloxwich	Staffordshire	Birmingham Canal Navigations (No. 10q1)	1
Bollington	Cheshire	Macclesfield Canal (No. 39c1)	1
Bolton	Lancashire	Manchester, Bolton, and Bury Canal (No. 55b)	1
Boston	Lincolnshire	Black Sluice Drainage and Navigation (No. 12)	1
		River Witham (No. 124), and	1
		Witham Drainage General Commissioners Navigable Drains (No. 125d)	1
Bradford	Yorkshire, West Riding	Bradford Canal (No. 13)	1
Bradford-on-Avon	Wiltshire	Kennet and Avon Navigation (No. 43a)	1
Brecon	Brecon	Brecon and Abergavenny Canal (No. 43h)	23
Brentford	Middlesex	Grand Junction Canal (No. 38a1), and	1
		River Thames (No. 107a)	1
Bridgwater	Somersetshire	Bridgwater and Taunton Canal (No. 43e), and	22
		River Parrett (No. 84)	22
Brierley Hill	Staffordshire	Birmingham Canal Navigations (No. 10f1)	1
Brigg	Lincolnshire	River Ancholme Drainage and Navigation (No. 5)	1
Brighouse	Yorkshire, West Riding	Calder and Hebble Navigation (No. 17a)	1
Bristol	Gloucestershire	River Avon (Bristol) (No. 7)	1
Briton Ferry	Glamorganshire	Giant's Grave and Briton Ferry Canal (No. 52a)	25
Buckingham	Buckinghamshire	Grand Junction Canal (No. 38a4)	1
Bude	Cornwall	Bude Canal (No. 15)	20
Bungay	Suffolk	River Waveney (No. 117a)	6
Burnham	Somersetshire	River Brue—River Parrett (No. 84)	22
Burnley	Lancashire	Leeds and Liverpool Canal (No. 58a)	1
Burslem	Staffordshire	Trent and Mersey Canal (No. 76d)	1
Burton-upon-Trent	Staffordshire	Trent and Mersey Canal (No. 76a)	1
Bury	Lancashire	Manchester, Bolton, and Bury Canal (No. 55a)	1

(13)—INDEX OF PRINCIPAL PLACES AND TOWNS TO WHICH THERE IS WATER
COMMUNICATION—*continued.*

Place.	County.	Name and No. of Navigation.	No. of Group. Section 12.
Cambridge	Cambridgeshire	River Cam (No. 18a)	1
Cannock	Staffordshire	Birmingham Canal Navigations (No. 10r)	1
Cardiff	Glamorganshire	Glamorganshire Canal (No. 36a)	24
Carnforth	Lancashire	Lancaster Canal (No. 61c1)	26
Castleford	Yorkshire, West Riding	Aire and Calder Navigation (Nos. 3a1, 3a2, and 3a3)	1
Castleton	Lancashire	Rochdale Canal (No. 87a)	1
Chatham	Kent	River Medway (No. 67)	11
Chatteris	Cambridgeshire	Middle Level Navigations (No. 69m)	1
Chelmsford	Essex	Chelmer and Blackwater Navigation (No. 19)	10
Chepstow	Monmouthshire	River Wye (No. 127)	1
Chertsey	Surrey	River Thames (No. 107a)	1
Cheshunt	Hertfordshire	River Lee (No. 57a)	1
Chester	Cheshire	River Dee (No. 26), and	1
		Shropshire Union Canals (Nos. 92b1, 92c1, and 92c2)	1
Chesterfield	Derbyshire	Chesterfield Canal (No. 39d.)	1
Chichester	Sussex	Chichester Canal (No. 21)	16
Chorley	Lancashire	Leeds and Liverpool Canal (No. 58a)	1
Cirencester	Gloucestershire	Thames and Severn Canal (No. 108b)	1
Colchester	Essex	River Colne (No. 23)	9
Congleton	Cheshire	Macclesfield Canal (No. 39c1)	1
Conisbrough	Yorkshire, West Riding	Sheffield and South Yorkshire Navigation (No. 91b1)	1
Coseley	Staffordshire	Birmingham Canal Navigations (No. 10a1)	1
Coventry	Warwickshire	Coventry Canal (No. 24)	1
Cricklade	Wiltshire	River Thames (No. 107a), and	1
		Thames and Severn Canal (No. 108a)	1
Crowland	Lincolnshire	River Welland (No. 119)	5
Crowle	Lincolnshire	Sheffield and South Yorkshire Navigation (No. 91c)	1
Darlaston	Staffordshire	Birmingham Canal Navigations (No. 10k1)	1
Dartford	Kent	Dartford and Crayford Navigation (No. 25a)	1
Dedham	Essex	River Stour (Suffolk) (No. 98)	8
Derby	Derbyshire	Derby Canal (Nos. 27a, 27b, and 27c)	1
Devizes	Wiltshire	Kennet and Avon Navigation (No. 43a)	1
Devonport	Devonshire	River Tamar (No. 103)	19
Dewsbury	Yorkshire, West Riding	Aire and Calder Navigation (No. 3e)	1
Doncaster	Yorkshire, West Riding	Sheffield and South Yorkshire Navigation (No. 91b1)	1
Downham Market	Norfolk	River Ouse (Bedford) (No. 79a)	1
Driffield	Yorkshire, East Riding	Driffield Navigation (No. 29a)	1
Droitwich	Worcestershire	Droitwich Junction Canal (No. 90c), and	1
		Droitwich Canal (No. 90d)	1
Droylsden	Lancashire	Ashton Canal (No. 39a4)	1
Dudley	Worcestershire	Birmingham Canal Navigations (No. 10c1)	1
Dunkinfield	Cheshire	Peak Forest Canal (No. 39b1)	1
Earlestown	Lancashire	St. Helens Canal (No. 61d1)	1
Eastham	Cheshire	Manchester Ship Canal (No. 64a), and	1
		River Mersey (No. 68)	1
Eccles	Lancashire	Manchester Ship Canal (No. 64a)	1
Edgbaston	Warwickshire	Worcester and Birmingham Canal (No. 90b)	1
Elland	Yorkshire, West Riding	Calder and Hebble Navigation (No. 17a)	1
Ellesmere	Shropshire	Shropshire Union Canals (No. 92d4)	1
Ellesmere Port	Cheshire	Manchester Ship Canal (No. 64a), and	1
		Shropshire Union Canals (No. 92c1)	1
Ely	Cambridgeshire	River Ouse (Bedford) (No. 77b)	1
Erith	Kent	River Thames (No. 107a)	1
Eton	Buckinghamshire	River Thames (No. 107a)	1
Evesham	Worcestershire	River Avon (Warwickshire) Lower Navigation (No. 8)	1
Exeter	Devonshire	Exeter Ship Canal (No. 31)	17
Failsworth	Lancashire	Rochdale Canal (No. 87a)	1
Gainsborough	Lincolnshire	River Trent (No. 112a)	1
Garston	Lancashire	River Mersey (No. 68)	1
Gateshead	Durham	River Tyne (No. 113a)	2
Glasson Dock	Lancashire	Lancaster Canal (No. 61c2)	26
Gloucester	Gloucestershire	River Severn (Nos. 89a and 89b), and	1
		Gloucester and Berkeley Ship Canal (No. 90a)	1
Godalming	Surrey	River Wey (No. 121)	1
Godmanchester	Huntingdonshire	River Ouse (Bedford) (No. 79a)	1
Golcar	Yorkshire, West Riding	Huddersfield Narrow Canal (No. 61b)	1
Goole	Yorkshire, West Riding	Aire and Calder Navigation (No. 3a3)	1
		River Don (No. 28), and	1
		River Ouse (York) (No. 81)	1
Gorton	Lancashire	Ashton Canal (No. 39a3)	1
Grantham	Lincolnshire	Grantham Canal (No. 41a)	1

DD

(13)—Index of Principal Places and Towns to which there is Water Communication—*continued.*

Place.	County.	Name and No. of Navigation.	No. of Group. Section 12.
Gravesend	Kent	Gravesend and Rochester Canal (No. 94), and	1
		River Thames (No. 107a)	1
Guildford	Surrey	River Wey (No. 121)	1
Halesowen	Worcestershire	Birmingham Canal Navigations (No. 10f2)	1
Halifax	Yorkshire, West Riding	Calder and Hebble Navigation (No. 17b)	1
Hampton	Middlesex	River Thames (No. 107a)	1
Hampton Court	Middlesex	River Thames (No. 107a)	1
Hanley	Staffordshire	Trent and Mersey Canal (No. 76c1)	1
Hanwell	Middlesex	Grand Junction Canal (No. 38a1)	1
Harlow	Essex	River Stort (No. 96)	1
Hebburn	Durham	River Tyne (No. 113a)	2
Hebden Bridge	Yorkshire, West Riding	Rochdale Canal (No. 87a)	1
Hednesford	Staffordshire	Birmingham Canal Navigations (No. 10r)	1
Henley	Oxfordshire	River Thames (No. 107a)	1
Hertford	Hertfordshire	River Lee (No. 57a)	1
Heywood	Lancashire	Rochdale Canal (No. 87c)	1
Hollinwood	Lancashire	Ashton Canal (No. 39a4)	1
Horbury	Yorkshire, West Riding	Calder and Hebble Navigation (No. 17a)	1
Huddersfield	Yorkshire, West Riding	Huddersfield Broad Canal (No. 61a), and	1
		Huddersfield Narrow Canal (No. 61b)	1
Hull	Yorkshire, East Riding	River Hull (No. 48a), and	1
		River Humber (No. 49)	1
Hungerford	Berkshire	Kennet and Avon Navigation (No. 43a)	1
Huntingdon	Huntingdonshire	River Ouse (Bedford) (No. 79a)	1
Hyde	Cheshire	Peak Forest Canal (No. 39b1)	1
Ilford	Essex	River Roding (No. 88)	1
Ipswich	Suffolk	Ipswich and Stowmarket Navigation (No. 51)	7
Jarrow	Durham	River Tyne (No. 113a)	2
Kegworth	Leicestershire	Loughborough Navigation (No. 62)	1
Kendal	Westmorland	Lancaster Canal (No. 61c1)	26
Kidderminster	Worcestershire	Staffordshire and Worcestershire Canal(No.95a)	1
King's Lynn	Norfolk	River Ouse (Bedford) (No. 79a)	1
King's Norton	Worcestershire	Stratford-on-Avon Canal (No. 43b1), and	1
		Worcester and Birmingham Canal (No. 90b)	1
Kingston	Surrey	River Thames (No. 107a)	1
Kippax	Yorkshire, West Riding	Aire and Calder Navigation (No. 3a1)	1
Knottingley	Yorkshire, West Riding	Aire and Calder Navigation (No. 3a3)	1
Lancaster	Lancashire	Lancaster Canal (No. 61c1)	26
Leamington	Warwickshire	Warwick and Napton Canal (No. 116)	1
Lechlade	Gloucestershire	River Thames (No. 107a)	1
Leeds	Yorkshire, West Riding	Aire and Calder Navigation (No. 3a1), and	1
		Leeds and Liverpool Canal (No. 58a)	1
Leek	Staffordshire	Trent and Mersey Canal (No. 76c2)	1
Leicester	Leicestershire	Grand Junction Canal (No. 38b1), and	1
		Leicester Navigation (No. 59)	1
Leigh	Lancashire	Leeds and Liverpool Canal (No. 58d), and	1
		Bridgewater Canal (No. 64b3)	1
Leighton Buzzard	Bedfordshire	Grand Junction Canal (No. 38a1)	1
Lewes	Sussex	River Ouse (Sussex) (No. 80)	13
Lichfield	Staffordshire	Birmingham Canal Navigations (No. 10q1)	1
Lincoln	Lincolnshire	Fossdyke Canal (No. 42), and	1
		River Witham (No. 124)	1
Littleborough	Lancashire	Rochdale Canal (No. 87a)	1
Littlehampton	Sussex	River Arun (No. 6)	15
Liverpool	Lancashire	Leeds and Liverpool Canal (Nos. 58a and 58f), and	1
		River Mersey (No. 68)	1
Llandaff	Glamorganshire	Glamorganshire Canal (No. 36a)	24
Llangollen	Denbighshire	Shropshire Union Canals (No. 92d5)	1
London		Grand Junction Canal (No. 38a8),	1
		Grosvenor Canal (No. 45),	1
		River Lee (Nos. 57a, 57b, 57c, 57d, 57e, and 57f)	1
		Regents Canal (Nos. 86a, 86b, 86c, and 86d),	1
		Surrey Canal (Nos. 101a and 101b),	1
		River Thames (Nos. 107a, 107e, and 107f), and	1
		Kensington Canal (No. 120)	1
Long Eaton	Derbyshire	Erewash Canal (No. 30)	1
Loughborough	Leicestershire	Leicester Navigation (No. 59), and	1
		Loughborough Navigation (No. 62)	1
Louth	Lincolnshire	Louth Navigation (No. 63)	4
Lowestoft	Suffolk	Navigation from the River Waveney to Lowestoft (No. 40b)	6
Macclesfield	Cheshire	Macclesfield Canal (No. 39c1)	1
Maidenhead	Berkshire	River Thames (No. 107a)	1
Maidstone	Kent	River Medway (No. 67)	11
Malton	Yorkshire, North Riding	River Derwent (No. 75a)	1

(13)—INDEX OF PRINCIPAL PLACES AND TOWNS TO WHICH THERE IS WATER COMMUNICATION—*continued.*

Place.	County.	Name and No. of Navigation.	No. of Group. Section 12.
Manchester	Lancashire	Ashton Canal (No. 39a1),	1
		Manchester Ship Canal (Nos. 64a, 64d4, and 64e)	1
		Bridgewater Canal (Nos. 64b1, and 64b2),	1
		Rochdale Canal (No. 87a), and	1
		See also Salford (Manchester)	
Manningtree	Essex	River Stour (Suffolk) (No. 98)	8
March	Cambridgeshire	Middle Level Navigations (No. 69f)	1
Market Drayton	Shropshire	Shropshire Union Canals (No. 92a1)	1
Market Harborough	Leicestershire	Grand Junction Canal (No. 38b3)	1
Marlow	Buckinghamshire	River Thames (No. 107a)	1
Marple	Cheshire	Peak Forest Canal (No. 39b1), and	1
		Macclesfield Canal (No. 39c1)	1
Merthyr Tydfil	Glamorganshire	Glamorganshire Canal (No. 36a)	24
Mexborough	Yorkshire, West Riding	Sheffield and South Yorkshire Navigation (No. 91b1)	1
Middlesbrough	Yorkshire, North Riding	River Tees (No. 104)	3
Middlewich	Cheshire	Trent and Mersey Canal (Nos. 76a and 76f), and	1
		Shropshire Union Canals (No. 92b2)	1
Mildenhall	Suffolk	River Larke (No. 56a)	1
Milnsbridge	Yorkshire, West Riding	Huddersfield Narrow Canal (No. 61b)	1
Mirfield	Yorkshire, West Riding	Calder and Hebble Navigation (No. 17a)	1
Mistley	Essex	River Stour (Suffolk) (No. 98)	8
Mountain Ash	Glamorganshire	Aberdare Canal (No. 36b)	24
Mount Sorrel	Leicestershire	Leicester Navigation (No. 59)	1
Nantwich	Cheshire	Shropshire Union Canals (Nos. 92a1 and 92b1)	1
Neath	Glamorganshire	Neath Canal (No. 72)	25
		River Neath (No. 73), and	25
		Tennant Canal (No. 106a)	25
Nelson	Lancashire	Leeds and Liverpool Canal (No. 58a)	1
Newark	Nottinghamshire	River Trent (No. 112a)	1
Newbury	Berkshire	Kennet and Avon Navigation (No. 43a)	1
Newcastle-on-Tyne	Northumberland	River Tyne (No. 113a)	2
Newcastle-under-Lyme	Staffordshire	Trent and Mersey Canal (No. 76b)	1
Newhaven	Sussex	River Ouse (Sussex) (No. 80)	13
Newnham	Gloucestershire	River Severn (No. 89a)	1
Newport	Monmouthshire	Monmouthshire Canal (No. 43i1)	23
Newport	Shropshire	Shropshire Union Canals (No. 92a2)	1
Newton Abbot	Devonshire	Stover Canal (No. 43g), and	18
		River Teign (Nos. 105a and 105b)	18
Newton Heath	Lancashire	Rochdale Canal (No. 87a)	1
Newtown	Montgomeryshire	Shropshire Union Canals (No. 92f)	1
Northampton	Northamptonshire	Grand Junction Canal (No. 38a3), and	1
		River Nene (Nos. 74a and 74b)	1
Northfleet	Kent	River Thames (No. 107a)	1
North Shields	Northumberland	River Tyne (No. 113a)	2
North Walsham	Norfolk	North Walsham and Dilham Canal (No. 77)	6
Northwich	Cheshire	River Weaver (No. 118a)	1
Norwich	Norfolk	River Yare (No. 128a)	6
Nottingham	Nottinghamshire	Grantham Canal (No. 41a)	1
		Nottingham Canal (Nos. 41b1, 41b2, and 41b3)	1
		Earl Manvers' Canal (No. 65), and	1
		River Trent (Nos. 112a and 112c)	1
Nuneaton	Warwickshire	Coventry Canal (No. 24)	1
Oldbury	Worcestershire	Birmingham Canal Navigations (Nos. 10c1 and 10c5)	1
Openshaw	Lancashire	Ashton Canal (No. 39a3)	1
Oundle	Northamptonshire	River Nene (No. 74a)	1
Oxford	Oxfordshire	Oxford Canal (Nos. 82a and 82h), and	1
		River Thames (Nos. 107a and 107b)	1
Penkridge	Staffordshire	Staffordshire and Worcestershire Canal (No. 95a)	1
Pershore	Worcestershire	River Avon (Warwickshire) Lower Navigation (No. 8)	1
Peterborough	Northamptonshire	River Nene (No. 74a)	1
Plymouth	Devonshire	River Tamar (No. 103)	19
Pontypool	Monmouthshire	Brecon and Abergavenny Canal (No. 43h), and	23
		Monmouthshire Canal (No. 43i1)	23
Pontypridd	Glamorganshire	Glamorganshire Canal (No. 36a)	24
Preston	Lancashire	Lancaster Canal (No. 61c1)	26
Preston Brook	Cheshire	Bridgewater Canal (No. 64b4), and	1
		Trent and Mersey Canal (No. 76a)	1
Radcliffe	Lancashire	Manchester, Bolton and Bury Canal (No. 55a)	1
Ramsey	Huntingdonshire	Middle Level Navigations (No. 69h)	1
Ravensthorpe	Yorkshire, West Riding	Calder and Hebble Navigation (No. 17a)	1
Reading	Berkshire	Kennet and Avon Navigation (No. 43a), and	1
		River Thames (Nos. 107a and 107c)	1
Retford	Nottinghamshire	Chesterfield Canal (No. 39d)	1

(13)—Index of Principal Places and Towns to which there is Water Communication—*continued.*

Place.	County.	Name and No. of Navigation.	No. of Group. Section 12.
Richmond	Surrey	River Thames (No. 107a)	1
Rickmansworth	Hertfordshire	Grand Junction Canal (No. 38a1)	1
Ripon	Yorkshire, West Riding	River Ure Navigation (No. 75c)	1
Rochdale	Lancashire	Rochdale Canal (Nos. 87a and 87b)	1
Rochester	Kent	River Medway (No. 67)	11
Romiley	Cheshire	Peak Forest Canal (No. 39b1)	1
Rotherham	Yorkshire, West Riding	Sheffield and South Yorkshire Navigation (Nos. 91b1 and 91b2)	1
Rugby	Warwickshire	Oxford Canal (No. 82e)	1
Rugeley	Staffordshire	Trent and Mersey Canal (No. 76a)	1
Runcorn	Cheshire	Manchester Ship Canal (No. 64a)	1
		Bridgewater Canal (Nos. 64b1 and 64c), and	1
		River Mersey (No. 68)	1
Ryton	Durham	River Tyne (No. 113a)	2
Saddleworth	Lancashire	Huddersfield Narrow Canal (No. 61b)	1
St. Helens	Lancashire	St. Helens Canal (Nos. 61d1, 61d2, 61d3 & 61d4)	1
St. Ives	Huntingdonshire	River Ouse (Bedford) (No. 79a)	1
St. Neots	Huntingdonshire	River Ouse (Bedford) (No. 79a)	1
Sale	Cheshire	Bridgewater Canal (No. 64b1)	1
Salford (Manchester)	Lancashire	Manchester, Bolton and Bury Canal (No. 55a), and	1
		Manchester Ship Canal (Nos. 64a and 64d4)	1
Saltash	Cornwall	River Tamar (No. 103)	19
Sandwich	Kent	River Stour (Kent) (No. 97)	12
Sawbridgeworth	Hertfordshire	River Stort (No. 96)	1
Selby	Yorkshire, West Riding	Aire and Calder Navigation (No. 3c), and	1
		River Ouse (York) (No. 81)	1
Selly Oak	Worcestershire	Birmingham Canal Navigations (No. 10f2), and	1
		Worcester and Birmingham Canal (No. 90b)	1
Sharpness	Gloucestershire	River Severn (No. 89a), and	1
		Gloucester and Berkeley Ship Canal (No. 90a)	1
Sheerness	Kent	River Medway (No. 67)	11
Sheffield	Yorkshire, West Riding	Sheffield and South Yorkshire Navigation (No. 91a)	1
Shipley	Yorkshire, West Riding	Leeds and Liverpool Canal (No. 58a)	1
Shoreham	Sussex	River Adur (No. 1)	14
Shrewsbury	Shropshire	Shropshire Union Canals (No. 92g)	1
Skipton	Yorkshire, West Riding	Leeds and Liverpool Canal (No. 58a)	1
Slaithwaite	Yorkshire, West Riding	Huddersfield Narrow Canal (No. 61b)	1
Slough	Buckinghamshire	Grand Junction Canal (No. 38a7)	1
Smethwick	Staffordshire	Birmingham Canal Navigations (Nos. 10a1, 10c1 and 10c2)	1
Snaith	Yorkshire, West Riding	River Aire (No. 2)	1
Snodland	Kent	River Medway (No. 67)	11
Solihull	Warwickshire	Warwick and Birmingham Canal (No. 115)	1
Southall	Middlesex	Grand Junction Canal (No. 38a8)	1
Southend	Essex	River Thames (No. 107a)	1
South Shields	Durham	River Tyne (No. 113a)	2
Sowerby Bridge	Yorkshire, West Riding	Calder and Hebble Navigation (No. 17a), and	1
		Rochdale Canal (No. 87a)	1
Spalding	Lincolnshire	River Welland (No. 119)	5
Stafford	Staffordshire	Staffordshire and Worcestershire Canal (No. 95d)	1
Staines	Middlesex	River Thames (No. 107a)	1
Stalybridge	Cheshire	Huddersfield Narrow Canal (No. 61b)	1
Staveley	Derbyshire	Chesterfield Canal (No. 39d)	1
Stockport	Cheshire	Ashton Canal (No. 39a3)	1
Stockton	Durham	River Tees (No. 104)	3
Stoke Prior	Worcestershire	Worcester and Birmingham Canal (No. 90b)	1
Stoke-upon-Trent	Staffordshire	Trent and Mersey Canal (Nos. 76a and 76b)	1
Stone	Staffordshire	Trent and Mersey Canal (No. 76a)	1
Stonehouse	Gloucestershire	Stroudwater Canal (No, 100)	1
Stourbridge	Worcestershire	Stourbridge Canal (No. 99)	1
Stourport	Worcestershire	River Severn (No. 89a), and	1
		Staffordshire and Worcestershire Canal (No. 95a)	1
Stowmarket	Suffolk	Ipswich and Stowmarket Navigation (No. 51)	7
Stratford-on-Avon	Warwickshire	Stratford-on-Avon Canal (No. 43b1)	1
Stretford	Lancashire	Bridgewater Canal (Nos. 64b1 and 64b3)	1
Strood	Kent	River Medway (No. 67)	11
Stroud	Gloucestershire	Stroudwater Canal (No. 100), and	1
		Thames and Severn Canal (No. 108a)	1
Sudbury	Suffolk	River Stour (Suffolk) No. 98)	8
Swansea	Glamorganshire	Swansea Canal (Nos. 43j1 and 43j2), and	25
		Tennant Canal (No. 106a)	25
Swinton	Yorkshire, West Riding	Sheffield and South Yorkshire Navigation (Nos. 91b1 and 91d1)	1
Tadcaster	Yorkshire, West Riding	River Wharfe (No. 122)	1

(13)—Index of Principal Places and Towns to which there is Water Communication—*continued.*

Place.	County.	Name and No. of Navigation.	No. of Group. Section 12.
Taunton	Somersetshire	River Tone Navigation (No. 43d), and	22
		Bridgwater and Taunton Canal (No. 43e)	22
Teddington	Middlesex	River Thames (No. 107a)	1
Teignmouth	Devonshire	River Teign (No. 105a)	18
Tewkesbury	Gloucestershire	River Avon (Warwickshire) Lower Navigation (No. 8), and	1
		River Severn (No. 89a)	1
Thetford	Norfolk	Brandon River (No. 14)	1
Thornaby	Yorkshire, North Riding	River Tees (No. 104)	3
Thorne	Yorkshire, West Riding	Sheffield and South Yorkshire Navigation (No. 91c)	1
Thorney	Cambridgeshire	Thorney River (No. 110)	1
Thornhill	Yorkshire, West Riding	Calder and Hebble Navigation (No. 17a)	1
Thrapston	Northamptonshire	River Nene (No. 74a)	1
Tipton	Staffordshire	Birmingham Canal Navigations (Nos. 10a1, 10c1, 10f1, and 10i)	1
Tiverton	Devonshire	Grand Western Canal (No. 43f)	21
Todmorden	Yorkshire, West Riding	Rochdale Canal (No. 87a)	1
Tonbridge	Kent	River Medway (No. 67)	11
Topsham	Devonshire	Exeter Ship Canal (No. 31)	17
Treforest	Glamorganshire	Glamorganshire Canal (No. 36a), and	24
		Dr. Thomas's Canal (No. 109)	24
Tunstall	Staffordshire	Trent and Mersey Canal (No. 76a)	1
Twickenham	Middlesex	River Thames (No. 107a)	1
Tynemouth	Northumberland	River Tyne (No. 113a)	2
Ulverston	Lancashire	Ulverston Canal (No. 35)	27
Upton-on-Severn	Worcestershire	River Severn (No. 89a)	1
Uxbridge	Middlesex	Grand Junction Canal (No. 38a1)	1
Wakefield	Yorkshire, West Riding	Aire and Calder Navigation (No. 3a2), and	1
		Calder and Hebble Navigation (No. 17a)	1
Walker	Northumberland	River Tyne (No. 113a)	2
Wallingford	Berkshire	River Thames (No. 107a)	1
Wallsend	Northumberland	River Tyne (No. 113a)	2
Walsall	Staffordshire	Birmingham Canal Navigations (Nos. 10k1 and 101)	1
Waltham	Essex	River Lee (No. 57a)	1
Walton	Surrey	River Thames (No. 107a)	1
Ware	Hertfordshire	River Lee (No. 57a)	1
Warrington	Lancashire	St. Helens Canal (No. 61d1)	1
		Mersey and Irwell Navigation (Nos. 64d1 and 64d2), and	1
		River Mersey (No. 68)	1
Warwick	Warwickshire	Warwick and Birmingham Canal (No. 115)	1
Watford	Hertfordshire	Grand Junction Canal (No. 38a1)	1
Wath	Yorkshire, West Riding	Sheffield and South Yorkshire Navigation (No. 91d1)	1
Wednesbury	Staffordshire	Birmingham Canal Navigations (No. 10k6)	1
Wednesfield	Staffordshire	Birmingham Canal Navigations (Nos. 10m1 and 10q1)	1
Wellingborough	Northamptonshire	River Nene (No. 74a)	1
Welshpool	Montgomeryshire	Shropshire Union Canals (No. 92e1)	1
Weybridge	Surrey	River Thames (No. 107a) and	1
		River Wey (No. 121)	1
Whitchurch	Shropshire	Shropshire Union Canals (No. 92d2)	1
Widnes	Lancashire	St. Helens Canal (No. 61d1), and	1
		River Mersey (No. 68)	1
Wigan	Lancashire	Leeds and Liverpool Canal (Nos. 58a and 58d)	1
Windsor	Berkshire	River Thames (No. 107a)	1
Winsford	Cheshire	River Weaver (No. 118a)	1
Wisbech	Cambridgeshire	River Nene (No. 74a) and	1
		Wisbech Canal (No. 123)	1
Wivenhoe	Essex	River Colne (No. 23)	9
Woking	Surrey	Woking Aldershot and Basingstoke Canal, (No. 126)	1
Wolverhampton	Staffordshire	Birmingham Canal Navigations (No. 10a1)	1
Wombwell	Yorkshire, West Riding	Sheffield and South Yorkshire Navigation (No. 91d1)	1
Woolwich	Kent	River Thames (No. 107a)	1
Worcester	Worcestershire	River Severn (No. 89a), and	1
		Worcester and Birmingham Canal (No. 90b)	1
Worksop	Nottinghamshire	Chesterfield Canal (No. 39d)	1
Yarm	Yorkshire, North Riding	River Tees (No. 104)	3
Yarmouth	Norfolk	River Bure (No. 16), and	6
		River Yare (No. 128a)	6
York	Yorkshire	River Foss (No. 33), and	1
		River Ouse (York) (No. 81)	1

(14)—GLOSSARY OF CANAL TERMS.

AEGRE, a tidal wave. *See* Section 8—Tides.

ANIMALS, a boatman's name for donkeys, which are much in use for towing purposes on the canals tributary to the River Severn, a pair of them taking the place of one horse.

BALANCE BEAM, or BALANCE, the beam projecting from a lock gate, which balances its weight, and by pushing against which the gate is closed or opened.

BARGE, a term including a variety of vessels, both sailing and non-sailing, in use for canal and river traffic, whose beam is approximately twice that of a narrow boat. The name barge is often applied erroneously to all vessels carrying goods on a canal or river, whether barge, wide boat, narrow boat, lighter, or any other vessel. *See* Section 9—Types of Vessels.

BECK, a dike or drain.

BORE, a tidal wave. *See* Section 8—Tides.

BOBBINS, short hollow wooden rollers, several of which are usually threaded on to each of the traces of horses engaged in towing, to prevent the traces chafing.

BOW HAULING, hauling by men, in distinction to the more usual method of hauling by horses. *See* Section 3—Haulage.

BREAST of a lock gate, the vertical post of the gate furthest from its hanging ; where the gates are in pairs the two breasts are usually mitred to bed against each other when shut, and in this case are often termed " mitre posts."

BROAD (Norfolk), a wide expanse of water, or lake.

BUTTY BOAT, a boat working in company with another boat. The term is generally applied to a boat towed by a steamer.

BYE TRADER, a term used to designate any trader on a canal other than a canal company itself when carriers. All canal companies are not carriers themselves, some merely providing the waterway, and taking toll for its use.

CHALICO, a mixture of tar, cow hair, and horse dung made hot, used for filling up interstices in old wooden boats.

CLOUGH.—*see* Paddle.

COCK BOAT, a small boat used as a shore boat or tender to a larger vessel.

COMPARTMENT BOAT, commonly called a " Tom Pudding," a type of boat in use on the Aire and Calder Navigation, which is worked in trains with other similar boats. *See* Section 9—Types of Vessels.

COTTING, a Fen term, taking out the roots of rushes or weeds growing in a river or dike. *See* Roding.

CRANK—*see* Windlass.

(14)—GLOSSARY OF CANAL TERMS—*continued.*

CRATCHES are the supports of the gang planks of a narrow boat at the fore end of the boat. The deck cratch is placed at the point where the fore deck terminates and the cargo space begins, the false cratch being situated a short distance abaft the deck cratch. *See* also gang planks.

CUT, a boatman's name for canal, so applied on account of canals having been originally cut or constructed in distinction to rivers, which are natural channels. " A narrow cut," a narrow boat canal.

DAY BOATS—*see* Open Boats.

DOORS, a Fen term for gates ; in the Fens all lock gates are called " sluice doors."

DRAW, to draw a paddle, slacker, slat, weir, or staunch, is to open it in order to allow the water to escape. The reverse is to " lower." " drop," or " shut in," or in the case of a staunch to " set."

DUMMY BOWS—*see* Aire and Calder Navigation compartment boats— Section 9—Types of Vessels.

DYDLE (Norfolk), to dredge, to clean out.

EBB, the tide is said to "ebb" when it is falling, and to " flow" when rising.

EYE, a Fen term, the opening closed by a slat. *See* paddle.

FEST ROPES, a pair of ropes attached one to each side of a Fen lighter, the loose ends being passed round the steering pole to steady it when in use. *See* Fen Lighters, Section 9—Types of vessels.

FLASH or FLUSH, a body of accumulated water suddenly released, used for the purpose of assisting navigation on rivers. On the Upper Thames certain days in the week are from time to time appointed on which flashes may be drawn. *See* Section 2—Canal Navigations and River Navigations.

FLASH (Cheshire), an inland lake caused by subsidence of the ground, due to salt mining operations.

FLASHERS—*see* Paddle.

FLASH LOCK—*see* Lock.

FLAT, a Mersey flat is a type of vessel which conducts the bulk of the trade on that river and neighbouring canals. A black flat is a larger vessel for trading between Liverpool and the River Weaver. *See* Section 9—Types of Vessels. The term " flat " is sometimes used to denote a shallow punt or raft, used for such purposes as painting or repairing the sides of a larger vessel.

FLEET (Norfolk), shallow.

FLOW—*see* Ebb.

FLY PADDLES—*see* Paddles.

FRESHET, an increase in the flow of a river due to rain.

(14)—GLOSSARY OF CANAL TERMS—*continued.*

GALLEY BEAM, a beam uniting across the top the gate posts of a pair of lock gates of the old fashioned river type hung on hooks and rides. The galley beam serves to keep the gate posts in place, and prevents them from falling inwards towards each other, which the weight of the lock gates would otherwise encourage, this type of gate being wholly unbalanced. Galley beams can still be seen on the rivers Larke, Stort, and Stour (Suffolk).

GANG, the number of Fen lighters, or River Stour (Suffolk) lighters, chained together for travelling with each other. In the case of Fen lighters the number in a gang is about five, and in the case of the Stour lighters always two. *See* Section 9—Types of Vessels.

GANG PLANKS, removable planks used to afford a means of passing from one end of a narrow boat to the other; when in place they run from the top of the cabin aft to the deck cratch forward, being supported in between by upright supports called stands. These stands, which are also removable, fit into mortices in the stretchers and boat's floor, and have the gang planks tightly lashed down to them.

GAUGING, means of ascertaining by the draught of a vessel the weight of cargo on board for the purpose of taking tolls. The first gauging of canal boats is carried out at a weigh dock, where particulars of the boat's draught are taken when empty, and when fully loaded, and at intermediate points, such as at every ton of loading. The boat is loaded with weights kept for the purpose, which are lifted in and out by cranes; the result arrived at is then either transferred to graduated scales fixed to the boat's sides, which can be read at any time, or the particulars of each vessel are furnished to each toll office in a book, from which on gauging the immersion of the boat at any time the number of tons on board can at once be ascertained. The usual method of gauging a boat for immersion is to take what is called the "dry inches" that is,—the freeboard— at four points, at one point each side near the bows and at one point each side near the stern. This is done by an instrument consisting of a float in a tube, having a bracket projecting from the side of the tube. The bracket is rested on the boat's gun-whale, and the float indicates the number of inches between that and the level of the water in the canal. The four readings are then added together and divided by four, which gives the average for the whole boat. On the Glamorganshire Canal at North Road Lock, Cardiff, boats are gauged in the first instance by being weighed, both empty and loaded, on a weighing machine. The boats to be weighed are floated into a dock over a large cradle or scale pan, the water is then let out of the dock and the boat settles down on the cradle high and dry. The scale beam connected with the cradle is of much less length from the cradle to the fulcrum than from the fulcrum to the scale pan in which the weights are placed for reading the result, thus enabling these weights to be proportionately lighter than the actual dead weights. A similar machine was also in use at Midford on the Somersetshire Coal Canal up to the time of its becoming unnavigable.

(14)—Glossary of Canal Terms—*continued.*

Gongoozler, an idle and inquisitive person who stands staring for prolonged periods at anything out of the common. This word is believed to have its origin in the Lake District of England.

Ground Paddles—*see* Paddle.

Handspike, a bar of wood used as a lever ; on some of the old-fashioned navigations a handspike is still required for working the lock paddles, instead of rack and pinion gear. A handspike is also often used for working the roller for getting up the anchor on River Barges.

Hane (Norfolk), higher. " The water is hane to-day," that is, the water is higher to-day.

Haling Way, a Fen term, a towing-path.

Hauling Path, a towing-path.

Heel Post, the vertical post of a lock gate nearest to its hanging, and the axis on which the gate turns, being rounded at the back to fit into the hollow quoin, in which it partially revolves.

Henhouse Rangers, a term applied in the neighbourhood of Hull to a class of men who go fishing in small decked boats.

Hold In, Hold Out, are boatman's terms used as directions for steering, the expressions having reference to the position of the towing-path. " Hold in " means hold the boat in to the towing-path side of the canal, and " hold out " consequently the reverse.

Hollow Quoin, the recess into which the heel post of a lock gate is fitted, and in which it partially revolves when being opened and closed.

Horse Boat, a small open boat for ferrying over towing horses from one side of a river to the other, used in the Fens and neighbourhood on account of the long distances which in many cases would have to be travelled by the horse and driver alone if crossed over by the nearest bridge. The horse boat is usually towed astern of the last lighter in the gang.

Horse Marines (Yorkshire), men who contract for the haulage of vessels by horses on canals.

House Lighter, a Fen term, used to denote a lighter provided with a cabin.

(14)—GLOSSARY OF CANAL TERMS—*continued*.

INVERT, an inverted arch of brickwork or masonry, used chiefly as regards canal work to form the bottom of locks and tunnels in cases where, owing to the nature of the soil, lateral or upward pressure has to be sustained.

JACK CLOUGH—*see* Paddle.

JAMBING POLE, the pole projecting from the bows of all Fen lighters forming a gang except the first and second ; the first lighter carrying no pole and the second the steering pole, which is longer than a jambing pole. *See* Fen Lighters, Section 9—Types of Vessels.

JOSHER, a term used by boatmen to signify a boat belonging to Fellows. Morton, and Clayton Ltd., Canal Carriers ; the Christian name of the late Mr. Fellows having been Joshua.

KEB, an iron rake used for fishing up coal or other articles from the bottom of a canal.

KEEL, a type of vessel in extensive use on the rivers and canals of Yorkshire and district. *See* Section 9—Types of Vessels. There also used to be a type of vessel called a keel on the Tyne and Tees, but it is now nearly extinct.

LAND WATER, a term used to denote the water in a river brought down from up country in distinction to the water set up by the flood tide from seawards.

LEE BOARDS, boards used by sailing barges which can be lowered into the water or raised at will, for the purpose of decreasing the lee-way made by the vessel when sailing close-hauled. These boards are fitted in pairs, one on each side of the vessel, and when in use act as a keel.

LEGGING, a method used to propel vessels through tunnels. *See* Section 5 —Tunnels.

LET OFF, an appliance for getting rid of some of the water from a canal in rainy weather so that it may not overflow its banks. The old fashioned let-off was a trap door sluice in the bottom of the canal pulled up by a chain, but modern patterns more closely resemble the ordinary lock paddle, being sometimes made to work with a windlass, having a different shaped socket to those for working the locks.

LEVEL, when two reaches of water, one on each side of a lock or weir, from the flow of the tide or other cause become level, a level is said to be made. *See* Section 8—Tides.

LIGHTER, a term including a variety of vessels ; such as a Thames lighter or punt, a Fen lighter, a River Stour (Suffolk) lighter, a Bridgewater Canal lighter, &c. *See* Section 9—Types of Vessels.

(14)—GLOSSARY OF CANAL TERMS—*continued.*

LOCK, an appliance for overcoming changes of level in the navigation of rivers and canals. A lock consists of a chamber built generally of brick or masonry, and provided at both ends with a gate or gates and the necessary paddles or valves for controlling the ingress and egress of the water. *See* Section 4—(*a*) Locks.

The term " pound lock " is sometimes applied to the ordinary lock in distinction to the term " flash lock," another name for a staunch or navigation weir.

LOCK TO, to work a vessel through a lock.

LOODEL, a staff used to form a vertical extension of the tiller of a barge for the purpose of steering the barge when loaded with high loads, such as hay or straw. The loodel when required is inserted in a mortice in the fore end of the tiller.

MARINES, HORSE—*see* Horse Marines.

MITRE POST—*see* Breast.

MONKEY BOAT—*see* Narrow boat.

NARROW BOAT, a type of boat in extensive use on canals, commonly called " a boat." *See* Section 9—Types of Vessels.

NIP (River Trent), a narrow place.

NUMBER ONES, boats owned by the boatmen who work them, and who are consequently their own masters, in distinction to boats owned by a firm or company.

OPEN BOATS, boats without cabins, used in working short-distance traffic, and on which there is no sleeping accommodation; also called DAY BOATS.

PADDLE, a sluice valve, by opening or closing which water can either be allowed to pass or be retained—synonym SLACKER, also CLOUGH in the north of England, as on Leeds and Liverpool Canal; the word clough, however, in the Fen Country is generally used to denote the large shutter closing the navigation opening of a staunch— *see* Section 4, (*b*) Navigation Weirs or Staunches. Also SLAT, a Fen term for a paddle, *e.g.*, " Slats and Eyes," the eye being the opening closed by the slat.

GROUND PADDLES at the head of a lock are those that admit water to the lock by culverts or sluiceways built in the ground in distinction to paddles in the lock gates. The ground paddles of the Grand Junction Canal Locks answer to what are termed JACK CLOUGHS on the Leeds and Liverpool Canal. Some of the locks on the older canals have only ground paddles to fill them, but usually there are other paddles in addition fitted in the top gates which help to fill the lock quickly. These are variously termed, in different localities, FLY PADDLES, RANTERS, and FLASHERS.

(14)—Glossary of Canal Terms—*continued.*

Pen, a Lock Pen, a Fen term, a lock chamber.

Pen, to, a Fen term, to lock or to work a vessel through a lock, *e.g.,* " a narrow boat is too long to pen at Stanground," that is, too long to lock at Stanground (called Stanground Sluice in Fen language).

Pound, the stretch of water on a canal between two locks.

Pound Lock—*see* Lock.

Puddle, clay worked up with water and spread in layers on the bottom and sides of a canal or reservoir when situated in porous strata, for the purpose of making it watertight.

Punt, another name for a Thames lighter. *See* Section 9—Types of Vessels.

Quant (Norfolk and District), a pole or shaft.

Quant, to, to propel a vessel by means of a quant.

Quarter Bits, a pair of ropes attached from the fore-end of the jambing pole of a Fen lighter, one to each quarter of the lighter immediately in front. *See* Fen Lighters, Section 9—Types of Vessels.

Quoins, Hollow—*see* Hollow Quoins.

Rate, charges payable to a canal company if carriers, or to a carrier or bye-trader by any person sending goods, as payment for carrying them from one place to another. Rate, therefore, equals toll plus haulage. *See* Toll.

Ranters—*see* Paddle.

Reach, a reach of a river is the stretch of water between two locks, or in the case of the tidal portion of a river between two bends or other landmarks, as the lower reaches of the Thames and Medway, all of which have names.

Rimers, the posts in the removable portions of weirs on the Upper Thames, against which the weir paddles are placed.

Risers—*see* Staircase Locks, and Section 4—(*a*) Locks.

Roding, a Fen term, cutting rushes or weeds growing in a river or dike. *See* Cotting.

Roving Bridge, or Turn Over Bridge, a bridge situated at the point where the towing-path changes from one side of a canal to the other, and over which all horses engaged in towing have to pass.

Screw, a boatman's term for a vessel driven by a screw propeller.

(14)—Glossary of Canal Terms—*continued.*

Seizing Chain, the chain by which two Fen lighters are fastened to each other, stem and stern, when forming part of a gang. *See* Fen Lighters, Section 9—Types of Vessels.

Set, to, to set a staunch is to close it in order to allow the water to accumulate. *See* Section 4—(*b*) Navigation Weirs or Staunches.

Shafting, propelling a vessel with a long shaft or pole, a method sometimes used in tunnels. *See* Section 5—Tunnels.

Slacker—*see* Paddle.

Slat—*see* Paddle.

Sluice, the Fen term for a lock. All locks in the Fens are called sluices.

Soar Pin—*see* Stud.

Spread or Sprit, a Fen term for a pole, shaft, or quant.

Staircase Locks, also called " Risers," a flight or series of locks so arranged that the top gate or gates of each lock, except the highest one, also form the bottom gate or gates of the lock above. *See* Section 4—(*a*) Locks.

Staith, in the Midlands and north of England a staith generally signifies a place where coal is loaded into vessels ; in the Norfolk district the word is used to denote a wharf, being a place where any kind of goods can be loaded or unloaded.

Stands. the intermediate supports for the gang planks of a narrow boat. *See* Gang Planks.

Stank, a temporary watertight dam constructed of sheet piling, from the interior of which the water is pumped out, so as to enable foundations or other works contained therein, which are normally under water, to be laid bare.

Staunch, an appliance for overcoming changes of level on a navigable river, also in different localities termed a " navigation weir " and a " flash lock." *See* Section 4—(*b*) Navigation Weirs or Staunches.

Steering Pole, the pole projecting from the bows of the second lighter forming a gang of Fen lighters, or River Stour (Suffolk) lighters, by which the whole gang is steered. *See* Fen Lighters, Section 9—Types of Vessels.

Stop, a stop or stop lock is generally a lock or gates, erected at the junction of one canal with another, to prevent loss of water from one to another if necessary, normally there being little or no change of level. There is generally a Toll Office at a stop lock where cargoes are declared, boats gauged, tolls paid, &c. The term stop is also used to denote a Toll Office not adjoining another Canal Co.'s property, as on the Birmingham Canal Navigations.

(14)—Glossary of Canal Terms—*continued.*

Stop Gates answer the same purpose as stop grooves and planks, but are made in the form of lock gates, and are always kept open except when required for use. In long canal pounds it is usual for stop gates to be fitted at intervals, so that in the event of a leak or burst the escape of water may be confined to that portion of the pound between the nearest stop gates on either side.

Stop Grooves, vertical grooves, usually provided at the head and tail of each lock, and in other situations as required, into which stop planks can be inserted so as to form a temporary dam or stank.

Stop Planks—*see* Stop Grooves.

Strap, a rope used for the purpose of stopping a vessel, one end being made fast on board and the other twisted round a stump, bollard, or other object on shore.

Stud, a loose iron pin with a T head fitting into a socket, in use on narrow boats, to which towing and mooring lines are made fast.

Studs are named according to their position on the boat: fore studs, stern studs, and towing studs.

Towing studs fit into a socket on the cabin top, and are used for attaching the long tow line necessary on some rivers, or when in tow of a steamer. This position for the towing stud is selected in order that the line may be under the immediate control of the steerer.

Before towing studs were brought into use, straight pins with a shoulder, called " Soar Pins," were used in the same position for the same purpose. The disadvantage of soar pins was that their use necessitated the towing line being fastened round the pin, inside the cabin, as well as outside, thereby chafing the combing of the cabin hatchway.

Summit Level, the highest pound of water in a canal, from which, if a portion of a through route, the canal descends in both directions, or if the termination of the canal in one direction only. The summit level being the highest pound is the one into which the main supply of water for the purpose of working the locks has to be delivered, and is consequently, in dry weather, the first pound to be affected as regards deficiency of navigable depth. The highest summit level in England is that of the Huddersfield Narrow Canal, which is $4\frac{1}{4}$ miles long from Diggle to Marsden, and is 644ft. 9in. above Ordnance Datum. For $3\frac{1}{4}$ miles of this summit level the course of the canal is through Standedge Tunnel, the longest canal tunnel in England.

Sweep, a large oar.

Tackle, a boatman's name for the harness of a boat horse.

(14)—GLOSSARY OF CANAL TERMS—*continued*.

TOLL, also called TONNAGE, the charge payable to a canal company for the use of the canal by a trader or other person doing his own haulage, that is, carrying goods in his own boat, worked by his own crew and horse. *See* Rate.

TOWING-PATH, the path by the side of a navigation for the use of the towing horses. Also called in various localities HAULING-PATH, and HALING-WAY, the latter being a Fen term. *See* Section 3—(*a*) Haulage.

TROW, a type of vessel in use on the River Severn. *See* Section 9—Types of Vessels.

TUB BOATS, small box boats carrying from three to five tons, some of which are still in use in Shropshire and Cornwall. *See* Section 9— Types of Vessels.

TURN OVER BRIDGE—*see* Roving Bridge.

TURNS, WAITING TURNS or WORKING TURNS, is a system often adopted at a flight of canal locks in dry weather in order to make the utmost use of the water. Each boat requiring to proceed either up or down the locks has to wait for the arrival of a boat coming in the opposite direction, thus making sure that the maximum amount of traffic is passed for the water consumed.

TYING POINT, the shallowest point in a navigation or route of navigation. For instance, the bottom sill of Cranfleet Lock, better known to boatmen as Old Sal's Lock, was previous to 1897, when alterations were made, the tying point on the River Trent between Nottingham and the junctions with the Erewash Canal and Loughborough Navigation ; that is to say, any vessel that could float over this sill could find enough water everywhere else between these places.

WASH LANDS or WASHES, lands adjoining a river, so embanked that the river can overflow on to them when in flood, thus forming a compensation reservoir from which the flood water can be discharged gradually to the sea. Wash Lands are generally a strip of land by the side of the river between its summer channel and the flood bank, which is set back on purpose. The embanked area of land between the old and new Bedford Rivers (River Ouse, Bedford), comprising about 5000 acres, is all wash land. In times of flood, when the water in the river rises to 4ft. 6in. above the level of this land, it is admitted to these washes by a sluice at Earith, discharging on the subsidence of the flood through Welmore Lake Sluice into New Bedford River near Denver.

WEIGH DOCK, a dock used for the purpose of gauging the cargo-carrying capacity of vessels trading on canals. *See* Gauging.

(14)—GLOSSARY OF CANAL TERMS—*continued.*

WEIR, an artificial barrier or dam across a river holding up the water for navigation purposes, the change of level thus involved being usually surmounted by a lock.   *See* Section 4—(*a*) Locks.

In a few cases vessels, instead of passing by a lock, are navigated through an opening in the weir constructed for the purpose so as to be capable of being shut when required.   The weir then becomes a navigation weir, staunch, or flash lock.   *See* Section 4—(*b*) Navigation Weirs or Staunches.

WHERRY, the name given to the sailing vessels which conduct the trade on the Rivers Bure, Yare, and Waveney, and connecting Dikes and Broads, also to another class of vessel in use on the Tyne. *See* Section 9—Types of Vessels.

WIDE BOAT, a type of boat in use on canals of a size intermediate between that of a narrow boat and a barge.   *See* Section 9—Types of Vessels.

WIND, TO, to wind a boat is to turn a boat round.

WINDING PLACE, WINDING HOLE, WINNING PLACE, or WINNING HOLE, is a wide place in a canal provided for the purpose of turning a boat round.

WINDLASS, also called in some districts CRANK, is a handle or key for opening and closing lock paddles, shaped in the form of the letter L, and having a square socket at one end to fit on the square of the spindle operating the paddle gear.

WINGS, flat pieces of board rigged for the purpose of legging in tunnels when the tunnel is too wide to permit of the leggers reaching the side walls with their feet from the boat's deck.   *See* Section 5— Tunnels.

A fully equipped narrow boat would carry two pairs of wings, a pair of " Narrow Cut Wings " and a pair of " Broad Cut Wings;" that is, a pair of wings suitable for the full-sized tunnel of a narrow boat canal, and also a pair suitable for the tunnels of barge canals, the broad cut wings being, of course, the longer ones.